The
New International
Lesson Annual

2008–2009

September–August

Abingdon Press
Nashville

THE NEW INTERNATIONAL LESSON ANNUAL 2008–2009

Copyright © 2008 by Abingdon Press

This book is printed on acid-free paper.

All scripture quotations unless noted otherwise are from the *New Revised Standard Version of the Bible,* copyright 1989, Division of Christian Education of the National Council of the Churches of Christ in the United States of America. Used by permission. All rights reserved.

Scripture quotations marked NIV are taken from the Holy Bible, NEW INTERNATIONAL VERSION®. Copyright © 1973, 1978, 1984 by International Bible Society. All rights reserved throughout the world. Used by permission of International Bible Society.

Scripture quotations marked KJV are from the King James or Authorized Version of the Bible.

ISBN 978-0-687-49177-3

ISSN 1084-872X

08 09 10 11 12 13 14 15 16 17—10 9 8 7 6 5 4 3 2 1

MANUFACTURED IN THE UNITED STATES OF AMERICA

PREFACE

Welcome aboard! We're so pleased that you have chosen to journey with us during 2008–2009. Together, we seek to understand God's Word and recognize how it impacts our lives. This year we will engage in a survey of the New Testament as we consider the theme of community; explore the lives of people who surrounded Jesus' birth and figures throughout the Old Testament to discern how they made and kept their commitments to God; examine the promise, path, and way of new life; and recognize God's call on the covenant community heard in the books of Exodus, Leviticus, Numbers, and Deuteronomy. As you study each week, you will join countless Bible students around the world who use resources based on the work of the Committee on the Uniform Series, known by many as the International Lesson Series.

Although adult learners often use *The New International Lesson Annual*, it is mainly designed for teachers of adults who want a solid biblical basis for each session and a teaching plan that will help them lead their classes. The following features are especially valuable for busy teachers who want to provide in-depth Bible study experiences for their students. Each lesson includes the following sections:

Previewing the Lesson highlights the background and lesson Scriptures, focus of the lesson, three goals for the learners, a pronunciation guide in lessons where you may find unfamiliar words or names, and supplies you will need to teach.

Reading the Scripture includes the Scripture lesson printed in both the *New Revised Standard Version* and the *New International Version*. By printing these two highly respected translations in parallel columns, you can easily compare them for in-depth study. If your own Bible is another version, you will then have three translations to explore as you prepare each lesson.

Understanding the Scripture closely analyzes the background Scripture by looking at each verse. Here you will find help in understanding concepts, ideas, places, and persons pertinent to each week's lesson. You may also find explanations of Greek or Hebrew words that are essential for understanding the text.

Interpreting the Scripture looks at the lesson Scripture, delves into its meaning, and relates it to contemporary life.

Sharing the Scripture provides you with a detailed teaching plan. It is divided into two major sections: *Preparing to Teach* and *Leading the Class*.

In the *Preparing to Teach* section, you will find a devotional reading related to the lesson for your own spiritual enrichment and a "to do" list to prepare your mind and classroom for the session.

The *Leading the Class* portion begins with "Gather to Learn" activities designed to welcome the students and draw them into the lesson. Here, the students' stories and experiences or other contemporary stories are highlighted as preparation for the Bible story. The next three headings of *Leading the Class* are the three "Goals for the Learners." The first goal always focuses on the Bible story itself. The second goal relates the Bible story to the lives of the adults in your class. The third goal prompts the students to take action on what they have learned. You will find a variety of activities under each of these goals to help the learners fulfill them. The activities are diverse in nature and may include among other strategies: listening, reading, writing, speaking, singing, drawing, interacting with others, and meditating. The lesson ends with "Continue the Journey," where you will find closing activities, preparation for the following week, and ideas for students to commit themselves to action during the week, based on what they have learned.

In addition to these weekly features, each quarter begins with the following helps:

- **Introduction to the Quarter** provides you with a quick survey of each lesson to be studied during the quarter. You will find the title, background Scripture, date, and a brief summary of each week's basic thrust. This feature is the first page of each quarter.
- **Meet Our Writer,** which follows the quarterly introduction, provides biographical information about each writer, including education, pastoral and/or academic teaching experience, previous publications, and family information.
- The **Big Picture**, written by the same writer who authored the quarter's lessons, is designed to give you a broader scope of the materials to be covered than is possible in each weekly lesson. You will find this background article immediately following the writer's biography.
- **Close-up** gives you some focused information, such as a timeline, chart, overview, short article, or list that you may choose to use anytime during the quarter, perhaps even repeatedly.
- **Faith in Action** provides ideas related to the broad sweep of the quarter that the students can use individually or as a class to act on what they have been studying. These ideas are usually intended for use beyond the classroom.

Finally, two annual features are included:

- **The list of background scriptures** is offered especially for those of you who keep back copies of *The New International Lesson Annual*. This feature, which follows the contents, will enable you to locate Bible background passages used during the current year at some future date.
- **The teacher enrichment article** is intended to be useful throughout the year, so we hope you will read it immediately and refer to it often. The article in this volume, "For Just Such a Time as This" examines current trends in postmodernism, biblical illiteracy, and globalism that impact how the gospel is shared and heard. You will find the article after the list of background scriptures.

Your feedback is very important to us. If you ever have any questions or comments, please write to me and include your e-mail address or phone number. I will respond as soon as your message reaches my home office in Maryland.

Dr. Nan Duerling
Abingdon Press
PO Box 801
Nashville, TN 37202

We are so glad that you are part of *The New International Lesson Annual* community. May God grant you wisdom and grace as you study and lead others to a broader understanding of the Bible and a deeper relationship with our Lord Jesus Christ.

Nan Duerling, Ph.D.
Editor, *The New International Lesson Annual*

Contents

FIRST QUARTER

The New Testament Community
September 7–November 30, 2008

UNIT 1: THE BIRTH OF A NEW COMMUNITY
(September 7-28)

UNIT 2: THE DEVELOPMENT AND WORK OF THE NEW COMMUNITY
(October 5-26)

UNIT 3: THE NEW COMMUNITY FACES GROWING PAINS
(November 2-30)

SECOND QUARTER

Human Commitment
December 7, 2008–February 22, 2009

UNIT 1: COMMITMENT TO THE MESSIAH
(December 7-28)

UNIT 2: OLD TESTAMENT PEOPLE OF COMMITMENT
(January 4-February 22)

THIRD QUARTER

New Creation in Christ
March 1–May 31, 2009

UNIT 1: THE PROMISE OF NEW LIFE
(March 1-29)

UNIT 2: THE PATH TO NEW LIFE
(April 5-26)

UNIT 3: THE WAY OF NEW LIFE
(May 3-31)

FOURTH QUARTER

Call Sealed With Promise
June 7–August 30, 2009

UNIT 1: CALLED OUT OF EGYPT
(June 7-28)

UNIT 2: CALLED TO BE GOD'S PEOPLE
(July 5-26)

UNIT 3: CALLED TO CHOOSE LIFE
(August 2-30)

List of Background Scriptures, 2008–2009

Old Testament

New Testament

TEACHER ENRICHMENT: FOR JUST SUCH A TIME AS THIS

NAN DUERLING

In the lesson for February 15, Mordecai urges Queen Esther to risk her life to go before the king because "perhaps [she has] come to royal dignity for just such a time as this" (Esther 4:14). This time is one of great peril, for a decree has been issued for the destruction of the Jews (3:8-10, 13). Maybe, just maybe, this favored wife of King Ahasuerus could intervene and save her people. As the Chinese sign for the word "crisis" so elegantly portrays, there is both danger and opportunity awaiting Esther.

In the church today, we too face crises that are both fraught with danger and brimming with opportunity. What happens will depend, as it did in Esther's case, on our clear reading and understanding of the situation as well as our willingness to take a risk, to conduct business in a highly unusual way. Admittedly, there is no governmental decree threatening the lives of all Christians in the United States, but there are many conditions in our world that, if not handled with care, could be just as devastating to the church as the king's order was to Esther's Jewish people. These are issues that you and your class members need to confront. How you perceive and respond to them could make all the difference in the future of your congregation.

Postmodernism

For almost two thousand years, the church has had a story to tell that people who claimed to be Christian "bought into" almost without question. This narrative of Christ's prophesied coming, birth, life and ministry, death, and resurrection were widely accepted. In the United States, the Bible story was very much linked with our national history, goals, and values. Although the terms "postmodern" and "postmodernism" are applied to numerous disciplines with varying meanings, the simplest definition with respect to the church and Christianity is a rejection of all metanarratives—the big stories that have dominated our thinking for millennia. The church is faced with a challenge: Many people question whether Christ actually lived, dismiss the notion of resurrection, do not accept the need for a Savior, and, perhaps most challenging of all, perceive the Christian faith as totally irrelevant to their daily lives. The story of our faith that has so long been accepted as truth is now questioned by many. Unbelief is not really the issue. Instead, people see multiple truths running on parallel tracks that can never intersect. The Christian story has become just one story among many.

This way of thinking is a seismic shift for the church because it means that we can no longer assume that for most people "Jesus is the answer." They are not even asking questions that would lead them to him. Yes, they may talk about spirituality, they may want to be part of a fellowship of people where they can feel a sense of belonging, and they might support causes that many churches respond to as a biblical mandate, such as feeding the hungry, caring for the poor and vulnerable, or advocating for the powerless. But, these sincere seekers and doers have no need to accept a two-thousand-year-old story that makes no sense to them within the context of their own lives. An individual seen as truly God and truly human is an impossible stretch for many people. Others wonder what kind of a God has a Son crucified—and if they want to worship one so violent. Many people are aware of the checkered history of the church that includes wars fought in God's name, assent to ecological damage as humans are encouraged to "have dominion over" the earth (Genesis 1:26), and abuse committed by clergy. To them the church has "talked the talk" but not "walked the walk." We have, from their perspective, been part of the problem, not part of the solution. While those of us within the church work to make it better and recognize that these sinful abuses of power are not God's will, those outside see hypocrisy and simply steer clear. The story becomes even less believable to them because they cannot see it enacted.

The bottom line is that the story that many of us grew up with is no longer known or cared about by significant numbers of people, especially among younger generations. And, unless we learn to live the story more faithfully as the servant-church, we have no hope of reaching those who may be searching, even if they cannot name the One they seek. This is a major challenge for us in "such a time as this."

Biblical Illiteracy

Even people who were not "religious superstars" used to be able to discern references to the Bible in art, music, and literature. That skill is becoming increasingly rare. Why? More and more people, even those who profess Christ, are biblically illiterate.

You will often hear people claim that because the United States was founded on Judeo-Christian principles we are a Christian country. Yet, when host Jay Leno asked several basic Bible questions during his television show—things like name one of the Ten Commandments, name one of the apostles—no one in the audience could do so. According to a Gallup survey only two in ten (yes, you read that correctly) people knew that Jesus delivered the Sermon on the Mount. Even in a church setting in Michigan, where a pastor also asked about the Ten Commandments, people could name no more than three or four. A simple quiz of Bible facts in a church netted average scores of 40 percent. While we may say that those who attended a Leno show or participated in a Gallup poll were not necessarily Christian and cannot be expected to have known the answers, surely people who attend church should have some basic knowledge.

Yet, I would venture to say that even in your own class, where members have perhaps been studying for years and may be part of the 16 percent of Gallup poll respondents who say they read their Bibles daily, you may find that the learners have a difficult time putting together a chronology of biblical events or understanding the causes of those events. The Bible books and stories are not in chronological order, so readers are challenged to figure out which prophet goes with which king, or to realize that 1 Thessalonians was written decades before Matthew, the first book listed in the New Testament. Particularly in the Old Testament, once you get beyond the familiar few names, many students really don't know the figures of the Bible or why they are important.

And yet, at least in our classes they come and try to absorb the biblical message and make it a rod by which to measure their lives. Still, as we teach and talk together we cannot assume that everyone in the room, including some of those who have been sitting in the same chairs for years, really have a handle on the wide sweep of biblical history or an understanding of what this all means to them at the beginning of the twenty-first century. Since many newcomers have not attended Sunday school as children, they may be totally lost when you refer to Jonah or the flood or Joseph and his coat of many colors. You and I may have grown up knowing these stories, but many people trying to connect with the church today simply do not have that background. So, what do you do, in addition to leading this class?

Some major programs, such as DISCIPLE (which I highly recommend), are addressing the problem of biblical illiteracy. Admittedly, those who participate must be highly motivated to devote a lot of time, energy, and study to an intensive investigation. Several years ago, my own Sunday school class made a huge commitment to meet two and a half hours on Sunday morning and then attend worship over the course of thirty weeks in order to work through *Jesus in the Gospels*. The adults in my class are vital Christians and active members of our congregation who have been deeply involved in the church for decades. Yet, we all finished this study feeling that we had learned so much more about Jesus and the way the Gospel writers portrayed him. Our vision had been enlarged, and we are better prepared for the next legs of our own spiritual journeys in "such a time as this."

Engaging the Global Community

Do you know that worldwide there are an estimated 2.1 billion Christians (33 percent of the earth's population), 1.3 billion Muslims (21 percent), 900 million Hindus (14 percent), 376 million Buddhists (6 percent), 14 million Jews (0.022 percent), and millions of adherents of other faiths? Only 16 percent of the world's population claims to have no religious preference or an atheistic view.

At one time, adherents of one faith tended to be located in specific areas. Even within a country such as the United States, enclaves of Jews, for example, tended to live together. To a certain extent, that is still true as we consider the world's population. But, globally we are seeing culture clashes as groups who are intolerant of each other's religions now have the communication and technology available not only to refuse to listen but also to try to destroy the "other." We often refer to "hardliners" as fundamentalists, but remember that these folks may be Christian, Jewish, Muslim, or another religion. No one belief system has a corner on the market of righteous claims of knowing, without question, the will of God. Unfortunately, when people insist that they are fully aware of God's will and refuse to dialogue with or tolerate other viewpoints, violence, bloodshed, and the loss of innocent life is often the result. Perhaps nothing more graphically and tragically illustrates this propensity than the Holocaust during World War II—or the Crusades. And lest we become smug, recall that these atrocities were perpetrated by those claiming to be Christians.

As Christians, we can no longer hide our heads in the sand and say that we live in a "Christian country" without recognizing that more and more people who have no Christian tradition—or a marginal one at best—now live among us. We need to learn to be in dialogue with the "other," to learn about how they approach God, by whatever name this deity is called. Does that mean that we relinquish our long-cherished beliefs? Of course not! But it does mean that our burgeoning world population that has truly become international must learn to live together in peace with understanding. Does this mean I cannot share my beliefs? Of course not! But it does mean that we have to learn to do that in a winsome way, wooing people to Christ, not denigrating their beliefs or insisting that they are on the way to eternal damnation. Only one place in the Bible (John 14:6) states, "No one comes to the Father except through me [Jesus]." While we Christians do come to the Father through Jesus, we need to be careful about insisting that *all* people must do so. Jesus also said, "I have other sheep that do not belong to this fold. I must bring them also, and they will listen to my voice. So there will be one flock, one shepherd" (John 10:16). Which of us can say with certainty who these people are? God knows, but we do not. They could possibly be some of these "other" neighbors whose beliefs do not reflect our own, so we need to tread lightly and with humility.

We need to learn how to be in dialogue with the "other." Dialogue requires a mutual sharing and an attempt to understand the other's point of view, whether we can agree with it or not. To do that we need to be willing to listen and learn. My husband and I and a couple we are very close to relish the time we spend talking about our faith. We are United Methodists; they are Conservative Jews. We have learned much from each other as to how God acts in the world, for we certainly do worship the same God. We have clarified our own thinking about matters of faith. We have heard how someone else views Christianity by the questions they ask and the observations they make. We have enriched our own spiritual lives by caring for one another, seeking common ground, respecting differences, and recognizing that they will never be Christian just as we will never be Jewish. But, we have seen the God of Abraham in them, and they, we believe, have seen Christ in us, and that is a precious gift. In an age when so much violence is done for the sake of one's religious beliefs, it is comforting to know that people can open their hearts and minds to one another in a respectful way. God can speak through these relationships. Do you know people who approach God through a different religious tradition with whom you could talk about their faith and yours? Telling our stories of faith and listening to the stories of others enables us to see God at work and mature in faith in ways that talking with other like-minded believers cannot.

To engage in fruitful dialogue we need to know who we are and whose we are. In our Sunday school classes we can prepare to dialogue by developing a clear understanding of what it means to claim the name of Christ. We need not fear an honest discussion with the "other" if we can state our own beliefs—and live them consistently, with integrity. We need to ask ourselves: What does God expect of us? What do we believe? How are we to act? How do our own stories intersect with the Bible's stories and teachings? What can we take from our own experience that can help someone else? When people are hurting, we have an opportunity to share God's love with them in a meaningful way. What have other people witnessed in my life that can help them? Platitudes are not useful, but a relationship with the living Christ that empowers me to live as a person of faith cannot help but draw others to Christ as they encounter the challenges and crises of life. Is your class helping members to grow in their relationship with Christ so as to be able to speak and act in ways that clearly reflect Christ living in each of you? If not, what steps do you need to take to help people engage others about faith in a meaningful way?

Furthermore, we can make our congregations sanctuaries where all are welcomed. We can work together to reach out to those in need so that our words and witness may conform to those of Jesus. In doing so, we can truly live out the Great Commandment to love God and neighbor as we love ourselves. I can't think of a better way to draw people to Christ while still respecting who they are and their understandings of the Holy. Like Esther, we are here "for just such a time as this" to share God's love with all people.

FIRST QUARTER
The New Testament Community

SEPTEMBER 7, 2008–NOVEMBER 30, 2008

The 2008–2009 Sunday school year begins with a survey of the New Testament that explores the theme of community. Our study will include lessons from Matthew and Mark as well as sessions from Acts, the history book of the early church, and letters, which were often written to discuss particular problems and challenges in the early faith communities.

Unit 1, "The Birth of a New Community," is a four-lesson examination of the new community as depicted in Matthew and Mark. "A New Community," the opening lesson on September 7 based on Mark 1:1-8 and Matthew 3:1-12, considers how repentance, as proclaimed by John the Baptizer, leads to community. Matthew 1:18–2:23 provides the background for "The Birth of a New Community," the lesson for September 14 that considers who Jesus is and the role he will play in the new community. On September 21 we move to the familiar Sermon on the Mount of Matthew 5:1–7:29 to investigate "Core Values of the New Community," where Jesus teaches us what it means to be happy or blessed. This unit ends on September 28 with a study of Matthew 20:1-28 and Mark 10:35-45 in a lesson entitled "Creating a Community of Servants," in which Jesus teaches about true greatness.

Unit 2, "The Development and Work of the New Community," includes four lessons that focus on the ministry of the new community. "Empowered to Be a Community," the session for October 5 that delves into Acts 2, looks at how the community is united by the Holy Spirit that comes in power on the day of Pentecost. On October 12, we turn to Acts 6:1-15 and 8:1-8 to see the "Expansion of the Community" as the church selects servant leaders who can delegate responsibilities and handle conflict. "Transformed to Witness to the Community," the lesson for October 19 from Acts 9:1-31, recounts Paul's life-changing experience on the Damascus road. In Acts 13 on October 26, we see Barnabas and Saul "Commissioned by the Community" for the work to which the Holy Spirit had called them.

The five lessons of Unit 3, "The New Community Faces Growing Pains," highlight some of the struggles of the early Christian community. The background for November 2 from 1 Corinthians 12:3-21 and Ephesians 4:1-16 illustrates diverse people "Fitting Into the Community." We explore another epistle, Galatians 2:11–3:29, on November 9 as we witness "Conflict in the Community." "Communion With God in the Midst of Struggle," the lesson from Philippians 3:3–4:9 on November 16, encourages Christians to support one another. On November 23, we examine 2 Timothy 2:1-3 and 4:1-5 in the lesson "Witness of the Community" to spotlight the need for a strong Christian witness. The unit concludes on November 30 with "Persecution Within the Community," a session based on 2 Corinthians 11:16–12:10 that explores the inevitability of facing difficulties in the Christian life and the reliability of God's grace.

MEET OUR WRITER

THE REVEREND JOHN INDERMARK

John Indermark received a B.A. in history from St. Louis University and a Master of Divinity degree from Eden Seminary. He now lives in southwest Washington state with his wife, Judy. John retired from pastoral ministry in the United Church of Christ to pursue a ministry of writing full time. He writes for several Christian education curriculum resources, *The New International Lesson Annual* and *Seasons of the Spirit* among others, and authors devotional books for Upper Room Books. Tentatively entitled *Hope: Our Longing for Home,* John's most recent book will be published in the fall of 2008.

THE BIG PICTURE:
THE NEW TESTAMENT
COMMUNITY

The course title may be slightly misleading, if in reading it you enter this quarter presuming the New Testament arises out of or reflects the experience of only one community. Even if we were to rephrase the title as "The New Testament Church," we might also imagine the Gospels and Epistles grew out of and addressed a unified community that did not change or reveal divisions until much later. It is not so.

The New Testament Community and Judaism

To begin with, the foundational community from which the church arose and with which it was in ongoing dialogue is first-century Judaism. Jesus was born a Jew, not a Christian. The initial two lessons of this quarter (more on them later) make strong associations with that Jewish past with the ministry of John the Baptizer and Matthew's relating the birth narrative of Jesus through the prism of Hebrew Scriptures fulfilled. When the second unit explores the story of Acts, the dynamic relationship between church and synagogue (not as yet separated) forms a key undercurrent. Again, more will be said of this later in this introduction.

So, to speak of the New Testament community or church is to first and foremost place it in the context of its Jewish moorings and traditions. Paul almost always initiates his mission activity, even in Gentile territories, among the Diaspora ("scattered") Jews in their eastern Mediterranean synagogues.

The first four of our lessons all include passages from the Gospel of Matthew. Christian scholarship has been advanced by the recognition that the Gospels themselves were addressed to particular Christian communities. The needs and issues faced by those communities find reflection in the differing styles and themes of each Gospel. For example, Matthew's Gospel reveals more than any other a profound interest in identifying Jesus as the fulfillment of Hebrew Scriptures and sometimes even Hebrew characters. So it is that Matthew portrays Jesus as a new "Moses" in the teaching of a new "law" in the Sermon on the Mount (parallel to Moses' ascending Sinai to receive the commandments).

Does that merely indicate Matthew has a personal obsession with things Jewish—or, more likely, is it an indicator that Matthew sees his community needing to establish their understanding of faith and covenant in continuity with the faith and covenant of Israel? Some scholars see Matthew's community as locked in a fervent debate with synagogue Judaism after the destruction of the Temple and the failure of the Zealot revolt over the future of Judaism. It was not a given that the church and synagogue must separate. In contrast, Luke shows little corresponding interest with connections to Judaism while frequently providing stories where Jesus ministers to and accepts outsiders, whether women or Samaritans or even Gentiles (for example, the centurion at the crucifixion who confesses Jesus' innocence). Based on such evidence, many commentators suggest that Luke's community was far less influenced by ties with Judaism, likely a largely Gentile community that hoped to establish positive relations within the Roman Empire.

The First-Generation New Testament Communities

The earliest Christian communities were not those addressed by the Gospels. Most scholarship attributes the earliest Gospel compilation (most likely Mark) to somewhere in the early 60s to about 70 of the first century, with the other three coming after the destruction of Jerusalem in the year 70. Some scholars contend Matthew and John were not written or compiled until much closer to the end of the first century. By then, the eyewitnesses to the life and ministry of Jesus had largely passed on, and the church was in its second and even third generation of followers. Indeed, one of the forces for gathering stories of the life and teachings of Jesus would have been the simple desire to preserve an oral tradition whose original speakers had long since passed.

And while the Book of Acts tells the story of the church's beginnings and early years, it too would have been compiled sometime after Paul's imprisonment and most likely after his death in the mid-60s of the first century—and perhaps, like the later Gospels, not until after the destruction of the Temple and the rise of synagogue Judaism. So the earliest writings are the epistles of Paul—and the earliest Christian communities are those to whom his letters were addressed.

In this quarter, the unit on Acts precedes the unit drawn from a variety of writings by or at least attributed to Paul. The excerpts taken from Acts in the second unit all narrate the period before Paul would have been writing. But it is important to remember that the "snapshots" of Christian communities in Ephesus or Galatia or Philippi or Corinth all come from times preceding the time when Acts was finally put together.

The diverse nature of those communities is evidenced in Paul's different styles in addressing them. The Galatian churches (and they likely were more than one community) tested Paul's patience. The polite introductions and words of thanksgiving that usually take up the entire first chapters in Paul's other correspondence are given a cursory note in the first five verses of Galatians. For already in verse 6 of Galatians 1, Paul wades into the controversies and conflicts that generated its writing: "I am astonished that you are so quickly deserting the one who called you in the grace of Christ and are turning to a different gospel." Philippians, on the other hand, is a largely endearing letter written to a community to whom Paul is closely attached. His letter to Corinth, particularly the portion used in this unit, is filled with sarcasm and a style of boasting that can be extremely off-putting if not held in context with the level of opposition and personal attack he is addressing.

So what does all this mean? Care needs to be taken about too easily characterizing the early Christian community as everywhere and always the same. It was not. Or, should I say, *they* were not. The Christian communities even at these early times reveal a remarkable diversity of character and interests—and, yes, errors. For example, Ephesians 4 would not need to dwell on the church as the body of Christ where all parts worked together and all members exercised their particular gifts if that metaphor of community were already perfectly engaged.

The very diversity of that early church makes these writings and the communities who evoked them so relevant to our own times. For when Paul or John the Baptizer or Jesus addresses the community who would respond to the gospel, those words are not spoken to idealized gatherings that have nothing in common with our all-too-human experiences of church and community. Rather, those words and stories directly engage our own struggles, as they did the folks in those formative times.

But for now, let us turn to each of the units to be covered, along with the texts and themes with which they will explore "The New Testament Community"—and our communities.

The Birth of a New Community

The four lessons in this unit use texts drawn primarily from Matthew's Gospel to explore the beginnings of Christian community. But please note: This does not mean the unit leads off with the story of Pentecost and what is often termed as the birth of the church. Instead, it opens with the voice of John the Baptizer crying out in the wilderness. The fundamental word of this prophet who prepares the way for the Christ and the community who would follow is "repent." Christian community begins in a turning away and a turning toward. The Greek word for repent literally means "a change in mind." Christian community finds its first stirrings in a willingness to change our minds from the status quo to the new ways of God among us—whether in first-century Israel or twenty-first-century America.

The remaining lessons in this unit lift up the birth and teachings of Jesus. Christian community is not a theoretical construct of community relationships. It is, first and foremost, a relationship with the God who has come and been revealed to us in Jesus of Nazareth. The birth story reminds us that Christian community, as with the One we follow, has humble origins. Pride and privilege stand in opposition to the nature of life in Christian community. That theme continues in the exploration of Jesus' Beatitudes. The ones Jesus reveals to be blessed of God bear little resemblance to the ones the wider culture, then and now, considers blessed. Christian community is called to a dramatic new view and practice of what constitutes the much misunderstood term of "happiness." The unit closes with an exclamation point to the humility and countercultural understandings of community in Christ by narrating an encounter between Jesus and the disciples over what makes for "greatness" in such community: service.

The Development and Work of the New Community

This second unit turns to narratives from the Acts to look at how the Christian community developed and ministered after Jesus' ascension. Some have wisely noted that Acts of the Apostles, as this book is called, might rightly be renamed Acts of the Spirit. For constant through all of its texts, including but not limited to those used in the four lessons of this unit, is the witness to the workings of God's Spirit in and through the early Christian communities in Jerusalem and beyond.

The first lesson, understandably in a study on Christian community, takes up the narrative of Pentecost. Empowerment of community by the Spirit is the theme of this lesson. The next lesson skips ahead to portions of the story about the setting aside of deacons to assist the apostles and, in particular, the work and person of Stephen. The theme of this session touches not only upon the expansion of the community that makes such divisions of labor necessary but also the qualities of leadership in the community as exemplified by Stephen. The third lesson, in one sense, returns to the quarter's opening text on repentance. It explores the story of Saul's conversion on the road to Damascus. Christian community, because of the experience of repentance ("change of mind") and the work of Spirit, is fundamentally transformative. Our lives are meant to be changed by encounter with Christ and empowerment by the Spirit. Christian community is continually renewed and changed itself by incorporation of those who have been (and are being!) transformed. The final session reveals a fundamental truth about Christian community: We do not live to merely be gathered in—we live to be sent out. The life of Christian community is never for its own sake alone but for the sake of bringing the gospel's word and hope and grace and service to the world around us. We are commissioned.

The selection of these texts from Acts reveals steady expansion of the gospel, fulfilling the words spoken by Jesus in Acts 1:8 to be "witnesses" to "the ends of the earth." By the time Acts concludes, Paul will have arrived at the center of the then-known world, Rome. But between the stories selected, and even between their lines, it is clear that such expansion and witness and community do not come easily, nor without controversy or conflict. Sometimes the difficulties arise from other communities: the Roman Empire and its culture of power; growing dissension with some in Judaism; and last but not least, by divisions within the church(es) of Christ. All of which leads to our concluding unit.

The New Community Faces Growing Pains

The concluding five lessons of this quarter focus on struggles experienced by and within the early Christian communities. Each of these lessons uses a passage from one of Paul's Epistles to look at a different dimension of such struggles. A word is in order about the five epistles from which these texts are drawn. Paul did not sit down and write his epistles at one time. They come from different times in his ministry. And the nature of the communities addressed differs as well. Philippians appears to be addressed to a particular congregation. The Corinthian correspondence, while consisting of two epistles, is considered by some to be composed of at least four and maybe five separate letters addressed to one or more congregations in that locale. Galatians was written to a collection of churches in a region. Ephesians is widely viewed as a "cover" letter to be circulated among various churches (some early manuscripts of the epistle omit the opening verse, which is the only reference specific to Ephesus). Timothy was addressed to an individual—and while some question its Pauline authorship, the very personal nature of some of its passages weigh in to support at least their origin with Paul.

The lessons based on the Ephesian and Philippian passages have the least amount of overt conflict apparent in the narrative. Rather, they offer guidelines for the interconnection of Christian community, the importance of exercising our Spirit-given gifts, and the significance of communion with God in living out the call of Christian community. The lesson based on the Timothy passage deals in largely positive terms with the call to serve as a faithful witness, though it does lift up the experience of finding that witness opposed by those who seek a religion centered more on selfish desires. The other two lessons, from Galatians and 2 Corinthians, deal with conflict and controversy in Christian community far more bluntly. While leaving the opponents (one also might say rival communities) unnamed, these epistles mince no words in the importance of holding to matters of principle in faith, precisely for the sake of community.

In Conclusion

These narratives and explorations of "The New Testament Community" are interesting and fascinating. However, the point of these studies is *not* to make you and those who will be joining you in these studies more knowledgeable students of first-century Christianity. Rather, the importance of this quarter is to draw the experiences of early Christian community(ies) into the community of faith in which you and your companions are immersed, both in terms of local congregation and the church in its wider connections.

There is an adage that those who do not learn from history will be doomed to repeat its mistakes. This quarter's corollary to that, more positively stated, is deepening our understanding of the New Testament community(ies) may provide critical insights into life and renewal in twenty-first-century Christian community. Local churches and the body of Christ today benefit from remembering where—and who—we have come from. The birthing of Christian community continues among us. The development and work of the church remains our calling as Christ's followers and servants. And while growing pains in Christian community will likely be with us until the coming of God's sovereign realm, we need not lose heart. Such struggles are signs not to give up, but to press on: in service, toward renewal, energized by the Spirit of hope given to us in Jesus Christ.

CLOSE-UP:
CREATING AND SUSTAINING
COMMUNITY

All of this quarter's sessions emphasize the theme of community in the context of the New Testament. "Community" was hardly a new idea, but the values and relationships within the Christian community would contrast sharply with those of the surrounding culture.

In the first unit, we see how John the Baptizer announced the values of the coming community, one that would truly be the kingdom of heaven come near to us on earth in the person of Jesus. As the one who is "God with us," Jesus becomes the shepherd of this new community, to lead by example and ultimately to be the one to save us from our sins. He teaches that the way we can find true happiness is to seek first God's kingdom and righteousness. The way we do this, however, is not self-aggrandizing or self-serving. Privilege, power, and status are definitely not valued in this community. Rather, as members of Christ's community, the path to greatness is trod by serving others.

At Christ's ascension, he promises that the Holy Spirit will empower his disciples (Acts 1:8). And, it is in the sending of the Spirit on Pentecost, as we explore in the second unit, that the community really begins to form. Timid disciples, once hiding for fear that they would meet the same fate as Jesus, are now proclaiming to all who will listen—even in their own native languages—the wonderful deeds of God. Listeners are so captivated by the message that they commit themselves to Christ. They too want to share in this fellowship. They too want to use their gifts for whatever ministry the Holy Spirit calls and equips them to undertake. Even the persecutor Saul is overcome by the Spirit to the point that he completely devotes the remainder of his life to the upbuilding of the community. The community commissions Saul, soon to be known as Paul, and Barnabas to go forth in the name of the community for the sake of Christ to spread the good news.

As the community grows, it faces challenges, as we see in the third unit. It becomes more diverse. Differences of opinion and conflicts arise, but the bottom line is that within this community, known as the body of Christ, there is unity in the midst of diversity. Members realize the value of supporting one another, even as strife swirls around them. Some tension, of course, buffets from outside the church, but other conflict is rooted within the faith community. Sincere Christians then, as now, have different perspectives on issues and sometimes, as now, have trouble settling their disputes and moving forward. But they obviously learn their lessons—or the church would not exist two millennia later. A major reason why the church continues to thrive is that people kept telling the story around the globe and across generational lines. And the church continues to be blessed with the "Pauls" throughout the ages who willingly suffer for the faith and for the Savior in whom they entrust their mortal and eternal lives.

Provide an opportunity for the students to discuss how they perceive their own faith community to be sustaining itself and inviting others into the fold.

FAITH IN ACTION: LIVING IN THE CRISTIAN COMMUNITY

As we see in the sessions for this quarter, the Christian community is not something that *we* have created; but rather Jesus himself created it. He is the head of it, even as we are the body. The community is empowered by the Holy Spirit and called to live in unity as it spreads the gospel message to all and encourages them to respond as committed disciples. Even so, it is clear throughout the church's history from its beginning until today that community members are a diverse lot who not only use their gifts for witness and ministry but also must face internal conflict and persecution from the world.

How, then, can we live in community today? Consider this checklist to evaluate your own faith community. What other ideas would you add? Are there any you need to delete or modify? Work with the class to create a covenant for living together in community based on these ideas or others you have brainstormed. Note that the list is in no particular order; one idea is not intended to be more or less important than another. You and the class will need to decide how you want to word and order your own covenant.

We acknowledge that Christ is Lord of our individual lives and of this faith community.

We hold our commitment to Christ above all else.

We welcome all people, just as Christ did, and invite them to participate fully in the life of our congregation.

We educate our children, youth, and adults so that they may be biblically literate and aware of God's call on their lives.

We practice spiritual disciplines and other activities that enable us to become spiritually formed in the image of Christ.

We pattern our individual and corporate life as a church after the example of Christ.

We live as servant-leaders who extend hospitality and care to all.

We preach good news not only to those within our fold but also to those outside who need to hear good news: the poor and oppressed, the widow and the orphan.

We work to create peace and justice within our society.

We practice the great commandments Jesus teaches in Mark 12:29-31: to love God with all our heart, soul, mind, and strength, and to love our neighbors as ourselves.

We help one another to identify and use the gifts God has given us for the purpose of building up the kingdom.

We value the time, talents, and resources that each person has to share, for we know that all members are essential to the well-being of the whole body of Christ.

We pray for one another.

We rejoice with those who rejoice and weep with those who weep.

We treat one another with care and respect, even in the midst of conflict.

We live together with integrity so that what we profess we believe may be seen enacted in our daily lives.

UNIT 1: THE BIRTH OF A NEW COMMUNITY
A NEW COMMUNITY

PREVIEWING THE LESSON

Lesson Scripture: Mark 1:1-8; Matthew 3:1-3
Background Scripture: Mark 1:1-8; Matthew 3:1-12
Key Verse: Matthew 3:2

Focus of the Lesson:
People look for a place where they can belong. What kind of community fosters a sense of belonging? The new community about which John talked and to which Jesus called people was a community of love, acceptance, repentance, and forgiveness.

Goals for the Learners:
(1) to explore the beginnings of a new community that was announced by John and pioneered by Jesus.
(2) to recognize that the community of faith is a place where they belong or fit in.
(3) to identify ways they can be involved in this community and commit to take action.

Pronunciation Guide:
euaggelion (yoo ang ghel' ee on)
shub (shoob)

Supplies:
Bibles, newsprint and marker, paper and pencils, hymnals, optional colored pencils or crayons

---

READING THE SCRIPTURE

NRSV
Mark 1:1-8
¹The beginning of the good news of Jesus Christ, the Son of God.
²As it is written in the prophet Isaiah,
"See, I am sending my messenger ahead of you,
who will prepare your way;

NIV
Mark 1:1-8
¹The beginning of the gospel about Jesus Christ, the Son of God.
²It is written in Isaiah the prophet:
"I will send my messenger ahead of you,
who will prepare your way"—
³"a voice of one calling in the desert,

3 the voice of one crying out in the
  wilderness:
  'Prepare the way of the Lord,
  make his paths straight,' "
4John the baptizer appeared in the wilderness, proclaiming a baptism of repentance for the forgiveness of sins. 5And people from the whole Judean countryside and all the people of Jerusalem were going out to him, and were baptized by him in the river Jordan, confessing their sins. 6Now John was clothed with camel's hair, with a leather belt around his waist, and he ate locusts and wild honey. 7He proclaimed, "The one who is more powerful than I is coming after me; I am not worthy to stoop down and untie the thong of his sandals. 8I have baptized you with water; but he will baptize you with the Holy Spirit."

Matthew 3:1-3

1In those days John the Baptist appeared in the wilderness of Judea, proclaiming, 2**"Repent, for the kingdom of heaven has come near."** 3This is the one of whom the prophet Isaiah spoke when he said,
  "The voice of one crying out in
  the wilderness:
  'Prepare the way of the Lord,
  make his paths straight.' "

'Prepare the way for the Lord,
  make straight paths for him.' "

4And so John came, baptizing in the desert region and preaching a baptism of repentance for the forgiveness of sins. 5The whole Judean countryside and all the people of Jerusalem went out to him. Confessing their sins, they were baptized by him in the Jordan River. 6John wore clothing made of camel's hair, with a leather belt around his waist, and he ate locusts and wild honey. 7And this was his message: "After me will come one more powerful than I, the thongs of whose sandals I am not worthy to stoop down and untie. 8I baptize you with water, but he will baptize you with the Holy Spirit."

Matthew 3:1-3

1In those days John the Baptist came, preaching in the Desert of Judea 2and saying, **"Repent, for the kingdom of heaven is near."** 3This is he who was spoken of through the prophet Isaiah:

  "A voice of one calling in the desert,
  'Prepare the way for the Lord,
  make straight paths for him.' "

UNDERSTANDING THE SCRIPTURE

Mark 1:1. The Gospels of Mark and John do not begin with stories announcing or narrating Jesus' birth. Interestingly, Mark's first word is one of the first words in John: "beginning." In John, the "beginning" is the "Word." In Mark, the "beginning" is "good news" (in Greek, *euaggellion*, from which we get the English root *evangel-*). As Mark develops the meaning of this good news, he bears witness to the writing of prophets (1:2-3) as well as the proclamation of John (1:4) and Jesus (1:14-15). Note that some

manuscripts of Mark do not contain the closing phrase, "the Son of God."

Mark 1:2-3. In some ancient manuscripts of Mark, the attribution of the following quotation to Isaiah is broadened to "as it is written in the prophets." And while verse 3 is a quotation of Isaiah 40:3, verse 2 is not from Isaiah. The closest parallel is Malachi 3:1. By this time, Judaism had expectations of Elijah's return to usher in God's kingdom or prepare for God's Messiah. Associations of John the Baptizer (Matthew 11:13) or even

Jesus (Mark 6:15) with Elijah occur in the Gospels. "Wilderness" plays a large role in the Hebrew Scriptures. It is the place where Israel sojourned for forty years after the exodus, a place of preparation. It is also the place where God promised to lead the people through safely to bring deliverance after exile (Isaiah 40:3-4). Those links of wilderness with preparation and deliverance both play into this verse's function to introduce John's ministry.

Mark 1:4. To say John "appeared" brings the connotation of suddenness or surprise that will also hold consistent with Mark's narrating of Jesus' ministry. Mark gives John the honor of being the first to "proclaim"—elsewhere in Mark, that verb is largely used in reference to Jesus. It is an important recognition of John's place in the beginnings of Christian community. For in later years, both Jesus and John had communities that identified with them. To place John at the outset of the narrative as one who, like Jesus, proclaims strongly signals that Mark sought to establish continuity, not conflict, with those who still identified with John. Baptism as a washing with water that symbolically dealt with sin was not unique to John. Communities that we now associate with the Dead Sea Scrolls practiced ritual washings. The major difference is that, for John, the washing was a one-time event rather than a daily discipline. "Repentance" translates a Greek word that literally means "a change of mind." However, its parallel word in Hebrew and Old Testament texts simply means "to turn."

Mark 1:5-6. The wilderness of the Jordan River descended to the east of Judea and Jerusalem in a deep valley beneath sea level where the Jordan River empties into the Dead Sea. Mark does not distinguish here the identity of those who sought out John for baptism. The details of his rough dress may be another allusion to Elijah (see 2 Kings 1:8). Others suggest that the dress and especially John's diet represent what a poor nomad in the desert would have available.

Mark 1:7-8. John's proclamation now turns to the One whose way he has come to prepare, in keeping with the quotation of 1:2-3. Strength and might identify this coming One. John's confessed unworthiness may be heard to imply a purity and greatness about this other One. The final distinction has to do with baptism, the hallmark of John's ministry. To say that this other one will baptize with the Holy Spirit is open to various interpretations. The Old Testament prophets were associated with the movement of God's Spirit, and this may echo such connections. Yet, to baptize "with" the Holy Spirit suggests some directing of the Spirit. Even the prophets could not do that—it was the other way around. So this can also be heard as affirming something— and someone—never before encountered.

Matthew 3:1-3. *Please note: Today's texts closely parallel one another. The comments made now on Matthew's text will not repeat what has already been said regarding Mark. Rather, they will comment on where Matthew diverges from or adds to Mark.* Matthew has already narrated genealogy and then a birth account of Jesus. However, as in Mark, Matthew precedes the public ministry of Jesus with that of John the Baptizer. In verse 2, John's proclamation is linked with the nearness of "the kingdom of heaven." This is Matthew's choice of phrase for what in Mark and Luke is typically rendered "the kingdom of God." In Mark, that announcement of the nearness of God's kingdom had been made by Jesus (1:15). There, Jesus announces the Kingdom's nearness and then issues the call to repent. In Matthew 3:2, John reverses the order: "repent" comes first, then the news of the Kingdom's nearness.

Matthew 3:4-7. Initially, Matthew follows Mark almost verbatim. But Matthew diverges when he singles out the Pharisees and Sadducees. Pharisees represented those who looked to the tradition of law as the guide for life. The Sadducees were more closely associated with the ritual of the Temple. They certainly had differences between them. The strong language used against them by John ("brood of vipers") and repeated later by Jesus (Matthew 23:33) may also reflect the later animosity between Matthew's community and the Jewish community contemporary to it.

Matthew 3:8-10. The narrative of conflict continues as the theme of repentance is now linked to the works ("fruits") that follow it. The critique by John of the religious leadership centers on reliance on ancestry apart from works. In some ways, the critique John offers is one many Pharisees would have shared. Their meticulous concern for the

law sought to ensure a keeping of the law, not just in word but also in deed. The ancestry argument of John may actually be more accurate about the Sadducees, a party closely associated with the priests whose offices were hereditary.

Matthew 3:11-12. The harvest imagery John had used in the encouragement to "bear fruit" now comes to a stark warning. The one who is to come is the harvester. Wheat will be gathered. Chaff will be burned. The stakes of repentance take on a harsh tone.

INTERPRETING THE SCRIPTURE

The Beginning

Those who seek to work in words, written or spoken, understand the importance of the first words you offer. The best of such opening words set the stage for whatever else may follow. Readers and listeners will attend to such words and how they are—or are not—kept.

Mark does not open by telling the birth of the baby Jesus in ways, like Luke, that will portend the mission of this child and those among whom he will go. Mark begins with what the core of this Gospel will be about: good news. And not just any good news: It will be "the good news of Jesus Christ" (remembering that "Christ" is not Jesus' last name, but the title in Greek that corresponds to Messiah). It is no secret at the beginning who Jesus is, at least to the reader or listener. Mark's beginning also asserts that the preparation for this good news has been a poorly kept secret all along. Prophets like Isaiah were given to see it, and proclaim it, and write it, hundreds of years before. John the Baptizer holding forth in the wilderness is just one in a long line of reminders—only now, the time of promise

edges on that of fulfillment. That is why the "nearness" of the Kingdom is the key to John's and then Jesus' proclamation. The secret's not just out, it's here. It's beginning.

And it's still beginning, here and now. This "good news" is not just old news. If it is news at all, it is because gospel is being preached and prepared, lived and hoped today. Readers and listeners—and watchers—still wait to see if the church lives up to its beginning words . . . if it still has good news.

Turning and Baptism

Maybe you have seen them too. A cartoon pictures a robed and bearded man with a sandwich board strapped across the shoulders. "Repent, the end is near," it usually says. Walking in a crowded urban street, the figure looks like the loneliest one in town.

If that is your view of John the Baptizer, get over it. Even though he ministered in one of the most isolated and hard-to-get-to places in his country, he was by no means alone. The crowds came to him. Repentance was about not the end but the beginning of life.

"Repentance." As noted in Understanding the Scripture, its literal meaning is "a change of mind." But this is not the change of mind akin to a decision to wear a blue tie to the dinner rather than the red one I first thought of donning. This "change of mind" is more like an "ex-change of mind." A new mind, a fresh perspective—the way in which Paul would counsel: "Let the same mind be in you that was in Christ Jesus" (Philippians 2:5).

The word in Hebrew that is translated as or associated with repentance (*shub*) means "to turn." To change one's mind is not just an attitude adjustment. It is to turn one's life around. That becomes clearer in Luke's account of John's preaching, where John's instructions to those who come to be baptized get very practical. He counsels tax collectors and soldiers how to conduct their vocations and ordinary individuals how to share.

For John, what we call baptism is the ritual act that symbolized such turning. Two directions are always involved in turning. To turn away from one direction is by necessity to turn toward another. John does not counsel turning from some sins toward others. John baptizes as a symbol of turning from sin toward God. Faith is never limited or exhausted by what we turn from. The key is what (or whom) we turn toward. Turning toward defines what the new life will be, what the new mind will see and choose. John baptizes and turns folks toward the One whose way he prepares.

Repentance still does the same for us today.

Re-forming Community

This session in its title and focus aims at the theme of community. What do we see as the marks of that community in our passages? Two things stand out.

For starters, it is a community whose basis is good news. That is an important point, because you and I know some com-

munities get bogged down in bad news. Budgets. Declining memberships. This new generation. Blah. Blah. Blah. They say misery loves company, so perhaps a community grounded in bad news does have growth potential. But it will not be the good news community of John and Jesus.

That is not to say that Christian community must be "happy face" and see the world only through rose-colored glasses. Christian community is grounded in this world's realities—but it is also driven by the hope that John and Jesus are right about the nearness of God's realm. For in that nearness, our call is to live joyful and faithful lives in the midst of it all.

Second, ours is a community that is about repentance in the Hebrew sense of "turning" and the Greek meaning of "a change of mind." We are not static. Neither our feet nor our structures nor our ideas need cement piers holding us from any movement, as if inertia is the point of being church. We are followers, which means we are on the move. And on the change. We need to be open, as individuals and communities, to turnings. It's not just initiates who need turning from old ways and sin. Sometimes, they are the very ones who remind us that *we* need to consider God's call to repent and turn and take a new direction. Why? God is on the move, not in a religious museum.

The One Who Is Coming

God is on the move.

In *The Lion, the Witch, and the Wardrobe*, a book (and now movie) from C. S. Lewis's *Chronicles of Narnia*, the hope racing through the land and seen in the signs of winter changing to spring is that Aslan is on the move.

John the Baptizer understands and proclaims hope in just the same way: "The one who is more powerful than I is coming after me" (Mark 1:7). Faith is about hope, and it is about hope in something and someone larger than we are. For those of us with messiah complexes, who think the fate of the world rests on our shoulders, it is a humbling and comforting word. For those of us who think we run the world and get to have things our way without regard for ethics or love or the consequences levied upon future generations who follow our mischief and worse, it is a confrontational word.

Who is that One who is coming? What will be the qualities and characteristics of the realm that One brings then and seeks from us now in our practice of faith? Well, that is what the gospel, whose beginning you have just now touched on, goes on to reveal. For more details, attend to the words Jesus speaks and the actions Jesus does and the ways Jesus rebukes and the ones whom Jesus embraces. For in those stories, and in the choices all around us, we may encounter the One who has come, and comes now, and will come yet again.

SHARING THE SCRIPTURE

Preparing Our Hearts

Meditate on this week's devotional reading, found in 1 Peter 2:1-10. Here we see Peter's vision of what the church should be—"a chosen race, a royal priesthood, a holy nation" (2:9). Compare Peter's concept with churches you know. How does your church reflect Peter's vision? Where does it miss the mark? What can you do to make your church a more "spiritual house"?

Pray that you and the adult learners will be aware of what the church is supposed to be and then do all in your power to help it live into that vision.

Preparing Our Minds

Study the background from Mark 1:1-8 and Matthew 3:1-12 and the lesson Scripture from Mark 1:1-8 and Matthew 3:1-3. As you prepare, consider the kind of community that fosters a sense of belonging.

Write on newsprint:
❑ information for next week's lesson, found under "Continue the Journey."
❑ activities for further spiritual growth in "Continue the Journey."

Plan the optional lecture if you choose to use it for "Explore the Beginnings of a New Community That Was Announced by John and Pioneered by Jesus."

Locate art supplies if you choose to do the optional activity under "Explore the Beginnings of a New Community That Was Announced by John and Pioneered by Jesus."

Read the "Introduction" to the quarter, "The Big Picture," "Close-up," and "Faith in Action." Consider how you will use these supplements throughout the quarter.

LEADING THE CLASS

(1) Gather to Learn

❖ Welcome the class members and introduce any guests.

❖ Pray that all who have come today will experience a sense of belonging in this community of faith.

❖ Post a sheet of newsprint. Head the left side "I'm in" and the right side "I'm out." Encourage the students to brainstorm examples of attitudes and behaviors of other people that help them feel as if they belong and list those ideas on the left. Also ask the students to give examples of attitudes and behaviors exhibited that make them feel excluded from the community. List those on the right side.

❖ Ask these two questions:

(1) Which of these attitudes and behaviors, from either side of the list, most often characterize the

church? (Place a check next to each identified item.)

(2) How do these characteristics draw people to God—or push them away?

❖ Read aloud today's focus statement: **People look for a place where they can belong. What kind of community fosters a sense of belonging? The new community about which John talked and to which Jesus called people was a community of love, acceptance, repentance, and forgiveness.**

(2) Explore the Beginnings of a New Community That Was Announced by John and Pioneered by Jesus

❖ Choose a volunteer to read Mark 1:1-3 and someone else to read Matthew 3:1-3.

❖ Note similarities and differences between these two passages by reading or retelling information for Mark 1:1, 2-3 and Matthew 3:1-3 in Understanding the Scripture.

❖ Select someone to read Mark 1:4-8.

❖ Complete this chart with the class, or do so yourself in an optional lecture. If the class is large, assign a group to each question and ask them to report to the total class.

Who was John?	Where was he?
Why did he come?	What was his message?
How was he received?	

❖ Zoom in on the idea of "repentance" by reading or retelling "Turning and Baptism."

❖ **Option:** Distribute paper and colored pencils or crayons. Ask the students to use abstract images and colors to illustrate how repentance feels to them.

❖ Conclude this portion of the lesson by inviting the students to talk about how the community of faith fosters a sense of belonging. You may wish to look again at the ideas brainstormed in "Gather to Learn" to affirm those behaviors and attitudes that draw people into the church and consider ways of changing those behaviors and attitudes that push people away from the church.

(3) Recognize That the Community of Faith Is a Place Where They Belong or Fit In

❖ Invite class members to tell stories about how they became involved in this particular congregation. Some may be life-long members, but others may have visited at one time and decided to stay. Encourage each person to explain why he or she feels at home here.

❖ Work together or in groups to brainstorm ways that this class and congregation can make newcomers feel welcomed. List the ideas on newsprint. Here are some suggestions: *greet people they do not know; give a small gift from the church to visitors; send a "thank you letter" to visitors; make a visit in the home to someone new to the church.*

❖ Wrap up this section by pointing out that when we feel that we belong to the congregation we are able to extend hospitality to others so as to make them feel included as well.

(4) Identify Ways They Can Be Involved in This Community and Commit to Take Action

❖ Note that when people say a church is "cold" or "unfriendly," often the root of the problem is that they have not taken the time to get to know people or participate in activities beyond worship. Every church has to find ways to help its members—new and established—feel a part of the congregation.

❖ Distribute paper and pencils. Ask the students to list ways in which they participate in the life of the church. Certainly their involvement in this class is a place to start. They are not to sign their names.

❖ Collect the papers, shuffle them, and begin reading activities, perhaps two or three from each sheet, and more if time permits. This activity will help students become aware of opportunities for ministry and fellowship, including some that may be unfamiliar to them. It will also help the adults recognize the gifts and talents of classmates.

❖ Invite students who are willing to commit themselves to new or continued involvement in the life of this faith community to raise their hands. Ask volunteers to state at least one action they will take on behalf of the community.

(5) Continue the Journey

❖ Pray that the students will go forth knowing that they are loved and accepted in this faith community and that their participation is crucial to the life of it.

❖ Read aloud this preparation for next week's lesson. You may also want to post it on newsprint for the students to copy.

- **Title: The Birth of a New Community**
- **Background Scripture: Matthew 1:18–2:23**
- **Lesson Scripture: Matthew 1:18-25; 2:13-15**
- **Focus of the Lesson: Regardless of the nature of our humble beginnings, we want to know that life has significance and value. What** community offers value and significance to those who, in the world's eyes, may seem insignificant? The new community, as exemplified in Jesus, provides a place where all people have value and significance.

❖ Challenge the students to complete one or more of these activities for further spiritual growth, which you will write on newsprint for the students to copy.

(1) **Think about repentance as a "change of mind." How does your mind need to be changed in order to be more Christ-like? What action will you take?**

(2) **Do whatever you can to draw a new member or visitor into the life of your congregation. Help this person feel welcomed and included.**

(3) **Participate in a church activity this week. Evaluate how such an activity enables you to feel connected to the faith community.**

❖ Sing or read aloud "We Are the Church."

❖ Conclude today's session by leading the class in this benediction, adapted from Ephesians 4:4-6: **Let us now depart rejoicing in the community we share, united as one body, with one Spirit, one Lord, one faith, one baptism, and one God and Father of all.**

UNIT 1: THE BIRTH OF A NEW COMMUNITY

THE BIRTH OF A NEW COMMUNITY

PREVIEWING THE LESSON

Lesson Scripture: Matthew 1:18-25; 2:13-15
Background Scripture: Matthew 1:18–2:23
Key Verse: Matthew 2:6

Focus of the Lesson:
Regardless of the nature of our humble beginnings, we want to know that life has significance and value. What community offers value and significance to those who, in the world's eyes, may seem insignificant? The new community, as exemplified in Jesus, provides a place where all people have value and significance.

Goals for the Learners:
(1) to review the story of Jesus' birth as the beginning of the new community.
(2) to discover their value and significance in the community of faith.
(3) to identify their unique gifts and use them in service in the community.

Pronunciation Guide:
Ahaz (ay' haz)   Ramah (ray' muh)
almah (al maw')   *Yeshua* (yesh oo' aw)
Archelaus (ahr kuh lay' uhs)   Zealot (zel' uht)
Balaam (bay' luhm)   Zoroastrian (zoh roh as' tree uhn)

Supplies:
Bibles, newsprint and marker, paper and pencils, hymnals

READING THE SCRIPTURE

NRSV
Matthew 1:18-25

¹⁸Now the birth of Jesus the Messiah took place in this way. When his mother Mary had been engaged to Joseph, but before they

NIV
Matthew 1:18-25

¹⁸This is how the birth of Jesus Christ came about: His mother Mary was pledged to be married to Joseph, but before they

lived together, she was found to be with child from the Holy Spirit. [19]Her husband Joseph, being a righteous man and unwilling to expose her to public disgrace, planned to dismiss her quietly. [20]But just when he had resolved to do this, an angel of the Lord appeared to him in a dream and said, "Joseph, son of David, do not be afraid to take Mary as your wife, for the child conceived in her is from the Holy Spirit. [21]She will bear a son, and you are to name him Jesus, for he will save his people from their sins." [22]All this took place to fulfill what had been spoken by the Lord through the prophet:
[23] "Look, the virgin shall conceive
    and bear a son,
    and they shall name him Emmanuel,"
which means, "God is with us." [24]When Joseph awoke from sleep, he did as the angel of the Lord commanded him; he took her as his wife, [25]but had no marital relations with her until she had borne a son; and he named him Jesus.

Matthew 2:6, 13-15
[6] 'And you, Bethlehem, in the land
        of Judah,
    are by no means least among the
        rulers of Judah;
    for from you shall come a ruler
        who is to shepherd my
        people Israel.'"
[13]Now after they had left, an angel of the Lord appeared to Joseph in a dream and said, "Get up, take the child and his mother, and flee to Egypt, and remain there until I tell you; for Herod is about to search for the child, to destroy him." [14]Then Joseph got up, took the child and his mother by night, and went to Egypt, [15]and remained there until the death of Herod. This was to fulfill what had been spoken by the Lord through the prophet, "Out of Egypt I have called my son."

came together, she was found to be with child through the Holy Spirit. [19]Because Joseph her husband was a righteous man and did not want to expose her to public disgrace, he had in mind to divorce her quietly.

[20]But after he had considered this, an angel of the Lord appeared to him in a dream and said, "Joseph son of David, do not be afraid to take Mary home as your wife, because what is conceived in her is from the Holy Spirit. [21]She will give birth to a son, and you are to give him the name Jesus, because he will save his people from their sins."

[22]All this took place to fulfill what the Lord had said through the prophet: [23]"The virgin will be with child and will give birth to a son, and they will call him Immanuel"— which means, "God with us."

[24]When Joseph woke up, he did what the angel of the Lord had commanded him and took Mary home as his wife. [25]But he had no union with her until she gave birth to a son. And he gave him the name Jesus.

Matthew 2:6, 13-15
[6] " 'But you, Bethlehem, in the land of
        Judah,
    are by no means least among the
        rulers of Judah;
    for out of you will come a ruler
        who will be the shepherd of my
        people Israel.'"
[13]When they had gone, an angel of the Lord appeared to Joseph in a dream. "Get up," he said, "take the child and his mother and escape to Egypt. Stay there until I tell you, for Herod is going to search for the child to kill him."

[14]So he got up, took the child and his mother during the night and left for Egypt, [15]where he stayed until the death of Herod. And so was fulfilled what the Lord had said through the prophet: "Out of Egypt I called my son."

UNDERSTANDING THE SCRIPTURE

Matthew 1:18-21. Matthew shows the greatest interest among the four Gospels in portraying the life and ministry of Jesus as fulfilling the Hebrew Scriptures. Here, Matthew opens the birth narrative by identifying Jesus as the Messiah. The title comes from a Hebrew word meaning "anointed one." Anointing was a ritual associated with kings in Judaism. The Jewish expectations of Messiah mingled political and military hopes of a promised leader who would usher in God's realm. The betrothal or engagement between Mary and Joseph was a formal relationship prior to marriage. Infidelity by one of the partners during the time of betrothal was equivalent to adultery, and could be punished with death. Joseph's decision to not expose Mary to disgrace indicates righteousness that moves beyond the letter of the law to its life-seeking spirit. The (first) dream of Joseph evokes remembrance of his namesake in the Hebrew Scriptures. The name Jesus comes from the Hebrew *Yeshua*, whose meaning is "Yahweh saves or helps."

Matthew 1:22-25. Verses 22-23 serve as the first of many quotations and allusions in Matthew from the Hebrew Scriptures. The source is Isaiah 7:14. The original context had to do with a promise to King Ahaz that Judah would be delivered from a threat posed by war (Isaiah 7:15-16). Ironically, this promise was given because the king refused to ask for a sign that would evoke his trust in God. Much controversy surrounds the meaning of the Hebrew word *almah*, translated variously as "virgin" or "young woman." It can mean either. Matthew's extensive use of Hebrew Scriptures in his Gospel might be both to familiarize his community with Jesus' moorings in the Hebrew Scriptures and to make the point to some Jewish opponents that the community who followed Jesus stood solidly within the traditions of Judaism.

Matthew 2:1-8. Several Herods appear in the Gospels and later in Acts. This is the first of them, Herod the Great. King Herod was renowned for his building program in Judah, including the Temple of Jesus' day. Herod was also ruthless in his elimination of enemies, even when it came to his own family members. "Wise men" translates *magi*. Magi were not kings, but priests, astrologers, and perhaps Zoroastrians from Persia. The association of a star with a Jewish king may have come from Numbers 24:17, wherein Balaam states in an oracle, "a star shall come out of Jacob." Herod's fear would be of a rival to the throne. The fear of "all Jerusalem with him" would likely be spurred by concern over how far Herod's reprisal against such a threat to the throne might reach. Verses 5-6 quote Micah 5:2, a passage that had come to be interpreted by this time with the promise of God's Messiah. The secrecy of Herod's call for the magi (2:7) hints that his expressed words are not all what they seem.

Matthew 2:9-12. The passage now moves into the realm of mystery. What does it mean for the "star" to stop over the location of Jesus? And was this a star, or as some have argued, an unusual planetary conjunction? And how exactly did the magi recognize the child, or understand that the star singled out one particular house? Matthew does not give us explanations. He offers witness. And the witness is that these Gentile visitors (a key point in this Gospel dominated by Jewish thought) come and worship Jesus. The number of gifts may be the source for later attempts to number the magi at three, a detail Matthew does not provide. More clear than the number of magi is the symbolism of their gifts. Gold, then as now, was a symbol of wealth. Frankincense was a resin burned as incense in worship. Myrrh was used in embalming. Their dream of warning is the second of six times (1:20; 2:12, 13, 19, 22; 27:19) in which dreams play key roles in the narrative of Matthew. Ironically, the one time a dream is not followed is Matthew 27:19, where Pilate ignores the dream of his wife to have nothing to do with the condemnation of Jesus.

Matthew 2:13-15. These verses describe what has sometimes been labeled the "flight to Egypt." On the surface, it appears to simply allow for the inclusion of the quotation in verse 15 from Hosea 11:1. More ominously, it sets the stage to explain why Herod's murderous actions in the following verses do not succeed.

Matthew 2:16. This verse relates the account of the "slaughter of the innocents." There is no attestation to this event outside of this verse in Matthew. On the other hand, there is absolutely nothing in this verse that contradicts the character of Herod. The murder of one wife and several sons reveals the capability of Herod to order the murders of some peasant children in a small town out of the public's eye. The detail of "two years old or under" makes clear that the magi did not show up right after the shepherds left, as Christmas pageants sometimes imply. The provisioning for such a long journey, plus the trip itself, would have taken many months, even after a decision to do so had been finally reached.

Matthew 2:17-23. The opening quotation is from Jeremiah 31:15. Rachel had been the mother of Joseph. She had died after giving birth to Benjamin. Jeremiah's original context for this verse was to symbolically express Rachel's grieving for her "children" led away into captivity and exile in Jeremiah's time. Ramah is, according to one tradition, the site of Rachel's burial. Another two dreams of Joseph, the husband of Mary, move the narrative forward. The first signals the return from Egypt made possible by the death of Herod. Herod died in 4 B.C., which reading back from the "two years old or younger" detail in the earlier verse would place Jesus' birth sometime around the year 7 or 6 B.C. The second dream directs Joseph and Mary to settle with the child in Galilee. Their home in Nazareth allows for the closing quotation, although the exact source remains unclear.

INTERPRETING THE SCRIPTURE

Birth Stories

Birth stories, then and now, sometimes are told in a way to hint at qualities of character yet to come. In the prelude to this birth, the story reveals that Joseph faces a predicament. His betrothed has, to all appearances, betrayed him sexually. She is pregnant. The law called for her to be stoned to death (Deuteronomy 22:23-27). Compassion called for her to be quietly dismissed without a scandal, which is the direction toward which Joseph is generously headed. Grace speaks to Joseph in a dream and says "do not be afraid" (1:20). In the end, Joseph acts graciously. In doing so, we find a clue as to how this child will one day act.

Birth stories are also about naming. Naming in the Hebrew tradition was strikingly important. Naming could reflect if not at times bestow identity. Naming could open the possibility of being called by another, as in God's critical decision to disclose the Holy Name to Moses at the burning bush, so that Israel could know and call on the name of the One who would deliver them (Exodus 3:14). The naming of this child is simple but profound. *Yeshua* was a common name in first-century Judaism. Perhaps it was common because of the hope it literally meant: "Yahweh helps" or "Yahweh saves." The importance of this name for Joseph and Mary's child is not its uniqueness but its shared dream of God's deliverance. And dreams, as we shall see, loom large in Matthew, for out of the following of dreams comes life.

Messiah and Emmanuel

Sometimes we say "Jesus Christ" as if "Christ" were his last name. It is not. "Christ" is the Greek word that corresponds to the Hebrew "Messiah." In the opening verse of today's narrative, Matthew affirms Jesus to be the Messiah, the Christ.

And who was the Messiah? Judaism expected a promised leader who would deliver them from their enemies and usher in God's realm. Traditions also connected this figure with the Davidic line of kingship. In first-century Judaism, expectations of Messiah were multiple. Groups such as the Zealots anticipated a military leader who would violently throw out the Romans and establish an independent Jewish state. Some Jews separated themselves from the religious establishment in Jerusalem and created communities in the Dead Sea wilderness. Among them, as reflected in some of their writings discovered in the Dead Sea Scrolls, expectations of Messiah sometimes blended those militaristic views along with ritualistic purity.

All hopes of Messiah centered on God's future reign. The differences arose in what Messiah would do to accomplish that. Those divergent opinions may contribute to why Jesus often sought to stifle the word that he is the Messiah, for the title meant many things to many people. In some ways, the title would lock Jesus into a particular identity that was not truly his. Jesus' life and ministry dictated who Messiah is, not the other way around.

The other title Matthew links to Jesus in the birth narrative is "Emmanuel," "God with us." The title comes from Isaiah 7. There, the promise of Emmanuel offered the promise of God's presence in a time of crisis in Judah's life. The presence of God had been experienced in various ways in Israel's stories: the burning bush, the cloud and fire that led Israel through the wilderness, the ark of the covenant. So Emmanuel, for Isaiah, comes from a long tradition of understanding how God comes among the people.

The birth story in Matthew draws on that tradition to identify Jesus as Emmanuel, the promise of God with us. How exactly will God be with us in Jesus; what will Jesus do as Messiah? Those are the matters that Matthew takes up in the narratives of Jesus' life and ministry, death and raising. For the time being, Matthew simply names what—and who—those narratives will reveal.

Following Dreams

The promise of "God with us" may help explain a curious but critical set of occurrences in the infancy and childhood stories of Jesus: dreams. Joseph dreams and takes Mary as his wife. The magi dream and spoil Herod's plan. Joseph dreams again and saves the child from Herod. Joseph dreams again and returns to Israel. Joseph dreams again and settles in Galilee to escape Herod's son Archelaus. Why dreams?

Following dreams has roots in the Hebrew Scriptures, and Matthew is prone to relate his Gospel in the light of its precedents. Joseph (of the coat of many colors) dreamed and rose to power in Egypt to be in a position to save life. Daniel dreamed and found his life delivered by God.

Dreams represent a time when we are not in control. They are a time when minds and spirits drift—and may in ways we are not aware of be even more open to the presence of God with us. In Matthew's Gospel, dreams become the vehicle for God to enter this drama and move the characters in saving ways.

In our time, we unfortunately view the word "dreamer" too often as someone with his or her head in the clouds, out of touch with reality. Biblically speaking, though, a dreamer is one who is, in truth, in touch with the Holy. And those who follow dreams prove to be the wisest of all, for they entrust themselves and those they love to the guidance and safe-keeping of God.

Community

The theme of this session is about a community, even as it illustrates its humble beginning in Jesus. "Humble" is an apt word. At the beginning, the faithful community is composed of a would-be husband who ignores the law's demands for justice to follow a dream of acceptance and grace. The faithful community is then joined by the outsiders not only to the Jewish nation but even to Judaism itself. Foreign Gentile magi are, in Matthew, the first to worship Jesus and then, like Joseph, follow a dream rather than obey a tyrant.

And even though Matthew 2:16-18 is omitted in today's lesson Scripture, make no mistake: The faithful community is then joined by the innocents of Bethlehem, martyred by Herod's infantile rage. To overlook them is to ignore the Gospel's harder questions for community. Where is God when innocents suffer? What can the community of Jesus do in subsequent times when innocents are threatened? What dreams must be followed, or risked, then?

The beginning is humble: explicitly for Jesus, implicitly for the community who will follow him. Jesus does not return from Egypt to assume the throne in Jerusalem. He goes to live in a minor town (Nazareth) in an isolated province (Galilee). John's Gospel records the incident where Nathaniel says, in hearing where Jesus hails from, "Can anything good come out of Nazareth?" (John 1:46). It is a legitimate question of Jesus, of Jesus' community: Can anything good come out of [fill in the name of your church]? The benefit of humble beginnings is that they provide the possibility for startling and surprising developments. So it is with Jesus, and that becomes the gist of Matthew's narrative. Is it so with us? Our lives and communities will yield the answer.

SHARING THE SCRIPTURE

Preparing Our Hearts

Meditate on this week's devotional reading, found in Hosea 11:1-4. Here the prophet recalls Israel's sojourn in the wilderness by speaking of God as a parent who called Israel "out of Egypt." This idea echoes in Matthew's nativity story that we will study today. Ponder this image in verses 1-4. How might it prompt you to see God differently than you normally do? What layers of meaning does this image add to Matthew's account of Jesus' birth?

Pray that you and the adult learners will give thanks for Emmanuel, God with us, whose incarnation makes all the difference in people's lives.

Preparing Our Minds

Study the background from Matthew 1:18–2:23 and the lesson Scripture from Matthew 1:18-25 and 2:13-15. As you explore this session, think about a community that offers value and significance to those who, in the world's eyes, may seem insignificant.

Write on newsprint:
- ❏ information for next week's lesson, found under "Continue the Journey."
- ❏ activities for further spiritual growth in "Continue the Journey."

Prepare information from Matthew 2:1-12 from Understanding the Scripture to present as a lecture under "Review the Story of Jesus' Birth as the Beginning of the New Community."

LEADING THE CLASS

(1) Gather to Learn

❖ Welcome the class members and introduce any guests.

❖ Pray that all who have come today will feel connected to this church class.

❖ Read this story, which may be familiar to some students: **The ocean current washed up thousands of little sea horses on the beach. A child began throwing them back one at a time. Someone saw the youngster walking along the beach and throwing them back and asked, "What difference can you make among so many thousand?" The child picked up one sea horse, threw it in the water, and said, "A lot of difference for that one."**

❖ Discuss this question: **Where else do you see people acting in seemingly small but significant ways to make a difference in someone's life?**

❖ Read aloud today's focus statement: **Regardless of the nature of our humble beginnings, we want to know that life has significance and value. What community offers value and significance to those who, in the world's eyes, may seem insignificant? The new community, as exemplified in Jesus, provides a place where all people have value and significance.**

(2) Review the Story of Jesus' Birth as the Beginning of the New Community

❖ Choose a volunteer to read the nativity story from Matthew 1:18-25.

❖ Encourage the students to listen for a word a phrase that in some way touches them or makes the story come alive for them. After the reader has finished, invite the students to talk with the class or a small group about the phrases they selected and why these seemed so meaningful.

❖ Invite the students to look again at the passage to discern information about who this child was to be and what he was to do. Discuss their ideas.

❖ Read or retell "Messiah and Emmanuel" from Interpreting the Scripture.

❖ Use information for Matthew 2:1-12 from Understanding the Scripture as a brief lecture to fill in the blanks between the nativity story and the story of the flight to Egypt.

❖ Select someone to read Matthew 2:13-15.

- ■ Ask the class to call to mind other stories related to Egypt. (They may recall Joseph acting as the second in command to Pharaoh during seven years of plenty and seven years of famine [Genesis 41–47], the exodus from Egypt, and Hosea 11:1, which is quoted in Matthew 2:15.)
- ■ Invite the class to share their own experiences and beliefs about how God may guide us in dreams.

❖ Wrap up this portion of the session by pointing out that it was through the humble birth of Jesus that God began to do a new thing. Not only was a child born but also a community led by this child would soon take shape.

(3) Discover One's Value and Significance in the Community of Faith

❖ Note that when Jesus was born, most people had no idea that anyone of significance had come into the world. Likewise, we tend to think of ourselves as insignificant.

❖ **Option 1** (for classes where everyone knows one another): Divide into groups or work with the whole class if it is less than eight members. Hand out paper and pencils. Ask each adult to write his or her name at the top of the paper and then pass the paper to the left. Each person will write a gift that the person named on the paper exhibits or write a brief example to show how this person has made a difference in the lives of others. Follow the same process until the paper returns to its owner. Provide quiet time for each person to read and reflect on what has been written about him or her. The purpose of this activity is to remind students that they have significance for the church, even though they may not recognize their own value.

❖ **Option 2** (for large classes or classes where members are not well acquainted): Read the angel's words to Joseph: "Do not be afraid" (1:20). Talk in small groups about how the church, the community of faith, provides a safe place for people to interact and respond to God's grace. Invite the students to state how they are trying to use their own God-given gifts to make the church a place where people want to come and feel as if they belong because they have something to offer.

❖ Conclude this portion of the lesson by affirming that everyone is important to the community of faith.

(4) Identify Each Learner's Unique Gifts and Use Them in Service in the Community

❖ Distribute paper and pencils if you have not already done so. Ask each student to write at least two gifts that he or she feels has been given by God to build up the faith community. (If Option 1 in the previous section was used, the adults will already have some gifts listed on their sheets.)

❖ Ask the students to write a few words stating how they are currently using each of their gifts.

❖ Work in small groups to help the students add to their lists ways that their gifts can be used to glorify God within the church.

❖ Challenge each student to write a sentence or two stating how he or she is using and intends to use the gifts God has given. Encourage as many students as possible to include opportunities for ministries that are new to them.

❖ Provide time for students to seal these commitments by reading them to at least one other class member.

(5) Continue the Journey

❖ Pray that the participants will recognize that Jesus' humble birth led to the beginning of a new community of faith—the church—that we are called to participate in.

❖ Read aloud this preparation for next week's lesson. You may also want to post it on newsprint for the students to copy.

- ■ **Title: Core Values of the New Community**
- ■ **Background Scripture: Matthew 5:1–7:29**
- ■ **Lesson Scripture: Matthew 5:1-16**
- ■ **Focus of the Lesson: People search for happiness in many places, but they often find the opposite due to their wrong choices. Who teaches us to know true and lasting happiness? Through his teachings, Jesus described how to find true happiness.**

❖ Challenge the students to complete one or more of these activities for further spiritual growth, which you will write on newsprint for the students to copy.

(1) Check news media for stories demonstrating the interplay between faith and politics. How does faith challenge politics, just as Jesus' birth challenged Herod?

(2) Write in your spiritual journal about your understanding of "God with us." How is God present with you on a daily basis? How do you respond to God's presence?

(3) Formulate a mission statement for your life. Why are you here? What significance does your life have? How are you fulfilling your life's mission?

❖ Sing or read aloud "Emmanuel, Emmanuel."

❖ Conclude today's session by leading the class in this benediction, adapted from Ephesians 4:4-6: **Let us now depart rejoicing in the community we share, united as one body, with one Spirit, one Lord, one faith, one baptism, and one God and Father of all.**

UNIT 1: THE BIRTH OF A NEW COMMUNITY
CORE VALUES OF THE NEW COMMUNITY

PREVIEWING THE LESSON

Lesson Scripture: Matthew 5:1-16
Background Scripture: Matthew 5:1–7:29
Key Verse: Matthew 6:33

Focus of the Lesson:
People search for happiness in many places, but they often find the opposite due to their wrong choices. Who teaches us to know true and lasting happiness? Through his teachings, Jesus described how to find true happiness.

Goals for the Learners:
(1) to investigate Jesus' teachings about happiness.
(2) to relate Jesus' teachings on happiness to the definitions they often encounter.
(3) to identify one of Jesus' teachings and decide how to put it into practice.

Supplies:
Bibles, newsprint and marker, paper and pencils, hymnals, pictures of things that make people happy, tape or pushpins, optional Bible commentaries

---

READING THE SCRIPTURE

NRSV
Matthew 5:1-16
¹When Jesus saw the crowds, he went up the mountain; and after he sat down, his disciples came to him. ²Then he began to speak, and taught them, saying:
³"Blessed are the poor in spirit, for theirs is the kingdom of heaven.
⁴"Blessed are those who mourn, for they will be comforted.

NIV
Matthew 5:1-16
¹Now when he saw the crowds, he went up on a mountainside and sat down. His disciples came to him, ²and he began to teach them, saying:
³"Blessed are the poor in spirit,
    for theirs is the kingdom of heaven.
⁴Blessed are those who mourn,
    for they will be comforted.

5"Blessed are the meek, for they will inherit the earth.

6"Blessed are those who hunger and thirst for righteousness, for they will be filled.

7"Blessed are the merciful, for they will receive mercy.

8"Blessed are the pure in heart, for they will see God.

9"Blessed are the peacemakers, for they will be called children of God.

10"Blessed are those who are persecuted for righteousness' sake, for theirs is the kingdom of heaven.

11"Blessed are you when people revile you and persecute you and utter all kinds of evil against you falsely on my account. 12Rejoice and be glad, for your reward is great in heaven, for in the same way they persecuted the prophets who were before you.

13"You are the salt of the earth; but if salt has lost its taste, how can its saltiness be restored? It is no longer good for anything, but is thrown out and trampled under foot.

14"You are the light of the world. A city built on a hill cannot be hid. 15No one after lighting a lamp puts it under the bushel basket, but on the lampstand, and it gives light to all in the house. 16In the same way, let your light shine before others, so that they may see your good works and give glory to your Father in heaven.

Matthew 6:33

33But strive first for the kingdom of God and his righteousness, and all these things will be given to you as well.

5Blessed are the meek,
    for they will inherit the earth.
6Blessed are those who hunger and
        thirst for righteousness,
    for they will be filled.
7Blessed are the merciful,
    for they will be shown mercy.
8Blessed are the pure in heart,
    for they will see God.
9Blessed are the peacemakers,
    for they will be called sons of God.
10Blessed are those who are persecuted
        because of righteousness,
    for theirs is the kingdom of heaven.

11"Blessed are you when people insult you, persecute you and falsely say all kinds of evil against you because of me. 12Rejoice and be glad, because great is your reward in heaven, for in the same way they persecuted the prophets who were before you.

13"You are the salt of the earth. But if the salt loses its saltiness, how can it be made salty again? It is no longer good for anything, except to be thrown out and trampled by men.

14"You are the light of the world. A city on a hill cannot be hidden. 15Neither do people light a lamp and put it under a bowl. Instead they put it on its stand, and it gives light to everyone in the house. 16In the same way, let your light shine before men, that they may see your good deeds and praise your Father in heaven.

Matthew 6:33

33But seek first his kingdom and his righteousness, and all these things will be given to you as well.

UNDERSTANDING THE SCRIPTURE

Matthew 5:1-2. The "sermon" is not actually a sermon but an extended teaching by Jesus. Matthew's interest in connecting Jesus with Old Testament parallels is done subtly in these opening verses. Moses had ascended Mount Sinai and received God's Torah for Israel. Jesus ascends this mount in order to teach a new way to the people of

God. Two possible audiences are identified: the crowd at large, and the disciples who come to Jesus. This teaching on the mount in Matthew parallels Jesus' teaching on the plain or "level place" in Luke 6:17 with significant differences beyond the physical setting.

Matthew 5:3-12. "Beatitudes" comes from a Latin word related to blessing. The Greek word translated as "blessed" in these verses has a range of meanings from "happy" to "privileged" to "blessed." Matthew records eight Beatitudes (with an apparent ninth one in verse 11 emphasizing the eighth one in verse 10), whereas Luke records four. Two of those that appear in both Gospels vary in key ways. Matthew has "poor in spirit" and "hunger and thirst for righteousness," while Luke has Jesus simply pronounce the accompanying blessings upon the "poor" and those who "are hungry now." Common to all of these blessings in Matthew and Luke is the declaring of God's blessing upon those in situations that conventional wisdom sees as anything but blessed.

Matthew 5:13-16. The address of the teaching moves from third person plural ("blessed are *they*") to second person plural ("*You* are the salt of the earth . . . light of the world"). Salt had great value in the ancient world. The English word "salary" derives from the ration of salt given to Roman soldiers. In a theme that Matthew will return to not only in this teaching narrative but also later in the Gospel, "good works" (5:16) are at the center of how one faithfully responds to the teaching of Jesus and the coming kingdom of heaven. (Matthew uses the phrase "kingdom of heaven" in contrast to Mark and Luke, who use "kingdom of God.")

Matthew 5:17-20. Matthew stresses Jesus' roots in the Hebrew traditions by relating Jesus' assertion that he has come to fulfill the Law and the Prophets. At this time in the development of the Hebrew Scriptures, the books of the Law and Prophets had been established. It would not be until the turn of the first century that the third category of Jewish Scripture, the Writings, would be (mostly) settled upon. The scribes and the Pharisees were those groups in first-century Judaism most closely associated with the keeping of the written and oral laws as the basis for Jewish identity. To "exceed" their observance of Torah roots Jesus' teaching within those traditions.

Matthew 5:21-48. What Jesus meant by exceeding the righteousness of those others finds examples in this series of illustrations. The formula is clear: "You have heard that it was said . . . but I say to you." Jesus does not set aside the older Torah traditions but calls for a more rigorous observance of them that goes to their heart and motive. What is intriguing about this passage in light of this study unit, "The Birth of a New Community," is that almost every example involves how one lives in relationship with others. While each one of these new interpretations and applications of traditions is demanding, perhaps none is more so than the final one: "Love your enemies." The ethic of love that Jesus taught is not simply for relationships within circles of family and church and friends. The closing admonition to be "perfect" is not in the sense of the impossible ideal of being without flaw in word or thought or deed. Rather, as suggested in *The New Interpreter's Bible*, the Hebrew word Matthew has in mind here has to do with "wholeness" and integrity.

Matthew 6:1-18. In these verses, Jesus reinterprets traditions surrounding three chief actions of piety in Judaism: the giving of alms, prayer, and fasting. Consistent in all of Jesus' teachings is a movement away from "show." The practice is to focus upon relationship with God rather than honor or acclaim from the community. At the heart of this section is the example of prayer Jesus gives that has come to be known as the Lord's Prayer. Note that the one section of the prayer to which Jesus adds additional interpretation is forgiveness. Forgiveness is critical in community, not simply with God, but within human community. The stakes are made higher by Jesus' pronouncement that those who do not forgive will not be forgiven.

Matthew 6:19-34. This section reads like wisdom teachings and proverbs. It also relies on "either/or" choices of aligning oneself with God or something other than God. The most extended teaching here has to do with not being anxious. Basic to Jesus' teaching is trust in the providence of God, a providence seen in nature (birds, lilies, grass of the field). The clear focus is upon today, a focus consistent with doing the good works of God in the day given to do them.

Matthew 7:1-27. The warning against judging reinforces a critical quality for life lived in the close quarters of community. Midway through this section is what we call the "Golden Rule" (7:12). The emphasis is faith expressed and community formed through action. An important reminder is that Jesus does not say to treat others as they treat you, which would create a very different ethic than love of enemy. Rather, the injunction is to treat others as you would *want* them to treat you. Jesus' teachings close with a parable that cements the critical nature of the doing of faith. It is not what (or who) we hear that transforms us in and of itself. Rather, it is what we do in response to what and who has been heard.

Matthew 7:28-29. Scribal authority in teaching relied on establishing precedent. Jesus has not broken with tradition or denied precedent but has instead made the authority of his teaching more personal: "but *I* say to you." Astonishment is the reaction by the crowds. What remains to be seen is whether astonishment on the part of the crowds, or the disciples, will lead to heeding of these words.

INTERPRETING THE SCRIPTURE

A Taught Community

While scholars may debate whether those to whom Jesus addresses these words are the crowds who gather or the disciples who come to him, the basic action here is that Jesus *teaches*. And from that teaching arises the possibility of community.

The fundamental identity of the church as those who are *taught* by Jesus invites reflection. For, to be a taught community is to place a high premium on the act of teaching—and the importance of learning. Sometimes, the church has overlooked this in order to emphasize the role of preaching and worship in forming community, or the place of service and mission in expressing community. All of those are important. But likewise, all of those are apt to fall short or ring hollow if we make teaching secondary at best.

Ordination vows may still include the commissioning to be a pastor and teacher. But at times we have weighed so much else on the pastoral office, from routine maintenance issues to social activities coordinator, that many pastors find it difficult to devote time to this calling. And many congregations no longer expect it. Too often, we have exchanged the identity of the church as a taught community for that of an entertained community.

Yet consider how Jesus forms community through teaching in Matthew 5–7 in general, and the Beatitudes in particular. Teaching challenges folks to see the blessings of God in a radically new way. Teaching commissions and instructs the community on its true functions (salt and light—more on these later). Teaching lays the groundwork for community action. Teaching reinterprets the traditions that are kept in liturgy.

Consider your own community of faith.

The fact that you are participating in this study suggests you are part of a "taught community." Is it a high priority for youth, for children, for adults? Do you expect as much pastoral leadership and involvement in the educational ministry as you do, say, in administrative meetings or social functions?

Our calling remains to be a community much like the one who gathered on that mount long ago: to be a taught community.

True Happiness

Let us be clear on one point at the outset. The blessedness or "happiness" pronounced in the Beatitudes is far from what passes for "happiness" in our time. "Happiness" has come to mean something like a state of glee: buttons with smiling faces and the like. "Happy" and "carefree" have become synonyms. But listen to those pronounced as blessed by God. Those who mourn. Those who hunger and thirst. Those who are persecuted. Such conditions are not what conventional wisdom, in Jesus' day or our own, would call happy. Consider also the types of persons called blessed. The meek. The poor, in spirit or in resources. The pure. The peacemakers. These are the happy ones? Have you ever tried peacemaking in a community, in a family?

True happiness, according to Jesus' Beatitudes, does not reside in the conditions that befall us in life. Our happiness does not rely on us being able to avoid cares or grief. Our happiness relies on the action of God to bring blessing, even in the midst of situations that others might see as anything but the setting for being happy. Our happiness relies on the grace of God in Jesus Christ that enables us to be the merciful, to engage in the peacemaking, to practice humility of spirit when the spirit of this age is all about pride and self-advancement.

Are you truly happy? Don't try to measure that by how emotionally pumped you may or may not feel. Don't try to measure that by how much stuff you may or may not call your own. True happiness comes in knowing oneself loved and blessed by God, regardless of the outward circumstances of life. True happiness comes in trusting ourselves to the One whose blessing is not a passing state of mind, but a promised state of grace.

The Now and Not Yet of Blessing

Besides "blessed," there are two other words that dominate Jesus' Beatitudes: "are" and "will." "Blessed are the . . . for they will. . . ." And already, the tension of living one's life according to these blessings appears. Namely, the blessing is offered now. The poor, the meek, the peacemakers, and all the others: All *are* blessed now. That word of assurance can be carried with them back into those circumstances that try, and into those vocations of being merciful and making peace that might otherwise drain us. We *are* blessed of God.

But the fullness of those blessings awaits promises that stretch into the future. Inheritance of the earth. Comfort. Filling. None of these are guaranteed fulfillment now. Does that mean, then, that the blessings are impotent? No, it simply means that is where and why trust comes in.

"Faith," remember, does not simply mean "belief," or a set of principles I give assent to. Faith is active. As in the letter to the Hebrews, faith trusts in the things not yet seen.

The blessings pronounced here—in their now and not yet dimensions—are something like the very promise of God's sovereign realm. Jesus taught that the kingdom of God is among us. But even the most casual reading of any newspaper or Internet news source will quickly reveal that we do not yet live in the fullness of God's realm. It is here, but it is also coming. The church lives in between those times of promise and fulfillment. And blessed are those who trust in God to keep the promises. And blessed are those, as we now shall see, who reorder our lives and values in light of those things and those ones whom God through Jesus pronounces to be blessed.

The Function of Christian Community

"You are the salt of the earth. . . . You are the light of the world." As noted in the comments on Matthew 5:13-16, the "you" in these verses is plural. Jesus speaks not of individuals here, but of the community that heeds these teachings, the church. We are to be salt that seasons the world with grace. We are to be light that sheds light, not darkness, in this world.

The church has not always had a good track record in these callings. Sometimes, so as not to offend (especially the powers that be) we have become bland, a religious version of a mutual admiration society that is great for the insiders but not of much help for those outside our walls. And the images of both salt and light presume influence on that which is other than salt and light—that is, the world. Salt *of the earth.* Light *of the world.* The church exists for the sake of others. The church exists to make a difference for the good of this world, not just to produce an annual budget and carry on the local traditions and keep the doors open.

We season the earth and enlighten the world around us when our lives not only trust but also give evidence to the ways and ones God blesses. When we practice mercy and make for peace, when we become the vehicles of God's comforting of those who mourn and God's filling of those who are without: We live out our call to be the people of God blessed to know and practice the grace of God.

SHARING THE SCRIPTURE

Preparing Our Hearts

Meditate on this week's devotional reading, found in Numbers 6:22-27. Note that this familiar benediction was found on two silver cylinders, dating to 600 B.C. What do these words say to you about what God wants for you? How do you respond to this relationship that God offers to you?

Pray that you and the adult learners will be aware of and thankful for God's blessings in your lives.

Preparing Our Minds

Study the background from Matthew 5:1–7:29 and the lesson Scripture from Matthew 5:1-16. As you read these words from the Sermon on the Mount, ponder who teaches us to know true and lasting happiness.

Write on newsprint:
❑ information for next week's lesson, found under "Continue the Journey."
❑ activities for further spiritual growth in "Continue the Journey."

Locate pictures of things, activities, and people (for example, a family) that often make people happy. Prior to class, affix these to a bulletin board or tape them to the wall.

LEADING THE CLASS

(1) Gather to Learn

❖ Welcome the class members and introduce any guests.
❖ Pray that all of the students will embrace values that lead them in the way of true happiness.
❖ Direct the students' attention to the

picture display showing things, activities, and people that often make people happy. Invite the students to talk in small groups about these pictures, noting which ones represent something that makes them happy.

❖ Assemble everyone and ask: **Which of these will bring lasting happiness?**

❖ Read aloud today's focus statement: **People search for happiness in many places, but they often find the opposite due to their wrong choices. Who teaches us to know true and lasting happiness? Through his teachings, Jesus described how to find true happiness.**

(2) Investigate Jesus' Teachings About Happiness

❖ Invite the class to join you in reading today's Scripture lesson. You read Matthew 5:1-2, and the first part of verses 3-10. Ask the students to finish those verses beginning with the word "for." Read in unison verses 11-12.

❖ Discuss these questions:
   (1) **How would you characterize the people described in the first half of these verses?**
   (2) **Why is the second half of these verses so surprising?**
   (3) **What does Jesus' teaching reveal about the way God works in the world?**
   (4) **What do these teachings reveal about what God expects of us?**

❖ Work together as a class, or in small groups if the class is large, to write a contemporary version of several Beatitudes. Choose a specific audience, such as young adults, older adults, or women, for example, and write using language and images that would be familiar to the group that you have selected. Record the ideas on newsprint and then read in unison what the group has written.

❖ Choose a volunteer to read Matthew 5:13 and another to read 5:14-16.

■ Use information for these verses in Understanding the Scripture to dig deeper into their meaning.

■ Talk about ways that the students see the church (remember, the "you" here is plural) as being "salt of the earth" and "light of the world."

■ Consider ways in which we as a community have strayed from these core values, thus becoming tasteless or living with our light hidden.

■ **Option:** Read "The Function of Christian Community" from Interpreting the Scripture.

■ Ask: **What steps can we take together to enable nonchurched people to experience the faith community as salt and light?**

(3) Relate Jesus' Teachings on Happiness to Definitions Learners Often Encounter

❖ Ask the learners to complete this sentence: "Happiness is . . ." as they would personally define "happiness." Write their ideas on newsprint.

❖ Read "True Happiness" from Interpreting the Scripture.

❖ Talk about how the world defines "happiness." (You might consider the money, prestige, power, and fame that one supposedly needs in order to be happy.)

❖ Consider how Jesus defines "happiness," based on the Beatitudes.

❖ Brainstorm ideas with the class to answer these questions:
   (1) **If the people of the world began to take Jesus' teachings on happiness seriously, how would the world be different?**
   (2) **What barriers prevent us from taking Jesus' teachings seriously now?**
   (3) **How might we redefine "happiness" so as to be more in keeping with Jesus' teachings?**

(4) Identify One of Jesus' Teachings and Decide How to Put It Into Practice

❖ Distribute paper and pencils. Ask each student to select one of the Beatitudes and copy it onto their paper.

❖ Suggest that they read this Beatitude several times silently until they have memorized it.

■ **Option:** Provide commentaries so that the students may research the meaning of their selected verse.

❖ Encourage the students to think of a situation in their own lives in which this Beatitude could make a difference, if it were practiced.

❖ Conclude this portion of the lesson by doing a guided imagery activity with the students.

■ **See yourself in whatever situation you have imagined in which your Beatitude could make a difference. Notice details such as where you are, who is with you, what is being said and done that makes this a difficult situation.** (pause)

■ **Envision yourself putting this Beatitude into practice. Note what you are now saying and doing. How are your actions making a difference in the people and situations?** (pause)

■ **Tell Jesus, who has been present and watching, what you plan to do now to turn this negative situation into a positive one by putting your Beatitude into practice.** (pause)

❖ Invite anyone who would care to do so to share any insights they received as you walked through this activity.

❖ Conclude by reading in unison today's key verse, Matthew 6:33.

(5) Continue the Journey

❖ Pray that all of the participants will embrace Jesus' teachings so as to live a blessed life as part of God's kingdom.

❖ Read aloud this preparation for next week's lesson. You may also want to post it on newsprint for the students to copy.

■ **Title: Creating a Community of Servants**

■ **Background Scripture: Matthew 20:1-28; Mark 10:35-45**

■ **Lesson Scripture: Matthew 20:17-28**

■ **Focus of the Lesson: Everyone yearns to be recognized as important in the eyes of others. How does one achieve greatness? Jesus taught that if we wish to be great we must become servants and follow his example of service to others.**

❖ Challenge the students to complete one or more of these activities for further spiritual growth, which you will write on newsprint for the students to copy:

(1) Think about Jesus' Beatitudes in light of a current local or world situation. Ponder how this situation could be different if people espoused Jesus' teaching. Take whatever steps you can to try to improve this situation.

(2) Choose a favorite hymn tune and write a verse that expresses the theme of blessing. Sing this song often.

(3) Recall the Beatitude you chose to focus on in class and find ways to put it into practice this week.

❖ Sing or read aloud "Seek Ye First," which is based in part on today's key verse.

❖ Conclude today's session by leading the class in this benediction, adapted from Ephesians 4:4-6: **Let us now depart rejoicing in the community we share, united as one body, with one Spirit, one Lord, one faith, one baptism, and one God and Father of all.**

UNIT 1: THE BIRTH OF A NEW COMMUNITY
CREATING A COMMUNITY OF SERVANTS

PREVIEWING THE LESSON

Lesson Scripture: Matthew 20:17-28
Background Scripture: Matthew 20:1-28; Mark 10:35-45
Key Verse: Matthew 20:28

Focus of the Lesson:
Everyone yearns to be recognized as important in the eyes of others. How does one achieve greatness? Jesus taught that if we wish to be great we must become servants and follow his example of service to others.

Goals for the Learners:
(1) to delve into Jesus' teaching about greatness.
(2) to recognize the responsibility and value of being a servant.
(3) to develop and act on a plan to serve others.

Pronunciation Guide:
denarius (di nair' ee uhs)
diakonos (dee ak' on os)
Zebedee (zeb' uh dee)

Supplies:
Bibles, newsprint and marker, paper and pencils, hymnals

READING THE SCRIPTURE

NRSV
Matthew 20:17-28

¹⁷While Jesus was going up to Jerusalem, he took the twelve disciples aside by themselves, and said to them on the way, ¹⁸"See, we are going up to Jerusalem, and the Son of Man will be handed over to the chief priests

NIV
Matthew 20:17-28

¹⁷Now as Jesus was going up to Jerusalem, he took the twelve disciples aside and said to them, ¹⁸"We are going up to Jerusalem, and the Son of Man will be betrayed to the chief priests and the teachers

and scribes, and they will condemn him to death; [19]then they will hand him over to the Gentiles to be mocked and flogged and crucified; and on the third day he will be raised."

[20]Then the mother of the sons of Zebedee came to him with her sons, and kneeling before him, she asked a favor of him. [21]And he said to her, "What do you want?" She said to him, "Declare that these two sons of mine will sit, one at your right hand and one at your left, in your kingdom." [22]But Jesus answered, "You do not know what you are asking. Are you able to drink the cup that I am about to drink?" They said to him, "We are able." [23]He said to them, "You will indeed drink my cup, but to sit at my right hand and at my left, this is not mine to grant, but it is for those for whom it has been prepared by my Father."

[24]When the ten heard it, they were angry with the two brothers. [25]But Jesus called them to him and said, "You know that the rulers of the Gentiles lord it over them, and their great ones are tyrants over them. [26]It will not be so among you; but whoever wishes to be great among you must be your servant, [27]and whoever wishes to be first among you must be your slave; [28]just as **the Son of Man came not to be served but to serve, and to give his life a ransom for many."**

of the law. They will condemn him to death [19]and will turn him over to the Gentiles to be mocked and flogged and crucified. On the third day he will be raised to life!"

[20]Then the mother of Zebedee's sons came to Jesus with her sons and, kneeling down, asked a favor of him.

[21]"What is it you want?" he asked.

She said, "Grant that one of these two sons of mine may sit at your right and the other at your left in your kingdom."

[22]"You don't know what you are asking," Jesus said to them. "Can you drink the cup I am going to drink?"

"We can," they answered.

[23]Jesus said to them, "You will indeed drink from my cup, but to sit at my right or left is not for me to grant. These places belong to those for whom they have been prepared by my Father."

[24]When the ten heard about this, they were indignant with the two brothers. [25]Jesus called them together and said, "You know that the rulers of the Gentiles lord it over them, and their high officials exercise authority over them. [26]Not so with you. Instead, whoever wants to become great among you must be your servant, [27]and whoever wants to be first must be your slave—[28]just as **the Son of Man did not come to be served, but to serve, and to give his life as a ransom for many."**

UNDERSTANDING THE SCRIPTURE

Matthew 20:1-7. This parable is among several (for example, unmerciful servant with great debt, talents) that appear only in Matthew's Gospel. This initial scene of the parable corresponds with usual labor practices in first-century Palestine. Day laborers would be hired. If the harvest was large, or inclement weather threatened, multiple hirings throughout the day might occur. The amount agreed upon with the first workers—one denarius for the day's work—was customary for that time. The fact that the parable does not specify what the owner discusses as payment with the later workers sets up the surprise that will occur at the parable's conclusion.

Matthew 20:8-16. The Torah specified that day laborers were to be paid on the day of their service (Deuteronomy 24:15) as a matter of justice. The observance of this tradition suggests that the owner is a man of justice. But the parable soon goes beyond matters of justice. Paying the last laborers first is an important detail. Otherwise, if the first laborers had been paid at the beginning, they might not have been around to see that others were being paid the same customary wage that they had agreed upon. This imbalance at first creates hope in those who labored all day that they will receive more. They do not. The owner keeps his word. The parable concludes with the open-ended question regarding the freedom of the owner to be generous. The final words attached to the end of the story link it back to the previous passage, which concerned the disciples' reaction to the encounter between a rich young man and Jesus (19:16-30).

Matthew 20:17-19. This is Jesus' third and final prediction about the passion (see also 16:21; 17:22-23). Several small details are worth noting. In the first two predictions, Jesus spoke of being "killed." Here, he specifies "crucified." Similarly, the first passage indicates only the role played by the Jewish leaders. The second passage does not specify a particular group, but uses the general term, "human hands." In Jesus' third prediction according to Matthew, the Jewish leaders and unspecified persons are joined by the "Gentiles." Crucifixion was a Roman form of execution. Had this been an act carried out only under Jewish auspices, stoning would have been the method. The details make clear that later condemnations of Jews as "Christ-killers" are unjustified. Jesus was killed by non-Jews under orders from Roman authority.

Matthew 20:20-21. The word "then" serves to place this episode immediately after the final passion prediction, which makes the request even more incredulous and Jesus' responses even more crucial. The mother of the sons of Zebedee is mentioned only here and among the witnesses to the crucifixion who had followed Jesus from Galilee (27:56). The request she makes—invited by Jesus' question, "what do you want?"—has to do with places of honor for her sons. "Your kingdom" asserts belief in Jesus attaining a position of royal power. The places to the immediate right and left of those in such power typically were granted only to those most trusted by them.

Matthew 20:22-23. The "you" in Jesus' response to this request is plural. It is aimed not at the mother but at her sons. Two issues come to the forefront: knowledge of what is being asked and ability to drink Jesus' "cup." "Cup" in Hebrew tradition has a range of symbolic meanings, the most likely ones here being suffering and/or death. The bravado of James and John ("We are able") is ironic, in light of their desertion when Gethsemane changed from a place of prayer into one of arrest. It is not unlike Peter's later assertion that he would not deny Jesus (26:35) shortly before doing just that. "We are able" will have to wait until empowerment by resurrection and Spirit.

Matthew 20:24-28. The anger of the disciples at James and John translates a word that can also be translated as "indignant." It is to this division in community resulting from the request that Jesus now directs his remarks. "Lord it over" and "are tyrants over them" translate two verbs that convey power rooted in privilege. The "rulers" and "great ones" who exercise such dominance in the world at large are contrasted with those who seek to be "great" and "first" in Christian community. The critical noun and verb here is *diakonos/diakoneo*: servant, and serve. This word family at this time literally meant domestic servants who waited on the tables. "Ransom" is a word that originally referred to payment made to secure the release of one who was indebted or held captive.

Mark 10:35-45. This passage in Mark parallels Matthew 20:20-28. Like the Matthew passage, it is preceded by the story of the rich young man and the final passion prediction. There are several places where the two accounts differ that will be noted below. First, in Mark, it is James and John themselves, not their mother, who request places of honor. Some view Matthew as "protecting" the reputation of the disciples. Another difference in Mark is Jesus' question to these two: "Are you able to drink the cup that I drink, *or be baptized with the baptism that I am baptized with?*" (10:38, italics added). There is no mention in Matthew of baptism. Many interpreters see the "cup" as referring in general to suffering, while Jesus' "baptism" specifies death or martyrdom. One interpretation is that "baptism" is included to reflect what happened with James, whose martyrdom was well-known in the early church (Acts 12:2). A third point to be noted, common to both Mark and Matthew, is the understanding of "many" in reference to those for whom Christ gave his life as ransom. Some hear "many" to imply "but not all." However, "many" can and sometimes does serve as a synonym for "all" (see 1 Corinthians 10:17). See 1 Timothy 2:5-6 for an assertion that Christ's ransom was indeed for all.

INTERPRETING THE SCRIPTURE

Teaching the Cross

There is an old theory of preaching (and teaching) that goes like this: Tell them what you're going to tell them, tell them, then tell them what you told them. If it sounds repetitive, it is.

But sometimes, repetition is needed—especially if the subject is something that is difficult to grasp or cuts against the grain of accepted wisdom. As noted in the preceding commentary, this is the third time Jesus has taught the disciples about the suffering he will face in Jerusalem. The first time, Jesus faced outright rebellion. "God forbid it, Lord!" was Peter's response (Matthew 16:22). The second time, Matthew tells us that the disciples were "greatly distressed" (17:23). This third time (20:17-19), there is no indication of a response. Do they finally get it? Is it finally understood—not only in terms of Jesus but also in terms of their own discipleship? According to Matthew (and Mark), the answer comes implied in the immediately ensuing request for a favor: discipleship as privileged position.

Now before we throw up our hands in wonderment that the church ever got off the ground with followers like these, we should ask the question: Do we get it? Let's face it. The teaching of cross and discipleship is not exactly a secret in the church. The yearly rhythm of Lent's remembrance of these things means we have had the opportunity not only of three passion predictions but at least annual reminders.

And do some still confuse discipleship with privileged position? Do some still conceive of Messiah, past or future, as a conquering military whirlwind instead of as a loving redeemer of all whose coming is to save life, not inflict death?

Some teachings do need repetition. Because even if we have heard it all before, the point is not in the hearing, but in the living.

What Do You Want?

Those are dangerous words, at least if they leave the impression that you can get whatever you ask of Jesus. And some folks do proceed on that presumption, often in the guise of asking in Jesus' name. But we quickly learn in this episode that Jesus' asking "what do you want" is worlds apart from Jesus' saying "you can have whatever you want."

The question is not a blank check to fill in with whatever is wished. The question is more of a reality check. It is to find out what is on the mind of the one who asks it—or in the case of Mark's record of this episode, of the two who come asking. It is a reality check because, remember, Jesus has just finished teaching about the cross. And the first thing asked in the wake of sacrifice is: What's in it for me?

By asking the question, though, Jesus puts the ball back in our court. It is a bit like an earlier episode on the road to Caesarea Philippi, where the disciples report to Jesus about all the gossip flying around about who or what Jesus is. It's all very interesting conjecture—but Jesus cut to the chase then by asking, "But who do *you* say that I am?" (Matthew 16:15, italics added).

Faith is not a matter of what other people think. It is a personal decision and commitment. And here, after teaching the disciples about what is on his mind regarding Jerusalem and suffering, cross and raising, Jesus asks what is on the mind—and in the desires—of the one or ones who come seeking. *What do you want?*

Maybe that is the question the church should be asking more often of its members. When you come to worship: What are you looking for, *what do you want?* When opportunities arise for service and ministry: What are you willing to do, *what do you want?* When it comes to conflicts with the pastor or within the parish: Come on now, *what do you want?*

And the discipline of discipleship comes in remembering that when these two disciples (or their mother) declare their wish, Jesus says no. Jesus may be the yes to all of God's promises, but Jesus is not the yes to everything we think we want. The question is asked not to trick us but to mature us.

A Different Way

This is one of the few passages in which Jesus gives the disciples organizational advice. He doesn't say whether he favors popes or bishops, presbyters or congregations, as the embodiment of church authority. He doesn't say whether leaders should be married or celibate, male or female. Jesus only insists, or I should say *demands*, this one standard: If you want to be first, you must be a servant.

The reason Jesus states this so emphatically, as his prior words make clear, is that authority is not usually or even normally viewed that way in society at large. Leadership and authority in the outside world is a matter of privilege and prerogative. In the language of the text, secular power consists of people in charge who stake out their positions and hold them at all cost, never forgetting to remind others of where authority resides and what the cost of breaching it might be.

This is a text that has a natural connection with the theme of re-forming the church and, in particular, renewing how the church views and exercises power. The great hindrance to re-forming the church is not necessarily resistance to change, although that can certainly be a factor. The more insidious hindrance to re-forming the church and how we structure ourselves is that we try to go about it in the wrong way. We fall into the habit of using secular models of institutions so that we might become more "cost-effective" or more "competitive," or whatever successful businesses and institutions tell us is needed to survive these days. Such comparative studies can be helpful, but they collapse on one critical point: the role of authority and power, for in the community Jesus would form—and re-form—the bottom line is not power brokers or arm-twisters. The bottom line is servanthood.

Servant Christ, Servant Community

The body of Christ draws its identity and mission directly from the example of Christ. We are a servant community because the

One we follow was a servant among us. Servanthood is the principle of power and authority that is to shape Christian community every bit as much as Christian individuals.

Please do not mistake "servant" for "servile." Too often, the church has miscommunicated this point, especially to women and minorities. Servanthood as Jesus speaks of it is not a denial of human worth or a removal of power. Servanthood is the exercise of power for the sake of others. Servanthood values human worth, including one's own, so

much as to risk self to affirm that worth. So Christ came—and so Christ sends us.

We see Jesus modeling this and calling us to such life-affirming servanthood time and again. Jesus washed the feet of the disciples. Even Jesus' teaching of the cross became, in the first passion prediction, the occasion for teaching discipleship as the taking up of the cross (16:24). We live in the example of Jesus even as our lives, individually and collectively, are to bear witness to Jesus' ways. Ways of grace and compassion, ways of justice and inclusion: ways of the servant.

SHARING THE SCRIPTURE

Preparing Our Hearts

Meditate on this week's devotional reading, found in Philippians 2:1-11. What do you learn about the mind of Jesus from this passage? How did God respond to Jesus' willingness to humble himself and become a servant? What clues can you gain from this passage about Jesus' definition of greatness? Ponder how you can be great in the sight of God.

Pray that you and the adult learners will recognize that service in the Kingdom is the key to greatness.

Preparing Our Minds

Study the background from Matthew 20:1-28 and Mark 10:35-45 and the lesson Scripture from Matthew 20:17-28. Ponder how one achieves greatness.

Write on newsprint:

❑ information for next week's lesson, found under "Continue the Journey."
❑ activities for further spiritual growth in "Continue the Journey."

LEADING THE CLASS

(1) Gather to Learn

❖ Welcome the class members and introduce any guests.

❖ Pray that all who have come today will open their hearts and minds to the Spirit's leading.

❖ Encourage the students to brainstorm names of people who in their eyes have achieved greatness. Unless a famous figure is named, ask the adults to explain briefly why the people they have identified are great. Jot down names and reasons on newsprint. Ask the class to discern common themes that run throughout all of their choices.

❖ Read aloud today's focus statement: **Everyone yearns to be recognized as important in the eyes of others. How does one achieve greatness? Jesus taught that if we wish to be great we must become servants and follow his example of service to others.**

(2) Delve Into Jesus' Teaching About Greatness

❖ Set the stage for a study of Matthew 20:17-19 by reading aloud the first (16:21) and second (17:22-23) predictions Jesus made about his passion.

■ Choose a volunteer to read Matthew 20:17-19.

■ Compare and contrast the three accounts. You will find information to help you do this in Understanding the Scripture for verses 17-19 and also under "Teaching the Cross" in Interpreting the Scripture.

❖ Select a cast to read the parts of Jesus, James, John, their mother, and a narrator in Matthew 20:20-23.

■ Encourage the students to imagine themselves as observers of this conversation. Individuals may choose to see themselves as among the disciples or simply as bystanders. Discuss with them what they see and hear in terms of facial expressions, body language, and tone of voice of those involved in this conversation.

■ Ask this question: **What does this conversation reveal about the priorities and expectations of James and John (and their mother)?**

❖ Choose someone to read Matthew 20:24-28.

■ Use information for these verses from Understanding the Scripture to help unpack their meaning.

■ Read or retell "A Different Way" in Understanding the Scripture.

■ Talk about how Jesus' teachings on greatness might be received in the White House or a corporate boardroom.

■ Ask: **How does Jesus' teaching turn conventional wisdom on its head? Does his way work? What evidence do you have to support your answer?**

(3) Recognize the Responsibility and Value of Being a Servant

❖ Note that in the church we often tend to think of service in terms of the work we do for the church as an organization: serve on committees, teach Sunday school, sing in the choir, usher, and so on. Jesus, however, did not limit service to the "insiders." We know from his talk—and action—that service is difficult and may involve suffering.

❖ Read aloud this story: **Father Lawrence, pastor of Our Lady of Lourdes Church in a poor section of Malad West, India, noticed hundreds of people running from their homes into the narrow, rain-drenched roads. A ravine had overflowed and the gushing water was submerging homes. Father Lawrence asked the police to help, but they said they could not do anything. A Navy boat arrived much later, but was unable to rescue even one person. Lawrence and a team of youth rescued 2,500 people by wading into the polluted, chest-high water, carrying children on their shoulders and leading others to the safety of the church compound. Nearby neighbors immediately pitched in with food. For several days after the disaster, people came from the surrounding region with food, supplies, and clothing. According to Lawrence, most of the residents earned daily wages by making crafts, and the raw materials for their work were destroyed in the flood. Father Lawrence is working with volunteers and non-profit organizations to help these people get back on their feet.**

❖ Discuss this question: **How does Father Lawrence demonstrate the responsibility and value of being a servant?**

❖ **Option:** Invite the students to tell stories to the class or to small groups about people who stepped into challenging situations and served others.

❖ **Option:** Read "Servant Christ, Servant Community" to help the students understand the church as a servant community.

(4) Develop and Act on a Plan to Serve Others

❖ Divide the class into groups, and give each group a sheet of newsprint and a marker. Challenge the adults to brainstorm groups of people in your community who need someone to care for them. Have a recorder note ideas on newsprint. (Here are some possibilities: *children in need of a big brother or sister or foster grandparent; HIV/AIDS patients; homebound; poor; hungry; those without proper shelter; elderly and unable to get out to shop*).

❖ Post the sheets of newsprint and provide time for class members to circulate around the room. Invite them to stand next to a paper containing an idea of interest.

❖ Regroup the class so that those who are interested in the same thing are seated together. Give each group newsprint and a marker and encourage them to develop a plan to serve whomever they have chosen, for example, offering transportation to those who need to get to medical appointments.

❖ Call the class back together and hear the plans that each group has devised.

❖ End this portion of the lesson by distributing paper and pencils to each individual. Ask them to write a sentence or two stating who they will work with, what they will do, and why this arena of service is important to them.

(5) Continue the Journey

❖ Pray that all who have come together this day will go forth as empowered servants.

❖ Read aloud this preparation for next week's lesson. You may also want to post it on newsprint for the students to copy.

■ **Title: Empowered to Be a Community**
■ **Background Scripture: Acts 2**
■ **Lesson Scripture: Acts 2:1-17**
■ **Focus of the Lesson: In our individualistic society, many people long for a sense of community. Where can we find resources to develop such community? At Pentecost, God provided spiritual power that brings together life's disjointed elements and bridges the gaps that divide people.**

❖ Challenge the students to complete one or more of these activities for further spiritual growth, which you will write on newsprint for the students to copy:

(1) **Offer to provide service to someone in your congregation or community who has a special need.**

(2) **Make it a point to recognize and thank someone in your church who is an unsung hero, that is, one who works behind the scenes with little acknowledgement.**

(3) **Look at the leaders in your congregation. Which ones are examples of true servant-leaders? What traits set them apart from leaders who may want power, privilege, and accolades for their work? Send a note or in some other way acknowledge the servant-leaders as role models for the congregation.**

❖ Sing or read aloud "Jesu, Jesu."

❖ Conclude today's session by leading the class in this benediction, adapted from Ephesians 4:4-6: **Let us now depart rejoicing in the community we share, united as one body, with one Spirit, one Lord, one faith, one baptism, and one God and Father of all.**

UNIT 2: THE DEVELOPMENT AND
WORK OF THE NEW COMMUNITY

EMPOWERED TO BE A COMMUNITY

PREVIEWING THE LESSON

Lesson Scripture: Acts 2:1-17
Background Scripture: Acts 2
Key Verse: Acts 2:4

Focus of the Lesson:

In our individualistic society, many people long for a sense of community. Where can we find resources to develop such community? At Pentecost, God provided spiritual power that brings together life's disjointed elements and bridges the gaps that divide people.

Goals for the Learners:

(1) to introduce the events surrounding the coming of the Holy Spirit on the day of Pentecost.
(2) to consider how the coming of the Holy Spirit has affected their lives.
(3) to take steps to spread the gospel through the power of the Spirit.

Pronunciation Guide:

Cappadocia (kap uh doh' shee uh)
Cretan (kree' tuhn)
Cyrene (si ree' nee)
Elamite (ee' luh mite)
Libya (lib' ee uh)
Mede (meed)
Pamphylia (pam fil' ee uh)
Parthian (pahr' thee uhn)
Phrygia (frij' ee uh)
Pontus (pon' tuhs)
proselyte (pros' uh lite)

Supplies:

Bibles, newsprint and marker, paper and pencils, hymnals, optional meditative music and appropriate player

READING THE SCRIPTURE

NRSV
Acts 2:1-17

¹When the day of Pentecost had come, they were all together in one place. ²And suddenly from heaven there came a sound like the rush of a violent wind, and it filled the entire house where they were sitting. ³Divided tongues, as of fire, appeared among them, and a tongue rested on each of them. **⁴All of them were filled with the Holy Spirit and began to speak in other languages, as the Spirit gave them ability.**

⁵Now there were devout Jews from every nation under heaven living in Jerusalem. ⁶And at this sound the crowd gathered and was bewildered, because each one heard them speaking in the native language of each. ⁷Amazed and astonished, they asked, "Are not all these who are speaking Galileans? ⁸And how is it that we hear, each of us, in our own native language? ⁹Parthians, Medes, Elamites, and residents of Mesopotamia, Judea and Cappadocia, Pontus and Asia, ¹⁰Phrygia and Pamphylia, Egypt and the parts of Libya belonging to Cyrene, and visitors from Rome, both Jews and proselytes, ¹¹Cretans and Arabs—in our own languages we hear them speaking about God's deeds of power." ¹²All were amazed and perplexed, saying to one another, "What does this mean?" ¹³But others sneered and said, "They are filled with new wine."

¹⁴But Peter, standing with the eleven, raised his voice and addressed them, "Men of Judea and all who live in Jerusalem, let this be known to you, and listen to what I say. ¹⁵Indeed, these are not drunk, as you suppose, for it is only nine o'clock in the morning. ¹⁶No, this is what was spoken through the prophet Joel:
¹⁷ 'In the last days it will be, God declares, that I will pour out my Spirit upon all flesh.' "

NIV
Acts 2:1-17

¹When the day of Pentecost came, they were all together in one place. ²Suddenly a sound like the blowing of a violent wind came from heaven and filled the whole house where they were sitting. ³They saw what seemed to be tongues of fire that separated and came to rest on each of them. **⁴All of them were filled with the Holy Spirit and began to speak in other tongues as the Spirit enabled them.**

⁵Now there were staying in Jerusalem God-fearing Jews from every nation under heaven. ⁶When they heard this sound, a crowd came together in bewilderment, because each one heard them speaking in his own language. ⁷Utterly amazed, they asked: "Are not all these men who are speaking Galileans? ⁸Then how is it that each of us hears them in his own native language? ⁹Parthians, Medes and Elamites; residents of Mesopotamia, Judea and Cappadocia, Pontus and Asia, ¹⁰Phrygia and Pamphylia, Egypt and the parts of Libya near Cyrene; visitors from Rome ¹¹(both Jews and converts to Judaism); Cretans and Arabs—we hear them declaring the wonders of God in our own tongues!" ¹²Amazed and perplexed, they asked one another, "What does this mean?"

¹³Some, however, made fun of them and said, "They have had too much wine."

¹⁴Then Peter stood up with the Eleven, raised his voice and addressed the crowd: "Fellow Jews and all of you who live in Jerusalem, let me explain this to you; listen carefully to what I say. ¹⁵These men are not drunk, as you suppose. It's only nine in the morning! ¹⁶No, this is what was spoken by the prophet Joel:
¹⁷ " 'In the last days, God says, I will pour out my Spirit on all people.' "

UNDERSTANDING THE SCRIPTURE

Acts 2:1-4. "Pentecost," a Greek word that literally means "fiftieth day," had come to refer to a Jewish harvest festival known as "Feast of Weeks." "Fiftieth" comes from the number of days following Passover on which this festival was set. Besides its harvest connections, Pentecost also later commemorated God's giving of Torah to Moses on Sinai. The "they" whom Luke says were "all together" likely refers not simply to the twelve apostles (Matthias had by now taken Judas's place) but the 120 identified as the "believers" in Acts 1:15. Jesus had earlier promised the Spirit's gift before his ascension (Acts 1:4-5). The relatively brief account of the Spirit's gift here focuses on three elements: sound, sight, and speech. Comparing the sound to "wind" (and a violent one at that) plays on the same word meaning "wind" and "spirit" (and "breath") in Greek and Hebrew. The sight (tongues of fire) recalls John the Baptizer's prophecy that linked the Spirit's baptism with fire (Luke 3:16). The speech in different dialects recalls the ancient story of Babel (Genesis 11:1-9). There, the multiplicity of languages resulted in the dispersion of community. Here, the different dialects result in the gathering of community.

Acts 2:5-11. After the time of the Babylonian exile, increasing numbers of Jews lived outside of Judea and Galilee. Pilgrimage feasts such as Pentecost encouraged those who were able to return to Jerusalem and the Temple for worship there. In fact, the law mandated such festival pilgrimages for "all males" (Exodus 23:14-17). "Proselytes," mentioned in verse 10, would have been Gentile converts to Judaism. Luke portrays their reaction to hearing their native tongues spoken by Galileans in strong terms: "bewildered," "amazed," "astonished." The list of nations in verses 9-11 is intriguing. At least one is an ethnic group rather than a nationality (Arabian). Several others listed among the nations had ceased to exist as such long before this time (Parthians, Elamites). The phrase "living in Jerusalem" (2:5) may indicate these are not all or even mostly pilgrims. Some may have taken up residence in Jerusalem.

Acts 2:12-21. The response of the crowd continues to be pronounced: "amazed and perplexed." The attribution of the diverse languages to getting drunk on new wine attempts to stifle the signs of God's Spirit, similar to how the charge that Jesus' disciples had stolen his body had attempted to stifle the proclamation of resurrection. This is the first of several speeches/sermons by Peter in Acts (later the book will shift to the public proclamations of the gospel by Paul). Peter had earlier addressed the 120 believers with the proposal that another disciple be chosen to take the place of Judas (Acts 1:15-22). The mention of the eleven (now including Matthias, 1:26) along with Peter presents an image of the church's early leaders united at this "birthing" time of the church. Peter counters the charge of drunkenness with another explanation. In verses 17-21, he quotes a prophecy from Joel 2:28-32 about a promise of the "last days," when God's Spirit would be poured out across boundaries of age and gender and class. Significantly for where this sermon is headed, it is a prophecy that promises salvation to "everyone who calls on the name of the Lord" (2:21).

Acts 2:22-24. "Israelite" is not a term of geography or even ethnicity, but—given the diversity of folks in the crowd—a term of covenantal community that all there are part of. The language shifts to a tone that brings the listeners directly into the story of "Jesus of Nazareth." The second-person voice makes this clear: "attested to you by God . . . you yourselves know . . . handed over to you . . . you crucified and killed." The church needs to exercise care and self-examination in these words. Their heart is not anti-Semitism, as the speaker is not only a Jew but also one whose hand in denial is clear. "You" is not a pejorative condemnation of the Jews. "You" evokes *our* acknowledgment of how *our* lives handle and too often hand over Christ among us. In contrast to the "you" language of suffering is the "God" affirmation of resurrection in verse 24.

Acts 2:25-36. In these verses, Peter engages several psalms in service of his argument and sermon. Verses 25-28 come from Psalm 16:8-11. Verse 30, while not a direct quotation, is based upon Psalm 132:11. Verse 31 returns to Psalm 16:10, while verses 34-35 quote Psalm 110:1. Combined with the earlier passage from Joel, the sermon of Peter—and the author of Acts—clearly understands the proclamation of gospel as a continuation of God's saving works and words from the Hebrew Scriptures. The followers of Jesus, and the soon-to-be Spirit-birthed church, remain within Judaism. This detail is not merely textual, but a reflection of the community to which Acts was addressed. For even in those later times when the relationship between church and synagogue became strained and conflicted, Acts maintained a witness to the continuity between those communities.

Acts 2:37-41. The address of Peter and the others as "brothers" indicates a receptivity to the message and a recognition of community as well as authority. "Repent/repentance" is a compound word that literally means "a change of mind." But mind, in Judaism, was not merely thought process. It involved what we might call will. The consequences of such change led to action as well as attitude, as indicated in the preaching of repentance by John the Baptizer (see Luke 3:10-14). The promise of verse 39 combines in thought the promise of Joel 2:32 with Isaiah 57:19. The results of this sermon among the crowd are as astounding as the sights and sounds that attracted their attention in the first place.

Acts 2:42-47. This is the first of several "summaries" of the early church in Jerusalem (see also 4:32-37 and 6:1-7). The emphasis is clearly upon community as life lived in common: not only in terms of devotion and fellowship but even economy (2:42). A seamless weave between faith, practice, need, and provision is portrayed. (See Acts 5:1-11 for a cautionary tale when the weave is broken.) The witness of Pentecost now is joined by the witness of the goodwill generated by the community's very life (2:47). And by sermons unrecorded of that goodwill, God brings continued growth (2:47).

INTERPRETING THE SCRIPTURE

When Spirit Comes

"When Spirit comes" is not only about the festival of Pentecost in Jerusalem. "When Spirit comes" in this story is also about the detail, "they were all together in one place" (2:1). Pentecostal power did not fall on individual believers closeted by themselves at home. Spirit descended upon the community gathered together. Spirit still descends when community gathers—

"together." When we are united with one another (understanding, of course, that "unity" and "uniformity" are not synonyms), great things can happen. We open ourselves to the ongoing movement of God's Spirit, whether the gatherings be worship or prayer or service. As we learn from The Acts of the Apostles, Spirit is all about gathering and empowering and transforming community.

This is not to say that all we need to do is

convene a meeting, hold hands, and then the Spirit will come at our beck and call (and do what we expect). The details of violent wind and tongues as of fire point not only to the Spirit's power but also to the Spirit's freedom. In the Gospel of John, Jesus taught, "The wind [remember "wind" and "Spirit" are the same word] blows where it chooses, and you hear the sound of it, but you do not know where it comes from or where it goes" (John 3:8). Neither individuals nor communities of faith control the movement of God's Spirit. It is the other way around.

"When Spirit comes" is not a task for us to manage. It is a gift for us to invoke for the sake of renewal.

The Miracle of Hearing in Tongues

I know, I know—everybody wants to talk about this speaking in other languages thing. The Pentecostals wonder why we don't get the gift, figuratively and literally. The rest of us wonder why this practice exists (although some scholars make a clear distinction between the gift of languages and speaking in tongues).

Perhaps both sides could benefit from what may be even the larger miracle here: not the speaking, but the *hearing*. Once we get into the reaction of the crowd, that is what the author of Acts focuses on. Verses 5-11 mention "speaking" twice, but "hear/hearing" three times. That is what bewilders and amazes these folks: "because each one *heard* them . . . how is it that we *hear* . . . in our own languages we *hear* them."

The church has rarely in its history been at a loss for speaking. The real crisis all along has been hearing. In truth, it is a crisis that predates Pentecost by countless centuries. In Hebrew, the word for "hear" and the word for "obey" is the same. The call of Deuteronomy 6:4 to "hear, O Israel" is not merely a summons to activate the auditory organs so that certain sonic vibrations will

cause one's eardrum to pick up the signal. To "hear" is an invitation to follow, to heed, the Word to be spoken.

So, while not dismissing the rather startling experience of hearing your native tongue sounding in your ear in a foreign land, the account of Pentecost is also about the deeper hearing made possible by Spirit (but still dependent on human decision) to *respond* to that word.

Anybody can listen to something, or someone, and walk away unaffected. The scoffers in the Pentecost crowd who suggested a few too many early morning martinis as the cause of the uproar had listened to what was said . . . but apparently didn't *hear* it.

Hearing something or someone, *truly* hearing, summons response. Note how the Pentecost story concludes: At the end of the sermon, the author notes, "Now when they *heard* this . . . 'what should we do?'" (2:37, italics added). The miracle of hearing comes in the change that can be evoked, in the lives that can be transformed, in the communities that can be brought into being.

Spirited Geography

It may be that, at first glance, our response to the list in verses 9-11 is not unlike our response to the long list of names in genealogies. We skip over it to get back to the real story.

But in significant ways, this list *is* integral to the story. The author of Acts alludes to that by indicating the crowd was made up of individuals "from every nation under heaven" (2:5). Clearly, even this somewhat lengthy (and occasionally hard to pronounce) list of places and peoples doesn't come close to an exhaustive list of every nation, even every nation that existed at that time. So, one might think that the names provided offer some other significance.

Some see in the listing a certain geographical progression, from east to west. Others see in providing this list that the gospel is making inroads across the then-known world—although, to be fair, the mission to the Gentiles awaits later chapters. The author clearly indicates at the end of the list that these are Jews and "proselytes"—meaning Gentiles who have converted to Judaism.

An even more intriguing aspect of this list is that it includes nations (Parthians and Elamites, for example) that were ancient history. Literally. They had ceased to exist centuries before. Why include them? Luke/Acts doesn't say. But why link them with God's Spirit—a Spirit who fashions community here, a Spirit whom, in the even older stories of Ezekiel, God breathes to give life to dead bones as a means of breathing hope into Israel who in exile had given up a lot of things for dead?

I would like to think these nations are a reminder of the ability of God's Spirit to still breathe life into persons and communities given up by the rest of us as dead. Without hope. Some have rendered that judgment upon the church itself. And the truth of the matter is that without God's Spirit renewing and transforming us, the church, like any other institution, has a tendency to grow brittle over time. The inclusion of Parthians and Elamites reminds us that God doesn't give up on us as easily as we do.

In the Eye (and Ear) of the Beholder

As noted already, marvel at the Pentecost event was not the universal response. Some saw it as too much wine too early in the day. Same event, drastically different views, and the story continues today. Consider the last time your church explored a new way of doing things, whether in worship or education or service. Chances are, sides formed. *It's progress. It's regress. It's the wave of the future. It's a shortcut to disaster. It's a wise investment. It's a foolish waste.*

You might think that such inevitable differences will mean the church can never find a way forward.

Pentecost says otherwise.

Even in the face of disagreement, where the same event is interpreted in radically different ways, God's Spirit brings transformation. Now, it may or may not involve transformation of the opposing opinion—there is nothing to indicate the scoffers were won over. Then again, there is nothing to indicate they were not.

Disagreements will come in the church, different interpretations of the same event or program or pastor are just part of the playing field. It is the church's task not to ensure there are no differences but to see and then follow where the Spirit is leading.

SHARING THE SCRIPTURE

Preparing Our Hearts

Meditate on this week's devotional reading, found in Ephesians 2:11-22. As Paul writes about the oneness we have in Christ, he notes in verse 18 that both Jews and Gentiles "have access in one Spirit to the Father." What does it mean to you to know that you can approach God through the Holy Spirit? Ponder the idea of being one in Christ. How is this oneness manifested in your life, in your congregation, and among Christians of all denominations?

Pray that you and the adult learners will seek God through the Spirit.

Preparing Our Minds

Study the background from Acts 2 and the lesson Scripture from Acts 2:1-17. Think about where we can find resources to develop a sense of community.

Write on newsprint:

❏ information for next week's lesson, found under "Continue the Journey."
❏ activities for further spiritual growth in "Continue the Journey."

Option: Call students who may have Bibles in a language other than English and ask them to bring those Bibles and be prepared to read Acts 2:1-4 aloud.

Prepare to read Acts 2:1-17 aloud. Use the Pronunciation Guide to help you.

Option: Select meditative music and locate a player if you choose for an activity under "Take Steps to Spread the Gospel Through the Power of the Spirit."

LEADING THE CLASS

(1) Gather to Learn

❖ Welcome the class members and introduce any guests.

❖ Pray that all who have come today will feel welcome and part of this class.

❖ Brainstorm with the class a list of places and organizations that people in your area turn toward in order to find a sense of community, a place where they can belong and feel accepted.

❖ Place a one (1) by the place or organization that seems most popular, a two (2) by the next most popular place, and so on.

❖ Ask: **Where does our church rank? If we are not at the top of the list, why do you think that the church has a lower ranking?**

❖ Read aloud today's focus statement: **In our individualistic society, many people long for a sense of community. Where can we find resources to develop such community? At Pentecost, God provided spiritual power that brings together life's disjointed elements and bridges the gaps that divide people.**

(2) Introduce the Events Surrounding the Coming of the Holy Spirit on the Day of Pentecost

❖ Introduce the story of Pentecost by reading or retelling information for Acts 2:1-4 found in Understanding the Scripture.

❖ **Option:** Invite students whom you have contacted in advance to read Acts 2:1-4 from a Bible written in a language other than English. Finish the story by reading verses 5-17 yourself.

❖ Read aloud Acts 2:1-17 yourself if you did not choose the previous option.

❖ Encourage the students to discuss what they envisioned, heard, tasted, touched, or smelled as these verses were being read aloud.

❖ Ask: **Suppose you had been in the crowd and heard in your own language a witness to "God's deeds of power" (2:11). How would you have responded?** (Students may want to discuss their answers, but also invite them to show their responses by facial expressions or movement.)

❖ Investigate the responses of the people originally present at Pentecost. Note especially Acts 2:5-13.

❖ Read about these responses as described in "The Miracle of Hearing in Tongues" in Interpreting the Scripture. Invite the learners to add their own observations.

❖ Conclude this portion of the lesson by asking: **What response do you think God is calling the church to make right now as we hear the gospel?**

(3) Consider How the Coming of the Holy Spirit Has Affected the Learners' Lives

❖ Recall that the same Peter who had denied Jesus three times before the crucifixion was able to proclaim his faith publicly when the Spirit came. Clearly, the presence of the Spirit had made a tremendous difference in Peter's life.

❖ Suggest that the students work in small groups to tell stories of how the Holy Spirit has worked in their own lives. They may bear witness to Spirit-led guidance, healing, comfort, empowerment, or some other movement of the Spirit.

❖ Consider together what life would be like without the presence of the Holy Spirit. Discern what might be missing in the learners' lives if the Spirit had not been given to all believers on Pentecost.

❖ Brainstorm with the class the answer to this question: **How do you see the Holy Spirit at work in our congregation?** List their ideas on newsprint. (If the class has difficulty perceiving the Spirit at work, talk about why they think there is so little spiritual presence within their church.)

(4) Take Steps to Spread the Gospel Through the Power of the Spirit

❖ Refocus the prior discussion by asking these questions. Write ideas on newsprint.

(1) **How can we build on our strengths as individuals and as a congregation to continue to spread the good news?**

(2) **If we perceive that the Spirit is not working mightily in our midst, what can we do to overcome the barriers that inhibit the Spirit's presence?**

❖ Distribute paper and pencil. Challenge the students to listen for the voice of the Holy Spirit speaking to them. Suggest that they ask the Spirit how they can spread the good news of Jesus Christ. Encourage them to jot down any names or situations that come to mind. Have them pray for opportunities to respond. While the students are meditating, you may wish to play some quiet instrumental music in the background.

❖ Call the students back together. Enlist volunteers to present any insights they have gained.

(5) Continue the Journey

❖ Pray that all who have participated in today's session will go forth recognizing that the Spirit empowers them to be a united community of faith.

❖ Read aloud this preparation for next week's lesson. You may also want to post it on newsprint for the students to copy.

■ **Title: Expansion of the Community**

■ **Background Scripture: Acts 6:1-15; 8:1-8**

■ **Lesson Scripture: Acts 6:1-5, 8-15**

■ **Focus of the Lesson: Increased responsibilities in our personal and professional lives cause us to experience stress and conflict. How do people of faith handle these responsibilities in order to reduce conflict? The expansion of the early church provides a model for delegating responsibilities and handling conflict through its selection of the first servants of the church.**

❖ Challenge the students to complete one or more of these activities for further spiritual growth, which you will write on newsprint for the students to copy.

(1) **Research the Jewish background of Pentecost. Note that this was one of the three festivals that the law required Jewish males to attend. You may also want to locate the homelands of the different groups mentioned in Acts 2:9-11.**

(2) **Ponder how the unity amid the great diversity of the early church can be a model for the contemporary church. What steps can you take to help anyone who comes into your congregation feel welcomed?**

(3) **Make a bold statement of faith in the world beyond the confines of the church, just as Peter did. What fruit are you able to see your witness bearing?**

❖ Sing or read aloud "O Church of God, United," which is based on Acts 2:5-11.

❖ Conclude today's session by leading the class in this benediction, adapted from Ephesians 4:4-6: **Let us now depart rejoicing in the community we share, united as one body, with one Spirit, one Lord, one faith, one baptism, and one God and Father of all.**

UNIT 2: THE DEVELOPMENT AND
WORK OF THE NEW COMMUNITY

EXPANSION OF THE COMMUNITY

PREVIEWING THE LESSON

Lesson Scripture: Acts 6:1-5, 8-15
Background Scripture: Acts 6:1-15; 8:1-8
Key Verse: Acts 6:7

Focus of the Lesson:

Increased responsibilities in our personal and professional lives cause us to experience stress and conflict. How do people of faith handle these responsibilities in order to reduce conflict? The expansion of the early church provides a model for delegating responsibilities and handling conflict through its selection of the first servants of the church.

Goals for the Learners:

(1) to investigate the cause of the Hellenists' complaint regarding the neglect of their widows in the daily distribution of food.
(2) to examine their roles as servant-leaders.
(3) to develop tools for defusing potentially defusing conflict within the church.

Pronunciation Guide:

Alexandrian (al ig zan' dree uhn)
Cilicia (suh lish' ee uh)
Cyrenian (si ree' nee uhn)
diakonia (dee ak on ee' ah)
Hellenist (hel' uh nist)
martureo (mar too reh' o)

Nicanor (ni kay' nuhr)
Nicolaus (nik uh lay' uhs)
Parmenas (pahr' muh nuhs)
Prochorus (prok' uh ruhs)
Sanhedrin (san hee' druhn)
Timon (ti' muhn)

Supplies:

Bibles, newsprint and marker, paper and pencils, hymnals

READING THE SCRIPTURE

NRSV
Acts 6:1-5, 7-15
  ¹Now during those days, when the disciples were increasing in number, the

NIV
Acts 6:1-5, 7-15
  ¹In those days when the number of disciples was increasing, the Grecian Jews among

Hellenists complained against the Hebrews because their widows were being neglected in the daily distribution of food. [2]And the twelve called together the whole community of the disciples and said, "It is not right that we should neglect the word of God in order to wait on tables. [3]Therefore, friends, select from among yourselves seven men of good standing, full of the Spirit and of wisdom, whom we may appoint to this task, [4]while we, for our part, will devote ourselves to prayer and to serving the word." [5]What they said pleased the whole community, and they chose Stephen, a man full of faith and the Holy Spirit, together with Philip, Prochorus, Nicanor, Timon, Parmenas, and Nicolaus, a proselyte of Antioch.

[7]The word of God continued to spread; the number of the disciples increased greatly in Jerusalem.

[8]Stephen, full of grace and power, did great wonders and signs among the people. [9]Then some of those who belonged to the synagogue of the Freedmen (as it was called), Cyrenians, Alexandrians, and others of those from Cilicia and Asia, stood up and argued with Stephen. [10]But they could not withstand the wisdom and the Spirit with which he spoke. [11]Then they secretly instigated some men to say, "We have heard him speak blasphemous words against Moses and God." [12]They stirred up the people as well as the elders and the scribes; then they suddenly confronted him, seized him, and brought him before the council. [13]They set up false witnesses who said, "This man never stops saying things against this holy place and the law; [14]for we have heard him say that this Jesus of Nazareth will destroy this place and will change the customs that Moses handed on to us." [15]And all who sat in the council looked intently at him, and they saw that his face was like the face of an angel.

them complained against the Hebraic Jews because their widows were being overlooked in the daily distribution of food. [2]So the Twelve gathered all the disciples together and said, "It would not be right for us to neglect the ministry of the word of God in order to wait on tables. [3]Brothers, choose seven men from among you who are known to be full of the Spirit and wisdom. We will turn this responsibility over to them [4]and will give our attention to prayer and the ministry of the word."

[5]This proposal pleased the whole group. They chose Stephen, a man full of faith and of the Holy Spirit; also Philip, Procorus, Nicanor, Timon, Parmenas, and Nicolas from Antioch, a convert to Judaism.

[7]So the word of God spread. The number of disciples in Jerusalem increased rapidly.

[8]Now Stephen, a man full of God's grace and power, did great wonders and miraculous signs among the people. [9]Opposition arose, however, from members of the Synagogue of the Freedmen (as it was called)—Jews of Cyrene and Alexandria as well as the provinces of Cilicia and Asia. These men began to argue with Stephen, [10]but they could not stand up against his wisdom or the Spirit by whom he spoke.

[11]Then they secretly persuaded some men to say, "We have heard Stephen speak words of blasphemy against Moses and against God."

[12]So they stirred up the people and the elders and the teachers of the law. They seized Stephen and brought him before the Sanhedrin. [13]They produced false witnesses, who testified, "This fellow never stops speaking against this holy place and against the law. [14]For we have heard him say that this Jesus of Nazareth will destroy this place and change the customs Moses handed down to us."

[15]All who were sitting in the Sanhedrin looked intently at Stephen, and they saw that his face was like the face of an angel.

UNDERSTANDING THE SCRIPTURE

Acts 6:1. "Hellenists" refers not to Gentile Christians but rather to ethnic Jews and some Gentile proselytes (converts) to Judaism who lived in the eastern Mediterranean (see also Acts 2:9-11). "Complained" elicits memories of the Hebrews murmuring in the wilderness. The verb also occurs in Luke's Gospel to register negative reactions to Jesus' ministry among tax collectors and sinners (Luke 5:30; 15:2; 19:7). The problem of such complaint is the creation of division in the community. The cause of the complaint here is the "neglect" (a more literal rendering of this word might be "overlook") of the widows identified with the Hellenists. Care of widows was fundamental in Jewish law and tradition, and that attitude carried over into the early church. A clue to what is about to unfold comes in the way in which that neglect has shown itself: in the "daily distribution of food." The Greek word translated as "distribution" is *diakonia*. That word's original association with the servant who waits on tables came to be used in the church as a synonym for ministry.

Acts 6:2-4. The complaint that threatens division in community results in those charged with leadership (the Twelve) gathering the whole community, rather than making a decision independent of community. "Wait on tables" in Greek is *diakoneo*, the verb form of the word identified previously. The role of the community as a whole is underscored by the apostles' entrusting the community with the selection of those to be appointed to this task (in Greek, the word for "task" can also mean "need"). One key characteristic of those to be selected is that they are to be "of good standing." The Greek word is *martureo*. Its original meaning was "to witness" or "testify" (thus, these individuals were to be well spoken of in the community). Ironically, one of those selected would become the first of the church's martyrs in the ensuing meaning of

that word of one who dies for faith's testimony. In another irony, when the Twelve go on to describe what their continuing responsibilities will be, devotion to prayer is joined with "serving" (*diakonia*) the Word.

Acts 6:5-7. The emphasis on the healing of the division threatened by the complaining comes in the affirmation that the "whole" community chose Stephen and the others. All of those selected bear Greek rather than Jewish names, strongly asserting that the community sought to redress the neglect by selecting individuals from the segment of the community that had felt overlooked. Empowerment follows inclusion. The other name on the list that will play a role later in this text and another key episode in Acts is Philip (Acts 8:26-40). The laying on of hands has its roots in Jewish rituals of investing an office. It was part of the rite for consecrating the Levites (Numbers 8:10). When it came time for Moses to pass on leadership to Joshua, God instructed Moses to lay his hands upon Joshua before Israel to commission him (Numbers 27:18-19). Elsewhere in Acts, the laying on of hands accompanies healing (9:17), ordination or commissioning (13:3), and the Spirit's gift following baptism (8:17). The brief reference to the response of the "priests" may hint at the growing tension between this new messianic community and the Jewish Temple establishment.

Acts 6:8-10. The qualities and actions attributed to Stephen connect to earlier affirmations made about the apostles and the community gathered around them. "Grace" and "power" had been used in 4:33 to depict the apostles' testimony and the state enjoyed by the community. This pairing of words appears elsewhere in Pauline Epistles to affirm the works and gift of Christ (Romans 1:4-5) as well as in Paul's confession about how he faces weakness in his own life and troubles from outside (2 Corinthians 12:9-10).

Synagogues had been developed during the Babylonian exile (and Diaspora to other lands) as a way of maintaining Jewish community without the existence of a temple. Even after the Temple's reconstruction, the synagogue grew in importance along with the parties associated with it (Pharisees and scribes). "Freedmen" suggests, but does not prove, a group composed of former Roman slaves. The locations with which they are identified more clearly indicate they, too, are Hellenists. As parties vied within Judaism for dominance (Zealots, Sadducees, Pharisees, Essenes) so apparently were the Hellenists divided. And it is Hellenist Jews, not Hebrew/Judean ones, who come into conflict with Stephen for reasons not identified.

Acts 6:11-15. The plot that hatches against Stephen bears close parallels to that which ensnared Jesus. The movement begins not in the public's eye, but in secrecy (Luke 19:47-48; 22:6). Charges of blasphemy are laid (Matthew 26:65). False witnesses are produced who charge Stephen with speaking against the Temple (Mark 14:55-58). "Council" refers to the Jewish Sanhedrin, a body of elders numbering seventy plus the high priest. Much controversy surrounds what the Sanhedrin could and could not do,

especially in terms of capital offenses (John 18:31-32). Disagreement is equally pronounced over how the Sanhedrin is depicted as functioning in the New Testament, as trials by night or on the spur of the moment were not the normal operating procedure. Our passage ends before the story eventually plays out in the stoning of Stephen, whose dying words closely parallel those of Jesus.

Acts 8:1-8. Saul had appeared in the stoning scene (7:58) as the one at whose feet the cloaks of the executioners were placed. Saul now moves from witness to one who approves the killing and will later be identified with the persecution unleashed on the church (9:1-2). The scattering by violence could be seen as a "seeding," whose results will be entirely opposite of what the persecutors intended. Such is the meaning of the second half of this passage. Philip, one of those "ordained" with Stephen, ends up in Samaria. As the Samaritans had earlier proved hospitable to Jesus (John 4:40-42), so now do they respond to Philip. The gospel spreads from Judea to Samaria, a region and people viewed as out of bounds by respectable religious folks. It is the first of many boundary crossings the gospel will make in Acts . . . and beyond.

INTERPRETING THE SCRIPTURE

Ministry as Distribution

Sometimes ministry is regarded primarily in terms of a structure or hierarchy within the church. Today's passage, among others, strongly reminds us that ministry must also be lifted up in dynamic terms—that is, what it does. The New Testament's adoption of *diakonia* ("table servants") as its chief word for ministry reminds us that ministry was rooted in action before it became structured. Or, to borrow a phrase often used in reference to architecture but

equally telling on ministry: form follows function.

As passages like 1 Corinthians 12:4-11 remind us, ministry may take many forms or functions. But for the moment, let us follow the one that takes center stage in Acts 6: ministry as distribution.

Think of ministry as distribution in its literal sense here. A crisis arose in ministry because some were being neglected in the distribution (again, that word *diakonia*) of food. But consider the form of ministry related to "distribution." Vital ministry meets the needs of those it is charged to care for. Both pastoral and prophetic ministry today rely on distributing what individuals and congregations most need for life, whether in word or in action.

Another key element of ministry as distribution takes shape in what the apostles do. They do not cling to the identified need in the community and add it to already growing lists of responsibilities. Rather, they engage a process that "distributes" the ministry tasks to others. Ministry is not the possession of the few. It is the calling of the whole community. Burnout and unrealistic expectations on clergy are but two signs of ministry not being distributed. The opening verses of Acts 6 remind us that ministry functions best when needs are identified *and* responsibilities are distributed for the good of the whole.

Leadership Marks

Bookstore shelves are filled with works on leadership these days. Christian bookstores likewise have no shortage of similar works. Before we rush out and jump on the latest bandwagon and enrich the royalty revenue of someone who may not know you or your congregation from Adam, we might want to reflect on what this passage identifies as leadership marks of those selected—and, in particular, of Stephen.

"Of good standing" (6:3) is a prerequisite of character the apostles identify to preface the community's selection. As noted in the comments on verse 3 in Understanding the Scripture, the phrase translates a word that basically means "testify" or "witness." In other words, choose someone whom others can vouch for. It remains good advice in the secular world and in the church. Listen to references. Leadership is not something to be gauged simply by how someone appears in an interview or what they say they can or cannot do. Leadership is recognized by experience of others. If others are willing to put their word on the line to speak for someone, their witness is worth hearing.

When Stephen is chosen, Acts notes that he is "full of faith and the Holy Spirit" (6:5). Leaders are not made simply by the possession of skills to be checked off on a job inventory. Leadership goes deeper. In the case of the church, faith and Spirit are requisites for leadership because they speak to that deeper need of leaders not simply to know the job but to be part of what gives life to the community. Spirit gave life to this community on Pentecost and continues to do so. And faith? Faith trusts God's continuing presence and movement. Faith understands that the church is more than a collection of pious (and often not so pious) individuals. And remember: The opposite of faith is not doubt in the New Testament. Faith's opposite is fear. The faith of Stephen becomes clearest, not in any doctrinal statement he offers (though Acts 7 will reveal he can preach); rather, Stephen's faith shines clearest at the time of his martyrdom. For even in that extreme circumstance, fear finds no room in his trust of God.

Such faith and Spirit lead to the concluding assessment of Stephen's leadership qualities in verse 8: "full of grace and power." The author leaves undisclosed what power his leadership exercises, beyond a summary of his doing "wonders and signs" (6:8). But grace is different. Full of grace is not only a testament to what fills Stephen's life and makes him a leader. Full of grace is also how Stephen lives his life in the exercise of leadership. For what other than grace can explain Stephen forgiving those who rain down stones on him (Acts 7:60)? Grace in a leader is what enables seeking the community's good, even the good of those who don't have a clue about grace. That is, until they are *led* to see it in action.

Putting a Face on Angels

"They saw that [Stephen's] face was like the face of an angel" (Acts 6:15).

Be truthful now: What does that conjure in your mind that Stephen's face looked like?

That he was cherubic? That he was benignly smiling, or glowing, or some other such thing? What does an angel look like anyway?

The text really does not explain at all what was meant by this. We are left to draw our own conclusions, or exercise our own imaginations, as to the face of an angel.

But maybe it would help to remember what angels *do* in the biblical witness. The English word "angel" comes from the Greek and originated as a reference to a messenger. And that is mostly what angels do in both Old and New Testaments. They bring messages. An angel greets Mary and announces the news of God's favor. An angel greets shepherds on the Bethlehem hillside to tell them news of a great joy for all people. An angel (or two angels, depending on which Gospel you read) greets women outside the tomb with the news that Jesus was not there because God has raised him from death.

At least two things are common in those three angel episodes that may help us see why those folks saw in Stephen the face of an angel. First, in all three cases, the news brought by angels was extraordinary and life-changing. What Stephen has done, and is about to say to them in Chapter 7, is nothing less than the same. Second, in all three cases, the news brought by angels resulted first in fear. The problem that follows in Acts 7 is that the fear of this "angel" builds to a killing crescendo.

And lest we get too comfortable in our disgust at these council members, let us remember that attempting to squelch unwelcome news or messages by squelching the messengers (literally, "angels") remains standard operating procedure in many quarters today. That is, we do not like what we hear so we turn our ire on who we hear it from.

"They saw that his face was like the face of an angel" (6:15). Maybe the question is not so much what the face of an angel might look like today but what the words of an angel might be.

SHARING THE SCRIPTURE

Preparing Our Hearts

Meditate on this week's devotional reading, found in Acts 1:3-11. "You will receive power . . . you will be my witnesses" (1:8). How has the Holy Spirit empowered you to witness for Jesus? What has it cost you to be a witness? What have been the fruits of your witness? Keep your own experiences in mind as you read today's passage and consider the witness Stephen made that cost him his life.

Pray that you and the adult learners will be ready to act through the empowerment of the Spirit to speak a word and do a deed according to the Spirit's leading.

Preparing Our Minds

Study the background from Acts 6:1-15 and 8:1-8 and the lesson Scripture from Acts 6:1-5, 8-15. Think about how people of faith handle personal and professional responsibilities in order to reduce conflict.

Write on newsprint:
❑ information for next week's lesson, found under "Continue the Journey."
❑ activities for further spiritual growth in "Continue the Journey."

Prepare to read aloud Acts 6:1-5. You will find the Pronunciation Guide to be helpful.

LEADING THE CLASS

(1) Gather to Learn

❖ Welcome the class members and introduce any guests.
❖ Pray that all who have come today

will be energized by the Spirit to serve Christ according to their gifts and the needs of the church.

❖ Read this case study: **Mr. Arnett owns a business. He has competent people in all departments but feels that he must be involved in every little detail of the operation. The work is too much for him, but because he won't let go of any aspect of the business, he is getting extremely stressed and irritable. His employees are also frustrated and some have quit because they are given menial tasks that do not engage their skills and talents. Mr. Arnett has hired you as a business consultant to help him figure out what to do. What suggestions would you make to him?**

❖ Read aloud today's focus statement: **Increased responsibilities in our personal and professional lives cause us to experience stress and conflict. How do people of faith handle these responsibilities in order to reduce conflict? The expansion of the early church provides a model for delegating responsibilities and handling conflict through its selection of the first servants of the church.**

(2) Investigate the Cause of the Hellenists' Complaint Regarding the Neglect of Their Widows in the Daily Distribution of Food

❖ Read aloud Acts 6:1-5 and then discuss these questions:
  (1) **What was the problem that was causing the Hellenists to complain?**
  (2) **How was the problem solved?**
  (3) **What traits were considered necessary for those who would assume the newly assigned tasks?** (List ideas on newsprint.)
  (4) **How were these men commissioned?**
  (5) **What examples can you think of in your own congregation where a problem was solved by the delegation of tasks?**

❖ Select a volunteer to read Acts 6:8-15.
  ■ Use information for these verses from Understanding the Scripture to explore Stephen's opponents and their plot against him.
  ■ Try to draw comparisons between the way Stephen was treated and the way Jesus was treated just prior to his crucifixion.
  ■ Ask: **How can the way Stephen handled this church confrontation, which resulted in his death, be a model for you?**

(3) Examine the Learners' Roles as Servant-Leaders

❖ Read or retell "Leadership Marks" from Interpreting the Scripture.

❖ Refer to the list you made of traits necessary for leadership. Invite the students to compare the list used by the early church with the spoken or unspoken list used to choose leaders in your congregation.

❖ Discuss these questions:
  (1) **As a church, are we looking for leaders with the spiritual qualities of the early church or do we have other criteria? If so, what are these other criteria?**
  (2) **Do you think we ask too much—or too little—of our leaders in terms of their spiritual preparation for and commitment to their jobs? What changes could we make in the way we recruit and train our leaders?**

❖ Distribute paper and pencils. Tell the students that since what you will ask them to write is for their eyes only, they should be as honest as possible. Invite them to do three things. First, list the traits they possess as servant-leaders. Next, list work that they do as servant-leaders on behalf of our Lord, either within or outside the church. Finally, evaluate themselves as to whether they are using their gifts and talents in accordance with God's will for their lives.

❖ Call time and suggest that the adults put these sheets in their Bible where they can refer back to them to see how well they are fulfilling their roles as servant-leaders.

(4) Develop Tools for Defusing Potentially Divisive Conflict Within the Church

❖ Recall the problem addressed in Acts 6 *(widows were not receiving food)* and its solution *(the leaders called the whole church together and suggested that the church select "men of good standing" [6:3] who would oversee this task).*

❖ Talk with the class for a few moments about how effective they believe such a process was.

❖ Invite the students to discuss how their congregation generally handles conflict.

❖ Ask these questions. Use the answers to develop a written plan for conflict resolution.

(1) **Does our preferred way of handling conflict as a congregation tend to heal us or drive us apart? Why?**

(2) **If our method is not working, what strategies could we use to resolve conflict in a healthy way, that is, in a way that solves the problem but does not create hard feelings and division?**

(3) **What lessons can we learn from the early church about resolving conflict?** (Note these points: The leadership took the complaint seriously; the problem was brought out into the open and discussed; all were invited to participate in the resolution; people paid attention to their leaders; delegation of tasks helped all involved; people recognized gifts in others that would allow them to deal successfully with the problem.)

(5) Continue the Journey

❖ Pray that all who have come today will be open to discerning gifts for leadership in themselves and others, and then act so as to use these gifts.

❖ Read aloud this preparation for next week's lesson. You may also want to post it on newsprint for the students to copy.

■ **Title: Transformed to Witness to the Community**
■ **Background Scripture: Acts 9:1-31**
■ **Lesson Scripture: Acts 9:1-11, 16-19**
■ **Focus of the Lesson: Human beings are sometimes involved in destructive patterns of behavior. What help is available that would rechannel our energy in a positive direction? The story of Saul's conversion from a persecutor to a preacher provides for the faith community a positive example of transformation in Christ.**

❖ Challenge the students to complete one or more of these activities for further spiritual growth, which you will write on newsprint for the students to copy.

(1) **Think of at least one way that you can be a servant-leader this week. Identify a person or group that needs assistance and use your gifts on their behalf.**

(2) **Identify someone you believe has the gifts and graces for a particular ministry. Encourage this person to use these gifts, which he or she may not even recognize.**

(3) **Refer to your personal list of servant-leader traits. Be alert for opportunities to use these traits to serve others.**

❖ Sing or read aloud "O Master, Let Me Walk With Thee."

❖ Conclude today's session by leading the class in this benediction, adapted from Ephesians 4:4-6: **Let us now depart rejoicing in the community we share, united as one body, with one Spirit, one Lord, one faith, one baptism, and one God and Father of all.**

UNIT 2: THE DEVELOPMENT AND
WORK OF THE NEW COMMUNITY

TRANSFORMED TO WITNESS TO THE COMMUNITY

PREVIEWING THE LESSON

Lesson Scripture: Acts 9:1-11, 16-19
Background Scripture: Acts 9:1-31
Key Verse: Acts 9:17

Focus of the Lesson:
Human beings are sometimes involved in destructive patterns of behavior. What help is available that would rechannel our energy in a positive direction? The story of Saul's conversion from a persecutor to a preacher provides for the faith community a positive example of transformation in Christ.

Goals for the Learners:
(1) to introduce the story of Saul's dramatic conversion experience on the road to Damascus.
(2) to recognize how Christ is transforming them to be witnesses.
(3) to develop and implement a strategy for witnessing to others about the transforming power of Christ.

Pronunciation Guide:
Ananias (an uh ni' uhs)   Hellenist (hel' uh nist)
Barnabas (bahr' nuh buhs)   Tarsus (tahr' suhs)
Cesaerea (ses uh ree' uh)   theophany (thee of' uh nee)

Supplies:
Bibles, newsprint and markers, paper and pencils, hymnals

READING THE SCRIPTURE

NRSV
Acts 9:1-11, 16-19
¹Meanwhile Saul, still breathing threats and murder against the disciples of the Lord,

NIV
Acts 9:1-11, 16-19
¹Meanwhile, Saul was still breathing out murderous threats against the Lord's disciples.

went to the high priest ²and asked him for letters to the synagogues at Damascus, so that if he found any who belonged to the Way, men or women, he might bring them bound to Jerusalem. ³Now as he was going along and approaching Damascus, suddenly a light from heaven flashed around him. ⁴He fell to the ground and heard a voice saying to him, "Saul, Saul, why do you persecute me?" ⁵He asked, "Who are you, Lord?" The reply came, "I am Jesus, whom you are persecuting. ⁶But get up and enter the city, and you will be told what you are to do." ⁷The men who were traveling with him stood speechless because they heard the voice but saw no one. ⁸Saul got up from the ground, and though his eyes were open, he could see nothing; so they led him by the hand and brought him into Damascus. ⁹For three days he was without sight, and neither ate nor drank.

¹⁰Now there was a disciple in Damascus named Ananias. The Lord said to him in a vision, "Ananias." He answered, "Here I am, Lord." ¹¹The Lord said to him, "Get up and go to the street called Straight, and at the house of Judas look for a man of Tarsus named Saul. At this moment he is praying. . . . ¹⁶I myself will show him how much he must suffer for the sake of my name." ¹⁷So Ananias went and entered the house. He laid his hands on Saul and said, "Brother Saul, **the Lord Jesus, who appeared to you on your way here, has sent me so that you may regain your sight and be filled with the Holy Spirit."** ¹⁸And immediately something like scales fell from his eyes, and his sight was restored. Then he got up and was baptized, ¹⁹and after taking some food, he regained his strength.

He went to the high priest ²and asked him for letters to the synagogues in Damascus, so that if he found any there who belonged to the Way, whether men or women, he might take them as prisoners to Jerusalem. ³As he neared Damascus on his journey, suddenly a light from heaven flashed around him. ⁴He fell to the ground and heard a voice say to him, "Saul, Saul, why do you persecute me?"

⁵"Who are you, Lord?" Saul asked.

"I am Jesus, whom you are persecuting," he replied. ⁶"Now get up and go into the city, and you will be told what you must do."

⁷The men traveling with Saul stood there speechless; they heard the sound but did not see anyone. ⁸Saul got up from the ground, but when he opened his eyes he could see nothing. So they led him by the hand into Damascus. ⁹For three days he was blind, and did not eat or drink anything.

¹⁰In Damascus there was a disciple named Ananias. The Lord called to him in a vision, "Ananias!"

"Yes, Lord," he answered.

¹¹The Lord told him, "Go to the house of Judas on Straight Street and ask for a man from Tarsus named Saul, for he is praying.

¹⁶I will show him how much he must suffer for my name."

¹⁷Then Ananias went to the house and entered it. Placing his hands on Saul, he said, "Brother Saul, **the Lord—Jesus, who appeared to you on the road as you were coming here—has sent me so that you may see again and be filled with the Holy Spirit."** ¹⁸Immediately, something like scales fell from Saul's eyes, and he could see again. He got up and was baptized, ¹⁹and after taking some food, he regained his strength.

UNDERSTANDING THE SCRIPTURE

Acts 9:1-2. This passage relates the first of three separate accounts in Acts of the conversion of Saul/Paul (see also 22:3-16; 26:4-

23). "Still" in verse 1 suggests this narrative continues the persecution unleashed in the wake of Stephen's martyrdom (8:1). It also links Saul's activity in this persecution with his previous approval of Stephen's death (8:1; see also 7:58). Letters from the high priest in Jerusalem would have provided Saul with a religious/legal foundation for his work in a city well to the north of Jerusalem (about 133 miles). Verse 2 provides the first of several references in Acts to the Christian movement as the "Way." The term is not without irony. "Torah," whose observance formed the core of Pharisaic Judaism, had a meaning closely akin to "guidance" or even "path."

Acts 9:3-9. The burst of light has the marks of an Old Testament theophany (encounter with God) story, such as Israel before Sinai (Exodus 19:16) or Ezekiel's vision of the throne chariot (Ezekiel 1:4 and following). The text suggests that Saul's falling to the ground is his own doing and choice, rather than the light somehow knocking him to the ground. Falling to the ground can be an act of fearful respect or worship (the literal meaning of the Greek word for "worship" is "to bend the knee"). To attribute worship to Saul at this early point in the episode would be too much, even as his addressing of the voice as "Lord" is not yet a confession of faith. Saul's act of falling and speaking of "Lord" does, however, suggest he understands himself to be in a situation of encounter with God. In this passage, Saul's companions hear the voice. In the account given by 22:3-16, the companions see the light but do not hear the voice. The message given to Saul here is simply to enter the city and wait to find out what is to be done. In the account given by 26:4-23, the voice discloses to Saul not only the promise of deliverance but also his call to the Gentile mission.

Acts 9:10-16. Ananias appears only here and in the account of Saul's conversion in 22:12. The text does not indicate how this disciple of Jesus (not to mention the Christian community Saul had initially sought out) got to Damascus in the first place. The placement of this story after the accounts of the "scattering" of the church that became a planting

of it in far-reaching territories suggests that as a possibility, though it cannot be proven. Both Ananias and Saul are described as having visions. Visions will continue to play an important role through Acts in general, and in the ministry of Saul/Paul in particular (16:9; 18:9). Without specifying exactly what they consist of, visions accentuate the role of God and the Spirit in moving forward the actions of the apostles and others. Prayer (9:11) likewise will become an important theme and action throughout Acts. Prayer often serves as a prelude, as it does here, for action carried out or made possible by God's Spirit (21:14; 10:2, 9).

Acts 9:17-19. The laying on of hands, as noted in the previous session (Acts 6:6), was related not only to healing but also to commissioning. Both meanings seem evident here (and in 9:12, 15). The healing Ananias is asked to do will result in the issuing of a call. Ananias addresses Saul as "brother," a subtle indication of his recognition of Saul as part of the community. That recognition seems even more explicit when Ananias follows words concerning healing with those that invoke the gift of the Spirit at the end of verse 17. In Acts, the order of the Spirit's infilling and baptism can differ. Here, Spirit precedes baptism. Elsewhere it is the reverse (8:16). Verse 19 indicates that Saul "got up" after his healing. It is the same verb used in verse 6 when Jesus orders Saul to "get up." This same word is the verb used for resurrection in Luke and the other Gospels. After the encounter, after healing, Saul "rises" to new life.

Acts 9:19-25. This portion narrates Saul's time and ministry in Damascus. "Synagogues" (plural) indicate that Damascus had a substantial Jewish population. The reaction to Saul's proclamation of Jesus as the Son of God is amazement—the same word used to describe the reaction of the crowds at Pentecost (2:7, 12). The wonderings (9:21) about Saul leave it unclear whether they are positive or negative reactions to this change. Opposition to Saul arises among the Jewish community, though it is not indicated whether this was widespread or the reactions of a few whose own power may have been threatened by Saul's becoming "increasingly more powerful" (9:22). As Saul had been healed by Ananias, so does he find deliverance from actions taken by the community. His lowering in a "basket" may have ironic undertones of Moses' deliverance in a basket (Exodus 2:3).

Acts 9:26-30. A parallel to Saul's time in Damascus is now followed by an account of his time in Jerusalem. The first negative reaction comes from the Christian community. The intervention of Barnabas, a future missionary partner of Saul (Acts 13:2), brought Saul's acceptance into the community. Once again, conflict quickly ensued. The opposition is now led by the Hellenists, quite likely the same group who took on Stephen (6:9-14). Once again, Saul is the beneficiary of the community's protection. They arrange for his escape to Caesarea, an imperial seaport, and then on to Tarsus, Saul's home city, located close to what is today southeastern Turkey.

Acts 9:31. Another summary statement about the church (2:42-47; 4:32-35) affirms God's purposes continue to move forward. In spite of opposition, the church enjoys peace and continues to multiply. The verse serves to close the door on the crisis of martyrdom and persecution with Saul waiting in the wings. In doing so, it sets the stage for the next major upheaval brought by the Spirit's expanding work: the inclusion of Gentiles in God's community (10:1 and following), first by the work of Peter and then by the apostle to the Gentiles, Saul soon to be known as Paul.

INTERPRETING THE SCRIPTURE

Bad Starts and Second Chances

"You never get a second chance to make a first impression." The truth of that sounds throughout the second half of today's passage. The history of Saul/Paul set up huge roadblocks to his acceptance by the church. But the story of the transformation of Saul/Paul counters with the gospel's grace that none of us is consigned to dwell forever in those first (or second) impressions. Change can come.

For all appearances, Saul is hopeless. He is a religious zealot—and some would rightly argue, a religious bigot. "Breathing threats and murder" (9:1) summons a powerful image of just how deeply Saul has fallen into the pit of hatred. In the days before cardiac monitors and machines that detected brain wave activity, breath was the sign of life. Only in Saul's case, breath betrayed the stench of death levied and sought against others, purely on the basis of religious belief.

Surely such a one was outside the bounds of grace! Then again, surely was a thief in the midst of crucifixion, who admitted his deserving of such a torturous death, outside the bounds of grace. Similar "certainties" in Jesus' day surrounded tax collectors and Samaritans and sinners of various sorts and sordid pasts. Yet to one the promise of that day's end in paradise is given, and to others the call to discipleship, and to others the welcome of table fellowship—all by the grace enacted in the words and actions of Jesus. For the worst of starts cannot rule out the possibility of gracious transformation.

These stories, Saul/Paul only one among many, bear hearing in the church. Some among us are quick to rule this group out of bounds, and that individual out of luck, because what they do offends us. Sometimes, we are right to be offended.

Sometimes, we are far off-target in our own bias. But always, those we view as bad starts—or bad ones—are apt to be claimed by grace. Grace breathes life and offers second chances to all—even, if the truth be told (or known), to us.

Stopped in Our Tracks

Some factions in the church would insist Saul's dramatic conversion to be the norm and pattern for all: a singular event that happens at a specific time, where before one was "outside" and after one was "inside." Nowhere does Saul (later Paul) make that claim. In Acts, the accounts are as much concerned with the commissioning that follows as with the precise sequence of light, fall, voice, rise, and so on.

That is not to say, however, that coming to faith—which can be a long process rather than a once-in-a-lifetime moment—is without times of stark turning . . . or being stopped in our tracks by the grace, call, and awareness of God.

Consider this study group you lead and are part of. Hopefully, this is not a program simply to impart holy information so that we all may be better "informed" about God. Are there not times in study, within the group or apart, that something strikes us so hard that we are brought to new insight about faith? The same hope applies to experiences of worship. Hopefully, we do not gather simply to repeat liturgies that are familiar to us or hear the eloquence (or lack thereof) of our ministers. Hopefully, from time to time, something happens that reminds us we stand on holy ground. Faith is *not* always and everywhere about continuity and routine. Sometimes, God's Spirit evokes change of direction—in individuals, in communities. Sometimes we do need to stop treading the path we have been following and strike out on a new one.

Sometimes, we stand in need of a Damascus Road experience to stop us in our tracks and restore us to God's tracks.

"Here I Am"

Ananias is a saint.

Ananias is remarkably open to God. He responds to God's speaking his name with "Here I am" (9:10). It is not "why me?" It is not "come back later!" It is a word that opens Ananias to God in the moment. Now.

Ananias is remarkably frank with God. After hearing the call to go and heal Saul, Ananias raises hard issues with God. About the kind of man Saul is. About the evil things Saul has done. About the threat Saul brings to the community and, without saying so, to himself. Ananias does not hold these things inside and unspoken, allowing them to churn in his heart and sabotage honesty with deception. Ananias speaks truthfully to God about the problem with what God has said—or should I say, about the problem with *whom* God has said. Like the laments of the Psalms, Ananias airs the complaint.

And Ananias is remarkably trusting and faithful, for once the complaint is given response, Ananias steps out of his comfort zone and does what is called for. To an enemy, in the name of Christ, he offers healing. And he offers baptism, which is another way of saying he offered entrance into the very community Saul had so earnestly sought to eliminate.

Would that every church had an Ananias!

Would that every church had someone so remarkably open to God as to be able to say without pause or fear, "Here I am." "Here we are. Now. What would you have us do?"

Would that every church had someone so remarkably frank with God. "God, do you see the suffering over there?" "God, do you know what kind of people those are . . . and I am?" Frankness with God is the best way to receive God's reply, "Yes, I do. I can even see what kind of people they could become. So can I work through you to help?"

Would that every church had someone so remarkably trusting or faithful. "You want us to minister to those ones we always considered your enemies as well as ours? To call them not the usual names and labels but brother or sister? Here I am."

In truth, every church *does* have someone like Ananias, at least someone called to be an Ananias. I can even name that one: you.

Restoration and Vocation

The goal of Christian faith is not to *get* saved. The goal of Christian faith is to *live* saved. A friend of mine reminded me of that truth in a class the other day on Nicodemus. Birth (as in "born again" or "born anew") is the starting point in life, not its end.

The conversion of Saul does not end the story of Acts, or his portion in it. It simply opens the door to a life lived now in recognition and faithfulness to the One Saul encountered on the road.

Saul's restoration to health, a physical expression of his saving, becomes prelude to his vocation. In each of the accounts of his conversion, vocation is a part of the story, but by the third time it is related (the second time from Saul's own lips), his call to ministry is not only made more explicit but also attributed to the words of Jesus even while Saul was still on the ground.

That is why the title of this book we now study is so appropriate: The *Acts* of the Apostles. The apostles, Saul/Paul among them, do not put in for a retirement check once salvation comes. Rather, that encounter with grace became the summons to ministry and service and witness.

It still does.

SHARING THE SCRIPTURE

Preparing Our Hearts

Meditate on this week's devotional reading, found in Galatians 1:11-24. Here Paul writes of his earlier life, of his persecution of the church, and of his life-changing experience. He wants his readers to understand that what he writes comes from God, not from him. Recall a transformation in your own life. Write about it in your journal. What was the catalyst that sparked this transformation? How did this change really affect your life?

Pray that you and the adult learners will be open to transforming experiences, especially ones that empower you to be a more faithful witness for Jesus Christ.

Preparing Our Minds

Study the background from Acts 9:1-31 and the lesson Scripture from Acts 9:1-11, 16-19. Think about the kind of help that is available to rechannel our energy in a positive direction when we are involved in destructive patterns of behavior.

Write on newsprint:
❏ information for next week's lesson, found under "Continue the Journey."
❏ activities for further spiritual growth in "Continue the Journey."

LEADING THE CLASS

(1) Gather to Learn

❖ Welcome the class members and introduce any guests.

❖ Pray that the participants will be open to a deeper relationship with Christ.

❖ Read this information aloud: **In 1985, a Lutheran congregation was formed for persons incarcerated in the state prisons in Maryland. Called Saint Dysmas, the traditional name of the thief on the cross with Jesus, this is a real congregation that bap-**

tizes members, serves weekly Holy Communion, conducts worship, and offers Bible studies. It ministers in medium and maximum security facilities for both men and women. At Saint Dysmas, those on the inside encounter volunteers from the outside and touch one another's lives. Only a fraction of Saint Dysmas members return to prison, whereas the general rate of recidivism is about 70 percent.

❖ Discuss these questions:

(1) Do you believe that it is possible for people engaged in destructive behavior patterns, including crime, to be transformed? Explain your answer.

(2) How do you imagine the Saint Dysmas congregation facilitates life-changing experiences?

❖ Read aloud today's focus statement: **Human beings are sometimes involved in destructive patterns of behavior. What help is available that would rechannel our energy in a positive direction? The story of Saul's conversion from a persecutor to a preacher provides for the faith community a positive example of transformation in Christ.**

(2) Introduce the Story of Saul's Dramatic Conversion Experience on the Road to Damascus

❖ Choose a volunteer to read Acts 9:1-11, 16-19. Invite two volunteers to pantomime the roles of Saul and Ananias. (If falling to the ground is not a good option for the "Saul" volunteer, ask him to slump in a chair, perhaps with his head on a table.)

❖ Encourage the adults to respond to the pantomime by stating how they would have felt and acted had they been Saul and how they would have felt and acted had they been Ananias.

❖ Divide the class into two groups. Give each group newsprint and a marker. One group will list all they can discern from this text about Saul. The other group will do the same for Ananias. (If the class is large, use multiple groups, assigning half to Saul and half to Ananias.) Word choices in different translations of the Bible may provide nuances to these two men's actions and attitudes.

❖ Call the groups together and ask a reporter for each one to report their findings and post the newsprint. Be prepared to add germane information from Understanding the Scripture.

❖ Conclude this portion by asking these questions:

(1) What does this passage say to you about how we are called to new life?

(2) What role do others in the faith community play in assisting us in this transformation? (If time permits, you may want to consider the importance of the faith community, for while some people insist that they can be spiritual Lone Rangers, the biblical record makes clear that we need each other.)

(3) Recognize How Christ Is Transforming the Learners to Be Witnesses

❖ Distribute paper and pencils. Ask the students to draw a line horizontally across the paper. Suggest that they put the date of their birth at the far left and today's date at the far right. Encourage them to mark places along their faith journey where they believe Christ has moved in transforming, though not necessarily spectacular, ways.

❖ Provide a few moments of quiet time for the adults to give thanks for these opportunities to better reflect the likeness of Christ.

❖ Call on volunteers who are willing to share briefly a meaningful event in their faith journey.

(4) Develop and Implement a Strategy for Witnessing to Others About the Transforming Power of Christ

❖ Read aloud "Here I Am" from Interpreting the Scripture. Invite the students to comment on how Ananias is a mentor for Saul and a role model for us as people who seek to help others grow into the likeness of Christ.

❖ Note that, as the last paragraph points out, every church has an Ananias and that you (that is, each one of us) are that person.

❖ Distribute paper and pencils if you have not already done so. Encourage the adults to name at least one person they could witness to, mentor, and possibly draw into the church. Suggest that they outline steps they will take to contact this person and speak to him or her about faith in Christ and his saving power.

❖ Commission one another to act by asking each adult to turn to a neighbor and state the steps he or she will take this week to reach someone for Christ.

(5) Continue the Journey

❖ Pray that all who have participated today will continue to grow in God's grace and witness to others about the Lord Jesus Christ.

❖ Read aloud this preparation for next week's lesson. You may also want to post it on newsprint for the students to copy.

- ■ **Title: Commissioned by the Community**
- ■ **Background Scripture: Acts 13**
- ■ **Lesson Scripture: Acts 13:1-12**
- ■ **Focus of the Lesson: Purposeful involvement in a community gives us a sense of satisfaction. Where**

can we find a community to which we want to dedicate our lives? The commissioning of Barnabas and Saul/Paul by the church at Antioch shows how the Holy Spirit motivates persons to represent the cause of Christ in the world.

❖ Challenge the students to complete one or more of these activities for further spiritual growth, which you will write on newsprint for the students to copy.

(1) **Talk with someone else about an experience that changed and somehow strengthened your relationship with Christ.**

(2) **Recall that Ananias acted as a mentor for Saul/Paul. To whom can you be a spiritual mentor? See what you can do to develop such a relationship.**

(3) **Notice that Ananias served as a reconciler within the Christian community. Where in your faith community is reconciliation needed? What can you do to build a bridge between people who are divided?**

❖ Sing or read aloud "Lord, Whose Love Through Humble Service."

❖ Conclude today's session by leading the class in this benediction, adapted from Ephesians 4:4-6: **Let us now depart rejoicing in the community we share, united as one body, with one Spirit, one Lord, one faith, one baptism, and one God and Father of all.**

UNIT 2: THE DEVELOPMENT AND
WORK OF THE NEW COMMUNITY

COMMISSIONED BY THE COMMUNITY

PREVIEWING THE LESSON

Lesson Scripture: Acts 13:1-12
Background Scripture: Acts 13
Key Verse: Acts 13:3

Focus of the Lesson:

Purposeful involvement in a community gives us a sense of satisfaction. Where can we find a community to which we want to dedicate our lives? The commissioning of Barnabas and Saul/Paul by the church at Antioch shows how the Holy Spirit motivates persons to represent the cause of Christ in the world.

Goals for the Learners:

(1) to summarize the account of the church's commissioning of Barnabas and Saul/Paul for the work to which the Holy Spirit had called them.
(2) to tell their own stories of being called to a task or ministry in the church.
(3) to make a commitment to answer God's call to work for the kingdom.

Pronunciation Guide:

Antioch (an' tee ok)
Barnabas (bahr' nuh buhs)
Elymas (el' uh muhs)
lectio divina (lek' tee oh di veen' a)
leiturgeo (li toorg eh' o)
Lucius of Cyrene (loo' shuhs of si ree' nee)
Manaen (man' ee uhn)

Niger (ni' guhr)
Pamphylia (pam fil' ee uh)
Paphos (pay' fos)
Salamis (sal' uh mis)
Seleucia (si loo' shuh)
Sergius Paulus (suhr' jee uhs paw' luhs)

Supplies:

Bibles, newsprint and marker, paper and pencils, hymnals, list of mission and ministry opportunities, optional map

READING THE SCRIPTURE

NRSV

Acts 13:1-12

¹Now in the church at Antioch there were prophets and teachers: Barnabas, Simeon who was called Niger, Lucius of Cyrene, Manaen a member of the court of Herod the ruler, and Saul. ²While they were worshiping the Lord and fasting, the Holy Spirit said, "Set apart for me Barnabas and Saul for the work to which I have called them." **³Then after fasting and praying they laid their hands on them and sent them off.**

⁴So, being sent out by the Holy Spirit, they went down to Seleucia; and from there they sailed to Cyprus. ⁵When they arrived at Salamis, they proclaimed the word of God in the synagogues of the Jews. And they had John also to assist them. ⁶When they had gone through the whole island as far as Paphos, they met a certain magician, a Jewish false prophet, named Bar-Jesus. ⁷He was with the proconsul, Sergius Paulus, an intelligent man, who summoned Barnabas and Saul and wanted to hear the word of God. ⁸But the magician Elymas (for that is the translation of his name) opposed them and tried to turn the proconsul away from the faith. ⁹But Saul, also known as Paul, filled with the Holy Spirit, looked intently at him ¹⁰and said, "You son of the devil, you enemy of all righteousness, full of all deceit and villainy, will you not stop making crooked the straight paths of the Lord? ¹¹And now listen—the hand of the Lord is against you, and you will be blind for a while, unable to see the sun." Immediately mist and darkness came over him, and he went about groping for someone to lead him by the hand. ¹²When the proconsul saw what had happened, he believed, for he was astonished at the teaching about the Lord.

NIV

Acts 13:1-12

¹In the church at Antioch there were prophets and teachers: Barnabas, Simeon called Niger, Lucius of Cyrene, Manaen (who had been brought up with Herod the tetrarch) and Saul. ²While they were worshiping the Lord and fasting, the Holy Spirit said, "Set apart for me Barnabas and Saul for the work to which I have called them." **³So after they had fasted and prayed, they placed their hands on them and sent them off.**

⁴The two of them, sent on their way by the Holy Spirit, went down to Seleucia and sailed from there to Cyprus. ⁵When they arrived at Salamis, they proclaimed the word of God in the Jewish synagogues. John was with them as their helper.

⁶They traveled through the whole island until they came to Paphos. There they met a Jewish sorcerer and false prophet named Bar-Jesus, ⁷who was an attendant of the proconsul, Sergius Paulus. The proconsul, an intelligent man, sent for Barnabas and Saul because he wanted to hear the word of God. ⁸But Elymas the sorcerer (for that is what his name means) opposed them and tried to turn the proconsul from the faith. ⁹Then Saul, who was also called Paul, filled with the Holy Spirit, looked straight at Elymas and said, ¹⁰"You are a child of the devil and an enemy of everything that is right! You are full of all kinds of deceit and trickery. Will you never stop perverting the right ways of the Lord? ¹¹Now the hand of the Lord is against you. You are going to be blind, and for a time you will be unable to see the light of the sun."

Immediately mist and darkness came over him, and he groped about, seeking someone to lead him by the hand. ¹²When the proconsul saw what had happened, he believed, for he was amazed at the teaching about the Lord.

UNDERSTANDING THE SCRIPTURE

Acts 13:1-3. "Prophets and teachers" suggests a developing set of offices in the apostolic church to go along with the earlier setting apart of deacons to relieve the apostles of some growing responsibilities. Barnabas was a Levite from the island of Cyprus. *Niger* is Latin for "black." Cyrene was an important city of a North African Roman province (modern-day Libya). "Member of the court" was a title given to youth who were raised as companions to royalty (in this case, Herod Antipas). *Leiturgeo* ("work of the people"), the root for the English word "liturgy," is translated here as "worshiping." Originally used in reference to the ritual done by the priests at the Temple, it became a synonym for public worship in the Christian community. "Fasting" as a spiritual discipline intends to focus one's life on things of the Spirit in hopes of creating greater openness to God's leading. It is coupled here with "praying," a key discipline of preparation throughout Acts. "Set apart" suggests designation to a special purpose. The Hebrew Scriptures spoke of setting apart clean from unclean. Here, the setting apart is for mission. Paul uses this same Greek word to relate his call as an apostle (Romans 1:1; Galatians 1:15).

Acts 13:4-12. These verses narrate the beginning of the first missionary journey of Saul called Paul (for the first time in Acts in verse 9). Salamis was a port city on the east coast of Cyprus. Paphos was the provincial capital of the island. Barnabas would have known those cities and their synagogues, as Cyprus was his home. The proconsul was the leading Roman administrator in a province. "Magician" translates the word *magos* (as in *magi* of the Matthew birth story). "False prophet" connects to traditions in the Hebrew Scriptures (Ezekiel 13:1-8) as well as threats faced in the early church (Matthew 7:15; 1 John 4:1). The action taken by Paul against Elymas is temporary ("for a while"). Its phys-ical effects bear close resemblance to what happened to Saul himself on the Damascus Road. Curiously, the proconsul comes to faith out of astonishment at the *teaching* rather than what befalls Elymas (or is that the teaching?). "Astonish" is the same word used in Luke 4:32 and Matthew 7:28 to describe the reaction of the crowds to Jesus' teaching.

Acts 13:13-15. "Paul and his companions" notes a significant shift. At the beginning of Chapter 13, Saul was listed last among those singled out in the Antioch church. The proconsul had summoned "Barnabas and Saul" to speak to him (13:7). Now, and from this point forward, the narrative of Acts centers on Paul and his primary role in the expansion of the church. Pamphylia was a district located in what is now south-central Turkey. The mention of John's (elsewhere called John Mark) departure here becomes an integral part of the later story of Paul and Barnabas's separation (15:36-41). The Antioch mentioned in verse 14 is an entirely different Antioch than the group's starting point in verse 1. The reputation of Paul and Barnabas apparently preceded them, as indicated by the synagogue leader's asking for them to speak in the Sabbath service.

Acts 13:16-25. "Others who fear God" likely referred to non-Hebrew worshipers. In this first half of Paul's "sermon" in the synagogue, he (like Stephen) offers a brief narration of Israel's sojourn from Egypt into the land, and from a tribal confederation to a monarchy. The transition to monarchy becomes a key juncture in the address, for Paul links the ascendancy of David with the lineage of Jesus ("of this man's posterity"). The quotation in verse 22 echoes 1 Samuel 13:14. The messianic associations with David find expression here in Paul's declaring of Jesus as "Savior." "Savior" had earlier been used as a title for the Emperor Augustus, especially in some Greek cities in Asia Minor (the general region in which

Paul and Barnabas now were). Paul's affirmation here of Jesus as "Savior" may be a subtle counterpoint to the imperial cult still strong in this region. The quotation attributed to John the Baptizer parallels closely the Gospels' reports of John's message. Besides serving to connect John's call to repentance with Paul's impending call to those he addresses, the quotation is an interesting example of the author of Acts "quoting" from oral or early written traditions, here about John, that will become the basis for the Gospels' compilations.

Acts 13:26-41. The second half of the sermon returns to a direct address of the audience in the synagogue (and the readers of Acts). The initial verses describe, as do other sermons in Acts, the failure of the leadership in Jerusalem to recognize Jesus and, instead, to kill him. In opposition to their plans, however, God intervenes—parallel to the sermon's opening affirmation of God's deliverance of Israel from Egypt. The sermon concludes with a series of four quotations from the Hebrew Scriptures (Psalm 2:7; Isaiah 55:3; Psalm 16:10; Habakkuk 1:5) with accompanying interpretation. Such use of quotations and then reflecting on them was an accepted and popular method of teaching in Judaism in this time. Some see it practiced also by Jesus ("You have heard that it was said. . . . But I say to you") in Matthew 5. The warning about scoffers in verse 41 forms a smooth transition into the opposition engendered by this sermon and all throughout this and later missionary journeys.

Acts 13:42-52. "The Jews" in verse 45 likely refers either to the synagogue leaders or to a group within it—after all, the passage clearly asserts the appeal of Paul and his message to many other Jews (13:42-44). The declaration of the mission to the Gentiles, accompanied by the quotation from Isaiah 49:6, while not new in Acts is certainly significant. The inciting of devout women is an intriguing line. It asserts the significance of women in this era's religious traditions. Later, such women will be drawn to the Christian movement. In Acts, as in Luke, the Gospel recognizes and emphasizes the role of women, even if at this juncture some of them form the opposition.

INTERPRETING THE SCRIPTURE

Community in Diversity

Tradition attributes the Gospel of Luke and The Acts of the Apostles to the same author. One common theme between these books is their witness to diversity of community.

In Luke, the characters swirling around Jesus in ministry and in teaching include Samaritans and women, shepherds and prodigals, in addition to disciples composed of fishers and publicans and Zealots. In Acts, that tradition continues. The crowds who heard Peter's sermon the day of Pentecost came from all parts of the then-known world. Here in Chapter 13, the author singles out the following prophets and teachers in the church at Antioch: a Cypriot and Levite, a North African, another who was called "Niger" (Latin for "black"), a member of the royal court, and a Hebrew and former enemy named Saul. Peter had earlier declared his understanding that God shows no "partiality" (Acts 10:34). In Antioch, the faces of the church are clearly diverse. Racially. Ethnically. Politically. Yet all find common grounding in the community of Jesus Christ, where common life is not just a slogan but a lifestyle of sharing (Acts 2:44-45; 4:33-35).

Diversity in community is honored in the

early church. Is that still true today? Here's a clue. Don't be satisfied with a church's talk. Watch its walk. Look at the folks who gather together. Perhaps even more important, look at those called to and vested in positions of leadership. Diversity makes for a great talking point, but its truth in community rests on practices that include those usually kept at arm's length. Like a member of Herod's court. Like a former persecutor of the church. Like racial minorities. Like . . . you fill in the blank that Acts 13:1 has only begun to complete.

Spiritual Disciplines

The last decade or two in the church has shown a resurgent interest in spiritual disciplines. It is not a new discovery. It is reclaiming an ancient tradition.

"Fasting and praying" (13:3, key verse) describe the disciplines engaged in by the community before they send Barnabas and Saul. Earlier in Acts, the community prays before reaching a decision on who should succeed Judas as one of the Twelve (1:24-25).

Note that in both of these cases spiritual disciplines are practiced by the whole community. This is not to devalue the importance of individual devotional practices. The ministry of Jesus is regularly punctuated with times of solitary retreat for prayer and renewal. But Acts affirms an equally important lesson for the practice of spiritual disciplines: They aim at strengthening the whole community.

What other practices constitute spiritual disciplines? Consider the aim of such disciplines: to bring us into deeper conscious awareness of God's presence around us and God's calling to us. What practices might enable you to do such things? Some practice journaling. Some use specific types of prayer. Some read Scripture in ways that have less to do with gaining information and more to do with "formation" by those words (for example, *lectio divina*).

Consider the disciplines encouraged and practiced by your own congregation. Sometimes, we place all of our eggs in one basket by making worship the only community discipline and private prayer the only individual discipline. Imagine what might result if individuals and groups in the church were encouraged to practice other forms of openness and responsiveness to God's presence and call. Acts tells the story of individuals and communities whose practice of spiritual disciplines draws them closer to God and one another even as it sends them farther into the world as witnesses.

Imagine that.

Set Apart and Sent

I have a vague childhood recollection of going to a party at my home church. It was for the children of a family who would soon be on their way to Japan. The mother was the daughter of our pastor. At the time, my main impression of the event was all the board games the children got (they would be traveling by ocean liner, not plane). Looking back, though, I wonder how it felt for my pastor and his wife to be sending off their daughter (and grandchildren!) to a place with no guarantees of a reunion.

Consider our text from Acts. Two of the five leaders singled out in the Antioch church are about to be sent off to do the work of God. Was there not enough godly work around Antioch? Were some wondering, "Couldn't we just set them apart to work among us without having to send them off?"

Acts doesn't tell us. Maybe it doesn't need to. Why? We already know those pulls on us. Think of it in terms of resources. Surely Barnabas and Saul were good resources. Why go sending them off to some faraway place when there was plenty to be done here? It's the same reasoning some use to justify reductions in support for global ministries for the sake of taking care of the local things first. Charity begins at home!

Or does it? In Acts, the movement is constantly outward. In Acts, the stage of the church is the world, not this or that particular locale, not even Jerusalem. Such a focus does not diminish what happens locally, whether local be Antioch or the name of your community. Rather, Acts reminds us of the connections we have—and the connections God sets us apart to make. Home is where the story begins, not ends. Not everyone, of course, goes on the road. But everyone does live in the world outside the sanctuary. That is where our witness resides, and that is where God sends us.

On the Way

Acts from this point forward almost exclusively narrates the missionary journeys of Paul and his experiences on the way. It is clear from the outset that the way will be marked by highs and lows. A false prophet named Elymas provides the first bump in the road. It is a curious encounter, troubling in how Paul dispatches his opponent. Is that an act of grace? It depends. Paul's words in verse 10 are not exactly gracious. But the condition that falls upon Elymas is almost precisely the same that fell upon Saul on the Damascus Road. Will

Elymas, like Saul, see his error? Acts does not say. Perhaps it is because conjecture about what others may or may not do in response to the gospel is not the point. The point is, how do we respond?

The positive half of the story comes in the response of the Roman official. Oddly, what astonishes this individual accustomed to wielding power is not Paul's display of power but his teaching. The thing one thinks would most impress him (the striking down of Elymas) does not. Teaching does. Consider the implications for the church's call today to be a teaching community. Sometimes, we'd rather go for the catchy displays that grab people's attention when, if the story is to be trusted, it is the teaching that matters. I wonder about this when modern church leaders seek to attract the crowds (and often succeed) by the spectacular or by gimmicks. What is it that is being taught? That the message is too dull to be trusted to attract attention? And what do we do next week to hold the attention? Goldfish swallowing? Celebrity testimonies?

The proconsul believed because of the teaching.

Do we believe that? Do we teach that?

SHARING THE SCRIPTURE

Preparing Our Hearts

Meditate on this week's devotional reading, found in Matthew 28:16-20. This familiar passage, often referred to as the Great Commission, points the disciples—and us—toward our task as disciple-makers. How do you perceive Jesus' words to be a personal commission to you? What action have you taken to fulfill this commission? What action can you take this week?

Pray that you and the adult learners will be aware of God's call on your lives to make disciples.

Preparing Our Minds

Study the background from Acts 13 and the lesson Scripture from verses 1-12. Think about where you can find a community to which you want to dedicate your life.

Write on newsprint:
❏ information for next week's lesson, found under "Continue the Journey."
❏ activities for further spiritual growth in "Continue the Journey."

Prepare to read aloud Acts 13:1-12. Since there are several unfamiliar names, you may want to consult the Pronunciation Guide prior to class.

Create the suggested lectures for Acts 1:1-3 and 1:4-12 under "Summarize the Account of the Church's Commissioning of Barnabas and Saul/Paul for the Work to Which the Holy Spirit Had Called Them."

Option: Locate a map that includes the places mentioned in today's reading.

Option: Invite someone—clergy or laity—to tell the class about an experience of being called to ministry and how the support of the community encouraged him or her in the call. Be sure to make clear where and when the class is held and set a time limit on the storytelling.

Talk with your pastor, program director, or layperson knowledgeable about the opportunities for mission and ministry within your congregation. Create or reproduce a list of current opportunities that you can post on newsprint or hand out to the class.

LEADING THE CLASS

(1) Gather to Learn

❖ Welcome the class members and introduce any guests.

❖ Pray that those who have gathered will commit themselves to the tasks that God has given them to do.

❖ Brainstorm with the class answers to this question: **If a new member were to ask me how he or she could become involved in our church, what ministries and groups would I suggest?**

❖ Encourage the students to speak briefly about how or why these ministries and groups provide opportunities for involvement in the church.

❖ Read aloud today's focus statement: **Purposeful involvement in a community gives us a sense of satisfaction. Where can we find a community to which we want to dedicate our lives? The commissioning of Barnabas and Saul/Paul by the church at Antioch shows how the Holy Spirit motivates persons to represent the cause of Christ in the world.**

(2) Summarize the Account of the Church's Commissioning of Barnabas and Saul/Paul for the Work to Which the Holy Spirit Had Called Them

❖ Read aloud today's passage from Acts 13:1-3.

■ Use information you have prepared from Acts 13:1-3 in Understanding the Scripture and "Community in Diversity" in Interpreting the Scripture to enable the class to see the range of people involved in the church at Antioch. As an option, locate on a map the cities mentioned.

■ Note that the spiritual disciplines of prayer and fasting are mentioned in our key verse, 13:3, prior to the commissioning of Barnabas and Saul. Ask: **What is your perception of the relationship between spiritual disciplines and God's commission for ministry? How have you experienced this relationship in your own life?**

❖ Read aloud the rest of the passage, verses 4-12. As an option, locate the cities mentioned.

■ Use information from verses 4-12 in Understanding the Scripture to help unpack these verses.

■ Invite several volunteers to act as a crowd of role-players who discuss Barnabas and Paul's encounter with Elymas and the effects of this encounter on Sergius Paulus, the proconsul.

■ Read aloud or retell the second paragraph of "On the Way," noting that Paul's teaching, not Elymas's sudden blindness, is what convinces Sergius Paulus to believe.

■ Consider how the current church tries to attract people's attention: **Do we rely on the teaching or gimmicks? If we do not rely on the teaching itself, what does that say about our perception of the gospel message?**

(3) Tell Personal Stories of Being Called to a Task or Ministry in the Church

❖ **Option:** If you invited a guest to talk about a call to ministry or specific tasks, introduce this person now. The individual may even be a class member who has gone on a mission trip or done something else that most students have not had an opportunity to experience. Encourage the speaker to talk about challenges and rewards of this ministry. Allow time for the class to ask questions. Perhaps the speaker can suggest ways that interested students can become involved in the same ministry or one similar to it.

❖ Invite class members to speak about a call they experienced to do something for God, either within the church or outside of its walls. If the class is large, divide into small groups so that more people can tell their stories. Suggest that the adults speak, without going into great detail, about the challenges and rewards they experienced in fulfilling this call.

(4) Make a Commitment to Answer God's Call to Work for the Kingdom

❖ Make known to the class the list of opportunities available to them through your congregation or denomination by passing out a list or posting it on newsprint. The students may be able to add to the list. Try for a variety of ways to participate that will include everyone.

❖ Ask each person to look through the list and select at least one project in which he or she can participate. Perhaps some projects will lend themselves to a small group effort. If so, those who are interested in the same project may want to meet together briefly to see how they can support one another.

(5) Continue the Journey

❖ Pray that those who have come today will go forth to answer God's call to do the work that is set before them.

❖ Read aloud this preparation for next week's lesson. You may also want to post it on newsprint for the students to copy.

■ **Title: Fitting Into the Community**
■ **Background Scripture: 1 Corinthians 12:3-21; Ephesians 4:1-16**
■ **Lesson Scripture: Ephesians 4:1-16**
■ **Focus of the Lesson: Diversity is a reality in every human community. In what ways is diversity important to the unity of the church? Paul's letter to the church at Ephesus challenges us to use our diverse identities and gifts to build up the Christian community.**

❖ Challenge the students to complete one or more of these activities for further spiritual growth, which you will write on newsprint for the students to copy.

(1) **Attend to a ministry task that you feel called to do. If possible, work with a small group so as to support one another and share the workload.**

(2) **Practice a spiritual discipline this week, perhaps one that you do not normally do. Consider fasting, tithing, journaling, or meditating on a Scripture passage.**

(3) **Encourage someone you know who appears to have appropriate gifts and graces to consider entering the ordained ministry.**

❖ Sing or read aloud "Go, Make of All Disciples."

❖ Conclude today's session by leading the class in this benediction, adapted from Ephesians 4:4-6: **Let us now depart rejoicing in the community we share, united as one body, with one Spirit, one Lord, one faith, one baptism, and one God and Father of all.**

UNIT 3: THE NEW COMMUNITY FACES GROWING PAINS
FITTING INTO THE COMMUNITY

PREVIEWING THE LESSON

Lesson Scripture: Ephesians 4:1-16
Background Scripture: 1 Corinthians 12:3-21; Ephesians 4:1-16
Key Verse: Ephesians 4:7

Focus of the Lesson:
Diversity is a reality in every human community. In what ways is diversity important to the unity of the church? Paul's letter to the church at Ephesus challenges us to use our diverse identities and gifts to build up the Christian community.

Goals for the Learners:
(1) to explore the concept of unity within diversity.
(2) to identify how gifts in their community contribute to building up Christian unity.
(3) to commit to using their gifts more effectively.

Pronunciation Guide:
agape (ah gah' pay)
charis (khar' ece)
glossalalia (gla sah la' le a)

Supplies:
Bibles, newsprint and marker, paper and pencils, hymnals

READING THE SCRIPTURE

NRSV
Ephesians 4:1-16

¹I therefore, the prisoner in the Lord, beg you to lead a life worthy of the calling to which you have been called, ²with all humility and gentleness, with patience, bearing with one another in love, ³making every effort to maintain the unity of the Spirit in the bond of peace. ⁴There is one body and

NIV
Ephesians 4:1-16

¹As a prisoner for the Lord, then, I urge you to live a life worthy of the calling you have received. ²Be completely humble and gentle; be patient, bearing with one another in love. ³Make every effort to keep the unity of the Spirit through the bond of peace. ⁴There is one body and one Spirit—just as

one Spirit, just as you were called to the one hope of your calling, [5]one Lord, one faith, one baptism, [6]one God and Father of all, who is above all and through all and in all.

[7]**But each of us was given grace according to the measure of Christ's gift.** [8]Therefore it is said,

"When he ascended on high he made
  captivity itself a captive;
he gave gifts to his people."

[9](When it says, "He ascended," what does it mean but that he had also descended into the lower parts of the earth? [10]He who descended is the same one who ascended far above all the heavens, so that he might fill all things.) [11]The gifts he gave were that some would be apostles, some prophets, some evangelists, some pastors and teachers, [12]to equip the saints for the work of ministry, for building up the body of Christ, [13]until all of us come to the unity of the faith and of the knowledge of the Son of God, to maturity, to the measure of the full stature of Christ. [14]We must no longer be children, tossed to and fro and blown about by every wind of doctrine, by people's trickery, by their craftiness in deceitful scheming. [15]But speaking the truth in love, we must grow up in every way into him who is the head, into Christ, [16]from whom the whole body, joined and knit together by every ligament with which it is equipped, as each part is working properly, promotes the body's growth in building itself up in love.

you were called to one hope when you were called—[5]one Lord, one faith, one baptism; [6]one God and Father of all, who is over all and through all and in all.

[7]**But to each one of us grace has been given as Christ apportioned it.** [8]This is why it says:

"When he ascended on high,
  he led captives in his train
  and gave gifts to men."

[9](What does "he ascended" mean except that he also descended to the lower, earthly regions? [10]He who descended is the very one who ascended higher than all the heavens, in order to fill the whole universe.) [11]It was he who gave some to be apostles, some to be prophets, some to be evangelists, and some to be pastors and teachers, [12]to prepare God's people for works of service, so that the body of Christ may be built up [13]until we all reach unity in the faith and in the knowledge of the Son of God and become mature, attaining to the whole measure of the fullness of Christ.

[14]Then we will no longer be infants, tossed back and forth by the waves, and blown here and there by every wind of teaching and by the cunning and craftiness of men in their deceitful scheming. [15]Instead, speaking the truth in love, we will in all things grow up into him who is the Head, that is, Christ. [16]From him the whole body, joined and held together by every supporting ligament, grows and builds itself up in love, as each part does its work.

UNDERSTANDING THE SCRIPTURE

1 Corinthians 12:3. First Corinthians was directed to a specific congregation addressing quite particular issues. Foremost among them was a lack of unity in the church. Earlier in this epistle, Paul addresses the lack of unity as it arises in regard to factions developing around leaders (3:1-9) and at

observances of the *agape* meal and Lord's Supper (11:17-34). In this chapter, Paul will address the issue by first laying a positive foundation for how diversity and unity may, and indeed must, coexist based on the gifts of the Spirit. Verse 3 states a basic premise: Anyone who confesses "Jesus is

Lord," believed to be the earliest and most primary Christian confession, does so by the Holy Spirit. In other words, in the context of Corinthians, if someone makes that confession, the judgment *cannot* be made that he or she lacks the gift of Spirit.

1 Corinthians 12:4-11. Two main themes emerge in this portion of the passage. The first is this: Spirit and Lord and God (perhaps a Trinitarian hint?) serve as the source of all the differences of gifts (*charisma*) and service and activities. The differences are not attributable to the superiority of some and inferiority of others in the community. Diversity is the Spirit's doing. Each is gifted, as Ephesians 4:7 affirmed, and the gifting has its purpose in the "common good." In 1 Corinthians 12:8-10, Paul lists such gifts. Unlike Ephesians, where the listing has to do with church functions, here the spiritual gifts are listed in terms of what are likely actual practices going on in the Corinthian church. It is probably not coincidental that Paul lists only at the end those two having to do with glossalalia or tongues (as he does with another list in verses 28-31). Tongues seemed to be the most sought after gift in Corinth (Chapter 14). Putting them at the end here and later may be a subtle indication of where Paul is eventually headed at the end of this chapter: "I will show you a still more excellent way" followed by Chapter 13's powerful rendering of love as the greatest gift of all.

1 Corinthians 12:12-21. The image of the church as the body of Christ with many members completes this passage. Verses 15-16 encourage those who have low opinions of their gifts or place. Verse 21 reminds those with a high opinion of themselves that a little more humility is in order, for the gifts are not our own, but God's. All are needed for the body to be whole.

Ephesians 4:1-3. Many early manuscripts of Ephesians omit "in Ephesus" in the first verse of this letter. For that reason, and from the absence of "local" references or issues of a particular congregation, it is believed Ephesians circulated as an epistle directed to a number of churches or even the church as a whole rather than one locale. Opinion is divided over Pauline authorship due to issues of language and style. This commentary will reference Paul as the author. For those who attribute this letter to Paul, it is included among the "captivity" epistles, written toward the end of Paul's life while he was imprisoned. The author's self-reference as "prisoner" in 4:1 had been made earlier in 3:1. Paul appeals to the hearers to adopt practices in keeping with their calling. Calling is important for Paul in identifying his own ministry. So here as well, the "calling" of the Christian community is to live in ways that maintain the unity of the Spirit in peace. "Love" is identified as the basis for life lived in community ("bearing with one another").

Ephesians 4:4-12. The foundation of community, from which such love and behavior arises, comes from the unity bestowed by God. Verses 4-6 emphasize this unity in God by the repeated uses of the word "one": one body, one Spirit, one hope, one Lord, one faith, one baptism, one God. How the Christian community finds itself empowered to live out such unity (and exhibit the practices urged in 4:1-3) is identified in verse 7: the grace we are given. "Grace" (*charis*) is one of Paul's most important words and contributions to understanding theology. Often it refers to the overarching favor with which God holds us, extended to us freely. Here, however, grace takes on a much narrower focus: Grace is the "gift" that God bestows upon members of the community. Development of that thought is put on hold by verses 8-10, where Psalm 68:18 is quoted and commented upon. At the end of those comments, verse 10 affirms Christ's purpose to "fill all things." That is not only an echo of Ephesians 1:10; it is an introduction to the purpose of these gifts. They are not for the sake of individuals. They are for the sake of the whole. The gifts Paul lists in verses 11-12 relate to functions in the early church. Some have noted that the first three ("apostles," "prophets," "evangelists") represented ministries that were itinerant in nature, while "pastors" and "teachers" suggest ministries exercised in individual congregations. Whatever the function, however, the shared strategies of those gifts are identified with equipping the saints (the whole community) and building up the body of Christ.

Ephesians 4:13-16. And what is the purpose of these gifts and their exercise? Unity, maturity, and growth. Unity was already mentioned in verse 3, identified there with the Spirit. "Maturity" is a word that connotes reaching completion or fulfillment.

The contrast Paul makes does not come across as strongly in English as in Greek. The word for children in verse 14 ("no longer be children") more accurately means a baby or one who is still nursing. The language parallels 1 Corinthians 3:1-3, where immaturity is intriguingly linked to lack of unity. "Love" makes two more key appearances in this passage in the final two verses. "Speaking the truth in love" is advanced as how growth occurs, even as we are "built up" in love. Notice in verse 15 that Paul twice speaks not of growing up *in* Christ, a favorite term of his elsewhere, but *into* Christ.

INTERPRETING THE SCRIPTURE

Spirited Unity

Years ago, a visiting Lutheran pastor caught our senior class at seminary off guard by telling us that unity in the church (and in our future congregations) was not ours to create. Unity was a given; it was God's doing. All we need to do is act on it.

Paul makes a similar point here. Make "every effort," he counsels in Ephesians 4:3, "to maintain the unity of the Spirit." Maintenance has to do with something already in existence. Unity is a given.

There is wisdom in that understanding of unity, whether on the local level or in the church universal. Sometimes, we try to enforce unity based on our favorite pieces of the theology game. So if you speak in tongues, or if you vote Democrat, or if you believe the Bible is literal and inerrant in doctrine and science, or if you read the Bible as only one of many books revealing God . . . if, if, if, then you are one of us. Of course, that also leads to the corollary that if you do *not* do as I do (or at least say), then you are not one of us.

All of those can be effective ways of elim-

inating dissent or enforcing homogeneity on the church, but none of them have anything to do with the unity of the Spirit in the bond of peace. Because unity in the Spirit is not ours to construct. It is a given. And if that puts us in uncomfortable company with folks we would rather have on the other side of the fence, well, perhaps that is why Paul speaks of this unity's peace involving a "bond." In Greek, the word "bond" shares the same root with Paul's opening identification of himself as a "prisoner." We are not "free" to pick and choose what unites us. God's Spirit has already done that for us. We are called into a community whose unity we have no need to create, only maintain. We are to make every effort to maintain not our idea of what the church should or should not be like. We are to make every effort to maintain the unity effected by the Spirit with and often without our consent.

Each Given Grace

Early on in ministry, I was informed about the 20/80 effect in congregational life. Twenty percent of the people do 80 percent of the work. The figure can also be applied to stewardship. Some pastors may whisper that 20 percent of the people create 80 percent of the conflicts. If you hear that, be sure to add that 20 percent of the pastors create 80 percent of the church's headaches for the laity. My latter points are tongue-in-cheek . . . I think.

Do you find those figures true in your experience?

If so (and many do), we need to revisit Paul's affirmation here that "each of us" was given grace (4:7). Remember that Paul here is not speaking so much about grace as that unearned favor that accepts us all. The other meaning of "grace" is "gift." In Greek, *charis* ("grace") is the root of the word *charisma* ("gifts"). That relationship between grace and gifts is especially clear in our other background Scripture (1 Corinthians 12:3-21), which constantly refers to the "gifts" (*charisma*) of the Spirit.

Each one of us is graced, not just 20 percent of us. To be sure, we are not gifted (graced) in the same way. Ephesians notes the differences of gifts in terms of functions in church offices, whereas 1 Corinthians does so more in terms of the actual practices associated with them. We are not gifted the same. But nowhere does Paul denigrate one gift and lift up another—with the exception of love! When we look at a few as the "gifted" among us, we run the risk of denigrating our own God-given gifts (and as a result not using them), *or* in viewing ourselves as the "gifted," we overlook and do not cultivate the gifts in others. Either way, the whole church suffers, for the gifts of the Spirit are for the *sake* of the whole. They are not individual badges or spiritual superiority or inferiority. They are marks of the Spirit intended for the common good. And *each one* of us is so gifted.

Maturity

If you have Internet access, do a Google search on "church growth," and be prepared to be inundated with references to literature and programs aimed at numerical increase of membership.

The second half of our passage from Ephesians likewise emphasizes growth, though you will find no mention of numbers. The "body language" here has to do with "equipping the saints," "building up" the body, "growing up," and finally ending on the note of promoting "the body's growth in building itself up in love." Some might say such goals are not opposed to numerical growth—and they are not. But numbers are not their focus. Being built up in love is. And, at the core of these verses, maturity is.

So what constitutes maturity in the church? The way Paul develops the idea, it begins by not being babies. Ouch!

That sounds harsh, but that is basically the meaning of verse 14. As Paul develops this idea, the focus falls on exercising the minds and wills God gave us with integrity to our beliefs and not becoming religious weather vanes who blow in whatever direction is the latest fad on the theological block—including nostalgia. As noted in Understanding the Scripture, Paul had resorted to such language in 1 Corinthians 3. The problem there had been personality cults in the church.

Maturity also involves engaging in speech that tells the truth in love. Love prevents this from becoming a judgmental activity of "Let me tell you what kind of a person you *really* are." Love engages in speech—and action—that seeks another's good and then is willing to be part of the journey toward that good. To speak the truth in love involves revisiting all those qualities that Paul urged back in verses 2 and 3. For when our words and actions reflect that kind of humility and gentleness and patience—and above all, love—speaking the truth will build up rather than tear down those we address.

And that's true even when we are looking in the mirror and speaking the truth that needs to be said.

Growing Up Into Christ

The final measure of what growth means comes in verse 15's affirmation that we are to grow up into Christ. To me, that is a peculiar turn of phrase. "Growing *in* Christ" seems more comfortable, or "growing *toward* Christ." But "growing *into* Christ"?

Clearly, Paul has no intention of arguing that we become Christ, as though we cease to be ourselves and become someone we are not. On the other hand, "growing up into Christ" reminds us of a truth inherent in this identification of the church as the "body" of Christ. Namely, we are to become persons and communities where others may encounter Christ through us. The flip side of the body of Christ metaphor is that we may become Christ's hands and feet and ears in this world.

All of this concern in Ephesians and Corinthians about the body of Christ is not simply so the church members get along with one another. The body of Christ is a missional image. We are in the world to embody the grace and love of Jesus Christ. Unity is not just for harmony. It is for service.

SHARING THE SCRIPTURE

Preparing Our Hearts

Meditate on this week's devotional reading, found in 1 Corinthians 12:4-20. This passage comprises the bulk of the 1 Corinthians portion of today's background Scripture. Notice the diversity of gifts given by the Spirit as well as the diversity of services to be rendered. How does the metaphor "body of Christ" help you to understand how you are connected to Christ and to all who call upon his name? Think about your own gifts and how you use them in service to Christ's body.

Pray that you and the adult learners will recognize the important role you have to play within the community of faith.

Preparing Our Minds

Study the background from 1 Corinthians 12:3-21 and Ephesians 4:1-16 and the lesson Scripture from Ephesians 4:1-16. Ask yourself: In what ways is diversity important to the unity of the church?

Write on newsprint:

❑ information for next week's lesson, found under "Continue the Journey."

❑ activities for further spiritual growth in "Continue the Journey."

LEADING THE CLASS

(1) Gather to Learn

❖ Welcome the class members and introduce any guests.

❖ Pray that all who have gathered today will honor the gifts that each one brings to the table.

❖ Encourage volunteers to name as many animals (or plants or nationalities of people) as possible. List them on newsprint.

❖ Ask: **What difference does it make to you individually and to the world at large as to whether each of these animals (or whichever group you have selected) continues to exist?** (Try to work into the discussion, if it is not mentioned, that diversity adds richness and variety. Life would be boring if everything and everyone were the same. Also note the interconnectedness of species.)

❖ Read aloud today's focus statement: **Diversity is a reality in every human community. In what ways is diversity impor-**

tant to the unity of the church? Paul's letter to the church at Ephesus challenges us to use our diverse identities and gifts to build up the Christian community.

(2) Explore the Concept of Unity Within Diversity

❖ Select two volunteers, one to read Ephesians 4:1-6 and the other to read verses 7-16.
    ❖ Invite the adults to look at their Bibles.
        ◼ Identify Paul's emphasis on unity. **What behaviors reveal our unity as a community of faith? In what ways are we unified? Should unity be understood to mean that we are all alike? Why or why not?**
        ◼ Identify Paul's emphasis on diversity. **In what ways is the church diversified? What is the purpose of this diversity?**
❖ Paul compares the church to the body of Christ. (If time permits, suggest that the learners review Paul's teaching in 1 Corinthians 12:12-31.) We surely understand that the human body has many parts that must function for the good of the whole. **What other images can you think of to describe the importance of diversity within unity?** (A computer may be an interesting contemporary example.)
❖ Paul warns the church not to act as children but rather to come to maturity. **In what areas do you see the church acting like a child? What needs to be changed to empower the church to act with maturity?**
❖ Provide a few moments for silent reflection on this question: **In what ways do I need to put away childish behaviors and attitudes and act as a mature Christian?**
❖ Break the silence by asking if anyone has any insights on how we can move beyond childishness and grow toward Christian maturity.

(3) Identify How Gifts in the Learners' Community Contribute to Building Up Christian Unity

❖ List on newsprint the gifts that Paul believes are given for the building up of the community, as noted in Ephesians 4:11, 1 Corinthians 12:8-10, and Romans 12:6-8. You may wish to ask one-third of the students to look at each of these lists, preferably from different translations, and then call out the words they find to describe the gifts.
❖ Make another list of gifts that the students believe are also vital to the contemporary community of faith but are not included in the biblical lists. Use contemporary terms where possible. (For example, Paul knew nothing about people who could organize church events or provide a music program or serve as webmaster for a church's website.)
❖ Create a third list in which the adults indicate how the diverse gifts they experience within their own congregation have been used to build up unity within their church. (For example, consider the many gifts required to go on a missions trip or to put together a vacation Bible school.)
❖ Discuss these questions:
    (1) Which gifts seem to be especially strong within our congregation? Where do we see them most often utilized?
    (2) Which gifts seem to be in short supply?
    (3) Who in our church has the gifts that we are lacking? How can we encourage these persons to contribute their gifts so as to build all of us up?

(4) Commit to Using Personal Gifts More Effectively

❖ Read aloud the first and second paragraphs of "Each Given Grace" in Interpreting the Scripture. Invite the adults to answer the question raised in the second paragraph.

❖ Distribute paper and pencils. Read this sentence: "Each one of us is graced, not just 20 percent of us." Invite the students to ponder what it means for them to know that they are graced with God's gifts and expected to help build up the body of Christ. Then suggest that they write on the paper two to four gifts that they believe they possess and how they are currently using these gifts to build up the body. They may also consider fresh ways in which they could be using their gifts.

❖ Read the following sentence aloud so that the learners may copy it on their papers and add their response: **With God's help I will use my gift(s) of _____ to help build up the body of Christ so that we may all grow toward maturity in Christ. To keep my commitment, I plan to** _____.

❖ Suggest that the adults put their papers in their Bibles and refer to them often this week as a reminder of what they have promised God they will do.

(5) Continue the Journey

❖ Pray that everyone who has participated today will recognize the importance of celebrating diversity within the unity of the body of Christ and will go forth to use the gifts they have identified.

❖ Read aloud this preparation for next week's lesson. You may also want to post it on newsprint for the students to copy.

- ■ **Title: Conflict in the Community**
- ■ **Background Scripture: Galatians 2:11–3:29**
- ■ **Lesson Scripture: Galatians 2:11-21**
- ■ **Focus of the Lesson: When we are**

afraid of what others might think about us, we sometimes behave in ways inconsistent with our beliefs. How can we live so that our lives witness to our beliefs? Through writing and example, Paul admonishes believers that our acceptance before God comes not by following the rules but through living faithfully to Christ.

❖ Challenge the students to complete one or more of these activities for further spiritual growth, which you will write on newsprint for the students to copy.

(1) Locate a book that includes a spiritual gifts inventory, such as *Rediscovering Our Spiritual Gifts* by Charles V. Bryant (Upper Room Books). Complete the inventory and then read ideas for using the gifts you have identified.

(2) Affirm the gifts of others in your class and congregation by expressing appreciation for the work that they do.

(3) Research the Turkish city of Ephesus as it existed in the first century. What do you learn about the diversity that existed in the city?

❖ Sing or read aloud "Many Gifts, One Spirit."

❖ Conclude today's session by leading the class in this benediction, adapted from Ephesians 4:4-6: **Let us now depart rejoicing in the community we share, united as one body, with one Spirit, one Lord, one faith, one baptism, and one God and Father of all.**

UNIT 3: THE NEW COMMUNITY FACES GROWING PAINS
CONFLICT IN THE COMMUNITY

PREVIEWING THE LESSON

Lesson Scripture: Galatians 2:11-21
Background Scripture: Galatians 2:11–3:29
Key Verse: Galatians 3:28

Focus of the Lesson:
When we are afraid of what others might think about us, we sometimes behave in ways inconsistent with our beliefs. How can we live so that our lives witness to our beliefs? Through writing and example, Paul admonishes believers that our acceptance before God comes not by following the rules but through living faithfully to Christ.

Goals for the Learners:
(1) to explore ways in which Paul stood firm in the face of conflicting views about the gospel.
(2) to identify situations in which they compromised their own principles (that is, acted insincerely with respect to their own judgment).
(3) to strategize ways to remain faithful to their belief in Christ's demands.

Pronunciation Guide:
Antioch (an' tee ok)
Barnabas (bahr' nuh buhs)
Cephas (see' fuhs)
hypokrites (hoop ok ree tace')

Supplies:
Bibles, newsprint and marker, paper and pencils, hymnals

READING THE SCRIPTURE

NRSV
Galatians 2:11-21

¹¹But when Cephas came to Antioch, I opposed him to his face, because he stood self-condemned; ¹²for until certain people came from James, he used to eat with the

NIV
Galatians 2:11-21

¹¹When Peter came to Antioch, I opposed him to his face, because he was clearly in the wrong. ¹²Before certain men came from James, he used to eat with the Gentiles. But

Gentiles. But after they came, he drew back and kept himself separate for fear of the circumcision faction. [13]And the other Jews joined him in this hypocrisy, so that even Barnabas was led astray by their hypocrisy. [14]But when I saw that they were not acting consistently with the truth of the gospel, I said to Cephas before them all, "If you, though a Jew, live like a Gentile and not like a Jew, how can you compel the Gentiles to live like Jews?"

[15]We ourselves are Jews by birth and not Gentile sinners; [16]yet we know that a person is justified not by the works of the law but through faith in Jesus Christ. And we have come to believe in Christ Jesus, so that we might be justified by faith in Christ, and not by doing the works of the law, because no one will be justified by the works of the law. [17]But if, in our effort to be justified in Christ, we ourselves have been found to be sinners, is Christ then a servant of sin? Certainly not! [18]But if I build up again the very things that I once tore down, then I demonstrate that I am a transgressor. [19]For through the law I died to the law, so that I might live to God. I have been crucified with Christ; [20]and it is no longer I who live, but it is Christ who lives in me. And the life I now live in the flesh I live by faith in the Son of God, who loved me and gave himself for me. [21]I do not nullify the grace of God; for if justification comes through the law, then Christ died for nothing.

Galatians 3:28

[28]**There is no longer Jew or Greek, there is no longer slave or free, there is no longer male and female; for all of you are one in Christ Jesus.**

when they arrived, he began to draw back and separate himself from the Gentiles because he was afraid of those who belonged to the circumcision group. [13]The other Jews joined him in his hypocrisy, so that by their hypocrisy even Barnabas was led astray.

[14]When I saw that they were not acting in line with the truth of the gospel, I said to Peter in front of them all, "You are a Jew, yet you live like a Gentile and not like a Jew. How is it, then, that you force Gentiles to follow Jewish customs?

[15]"We who are Jews by birth and not 'Gentile sinners' [16]know that a man is not justified by observing the law, but by faith in Jesus Christ. So we, too, have put our faith in Christ Jesus that we may be justified by faith in Christ and not by observing the law, because by observing the law no one will be justified.

[17]"If, while we seek to be justified in Christ, it becomes evident that we ourselves are sinners, does that mean that Christ promotes sin? Absolutely not! [18]If I rebuild what I destroyed, I prove that I am a lawbreaker. [19]For through the law I died to the law so that I might live for God. [20]I have been crucified with Christ and I no longer live, but Christ lives in me. The life I live in the body, I live by faith in the Son of God, who loved me and gave himself for me. [21]I do not set aside the grace of God, for if righteousness could be gained through the law, Christ died for nothing!"

Galatians 3:28

[28]**There is neither Jew nor Greek, slave nor free, male nor female, for you are all one in Christ Jesus.**

UNDERSTANDING THE SCRIPTURE

Galatians 2:11-14. The letter of Galatians is the most confrontational epistle of Paul's. The background of conflict comes to the fore in the passages highlighted in this lesson. The conflict with Cephas (the Aramaic word for "rock," corresponding to the Greek word *petros* or Peter) in verse 11 seems to reverse the détente reached in the Jerusalem meeting described in 2:1-10. One explanation is that while the issue of circumcision had been yielded to by Peter and the Jerusalem leaders, the issue of table fellowship with Gentiles had not. "James" (2:12) was the leader of the Jerusalem church. The mention of James's name implies his authority is at work in those who apparently swayed Peter's decision. The charge Paul makes against Peter is hypocrisy. In Greek, *hypokrites* referred to actors playing roles on stage. Over time, the word "hypocrisy" came to be used of insincere actions. The naming of Barnabas among those who followed Peter's lead is telling, as Barnabas had been Paul's missionary partner and long-time supporter (Acts 9:27 and following).

Galatians 2:15-16. Paul had earlier detailed his background as Jew and Pharisee (1:13-14) to set the stage for underscoring his calling as an apostle. This is likely his initial response to the "false believers" (2:4) who may have challenged Paul's credentials as an apostle, since he had not been one of the Twelve. Here in 2:15, Paul affirms his Jewish heritage to argue from within that perspective that it is not traditional observances such as table fellowship but faith in Christ that matters. "We" in verses 15-16 includes those who share Paul's position, probably his Gentile missionary partner Titus (2:3) among others. "Law" is mentioned six times in 2:15-21, and thirty-three times altogether in Galatians. Here and elsewhere, it is juxtaposed with faith (and later, promise). "Justify" and "justification" (2:16-17, 21) are not only terms that grow out of the courtroom in reference to "acquittal" or declaration of innocence. More broadly, especially in Old Testament texts, justification is related to God's vindication of those deemed righteous or just at the end of history. To be justified, then, is not simply to have right standing before God—it is a term

that points to inclusion in God's coming realm.

Galatians 2:17-21. Paul uses extremely strong language in verse 17 to make his point about our standing in Christ. "Servant" translates a term elsewhere translated as "minister." The truth that even those justified by Christ still may sin, however, does not excuse what Peter and the others seek to do by insisting on restoring old divisions in the community. The Greek word translated here as "build up" literally means "construct a home." The "home" of ethnic-related traditions that Peter *and* Paul had once observed as Jews is no longer in force in Christ. The return to discussion of the law in verse 19 is now further developed by the themes of living and dying in Christ. "In Christ" is one of Paul's most fundamental expressions for the life of faith. There is an interesting parallel in these verses ("the life I now live . . . I live by faith") with the earlier charge against Peter in verse 14 ("if you, though a Jew, live like a Gentile . . . how can you compel the Gentiles to live like Jews?"). Life in Christ is the basis for Paul's objections to Peter's inconsistency. The ultimate folly of that inconsistency comes to a head in Paul's argument in verse 21, where by implication it "nullifies the grace of God" and renders Christ's death "for nothing."

Galatians 3:1-5. "Bewitched" translates a Greek word that has to do with the casting of spells. Paul's argument for the Galatians not needing to become Jewish in order to be fully Christian in these verses focuses on their experience of the Spirit. Verse 2 contains the first reference to the Spirit in Galatians. From this point forward, Spirit becomes a dominant theme in the epistle. "Believing what you heard" (3:2, 5) is ambiguous in Greek. In light of Paul's insistence that it is not faith but grace that saves, a more likely translation would place the emphasis not on our act of believing but on the gift of God's message (the gospel) that evokes faith.

Galatians 3:6-18. Paul's argument on

faith versus works now summons a lengthy passage on Abraham as an example. The "gospel" declared to Abraham (3:8) in this context is not a revealing of Jesus but rather the blessing that will come to the Gentiles (see Genesis 12:3). To further bolster his argument, Paul quotes Habakkuk 2:4 in verse 11, which he also does in Romans 1:17 to open that letter's far more extensive treatment of the role of faith. In verses 15-18, Paul moves into a fairly technical metaphor about human wills or testaments (the Greek word can also be translated as "covenant"). The point is that the covenant with Abraham preceded the giving of the law to Moses so that the promises/blessings revealed to Abraham (in this case, in particular, the blessing Abraham would be to the Gentiles) cannot be abolished by a later "will" struck with Moses.

Galatians 3:19-26. Dominating these verses is a comparison of the law with a "disciplinarian." In that era a disciplinarian was a household slave whose charge was to watch over the children of a family. A key responsibility had to do with accompanying them and keeping them out of trouble. So the law, in Paul's view, served as an interim caretaker or guardian until "faith would be revealed" in Christ.

Galatians 3:27-29. Paul's concluding words are some of his most memorable in all of Scripture. The connection between baptism and clothing (3:27) likely reflects the baptismal practice in the early church of giving a new robe to the newly baptized (see also Colossians 3:9, 12). Note how the final verse joins Christ and Abraham. Paul in his mind remains true to the Jewish tradition, of which Abraham is often deemed the "father." The promises of God are the common denominator between Abraham and Christ. Those promises, and their grace-based freedom as well as unity, form the core of this entire epistle.

INTERPRETING THE SCRIPTURE

Taking a Stand in Conflict

Conflict is a given in community, even (and especially) in the church. Not everyone will agree on everything all the time. There are times when the disagreements are on matters inconsequential to the life and calling of Christian community. For example, splitting the church over what color the new pew cushions will be does not rise to a "here I stand, I can do no other" response. But does risking such confrontation over who gets to sit on those cushions (or preach from the pulpit before them) qualify?

In Galatians 2:11-14, Paul publicly gets in the face of Cephas (Peter) over the reversal of sharing table fellowship with Gentile Christians. For Paul, in this case, tranquility takes second place to integrity in terms of what makes for unity in the church. Far from a peripheral issue, Paul sees this conflict dealing directly with "the truth of the gospel" (2:14). As a result, Paul decides not only to bring the conflict out into the open but also to oppose Peter and (implicitly) James, who stood at the time at the pinnacle of church authorities.

Taking stands in the church today, not only in opposition to things seen in the wider society but also to things seen within the church, still takes its cue from Paul's example. When conflicts rise to the level of what is at stake in the gospel, stands need to be taken. Does this mean we will always be in agreement over the choice or timing of such actions? No. Different perspectives on what is central and what is secondary to the gospel continue to result in differing views of what merits compromise and what merits no compromise. Folks on all sides of issues in dispute within the church need to exercise discernment, within the context of community as well as individual conscience, to seek the leading of God's Spirit in such matters. But clearly from this text, what is right does not always equate with what established authorities declare or practice. In such times, as here, conflicts call for opposing stands for the sake of the gospel.

Hypocrisy

As noted in the comments on Galatians 2:11-14 in Understanding the Scripture, the term "hypocrite" came from Greek drama, where it was used to describe actors who played roles on stage. In Greek theater, those roles were accompanied by the wearing of masks, so that you would not see the actor's true face.

For Paul, Peter merited this pejorative use of "hypocrite" because he formerly ate with Gentiles but retreated from table fellowship with them when "certain people" came from the mother church in Jerusalem. These people, under the authority of James, probably observed the law strictly. Peter "masked" his former practice by refusing to eat with Gentiles when those he felt would not approve were present. This charge against Peter would have been especially harsh. The opening of the Gentile mission as described in Acts was accomplished by Peter, not Paul (Acts 10:1-48). And central to that action was Peter's vision of a sheet filled with all sorts of foods considered unclean by Jews, but declared made clean by God (10:15). At the end of that passage, Acts notes that the Gentile convert Cornelius invited Peter and his companions to stay with him several days, strongly implying they would have eaten together.

Hypocrisy remains a difficult obstacle for the church. Unless we live perfect lives, we cannot help at times doing things in contradiction to our beliefs and values. So in that sense it may be unavoidable. To a degree. But where hypocrisy takes its toll is in pride that blinds us to the lack of integrity in our actions or accepts such incongruities as givens. Jesus lambasted as hypocrites those who make shows of their own piety (Matthew 6:2-5) or whose religion is all talk (Matthew 15:7) or who become obsessed with irrelevant superficial minutiae while ignoring faith's calling to the weightier matters of justice and mercy and compassion (Matthew 23:25-29).

Such critiques speak hard but necessary words about hypocrisy to the church today. Do the matters that most concern our time and energies go to the heart of the gospel and the needs of people, or are they much ado about nothing? Do we exercise great care in pointing out the faults and errors of those with whom we disagree (on the right *or* the left), while neglecting our own need for transformation?

What say you?

Living by Fear

The power of fear is an amazing thing. Take Peter, for example. By this time, he has preached to the crowds on Pentecost and called them to repentance. He has been arrested by the Temple authorities, only to turn the tables and charge them with crucifying Jesus (Acts 4:10). He has been freed from jail by the intervention of an angel (5:19). He has gone to the home of a Gentile centurion and baptized him and his household and then faced criticism for that act (11:1-2). But now, suddenly, Peter reverses himself. And the only reason given is fear.

Lest we come down too hard on Peter, though, it would be better to read this story as our own. Truthfully, can we say we have never acted out of fear for the sake of the convenient or the line of least resistance or however we would justify or rationalize turning our back on the right?

Fear is a powerful persuader not only of

individuals but also of communities and even nations. Adolph Hitler may or may not have been a great orator, but he was exquisite in his use of fear to divide and conquer. Never mind that exaggerations or outright lies would be employed. If enough fear could be generated, truth would be a minor inconvenience easily sacrificed on the altar of national destiny or racial purity.

And purveyors of fear, religious and political, remain abroad. Fear, it would seem, has everything going for it. Save, in the instance of Galatians 2, truth. Save, in the perspective of the gospel as a whole, the love of God. ("There is no fear in love, but perfect love casts out fear," 1 John 4:18.)

The gospel provides a choice about living on a basis other than fear. Paul confronts Peter with that possibility, revealed by the love of God made known in Jesus Christ for all people.

Living in Christ

The alternative to living in fear for Paul is to live in Christ. "In Christ" is one of Paul's favorite phrases throughout this and the other epistles about the life of faith.

There is mystery in that phrase, as it points to but does not define the way in which Christ dwells in us and we live in Christ. Faith is not mere doctrinal assent or a behavioral marker. Faith is also spiritual experience: life in Christ.

There is community in that phrase as well, for remember that one of Paul's chief metaphors for the church is the "body of Christ." To live in Christ is also to live in community with others. The Galatian church (or churches, as it was likely written to a cluster of congregations rather than to an individual one) had its share of conflict that evoked this sharpest of Paul's Epistles. Yet Paul remains engaged with this community, because it is the body of Christ of which he is part.

Life in Christ is not a solitary venture. Life in Christ engages us with community; empowers us with Spirit; and experiences, in ways that often defy words, the presence and grace of Christ.

Thanks be to God!

SHARING THE SCRIPTURE

Preparing Our Hearts

Meditate on this week's devotional reading, found in Romans 10:5-17. Here Paul writes about the availability of salvation to all people, Jew and Gentile alike. The gospel message needs to go forth, but not everyone believes it or acts upon it. How do you, in word and deed, proclaim the gospel? In what ways do others see Christ in you? If you had to rate yourself on a scale of one to ten as to how well you live up to the gospel, what number would you give yourself? Why?

Pray that you and the adult learners will recognize that all people are called by God.

Preparing Our Minds

Study the background from Galatians 2:11–3:29 and the lesson Scripture from Galatians 2:11-21. As you prepare, think about how we can live so that our lives witness to our beliefs.

Write on newsprint:
❑ questions under "Identify Situations in Which the Learners Compromised Their Principles."
❑ information for next week's lesson, found under "Continue the Journey."
❑ activities for further spiritual growth in "Continue the Journey."

LEADING THE CLASS

(1) Gather to Learn

❖ Welcome the class members and introduce any guests.

❖ Pray that all who have come will open their hearts and minds to the message that the Holy Spirit has for them this day.

❖ Encourage the adults to identify some situations in which people may act in ways that are inconsistent with their beliefs and values. Here are some discussion starters if you need them.

■ A pastor who consistently spoke out against homosexuality was found to have engaged the services of a male prostitute.

■ A prominent business leader who touted the importance of high ethical practices was convicted of embezzling money from the company.

■ A layman who was a leader in his church committed heinous murders.

❖ Discuss briefly why the students think people's stated beliefs and actions are sometimes so at odds with each other.

❖ Read aloud today's focus statement: **When we are afraid of what others might think about us, we sometimes behave in ways inconsistent with our beliefs. How can we live so that our lives witness to our beliefs? Through writing and example, Paul admonishes believers that our acceptance before God comes not by following the rules but through living faithfully to Christ.**

(2) Explore Ways in Which Paul Stood Firm in the Face of Conflicting Views About the Gospel

❖ Select a volunteer to read Galatians 2:11-21.

❖ Discuss these questions:

(1) **What is at the root of the conflict between Peter and Paul?** (See verses 11-14 in Understanding the Scripture.)

(2) **We do not hear Peter's side of the argument. Is it possible that both Peter and Paul thought they were being true to God's will? Explain your answer.**

(3) **What is Paul's argument in light of those who insist that one must follow the law?** (See verses 15-16, 17-21 in Understanding the Scripture.)

❖ Invite the students to discuss these questions with a small group: **Had you heard this letter being read to your congregation in Galatia, how would you have perceived that Paul stood fast in light of what he believed? If you were to write a reply to him, what would you say?**

(3) Identify Situations in Which the Learners Compromised Their Principles

❖ Read aloud "Hypocrisy" in Interpreting the Scripture.

❖ Distribute paper and pencils. Ask the students to identify situations in which they have compromised their own values in order to conform to the standards of others. Suggest that they answer the following questions, which you will have written on newsprint. Set a time limit. Assure them that they will not be asked to share their answers with anyone else.

(1) **Under what circumstances have you set aside your own values?**

(2) **Is there a pattern to your behavior? If so, what is it? Are there certain people, for example, whose opinion is so important to you that you will compromise your own values? Are there certain places where you are willing to set aside your own integrity?**

(3) **What changes do you need to make in order to live with integrity in ways that you believe are consistent with the gospel message?**

(4) **What one step will you take this week to begin to make a change?**

❖ Call the class back together at the appointed time and move on to the next activity.

(4) Strategize Ways to Remain Faithful to Belief in Christ's Demands

❖ Point out that Paul became involved in a conflict with Peter because he believed Peter had acted hypocritically in light of the gospel on the issue of table fellowship. Paul chose to stand firm. We, too, are called to stand firm.

❖ Read aloud the third paragraph under "Taking a Stand in Conflict" in Interpreting the Scripture.

❖ Brainstorm answers to this question and write them on newsprint: **What issues are currently causing conflict within the church in general or in your particular denomination?** (Avoid confrontations about matters within your own congregation because you will not have time to hear all sides or to come to resolution.)

❖ Divide the class into groups and give each group a sheet of newsprint and marker. Ask each group to select one of the issues and discuss how Paul might approach it. What would be the faith issues involved? What strategies could be used to resolve the conflict while remaining true to the gospel?

❖ Bring the class together and call on each group to report its ideas. (Recognize that different people may sincerely disagree as to what it means to be faithful to the truth of the gospel.)

❖ Wrap up this portion of the lesson by encouraging class members to identify strategies for remaining faithful to the gospel that they found particularly useful. How might they apply these strategies to conflicts they face?

(5) Continue the Journey

❖ Pray that the participants will go forth better able to act with integrity when confronted by conflict.

❖ Read aloud this preparation for next week's lesson. You may also want to post it on newsprint for the students to copy.

■ **Title: Communion With God in the Midst of Struggle**

■ **Background Scripture: Philippians 3:3–4:9**

■ **Lesson Scripture: Philippians 3:17–4:9**

■ **Focus of the Lesson: During difficult times, people in community support one another and find reasons to give thanks. How do people in community come together in the midst of struggle? Paul exhorted the Philippians to follow examples of those who work together for the common good and to rejoice together.**

❖ Challenge the students to complete one or more of these activities for further spiritual growth, which you will write on newsprint for the students to copy.

(1) **Investigate the life of someone who you believe lived faithfully for Christ. Saint Francis of Assisi, Mother Teresa, and Corrie ten Boom are examples. What enabled this person's walk to match his or her talk?**

(2) **Identify a conflict within your own church. What action can you take to solve the problem while remaining true to your understanding of the gospel?**

(3) **Talk with someone whose theological perspective is different from your own. Even if you disagree, what can you both learn from a civil discourse?**

❖ Sing or read aloud "Christ, From Whom All Blessings Flow."

❖ Conclude today's session by leading the class in this benediction, adapted from Ephesians 4:4-6: **Let us now depart rejoicing in the community we share, united as one body, with one Spirit, one Lord, one faith, one baptism, and one God and Father of all.**

UNIT 3: THE NEW COMMUNITY FACES GROWING PAINS
COMMUNION WITH GOD IN THE MIDST OF STRUGGLE

PREVIEWING THE LESSON

Lesson Scripture: Philippians 3:17–4:9
Background Scripture: Philippians 3:3–4:9
Key Verse: Philippians 4:7

Focus of the Lesson:
During difficult times, people in community support one another and find reasons to give thanks. How do people in community come together in the midst of struggle? Paul exhorted the Philippians to follow examples of those who work together for the common good and to rejoice together.

Goals for the Learners:
(1) to investigate Paul's writing to the Philippians concerning support for one another.
(2) to recognize both the importance of building community and the personal support they receive from that community.
(3) to demonstrate how God's people can live together in community.

Pronunciation Guide:
Epaphroditus (i paf ruh di' tuhs)   *parakaleo* (par ak al eh' o)
Euodia (yoo oh' dee uh)   *phroneo* (fron eh' o)
koinonia (koy nohn ee' ah)   Syntyche (sin' ti kee)

Supplies:
Bibles, newsprint and marker, paper and pencils, hymnals

READING THE SCRIPTURE

NRSV
Philippians 3:17–4:9

[17]Brothers and sisters, join in imitating me, and observe those who live according to the example you have in us. [18]For many live as enemies of the cross of Christ; I have often

NIV
Philippians 3:17–4:9

[17]Join with others in following my example, brothers, and take note of those who live according to the pattern we gave you. [18]For, as I have often told you before and now say

told you of them, and now I tell you even with tears. [19]Their end is destruction; their god is the belly; and their glory is in their shame; their minds are set on earthly things. [20]But our citizenship is in heaven, and it is from there that we are expecting a Savior, the Lord Jesus Christ. [21]He will transform the body of our humiliation that it may be conformed to the body of his glory, by the power that also enables him to make all things subject to himself. [4:1]Therefore, my brothers and sisters, whom I love and long for, my joy and crown, stand firm in the Lord in this way, my beloved.

[2]I urge Euodia and I urge Syntyche to be of the same mind in the Lord. [3]Yes, and I ask you also, my loyal companion, help these women, for they have struggled beside me in the work of the gospel, together with Clement and the rest of my co-workers, whose names are in the book of life.

[4]Rejoice in the Lord always; again I will say, Rejoice. [5]Let your gentleness be known to everyone. The Lord is near. [6]Do not worry about anything, but in everything by prayer and supplication with thanksgiving let your requests be made known to God. [7]**And the peace of God, which surpasses all understanding, will guard your hearts and your minds in Christ Jesus.**

[8]Finally, beloved, whatever is true, whatever is honorable, whatever is just, whatever is pure, whatever is pleasing, whatever is commendable, if there is any excellence and if there is anything worthy of praise, think about these things. [9]Keep on doing the things that you have learned and received and heard and seen in me, and the God of peace will be with you.

again even with tears, many live as enemies of the cross of Christ. [19]Their destiny is destruction, their god is their stomach, and their glory is in their shame. Their mind is on earthly things. [20]But our citizenship is in heaven. And we eagerly await a Savior from there, the Lord Jesus Christ, [21]who, by the power that enables him to bring everything under his control, will transform our lowly bodies so that they will be like his glorious body.

[4:1]Therefore, my brothers, you whom I love and long for, my joy and crown, that is how you should stand firm in the Lord, dear friends!

[2]I plead with Euodia and I plead with Syntyche to agree with each other in the Lord. [3]Yes, and I ask you, loyal yokefellow, help these women who have contended at my side in the cause of the gospel, along with Clement and the rest of my fellow workers, whose names are in the book of life.

[4]Rejoice in the Lord always. I will say it again: Rejoice! [5]Let your gentleness be evident to all. The Lord is near. [6]Do not be anxious about anything, but in everything, by prayer and petition, with thanksgiving, present your requests to God. [7]**And the peace of God, which transcends all understanding, will guard your hearts and your minds in Christ Jesus.**

[8]Finally, brothers, whatever is true, whatever is noble, whatever is right, whatever is pure, whatever is lovely, whatever is admirable—if anything is excellent or praiseworthy—think about such things. [9]Whatever you have learned or received or heard from me, or seen in me—put it into practice. And the God of peace will be with you.

UNDERSTANDING THE SCRIPTURE

Philippians 3:3-6. The previous verse of this chapter sharply criticized opponents who, among other things, insisted on a physical "mutilation." While scholars disagree over the exact identity of the group (or groups) Paul had in mind, this last reference suggests Jewish Christians who insisted on circumcision for Gentiles. In that light, Paul's phrase of "we who are the circumcision" may be heard as an ironic statement of the church's inclusion in God's people by the gift of the Spirit rather than by the rite insisted on by Judaizers, who wanted Gentiles who accepted Christ to live according to Jewish teachings and ritual. To underscore Paul's qualifications to make such a break with tradition and place his confidence elsewhere, Paul continues on in verses 4-6 with a retelling of his own credentials in Judaism, similar to Galatians 1:13-14.

Philippians 3:7-11. The dominant language and imagery here is loss and gain, and Paul's overarching goal of knowing Christ. "Righteousness" and "law" (3:9) are familiar themes in the writings of Paul, developed most extensively in Romans. Verse 10 is the focal point of this section. In it, Paul makes an intriguing statement about "sharing" Christ's sufferings. The word for "sharing" in Greek is *koinonia*, translated elsewhere as "fellowship" or "community." In the background is Paul's imprisonment as the setting for this letter (1:14), where his captivity becomes an opportunity to experience such sharing with Christ—even as it becomes the occasion to renew his *koinonia* with the church at Philippi that he helped to found.

Philippians 3:12-16. As he does elsewhere (1 Corinthians 9:24-27; 2 Timothy 4:7-8), Paul turns to the language and imagery of the stadium and athletic competition to depict his efforts at faithfulness. The emphasis is upon faith lived in the "interim" between the gift of Christ and the consummation of God's sovereign realm. The concluding two verses suggest issues regarding the mind ("be of the same mind . . . if you think differently") that will be further pursued in 3:17–4:9.

Philippians 3:17-21. The invitation to "imitate" Paul and other unnamed supporters ("the example you have in us") is quickly contrasted with the way in which the still unidentified opponents live and think and hope. Again, Paul is not specific enough in his descriptions for us to draw any hard conclusions about just what their positions were. Paul's concluding word on them returns to the theme of "mind" broached in 3:15. *Phroneo*, translated as "mind set on" in verse 19, will occur again in 4:2, whereas the next-to-last verse in this overall passage (4:8) directs the "thinking" of the Philippians to those things worthy of praise. Philippians 3:20 identifies the "expectation" of Christ as Savior. Philippi was a Roman colony whose citizens enjoyed Roman citizenship. And not only some of the Roman gods but also the emperor himself were accorded the title of "Savior." Paul's use of that term here is likely a subtle reminder of the different allegiances between Roman citizenship and "our citizenship in heaven." The twice-repeated reference to "body" in verse 21 may call up reminders of Paul's use of this term to refer to Christian community as well as individual bodies.

Philippians 4:1-3. The reference to "crown" recalls the earlier imagery from athletic contests, as winners of the competitions would be given garlands for their head. The encouragement to "stand firm" in verse 1 echoes the same admonition as "hold fast" in 3:16. Euodia and Syntyche are women who are leaders in the Philippian Christian community, both of whom have worked with Paul and for whom he has high regard. We are given no indication of what issue may have caused them not to be of the same mind. Paul does not take sides between them, choosing one over the other. The "loyal companion" whom Paul charges to help these women is also unidentified. Some suggest it is Epaphroditus, whom Paul earlier identified as the one bearing this letter to the Philippian community (2:25-30). Or is Paul addressing the community as a whole, using the singular form of this word to underscore their unity? Both interpretive options are possible.

Philippians 4:4-7. A shift is made to a more general exhortation that returns to the theme of joy and rejoicing (see 1:25 and 2:17-18). "Always" is a remarkable word for Paul to attach to rejoice, given his own imprisonment and the Philippian community's concern for him (4:10). The expectation of Christ's return ("The Lord is near") had been part of Paul's earliest writings (1 Thessalonians 4:15). Here, that hope is directly related to the adoption of an attitude of trust. "Do not worry" about anything recalls the teaching of Jesus (Matthew 6:25-31).

Notice, again, that in this passage where the mind of the Philippians is so much at the forefront of Paul's writing, he closes what has become a frequently used benediction in the church with an expression invoking peace that guards "your hearts and your *minds*" (4:7, italics added).

Philippians 4:8-9. Scholars have noted that the list of qualities here have nothing intrinsically Christian about them. It is pos-sible Paul may have borrowed or adapted an existing list of Greco-Roman virtues—and with Philippi having such close ties to Rome, it would have been a connecting point to the wider culture, revealing that the Christian community did not seek to "over-throw" what it valued. Such matters, though, go beyond certainty. What is clear is that Paul encourages the Philippian com-munity to "think" about these things. But Jewish wisdom is never reduced to thought—and so Paul, maintaining those ties as well, moves from an encouragement to think on these things to action: "keep on doing the things" (4:9). Where the benedic-tion in verse 7 appealed to the "peace of God," now this closing commissioning of the community to action assures the Philippians that the "God of peace will be with you." The peace Paul seeks for the Philippian community flows from the God for whom peace is part of God's nature and action in Jesus Christ.

INTERPRETING THE SCRIPTURE

"A Mind Is a Terrible Thing to Waste"

The words above may be most familiar as the slogan of the United Negro College Fund for more than thirty years, but their under-lying wisdom stretches back much further.

The "mind" is a dominant theme throughout the whole of Philippians 3–4. Indeed, this letter's most memorable pas-sage urges the Philippian community: "Let the same *mind* be in you that was in Christ Jesus" (2:5, italics added).

Sometimes, the church fails to honor the importance of the mind in faith. We rightly focus on matters of the heart. But, a mindless Christianity is no more faithful to our cre-ation in the image of God or our calling as the body of Christ than a heartless Christianity. Those who occasionally suggest we leave our mind at the altar so that we can follow Jesus wholeheartedly misrepresent our creation as whole human beings. Heart and mind are not opposites but complements to each other. That tradition goes back to the core of Judaism and that core's affirmation by Jesus: "You shall love the Lord your God with all your heart, and with all your soul, and with all your mind, and with all your strength" (Mark 12:30). In fact, if you look at Deuteronomy 6:4, the verse of the Torah Jesus quotes in support of what he declares the "first" commandment, you will see that Jesus *adds* the word "mind" in his summary of the command to love God. Would Jesus add "mind" only so that his followers would make its exercise secondary to faith?

You may have already noticed in your reading of this passage that Paul uses "mind" in a variety of ways. Sometimes, it is to encourage unity (3:15; 4:2). Sometimes, it is to connect how one's actions and hopes flow from one's thoughts (3:19). Sometimes, it is to identify, along with the heart, what God's gift of peace seeks to guard (4:7). Our minds are not peripheral to our fashioning in the image of God. We have this God-given gift of mind to aid us in the choices we make and the trusts we exercise and the hopes and actions to which we commit ourselves. God has made us with heads whose use is not limited to hat racks. So let us be stewards of our minds as well as our hearts, as individually and together we seek the mind of Christ to guide our thinking and our faith.

Who Are These People?

Philippians 3:19 offers one of Paul's harshest critiques of any opponent in any of his epistles, including Galatians. As noted in the comments on this verse in Understanding the Scripture, we do not know exactly who he refers to. Perhaps that is just as well. If we had a specific name or group, we might easily dismiss the critique as limited to those folks back then. But we don't.

Instead, we have several hints about what Paul considers opposition to the cross.

"Their end is destruction" is the first of these. On the surface, that seems contradictory. Who would choose destruction for an end? But if Paul's emphasis, then and now, is on ends that lead to destructiveness, the possibilities open up. What attitudes and practices lead to destructiveness among us, inside and outside the church? Might not the decision to advance one's interests, political or social, by engaging in character assassination or fearmongering, qualify? Such strategies may succeed in the short run, but, in the long run, they only demean relationships and leave communities crippled by a lack of civil conversation. Their end is destructive, and destruction.

Or consider Paul's second mark of those who stand in opposition to to the gospel:

"Their god is the belly." Indulgence seems to be the order of the day here but not just in food. Paul would surely include other "appetites" driven and exaggerated when they go unchecked by reason or by recognition of the needs of others. Some today posit a link between faith and material prosperity. What does this verse suggest in that context? Even more controversial, what might this verse mean in the context of the vast majority of the world's population having barely enough to eat while a small percentage have access to food and luxuries unimaginable to those others—and too often indifferent to them as well? Have the Beatitudes of Luke 6:20-21 ("Blessed are you who are poor. . . . Blessed are you who are hungry.") or the Magnificat of Mary in Luke 1:53 ("[God] has filled the hungry with good things, / and sent the rich away empty") been forgotten as words spoken to *all*?

Paul finally says of those opponents at the end of Philippians 3:19: "Their glory is in their shame." So to continue the previous line of argument, is glorying in the abundance at one's disposal a fitting sign of our thanks for God's providence or a shameful ignoring of need in the face of God's justice? Setting minds on earthly things can be counterproductive to those whose citizenship is the realm of God's Savior Jesus Christ.

Helping Community

Euodia and Syntyche. They are not exactly household names. But through their names we encounter an ongoing need and call for Christ's household even today: Help them.

From the sound of it, a dissension has arisen between two pillars of the church. Have you ever experienced the kind of conflict that results when people you love and respect suddenly find themselves at odds with one another? Or, in truth, have you been in the position of one of those two, estranged from a friend and co-worker?

Several things are critical to notice in this passage. First, Paul does not choose sides.

We don't know what the difference between them was. Maybe it was something about which Paul had no feelings. Maybe he just heard there was trouble. Or maybe—just maybe—he felt passionately about it one way or the other but did not act in a way that would put one woman outside of community. "I urge," he says to both women (4:2). The word there is *parakaleo*. In the Gospel of John, the noun form of this verb is the main metaphor for the Holy Spirit (Paraclete). It literally means "call toward" but can also mean "advocate." Paul advocates for, and to, both women.

But Paul does not leave them on their own with only his urging to help. To "my loyal companion," he says, "help these women" (4:3). The comments on these verses in Understanding the Scripture note two possible meanings of who Paul had in mind: the letter's messenger (Epaphroditus) or the whole community. A third option is possible: Paul's plea could be aimed at whoever heard or read these words. In other words, the summons is to you: You help them.

Although Euodia and Syntyche may have resolved things in their day, others may have taken their place. In your church. In your life. Your role is to help. Agreed, you cannot solve every problem or conflict. But neither can you ignore every one and say it is someone else's business in the church. Community is everyone's business, for all are members of the body of Christ, and all, as Paul argued in 1 Corinthians 12:25, are to have "the same care for one another."

In the name, and for the sake, of Christ: Help them.

SHARING THE SCRIPTURE

Preparing Our Hearts

Meditate on this week's devotional reading, found in Psalm 46. On behalf of the community, the psalmist proclaims trust in God, who offers refuge for those who experience trouble. No matter where trouble is raging, we need not fear, for God is with us. What situations prompt you to seek refuge right now? What memories do you have of God as your refuge in the past that can give you confidence that God will again—and always—help you in times of trouble? Record these memories in your spiritual journal.

Pray that you and the adult learners will continue to be in close communion with God and trust God to support you no matter what.

Preparing Our Minds

Study the background from Philippians 3:3–4:9 and the lesson Scripture from Philippians 3:17–4:9. Think about how people in community come together in the midst of a struggle.

Write on newsprint:
- ❑ words that are underlined in "Recognize Both the Importance of Building Community and the Personal Support the Learners Receive From That Community."
- ❑ information for next week's lesson, found under "Continue the Journey."
- ❑ activities for further spiritual growth in "Continue the Journey."

Prepare a brief lecture from Understanding the Scripture for "Investigate Paul's Writing to the Philippians Concerning Support for One Another."

LEADING THE CLASS

(1) Gather to Learn

❖ Welcome the class members and introduce any guests.

❖ Pray that today's participants will offer mutual support to one another as they study and fellowship together.

❖ Challenge the class to identify one or more tragedies or conflicts within their community or country that cried out for people to support one another. (Examples include *natural catastrophe, closure or mass layoffs at a major business, school shootings, riots.*)

❖ Discuss with the group how they individually or corporately experienced support in this time of trouble. Note any common threads among the stories.

❖ Read aloud today's focus statement: **During difficult times, people in community support one another and find reasons to give thanks. How do people in community come together in the midst of struggle? Paul exhorted the Philippians to follow examples of those who work together for the common good and to rejoice together.**

(2) Investigate Paul's Writing to the Philippians Concerning Support for One Another

❖ Choose one or more volunteers to read Philippians 3:17–4:9.

❖ Use information from Understanding the Scripture to illuminate the meaning of these verses.

❖ Note Paul's call in verse 17 for people to imitate him and others who live Christ-centered lives. Ask:
(1) **How can role models support us as we seek to live like Christ?**
(2) **What dangers, if any, do you see in following someone else's example?**

❖ Invite the students to look again at Philippians 4:2-3. Note that we have no idea what has caused the dispute between two female pillars of the Philippian church, but we are aware that Paul is concerned about them. Ask these questions:
(1) **How would you describe Paul's apparent relationship with these two women?**

(2) **How does Paul handle the unexplained conflict?** (You may wish to read or retell "Helping Community" from Interpreting the Scripture to broaden the discussion.)
(3) **What kind of help do you think those around Euodia and Syntyche would be able to offer?**

❖ Look again at Philippians 4:4-9. Ask the class to imagine what a congregation that followed Paul's advice would act and feel like. Encourage the students to call out ideas.

❖ Discuss these questions:
(1) **What kind of witness do you think such a congregation would make for Christ?**
(2) **Do you think most contemporary congregations make that kind of witness? If so, give examples. If not, why do you suppose that we are not able to live up to Paul's expectations for us as the community of God's people?**

(3) Recognize Both the Importance of Building Community and the Personal Support the Learners Receive From That Community

❖ Read aloud this information, taken from the Baltimore-Washington Conference website, www.bwcumc.org: **The Baltimore-Washington Conference of The United Methodist Church has adopted a program,** *The Discipleship Adventure,* **so as to "seek to be like Christ as we call, equip, send and support spiritual leaders to make disciples and grow 600 Acts 2 congregations by 2012." Note how the steps on this adventure include building community and supporting one another:**
■ *Celebrate—worship. We celebrate the significance of God in our lives and live all of life as though it were the worship of God;*
■ *Connect—fellowship. First we connect with God and then with others to build up the body of Christ;*

■ *Develop—study*. Through Christian education and the development of spiritual insights, we grow in our understanding of God;

■ *Serve—mission and service*. Discover the purpose of one's life through justice and mercy ministries in the community and the world; and

■ *Share—evangelism*. We must witness to and share with others what God has done in our life.

❖ Divide the adults into small groups and distribute paper and pencils. Post newsprint showing the underlined words. Ask each group to consider specific ways in which these five steps could enable them to develop community and receive support from the community.

❖ Call the groups back together to report.

❖ Consider how the class or congregation could implement these suggestions.

(4) Demonstrate How God's People Can Live Together in Community

❖ Invite the students to read in unison today's key verse, Philippians 4:7.

❖ Encourage the adults to give examples of how God's peace dwells in them, even when they are facing conflict or trials. Think in terms of peace within individuals and also peace within the church.

❖ Read aloud Acts 2:42-47, which demonstrates the early church living together as a harmonious community.

❖ List on newsprint the things that the Acts community did, particularly as noted in verse 42. Also mention that, according to verse 47, the church was growing numerically as people were accepting Christ.

❖ Identify the kinds of activities that your congregation undertakes. List them on newsprint. Discuss how these activities afford those who participate an opportunity to live together in community.

(5) Continue the Journey

❖ Pray that those who have participated in today's session will continue to support and help one another.

❖ Read aloud this preparation for next week's lesson. You may also want to post it on newsprint for the students to copy.

■ **Title: Witness of the Community**
■ **Background Scripture: 2 Timothy 2:1-3; 4:1-5**
■ **Lesson Scripture: 2 Timothy 2:1-3; 4:1-5**
■ **Focus of the Lesson: Through constructive living, people have a positive influence on and set a good example for others in their community. What characterizes a good example? Paul wrote that living as Jesus did was a strong witness for others to follow in good times and bad and that this message should be shared with all who would listen.**

❖ Challenge the students to complete one or more of these activities for further spiritual growth, which you will write on newsprint for the students to copy.

(1) **Meditate on Paul's statement: "The Lord is near" (Philippians 4:5). How does God's nearness support you or challenge you or make you feel uncomfortable?**

(2) **Review Philippians 4:8-9. Where do you see these values being played out? How would our society be different if people took seriously Paul's exhortation to act with truth, honor, justice, and so on?**

(3) **Offer support to someone who needs a helping hand.**

❖ Sing or read aloud "Let There Be Peace on Earth."

❖ Conclude today's session by leading the class in this benediction, adapted from Ephesians 4:4-6: **Let us now depart rejoicing in the community we share, united as one body, with one Spirit, one Lord, one faith, one baptism, and one God and Father of all.**

UNIT 3: THE NEW COMMUNITY FACES GROWNG PAINS

WITNESS OF THE COMMUNITY

PREVIEWING THE LESSON

Lesson Scripture: 2 Timothy 2:1-3; 4:1-5
Background Scripture: 2 Timothy 2:1-3; 4:1-5
Key Verse: 2 Timothy 2:2

Focus of the Lesson:
Through constructive living, people have a positive influence on and set a good example for others in their community. What characterizes a good example? Paul wrote that living as Jesus did was a strong witness for others to follow in good times and bad and that this message should be shared with all who would listen.

Goals for the Learners:
(1) to examine Paul's writings about the need for strong Christian witness.
(2) to appreciate the necessity of telling others about their Christian faith and life.
(3) to dedicate themselves consistently to proclaiming and living their Christian witness.

Pronunciation Guide:
chronos (khron' os)
kairos (kahee ros')
logos (loh' gohs)
martus (mar' toos)

Supplies:
Bibles, newsprint and marker, paper and pencils, hymnals, optional Bible commentaries

---

READING THE SCRIPTURE

NRSV
2 Timothy 2:1-3

¹You then, my child, be strong in the grace that is in Christ Jesus; ²and **what you have heard from me through many witnesses entrust to faithful people who will be able**

NIV
2 Timothy 2:1-3

¹You then, my son, be strong in the grace that is in Christ Jesus. ²**And the things you have heard me say in the presence of many witnesses entrust to reliable men**

to teach others as well. ³Share in suffering like a good soldier of Christ Jesus.

2 Timothy 4:1-5

¹In the presence of God and of Christ Jesus, who is to judge the living and the dead, and in view of his appearing and his kingdom, I solemnly urge you: ²proclaim the message; be persistent whether the time is favorable or unfavorable; convince, rebuke, and encourage, with the utmost patience in teaching. ³For the time is coming when people will not put up with sound doctrine, but having itching ears, they will accumulate for themselves teachers to suit their own desires, ⁴and will turn away from listening to the truth and wander away to myths. ⁵As for you, always be sober, endure suffering, do the work of an evangelist, carry out your ministry fully.

who will also be qualified to teach others. ³Endure hardship with us like a good soldier of Christ Jesus.

2 Timothy 4:1-5

¹In the presence of God and of Christ Jesus, who will judge the living and the dead, and in view of his appearing and his kingdom, I give you this charge: ²Preach the Word; be prepared in season and out of season; correct, rebuke and encourage—with great patience and careful instruction. ³For the time will come when men will not put up with sound doctrine. Instead, to suit their own desires, they will gather around them a great number of teachers to say what their itching ears want to hear. ⁴They will turn their ears away from the truth and turn aside to myths. ⁵But you, keep your head in all situations, endure hardship, do the work of an evangelist, discharge all the duties of your ministry.

UNDERSTANDING THE SCRIPTURE

2 Timothy 2:1. Please refer to "The Big Picture: New Testament Community" for background material on 2 Timothy, especially on the discussion regarding Pauline and possible non-Pauline materials in the epistle. The address of Timothy as "my child" echoes the assertion made in 1 Timothy 1:18. Even those who support a non-Pauline editing or authoring of the epistle tend to attribute such personal addresses back to Paul. The relationship envisaged in this reference is something on the order of a mentor. The urging to "be strong" parallels Ephesians 6:10. There, however, such strength is associated with Christ's power. Here, strength derives from Christ's grace. Grace has been a foundational theme in practically all of the Pauline letters. Its varying shades of meaning share common ground in an affirmation of God's

actions for the sake of our salvation and reconciliation. The phrase "that is in Christ Jesus" is found elsewhere in the Timothy correspondence (1 Timothy 1:14, 3:13; 2 Timothy 1:13). It serves here to "locate" the grace that is our strength. Beyond that, it hints at Paul's frequent use of "in Christ" as a metaphor for the Christian life.

2 Timothy 2:2-3. The text is slightly unclear as to the function or identity of the "many witnesses." Is it saying Timothy has heard Paul's words or teachings from many others? Is it saying the relationship with Paul and the familiarity with his words have been underscored by similar witness borne by others? What is clear is the declaration that Paul's (or the author's) witness is shared by the wider community. Perhaps the mention of these other witnesses sets up the flow of the following phrase, namely, that what Timothy has heard is to be entrusted to individuals of faith who will then pass it on to others. "Entrust" carries the meaning of "commit" or "commend." It is the word Luke recalls Jesus speaking from the cross immediately prior to his death: "Father, into your hands I *commend* my spirit" (Luke 23:46, italics added). "Share in suffering" is a unique compound word used in verse 3, as it had been earlier in 1:8. The gospel is not an "escape valve" for avoiding suffering. Faithful witness (in Greek, *martus*, from which we get "martyr") may lead directly to suffering. The image of "soldier" is shortly followed with "athlete" (2:5) and "farmer" (2:6). Such vocations require discipline and patience and persistence, the same qualities evoked by the call to "share in suffering."

2 Timothy 4:1-2. The opening phrase ("in the presence of God and of Christ Jesus") had been used in 1 Timothy 5:21 toward the end of a chapter-long series of instructions concerning life and leadership in Christian community. It is asserted there as a warning "to keep these instructions." Now in 2 Timothy 4:1, the same phrase introduces a shorter section that counsels Timothy on his ministry. Christ as judge of the living and the dead (4:1) reflects earlier traditions surrounding the teachings of Peter (Acts 10:42). "Appearing" translates the word from which we get "epiphany." Paired together, "appearing" and "kingdom" may refer to Christ's incarnation (already accomplished) and Christ's reign (the future's hope). The church lives in between those times, drawing strength and witnessing to the truth and hope of both. Out of those assertions of Christ, Paul "solemnly urges" (the root of which in Greek is *martus*, or "witness") Timothy to a series of actions related to his teaching and preaching. "Message" in verse 2 is *logos*, "word." "Word" in the Timothy correspondence is a frequent metaphor for the word God reveals and the content of Christian proclamation (1 Timothy 4:6; 2 Timothy 2:9). "Time" in verse 2 (and later

in verse 3) has the distinct meaning of "season." The word used here is not the Greek word *chronos* (the root of our word "chronological"), which has to do with the succession of one moment after another. Rather, the word here has as its root *kairos*, a sense of time related to "fitting."

Verse 2 closes with a list of types of speech, whose differences balance on the exercise of patience (knowing when one is needed and others are not).

2 Timothy 4:3-4. *Kairos* again is the time word used, and here the "time" approaching is contrasted in its negativity with and even opposition to the "time" of Christ's appearing and kingdom. The "itching ear" imagery was apparently a familiar metaphor in these times for conveying the idea of impatience or intolerance that leads to seeking out only what is wanted to be heard. (Perhaps the closest allusion in English would be "an itch in need of scratching.") "Accumulation" suggests a consumer approach to teachers (and messages) that are welcomed, leaving unspoken but implied a disassociation with those that do not suit desires. The irony is the "turning away" that will occur, not from sin but from truth. The word "myths" carries a negative connotation in the Timothy correspondence (1 Timothy 1:4; 4:7). The author does not specify what such myths consist of in those earlier references or here. Clearly, though, the contrast is made between such words and the word that Timothy is called to proclaim (4:2).

2 Timothy 4:5. For the third time now in these passages considered (2:1; 4:1), the addressing of Timothy by the author is direct and personal: "you." What follows now as the conclusion of this charge is a series of three instructions. The word translated here as "sober" has a broader meaning of "self-controlled" or "disciplined" connected with a need for readiness (1 Thessalonians 5:6; 5:8). It does carry the idea of sobriety from intoxicants, but it is frequently used in a more symbolic sense of clearness of mind. "Endure suffering" reflects back on 2 Timothy 2:3. "Evangelist" is a precise function of ministry (Ephesians 4:11), while "your ministry" appears to have a wider context and practice of ministry in mind, especially when paired with the verb "to carry out fully"—as in exercise all of its components.

INTERPRETING THE SCRIPTURE

Strength in Grace

Strength through.... Take a look through today's headlines or listen to candidates vying for political office. How would they finish the phrase: "strength through . . ."?

Better yet, look back on your own life experience. In those times when you found yourself strengthened to face some difficult task, to speak a word you might have otherwise held to yourself, what gave you strength?

Paul's counsel to Timothy is to find strength in grace. Grace is, at its core, the recognition of what God does on our behalf. Grace recognizes that our strength resides somewhere other than our ingenuity or our physical prowess or our moral steadfastness or our innate ability to pull ourselves up by the bootstraps and proclaim we are self-made men and women.

None of this means we ought to discount the God-given gifts entrusted to us: gifts of intellect, gifts of compassion, gifts of character. Indeed, God has "graced" us with such qualities and attributes for the sake of their exercise, not their denial. But remembering that they are gifts, and that we are graced by them, reminds us that the strength they provide arises from somewhere beyond the sum total of who we are as individuals and even as communities. Our strength, our capability to speak and act faithfully and for the sake of justice and compassion, derives from the grace of God.

Be strong in that gift. Be empowered (a more literal meaning of this verb in Greek) in that grace. Why? Purely human strengths rise and then fall with age, with physical and mental abilities. Purely human strengths may wither in the face of opposition or ridicule in those times and places where taking a stand may mean standing for the moment in isolation. But the strength that is ours in Christ endures.

From Generation to Generation

The commentary in the *New Interpreter's Bible* by James D. G. Dunn on 2 Timothy 2:2 makes an intriguing point. It suggests this passage has in mind not simply Paul's and then Timothy's generation but up to four generations. There is Paul, the representative of the first-generation church. Then there is Timothy, a second-generation Christian who has been taken under Paul's wing even as he is now commissioned to carry on the work of Paul's generation. Then there are the "faithful people" to whom Timothy is to entrust what he has heard from Paul and others, the third generation of Christians. But it does not stop there. Paul encourages this entrusting of the message to them, for they "will be able to teach others as well."

This simple verse affords a powerful image of the gospel moving across generations, inviting and then entrusting and then commissioning each successive one into faith and service.

I suspect it is much like the community with which you gather. Unless you are a highly unusual person (and I have never met such a one), you did not come to faith all on your own. Others led you: by word, by example, by encouragement, maybe by challenge. Two generations. I would also venture to say that in that community, future leaders and participants in the church are being nurtured (hopefully)— folks who will take up the service and ministry you and others presently render. A third generation. But it does not end with them. They will take their place in faith to provide word and example and challenge for others to come. Four generations.

The key here is that all four generations, and more, blend and mingle in this present one. In our words and actions, in our witness and ministry. Past and present and future all merge into a common service of Christ Jesus. We never can act for our own sake alone. If we do, we deny the connections between us—the ones that bind us not only to our contemporaries but also to those who have gone before us and those who follow after us. That is the trust we are given and are to entrust.

Persistent Witness

"Whether the time is favorable or unfavorable" (4:2). Clearly, Paul did not perceive the preaching or living of the gospel as a weather vane. That is, follow the direction of the prevailing winds, be those prevailing winds dictated by culture or nation or local gossips.

It is likely not accidental that Paul includes this urging in a passage that includes challenges Timothy will encounter in presenting the gospel. The truth of the matter is this: A persistent witness is likely to cause you grief if it steps on the wrong toes or speaks what is deemed to be "out of turn."

This is not an excuse to say any old thing and then, when trouble comes, to attribute that to your being faithful to the gospel while the rest of the world doesn't get it. Paul's prior imperative clarifies what is to hold true in season and out: "proclaim the message," which is to say the word of Jesus

Christ. The word of God's grace. The word of God's compassion. The word of God's justice. We don't get to say any old thing we want. The word needs to be consistent with the word encountered in Jesus. It is that living Word that forms the measure of all the other words we speak. And it is faithfulness and integrity to the Word, who is Christ, that forms the message we are to speak and live in season and out.

Carry Out Your Ministry

What is your ministry? That is, what do you find yourself called to do in response to the God revealed to us in Jesus?

Let us be clear from the outset: Ministry is not a private club reserved for clergy with ordination documents. Ministry, as Paul spoke of it in 1 Corinthians 12:7, has to do with the whole people of God: "*Each* is given the manifestation of the Spirit for the common good" (italics added).

In the case of Timothy, it seems he had a particular calling as an evangelist. But even exercising that particular activity did not exhaust the whole of his ministry. While Paul encourages him to do that work, he adds at the close of our passage that Timothy is to carry out his ministry *fully*. Timothy was an evangelist, but that did not encompass the whole of who he was in the service of Christ and in the community of the church.

Think about that for yourself. Sometimes, and with good reason, we like to focus on particular callings and gifts that we have. I teach, or I sew, or I visit, or I pray. It is good and wise to know our particular gifts and callings and to exercise them for the good of the whole. But Paul's closing words may invite us to recognize that we are not valued and gifted for one thing only. Our ministry, our participation in community and service of others, moves in wider arcs than that. So, part of the church's task is to help individuals discover and practice those other "ministries" that we are as yet unaware of. And part of our task is to be open to the possibility of discovering that we have other gifts and graces than those we already know.

The opening and closing words of today's passages make for an intriguing benediction: Be strong in grace and carry out your ministry fully. That is the good news we are given and the good work to which we have been called.

SHARING THE SCRIPTURE

Preparing Our Hearts

Meditate on this week's devotional reading, found in Acts 4:13-20. (Begin at Chapter 3, verse 1, if you want to read the entire story.) The point in verses 13-20 relevant for today's lesson is that Peter and John were "bold" witnesses. Even when the religious officials demanded that they stop speaking in the name of Jesus, the two apostles responded, "we cannot keep from speaking about what we have seen and heard" (4:20). Think about your own witness. Are you so on fire for Christ that you will speak out, despite warnings and threats?

Pray that you and the adult learners will stand firm in making a bold witness for Christ.

Preparing Our Minds

Study the background and lesson Scripture, both found in 2 Timothy 2:1-3; 4:1-5. Think about what characterizes a good example.

Write on newsprint:

❑ words of commitment under "Dedicate Oneself Consistently to Proclaiming and Living the Christian Witness."

❑ information for next week's lesson, found under "Continue the Journey."

❑ activities for further spiritual growth in "Continue the Journey."

Plan the suggested lecture for "Examine Paul's Writings About the Need for Strong Christian Witness."

LEADING THE CLASS

(1) Gather to Learn

❖ Welcome the class members and introduce any guests.

❖ Pray that the participants will feel a sense of oneness as they gather in community today.

❖ Divide the students into small groups. Ask them to recount in their groups a memory of someone who set a good example for them. Encourage them to talk about how this example influenced them then and, perhaps, continues to influence them now.

❖ Bring the groups together and read aloud today's focus statement: **Through constructive living, people have a positive influence on and set a good example for others in their community. What characterizes a good example? Paul wrote that living as Jesus did was a strong witness for others to follow in good times and bad and that this message should be shared with all who would listen.**

(2) Examine Paul's Writings About the Need for Strong Christian Witness

❖ Select a volunteer to read 2 Timothy 2:1-3.

■ Present a lecture based on verses 1-3 from Understanding the Scripture and "Strength in Grace" from Interpreting the Scripture. Your purpose here will be to help the students understand what Paul means by being "strong in grace," entrusting the faith to others, and sharing in suffering.

- **Option:** Divide the class into groups and give each group at least one Bible commentary and paper and pencils. Challenge them to explore Paul's ideas on being "strong in grace," entrusting the faith to others, and sharing in suffering. Bring the class back together to hear what each group has discovered.
- Conclude this portion of the session by asking these questions:
  (1) **Do you agree with Paul?**
  (2) **If so, how are you entrusting the gospel to others?**
  (3) **How are you sharing in suffering because you are a Christian? If you are not personally suffering for the sake of the gospel, how do you support those who are?**

❖ Choose someone to read 2 Timothy 4:1-5.

- Make a list on newsprint of the things that Paul is urging Timothy to do in verse 2.
- Make another list of the traits that Paul wants Timothy to exhibit, as seen in verse 5.
- Talk about the challenges Timothy faces by using information from 4:3-4 in Understanding the Scripture.
- Use all of this information as a basis for talking with the adults about how they can carry out their own ministry fully (4:5). With the entire class or in groups, discuss these questions:
  (1) **What challenges do we face in bearing witness to the gospel? How are these challenges similar to and different from the ones Timothy faced?**
  (2) **In what ways are we proclaiming the message individually and as a congregation?**

  (3) **In what ways can we mentor others so that we not only bear a strong Christian witness ourselves but also encourage others to carry out their own ministries?**

(3) Appreciate the Necessity of Telling Others About the Learners' Christian Faith and Life

❖ Read aloud "From Generation to Generation" in Interpreting the Scripture.
  ❖ Discuss these questions:
  (1) **What does this commentary suggest to you regarding the importance of families teaching the faith?**
  (2) **What does this commentary suggest to you regarding the church's role in transmitting the faith?**
  (3) **In what ways are you as a congregation teaching and modeling the faith for people of all generations?** (List these ideas on newsprint.)
  (4) **What steps does your church need to take to better equip and empower people to tell others about the Christian faith and its importance in your life?** (List these ideas on newsprint.)

(4) Dedicate Oneself Consistently to Proclaiming and Living the Christian Witness

❖ Read the fourth and fifth paragraphs of "Carry Out Your Ministry" in Interpreting the Scripture.
  ❖ Distribute paper and pencils. Ask the students to look at the two lists brainstormed during the previous activity. Suggest that they write a few sentences or phrases stating how they can help to teach and model the faith and help the church to better equip people to do this.
  ❖ Call on volunteers to read or retell their ideas.
  ❖ Conclude this portion of the session by

asking the students to write these words, which you will post on newsprint, on their papers and sign their names, if they can honestly agree with this commitment. They will fill in the blank with whatever they feel called to do. Note that they will keep the papers and refer to them at home. **With God's help, I will make every effort to _____ so as to teach and model the faith and equip others to share the faith.**

(5) Continue the Journey

❖ Pray that those who have gathered today will go forth to set a good example and bear witness to the gospel of Jesus Christ.

❖ Read aloud this preparation for next week's lesson. You may also want to post it on newsprint for the students to copy.

- **Title: Persecution Within the Community**
- **Background Scripture: 2 Corinthians 11:16–12:10**
- **Lesson Scripture: 2 Corinthians 11:17, 21-30; 12:9-10**
- **Focus of the Lesson: People will face many trials in life from friend and foe as well as from expected and unexpected sources. How can one overcome such hardships? Paul says that through his weaknesses he finds strength in the grace of God.**

❖ Challenge the students to complete one or more of these activities for further spiritual growth, which you will write on newsprint for the students to copy.

(1) **Identify a situation in your church where you need to "be persistent whether the time is favorable or unfavorable" (4:2) in proclaiming a message or course of action consistent with the gospel. Do what you can to help the congregation to move forward.**

(2) **Interview at least one church member to see how he or she defines "Christian living." Ponder how this definition affirms or challenges your own definition.**

(3) **Recall that Paul was Timothy's mentor. Act as a mentor to someone else seeking to live the Christian life.**

❖ Sing or read aloud "I Want to Walk as a Child of the Light."

❖ Conclude today's session by leading the class in this benediction, adapted from Ephesians 4:4-6: **Let us now depart rejoicing in the community we share, united as one body, with one Spirit, one Lord, one faith, one baptism, and one God and Father of all.**

UNIT 3: THE NEW COMMUNITY FACES GROWING PAINS
PERSECUTION WITHIN THE COMMUNITY

PREVIEWING THE LESSON

Lesson Scripture: 2 Corinthians 11:17, 21-30; 12:9-10
Background Scripture: 2 Corinthians 11:16–12:10
Key Verse: 2 Corinthians 12:10

Focus of the Lesson:
People will face many trials in life from friend and foe as well as from expected and unexpected sources. How can one overcome such hardships? Paul says that through his weaknesses he finds strength in the grace of God.

Goals for the Learners:
(1) to consider Paul's writing about the inevitability of facing difficulties in the Christian life and the reliability of God's grace.
(2) to accept that being a Christian will not prevent them from facing persecution, even from some within the faith community.
(3) to support one another as they witness to their faith during difficult times.

Pronunciation Guide:
Aretas (air' uh tuhs)   Nabatea (nab uh tee' a)
eudokeo (yoo dok eh' o)   *skandalizo* (skan dal id' zo)
gnosis (noh' sis)

Supplies:
Bibles, newsprint and marker, paper and pencils, hymnals, articles/information related to current persecutions of Christians around the world, optional meditative music and appropriate player

---

READING THE SCRIPTURE

NRSV
2 Corinthians 11:17, 21-30
¹⁷What I am saying in regard to this boastful confidence, I am saying not with the Lord's authority, but as a fool.

NIV
2 Corinthians 11:17, 21-30
¹⁷In this self-confident boasting I am not talking as the Lord would, but as a fool.

21But whatever anyone dares to boast of—I am speaking as a fool—I also dare to boast of that. 22Are they Hebrews? So am I. Are they Israelites? So am I. Are they descendants of Abraham? So am I. 23Are they ministers of Christ? I am talking like a madman—I am a better one: with far greater labors, far more imprisonments, with countless floggings, and often near death. 24Five times I have received from the Jews the forty lashes minus one. 25Three times I was beaten with rods. Once I received a stoning. Three times I was shipwrecked; for a night and a day I was adrift at sea; 26on frequent journeys, in danger from rivers, danger from bandits, danger from my own people, danger from Gentiles, danger in the city, danger in the wilderness, danger at sea, danger from false brothers and sisters; 27in toil and hardship, through many a sleepless night, hungry and thirsty, often without food, cold and naked. 28And, besides other things, I am under daily pressure because of my anxiety for all the churches. 29Who is weak, and I am not weak? Who is made to stumble, and I am not indignant?

30If I must boast, I will boast of the things that show my weakness.

2 Corinthians 12:9-10

9[B]ut he said to me, "My grace is sufficient for you, for power is made perfect in weakness." So, I will boast all the more gladly of my weaknesses, so that the power of Christ may dwell in me. 10Therefore **I am content with weaknesses, insults, hardships, persecutions, and calamities for the sake of Christ; for whenever I am weak, then I am strong**.

21What anyone else dares to boast about—I am speaking as a fool—I also dare to boast about. 22Are they Hebrews? So am I. Are they Israelites? So am I. Are they Abraham's descendants? So am I. 23Are they servants of Christ? (I am out of my mind to talk like this.) I am more. I have worked much harder, been in prison more frequently, been flogged more severely, and been exposed to death again and again. 24Five times I received from the Jews the forty lashes minus one. 25Three times I was beaten with rods, once I was stoned, three times I was shipwrecked, I spent a night and a day in the open sea, 26I have been constantly on the move. I have been in danger from rivers, in danger from bandits, in danger from my own countrymen, in danger from Gentiles; in danger in the city, in danger in the country, in danger at sea; and in danger from false brothers. 27I have labored and toiled and have often gone without sleep; I have known hunger and thirst and have often gone without food; I have been cold and naked. 28Besides everything else, I face daily the pressure of my concern for all the churches. 29Who is weak, and I do not feel weak? Who is led into sin, and I do not inwardly burn?

30If I must boast, I will boast of the things that show my weakness.

2 Corinthians 12:9-10

9But he said to me, "My grace is sufficient for you, for my power is made perfect in weakness." Therefore I will boast all the more gladly about my weaknesses, so that Christ's power may rest on me. 10That is why, **for Christ's sake, I delight in weaknesses, in insults, in hardships, in persecutions, in difficulties. For when I am weak, then I am strong.**

UNDERSTANDING THE SCRIPTURE

2 Corinthians 11:16. Irony, sarcasm, and "boasting" form the style of Paul's language in this and following verses. This passage

drops us midstream into Paul's argument with opponents who work to undermine Paul's authority in the Corinthian community. Scholars view chapters 10–13 of 2 Corinthians as a later letter to the community evoked by the work of these opponents. In verse 5, Paul refers to these opponents as "super apostles," so there is some basis for assuming that they claimed to be Christian missionaries. While much debate has ensued as to precisely who these opponents were, the truth is that we really do not know. It is critical in listening to this and following verses to keep this context of conflict and challenge in mind. Otherwise, Paul's tactic of "boasting" and claiming the part of a "fool" may come across as self-serving pride, rather than a defense of his authority as an apostle.

2 Corinthians 11:17-21a. Paul occasionally clarifies, as he does in verse 17, that his words are spoken on his own authority rather than that of God (see also 1 Corinthians 7:12). The contrast made with his opponents in verse 18 sets up Paul's sarcastic critique of how the Corinthian community has allowed itself to be abused by those opponents in verse 20. His calling the community "wise" strongly echoes themes pronounced at the beginning of his first epistle to the community about the message of the cross being foolishness in the eyes of the "wise" (1 Corinthians 1:18-25). Paul concludes the critique with an admission of his "weakness" (and of those with whom he worked) that did not allow them to take advantage of the community. He will soon return to this positive view of "weakness."

2 Corinthians 11:21b-23. This passage provides one of the few clear insights into the identity of Paul's opponents: Hebrews, Israelites, descendants of Abraham. The terms can be interchangeable, although they might also underscore how Paul shares with them ethnicity, nationality, and a common faith tradition. He even suggests they are ministers of Christ. From casting himself as a fool, Paul now asserts he is about to talk as a "madman." And if we do not keep close in sight the opposition he faced and their apparent undercutting of his authority—we might well agree with Paul's assessment of himself. For on the surface, the boasting that now fol-

lows is not the most appealing or endearing of discourse to use about oneself—unless it is remembered that Paul is having to write in absentia in self-defense, when it sounds like no one else was standing up for him.

2 Corinthians 11:23-27. The litany of hardships Paul now recites is telling. Deuteronomy 25:3 called for forty lashes as punishment, and a tradition developed that thirty-nine be given lest the count be missed and someone receive more than the forty lashes. Stoning was a capital punishment, intended to kill rather than simply injure. The overall thrust of this passage comes in the repetition of the word "danger," no less than eight times. It is unclear whether Paul's opponents had laid claim to authority based on hardships they had experienced. But from Paul's recital, it is clear he intended to show that his faith came at risk and cost.

2 Corinthians 11:28-30. In his First Epistle to the Corinthians (12:26), Paul had depicted church life as the sharing of one another's lives. The theology of that passage now becomes the lived experience of the apostle. The weakness of others becomes his weakness. "Made to stumble" translates the Greek word *skandalizo*—so, in a literal sense, when another is scandalized it is Paul who is indignant at their treatment. The weight of "all" the churches is upon him. Paul closes by once again returning to the theme of weakness, only here identified with what causes Paul to boast, in contrast to those opponents who "boast according to human standards" (11:18).

2 Corinthians 11:31-33. The episode alluded to here is also reported in Acts 9:23-25. There, however, the opposition to Paul was identified with some of the Jewish leaders rather than the governing authorities of the city. King Aretas ruled the region of Nabatea, which was located southeast of Palestine. Damascus is north of Palestine, in modern-day Syria. There is some dispute about whether (or why) Damascus would be under his rule.

2 Corinthians 12:1-6. Now comes one of

the most intriguing of the epistle's passages. Paul speaks in third person of an individual who has this mystical experience. Many suggest the one of whom he speaks is himself. The repeated "I know / I do not know / God knows" adds both mystery and confusion. It may also have been a hint to some that Paul was addressing early gnostics, that is, those who purportedly had special "knowledge" (that is what the word *gnosis* literally means). The levels of heaven and hearing things not to be told are familiar themes in Jewish mysticism of this and later centuries. Paul's witness, however—even if this mystical experience is his own—is not in such private experiences but in what others see and hear in Paul.

2 Corinthians 12:7-10. On the heels of one mystery comes another: What exactly is the "thorn" in Paul's flesh? Some have taken it to mean a physical ailment. Or was it his anxiety over the church? We do not know. Paul notes that he called on God to remove it no less than three times. The answer to the prayer pushes Paul back onto reliance of God: grace, power brought to completion in weakness. Paul returns in verse 10 to a "shorthand" form of his hardships, noting that in all of them he is "content." The word *eudokeo* can also mean "consent" or "willing." Paul is not making a virtue of such experiences. Rather, he is acknowledging that the grace of God empowers life in the midst of such trying times. Verse 10's affirmation sounds in word and spirit very much like another of Paul's passages, attributed to his imprisonment: "for I have learned to be content with whatever I have" (Philippians 4:11).

INTERPRETING THE SCRIPTURE

The Myth of Pristine Christianity

At various points in the church's history, people have sought to return the church to perceived earlier states of innocence or purity. Sometimes such movements have merely sought to go back to the previous generation, where it seemed all was well and life was simpler. At other times, those movements have pushed for restoration to apostolic times, where such summaries as Acts 4:32-37 made it appear as if life in community was not stained by division. Yet we may forget that the Acts 4 summary of "not a needy person among them" was followed immediately by the story of Ananias and Sapphira in Acts 5.

Paul's correspondence with the Corinthian church also sets the record straight about idealizing first-generation Christianity. The whole of our passage grows out of opposition to Paul's ministry that seems to have used personal attack to undermine his authority. Between the lines of Paul's sarcasm and boasting is the voice of one seeking to stand in the face of such antagonism and, in doing so, to correct the community he had played such a large role in shaping.

Opposition and conflict hurt most when they arise from within one's community. That was Paul's experience. It is a truth, and experience, known in our day as well. Church unity and the call to love one another face their greatest testing, not so much when folks outside the church community critique (sometimes rightfully so) our life or integrity but when differences between us lead to recriminations against one another. In those times, faithfulness is not found in returning to some imagined innocent state of the church in the past. Rather, God's Spirit beckons us to find our way forward by speaking the truth in love—and practicing Jesus' counsel to love one's enemies—even when those who oppose us or our positions come from within the very community we cherish.

A Dangerous Faith

It is not likely that 2 Corinthians 11:24-27 gets used in new-member classes. Nor is it likely a text that the church nominating committee presents to prospective candidates for office about what their service on the trustees or committees or boards might involve. After all, who wants to use this litany of extraordinary hardships as an invitation to community life?

Then again, how often do we want to invoke "taking up your cross" when speaking of joining Christian community or participating in its responsibilities?

Beneath the boasting and "one-upmanship" of Paul's words here is the unsettling truth that Christian faith does hold the potential for danger when its call is heeded regardless of consequences. Some of what Paul depicts are hazards of travel in his day. But many of the hardships listed trace to offending folks in positions of power. Imprisonment. Flogging. Stoning. Lashings. Even danger from those who are brothers and sisters. Paul's litany here can be a wake-up call to faith and faith communities that have confused the following of Jesus with being a country club where no one speaks or acts in troubling ways. Why is it dangerous? In a world where violence is so often the first resort to settle disputes, personally or nationally, it is dangerous to speak of resolving conflict in nonviolent ways. In a world where resources are so unequally distributed, it is dangerous to speak and act in ways that seek equity.

Perhaps we read Paul's words and wonder how in the world he could get into so much trouble. If so, perhaps we should look at the injustices and inequities and hatreds around and among us and wonder why individuals and communities of faith aren't getting into more trouble about the things that *really* matter in the sight of God.

Taking the Community to Heart

"I am under daily pressure because of my anxiety for all the churches" (2 Corinthians 11:28). The words are Paul's. Are they ours as well? Do we carry the community of Christ so close to our hearts?

There is, to be sure, a limit to what might constitute healthy anxiety. A literal understanding of Jesus' words in Matthew 6:25 might even make it seem that any anxiety in our lives is out of order. But clearly, to be concerned for others—to be concerned for the community at large—has a place. Paul goes on here to describe the empathy he has for others in terms of sharing weakness and indignation when another is "scandalized" (see the note on 2 Corinthians 11:28-30 in Understanding the Scripture). You might want to pause here and consider when you have had such experiences in the faith community, where the mere word of another's illness or joy has markedly affected you. That is the nature of genuine community. We are not an isolated collection of individuals who merely share time together in worship or service or fellowship. Those times and the experiences they bring bind us to one another in deep ways. And the more we allow ourselves to be touched by the lives of others, and vice versa, the more we grow in community and in the experience of the church as the body of Christ.

Weakness and Strength

When we experience weakness in our lives, two things may happen.

One is that we can become defensive, either denying that we are weak or retreating into some isolation so that others do not see us. In such ways, the weakness may grow in its influence, for separated from others it looms larger and larger, and our inability to deal with it becomes ever more evident.

But another response to weakness can be opening ourselves to the strength of others.

Experiences of loss and grief can trigger such a response. In our tears, in our sadness, we open ourselves to the leading and support of others.

For Paul, the awareness of his weakness did not become a source of despair. Rather, his weakness steered him into reliance on the grace of God. His prayer to be released from a particular though unidentified weakness in his life not once but three times clearly indicates he did not see it as a good thing. But as he earlier wrote in Romans 8:28, "All things work together for good for those who love God." Grace brought good out of this condition.

That is a critical insight into our own experience of weakness. It is not that God levies conditions on us so that somehow we will learn from them. Rather, in the weakness that does beset us, God offers grace that allows us to live through it. Sometimes healing comes. Sometimes, though, as in Paul's case, healing doesn't. But grace endures and provides the way for us to live in the midst of whatever comes our way. The good is not in those conditions that come our way—the good is in the God whose grace accompanies us through them.

It is from the realization of God's abiding grace that weakness, in Paul's experience, can become strength. The strength of knowing and trusting God's presence. The strength of experiencing the love of Christ even in the midst of unlovely times. The contentment Paul speaks of in 12:10 is not a passive "oh well, nothing to be done about it anyway" attitude. Rather, it is the contentment (and the word can also mean "willingness") to accept life as it comes in the knowledge that God's strength and grace will be sufficient.

As it is for Paul, so it can be for us.

SHARING THE SCRIPTURE

Preparing Our Hearts

Meditate on this week's devotional reading, found in 1 Corinthians 1:18-25. Here we see that Christ, not the world, embodies the wisdom and power of God. Paul claims in verse 18 that whereas the world views the cross as foolishness, those who are saved recognize God's power there. Where do you seek wisdom? Where do you seek strength? Do you need to re-adjust your focus?

Pray that you and the adult learners will set aside the foolishness of the world to seek God's strength and wisdom.

Preparing Our Minds

Study the background from 2 Corinthians 11:16–12:10 and the lesson Scripture from 2 Corinthians 11:17, 21-30; 12:9-10. Consider how one can overcome trials in life from friend and foe as well as from expected and unexpected sources.

Write on newsprint:
- ❏ information for next week's lesson, found under "Continue the Journey."
- ❏ activities for further spiritual growth in "Continue the Journey."

Do some research concerning current persecutions of Christians around the world. You will likely find news articles on the Internet. Palestine, Egypt, Iraq, North Korea, Pakistan, Myanmar (formerly Burma), Somalia, and the Maldives are some places where such persecution exists as this lesson is being written. Print out these articles for group use during class or prepare a lecture based on the articles.

Option: Locate meditative music and an

appropriate player if you choose to use that in the "Accept That Being a Christian Will Not Prevent Persecution, Even From Some Within the Faith Community" portion of the lesson.

LEADING THE CLASS

(1) Gather to Learn

❖ Welcome the class members and introduce any guests.

❖ Pray that those who attend today will invite the Holy Spirit to lead and teach them through this lesson.

❖ Read aloud this story: **On April 16, 2007, the deadliest massacre ever perpetrated by a single killer in the United States occurred on the campus of Virginia Tech in Blacksburg, Virginia. Professors and students peacefully attending classes, as well as two students in a dorm—thirty-two in all—were gunned down by a young man who had so carefully orchestrated this carnage that he even sent a packet of information to NBC News about the crime. The young man who committed this heinous act was not a terrorist or escaped criminal. No, he was a student at the very university where his guns snuffed out the lives of innocent victims and then took his own.**

❖ Invite the adults to reflect on how such a catastrophic betrayal of trust and confidence by one of their own can affect a community, in this case, an entire university.

❖ Read aloud today's focus statement: **People will face many trials in life from friend and foe as well as from expected and unexpected sources. How can one overcome such hardships? Paul says that through his weaknesses he finds strength in the grace of God.**

(2) Consider Paul's Writing About the Inevitability of Facing Difficulties in the Christian Life and the Reliability of God's Grace

❖ Set the stage for today's biblical text by reading or retelling information for 2 Cor-

inthians 11:16 from Understanding the Scripture.

❖ Select a volunteer to read 2 Corinthians 11:17, 21-30. Ask someone else to read 2 Corinthians 12:9-10.

❖ Encourage the students to discuss how Paul viewed the punishments inflicted upon him for his Christian witness. Ask: **Could you have viewed these punishments as he did? Why or why not?**

❖ Note that Paul has hardly been the only person to suffer for the faith. Many named and unnamed believers have been persecuted and killed because they claimed the name of Christ.

❖ Divide into groups and distribute any articles you have found related to current persecutions of Christians around the world. Allow time for the groups to digest their articles and report back to the rest of the class.

❖ **Option:** Present a brief lecture to the class based on the research regarding persecution that you have done, if you do not choose to work in groups.

❖ Conclude with these questions for the entire class:

   (1) Based on what you know about each situation, how do you see God's grace at work?

   (2) In what ways are other Christians, including us, supporting these suffering brothers and sisters?

(3) Accept That Being a Christian Will Not Prevent Persecution, Even From Some Within the Faith Community

❖ Read the following information: **Many people are familiar with the comment attributed to Joseph P. Kennedy and later popularized in a 1986 hit by Billy Ocean, "When the going gets tough, the tough get going."**

   (1) What do you understand this quotation to mean? (Here are two possible ways among many to rephrase the quotation: [a] In times of trouble, people become bold and willing to act. [b] When adversity strikes, people try hard to overcome it.)

(2) How does this quotation relate to difficulties that we experience as Christians, even within the church, and our response to those problems?

❖ Read aloud "The Myth of Pristine Christianity" in Interpreting the Scripture. Encourage the adults to respond to the observations made there.

❖ Distribute paper and pencils. Invite the adults to write about a time when they felt criticized within the church. What caused the problem? How did they resolve it? Can they honestly say that they stood up to this adversity, buoyed by the power of God? Or did they choose to ignore the situation, perhaps by backing away from it? Assure the students that they will not be asked to share their thoughts.

❖ **Option:** Play some meditative music as the students write.

(4) Support One Another as the Learners Witness to Their Faith During Difficult Times

❖ Read the last paragraph of "A Dangerous Faith" in Interpreting the Scripture.

❖ Discuss these questions:

(1) Why do you suppose that individuals and the community of faith as a body are not getting into more trouble about things that really matter?

(2) What issues should we Christians be taking stands on today that may create difficulties for us in the society at large and possibly even within the church itself?

(3) What steps can we take to support one another as we deal with the difficulties that may arise if we are courageous enough to take a stand for Christ?

(5) Continue the Journey

❖ Pray that those who have participated in today's class will go forth recognizing that God's grace and strength are sufficient, even in the midst of strife.

❖ Read aloud this preparation for next week's lesson. You may also want to post it on newsprint for the students to copy.

■ **Title: Mary's Commitment**
■ **Background Scripture: Luke 1:26-38, 46-55**
■ **Lesson Scripture: Luke 1:46-55**
■ **Focus of the Lesson: Many people encounter someone or something so charismatic and powerful that it demands their complete commitment. Who or what is able to command such a commitment? Mary recognized the glory of God and made her total commitment to God.**

❖ Challenge the students to complete one or more of these activities for further spiritual growth, which you will write on newsprint for the students to copy.

(1) Ponder Paul's remark in 2 Corinthians 12:9: "Power is made perfect in weakness." What does this statement suggest to you about the value of the nonviolent approach to social change advocated by such people as Ghandi and Dr. Martin Luther King, Jr.?

(2) Identify a weakness with which you are struggling. How does this weakness affect your faith?

(3) Recall a difficulty that your church community faced. What were the advantages and disadvantages of struggling with this difficulty together?

❖ Sing or read aloud "Stand By Me."

❖ Conclude today's session by leading the class in this benediction, adapted from Ephesians 4:4-6: **Let us now depart rejoicing in the community we share, united as one body, with one Spirit, one Lord, one faith, one baptism, and one God and Father of all.**

SECOND QUARTER
Human Commitment

DECEMBER 7, 2008–FEBRUARY 22, 2009

During the winter quarter, we will encounter people who each heard God's call and made a commitment to respond. In Unit 1, those people all made commitments to Jesus as the world was being prepared for his arrival. In the second unit, the Old Testament characters we meet have been selected by God for specific work in a specific time and place. Although we will never be called to do exactly what any of these figures has been asked to do, we can learn much from them if we view them as role models.

The four lessons for Unit 1, "Commitment to the Messiah," are all drawn from Luke's Gospel. Our background Scripture for "Mary's Commitment," the lesson for December 7 is Luke 1:26-38, 46-55, which includes Mary's glorious song of praise for the favor God has shown her. In "Elizabeth's Commitment" on December 14, Luke 1:5-24, 39-45 introduces us to Elizabeth, mother of John the Baptizer, who makes a commitment to raise her son as one devoted to God as well as a commitment to Mary's unborn son. Luke 2:1-20, our background for December 21 for "Shepherds Glorify God," points us toward the shepherds who hear good news from angels and rush to commit themselves to the baby Jesus. The unit ends on December 28 with a lesson from Luke 3:1-20, where "John the Baptizer Proclaims God's Message."

Unit 2, "Old Testament People of Commitment," opens on January 4 with "Midwives Serve God," an exploration of Exodus 1:8-21 concerning two midwives, Shiphrah and Puah, who risk Pharaoh's wrath by choosing to serve God. Joshua 2 and 6:22-25, which we will study on January 11 in a lesson titled "Rahab Helps Israel," portray another woman, Rahab of Jericho, who risked her life by siding with God's people. As we will learn on January 18 in "Joshua Leads Israel," Joshua not only committed himself to lead but was also endowed with many resources to do the job God had called him to do, as recorded in Joshua 3. In "Samson's Mother Prepares for His Birth," the session for January 25 from Judges 13, we hear God's angel give the unnamed woman directions as to how she is to prepare herself and her son for the work that God is calling him to do. We meet another unnamed woman, this one from Shunem, who serves God by providing lodging for the prophet Elisha, as we read in "A Shunammite Woman Helps" from 2 Kings 4:8-17 on February 1. Second Samuel 12:1-15 is the background for our session on February 8, "Nathan Challenges David," when the prophet Nathan boldly tells King David a parable to illustrate the magnitude of his sin with Bathsheba. As we shall see on February 15 in "Esther Risks Her Life," Esther 4–5 tells the story of a young Jewish woman, a favorite of the king, who risked her life to save her Jewish people, who were under a death warrant. Our unit concludes on February 22 with the beloved vision of Isaiah in the Temple, found in Isaiah 6, where we witness this prophet's absolute surrender to God's will for his life in "Isaiah Answers God's Call."

MEET OUR WRITER

DR. GAYLE CARLTON FELTON

Gayle Carlton Felton is an elder in the North Carolina Annual Conference of The United Methodist Church. She has a B.A. degree summa cum laude from North Carolina Wesleyan College (1964), where she majored in American history. Her master of divinity is from Duke Divinity School (1982), and her Ph.D., with concentration in the history of Christianity, is from Duke University (1987). She has served on the faculties of Meredith College and Duke Divinity School.

Gayle was a member of the denomination's Committee to Study Baptism (1989–1996), wrote the final version of *By Water and the Spirit: A United Methodist Understanding of Baptism*, and presented the document to the 1992 and 1996 General Conferences. She continued as a member of an advisory team of the General Board of Discipleship that worked to reconcile the provisions of the *Discipline* with this document and with the ritual. She is the principal writer for *This Holy Mystery: A United Methodist Understanding of Holy Communion*, which is an exposition of that sacrament comparable to the earlier work on baptism. *This Holy Mystery* was presented to the 2004 General Conference and approved. These documents now constitute the denomination's official interpretive positions on the sacraments.

Gayle is the author of *This Gift of Water: The Practice and Theology of Baptism Among Methodists in America* (1992), *By Water and the Spirit: Making Connections for Identity and Ministry* (1997, 1998), *The Coming of Jesus* (2000), *This Holy Mystery: A United Methodist Understanding of Holy Communion, What United Methodists Believe About the Sacraments* (2007), and a variety of articles on Methodism, sacraments, and the teaching ministry of the church. She is the editor of *How United Methodists Study Scripture* (1999) and a regular contributor to *The New International Lesson Annual*.

Gayle serves as Minister of Christian Formation at Calvary UMC in Durham, North Carolina, and as an adjunct member of the faculty at Garrett-Evangelical Theological Seminary. She is active as a speaker, teacher, and preacher in The United Methodist Church from the local to the general church level.

THE BIG PICTURE:
GOD'S COVENANT;
OUR COMMITMENT

The God of the Bible craves relationships. This is essentially what it means to say that God is love. Love does not exist in a vacuum. Love requires something, or better someone, to be the recipient of love. Originally, love existed as the relationship between the three persons of the Trinity. God includes three personalities within the divine self, and these three are related to each other by love. Love is the defining nature of the Godhead. God created the universe and humankind so as to have more recipients of divine love. Love is the reason for and the power behind creation. From the beginning God committed the divine self in covenant relationship with human creatures. God provided for their needs and enjoyed their fellowship. On their side, humans were expected to be obedient to the divine will and to share love harmoniously with God, with one another, and with the natural world of which they were residents. As we learn in Genesis 3, human beings proved incapable of faithful obedience to God and, as a result, all of their loving relationships were disrupted. The remainder of the Bible is the account of the divine efforts to restore humanity to the loving relationships for which we were created. Violation of this first covenant by human misuse of freedom of will motivates God to establish a series of covenant relationships through which God seeks to reconcile the brokenness caused by human sin. This process of sin, covenant, violation, and reconciliation is continually repeated since, as a Jewish writing reminds us, "Each of us has been the Adam of his own soul" (2 Baruch 54:19). God's commitment is always clear and firm; God always takes the initiative to reach out and offer saving relationship. The ultimate divine commitment is in the life, death, and resurrection of Jesus Christ.

Because God has created us with free will, all the divine efforts toward reconciliation may be fruitless without our cooperation. This is why human commitment is essential. These two units of lessons focus at this point. As the Introduction to the Uniform Lesson Cycle states, these lessons are concerned with "living out what it means to be part of the realm of God." Human beings do not consistently do very well with our side of the covenant. In the Old Testament, God initiated covenant relationships with the Hebrew people—especially through their great leaders such as Abraham, Moses, and David. Eventually all of these covenants failed due to the inability and unwillingness of humans to be faithful to them. In these lessons, we study some of the admirable examples of persons who, in spite of the pressures upon them, were able to be faithful. They offer inspiration and hope to us as we struggle with our own commitments.

The lessons in Unit 1 center on people who had major roles in the events related to the birth of Jesus, the Christ, the Messiah. We consider the commitments of Jesus' mother Mary and of Elizabeth, the mother of John the Baptizer. John's faithful ministry, which cost him his life, helped to prepare people for the ministry of Christ. The shepherds who were sent by angels to see the newborn Christ remind us that God calls into committed service persons of every rank and station of life. These lessons make it apparent that God's action in human history is through human beings who are receptive to and cooperative with the divine plan for salvation.

The eight lessons in Unit 2 consider selected persons from the Old Testament whose faithfulness to the God of the covenant led them to committed service even before knowing God through Jesus Christ. Six of these figures are women: Shiphrah and Puah, Rahab, Samson's mother, a Shunammite woman, and Queen Esther. This is surprising since we know that the roles of women were restricted in ancient Israelite society and that their opportunities to serve God were usually limited.

Some characteristics of the commitments presented in these lessons can be identified and can enable us to better comprehend the nature of commitment. Many of the individuals upon whom the lessons focus were surprised by God's intervention in their lives. They were not really ready for the commitments that they were called to, but they found within themselves the resources that they needed to respond. Mary was a young teenager who may have been dreaming of motherhood but certainly was not anticipating becoming "the mother of God." Elizabeth and Zechariah had surely resigned themselves to their fate of childlessness. The shepherds did not expect their calm evening to be intruded upon by angels. It was the same for many in the Old Testament. Rahab probably feared the threatened Israelite invasion of her city, but she did not expect to have any part in it. Certainly she would not have imagined that she might be called upon to facilitate it. Esther had settled into life as a part of the Persian king's harem. Being a hero by saving her people from massacre was beyond her wildest dreams. These examples, and the others in the lessons, remind us of the old addage, "If you want to make God laugh, tell him your plans." Christians must always be willing to follow where God directs, even when God surprises us and shakes us out of our accustomed lives.

A characteristic of the commitments to which God called persons in these lessons was that they involved risk. Courage was required. John the Baptizer undoubtedly realized that his preaching of sin and repentance would not be well received. Certainly he knew that his later condemnation of the immorality of a ruler was extremely dangerous, and so it proved to be. The midwives who deceived the Egyptian pharaoh in order to protect the Hebrew babies knew that their rather unlikely story might be exposed and their lives be taken. When he led the Israelite people across the Jordan and into Canaan, Joshua was well aware of the hostile situation they were entering and that dangerous conflicts lay ahead. The prophet Nathan, who approached a king who had already shown himself willing to have a man killed, was taking an enormous risk of his career as court prophet and even his life. Committing oneself to God is dangerous business. Fulfilling commitments carries a price, sometimes a steep price.

Another common theme in the commitments in these lessons is that they required action. But it was not simply one action or action in the moment. These commitments determined the courses of the entire future lives of these individuals. Life for Manoah's wife would never be the same after she became Samson's mother. Being the mother of a judge of Israel—particularly one who was often unfaithful to his calling—must have been painful. The Shunammite woman who provided for Elisha opened herself through her hospitality to actions of the prophet, which affected her life dramatically. Isaiah, after his call experience in the Temple, moved from the predictable ministry of a court prophet/priest, to the marginal lifestyle of one who confronted his people and his rulers with God's word of judgment. When Jesus spoke of denying oneself and taking up the cross and following him, he was speaking of this kind of life-altering commitment.

A final theme exemplified in all the lessons is that of faith. These were people who trusted God. They were able to accept the surprising calls, take the risks, have the courage, act decisively, and have their lives transformed. All this was because ultimately they trusted the God who called them to commitment. These commitments were not fundamentally to certain actions or roles; they were commitments to the God they worshiped and served.

Many religious thinkers, including Methodism's founder John Wesley, emphasize the divine action that is prerequisite to any human movement toward God. This is the meaning of Wesley's often-mentioned prevenient grace. God's grace comes before anything that we can do; God's grace makes possible any efforts that we make to reach God; God's grace is even what makes us realize that we need God. But having firmly established the requirement of divine initiative, Wesley considers the other side of the salvation equation: human response. We must accept divine grace, recognize and repent of our alienation from God, and trust in Christ for forgiveness and reconciliation. This is the first meaning of human commitment. If a person were truly desirous of coming into saving relationship with God, that desire would be evidenced by the fruits of his or her living. Those who are committed to seek God will avoid doing evil and, instead, do all the good possible. They will avail themselves of the avenues of grace that God has provided such as prayer, worship, and sacraments. This is the test of human commitment.

Our commitment to God is formally expressed in baptism. If the person's faith tradition is that of believer's baptism, the baptismal event is itself a public expression of the individual's commitment to Christ. In the traditions that practice infant baptism, the situation is more complex. The parents (or guardians, sponsors) of a child are the ones who are professing their faith and committing themselves to Christ and Christ's church. They also commit themselves to raise the child in the Christian faith and seek to nurture and form him or her into a person who desires commitment to Christ. The congregation also commits itself, promising to provide support in this process by word and example. When baptized children grow to an age when they can assume moral responsibility for themselves, they are further educated and shaped to be ready to make their own personal commitment. In the service that the church calls profession of faith/confirmation, that commitment is publicly made. Commitment always involves acceptance of God's offer of covenant relationship and the pledge to live out their obligations of it. Such commitment defines and directs all of life.

I find it telling that there are fifty-two entries under *Commitment* (almost all of them hymns) in the Index of Topics and Categories in the 1989 *United Methodist Hymnal*. I expect that similar results would be found in the contents of hymnals and songbooks of other denominations. This offers strong evidence of the significance of the theme in our theology. When we sing these hymns we recognize and affirm that whatever God does for us must be received by us through the commitment of ourselves. It is our commitments that give our lives meaning and direction. They determine who we are. We are the product of the commitments that we have made—those we break as well as those we keep.

To live as part of the realm of God, committed Christians must be concerned about the physical welfare of our fellow human beings and actively involved in efforts toward peace, justice, and provision for human need. God's commissioning of Christian people to address these kinds of sufferings comes from the pain in the loving heart of God. We are instruments of the divine to work for change. When we engage in acts of compassion and relief, we are not simply fulfilling our own Christian commitment; we are also helping people to know the love of Christ. We cooperate with God, but without divine empowerment, our efforts will be futile. It is only when we are engaged in that synergism of divine grace and human response that the world might be transformed. The living out of human commitments in work on earth inspired and empowered by God will shape the world increasingly into the image of the kingdom of God. Human effort alone will not bring in the fullness of the kingdom; only God can and will do that. But until the time that God acts to bring human history to consummation, it is the task of committed people to attack the conditions of violence, deprivation, and injustice, working always toward the ideal of God's perfect will.

In the midst of the struggle, commitments that were clear and shining may blur and tarnish. Simply because we are inconstant creatures, we often find it difficult to hold on to our commitments and continue to live them out with conviction and energy. If we are honest, we may even experience uncertainty and doubt. Surely there were moments in the lives of all the biblical characters that we are studying when they had second thoughts, when their conviction flagged, and when questions intruded. Dr. Rollo May has written, "The relationship between commitment and doubt is, by no means, an antagonistic one. Commitment is healthiest when it's not *without* doubt but *in spite* of doubt."

How else might we analyze the nature of commitment? Perhaps by considering the distinction between commitment and some other things that resemble it and, therefore, may distract us from it. A widely circulated quotation says, "There's a difference between interest and commitment. When you're interested in doing something, you do it only when circumstances permit. When you're committed to something, you accept no excuses, only results." Most of us have a wide variety of interests, all of which compete for our attention and resources. These may include our jobs, families, friends, hobbies, pets, recreations, organizations, and even church. But Christian commitment is unique. It always takes precedence over our other interests. This does not mean that all other interests must be eliminated. But, it does mean that they must be prioritized behind the one defining commitment of our life—our commitment to Christ.

It is important to recognize that the biblical commitments that we have studied during this quarter are commitments to a person, not to a cause. Of course, causes were advanced by these committed people. The births of the forerunner and of the Christ himself were among them. In the Old Testament, our committed characters contributed to the survival and progress of God's chosen people so that the divine plan of salvation might be furthered. But fundamentally, the commitment of all these characters was to God, not to other human beings, not to victories, not to self-interests, not even to alleviate suffering. Ultimate loyalty to God assured that causes would be advanced and individuals served. But even in the face of failure, when causes collapsed and individuals were not helped, ultimate loyalty to God was all that truly mattered.

Peter Drucker, the late business guru, emphasized that commitment is essential to action. Without commitment, there may be promises and hopes, but there are not plans. Commitment is focused; it does not approach problems casually or tentatively. It is prepared, organized, and equipped. It is attentive to the object of its commitment—God—and acts according to divine direction.

Christians do not have the alternative of standing on the sidelines and watching when called to commit ourselves to God and the action that God requires of us. We must commit ourselves to God and plunge in. Commitment to God requires no more than we have to give, but it never requires less.

CLOSE-UP:
COMMITTED CHRISTIANS

Throughout the winter quarter we are exploring the commitment of selected biblical characters. These people are role models for us. So are other believers who have shown great courage by taking risks and acting on their faith.

Use these short biographies to challenge the adults to recognize that they, too, can make significant commitments on behalf of God. Identify with the class what each of these believers risked and what they gained by making a commitment to Christ. Conclude by asking the adults to ponder what they are willing to risk.

- **Saint Francis of Assisi (1182–1226):** Having enjoyed a carefree childhood as the son of a wealthy merchant, this founder of the Franciscans was injured and captured during war. He was hospitalized for a year. When he returned to his home in Assisi, Francis vowed that he would live a life of poverty. Apparently Francis was too free with his father's resources, which he used to repair God's house as directed by a voice, and found himself in court. To sever his relationship with his family and their way of life, Francis stripped naked in court. Committed to poverty, the way of Francis and his followers stood in sharp contrast to the rest of the church.

- **Martin Luther (1483–1546):** Born into a poor German family, Luther became well-educated and was on the verge of entering law school when a bolt of lightning struck so close that he recognized his mortality and feared for his soul. This transforming experience prompted him to become an Augustinian monk and earn a doctorate in theology. Luther had believed that he had to work his way into heaven. Later, he recognized that we are made right with God (justified) by faith alone. A leader in the founding of the Protestant movement, Luther's life was on the line after he was excommunicated for burning a proclamation from the pope in 1521.

- **William Tyndale (about 1494–1536):** An Englishman educated at both Oxford and Cambridge, Tyndale was a reformer who translated the Greek New Testament into English. Published in Worms, Germany, in 1525, the English New Testament was burned by church authorities in England, but not before it had been widely distributed. Tyndale continued his work, creating a translation on which the King James Version was later modeled. He also translated the first five books of the Old Testament into English. Betrayed by a friend, Tyndale was found guilty of heresy and burned at the stake.

- **Dietrich Bonhoeffer (1906–1945):** One of the most influential theologians of the twentieth century, Dietrich Bonhoeffer became a martyr after resisting the Nazi regime and being involved in an attempt to assassinate Hitler. A prolific writer, Bonhoeffer's most widely known book is *The Cost of Discipleship*. He believed that personal piety was not enough. Instead, the church is "to exist for others." Discipleship is costly because it entails suffering. Bonhoeffer called upon Christians to be spiritually disciplined in order to enter into the suffering of God in the midst of a secular world.

FAITH IN ACTION: COMMITMENT TO ANSWER GOD'S CALL

All of the lessons in the winter quarter focus on God's call and human response. In essence, each lesson asks, What kind of commitment was this person willing to make for God? As we unpack the lessons, the question expands to read, What kind of commitment am I willing to make for God?

Follow these steps to help the class make a commitment to God.

❖ **Step 1:** Review on your own "The Big Picture: God's Covenant; Our Commitment" and list on newsprint the characteristics associated with commitment: *risk, courage, action, faith*. Encourage the adults to talk about how they see each of these characteristics as being related to commitment.

❖ **Step 2:** Read aloud this quotation: **"There's a difference between interest and commitment. When you're interested in doing something, you do it only when circumstances permit. When you're committed to something, you accept no excuses, only results."** Ask the students if they accept this distinction and, if not, how they would clarify the difference between "interest" and "commitment."

❖ **Step 3:** Encourage the participants to reflect quietly on what they believe God is calling them to commit themselves to now. Note that this call to commitment may relate to personal change, family, church, the workplace, efforts on behalf of a cause, or something else. It may be an emerging commitment or something that is ongoing.

❖ **Step 4:** Read this quotation from Peter Drucker: **"Unless commitment is made, there are only promises and hopes; but no plans."** Distribute paper and pencils. Invite the participants to sketch out a plan for fulfilling the commitment they feel God is calling them to make or renew. Suggest that they write the commitment in one sentence that includes what they will do, when, why, how, and for whom. Here's an example, though there are many ways to write such a sentence. **In response to God's call, I commit myself to serve children by volunteering at the church child-care center for three hours per week.** Here is another example: **To fulfill my calling to be a more faithful steward, I will commit 10 percent of my income and five hours of volunteer service to the church on Wednesdays.**

❖ **Step 5:** Invite the students to work in groups of three or four to read their statements of commitment and then hear affirmations and suggestions from the group.

❖ **Step 6:** Ask the adults to form a circle or several circles if the group is large. Go around each circle clockwise and ask each person to say a word or two that sums up the commitment, such as "serve by volunteering" or "be a faithful steward." Invite the other students to respond with these words, which you may want to post on newsprint: **We will surround you with prayer and the love of God as you seek to be faithful to the commitment to which God has called you.**

UNIT 1: COMMITMENT TO THE MESSIAH
MARY'S COMMITMENT

PREVIEWING THE LESSON

Lesson Scripture: Luke 1:46-55
Background Scripture: Luke 1:26-38, 46-55
Key Verses: Luke 1:46-47

Focus of the Lesson:

Many people encounter someone or something so charismatic and powerful that it demands their complete commitment. Who or what is able to command such a commitment? Mary recognized the glory of God and made her total commitment to God.

Goals for the Learners:

(1) to explore Mary's hymn of commitment to God.
(2) to consider the characteristics in another that may lead them to commitment.
(3) to make commitments to others and to God and strategize ways to be faithful to these commitments.

Pronunciation Guide:

Magnificat (mag nif' uh kat)

Supplies:

Bibles, newsprint and marker, paper and pencils, hymnals

READING THE SCRIPTURE

NRSV
Luke 1:46-55
⁴⁶And Mary said,
⁴⁷"My soul magnifies the Lord,
  and my spirit rejoices in God
  my Savior,
⁴⁸ for he has looked with favor on the
    lowliness of his servant.
  Surely, from now on all generations
    will call me blessed;

NIV
Luke 1:46-55
⁴⁶And Mary said:
  "My soul glorifies the Lord
⁴⁷   and my spirit rejoices in God
     my Savior,
⁴⁸ for he has been mindful
    of the humble state of his servant.
  From now on all generations will call
    me blessed,

[49] for the Mighty One has done great
  things for me,
 and holy is his name.
[50] His mercy is for those who fear him
 from generation to generation.
[51] He has shown strength with his arm;
 he has scattered the proud in
  the thoughts of their hearts.
[52] He has brought down the powerful
 from their thrones,
 and lifted up the lowly;
[53] he has filled the hungry with good
 things,
 and sent the rich away empty.
[54] He has helped his servant Israel,
 in remembrance of his mercy,
[55] according to the promise he made to
 our ancestors,
 to Abraham and to his descendants
 forever."

[49] for the Mighty One has done great
  things for me—
 holy is his name.
[50] His mercy extends to those who fear him,
 from generation to generation.
[51]He has performed mighty deeds with
 his arm;
 he has scattered those who are proud in
  their inmost thoughts.
[52] He has brought down rulers from their
 thrones
 but has lifted up the humble.
[53] He has filled the hungry with good things
 but has sent the rich away empty.
[54] He has helped his servant Israel,
 remembering to be merciful
[55]to Abraham and his descendants forever,
 even as he said to our fathers."

UNDERSTANDING THE SCRIPTURE

Luke 1:26. The sixth month refers to the pregnancy of Elizabeth who will be the mother of John the Baptizer. Gabriel is one of only three angels named in the Bible. (Michael is another. The fallen angel Satan is also mentioned by name.) Gabriel appears to Zechariah, the father of John the Baptizer, to foretell that child's birth in the first chapter of Luke. This angel is also mentioned in the Book of Daniel. Angels were understood as God's messengers. The name Gabriel means "man of God."

Galilee was a province in the northern part of the Holy Land. Mary's hometown of Nazareth was an obscure place, never mentioned in the Old Testament.

Luke 1:27. Mary and Joseph are betrothed but not yet married. It was customary for a girl's father to make arrangements for her marriage before she was of childbearing age. She continued to live with her family at least until puberty, when the groom would come for her and the wedding would be celebrated. Engagement was a legal arrangement that could be broken only by death. The couple was not to have sexual relations during this period.

Joseph, the legal father of Jesus, was a descendant of King David who had ruled the nation some one thousand years earlier. This is important because the Messiah was to be from the house—the family—of David.

This passage in Luke and Matthew 1:18-25 are the only places in the New Testament where what is usually called the virgin birth—more correctly, the virgin conception—is mentioned. This is the way that the nativity stories (found only in Matthew and Luke) seek to explain how Jesus was both fully human and fully divine. Whether or not the virgin conception should be understood as historical fact has long been controversial in Christianity and certainly remains so today. In the fundamentalist movement of the early twentieth century, the "virgin birth" was one of the five doctrinal assertions that were considered essential for orthodox Christianity. Other Christians see it as a poetic and traditional way of expressing the relationship between Jesus and God. Jesus' having been conceived through an act of the Holy Spirit does not necessarily mean that he had no human biological father. In the letters of Paul and the other epistle writers, there is no reference to the virgin birth, though some argue that Galatians 4:4 may be construed that way. Mark says nothing of Jesus' birth and understands his Sonship to be his adoption by God at his baptism. John's Gospel emphasizes that Christ existed with the Father before the creation of the world and took flesh in the man Jesus. This biblical evidence indicates that first-century Christians had different ways of interpreting how Jesus came to be the incarnation of God. It is not the biological process that is important, but the reality that in Jesus Christ, God came to us as a human person.

Luke 1:28-29. "Greetings" is rendered as *Ave* in the Latin Vulgate translation of the Bible, hence this verse is the source of *Ave Maria*. Some ancient scriptural texts include the line "Blessed are you among women." From this (and verse 42) comes the "Hail Mary" prayer often used by Roman Catholics and other Christians.

Luke 1:30-31. Almost always in biblical accounts, angels try to calm the fear of persons to whom they appear. Mary's reaction of confusion and fright is very natural. The name Jesus is the Greek form of Joshua and is usually understood to mean "one who saves."

Luke 1:32-33. The angel makes clear to Mary that her son will be no ordinary man. God is frequently referred to as "the Most High" in both the Old and New Testaments. The throne of David had been promised to

the coming Messiah in 2 Samuel 7:13, 16. Many of the Jewish people believed that God's promise to David was that an everlasting kingdom would be ruled by his descendants. The Davidic line of kings had been ended by the Babylonian conquest of Judah in the sixth century B.C. The Messiah was expected to restore it. Jacob was the father of twelve sons who were the progenitors of the twelve tribes that make up the Jewish people.

Luke 1:34-35. Mary was not so frightened as to be unable to ask the obvious question about the conception of the child. In reply, the angel makes it clear that the conception will be the result of the action of God. The description is similar to that of the Transfiguration in Luke 9:34-35 when the presence of God is said to have "overshadowed" the disciples in a cloud. The child will be holy—without sin and set apart for the use of God.

Luke 1:36-38. As a sign or evidence of the truth of what Mary has been told, the angel informs Mary of the miraculous pregnancy of her relative Elizabeth. The exact relationship between Mary and Elizabeth is unclear. Probably she was Mary's aunt or cousin. Mary is reminded, as were Abraham and Sarah in a somewhat similar situation (Genesis 18:14), that even the most incredible things are possible for God. Mary asks no more questions; she obediently agrees to God's will for her.

Luke 1:46-49. This beautiful hymn is called the Magnificat from its first word in Latin. It is heavily influenced by the prayer of Hannah, the mother of Samuel, recorded in 1 Samuel 2:1-10. The Magnificat is a joyous but revolutionary hymn. Mary magnifies—tells the greatness of—God for what God has done for her. While her son will be called Savior, Mary affirms that it is God who is the source of salvation.

Luke 1:50-51. What God has done for Mary, God will do for all of the lowly and oppressed people. It is not that all will experience miraculous divine visitations, but all will be liberated by divine action. God's arm is God's strength or power. It will be employed against those who are filled with pride and unrighteousness.

Luke 1:52-53. These verses describe the kind of reversal that will be typical of the actions and preaching of Jesus. The first are put last; the high-ranking toppled; the exploited given strength. Those who have suffered want are provided for, while those who had much are reduced to nothing. The political and socioeconomic order is transformed in accord with the divine values and purpose. Notice the tense of the verbs. There is so much confidence in the actions of God that they are proclaimed as if they have already happened.

Luke 1:54-55. God's actions on behalf of God's people fulfill the divine promises made to Abraham and his descendants in the Old Testament. God promised to make them a great nation and to be in covenant relationship with them.

INTERPRETING THE SCRIPTURE

To Whom Shall We Commit?

Psychologists tell us that there is a need within human beings to find something or someone greater than ourselves to which we can commit our lives. I am looking at a cartoon in a wonderful book by Ashleigh Brilliant entitled *I May Not Be Totally Perfect, But Parts of Me Are Excellent*. The cartoon shows a figure waving a white flag saying, "I'm ready to give up . . . but can't find anybody to surrender to." We will eventually surrender ourselves to some ultimate loyalty; we must choose carefully who or what we commit to, for that commitment will determine our destiny. In his book *Markings*, former Secretary General of the United Nations Dag Hammarskjöld wrote, "I don't know Who—or what—put the question, I don't know when it was put. I don't even remember answering. But at some moment I did answer *Yes* to Someone—or Something—and from that hour I was certain that existence is meaningful, and that, therefore, my life, in self-surrender, had a goal."

It is not then so much a question of whether or not we will commit ourselves. It is more a choice of to what or whom we commit. That is what will determine our destiny—in this life and beyond. Mary chose to commit herself to God.

"Let It Be With Me According to Your Word"

March 25 is commemorated in traditional churches as the date of the Annunciation—Gabriel's announcement to Mary of God's plan for her life. We can more fully appreciate Mary's response when we remember that she was probably thirteen or fourteen years old. The commitment that this young woman made was not an easy one. Imagine having to explain the situation to her parents, to her fiancé. Picture the reaction of the neighbors in her small town as the pregnancy of this unmarried girl becomes obvious. Try to feel the fear during a hard journey to Bethlehem and the birth of her child in a strange place with little help and few comforts.

Let us remember that Mary's commitment was not only to carry the Christ child in her womb and bring him to birth but also to be his mother for a lifetime, to raise this extraordinary child as God wanted, to feel confusion and concern about the decisions he would make, to suffer the anguish of his death, to rejoice in his resurrection. Mary would experience times of doubt. The

Gospels tell us that she and his brothers went to get Jesus at least once, apparently fearful and perplexed about what he was doing and saying (see Matthew 12:46-50; Mark 3:31-35). But we know that she was present at the cross, having followed him to the end, and in the upper room where his Spirit came upon her and the other disciples after his ascension. In many ways, Mary was a model of commitment and discipleship for us. A contemporary collect from *The Book of Common Prayer* praises her commitment and challenges us to emulate it:

> Father in heaven, by your grace the virgin mother of thy incarnate Son was blessed in bearing him, but still more blessed in keeping thy word: Grant us who honor the exaltation of her lowliness to follow the example of her devotion to thy will; through the same Jesus Christ our Lord, who liveth and reigneth with thee and the Holy Spirit, one God, for ever and ever.

There's a Revolution Coming

Mary's hymn of commitment and rejoicing, in verses 46-55, is called the Magnificat. As I have written in *The Coming of Jesus*, "The Magnificat is the great New Testament song of liberation, personal and social, moral and economic, a revolutionary document of intense conflict and victory. It praises God's liberating actions on behalf of the speaker, which are paradigmatic of all of God's actions on behalf of marginal and exploited people."

Luke probably did not compose this hymn but rather borrowed it from the Jewish culture of the day. It likely had been created among the poor people of the land who looked to God to deliver them from their oppression—political, economic, and social. Well aware of their own powerlessness, they anticipated with great joy the manifestation of divine power on their behalf.

The Magnificat is an expression of the faith and joy of Mary, whom Luke portrays as the first Christian disciple. It is also a communal affirmation of confidence in the action of God. Mary is a kind of model: What God has done for her, God will do for all who are poor, powerless, and oppressed.

It is necessary to remember that all the Jewish participants in the infancy narratives—the stories telling of events associated with the birth of Jesus—were from the lowly, exploited class of the society. They were likely peasants living in rural areas and small villages. Their ability to sustain themselves was being threatened by the oppressive power of the Roman Empire that ruled them. Particularly, they were burdened with heavy taxes, which consumed a large portion of what they produced. Many had to go deeply into debt, and as a result, often lost their land. The conglomeration of landless people with no means of support caused a huge rise in banditry. Travel was very dangerous because it made people targets and victims of these lawless elements.

The Magnificat must be viewed against this background. It is a passionate call for God's action to overthrow the forces of oppression and to establish conditions of economic, political, and social justice. Significantly, when Jesus preached his first public sermon in his hometown of Nazareth, he addressed these same themes. In Luke 4:16-21, Jesus proclaimed his calling in words reminiscent of his mother's song, as well as Isaiah:

> "The Spirit of the Lord is upon me,
>   because he has anointed me
>   to bring good news to the poor.
> He has sent me to proclaim release to the
>   captives
>   and recovery of sight to the blind,
> to let the oppressed go free,
>   to proclaim the year of the Lord's
>   favor."

Middle-class North American Christians can easily mislead ourselves about Mary's song, as I wrote in *The Coming of Jesus*:

We read Mary's powerful proclamation in the Magnificat and feel our hearts soar with praise for the mighty work of God. But, is the good news proclaimed here really good news for us? Do we truly want the proud to be scattered, the powerful brought down, "the rich sent away empty"?

The uncomfortable truth is that for most [of us] the Magnificat is not good news at all. It is a revolutionary document, and revolutions mean turnover in the power structure. For those of us who are on or near the top of this structure, change is not a promise but a threat.

Christians must be committed to changes for justice and peace in our social order, even though they threaten our comfortable ways of life.

SHARING THE SCRIPTURE

Preparing Our Hearts

Meditate on this week's devotional reading, found in 1 Samuel 2:1-10. As you read this prayer attributed to Hannah, notice what she prays for. How does she describe God? What reversals of fortune do you see here? How does this prayer affect you? Compare Hannah's prayer with Mary's Magnificat in Luke 1:46-55. What similarities and differences do you notice? Write these ideas in your spiritual journal.

Pray that you and the adult learners will be aware of how God's presence brings about justice.

Preparing Our Minds

Study the background from Luke 1:26-38, 46-55 and the lesson Scripture from Luke 1:46-55. As you prepare, think about who or what is so charismatic and powerful that people are willing to make a total commitment.

Write on newsprint:
❑ sentence completion for "Make Commitments to Others and to God and Strategize Ways to Be Faithful to These Commitments."
❑ information for next week's lesson, found under "Continue the Journey."
❑ activities for further spiritual growth in "Continue the Journey."

Read the "Introduction" to the quarter, "The Big Picture," "Close-up," and "Faith in Action." Consider how you will use these supplements throughout the quarter.

LEADING THE CLASS

(1) Gather to Learn

❖ Welcome the class members and introduce any guests.

❖ Pray that all who have come today will recognize commitments in others that will encourage them to make their own commitments.

❖ Read this information aloud: **When the second live album of the Grateful Dead was released in 1971, it included an invitation for fans to identify themselves if they wanted to be kept informed of news related to the band. Deadheads, as they were known, swelled in numbers during the 1970s from 350 to over 40,000. The band had a cultlike following, with Deadheads traveling to hear and record their concerts. Scholar Joseph Campbell, a Deadhead himself, referred to Deadheads as "the world's newest tribe." Blair Jackson, publicist for the band, stated "shows were the sacrament . . . rich and full of blissful, transcendent musical movements that moved the body and enriched the soul." Jackson further stated, "for many Deadheads, the band was a** medium that facilitated experiencing other planes of consciousness and tapping into deep, spiritual wells that were usually the province of organized religion."

❖ Discuss this question: **Why do you suppose that so many people committed themselves to this band with religiouslike fervor?**

❖ Read aloud today's focus statement: **Many people encounter someone or something so charismatic and powerful that it demands their complete commitment. Who or what is able to command such a commitment? Mary recognized the glory of God and made her total commitment to God**.

(2) Explore Mary's Hymn of Commitment to God

❖ **Option:** Use information from "The Big Picture: God's Covenant; Our Commitment" to introduce the themes for this quarter's lessons.

❖ Choose someone to read aloud Luke 1:46-55.

❖ **Option:** If you have access to a hymnal that includes the Magnificat as a responsive reading, divide the class in half and ask the adults to read responsively. (You will find this reading on page 199 of *The United Methodist Hymnal*.)

❖ Discuss these questions:
(1) **What does the Magnificat reveal to you about Mary?**
(2) **What does it say about God?**
(3) **What will happen to various social and economic classes?**
(4) **For whom is this Song of Mary good news?**
(5) **For whom is Mary's Song bad or frightening news?**

❖ Read aloud an excerpt from "There's a Revolution Coming" in Interpreting the Scripture, beginning with "The Magnificat is an expression of the faith" and concluding with "even though they threaten our comfortable ways of life."

❖ Provide a few moments of quiet time for the participants to reflect on this question: **How does the Magnificat comfort, frighten, or challenge you?**

❖ Encourage volunteers to share their reflections with the class.

(3) Consider the Characteristics in Another That May Lead the Learners to Commitment

❖ Discuss: **Speculate as to why Mary would commit herself to God when she had so much to lose in the eyes of her fiancé, her family, and her neighbors.** List these ideas on newsprint.

❖ Add to the list traits students can name that other highly committed people seem to embody.

❖ Read at least two of these quotations concerning commitment and invite the adults to comment on them, relating them where possible to the traits they have already listed. They may also want to consider how the quotation relates to Mary's commitment.

■ **I'm doing what I think I was put on this earth to do. And I'm really grateful to have something that I'm passionate about and that I think is profoundly important.** (Marian Wright Edelman, 1939–)

■ **Jesus did not say, "Come to me and get it over with." He said, "If any man would come after me, let him take up his cross daily and follow me." "Daily" is the key word. Our commitment to Christ, however genuine and wholehearted it may be today, must be renewed tomorrow . . . and the day after that . . . and the day after that . . . until the path comes at last to the river.** (Louis Cassels, 1922–1974)

■ **Say, "Yes," Son. I need your yes as I needed Mary's yes to come to earth. . . . Give all to me, abandon all to me. I need your yes to be united with you and to come** down to earth, I need your yes to continue saving the world. (Michel Quoist, 1921–)

❖ Ask: **How do others who have made commitments serve as a role model for you?**

(4) Make Commitments to Others and to God and Strategize Ways to Be Faithful to These Commitments

❖ Read the final paragraph of "To Whom Shall We Commit?" in Interpreting the Scripture.

❖ Distribute paper and pencils. Encourage the students to make a list of people and organizations to which they have committed themselves. Next to each person or group, they are to indicate how they fulfill their commitment. For example, perhaps they give money or assist with activities or nurture family.

❖ Invite the adults to talk about strategies they find useful for fulfilling these commitments. Do they, for example, schedule regular time to volunteer with a group or pledge a certain amount of money or set aside time to be with a loved one?

❖ Challenge the students to complete this sentence, which you will post on newsprint: **I will commit myself as a servant of God to . . .** Suggest that the adults may want to name a specific person or group and even set a start date or deadline for what they intend to do.

(5) Continue the Journey

❖ Pray that today's participants will be willing to make and honor commitments.

❖ Read aloud this preparation for next week's lesson. You may also want to post it on newsprint for the students to copy.

■ **Title: Elizabeth's Commitment**
■ **Background Scripture: Luke 1:5-24, 39-45**
■ **Lesson Scripture: Luke 1:39-45**
■ **Focus of the Lesson: Sometimes a commitment varies in its degree of complexity. How can a person make multiple commitments? Elizabeth remembered God's promise to her and to Zechariah, recognized the fulfillment of God's promise to Mary, and committed herself to the Messiah.**

❖ Challenge the students to complete one or more of these activities for further spiritual growth, which you will write on newsprint for the students to copy.

(1) **Fulfill a commitment that you have made to God. Perhaps this commitment will entail helping someone in need.**

(2) **Do some research on "Mary, Mother of God." Note art, literature, and music that honor Mary. Consider how the view of Mary in Roman Catholic and Orthodox faith communities is different from the status she has in Protestant circles.**

(3) **Think about how Mary can serve as a role model for all Christians, particularly for women, in terms of God's call on people to serve. How is Mary a role model for you?**

❖ Sing or read aloud "My Soul Gives Glory to My God," based on Luke 1:46-55.

❖ Conclude today's session by leading the class in this benediction, taken from Luke 1:38: **Here am I, the servant of the Lord; let it be with me according to your word.**

UNIT 1: COMMITMENT TO THE MESSIAH
ELIZABETH'S COMMITMENT

PREVIEWING THE LESSON

Lesson Scripture: Luke 1:39-45
Background Scripture: Luke 1:5-24, 39-45
Key Verses: Luke 1:41-42

Focus of the Lesson:
Sometimes a commitment varies in its degree of complexity. How can a person make multiple commitments? Elizabeth remembered God's promise to her and to Zechariah, recognized the fulfillment of God's promise to Mary, and committed herself to the Messiah.

Goals for the Learners:
(1) to explore Elizabeth's response to God's action in Mary's life.
(2) to evaluate the complexity of their own commitments.
(3) to recognize God's action in the lives of others and to respond by making their own commitment to God.

Pronunciation Guide:
Nazarite (naz' uh rite)
Zechariah (zek uh ri' uh)

Supplies:
Bibles, newsprint and marker, paper and pencils, hymnals, commentaries on Luke

---

READING THE SCRIPTURE

NRSV
Luke 1:39-45

³⁹In those days Mary set out and went with haste to a Judean town in the hill country, ⁴⁰where she entered the house of Zechariah and greeted Elizabeth. ⁴¹When Elizabeth heard Mary's greeting, the child

NIV
Luke 1:39-45

³⁹At that time Mary got ready and hurried to a town in the hill country of Judea, ⁴⁰where she entered Zechariah's home and greeted Elizabeth. ⁴¹When Elizabeth heard Mary's greeting, the baby leaped in her

leaped in her womb. And **Elizabeth was filled with the Holy Spirit** [42] and exclaimed with a loud cry, "Blessed are you among women, and blessed is the fruit of your womb. [43] And why has this happened to me, that the mother of my Lord comes to me? [44] For as soon as I heard the sound of your greeting, the child in my womb leaped for joy. [45] And blessed is she who believed that there would be a fulfillment of what was spoken to her by the Lord."

womb, and **Elizabeth was filled with the Holy Spirit.** [42] In a loud voice she exclaimed: "Blessed are you among women, and blessed is the child you will bear! [43] But why am I so favored, that the mother of my Lord should come to me? [44] As soon as the sound of your greeting reached my ears, the baby in my womb leaped for joy. [45] Blessed is she who has believed that what the Lord has said to her will be accomplished!"

UNDERSTANDING THE SCRIPTURE

Introduction. These verses selected from the first chapter of Luke tell the story of Zechariah and Elizabeth—the parents of John the Baptizer. This account precedes that of the Annunciation to Mary, which was the focus of Lesson 1. We will discuss John's ministry in the lesson on December 28, but here the focus is on the circumstances surrounding his conception and birth.

Luke 1:5. King Herod, who was called the Great, ruled the area from 37–4 B.C. It was he who built the magnificent Temple for the Jews in Jerusalem, as well as much other impressive construction. Herod owed his authority to the Roman Empire and may be thought of as a sort of puppet king, although he exercised great power. Herod was detested by the Jews as a foreigner and a threat.

Zechariah is introduced as a priest. At this time, there were thousands of Jewish priests. Most of them did not live in Jerusalem, as they were not employed full-time in Temple service. They traveled to the capital city when their particular family (or order) had its turn to serve. There were twenty-four priestly families (see 1 Chronicles 24:7-18). Each of them served in the Temple for two nonconsecutive weeks annually and during the three great

festivals of the religious year. Priests were paid a portion of the annual tithes collected in the Temple, and some were very poor. Zechariah's wife, Elizabeth, was also from a priestly family, tracing her ancestry back to Aaron—the brother of Moses and first high priest.

Luke 1:6-7. Zechariah and Elizabeth were obedient followers of the law of God—good people. So it was ironic that they had no children. Luke is making clear that Elizabeth's barrenness was not the result of God's disfavor, as was commonly thought at the time.

Luke 1:8-10. I have explained the pattern of priestly service in *The Coming of Jesus:*

> On a typical day, the priests who were on duty in the Temple divided their duties by casting lots. This way it was determined who would clean the altar, prepare the cereal offering, slaughter the lamb, sprinkle the blood on the altar, and perform each of the other tasks involved in offering sacrifices on behalf of the people. On the day that he was addressed by the angel, Zechariah had been chosen by lot to be one of the five priests presenting the incense offering. This would surely have been the highest moment of his life as a priest. After they had burned incense on the altar in the sanctuary of the Temple, the priests would come out on the steps and bless the gathered people.

Luke 1:11-12. People in the Bible are almost never pleased to see angels. Perhaps if we try to put ourselves in their place we can begin to imagine the deep fear that an angelic appearance evoked. It is important that this angel came to Zechariah in the heart of the Temple—the most holy place of Israel. Luke is preparing to locate Jesus in the context of earlier Hebrew history, as a continuation of God's saving work.

Luke 1:13-15. The angel told Zechariah the astounding news of the joyous impending birth of his and Elizabeth's son. This child will be filled with the Holy Spirit and "great in the sight of the Lord." He will live in the Nazarite tradition described in Numbers 6. Those who so separated themselves unto God lived simply, even ascetically, without luxuries. They avoided not only wine but also any grapes or grape products. They cut their hair only as a special sacrificial offering. The most familiar Nazarites from the Old Testament are Samuel and Samson. The announcements to their mothers of their coming births were quite similar to this announcement of John's birth.

Luke 1:16-17. There had been no prophet in the land since Malachi centuries earlier, but this was clearly a description of the work of a prophet. Luke is here using the very words of Malachi in 3:1 and 4:5-6 to explain the role that John will play in God's drama of salvation. John is likened to the mighty prophet Elijah whose story is told in 1 Kings 17–2 Kings 2:12.

Luke 1:18-20. Zechariah was skeptical of the angel's promise; even though he had been praying for a child, he was unable to believe that his prayers were to be answered. His question was a direct quotation of Abraham's in Genesis 15:8 when Abraham was told that he and Sarah would have a son. The angel answered Zechariah's comment, "I am an old man," with the response "I am Gabriel," which represents the power of the angel who stands in God's presence and has been sent as God's messenger. Zechariah would be unable to speak until the child was born.

Luke 1:21-24. The gathered people realized that Zechariah's muteness was the result of a powerful vision. The priest returned home after his period of service ended; his wife became pregnant and secluded herself for the first five months.

Luke 1:39-40. In the verses between 24 and 39, Luke records the Annunciation to Mary some six months into the period of Elizabeth's pregnancy. Told by Gabriel about Elizabeth, Mary left Nazareth and traveled to the Judean village where Zechariah and Elizabeth lived.

Luke 1:41-45. The Holy Spirit was powerfully at work in this encounter traditionally called the visitation. Both Elizabeth and her unborn child responded to Mary and the child she was carrying. The "leaping for joy" of the child in Elizabeth's womb was understood as a sign of the relationship that the two sons were to have in their lifetimes. Elizabeth's brief canticle praises Mary for her faith. One point in this story is the emphasis upon the priority of Mary's child. Although older, John will be secondary; it is he who responds to Jesus. Elizabeth's phrase "the mother of my Lord" is the first time that the term "Lord" was clearly applied to Jesus rather than to God.

It is in reply to Elizabeth's song that Mary delivers the beautiful Magnificat that we looked at last week.

INTERPRETING THE SCRIPTURE

When Commitments Collide

Elizabeth had a difficult task. God called her to complex and competing commitments. She was committed to her husband, Zechariah, and to her unborn son for whom she had waited so long. But, when Mary showed up at Elizabeth's home pregnant with the child who would be the Messiah, she had to add to her commitments. She committed herself to Mary, her young relative, and to the role that God had called Mary to play in the divine plan. Above all, she committed herself to Mary's child recognizing that he would be the Lord—God in flesh.

Life would be so much simpler if we had only a single commitment to fulfill. But, in reality, we usually find ourselves struggling to balance the competing claims upon our lives. Many of us have primary relationships with spouses or partners. We realize that these relationships will not flourish without nurture and attention, but there is so much competition. Middle-aged Americans are often referred to as the "sandwich generation" because they are caught between the needs of their own children on one hand and that of their parents and other older relatives on the other. Time, resources, energy, and attention are demanded from all directions, and we end up feeling squeezed and pulled. This problem will only worsen in the future. Increasingly, our parents are living much longer and needing care for many more years than was typical in the past. At the same time, our children are experiencing what is sometimes called "lengthened adolescence." Because of educational and occupational requirements, many have extended periods prior to being prepared for jobs in which they can support themselves. Many are returning to live at home as they try to launch their careers.

Most of us have our own careers to pursue. We have homes to maintain. We want to keep our bodies in good shape—to exercise regularly, eat healthily, and rest properly. Then there are good causes to be supported and good citizenship to be practiced. And, of course, we want to be faithful, active members of our churches. There is a lot pulling at us; we have colliding commitments. We are challenged to examine and acknowledge the multiple commitments in our lives and intentionally consider how we can handle them all.

Being Committed to Ourselves

In the tension and busyness of our colliding commitments, we sometimes devalue one that is extremely important: our commitment to ourselves. The Christian faith with its talk of sacrifice and self-denial can mislead us into believing that our own lives have no value. Historically, this has been a very potent, and dangerous, ideal, taught particularly to women. I want to argue that we have the duty to love ourselves. Jesus told us to love our neighbors *as we love ourselves*, not instead of ourselves. Before we can have a self worthy to give away in sacrifice and denial, our selves have to be valued and cultivated. The late-nineteenth–early-twentieth-century feminist leader Elizabeth Cady Stanton preached repeatedly to the women of her day that self-development was a higher value than self-sacrifice. God has given to each of us qualities and abilities that we are obliged to acknowledge and to develop. It is only out of healthy commitment to self that faithful commitments to others and to God can grow.

Notice that both Mary and Elizabeth honored their commitment to themselves. While submitting their wills to that of God, they understood and valued their ability to be faithful to the call of God on their lives. They embraced with joy the parts that they had been given. They were not crushed by the weight of the divine demand. They looked forward to the further self-development that being the mothers of extraordinary sons would require.

As we seek to perceive God's call on our lives, we should do so from a place of authentic commitment to the selves that we have developed. Even more, we are to be receptive to the self development that God seeks for us. After all, our selves are gifts from God.

Willingness Not to Be First

Elizabeth was thrilled about her unexpected late pregnancy and no doubt dreamed of the destined future of this special child. His conception had been announced to his father in a dramatic Temple vision; his name was chosen by the messenger of God. Still, Elizabeth proved herself willing to play the part assigned her in God's plan and, probably more difficult, to raise her son to understand both who he was and who he was not. Elizabeth knew that John's role was to be secondary to Jesus; he was the one whose job was to prepare the way for God's Chosen One. He would call the people to repentance in order that their hearts might be opened to Jesus' proclamation of the good news. It was Mary who would be mother of the Messiah. Her son would be the Savior, the Lord, the one whose coming had been anticipated for so long. Elizabeth was committed to her own role and to that of her son, but she was most deeply committed to God's larger plan for salvation. She was willing to accept a secondary place, a supporting role, and to see her son function as one who was unworthy to untie the sandals of Christ.

It is not always easy to perceive and honor God's action in the lives of other people. This is especially true when we think ourselves diminished and pushed off center stage by somebody else. But like Elizabeth, we are to be grateful for what God has given us and how God is using us, without needing always to be first and most important. Elizabeth was not ego-driven, self-centered, or insecure. She was comfortable and committed to God's intentions for her and for her son.

Unexpected Commitments

Commitments are not always something that we plan and choose. As a girl perhaps only fourteen years of age, Mary could not have imagined the direction that her life was to take. But, when God broke in, she was able to accept the divine plan and commit herself to it. As a woman beyond her childbearing years, Elizabeth surely expected to spend the remainder of her life caring for her husband and enjoying the quiet life of her village. But dramatically and startlingly, God intervened and turned her expectations upside down. Elizabeth submitted herself to God and changed her commitments to center on raising her son to fulfill his part in the divine drama of salvation.

For any of us, God may break into our lives quite unexpectedly and rearrange our plans radically. You have surely heard the old expression: "If you want to make God laugh, tell him your plans." We are to live lightly in the world, even somewhat tentatively, always ready to change and adapt as God has need of us. A part of being a faithful Christian is to be able to make unexpected commitments.

SHARING THE SCRIPTURE

Preparing Our Hearts

Meditate on this week's devotional reading, found in Isaiah 7:10-14. Here the prophet Isaiah gives King Ahaz a sign from God: A young woman will bear a child whose name will be Immanuel. What kinds of signs do you seek in determining where and how God is at work? How important are signs to you? Think about a major decision you have made. At the time, what prompted you to believe that this was the right decision? What signs, if any, were involved? How did these signs guide you?

Pray that you and the adult learners will be open to signs from God and willing to commit yourselves as you feel led.

Preparing Our Minds

Study the background from Luke 1:5-24, 39-45 and the lesson Scripture from Luke 1:39-45. Ponder this question: How can a person make multiple commitments?

Write on newsprint:

❑ questions under "Evaluate the Complexity of the Learners' Commitments."

❑ information for next week's lesson, found under "Continue the Journey."

❑ activities for further spiritual growth in "Continue the Journey."

Prepare to tell the story of Zechariah, found in today's background Scripture, Luke 1:5-24.

Locate several commentaries on the Gospel of Luke. Many public libraries have such books available. Also check your church library or talk with your pastor to see if you can borrow resources from him or her.

LEADING THE CLASS

(1) Gather to Learn

❖ Welcome the class members and introduce any guests.

❖ Pray that today's participants will be open to hearing God's Word for them and ready to make a commitment to do God's will.

❖ Read this story aloud: **In the August 15, 2003, edition of *Jewish News of Greater Phoenix*, Rabbi Shlomo Riskin tells the story of a young man who made a serious commitment to study Torah and observe its precepts. After only a year of study, the young man left school, giving this explanation: "As a non-religious Jew, I would get up each morning asking myself how I wished to spend the day; as a religious Jew, I must get up each morning asking myself how God wants me to spend the day. The pressure is simply too intense for me to take."**

❖ Discuss these questions:

(1) **What do these words say to you about commitment to God?** (Note that this story, although about a Jewish man, applies equally well to Christians.)

(2) **How would you respond to the student's concern that asking how God wants us to spend the day is too stressful?**

❖ Read aloud today's focus statement: **Sometimes a commitment varies in its degree of complexity. How can a person make multiple commitments? Elizabeth remembered God's promise to her and to Zechariah, recognized the fulfillment of God's promise to Mary, and committed herself to the Messiah.**

(2) Explore Elizabeth's Response to God's Action in Mary's Life

❖ Set the stage for today's lesson by retelling the story of Zechariah, found in Luke 1:5-24. You may wish to include information from Understanding the Scripture.

❖ Select a volunteer to read Luke 1:39-45. Or, you may wish to choose two readers, one to act as the narrator and one to read Elizabeth's words.

❖ Invite the students to comment on what this passage reveals to them about Elizabeth.

❖ Read "Willingness Not to Be First" from Interpreting the Scripture.

❖ Discuss this question: **What does Elizabeth's willingness not to be first suggest about her commitment to God?**

❖ Choose two volunteers to role-play a discussion between Mary and Elizabeth concerning how they hope to raise their sons in order to fulfill God's role for their lives. If time permits, several pairs may want to do their own version of this role-play.

❖ Divide the class into groups and give each group a commentary, paper, and pencils. Also ask the students who have study Bibles with footnotes to use these resources as well. Challenge the adults to learn what they can about this encounter between Elizabeth and Mary. Provide an opportunity for each group to report to the entire class.

(3) Evaluate the Complexity of the Learners' Commitments

❖ Read aloud "When Commitments Collide" from Interpreting the Scripture.

❖ Invite the students to respond to this reading, perhaps by telling stories of their own colliding commitments.

❖ Distribute paper and pencils if you have not already done so. Ask the adults to list all the commitments they have, possibly using the following categories as a guide:

self, church, work, family, education, community organizations, recreational activities. They may have other categories to add.

❖ Suggest that the students silently consider these questions, which you will post on newsprint, in light of their commitments:

    (1) Of what value or importance is this commitment in my life?

    (2) How does this commitment reflect my values and priorities?

    (3) Given all the commitments I have, are there some that I could eliminate? If so, what would happen if I no longer held them?

❖ Provide time for the learners to respond aloud to any of the questions or to share insights they have gleaned from this activity.

❖ Conclude this portion of the session by asking: **How do our multiple commitments collide with our commitment to God—or do they? How can we keep our priorities straight?**

(4) Recognize God's Action in the Lives of Others and Respond by Making a Commitment to God

❖ Read aloud this story about how God acted in one person's life: **The late Reverend Robert Drinan, a Roman Catholic priest and Massachusetts congressman, died in 2007 at the age of 86. A champion of human rights and justice, Drinan supported abortion rights. While his Roman Catholic faith and abortion stance were in conflict, Father Drinan tried to put the issue "in the context of a common concern for the well-being of women and children in a society racked by moral disagreement," according to Reverend John Langan. After five terms in Congress, Drinan was required by Pope John Paul II to make a choice between continuing to serve in politics or continuing as a priest. Drinan left Congress with "regret and pain," but enthusiastically continued for 26 years as professor of international** human rights, legal ethics, and constitutional law at Georgetown University Law Center.

❖ Discuss this question: **What lessons can we learn from Robert Drinan concerning how we deal with multiple commitments that sometimes collide?**

❖ Encourage the learners to look again at the commitments they listed in a prior activity. Suggest that they put an asterisk (*) beside at least one of these commitments that they perceive to be a commitment to God, though it may involve people or creation. Invite them to take action this week on the starred commitment.

(5) Continue the Journey

❖ Pray that those who have come today will cope with the multiple commitments in their lives in ways that are pleasing to God.

❖ Read aloud this preparation for next week's lesson. You may also want to post it on newsprint for the students to copy.

■ **Title: Shepherds Glorify God**

■ **Background Scripture: Luke 2:1-20**

■ **Lesson Scripture: Luke 2:8-20**

■ **Focus of the Lesson: People yearn to hear the good news of the fulfillment of promises. What results from our appreciation for promises that are kept? The shepherds**

glorified and praised God for the gift of the long-awaited Messiah and told others the good news.

❖ Challenge the students to complete one or more of these activities for further spiritual growth, which you will write on newsprint for the students to copy.

(1) **Review the list of commitments you made during this week's session. If you considered eliminating one or more, take steps this week to begin to close out this commitment. Remember that in most cases you will need to give notice to end a commitment.**

(2) **Do a Bible study in which you compare and contrast Hannah's experience (1 Samuel 1) with that of Zechariah and Elizabeth (Luke 1:5-24).**

(3) **Look for evidence of God's work in your life and the lives of those around you. What delights or surprises you about the way God works in human lives?**

❖ Sing or read aloud "Come, Thou Long-Expected Jesus."

❖ Conclude today's session by leading the class in this benediction, taken from Luke 1:38: **Here am I, the servant of the Lord; let it be with me according to your word.**

UNIT 1: COMMITMENT TO THE MESSIAH
SHEPHERDS GLORIFY GOD

PREVIEWING THE LESSON

Lesson Scripture: Luke 2:8-20
Background Scripture: Luke 2:1-20
Key Verse: Luke 2:20

Focus of the Lesson:
People yearn to hear the good news of the fulfillment of promises. What results from our appreciation for promises that are kept? The shepherds glorified and praised God for the gift of the long-awaited Messiah and told others the good news.

Goals for the Learners:
(1) to recount the angels' announcement to the shepherds and the shepherds' response.
(2) to consider how issues of proclamation, promises, and commitment relate to their lives.
(3) to demonstrate commitment to God in acts of praise.

Pronunciation Guide:
Adonai (ad oh ni')
Quirinius (kwi rin' ee uhs)
Yahweh (yah' weh)

Supplies:
Bibles; newsprint and marker; paper and pencils; hymnals; optional cookies, punch, coffee, napkins, and cups

---

READING THE SCRIPTURE

NRSV
Luke 2:8-20

⁸In that region there were shepherds living in the fields, keeping watch over their flock by night. ⁹Then an angel of the Lord stood before them, and the glory of the Lord shone around them, and they were terrified. ¹⁰But the angel said to them, "Do not be

NIV
Luke 2:8-20

⁸And there were shepherds living out in the fields nearby, keeping watch over their flocks at night. ⁹An angel of the Lord appeared to them, and the glory of the Lord shone around them, and they were terrified. ¹⁰But the angel said to them, "Do not be

afraid; for see—I am bringing you good news of great joy for all the people: [11]to you is born this day in the city of David a Savior, who is the Messiah, the Lord. [12]This will be a sign for you: you will find a child wrapped in bands of cloth and lying in a manger." [13]And suddenly there was with the angel a multitude of the heavenly host, praising God and saying,

[14]"Glory to God in the highest heaven,
    and on earth peace among those
      whom he favors!"

[15]When the angels had left them and gone into heaven, the shepherds said to one another, "Let us go now to Bethlehem and see this thing that has taken place, which the Lord has made known to us." [16]So they went with haste and found Mary and Joseph, and the child lying in the manger. [17]When they saw this, they made known what had been told them about this child; [18]and all who heard it were amazed at what the shepherds told them. [19]But Mary treasured all these words and pondered them in her heart. **[20]The shepherds returned, glorifying and praising God for all they had heard and seen, as it had been told them.**

afraid. I bring you good news of great joy that will be for all the people. [11]Today in the town of David a Savior has been born to you; he is Christ the Lord. [12]This will be a sign to you: You will find a baby wrapped in cloths and lying in a manger."

[13]Suddenly a great company of the heavenly host appeared with the angel, praising God and saying,

[14]"Glory to God in the highest,
    and on earth peace to men on whom
      his favor rests."

[15]When the angels had left them and gone into heaven, the shepherds said to one another, "Let's go to Bethlehem and see this thing that has happened, which the Lord has told us about."

[16]So they hurried off and found Mary and Joseph, and the baby, who was lying in the manger. [17]When they had seen him, they spread the word concerning what had been told them about this child, [18]and all who heard it were amazed at what the shepherds said to them. [19]But Mary treasured up all these things and pondered them in her heart. **[20]The shepherds returned, glorifying and praising God for all the things they had heard and seen, which were just as they had been told.**

UNDERSTANDING THE SCRIPTURE

Introduction to Luke 2. The stage had been set. As we saw in the first two lessons of this unit, Mary had conceived the Son of God, and Elizabeth had conceived John the Baptizer. The two mothers-to-be had met and recognized each other's role in the divine plan of salvation. They had rejoiced and praised God. Elizabeth's son had been born and named John, according to the direction of the angel. John's father, Zechariah, had been inspired by the Holy Spirit to utter the hymn we call the

Benedictus (Luke 1:67-79). It is now time for the birth of Jesus.

Luke 2:1-3. In Luke's typical manner, the birth was set within the context of world events. Perhaps it was because Luke himself was not a Jew. While he always linked Jesus to the story of God's actions in the Old Testament, he also portrayed him against the backdrop of the larger, secular world. For Luke and for his readers, the world was the Roman Empire; they knew and cared little about anything beyond that entity.

Unfortunately for those who are historically literalistic, Luke's account does not conform well to the historical record as we now know it, but for Luke that was not a pressing concern.

Augustus was emperor of the Roman Empire from 31 B.C. to A.D. 14. He was the ultimate authority in the political, social, and religious world into which Jesus was born. Palestine at that time was part of the Roman province of Syria, and Quirinius was identified by Luke as its military governor. While the Empire did periodically take censuses of its people, there is no record of persons having to return to their ancestral homes to register. For Luke, such an order served to explain why Mary and Joseph were in Bethlehem when she gave birth rather than in their hometown of Nazareth. In Matthew's account, Mary and Joseph are portrayed as residents of Bethlehem who go to Nazareth only when the family returns from refuge in Egypt.

Luke 2:4-5. Nazareth was located in Galilee in the northern area of Palestine, southwest of the Sea of Galilee. Judea was in the south, and, in it, Bethlehem was located only six miles southwest of Jerusalem. A journey on foot between Nazareth and Bethlehem would take several days. Bethlehem was called the city of David because it was the place where that great king had been born, as recorded in 1 Samuel 17:12. Joseph was explicitly identified as a descendant of David. He was accompanied on the journey by Mary. They were pledged to each other for marriage, although the official ceremony had not occurred, nor had the marriage been consummated. We can assume that they were unwilling to be apart with the birth of the child so imminent. Note that there is no mention in the story of Mary having ridden on a donkey. Probably later Christians imagined the journey that way in the hope that the mother of Jesus was provided at least some measure of comfort. There is also no mention of an inn.

Luke 2:6-7. The actual birth of Jesus is related in these two verses. Their brevity gives no hint of what the young mother must have suffered in the circumstances. The description of Jesus as Mary's "firstborn" son raises questions about the Roman Catholic doctrine of Mary's perpetual virginity. Did she subsequently have other children? There is no way to decide this conclusively. Later scriptural references do speak of Jesus' siblings, but it is possible that they were Mary's stepchildren, that is, the children of Joseph by a previous marriage.

Wrapping the child in strips of cloth to keep the limbs straight was the customary practice of the time. Interestingly, modern theory now emphasizes the security experienced by the infant who is snugly wrapped. The manger is the only indication that the birth was in a place associated with animals. Very early Christian tradition suggested that it was a cave. Caves in the soft rock were common in the area and often used to house livestock. The birth was just as likely to have been in the sleeping area of a house where troughs were cut at the edge of the floor so that the animals below could reach them.

Luke 2:8. Luke immediately shifts his story from the family to the fields. Today Shepherds' Field is a tourist site about two miles from Jerusalem, although no one knows the precise place of the angels' appearance. Shepherds were guards, protecting the sheep from predatory animals and thieves. It is possible that this flock was composed of animals reserved for Temple sacrifice. This verse contains the sole indication that Jesus' birth occurred at night.

Luke 2:9-10. The quiet of the night was abruptly shattered by the overpowering appearance of an angel, who was not identified by name, surrounded by the light of divine presence. As was the custom of human beings, the response of the shepherds was fear—intense fear, even terror. The angel tried, as was the custom of angels, to calm their fears and to assure them that the message it brought was one of joy, not only to the shepherds but to all people.

Luke 2:11-12. The good news was the birth in Bethlehem, on that very day, of one who would be Savior, Messiah, and Lord. The angelic announcement was to be confirmed by the sign of the wrapped child in a manger.

Luke 2:13-14. As if there were not splendor enough, a huge number of angels suddenly join the messenger, all singing praises to God. The angels' song is traditionally called the "Gloria in Excelsis Deo." In the period between the writing of the Old and New Testaments, Jewish thought had developed an elaborate view of a heaven of many levels with God at the top. The promise was peace—not the Pax Romana imposed by the power of the Empire, but God's deeper, lasting peace. The precise translation of the last phrase is not certain: Does "favor" describe those who receive peace, or is it the goodwill that God bestows? Probably we best understand this when we see those who

believe and obey as those God favors. They are favored not because of anything they deserve but because they are willing to receive what God offers.

Luke 2:15-18, 20. The shepherds apparently recovered from their shock quickly and hurried to the village to confirm what they had been told. When they arrived, they found things to be just as the angel had described. We do not know what they said to the Holy Family, but they rushed out to tell what had happened to all the people that they encountered. Apparently the shepherds' testimony was accepted as true and "all who heard it" joined in their amazement.

Luke 2:19. It is interesting that Luke inserted this quiet comment about the reaction of Mary to the shepherds' visit. She will have much more to ponder as this child grows up.

INTERPRETING THE SCRIPTURE

Promise and Fulfillment

The Hebrew people had learned through the events of their own history to trust the promises of God. As early as Abraham and Sarah, God promised the gifts of the land and of numerous descendants. These promises were repeated to Isaac and Rebekah and, in turn, to Jacob (Israel) and Rachel. Most important, God promised Abraham and his descendants that they would be in covenant relationship with God: They would be God's special people and God would be their own God. This did not, of course, mean that God did not care for the other peoples of the earth. The people of Israel were to be the special instrument through whom God's will for all humankind would be accomplished. In fulfillment of the promise, God had rescued the people of Israel from slavery in Egypt.

During the long decades of wandering in the desert, the Israelites were taught their covenant responsibilities as expressed in the law. Through hard times of conflict, conquest, and captivity, God remained faithful, even when Israel was not. As the Old Testament drew to its end, we read how God restored them to their land. By the beginning of the New Testament, the people (by then called Jewish) were again under the power of an oppressive conqueror—in this case, the Roman Empire. Through all their times of defeat, poverty, and suffering, the nation continued to look to God to fulfill the ancient divine promise.

The Shepherd King Comes to Shepherds

In the minds of many of the Jewish people, King David, who had ruled about a thousand years before the time of Christ, was a model for the deliverer whom they expected God to send. David had defeated their enemies, joined them together into a strong kingdom, and even conquered neighboring countries. David's reign was a time of power and prosperity that they looked back to with longing.

David had started out as a shepherd. The judge/prophet Samuel was sent by God to the house of David's father, Jesse, to seek out the one who would become king. After looking at all of Jesse's fine older sons, Samuel was told by God that none of them was the chosen one. Inquiring further, Samuel learned that the youth David was out tending the flocks. This shepherd boy was called in to be anointed as the nation's king. David's background as a shepherd probably influenced the writer of Psalm 23 and other sections of the Old Testament in which God is portrayed in this role.

The appearance of the angels to the shepherds in Luke 2 was another sign of the connection between David and the child born that night in David's city with a legal father of David's lineage. Jesus, grown to manhood, was often pictured by early Christians as the good shepherd of the sheep (see John 10 and Luke 15 for examples). The importance of shepherds in Luke's account is somewhat surprising in view of the low status they had in Palestinian society of the day. Shepherds had developed a rather unsavory reputation; they were stereotyped as dishonest, even as thieves. By making shepherds so prominent in the story of Jesus' birth, Luke was affirming that Christ came to and for the lowly, the rejected, and the marginalized. He did not come to a palace and sit on a throne; he came to a peasant home and lay in a manger.

Fulfillment Greater Than They Could Imagine

God's unfathomable commitment to humankind in the coming of Jesus can never be fully understood. Certainly Jesus

was very different from the expectations of those Jews who looked for a military messiah—one who would overthrow the power of Rome. There were a variety of hopes related to the Messiah in Jewish thought of that time, but none of them even came close to the reality of God's action in Christ. Luke helps us begin to grasp this reality when he uses three titles to describe Jesus in Luke 2:11.

To speak of Jesus as Savior was to attribute to him the role and work of God in the Old Testament. God had always been seen as the savior of the people of Israel—saving them from historical and spiritual destruction. Throughout the New Testament, Jesus is understood to have fulfilled God's promises in Israel's Scripture (Old Testament). He came to save human beings, all of whom are in some sense lost. He came first to the people of Israel, but his mission very soon was extended to all. The salvation that Jesus offers is not to be earned or deserved; it is available to sinners, to all who will receive it.

This newborn Savior, Luke continues, is the Christ, the Messiah. In English, "Messiah" means "anointed one." In the life of the Hebrew people, kings, priests, and prophets were anointed, meaning that they had oil poured over their heads as a sign of God's choice of them for special purposes. "Messiah" is the Hebrew term for the deliverer whom God had promised to send. "Christ" is the Greek term for this same expected ruler. Christ is the most common title applied to Jesus in Scripture, used so frequently that it became almost a surname. It is this title that most closely and clearly identifies Jesus as the one who has been sent to fulfill the promises of God.

Perhaps the most powerful title for Jesus was that of Lord because it is in the use of this term that the divinity of Jesus is claimed. Its roots go back to Moses' encounter with God at the burning bush in Exodus 3. God's reply to Moses' question about God's name is translated by the

NRSV and NIV as "I AM WHO I AM" (3:14). This name of God was rendered as YHWH in Hebrew. Over time, YHWH came to be considered so holy that it was not spoken aloud lest it be profaned. The Hebrew term "Adonai" was used as God's name instead. Scribes who worked with the Old Testament text later used the vowels from "Adonai" and inserted them into YHWH. This was easily done since Hebrew was written without vowels—consonants only. The two names were merged and the resulting name, Yahweh, used for God. In most English translations of the Old Testament, this name is written as LORD, with small capital letters. For early Jewish Christians, the use of this term for Jesus indicated that he was to be identified with God. For non-Jewish Christians the title was also familiar, since it was used in many of the so-called Greek mystery religions as a name for the god being worshiped. "Jesus is Lord" became the earliest Christian creed—a statement of faith in him as divine. More than Mark and Matthew, Luke uses "the Lord" quite freely as the designation for Jesus.

The fulfillment of the divine promise to human beings is still mysterious; it is literally beyond our capacity to grasp. Through his use of the three titles—Savior, Messiah, and Lord—Luke attempts to articulate to his readers who this newborn child was and what he was to do on earth.

SHARING THE SCRIPTURE

Preparing Our Hearts

Meditate on this week's devotional reading, found in Psalm 107:1-15. The psalmist gives thanks to God, who is good, for the steadfast love and care God has shown, particularly to those who are in distress. What echoes in this psalm of thanksgiving do you hear of Mary's Magnificat or Jesus' announcement of his mission in Luke 4:18-19? Write your own psalm of thanksgiving for God's action in your life.

Pray that you and the adult learners will recognize that just as God kept promises to people long ago, so God now continues to keep promises to us.

Preparing Our Minds

Study the background from Luke 2:1-20 and the lesson Scripture from Luke 2:8-20. As you read consider this question: What results from our appreciation for promises that are kept?

Write on newsprint:

❑ points concerning promises in "Consider How Issues of Proclamation, Promises, and Commitment Relate to the Learners' Lives."
❑ information for next week's lesson, found under "Continue the Journey."
❑ activities for further spiritual growth in "Continue the Journey."

Familiarize yourself with the information for Luke 2:1-3, 4-5, 6-7 in Understanding the Scripture. Decide whether you will read this information or present it in a brief lecture.

Research the role and status of shepherds in first-century Palestine. Be prepared to give a brief lecture on their work and place in society for the portion of the session entitled "Recount the Angels' Announcement to the Shepherds and the Shepherds' Response."

Option: Have cookies, punch, coffee, napkins, and cups on hand to celebrate the birth of Jesus. You may want to contact some students during the week to ask them to bring a contribution. Be aware that while some students may be away, others may have guests visiting with them.

LEADING THE CLASS

(1) Gather to Learn

❖ Welcome the class members and introduce any guests.

❖ Pray that those who are participating today will hear good news and share it with others.

❖ Invite the students to think of promises that politicians have made to them. List these on newsprint. Review the list by inviting the students to indicate how these promises have been fulfilled—or if they remain unfulfilled.

❖ Discuss these two questions:
   (1) How does it make you feel when someone in authority makes a promise and then does not keep it?
   (2) How do you respond when authority figures are true to their word?

❖ Read aloud today's focus statement: **People yearn to hear the good news of the fulfillment of promises. What results from our appreciation for promises that are kept? The shepherds glorified and praised God for the gift of the long-awaited Messiah and told others the good news.**

(2) Recount the Angels' Announcement to the Shepherds and the Shepherds' Response

❖ Set the stage for the Scripture by reading or retelling the information for Luke 2:1-3, 4-5, 6-7 in Understanding the Scripture.

❖ Choose volunteers to read the roles of the narrator, first angel (2:10b-12), and two shepherds (2:15b). Invite all of the class members to read the angel chorus of Luke 2:14 in unison. If the readers are able, suggest that they act out this story.

❖ Encourage the adults to discuss what they know about the role of shepherds and their place in first-century Palestinian society. Use "The Shepherd King Comes to Shepherds" in Interpreting the Scripture, Luke 2:8 in Understanding the Scripture,

and any other information you have located to augment the discussion. You may choose to give a brief lecture here.

❖ Point out that the Jewish people had been waiting for about one thousand years since the death of David and about four hundred years since the fall of Jerusalem in 587 B.C. for another shepherd king, who was to be from the house of David.

❖ Ask the students to assume that they are one of the shepherds as they answer these questions:
   (1) What would you have said to the other shepherds after the appearance of the angels?
   (2) What would you have said to Mary and Joseph? What questions would you have asked them?
   (3) What would you have said to others you met as you returned to your flocks?
   (4) How would your life have been changed by this encounter with the Christ child?
   (5) What would you think about God? (Many answers are possible, but be sure the students include that God can be counted on to keep promises.)

(3) Consider How Issues of Proclamation, Promises, and Commitment Relate to the Learners' Lives

❖ Recall with the students that the angels proclaimed the good news of Jesus' birth to the shepherds. This birth fulfilled God's promise. When the shepherds heard the news, they committed themselves to finding the Christ child and then telling others about him.

❖ Suggest that the adults talk with a partner or small group about a promise made to them. Ask them to consider the following points, which you will write on newsprint.
   ■ why this promise was important to them

■ how its fulfillment changed their lives

■ how, if the promise went unfulfilled, its brokenness affected them

❖ Invite the partners to share with the class any helpful insights.

❖ Wrap up this portion of the lesson by providing meditation time for the students to recall a promise they made to God or someone else. Suggest that they think about how they have fulfilled this promise. If it is not fulfilled, what steps are they willing to take in the next two to three weeks to begin to make this promise a reality?

(4) Demonstrate Commitment to God in Acts of Praise

❖ Distribute hymnals, paper, and pencils. Divide the class into groups of three or four. Ask each group to page through the hymnal and jot down page numbers and titles of hymns or responses that proclaim the coming of the promised Messiah. You may want to limit the search to Advent and Christmas music.

❖ Provide time for each group to report on the song(s) they have selected as an act of praise. Perhaps a hymn has special meaning to one or more group members.

❖ Plan to sing as many of the selected hymns as time will allow.

❖ **Option:** Provide time for fellowship and celebration by serving refreshments. If time is short, enjoy the refreshments while the groups talk.

(5) Continue the Journey

❖ Pray that the students will go forth praising God for keeping the promise to send the Messiah.

❖ Read aloud this preparation for next week's lesson. You may also want to post it on newsprint for the students to copy.

■ **Title: John the Baptist Proclaims God's Message**

■ **Background Scripture: Luke 3:1-20**

■ **Lesson Scripture: Luke 3:7-18**

■ **Focus of the Lesson: Making a commitment requires action to accompany verbal assent. What actions may be required to fulfill a commitment? When John took the message to the people about the coming of the Messiah, he challenged them to make a response.**

❖ Challenge the students to complete one or more of these activities for further spiritual growth, which you will write on newsprint for the students to copy.

(1) **Recall several biblical promises that are especially meaningful to you. How do you perceive that God has kept these promises in your life?**

(2) **Tell at least one other person the good news of Jesus' coming as God-in-the-flesh. Encourage this person to attend worship this week to hear more and to celebrate Jesus' birth.**

(3) **Read Psalm 23, Ezekiel 34, and John 10. How is God portrayed as the Good Shepherd? What is your response to the idea of being characterized as a sheep? You may want to do some research on sheep before you answer that question.**

❖ Sing or read aloud "While Shepherds Watched Their Flocks."

❖ Conclude today's session by leading the class in this benediction, taken from Luke 1:38: **Here am I, the servant of the Lord; let it be with me according to your word.**

UNIT 1: COMMITMENT TO THE MESSIAH
JOHN THE BAPTIST PROCLAIMS GOD'S MESSAGE

PREVIEWING THE LESSON

Lesson Scripture: Luke 3:7-18
Background Scripture: Luke 3:1-20
Key Verse: Luke 3:8

Focus of the Lesson:

Making a commitment requires action to accompany verbal assent. What actions may be required to fulfill a commitment? When John took the message to the people about the coming of the Messiah, he challenged them to make a response.

Goals for the Learners:

(1) to examine John's commitment to call people to repentance in preparation for the coming of the Messiah.
(2) to explore the range of possible actions required by commitment.
(3) to evaluate actions they have taken because of their commitment to God.

Pronunciation Guide:

Annas (an' uhs)   Herodias (hi roh' dee uhs)
Antipas (an' tee puhs)   Machaerus (muh kihr' uhs)
Caiaphas (kay' uh fuhs)

Supplies:

Bibles, newsprint and marker, paper and pencils, hymnals

READING THE SCRIPTURE

NRSV
Luke 3:7-18

⁷John said to the crowds that came out to be baptized by him, "You brood of vipers! Who warned you to flee from the wrath to come? **⁸Bear fruits worthy of repentance.**

NIV
Luke 3:7-18

⁷John said to the crowds coming out to be baptized by him, "You brood of vipers! Who warned you to flee from the coming wrath? **⁸Produce fruit in keeping with repentance.**

Do not begin to say to yourselves, 'We have Abraham as our ancestor'; for I tell you, God is able from these stones to raise up children to Abraham. ⁹Even now the ax is lying at the root of the trees; every tree therefore that does not bear good fruit is cut down and thrown into the fire."

¹⁰And the crowds asked him, "What then should we do?" ¹¹In reply he said to them, "Whoever has two coats must share with anyone who has none; and whoever has food must do likewise." ¹²Even tax collectors came to be baptized, and they asked him, "Teacher, what should we do?" ¹³He said to them, "Collect no more than the amount prescribed for you." ¹⁴Soldiers also asked him, "And we, what should we do?" He said to them, "Do not extort money from anyone by threats or false accusation, and be satisfied with your wages."

¹⁵As the people were filled with expectation, and all were questioning in their hearts concerning John, whether he might be the Messiah, ¹⁶John answered all of them by saying, "I baptize you with water; but one who is more powerful than I is coming; I am not worthy to untie the thong of his sandals. He will baptize you with the Holy Spirit and fire. ¹⁷His winnowing fork is in his hand, to clear his threshing floor and to gather the wheat into his granary; but the chaff he will burn with unquenchable fire."

¹⁸So, with many other exhortations, he proclaimed the good news to the people.

And do not begin to say to yourselves, 'We have Abraham as our father.' For I tell you that out of these stones God can raise up children for Abraham. ⁹The ax is already at the root of the trees, and every tree that does not produce good fruit will be cut down and thrown into the fire."

¹⁰"What should we do then?" the crowd asked.

¹¹John answered, "The man with two tunics should share with him who has none, and the one who has food should do the same."

¹²Tax collectors also came to be baptized. "Teacher," they asked, "what should we do?"

¹³"Don't collect any more than you are required to," he told them.

¹⁴Then some soldiers asked him, "And what should we do?"

He replied, "Don't extort money and don't accuse people falsely—be content with your pay."

¹⁵The people were waiting expectantly and were all wondering in their hearts if John might possibly be the Christ. ¹⁶John answered them all, "I baptize you with water. But one more powerful than I will come, the thongs of whose sandals I am not worthy to untie. He will baptize you with the Holy Spirit and with fire. ¹⁷His winnowing fork is in his hand to clear his threshing floor and to gather the wheat into his barn, but he will burn up the chaff with unquenchable fire." ¹⁸And with many other words John exhorted the people and preached the good news to them.

UNDERSTANDING THE SCRIPTURE

Luke 3:1-2. We have already looked at the accounts of the annunciation of John's birth to his father, Zechariah, and of the unborn John's response to the pregnant mother of Jesus. In the style that is characteristic of his Gospel, Luke begins his presentation of the ministry of John the Baptist (better, "the Baptizer") by placing it in a precise historical setting. The year was probably A.D. 28 or 29, and the area was still under Roman control. After the death of Herod the Great, his kingdom had been divided between two of his sons, Herod Antipas and Philip, to rule as puppet monarchs. Pilate was the Roman prefect or procurator—the chief officer—of Judea. The high priest was the preeminent authority among the Jewish people. Primarily a religious leader, he exercised significant political power as well, as long as he did not antagonize the Romans. Annas, the old high priest, was retired (probably removed by the Romans), but still very influential. The official high priest, was his son-in-law Caiaphas. In his trials, Jesus appeared before both of these priests.

The call of John the Baptizer was in the manner of that of the prophets of the Old Testament. Jeremiah 1:1-2 is an example: "Jeremiah . . . to whom the word of the LORD came in the days of King Josiah," as is Ezekiel 1:2-3: "On the fifth day of the month . . . the word of the LORD came to the priest Ezekiel." A prophet was one who spoke the word that God gave him. John was in a desolate, uninhabited area, which was similar to the places where the tribes of Israel had wandered during the period of their formation as a people after being delivered from Egypt.

Luke 3:3. John preached a message of sinfulness, of the need for repentance and receiving baptism. To repent was to turn around, to return to the way of God. Baptism symbolized recognition of one's sinfulness, broken relationship with God, and acceptance of forgiveness through God's mercy.

Luke 3:4-6. Luke uses the words of Isaiah 40:3-5 to explain the role of John in God's plan of salvation. In this culture, roads often had to be considerably improved prior to the travels of a king. This is the image used for the preparation for the coming of the Messiah. Luke was probably a Gentile himself, so it was particularly important to him to make clear that the Messiah came for both Jews and Gentiles.

Luke 3:7-9. The image of poisonous reptiles fleeing before the spreading fire is a powerful one, though highly uncomplimentary. John condemned the privileged Jews,

especially those who took undue pride in their heritage as God's people and believed that God would not punish them. He warned of the coming judgment, both the destruction of the Temple by the Romans in the year 70 and the final judgment. The only escape was through repentance and right living. With the image of the ax at the roots of the tree, John emphasized that the time was short; judgment was imminent. Fire is symbolic of the flames of judgment and also of the work of the Holy Spirit.

Luke 3:10-14. John's message was one of social ethics. Repentance was not only a theological category but also a change of heart expressed in changed actions. Those who have more clothing or food than they really need are to share with those who have less. Tax collectors were despised as agents of Rome who took advantage of their position fraudulently to enrich themselves at the expense of the people. Rather than squeezing all they could from the poor, they were to collect only what was legally required. The mention of soldiers probably refers to Jewish mercenaries who supported the Romans. They were not to use their status and weapons to frighten the people and take their money.

Luke 3:15-17. John answered the curiosity of the crowd by distinguishing himself from the coming Messiah by contrasting their ministries. Water baptism will be completed by the action of the Holy Spirit. The Messiah will separate the righteous from the evil. Continuing his characteristic use of powerful imagery, John proclaimed that the Messiah would figuratively use the kind of large, broad fork employed to separate grain from trash after the harvest. Grain was tossed into the air so that the wind would blow away the refuse. The righteous would be safely stored away, while the wicked would be destroyed. This image is used by Jesus in his parable of the weeds in the field (Matthew 13:36-43). It also provides the central metaphor of the popular Thanksgiving hymn "Come, Ye Thankful People, Come."

Luke 3:18. John's proclamation might not

have sounded like good news to his hearers, for it was a strong message of impending judgment. But, a new relationship with God was being made available. For those who would repent, receive the Messiah, and live according to his teachings, it was good news indeed that he was coming very soon.

Luke 3:19-20. While condemning the sin of his hearers, John had sharply criticized Herod Antipas for his evil actions. This son of Herod the Great had first married an Arabian princess but divorced her to marry Herodias, who was his niece and already the wife of his brother Philip. Antipas responded by having John arrested and imprisoned, probably at Machaerus, a fortress east of the Dead Sea. There John was later put to death.

INTERPRETING THE SCRIPTURE

Commitments Require Actions

The birth of John the Baptizer is traditionally celebrated by the church on June 24. One of Luke's consistent themes is continuity between the Old and New Testaments. As I wrote in *The Coming of Jesus:* "The ministry of John the Baptist is set as a continuation of the work of God in the salvation history of Israel and as a link to God's work in Christ. . . . John was a bridge between the old covenant and the new. He was the last of the Old Testament prophets and the first of the New Testament disciples."

Chapter 3 in the book of the prophet Malachi gives us an understanding of the role that John was to play in the drama of salvation:

> See, I am sending my messenger to prepare the way before me, and the Lord whom you seek will suddenly come to his temple. . . . But who can endure the day of his coming, and who can stand when he appears?
> For he is like a refiner's fire and like fullers' soap. . . .
> Then I will draw near to you for judgment. . . .
> . . . Return to me, and I will return to you, says the LORD of hosts. But you say, "How shall we return?"
> Will anyone rob God? Yet you are robbing me! . . .
> . . . Then once more you shall see the difference between the righteous and the wicked, between one who serves God and one who does not serve him.

The emphasis in Malachi and the other Old Testament prophets is on actions, not doctrines. It is the actions of the people that are displeasing to God, and only change of actions will please God. John reiterated this message, calling for his listeners to turn their lives around and behave differently. Only by so doing can they be prepared for the coming of the Messiah. Similar to the question in Malachi, John's audience asks, "What then should we do?" The question is one of doing, of acting, of behaving. Verbal agreement and even orthodox beliefs are not sufficient. Commitments require actions; only actions can prove genuine commitment. We have probably all heard the old expression, "What you do speaks so loudly that I cannot hear what you say." This is the message that God is speaking through John the Baptizer.

Commitment to Social Responsibility

John's answers to the question "What then should we do?" reveal his understanding of what God desires. He does not counsel rededication to right beliefs or more regular worship attendance or even a deeper resolve to accept Jesus as savior. Instead, he directs his hearers to actions of social responsibility. In this he is again like the Hebrew prophets of the Old Testament who talked very little about what to believe. These prophets proclaimed that God is most concerned with social justice—with treatment of the poor and powerless of the society. Mary's Magnificat, which we studied on December 7, has the same theme. John preached that God demands the sharing of material resources so that those who are needy receive what they lack from those who have more than enough. Notice that this admonition is not addressed only to the very rich. Anyone who has more than is absolutely needed is to give away half of what he or she has. This is a convicting and disconcerting word in our affluent, indulgent society.

John gave practical, ethical examples of the actions that God will consider as "fruits of repentance." Without such fruits, or evidence, repentance is not genuine. The people must demonstrate their concern for others by concrete acts of giving. Those in positions of authority, such as tax collectors and soldiers, must not exploit others but carry out their jobs honestly.

United Methodists are reminded of the teaching and work of our founder John Wesley, for whom social action for justice and charity was central. Wesley wrote, "There is no religion, but social religion; no holiness, but social holiness." A great deal of his energy went into providing for the needs of the poor and sick. Both in the institutions he established—such as medical dispensaries and employment agencies—and in his personal acts of charity, he exemplified his commitments through actions. Wesley insisted that the Methodists take seriously their responsibility for the less fortunate and give generously of their money and their time in what he called "works of mercy."

In his General Rules for the Methodist Societies, which is quoted in the "Doctrinal Standards" of the United Methodist *Book of Discipline*, Wesley stipulated that the only requirement was "'a desire to flee from the wrath to come, and to be saved from their sins.' But wherever this is really fixed in the soul it will be shown by its fruits." One of the essential evidences of this commitment was shown, "By doing good; by being in every kind merciful after their power; as they have opportunity, doing good of every possible sort, and, as far as possible, to all men."

Almost all Protestant denominations, as well as Roman Catholicism, have been and are deeply involved in the work of social justice. In 1907 the Federal Council of Churches (now National Council of Churches) was formed to coordinate and strengthen efforts to improve social conditions, especially in the factories and tenements of the cities.

The Church as Prophet

The mission of the Christian church is to continue the work of Christ in redeeming the world. God's work is not yet completed; the Kingdom has not yet come. John the Baptizer can serve as a role model for the church in its ongoing task of declaring what God is doing and what God desires in the contemporary world. John held before the people of his day a vision of the committed actions that God demanded. He challenged them to respond with repentance and to evidence that repentance in acts of justice and love. Is this not the present-day challenge to the church?

Unfortunately, the church often tends to accommodate itself to the culture around it and to lose its prophetic edge. Especially in churches made up of upper- and middle-class people, the prophetic message of social responsibility is often muted. It is not easy to hear God calling us to do things that we do not want to do. We turn away. We seek other ways of salving our consciences and fulfilling what we perceive to be our religious duties. The challenge to right use of wealth and power is no easier for us than it was for the Hebrew people, for those who heard John, for those who followed John Wesley. Indeed, the challenge is probably more difficult, for our resources are greater than those of these people in the past. But, the divine demand is the same: Exercise justice, seek peace, and give away your possessions to those who are poor.

The committed action that God requires of the church is twofold. It must practice justice and charity within itself. Christian people, individually and communally, must behave as John called his hearers to behave. In our actions we are to model the life of social holiness—repent, give, share, be fair and honest. If the church does not faithfully live out its commitment to love and justice, the world will surely not be impressed by our preaching. Second, the church is to call the world to accountability. In a nation rich beyond the imagination of most inhabitants of the globe, the church must be John the Baptizer. We must challenge and criticize, proclaim the wrongness of conditions, point out the coming of judgment in one form or another, call for repentance, and insist that repentance be expressed in changed actions.

SHARING THE SCRIPTURE

Preparing Our Hearts

Meditate on this week's devotional reading, found in Psalm 51:10-19. In this psalm, traditionally ascribed to David, we hear the king repent of his sin with Bathsheba. David wants a "clean heart," and "a new and right spirit" (51:10). In other words, David repented and committed himself to change. What needs to be confessed, repented of, and changed in your life? Spend time in prayer, asking God to help you root out that which is displeasing so that you may bear good fruit.

Pray that you and the adult learners will be willing to take action on the commitments they make.

Preparing Our Minds

Study the background from Luke 3:1-20 and the lesson Scripture from Luke 3:7-18. As you read, consider actions that may be required to fulfill a commitment.

Write on newsprint:

❑ Scripture passages for "Examine John's Commitment to Call People to Repentance in Preparation for the Coming of the Messiah."

❑ information for next week's lesson, found under "Continue the Journey."

❑ activities for further spiritual growth in "Continue the Journey."

Locate membership vows for your church. You will likely find them in your denominational hymnal.

LEADING THE CLASS

(1) Gather to Learn

❖ Welcome the class members and introduce any guests.

❖ Pray that all who have gathered today will be open to hearing and doing the Word of the Lord.

❖ Read this quotation from Anthony Robbins: **I believe life is constantly testing us for our level of commitment, and life's greatest rewards are reserved for those who demonstrate a never-ending commitment to act until they achieve. This level of resolve can move mountains, but it must be constant and consistent. As simplistic as this may sound, it is still the common denominator separating those who live their dreams from those who live in regret.**

❖ Ask: **Do you agree with Robbins that commitment and action go hand in hand in order to achieve results? Explain your position.**

❖ Read aloud today's focus statement: **Making a commitment requires action to accompany verbal assent. What actions may be required to fulfill a commitment?**

When John took the message to the people about the coming of the Messiah, he challenged them to make a response.

(2) Examine John's Commitment to Call People to Repentance in Preparation for the Coming of the Messiah

❖ Choose one person to read the words of John and another to act as the narrator for Luke 3:7-18. Ask the entire class to read the crowd's words in verse 10.

❖ **Option:** Read Luke 3:7-18 again yourself. This time, ask the learners to show by body language and facial expression how they are responding to John's message. This activity would be most effective if the students could see one another.

❖ Invite the adults to list on newsprint questions they would want to ask John had they been in his audience. Encourage them to answer these questions as they think John might have answered them.

❖ Use information from Understanding the Scripture to help the class delve into this passage, which some may view as difficult to comprehend.

❖ Note that the thrust of John's preaching is repentance. Divide the class into groups to read other passages from Luke on the theme of repentance. (Note that the concept of repentance runs throughout the entire Bible, but we are limiting our study to Luke.) Charge the groups with discerning what they can from their assigned passage concerning Jesus' teachings on repentance. You will want to list these passages on newsprint.

Luke 5:27-32	Luke 10:13-16
Luke 13:1-5	Luke 15:1-7
Luke 15:8-10	Luke 16:19-31
Luke 17:1-4	Luke 24:44-49

❖ Provide time for each group to report on its findings. Encourage the class to draw conclusions about what is meant by "repentance."

❖ Prompt the students to repeat in unison today's key verse, Luke 3:8: "Bear fruits worthy of repentance."

❖ Suggest that the learners turn to Galatians 5:22-23 and read silently the list of the fruit of the Spirit. Note that surely love, joy, peace, patience, kindness, generosity, faithfulness, gentleness, and self-control are also "fruits worthy of repentance."

❖ Challenge each class member to think of at least one tangible action that he or she could take to demonstrate the bearing of "fruits worthy of repentance." Some volunteers may be willing to state the action they plan to take.

(3) Explore the Range of Possible Actions Required by Commitment

❖ Read or retell "Commitment to Social Responsibility" in Interpreting the Scripture.

❖ Consider the actions required by commitments within your own denomination or congregation, based on the questions that follow. List on newsprint answers to these questions. You may want to add similar questions for other vulnerable groups of people.

(1) What commitments have we made to serve the poor?

(2) What commitments have we made to serve the sick?

(3) What are our commitments to children?

❖ Review the lists. Encourage the class to speculate on how Jesus might evaluate these commitments. Think especially about whether or not you are reaching out to enough people in need and whether or not your actions reflect your words.

❖ Challenge the students to consider ways to increase their commitments or take more action on the commitments the church has already made.

(4) Evaluate Actions the Learners Have Taken Because of Their Commitment to God

❖ Read this information. **When people decide to join a congregation, they are** asked to make some kind of commitment. For example, The United Methodist Church asks: "Will you be loyal to The United Methodist Church, and uphold it by your prayers, your presence, your gifts, and your service?" The members of the congregation respond by renewing their covenant. (Substitute or add your own denomination's pledge and response.)

❖ Distribute paper and pencils. Invite the adults individually to list key words of the pledge, such as "prayers," "presence," "gifts," and "service" (or ones from your own denomination). You may need to reread the pledge. Next to each key word, challenge them to write several actions they have taken to be faithful to this commitment.

❖ Do this guided imagery exercise. Suggest that the students may wish to get comfortable in their chairs and clear their minds.

■ Imagine that you are standing before Christ as he asks you to give an account of your life. What sights, sounds, and aromas grab your attention? (pause)

■ Silently read the list you have written. Explore how you feel about your level of faithfulness to the commitment. (pause)

■ Before Christ says anything to you, what will you say to him about how you have fulfilled your commitment? (pause)

■ Listen as he speaks to you about how you have acted on your commitments. (pause)

■ Meditate on any changes you need to make as a result of Christ's words to you. (pause)

(5) Continue the Journey

❖ Pray that each of today's participants will be faithful to the commitments they have made.

❖ Read aloud this preparation for next week's lesson. You may also want to post it on newsprint for the students to copy.

■ Title: Midwives Serve God
■ Background Scripture: Exodus 1:8-21
■ Lesson Scripture: Exodus 1:8-21
■ Focus of the Lesson: There are often competing demands for our commitment. How does one evaluate these competing claims and choose an appropriate course of action? The midwives knew they belonged to God's people and remained faithful to God while denying Pharaoh's edict.

❖ Challenge the students to complete one or more of these activities for further spiritual growth, which you will write on newsprint for the students to copy.

(1) Use a concordance to locate references to "repent" and its related words, such as "repentance." How do these verses speak to you about the need for and privilege of repentance?

(2) Talk with someone who has made a major commitment of time, money, and energy. Perhaps this person is a grandparent now raising grandchildren, or an adult caring for parents or other older family members, or a missionary who is willing to spread the good news even in remote and dangerous places. What can you learn from this person about commitment?

(3) Write at least one New Year's resolution that demonstrates a commitment to act on behalf of Christ.

❖ Sing or read aloud "When Jesus Came to Jordan."

❖ Conclude today's session by leading the class in this benediction, taken from Luke 1:38: **Here am I, the servant of the Lord; let it be with me according to your word.**

UNIT 2: OLD TESTAMENT PEOPLE OF COMMITMENT
MIDWIVES SERVE GOD

PREVIEWING THE LESSON

Lesson Scripture: Exodus 1:8-21
Background Scripture: Exodus 1:8-21
Key Verse: Exodus 1:17

Focus of the Lesson:
There are often competing demands for our commitment. How does one evaluate these competing claims and choose an appropriate course of action? The midwives knew they belonged to God's people and remained faithful to God while denying Pharaoh's edict.

Goals for the Learners:
(1) to tell how the midwives obeyed God rather than Pharaoh.
(2) to consider the competing demands they face in making appropriate commitments.
(3) to order their commitments around their primary loyalty to God and to the community of faith.

Pronunciation Guide:
Pithom (pi' thom)   Ramses (ram' seez)
Puah (pyoo' uh)   Shiphrah (shif' ruh)
Rameses (ram' uh seez)   Thebes (theebz)

Supplies:
Bibles, newsprint and marker, paper and pencils, hymnals

READING THE SCRIPTURE

NRSV
Exodus 1:8-21

⁸Now a new king arose over Egypt, who did not know Joseph. ⁹He said to his people, "Look, the Israelite people are more numerous and more powerful than we. ¹⁰Come, let us deal shrewdly with them, or they will increase and, in the event of war, join our

NIV
Exodus 1:8-21

⁸Then a new king, who did not know about Joseph, came to power in Egypt. ⁹"Look," he said to his people, "the Israelites have become much too numerous for us. ¹⁰Come, we must deal shrewdly with them or they will become even more numerous

enemies and fight against us and escape from the land." [11]Therefore they set taskmasters over them to oppress them with forced labor. They built supply cities, Pithom and Rameses, for Pharaoh. [12]But the more they were oppressed, the more they multiplied and spread, so that the Egyptians came to dread the Israelites. [13]The Egyptians became ruthless in imposing tasks on the Israelites, [14]and made their lives bitter with hard service in mortar and brick and in every kind of field labor. They were ruthless in all the tasks that they imposed on them.

[15]The king of Egypt said to the Hebrew midwives, one of whom was named Shiphrah and the other Puah, [16]"When you act as midwives to the Hebrew women, and see them on the birthstool, if it is a boy, kill him; but if it is a girl, she shall live." [17]**But the midwives feared God; they did not do as the king of Egypt commanded them, but they let the boys live.** [18]So the king of Egypt summoned the midwives and said to them, "Why have you done this, and allowed the boys to live?" [19]The midwives said to Pharaoh, "Because the Hebrew women are not like the Egyptian women; for they are vigorous and give birth before the midwife comes to them." [20]So God dealt well with the midwives; and the people multiplied and became very strong. [21]And because the midwives feared God, he gave them families.

and, if war breaks out, will join our enemies, fight against us and leave the country."

[11]So they put slave masters over them to oppress them with forced labor, and they built Pithom and Rameses as store cities for Pharaoh. [12]But the more they were oppressed, the more they multiplied and spread; so the Egyptians came to dread the Israelites [13]and worked them ruthlessly. [14]They made their lives bitter with hard labor in brick and mortar and with all kinds of work in the fields; in all their hard labor the Egyptians used them ruthlessly.

[15]The king of Egypt said to the Hebrew midwives, whose names were Shiphrah and Puah, [16]"When you help the Hebrew women in childbirth and observe them on the delivery stool, if it is a boy, kill him; but if it is a girl, let her live." [17]**The midwives, however, feared God and did not do what the king of Egypt had told them to do; they let the boys live.** [18]Then the king of Egypt summoned the midwives and asked them, "Why have you done this? Why have you let the boys live?"

[19]The midwives answered Pharaoh, "Hebrew women are not like Egyptian women; they are vigorous and give birth before the midwives arrive."

[20]So God was kind to the midwives and the people increased and became even more numerous. [21]And because the midwives feared God, he gave them families of their own.

UNDERSTANDING THE SCRIPTURE

Exodus 1:8. It is necessary to recall the story of Joseph in order to place this account in context. Joseph was the son of Jacob (also called Israel) and Rachel, the grandson of Isaac and Rebekah, and the great-grandson of Abraham and Sarah. He was the inheritor of the covenant promises that God had made to his ancestors. As a youth, Joseph had so offended his older brothers that they

had sold him into slavery and convinced his father that he was dead. Joseph had been brought to Egypt where, through the use of his God-given powers, he had risen to be Pharaoh's top official. Later, his father and brothers were forced to come to Egypt seeking food during a famine. Joseph astonished them by identifying himself. The family was reconciled and moved to Egypt, where they and their descendants lived and prospered for several centuries, as verse 7 indicates. Verse 8 tells of an abrupt change. Power in Egypt had been shifted from the family of rulers who dealt kindly with the Hebrews to a new dynasty. This was probably when Ramses I, considered by many to be the founder of the nineteenth dynasty, came to the throne. Historians differ greatly as to the exact year. The pharaoh is not named in the biblical text; the term means literally "great house" and was the title of the Egyptian kings. This pharaoh symbolizes opposition to God's plan for salvation through the Hebrew people. Not knowing Joseph meant that he did not know Joseph's God.

Exodus 1:9-10. The new king was frightened by the Hebrew people. Clearly God had blessed them during their time in Egypt, and Pharaoh feared that their large numbers made them a security threat. His words about escape anticipated the exodus that would occur later. He embarked on a national policy to control the Hebrews and diminish the threat. But, Pharaoh's plans for them conflicted with the plans of God.

Exodus 1:11. The Egyptian rulers were great builders, understanding their constructions to be permanent monuments to their power and grandeur. Ramses II (known as the Great) was famed for his building projects. He is also considered by many scholars to be the pharaoh who ruled during the exodus. The city of Rameses included the royal residence in the regions of the Nile Delta. The huge amount of work required to build Rameses and Pithom was done by forced labor gangs. The harsh treatment of the Hebrews would serve two purposes: to provide labor and to curb the danger that Pharaoh feared.

Exodus 1:12-14. Hard labor did not keep the Hebrew people from continuing to grow, and Pharaoh's fear of them increased. His paranoia is reminiscent of the terror of slave revolts in the antebellum South. Oppression affects both the oppressed and the oppressor; oppressors become increasingly cruel and fear-stricken. The rigor of slavery for the Hebrews was experienced in both building work and labor in the agricultural fields. This likely involved constructing irrigation systems for pumping water for crops, since Egypt has little rain. The bitterness of their oppression is commemorated to the present day in the Passover meal by the eating of bitter herbs (see Exodus 12:8).

Exodus 1:15-16. Terrified by the failure of his efforts to weaken the Hebrews, Pharaoh decided to launch a policy of genocide. This effort to exterminate the Jewish people was repeated many times throughout their history and reached its apex in the Holocaust of World War II. The New Testament counterpart of this story is the slaughter of the innocents by King Herod—the killing of male children in the area of and around Bethlehem after the birth of Jesus (Matthew 2:16-18).

As has been customary practice in most cultures, midwives assisted at the birth of children. The term translated "birthing stool" is literally "two stones" and doubtless came from the original place where women sat while giving birth. The midwives were probably Hebrews themselves; their names are Semitic rather than Egyptian.

In *Moses, Man of the Mountain*, Zora Neale Hurston comments on the king's appalling order and the fear that it must have engendered: "The birthing beds of Hebrews were matters of state. The Hebrew womb had fallen under the heel of Pharaoh." Hebrew women must have shuddered with terror at the indifference of their wombs to the Egyptian law.

Exodus 1:17-19. Heroically, the midwives became part of the resistance to the oppressor's power. At great danger to their own lives, they did not obey Pharaoh; their commitment was to God. We are reminded of the words of Peter and the other apostles in Acts 5:29: "We must obey God rather than any human authority." They claimed that the strength of Hebrew women enabled them to bear children with ease so that the births had already taken place before the midwives arrived, and they had no opportunity to kill the male babies. Too often we fail to recognize and appreciate the humor found in biblical stories. We need to picture these tales being told by fathers to sons around the campfires and by mothers to daughters around the grinding stones. This account is one that the Hebrew people would savor for centuries and retell with glee. Humorously, to the Hebrew hearers and readers of the story, the midwives make an unflattering comparison to Egyptian women. The king is amusingly naive and easily fooled—a figure of ridicule.

Exodus 1:20-21. God rewarded the midwives for their courage by making them mothers. God's plan was protected by their action, and the Hebrews continued to grow stronger and more numerous.

INTERPRETING THE SCRIPTURE

Subversion to Maintain Ultimate Loyalty

As Christians we must begin any thinking about loyalty by insisting that there is only one ultimate loyalty, and that is to God. The midwives in Exodus 1 are an excellent example. The Scripture tells us plainly that they "feared God" (1:17). To fear God in biblical language did not mean that they were scared of God and acted out of terror about what God might do to them. To fear God meant that they honored and revered God, that they were obedient to the divine commands. Obviously Pharaoh's order conflicted with God's will; they could not obey both. What were the midwives to do?

They solved their dilemma by using a tactic that we find often in the Bible but that usually makes us uncomfortable. The midwives decided to use subversion—to work secretly to undermine authority. To do this they had to lie. There is an old ethical dilemma that is sometimes posed for discussion: Suppose you were in a war zone and your home was invaded by enemies bent on revenge. They ask you if there is anyone else in the house. There are several children hidden up in the loft. Do you tell the truth or do you lie? Lying is not an action that we generally commend to God's people. We stress the importance of honesty.

We expect it of ourselves; we teach it to our children.

How then should we deal with the midwives' dishonesty, of which God obviously approved? I would argue that the tests of the moral quality of an action are motivation and results. In his play *Murder in the Cathedral*, T. S. Eliot writes, "the greatest treason: to do the right deed for the wrong reason." The midwives did what might be considered the wrong thing, but they did it for the right reason. The results of their action were to protect God's people and advance God's plan for salvation. They used subversion, even untruthfulness, to maintain their ultimate loyalty. Are there occasions in our lives when such action might be necessary? Is there danger here of believing that the ends always justify the means? I repeat my contention that it is both motivation and results that determine the moral quality of actions. Maintaining our ultimate loyalty to God is not always simple or easy.

Deceiving Women Who Served God

The midwives are not the only Old Testament women who found it necessary to use questionable methods in order to serve God. Commitment may require unusual, even disreputable, acts. In Genesis 27 we find the account of Rebekah instructing and helping her son Jacob fool his blind father. Her husband, Isaac, intended to give the blessing of the firstborn son to Esau who, having been born before Jacob, was the older of the twins. Rebekah initiated the deception. She had Jacob bring animals for her to cook Isaac's favorite food; she dressed Jacob in Esau's clothes; she covered his arms and neck with animal skins to make him feel hairy like his brother. Her plot succeeded. Jacob received the coveted blessing from his father and Esau was cheated out of it. Later, when she learned that Esau was planning to kill his brother, she contrived to send him away to her brother Laban's home. What a conniving, deceitful woman! Fooling her poor, blind husband and cheating her older son! But, there is no word of condemnation or even criticism of Rebekah in the story. There is no indication that God disapproved of her scheming. Indeed, it is quite the opposite, for it is through Jacob and his sons that the covenant promises of God are reaffirmed and that the Israelite nation will rise.

The results of Rebekah's deceit were to advance God's plan. What about her motivation? In an earlier chapter (Genesis 25:19-26) we read that when she was pregnant with her twin sons, Rebekah had become concerned because they seemed to be fighting in her womb, and she went to a holy place to ask God what was to happen. God had told her that her sons were to be the fathers of two different nations and that "the elder shall serve the younger." From this experience, Rebekah knew that Jacob was the child of the promise, the inheritor of the covenant relationship with God. Her elaborate deception of her husband and older son were motivated by her commitment to God and loyalty to God's plan.

Some years later, Rebekah's daughter-in-law Rachel was involved in a similar deception as a result of trying to maintain her ultimate loyalty. Jacob and all his wives,

children, flocks, and herds were leaving the home of his uncle Laban (where his mother had sent him). There was ill-feeling and mutual suspicion between Jacob and Laban, so Jacob and his caravan left while Laban was away. Laban was angry, chased them, and caught up with them. He was especially concerned about the theft of his household gods—images or idols. Jacob knew nothing about the gods and invited Laban to search the tents. When Laban entered his daughter Rachel's tent, she apologized for being unable to rise to honor him, as "the way of women is upon me" (31:35). Unable to find the gods Laban eventually gave up and returned home. As readers or hearers of the story, we are told clearly that Rachel had taken the gods, hidden them in a saddle, and was sitting on them when her father came to search. Was the favorite wife of Jacob a worshiper of false gods? Was she a common thief? No. Rachel knew that by the customs of the culture, possession of the household gods meant legal claim on property and leadership in the family. She was protecting the prerogatives of her husband, Jacob, and her son Joseph—the inheritors of God's covenant promise. Her deceitful actions contributed to God's ongoing plan of salvation. Again, maintaining ultimate loyalty required unexpected and compromising action.

Service Is Working With God

When we examine the subversive actions of the faithful midwives, as well as those of Rebekah and Rachel, we realize that the most significant thing about what they did was that they cooperated with God. This is always the work to which God's people are to be committed. The purpose of God's relationship with the Hebrew people was that God might work through the events of their history to bring salvation to the entire world. The purpose of the Christian church is to cooperate with God in the ongoing work of redeeming the world—continuing the work of Christ and bringing it to fulfillment.

Such a task will often bring us into conflict between the loyalty and obedience that we owe to other people and institutions and that which we owe to God. Life is complicated that way! Sometimes we can please others, please God, and even please ourselves. We may struggle to rank the various commitments that we have made and strive to fulfill them all. But often, we find that we have to choose. For Christians, as for the Hebrew midwives, there is always one ultimate loyalty. We may expose ourselves to loss of reputation, resources, even life. We may have to disobey some legitimate authorities and disappoint some who love us. But, we must remain faithful to our commitment to God. We serve God and others by cooperating with God in the work of the divine plan for salvation.

SHARING THE SCRIPTURE

Preparing Our Hearts

Meditate on this week's devotional reading, found in Proverbs 16:1-7. "Commit your work to the LORD," verse 3 begins. As we look this week at midwives in Egypt who were forced to make a commitment to either Pharaoh or God, we consider the challenges of making choices when commitments conflict with one another. What commitments are you struggling with right now? Are you making commitments based on what God wills for you, or that which you perceive to be best? Turn these choices over to God in prayer.

Pray that you and the adult learners will be ready to weigh your commitments in light of God's plan for your life and the lives of those you touch.

Preparing Our Minds

Study the background and lesson Scripture, both taken from Exodus 1:8-21. As you prepare, consider how you evaluate competing demands for your commitment and then choose the appropriate course of action.

Write on newsprint:
❑ steps for "Gather to Learn."
❑ information for next week's lesson, found under "Continue the Journey."
❑ activities for further spiritual growth in "Continue the Journey."

LEADING THE CLASS

(1) Gather to Learn

❖ Welcome the class members and introduce any guests.

❖ Pray that today's participants will not only listen for God's voice but also obey.

❖ Distribute paper and pencils. Invite the students to follow these steps, which you will have noted on newsprint:

◼ **Step 1:** List your commitments to family, friends, work, church, and self.

◼ **Step 2:** Prioritize each of these commitments in order of importance to you by placing a 1 to the left of the most important, 2 to the left of the second-most important, and so on.

◼ **Step 3:** Review your list. Think about how you actually spend your time and money. Do your actions match the priorities you have given to each commitment?

❖ Encourage volunteers to comment on any insights they have gleaned. Ask them to set these papers aside for use later in the session.

❖ Read aloud today's focus statement: **There are often competing demands for our commitment. How does one evaluate these competing claims and choose an appropriate course of action? The midwives knew they belonged to God's people and remained faithful to God while denying Pharaoh's edict.**

(2) Tell How the Midwives Obeyed God Rather Than Pharaoh

❖ Use information from Exodus 1:8 in Understanding the Scripture to set the stage for today's reading.

❖ Select three volunteers—one to read the king's words, one to read the midwives' words, and one to serve as the narrator. Ask the students to read Exodus 1:8-21 as dramatically as they can.

❖ Discuss these questions with the class.
   (1) **What problem(s) did the Egyptian king perceive?**
   (2) **How did he hope to resolve the situation?**
   (3) **How would you describe the dilemma that the midwives faced?** (Use any or all of "Subversion to Maintain Ultimate Loyalty" from Interpreting the Scripture to augment the discussion.)

❖ Select two people to role-play the following situation, which you will need to read aloud. If the class is large, you may wish to divide into groups and have several role-plays going on simultaneously.

You are discussing the story from Exodus 1 with a friend. He or she can understand why the midwives took the actions they did, but your friend is very upset by the deception and outright lies they told the king in order to avoid following his orders. How would you explain Shiphrah and Puah's actions? Do you believe that they served God, even though on first glance they appear to be deceptive schemers? Try to build a case in their defense.

❖ **Option:** Read aloud "Deceiving Women Who Served God" from Interpreting the Scripture.

❖ Wrap up this portion of the lesson by encouraging the students to comment on the risks and rewards of honoring one's commitments.

(3) Consider the Competing Demands the Learners Face in Making Appropriate Commitments

❖ Read aloud these questions, pausing to allow the adults time to think silently about their answers.
   (1) **Who sets my priorities? Do I get to do that, or does my family, work, church, or other group to which I belong determine how I focus my attention and use my gifts?**
   (2) **If I could rearrange any of my priorities, what would they look like?**
   (3) **Why is this new order preferable to my current priorities?**
   (4) **Who would be upset if I changed my priorities? Why? What could I do to help them accept the new order?**

❖ Divide the students into groups of three or four. Ask them to talk about the challenges they face in setting priorities and making choices among the commitments they have made or that seem to be made for them. Suggest that they share strategies or criteria that have helped them make appropriate choices.

❖ Bring the class together. Invite them to report on their small group discussions, particularly noting any strategies they have found useful in dealing with competing priorities.

(4) Order Commitments Around the Learners' Primary Loyalty to God and to the Community of Faith

❖ Brainstorm with the class answers to this question: **What are the characteristics** of a commitment made to God? List responses on newsprint. Answers may include: *renewable daily as we take up our cross, wholehearted, according to God's will, of positive value for the community of faith, made in love, demonstrates love and concern for neighbor.*

❖ Ask the students to look one more time at the list of commitments they made at the beginning of the session. Suggest that they try to discern which of these commitments demonstrates their loyalty to God.

❖ Note that some commitments are made to the church. Discuss the following questions:

(1) **Many churches have difficulty recruiting volunteers to take care of the work and ministry of the church. Is this a problem for us? Why?** (Consider such stumbling blocks as meetings that are too long, hastily called, or lacking a clear agenda. Also consider whether or not anything actually happens in the church that people feel passionately about.)

(2) **If so, what changes can we make to help people feel more welcome and able to participate?**

❖ Conclude with these questions for silent reflection: **Am I doing what God calls me to do on behalf of my congregation? If not, why not? What do I need to do to live out my commitment to God through the church more faithfully?**

(5) Continue the Journey

❖ Break the silence by praying that all who have participated today will go forth ready and willing to put their commitment to God above all else.

❖ Read aloud this preparation for next week's lesson. You may also want to post it on newsprint for the students to copy.

■ Title: Rahab Helps Israel
■ Background Scripture: Joshua 2; 6:22-25
■ Lesson Scripture: Joshua 2:1-4, 12-14; 6:22-25
■ Focus of the Lesson: Commitments may create conflicting priorities, require risks, and exact a cost. How does one balance the value of the different sides of a commitment? Rahab willingly faced great personal danger in order to save her family.

❖ Challenge the students to complete one or more of these activities for further spiritual growth, which you will write on newsprint for the students to copy.

(1) **Review the list of commitments created during the session. Honor these commitments in order of their priority to you. Note any change as compared to how you normally spend your time and energy.**

(2) **Think about the commitments your congregation has made to missionaries, outreach work, your local community. Cite specific examples of how the church is honoring these commitments. Which ones need more attention? What action will you take?**

(3) **Spend time in prayer and meditation, asking God to help you prioritize your commitments so that your actions will be in keeping with God's will for your life.**

❖ Sing or read aloud "Go Forth for God."

❖ Conclude today's session by leading the class in this benediction, taken from Luke 1:38: **Here am I, the servant of the Lord; let it be with me according to your word.**

UNIT 2: OLD TESTAMENT PEOPLE OF COMMITMENT
RAHAB HELPS ISRAEL

PREVIEWING THE LESSON

Lesson Scripture: Joshua 2:1-4, 12-14; 6:22-25
Background Scripture: Joshua 2; 6:22-25
Key Verses: Joshua 2:11-12

Focus of the Lesson:
Commitments may create conflicting priorities, require risks, and exact a cost. How does one balance the value of the different sides of a commitment? Rahab willingly faced great personal danger in order to save her family.

Goals for the Learners:
(1) to explore Rahab's commitment to saving her family.
(2) to consider the possible risks and costs of making a commitment.
(3) to weigh thoughtfully the demands of their own commitments and to make appropriate changes.

Pronunciation Guide:
Achan (ay' kan)   Rahab (ray' hab)
Ai (i)   Shittim (shi' tim)

Supplies:
Bibles, newsprint and marker, paper and pencils, hymnals, picture of Rahab

READING THE SCRIPTURE

NRSV
Joshua 2:1-4, 11-14

¹Then Joshua son of Nun sent two men secretly from Shittim as spies, saying, "Go, view the land, especially Jericho." So they went, and entered the house of a prostitute whose name was Rahab, and spent the night there. ²The king of Jericho was told, "Some Israelites have come here tonight to search

NIV
Joshua 2:1-4, 11-14

¹Then Joshua son of Nun secretly sent two spies from Shittim. "Go, look over the land," he said, "especially Jericho." So they went and entered the house of a prostitute named Rahab and stayed there.

²The king of Jericho was told, "Look! Some of the Israelites have come here

out the land." [3]Then the king of Jericho sent orders to Rahab, "Bring out the men who have come to you, who entered your house, for they have come only to search out the whole land." [4]But the woman took the two men and hid them. Then she said, "True, the men came to me, but I did not know where they came from.

[11] . . . **The LORD your God is indeed God in heaven above and on earth below. [12]Now then, since I have dealt kindly with you, swear to me by the LORD that you in turn will deal kindly with my family.** Give me a sign of good faith [13]that you will spare my father and mother, my brother and sisters, and all who belong to them, and deliver our lives from death." [14]The men said to her, "Our life for yours! If you do not tell this business of ours, then we will deal kindly and faithfully with you when the LORD gives us the land."

Joshua 6:22-25

[22]Joshua said to the two men who had spied out the land, "Go into the prostitute's house, and bring the woman out of it and all who belong to her, as you swore to her." [23]So the young men who had been spies went in and brought Rahab out, along with her father, her mother, her brothers, and all who belonged to her—they brought all her kindred out—and set them outside the camp of Israel. [24]They burned down the city, and everything in it; only the silver and gold, and the vessels of bronze and iron, they put into the treasury of the house of the LORD. [25]But Rahab the prostitute, with her family and all who belonged to her, Joshua spared. Her family has lived in Israel ever since. For she hid the messengers whom Joshua sent to spy out Jericho.

tonight to spy out the land." [3]So the king of Jericho sent this message to Rahab: "Bring out the men who came to you and entered your house, because they have come to spy out the whole land."

[4]But the woman had taken the two men and hidden them. She said, "Yes, the men came to me, but I did not know where they had come from.

[11] . . . **the LORD your God is God in heaven above and on the earth below. [12]Now then, please swear to me by the LORD that you will show kindness to my family, because I have shown kindness to you.** Give me a sure sign [13]that you will spare the lives of my father and mother, my brothers and sisters, and all who belong to them, and that you will save us from death."

[14]"Our lives for your lives!" the men assured her. "If you don't tell what we are doing, we will treat you kindly and faithfully when the LORD gives us the land."

Joshua 6:22-25

[22]Joshua said to the two men who had spied out the land, "Go into the prostitute's house and bring her out and all who belong to her, in accordance with your oath to her." [23]So the young men who had done the spying went in and brought out Rahab, her father and mother and brothers and all who belonged to her. They brought out her entire family and put them in a place outside the camp of Israel.

[24]Then they burned the whole city and everything in it, but they put the silver and gold and the articles of bronze and iron into the treasury of the LORD's house. [25]But Joshua spared Rahab the prostitute, with her family and all who belonged to her, because she hid the men Joshua had sent as spies to Jericho—and she lives among the Israelites to this day.

UNDERSTANDING THE SCRIPTURE

Joshua 2:1. The story of Rahab is one of the rich tales that culminate in the conquest

of Jericho in Chapter 6. The Israelites were encamped around Shittim, east of the

Jordan River, facing the river and the city of Jericho beyond it. Jericho was in Judea, about twenty-three miles east of Jerusalem. It was located only five miles west of the Jordan River. Jericho was a strongly fortified city with protective walls and abundant water supply. Joshua had become the Israelite leader after the death of Moses. He sent spies to gather information about Jericho that he might use in planning the attack on the city.

The text clearly identifies Rahab as a prostitute, although there was some attempt in later Jewish and Christian tradition to obscure this. The first-century Jewish historian Josephus wrote of her as an innkeeper, and other writers followed his suggestion. Obviously these later writers were uncomfortable with such a heroic role having been played by a prostitute. The Israelite spies spent the night in Rahab's brothel, and the Hebrew text suggests that they may have been her customers.

Joshua 2:2-3. Jericho, like each of the major Canaanite cities, was a small kingdom ruled by its own sovereign. The city was well guarded by authorities who closely observed any strangers who showed up. The king's security forces easily identified the Israelites as spies, and the king commanded Rahab to surrender them.

Joshua 2:4-5. Rahab hid the spies and deceived the king's men by telling them that the spies—whose identity she denied knowing—had left her house at dusk, in order to escape the city before the gates were closed. In a trick familiar to us from old Western movies, she urged the king's men to hurry out of the city themselves before the gates closed for the night so as to chase and catch the spies. It is not clear whether the Israelite spies had told Rahab who they were or whether she realized this when the king's agents came seeking them. Either way, she obviously decided to side with them.

Joshua 2:6-7. Flat rooftops are still used in Palestine for the drying of stalks and grain. Flax was harvested and laid out to dry just before the barley harvest, which marked the time of Passover. The king's men chased the spies unsuccessfully as far as the shallow crossing points of the Jordan River. They would not have been able to reenter Jericho until the gates were opened in the morning.

Joshua 2:8-9. In conversation with the Israelite spies, Rahab told them that she knew God was giving the land to them. She provided the valuable information that the people of the city were terrified of the Israelites' approach.

Joshua 2:10-11. The cause of that fear was news that had reached Jericho about what God was doing for the Israelites. These tales included accounts of the miraculous crossing of the sea when the Israelites left Egypt and their destruction of two powerful Canaanite cities (as related in Numbers 21). Rahab understood the nature and power of God and, so, had switched her loyalty from her city to the people of God.

Joshua 2:12-14. Rahab asked the spies to reward her protection of them by sparing her and her family when the Israelites won their inevitable victory over Jericho. Interestingly, she asked them to swear to her "by the LORD"—on the covenant faithfulness that God showed to God's people.

Joshua 2:15-16. Rahab's home was apparently built between the two parallel walls that surrounded the city. This location enabled her to help the spies escape when the gates were closed. The location may also be a symbol of the prostitute's marginal place in the society of her city. She instructed the men to hide in the opposite direction from their pursuers until it was safe to return to their camp.

Joshua 2:17-21. The spies stressed the conditions that Rahab and her extended family must meet if they were to be safe when the attack came. A crimson cord was to be tied in the window of the house; all family members were to stay inside; Rahab was not to betray them. Rahab agreed to these conditions and tied the cord in her window. The details about the red cord are not entirely clear to us. Perhaps the legitimate business by which Rahab supported her family was weaving, so strands of threads were lying about the house. The color of the cord may be a reminder of the blood of the Passover lambs with which the Hebrews/Israelites marked the doors of their houses in Egypt. Early Christian writers interpreted the crimson cord as a symbol of the atoning death of Christ.

Joshua 2:22-24. Following Rahab's advice, the spies went westward into the central mountain ridge of Palestine where the high hills had many caves that made excellent hiding places. When it was safe, they returned east to the Israelite camp across the river and reported to their leader, Joshua, the good news that the people of Jericho were terrified of them. They under-stood this as a compelling sign that God was guaranteeing their victory.

Joshua 6:22-25. In Chapters 3–5 we read about the various preparations that the Israelites made for war. Also in Chapter 3, as we shall study next week, the crossing of the Jordan River is recounted. As told in Chapter 5, they celebrated their first Passover in Canaan—the land that God had promised them. From that time on, God ceased to provide them with manna. Instead, they ate the produce of the land.

When the walls of Jericho fell, Joshua sent the two spies to rescue Rahab and her family and take them to safety in the Israelite camp. They dwelled among the Israelites from that time forward. The city was burned after its valuable metal vessels were looted for the Lord's treasury.

INTERPRETING THE SCRIPTURE

Dangerous Commitments

Few of us will ever be in positions as dangerous as Rahab's. She had to trust the faithfulness of men who were to her enemy spies. She had to take an enormous risk. Most commitments carry with them a certain amount of risk. If we commit to something or someone, we turn away from other alternatives. Some people even find themselves paralyzed by this dilemma—unable to choose, fearful of risks, afraid to surrender other possibilities. Sometimes we can hardly bear to think what we are risking, what we might lose.

Rahab is an example of decisiveness, of willingness to give up much in order to gain the lives of her family and herself. Her commitment was a very dangerous one, for if the king's men realized that she had deceived them, they would surely return for revenge. In the heat of the battle, the Israelite spies might forget her, or come too late to rescue her and her family. The crimson cord might not be visible amid the fallen walls of the city, and the Israelites would be unable to locate her. So many dire possibilities, so much risk, such intense danger.

She was able to do what she did only because she believed that God was giving Jericho to the Israelites. She quite literally bet her life. That is, of course, the key. We are not usually able to see the outcomes with certainty; risk in commitment is inescapable. This is a major reason why so many people today have great difficulty in making commitments. They want assurance, guarantees of what is going to happen. But in reality such guarantees usually do not exist. We simply cannot know the end of the journey when we take its first steps. We can make right, but dangerous and courageous, commitments only when we trust the God who directs us and promises to care for us. No other motive will sustain us.

Saved From the Ban

The story of Rahab is set in the context of several commitments, some honored, some betrayed, some admirable, some horrific. The people who wrote the accounts of Joshua's conquest of the land of Canaan believed that God desired the total annihilation of the Canaanites. The Canaanites represented the forces of evil, of opposition to God's will. They were a source of temptation of God's people to unfaithfulness. For these reasons, the people of Israel believed that "The city [Jericho] and all that is in it shall be devoted to the LORD for destruction" (Joshua 6:17).

In Chapter 7, a man named Achan has stolen some of the loot from Jericho, and suffering comes upon the whole people because of it. He had violated the commitment that, while abhorrent to us, was believed to be the divine will. When the deed was discovered, Achan, along with his family and all his possessions, were stoned and burned at Joshua's order. Joshua's commitment to obeying what he believed God demanded was total. After rooting out this evil, the Israelites again attacked the city of Ai, where they had been previously defeated. This time they were victorious and "Joshua did not draw back his hand, with which he stretched out the sword, until he had utterly destroyed all the inhabitants of Ai" (Joshua 8:26).

The ban—this commitment of Israel to destroy totally their enemies in obedience to God's command—seems to us misguided, even repulsive. We believe that they misunderstood the nature and will of God, for we know that the God revealed to us in Jesus Christ would not desire such action. Still, we can respect the depth and passion of the commitment and the fervor with which Israel sought to be faithful to it.

The account of the sparing of Rahab and her family was told as an instance when the ban was mitigated, when an exception was allowed. Perhaps it was used by the writer to suggest that the ban may have been morally questionable and that good results would come from practicing different commitments. There is a Jewish legend that says that Joshua and Rahab were married after her family joined the Israelites. Certainly this would indicate God's blessings. Joshua was blessed for his mitigating of the ban; Rahab was blessed for her risky faith in the God of Israel.

The early Christian church interpreted the Rahab story as a story of God's grace and redemption. All the Canaanites were under the divine order of destruction, destruction they deserved because of their evil ways. Yet, God made salvation available to this woman and her family because of her actions and faith. Similarly, as Paul presents the account of salvation, all human beings deserve destruction due to their sinfulness. Yet, in Jesus Christ, God makes salvation available for those who will accept it in faith as expressed in their living.

A Hero of Faith and Works

Rahab is respected and praised by New Testament writers more than one might expect in view of the relatively minor role she plays in the Old Testament. In the genealogy of Jesus in Matthew, she is identified as the mother of Boaz, whose father is said to be Salmon. According to the Book of Ruth, Boaz and Ruth were the parents of Obed who was the father of Jesse, David's father. This would mean that Rahab was the great-great-grandmother of King David. The purpose of Matthew's entire genealogy is to establish Jesus in the lineage of David. Rahab is one of the four women Matthew listed by name in Jesus' genealogy, all of whom had unorthodox sexual histories.

In Hebrews 11:31, Rahab is the only woman named in the parade of the heroes of faith: "By faith Rahab the prostitute did not perish with those who were disobedient, because she had received the spies in peace." Here it is her obedience which is the evidence of faith. Rahab is also cited in James 2:25: "Likewise, was not Rahab the prostitute also justified by works when she welcomed the messengers and sent them out by another road?" James is usually considered to be the epistle that emphasizes works whereas Hebrews belongs to the Pauline and deutero-Pauline letters that stress the importance of faith. In these texts, Rahab exemplifies the best of both. It was her faith in the God of Israel that motivated her to make the radical commitment to the spies and, therefore, to enabling the Israelites to win victory over her own city. It was her actions of hiding and guiding the spies that made it possible for them to return to their camp with the news that empowered Israel to believe in its coming victory. Commitments are made by faith and kept by faithful living.

SHARING THE SCRIPTURE

Preparing Our Hearts

Meditate on this week's devotional reading, found in Hebrews 11:23-31. In this chapter of Hebrews, examples of faithful people are lifted up. In the verses for today, Moses, his parents, the Israelites who crossed the Red Sea, and Rahab, whose story we encounter this week, are all touted as heroes of the faith. Who has been an example of faith to you? How are you an example of faith to others? Look for opportunities this week to act on the faith you profess.

Pray that you and the adult learners will make a commitment to act in faith for God, despite the risks.

Preparing Our Minds

Study the background from Joshua 2 and Joshua 6:22-25. The lesson Scripture focuses on Joshua 2:1-4, 12-14 and Joshua 6:22-25. As you prepare, think about how one balances the value of a commitment, especially when there are conflicting priorities, risks, and costs involved.

Write on newsprint:
❏ information for next week's lesson, found under "Continue the Journey."
❏ activities for further spiritual growth in "Continue the Journey."

Locate at least one picture of Rahab, either in a book or on the Internet. Many artists have illustrated scenes from Joshua 2. One helpful place to check is http://www.biblical-art.com/biblicalsubject.asp?id_biblicalsubject=122&pagenum=1.

LEADING THE CLASS

(1) Gather to Learn

❖ Welcome the class members and introduce any guests.

❖ Pray that those in attendance will allow the Holy Spirit to lead them into unfamiliar territory as God calls them.

❖ Read aloud this information, based on an article by Janice Price for *Seattle Volunteer* (1996). **KCSARA (pronounced "Kay-SARA") is the umbrella group of 14 volunteer organizations in King County, Washington, all of which are dedicated to search and rescue missions. Ron Ryals of the Sheriff's Department, who coordinates with KCSARA, praises the volunteers: "They are ready to go under the worst of conditions, and they don't give up." These specially trained volunteers, who buy their own equipment and pay their own expenses, may be called upon to search for someone who is lost in an urban area, locate a mountain climber, assist a skier** caught in an avalanche or other dangerous situation, rescue hikers lost in the wilderness, or find downed aircraft. The volunteers who commit themselves to this work come from all walks of life. Some team members are four-footed: dogs trained in search and rescue and horses who take riders into difficult terrain. Those who do this work put themselves in risky, uncomfortable situations in order to assist someone they do not know.

❖ Invite the adults to speculate on why people make such risky commitments. (The article notes that when asked why they volunteer for such difficult assignments, most people respond that they "want to give something back to [their] community.")

❖ Read aloud today's focus statement: **Commitments may create conflicting priorities, require risks, and exact a cost. How does one balance the value of the different sides of a commitment? Rahab willingly faced great personal danger in order to save her family.**

(2) Explore Rahab's Commitment to Saving Her Family

❖ Select a volunteer to read Joshua 2:1-4, 12-14 and another person to read Joshua 6:22-25.

❖ **Option:** Read Joshua 2 in its entirety yourself, if time permits, along with Joshua 6:22-25, so that the adults will hear the whole story.

❖ Show the picture(s) of Rahab you have located. Discuss questions such as these with the students:

(1) **What do Rahab's facial expressions and body language suggest about how she is feeling and what she is thinking?**

(2) **How do the colors (or lack thereof) heighten her emotions and add tension to the scene?**

(3) **If Rahab is speaking to other characters in the picture, what do**

you suppose they are saying to one another?

(4) **What words would you use to describe Rahab's personality, based on this art?**

❖ Read or retell "A Hero of Faith and Works" in Interpreting the Scripture to see how Rahab is perceived in the New Testament.

❖ Conclude this portion of the lesson by asking: **Why do you think that Rahab, who makes such a brief appearance in the Old Testament, is remembered in a positive light in the New Testament?**

(3) Consider the Possible Risks and Costs of Making a Commitment

❖ Discuss this question with the class: **In what situations have people taken risks to make a commitment?** (Students may have personal stories to tell. They may also give well-known examples, such as the Righteous Gentiles who aided Jews during the Holocaust; English interpreters who assisted American and British military during the war in Iraq; passengers on Flight 93 on September 11 who acted bravely against terrorists; rescue personnel who raced into the twin towers on September 11; soldiers risking their lives to save a fallen comrade.)

❖ Post a sheet of newsprint that you have divided into two columns, one side headed "Risks," the other side headed "Rewards." Invite the students to call out possible risks and rewards associated with making a commitment.

❖ Give the students paper and pencils. Pose this question for silent reflection: **When you see a situation that needs intervention, what criteria do you use to determine whether the possible rewards (or potential positive outcomes) outweigh the possible risks?** (Note that sometimes we act without weighing the pros or cons. We see a burning car, and we race to rescue occupants. At other times, however, the situation is serious but not urgent, and we can apply our criteria.)

❖ Invite the students to speak with a partner or small group about the criteria they use.

❖ Ask the groups to report back. List ideas on newsprint. Discern commonalities among the answers. Suggest that the adults be mindful of these ideas as they determine whether or not a particular risk is worth the taking.

(4) Weigh Thoughtfully the Demands of the Learners' Commitments and Make Appropriate Changes

❖ Recognize, as we discussed last week, that we all have many commitments to family, friends, work, church, and other groups. Sometimes these commitments are in conflict and we have to make choices.

❖ Suggest that the students fill in this sentence, using the back of the paper distributed for a prior activity: **I would like to make a commitment to _____ (name something you would like to do), but it would mean that I would have to _____ (identify a change that would need to be made).**

❖ Provide quiet time for the students to pray about this choice.

❖ End this activity by asking volunteers to comment on any changes they feel that God is calling them to make. Some adults may be willing to say that they need to make a change but may not choose to say what that change is. Respect that need for privacy.

(5) Continue the Journey

❖ Pray that those who have participated in today's class will be willing to take risks that God calls them to take.

❖ Read aloud this preparation for next week's lesson. You may also want to post it on newsprint for the students to copy.

■ **Title: Joshua Leads Israel**
■ **Background Scripture: Joshua 3**
■ **Lesson Scripture: Joshua 3:1-13**
■ **Focus of the Lesson: Sometimes people make commitments without assurance that resources to fulfill them are available. From where do the resources come for fulfilling commitments? Joshua committed himself to becoming a leader of the Israelites and received power from God to meet this commitment.**

❖ Challenge the students to complete one or more of these activities for further spiritual growth, which you will write on newsprint for the students to copy.

(1) **Be alert for news reports concerning someone who took a risk to do a good work. Think about how you might have responded in a similar situation.**

(2) **Research Harriet Tubman (1820–1913), who, at great peril, helped slaves escape through the Underground Railroad. Having escaped slavery herself, she risked her life and freedom to rescue seventy other slaves.**

(3) **Think about your own willingness to take risks in order to bring about good. (We are not talking here about thrill-seeking.) How would you rate yourself as a risk-taker? Pray that you will have faith to take risks to do what God calls you to do.**

❖ Sing or read aloud "God of Love and God of Power."

❖ Conclude today's session by leading the class in this benediction, taken from Luke 1:38: **Here am I, the servant of the Lord; let it be with me according to your word.**

UNIT 2: OLD TESTAMENT PEOPLE OF COMMITMENT
JOSHUA LEADS ISRAEL

PREVIEWING THE LESSON

Lesson Scripture: Joshua 3:1-13
Background Scripture: Joshua 3
Key Verse: Joshua 3:7

Focus of the Lesson:
Sometimes people make commitments without assurance that resources to fulfill them are available. From where do the resources come for fulfilling commitments? Joshua committed himself to becoming a leader of the Israelites and received power from God to meet this commitment.

Goals for the Learners:
(1) to examine Joshua's commitment to God.
(2) to explore issues of their own responsibility and resources for making and keeping commitments.
(3) to better use their resources for making and fulfilling their commitments.

Pronunciation Guide:
Amorite (am' uh rite)   Jebusite (jeb' yoo site)
Canaanite (kay' nuh nite)   levitical (li vit' i kuhl)
Girgashite (guhr' guh shite)   Moab (moh' ab)
Hittite (hit' tite)   Perizzite (per' uh zite)
Hivite (hiv' ite)   Shittim (shi' tim)

Supplies:
Bibles, newsprint and marker, paper and pencils, hymnals

READING THE SCRIPTURE

NRSV
Joshua 3:1-13

¹Early in the morning Joshua rose and set out from Shittim with all the Israelites, and they came to the Jordan. They camped there before crossing over. ²At the end of three

NIV
Joshua 3:1-13

¹Early in the morning Joshua and all the Israelites set out from Shittim and went to the Jordan, where they camped before crossing over. ²After three days the officers went

days the officers went through the camp [3]and commanded the people, "When you see the ark of the covenant of the LORD your God being carried by the levitical priests, then you shall set out from your place. Follow it, [4]so that you may know the way you should go, for you have not passed this way before. Yet there shall be a space between you and it, a distance of about two thousand cubits; do not come any nearer to it." [5]Then Joshua said to the people, "Sanctify yourselves; for tomorrow the LORD will do wonders among you." [6]To the priests Joshua said, "Take up the ark of the covenant, and pass on in front of the people." So they took up the ark of the covenant and went in front of the people. **[7]The LORD said to Joshua, "This day I will begin to exalt you in the sight of all Israel, so that they may know that I will be with you as I was with Moses.** [8]You are the one who shall command the priests who bear the ark of the covenant, 'When you come to the edge of the waters of the Jordan, you shall stand still in the Jordan.'" [9]Joshua then said to the Israelites, "Draw near and hear the words of the LORD your God." [10]Joshua said, "By this you shall know that among you is the living God who without fail will drive out from before you the Canaanites, Hittites, Hivites, Perizzites, Girgashites, Amorites, and Jebusites: [11]the ark of the covenant of the Lord of all the earth is going to pass before you into the Jordan. [12]So now select twelve men from the tribes of Israel, one from each tribe. [13]When the soles of the feet of the priests who bear the ark of the LORD, the Lord of all the earth, rest in the waters of the Jordan, the waters of the Jordan flowing from above shall be cut off; they shall stand in a single heap."

throughout the camp, [3]giving orders to the people: "When you see the ark of the covenant of the LORD your God, and the priests, who are Levites, carrying it, you are to move out from your positions and follow it. [4]Then you will know which way to go, since you have never been this way before. But keep a distance of about a thousand yards between you and the ark; do not go near it." [5]Joshua told the people, "Consecrate yourselves, for tomorrow the LORD will do amazing things among you." [6]Joshua said to the priests, "Take up the ark of the covenant and pass on ahead of the people." So they took it up and went ahead of them. **[7]And the LORD said to Joshua, "Today I will begin to exalt you in the eyes of all Israel, so they may know that I am with you as I was with Moses.** [8]Tell the priests who carry the ark of the covenant: 'When you reach the edge of the Jordan's waters, go and stand in the river.'" [9]Joshua said to the Israelites, "Come here and listen to the words of the LORD your God. [10]This is how you will know that the living God is among you and that he will certainly drive out before you the Canaanites, Hittites, Hivites, Perizzites, Girgashites, Amorites and Jebusites. [11]See, the ark of the covenant of the Lord of all the earth will go into the Jordan ahead of you. [12]Now then, choose twelve men from the tribes of Israel, one from each tribe. [13]And as soon as the priests who carry the ark of the LORD—the Lord of all the earth—set foot in the Jordan, its waters flowing downstream will be cut off and stand up in a heap."

UNDERSTANDING THE SCRIPTURE

Joshua 3:1. The Hebrews/Israelites had been living in tents, probably for several months, in the plains of Moab some miles east of the Jordan River. As Moses' death approached, God had said to him: "Your time to die is near; call Joshua and present yourselves in the tent of meeting, so that I may commission him." In that meeting, God told Joshua: "Be strong and bold, for you shall bring the Israelites into the land that I promised them; I will be with you" (Deuteronomy 31:14, 23). Joshua, who succeeded Moses as leader, had been planning and preparing for the invasion of Canaan, the land that God had promised to Abraham and his descendants. Some of the Israelite tribes had already settled east of the Jordan River and Joshua called upon them for help: "All the warriors among you shall cross over armed before your kindred and shall help them until . . . they too take possession of the land that the LORD your God is giving them" (Joshua 1:14-15). The Hebrew people had moved to camp at the edge of the desert east of the Jordan River, waiting for Joshua's command to cross the river and move into Canaan. In the lesson on January 11, we saw how the Hebrews gained information about Jericho, which was just beyond the river and the first city that they would have to conquer, through the spies who were protected by Rahab. The Hebrews were aware of the strength of the Canaanite city-states and made their plans for invasion carefully.

Joshua 3:2-3. After three days of camping just on the bank of the Jordan, Joshua's order came that it was time to move. The people were to follow the ark of the covenant, which would be carried by the priests from the tribe of Levi. According to 1 Chronicles 15:2, the ark was to be carried only by Levites, who had been chosen by God to serve as priests. At this time in Israel's history, it was probably a simple wooden chest, perhaps containing the stone tablets upon which God had written the Law and given to Moses.

Joshua 3:4. The ark was the sign of God's presence and would be the people's guide and protector. They were to treat it with reverence; they were not to get closer than 3000 feet to it as they passed through the river. A number of other Old Testament stories sug-

gest that the ark possessed supernatural powers and could even kill if it was handled wrongly (see 1 Chronicles 13; 15).

Joshua 3:5-6. In preparation for the momentous act of God in which they would participate the next day, Joshua demanded that the people sanctify themselves. This meant that they were to ritually cleanse themselves so as to be purified, consecrated, or set aside for God's use. A similar ritual was used in Exodus 19 when God commanded Moses to have the people sanctify themselves before encountering God at Mount Sinai. Consecration involved sexual abstinence and the washing of bodies and clothing (see Genesis 35:2 and 1 Samuel 21:4-6).

Joshua 3:7-8. One of the purposes of the miracle that God would work was to validate the leadership of Joshua, who some might not yet have fully accepted as the successor to the great Moses. Joshua was to send the priests bearing the ark of the covenant into the middle of the river. He himself was to stand in the edge of the water.

Joshua 3:9-11. Joshua told the people that what they were to experience would prove that God was working for them and would make them victorious over their enemies. The list of the peoples whom God would drive out includes those who are mentioned elsewhere in the Old Testament as enemies of Israel. We know from historical evidence that the Hebrew taking of the land was neither abrupt nor complete. It involved a long process of fighting, compromise, uneasy truces, and even assimilation.

Use of the titles "living God" and "Lord of all the earth" emphasized the awesome power of the God who was acting on Israel's behalf. This account may have been influenced by the ancient tradition of trial by ordeal. The power of Israel's God and the rightness of the Israelites' claim to the land would be proven by their passing safely through the water. God, as embodied in the ark, would enter the river first and remain there until all the people passed over.

Joshua 3:12-13. The Hebrew people

understood themselves to be divided into twelve tribal groups, each made up of the descendants of one of the twelve sons of Jacob. Apparently, each tribe was to choose one man who would be their leader as they went through the river. When the priests bearing the ark entered the river, the flow of water from the north would be blocked.

Joshua 3:14-16. This crossing was taking place during the harvest season—the time when the river was highest, due to the spring rains and the melting of snow and ice on Mount Hermon. By our calendar, it was during April-May. Apparently the water did not stop within sight of the Israelites, but backed up several miles away, while the Israelites walked across the riverbed and onto dry land close to the city of Jericho—their first target. The Dead Sea or Salt Sea is connected to the Sea of Galilee in the north by the Jordan River. Because it has no natural outlet, it has an extremely high concentration of minerals and cannot sustain either plant or animal life.

Joshua 3:17. The use of the Hebrew word for "nation" here may be intentionally indicating that the "people" who came out of Egypt and had traveled for decades through the desert wilderness had now become a "nation."

INTERPRETING THE SCRIPTURE

Keeping Commitments Requires Having Resources

A part of keeping our commitments to God and to other people is simply a matter of strength of will and determination. Realistically, however, these are usually not enough. We need a variety of resources, both tangible and intangible, to draw from if we are to succeed. Keeping commitments is not easy; we must have help beyond ourselves. Let us examine the resources that were available to Joshua for the keeping of his commitments as God's designated leader of the Israelites.

Most prominent of Joshua's resources was the ark of the covenant. The ark played an important part in the Old Testament story of God's dealing with the people of Israel. It is mentioned more than two hundred times. Apparently it originated during the period when the Hebrews were wandering in the desert wilderness after their escape from Egypt and before their entrance into Canaan. In Deuteronomy 10:1-5, Moses related his making of the ark and placing in it the stone tablets with the Ten Commandments: "So I made an ark of acacia wood, cut two tablets of stone like the former ones, and went up the mountain. . . . Then he wrote on the tablets the same words as before, the ten commandments. . . . So I turned and came down from the mountain, and put the tablets in the ark that I had made; and there they are, as the LORD commanded me." The ark traveled with the people in the wilderness and was kept in its own tent, sometimes called the tabernacle. Much later than Joshua's time, the ark was placed in the inner sanctuary of the Temple built by King Solomon.

The Israelites did not believe that God literally dwelled fully in the ark nor did they perceive it as an idol to be worshiped as divine. However, the ark was a potent manifestation of God's presence with them. It was more than a symbol; it embodied divinity and possessed some of the characteristics of divinity. It was highly significant that the ark was carried into the Jordan to stop its waters so that the Israelites could cross into the land of promise. There was no more powerful way of making clear that their crossing was the result of divine intervention.

Most scholars believe that the account of the crossing of the Jordan that we are studying in Joshua 3 is a liturgical adaptation of the event. We might say that it is a script for its reenactment in celebration. Quite likely such celebrations were held annually on the anniversary of the event. The Hebrew people believed strongly in regular commemorations of what God had done in their history. Their faith was based upon their history, and they recognized the importance of historical memory and passing on of traditions.

Resources From Experience

Another resource for Joshua was the fact that he had known Moses. Joshua was first mentioned in the Book of Exodus where he was described as one of the Israelite leaders in battle. He was identified as Moses' lieutenant and won his greatest fame as one of the spies whom Moses sent to spy out the land (see Numbers 13–14). Of the twelve spies who were sent, only Joshua and Caleb gave positive reports when they returned. Their optimism was based on their faith in God, not on weaknesses that they found among their enemies. As reward for their faith, God permitted only Joshua and Caleb to survive long enough to enter the Promised Land (see Numbers 14:28-30). Everyone over age twenty who lived in the period of the wilderness wandering, including Moses, died prior to the Israelites' entry into the land. Joshua had the advantage of his years with Moses and what he had experienced then. Moses was his hero, his mentor, his model.

Joshua had been a participant in the historical event that launched Israel on its path to becoming a nation—the exodus from Egypt under the leadership of Moses. In this famous "crossing of the Red Sea" (more correctly, Reed Sea), God had held back the waters to allow the Hebrews to escape Pharaoh's pursuing army (see Exodus 14). This powerful experience was the pattern for the crossing of the Jordan under the leadership of Joshua—the event that sent the Hebrews into the Promised Land to become a nation. Joshua's faith was based on his past experience. That experience was a powerful resource for faithfulness to his commitment to God and God's plan.

Crossing the Jordan

The crossing of the Jordan River into the Promised Land was a pivotal event in Israel's history. From this point forward, Israel ceased to be chiefly a nomadic, herding people and began to evolve into a settled, landed nation. This occasion was not only historically important; it has become deeply significant as a metaphor for physical death—passage to the Promised Land for Christians. This metaphorical meaning of crossing the Jordan River is expressed repeatedly in the lyrics of Christian music, especially in Negro spirituals. "Deep River" includes the words, "My home is over Jordan." "Swing Low, Sweet Chariot" says, "I looked over Jordan and what did I see / coming for to carry me home?" "Roll, Jordan, Roll" proclaims, "I want to go to heaven when I die, / to hear Jordan roll." In Charles Tindley's famous hymn, "Stand By Me," he prays,

> When I'm growing old and feeble,
> stand by me.
> When my life becomes a burden,
> and I'm nearing chilly Jordan,
> O thou Lily of the Valley,
> stand by me

Samuel Stennett employed the full metaphor when he wrote,

> On Jordan's stormy banks I stand,
> and cast a wishful eye
> to Canaan's fair and happy land,
> where my possessions lie.
> I am bound for the promised land,
> . . . .
> oh, who will come and go with me?
> I am bound for the promised land.

The metaphor is so well-known that it even appears in secular entertainment. Several years ago, NBC television launched a popular series entitled "Crossing Jordan." The lead character's name and the subject matter plainly reveal the connection: She is Dr. Jordan Cavanaugh, and the show focuses on the forensic work of coroners examining victims of murder.

On a much more pleasant note, this image of death portrays the beauty and joy of the Promised Land that awaits God's people. Passage through the river may be an ordeal—"The river Jordan is chilly and cold." But, beyond lies the fulfillment of God's promise. The land beyond the Jordan is the goal of those who journey in accord with God's plan.

All of this suggests that another resource for the faithful living out of our commitments is the biblical story and how it is brought to life in the worship life of the community of faith. Without knowledge of the account in Joshua 3, we could not apprehend the meaning of the powerful musical metaphors cited above. Without such passionate music, we would not so readily grasp the figurative language that brings us insight into the meaning of death. Such insight offers us confidence and assurance as we contemplate the reality of our own death and that of those we love.

SHARING THE SCRIPTURE

Preparing Our Hearts

Meditate on this week's devotional reading, found in Psalm 142. In this prayer for deliverance, David seeks God's protection from enemies. In verse 4, David claims "there is no one who takes notice of me; / . . . no one cares for me." Have you ever experienced such feelings? What were the circumstances? How did you move beyond them? Perhaps you are facing a difficult situation now. Are you willing to trust God to see you through it? Turn this matter over to God.

Pray that you and the adult learners will place your full faith and confidence in God, particularly when times are tough.

Preparing Our Minds

Study the background from Joshua 3 and the lesson Scripture from verses 1-13. Consider where people find the resources to fulfill commitments.

Write on newsprint:

❑ questions to close "Examine Joshua's Commitment to God."

❑ list of resources for "Explore Issues of the Learners' Responsibility and Resources for Making and Keeping Commitments."

❑ information for next week's lesson, found under "Continue the Journey."

❑ activities for further spiritual growth in "Continue the Journey."

LEADING THE CLASS

(1) Gather to Learn

❖ Welcome the class members and introduce any guests.

❖ Pray that those who have come today will open their hearts and minds to the resources God wants to give them.

❖ Read Luke 14:27-30 and discuss this question with the class: **Why is it so important to count the cost to be sure one has appropriate resources before making a commitment?**

❖ **Option:** Encourage the students to tell stories of times when they got involved in a project or situation without the resources to see it through. What happened?

❖ Read aloud today's focus statement: **Sometimes people make commitments without assurance that resources to fulfill them are available. From where do the resources come for fulfilling commitments? Joshua committed himself to becoming a leader of the Israelites and received power from God to meet this commitment.**

(2) Examine Joshua's Commitment to God

❖ Choose a volunteer to read aloud Joshua 3:1-13.

❖ Point out the sequence of events that Joshua says will occur.

- ■ 3:8—The people are to stand still in the water at the edge of the Jordan.
- ■ 3:11—The ark of the covenant is to pass before the people into the Jordan.
- ■ 3:13—As soon as the feet of the priests bearing the ark touch the water, the waters shall stop flowing and "stand in a single heap."

❖ Compare this sequence to Exodus 14:19-22. (Note that the presence of the Lord is seen in the "pillar of cloud" in Exodus, whereas the ark of the covenant is understood as God's presence as the people cross the Jordan.)

❖ List on newsprint characteristics of Joshua that the students can identify or infer from this passage. Here is a passage from a book in the Apocrypha that may expand the discussion: **Joshua son of Nun was mighty in war, and was the successor of Moses in the prophetic office. He became, as his name implies, a great savior of God's elect, to take vengeance on the enemies that rose against them, so that he might give Israel its inheritance** (Sirach 46:1).

❖ Compare the figures of Moses and Joshua. Here is a list taken from page 310 of *The New Interpreter's Study Bible*: Both men are called "servant of the LORD." Both men did the following acts: "leading the people across boundary waters; guiding them into

and through a new territory; sending out spies; engaging in military campaigns; ordering circumcision; celebrating the Passover; receiving the command to remove their sandals; delivering the Law (Moses) or writing a copy of it (Joshua); allocating territory to tribes; designating cities of refuge; and instituting a covenant ceremony." Also note that both men offered intercessory prayer for the people.

❖ Divide the class into groups and ask each one to answer these questions, which you will post on newsprint: **When Joshua made a commitment to act, what resources did he have? Would you have moved forward had you had the same resources? Why or why not?**

❖ Call the students back together to report on their ideas.

❖ Read or retell "Keeping Commitments Requires Having Resources" and "Resources From Experience," both from Interpreting the Scripture, to add to the discussion.

(3) Explore Issues of the Learners' Responsibility and Resources for Making and Keeping Commitments

❖ Distribute paper and pencils. Ask each adult to identify at least one recent commitment that he or she is striving to fulfill. Then, using the following list, which you will have posted on newsprint, the students are to indicate the resources available in each category (as appropriate) to fulfill this commitment.

- ■ Gifts, talents, and skills
- ■ Education
- ■ Passion for cause/project
- ■ Money
- ■ Facilities
- ■ People willing to work with you
- ■ Spiritual resources

❖ Invite the adults to talk with a partner or small group about the resources they have listed. Do the students feel they have sufficient resources to fulfill the commitment? If not, what else is necessary?

❖ Conclude this portion of the session by discussing how recognition of a variety of resources enables us to make and keep commitments.

(4) Use Resources for Making and Fulfilling Commitments

❖ Read this brief biography of Joanne Kathleen Rowling, better known as the author of the Harry Potter stories, J. K. Rowling. **Born to middle-class parents in Gloucestershire, England, July 31, 1965, J. K. Rowling started to write early during her happy childhood. Ms. Rowling attended Exeter University to study French and then worked for Amnesty International in French-speaking Africa. While riding the train from Manchester to London, she suddenly visualized Harry Potter. Although she had no writing materials with her, she was brimming with ideas that she wrote down as soon as possible. These ideas were the foundation for her books. In 1990, she taught English in Portugal, where she met her husband, married, gave birth to a daughter, and divorced. A single mom with a baby, she settled in Edinburgh, Scotland. Unable to afford child care, she was unable to work and had to live on public assistance for a year. To escape her unheated flat, she took her baby and went to Nicolson's Restaurant to write. It took five years from the time she conceived the idea until her first book was finished. Although her books are widely popular now, major publishers all rejected it. Finally, her agent notified her that Bloomsbury Press would publish it. Now, all seven of the books she had envisioned have been published. No longer dependent on public assistance, J. K. Rowling is reportedly richer than Queen Elizabeth II.**

❖ Ask: **What resources did J. K. Rowling have that she used to great advantage?** (You may want to use the list of categories from the prior activity.)

❖ Encourage volunteers to comment on how they, too, can use resources to better fulfill their commitments.

(5) Continue the Journey

❖ Pray that all who have participated today will recognize and use the resources God has given them.

❖ Read aloud this preparation for next week's lesson. You may also want to post it on newsprint for the students to copy.

■ **Title: Samson's Mother Prepares for His Birth**

■ **Background Scripture: Judges 13**

■ **Lesson Scripture: Judges 13:1-13, 24**

■ **Focus of the Lesson: Promise and commitment may arise out of great disappointment. How are people challenged to make new commitments? God sent an angel to prepare Samson's mother for his coming birth.**

❖ Challenge the students to complete one or more of these activities for further spiritual growth, which you will write on newsprint for the students to copy.

(1) **Focus on one commitment that you are having difficulty keeping. Pray that God will give you the resources you need to fulfill this.**

(2) **If you are taking on a new office in the church this year, talk with other people who know the job to familiarize yourself with it.**

(3) **Identify a fictional or historical character who, like Joshua, Moses, or J. K. Rowling, rose from ordinary status with apparently few resources to accomplish something great. What can you learn from this person?**

❖ Sing or read aloud "The God of Abraham Praise."

❖ Conclude today's session by leading the class in this benediction, taken from Luke 1:38: **Here am I, the servant of the Lord; let it be with me according to your word.**

UNIT 2: OLD TESTAMENT PEOPLE OF COMMITMENT

SAMSON'S MOTHER PREPARES FOR HIS BIRTH

PREVIEWING THE LESSON

Lesson Scripture: Judges 13:1-13, 24
Background Scripture: Judges 13
Key Verse: Judges 13:5

Focus of the Lesson:
Promise and commitment may arise out of great disappointment. How are people challenged to make new commitments? God sent an angel to prepare Samson's mother for his coming birth.

Goals for the Learners:
(1) to examine the circumstances surrounding Samson's birth.
(2) to sense God's promise amid disappointments.
(3) to accept new challenges and to act on them.

Pronunciation Guide:
Astarte (as tahr' tee)   Nazirite (naz' uh rite)
Baal (bay' uhl) or (bah ahl')   Philistine (fi lis' teen)
Danite (dan' ite)   Zorah (zor' uh)
Manoah (muh noh' uh)

Supplies:
Bibles, newsprint and marker, paper and pencils, hymnals, small candle for each participant, lighter

---

READING THE SCRIPTURE

NRSV
Judges 13:1-13, 24

¹The Israelites again did what was evil in the sight of the LORD, and the LORD gave them into the hand of the Philistines forty years.

NIV
Judges 13:1-13, 24

¹Again the Israelites did evil in the eyes of the LORD, so the LORD delivered them into the hands of the Philistines for forty years.

²There was a certain man of Zorah, of the tribe of the Danites, whose name was Manoah. His wife was barren, having borne no children. ³And the angel of the LORD appeared to the woman and said to her, "Although you are barren, having borne no children, you shall conceive and bear a son. ⁴Now be careful not to drink wine or strong drink, or to eat anything unclean, ⁵for **you shall conceive and bear a son. No razor is to come on his head, for the boy shall be a nazirite to God from birth. It is he who shall begin to deliver Israel from the hand of the Philistines."** ⁶Then the woman came and told her husband, "A man of God came to me, and his appearance was like that of an angel of God, most awe-inspiring; I did not ask him where he came from, and he did not tell me his name; ⁷but he said to me, 'You shall conceive and bear a son. . . .' "

⁸Then Manoah entreated the LORD, and said, "O, LORD, I pray, let the man of God whom you sent come to us again and teach us what we are to do concerning the boy who will be born." ⁹God listened to Manoah, and the angel of God came again to the woman as she sat in the field; but her husband Manoah was not with her. ¹⁰So the woman ran quickly and told her husband, "The man who came to me the other day has appeared to me." ¹¹Manoah got up and followed his wife, and came to the man and said to him, "Are you the man who spoke to this woman?" And he said, "I am." ¹²Then Manoah said, "Now when your words come true, what is to be the boy's rule of life; what is he to do?" ¹³The angel of the LORD said to Manoah, "Let the woman give heed to all that I said to her."

²⁴The woman bore a son, and named him Samson. The boy grew, and the LORD blessed him.

²A certain man of Zorah, named Manoah, from the clan of the Danites, had a wife who was sterile and remained childless. ³The angel of the LORD appeared to her and said, "You are sterile and childless, but you are going to conceive and have a son. ⁴Now see to it that you drink no wine or other fermented drink and that you do not eat anything unclean, ⁵because **you will conceive and give birth to a son. No razor may be used on his head, because the boy is to be a Nazirite, set apart to God from birth, and he will begin the deliverance of Israel from the hands of the Philistines."**

⁶Then the woman went to her husband and told him, "A man of God came to me. He looked like an angel of God, very awesome. I didn't ask him where he came from, and he didn't tell me his name. ⁷But he said to me, 'You will conceive and give birth to a son. . . .'"

⁸Then Manoah prayed to the LORD: "O Lord, I beg you, let the man of God you sent to us come again to teach us how to bring up the boy who is to be born."

⁹God heard Manoah, and the angel of God came again to the woman while she was out in the field; but her husband Manoah was not with her. ¹⁰The woman hurried to tell her husband, "He's here! The man who appeared to me the other day!"

¹¹Manoah got up and followed his wife. When he came to the man, he said, "Are you the one who talked to my wife?"

"I am," he said.

¹²So Manoah asked him, "When your words are fulfilled, what is to be the rule for the boy's life and work?"

¹³The angel of the LORD answered, "Your wife must do all that I have told her."

²⁴The woman gave birth to a boy and named him Samson. He grew and the LORD blessed him.

UNDERSTANDING THE SCRIPTURE

Judges 13:1. Years had passed since the Israelites crossed the Jordan River and entered the land of Canaan, as we studied on January 18. Joshua had died (Joshua

24:29; Judges 2:8). The Book of Judges makes it apparent that, despite the accounts of military victories in the Book of Joshua, the land was far from conquered. Conflict between the Israelites and various other peoples in Palestine was protracted and intense, and Israel was not consistently victorious. One cause of weakness was the lack of any central governing authority. Moses and Joshua had been strong enough to command the allegiance of all of the Israelites, but no leader arose after them who could continue such leadership. The loyalty of the people was divided among the twelve tribes (and some subtribes) that constituted Israel. Rather than having become a unified nation, Israel was a tribal confederacy that cooperated against common dangers but was very loosely structured. The theme of the Book of Judges is this recurring pattern: Israel ceased to be faithful to God; they were oppressed by their enemies; God delivered them from their enemies through the leadership of a charismatic judge whom God raised up; after a short period of faithfulness the people returned to sinful ways and the pattern was repeated. The various judges may have exercised some juridical authority, such as settling disputes among the people, but they were primarily military leaders. They are described as having been raised up by the spirit of God to undertake the task that Israel needed. Deborah and Gideon were two of the most familiar judges. Samson, whose birth is discussed in this lesson, was the last and best known of these deliverers. He was also the worst.

The opening verse of Chapter 13 reveals the continuing pattern of Israel's life as already explained. The phrase "did what was evil in the sight of the LORD" appears in Judges frequently. The evil committed by the Israelites was their unfaithfulness to God and their disobedience to the law that God had given them on Mount Sinai. They were seduced to the worship of the false gods of the Canaanites—the Baals and Astartes. In the process of adapting to an agricultural economy, they were particularly tempted by the alleged control that these fertility gods had over the success of crops.

The Philistines were a people who came into Canaan soon after the Israelites and quickly became their strongest rival. They were known as "the people of the sea" and settled along the Mediterranean coast of Palestine.

Judges 13:2. Zorah was a town on the border of the territories occupied by the tribes of Judah and Dan. Indicative of the patriarchal culture of the time, Manoah's wife is not named, even though she will be the main character in the story. The familiar biblical motif of the barren woman reappears here.

Judges 13:3-5. The angel's appearance to the woman reminds us of the similar experiences of Sarah, the wife of Abraham; Rebekah, the wife of Isaac; Rachel, the wife of Jacob; and Hannah, the mother of Samuel. From the New Testament, we recall Elizabeth, the mother of John the Baptizer. There is a further similarity to John in that the woman was told that her son, like Elizabeth's centuries later, was to be a Nazirite. Numbers 6:1-21 stipulated the conditions of life for one who was a Nazirite: no wine, no contact with the dead, and no cutting of one's hair. The name itself comes from the Hebrew for "dedicated" or "consecrated." A Nazirite was to live an ascetic lifestyle appropriate to one set apart for God's purpose. That the promised son was to be a Nazirite for life, rather than for a period of time, probably indicates the severity of Israel's need. Apparently the mother was herself to live as a Nazirite during her pregnancy. The task of the child was to begin the work of freeing Israel from Philistine control, although he would not be able to complete it.

Judges 13:6-14. The repetition and redundancy here are consistent with the style of a folklore tale passed down through the generations of Israel. Even though Samson would not be a moral paragon or a successful deliverer, his legend was popular in

Israel. When Manoah was told by his wife about the angel's words, he apparently wanted to hear the account himself. When the angel or "man of God" did return, Manoah questioned him about how the child was to be brought up and what his destiny would be. The angel stopped Manoah's inquiries by reminding him that his wife had already been told what to do.

Judges 13:15-18. Manoah asked the angel to stay and be honored by sharing a special meal of young goat. Such hospitality was characteristic of the culture. Manoah's request to learn the name of the angel was refused. To know one's name in that culture was to know one's nature and that would be too much for humans to receive.

Judges 13:19-23. When Manoah offered the sacrifice, the angel disappeared in the flame and Manoah realized that the visitor was divine. His fear of death for having seen God was soothed by his more practical wife.

Judges 13:24-25. The angelic prediction was fulfilled in the birth of the child, whom his mother named Samson. The boy grew and was favored by God. This verse is ironic and sad. Although verse 25 says, "The spirit of the LORD began to stir him," he did not live in accord with the divine spirit. If we read the next few chapters of Judges, we learn that Samson became a deeply flawed hero. He violated the Nazirite vow in every way. He had a dangerous weakness for Philistine women, even though the Philistines were Israel's enemy. Samson did not fulfill the leadership role for which God had designated him. The next leader, Samuel, would have to continue that fight; he also would be a Nazirite for life (1 Samuel 1:11).

INTERPRETING THE SCRIPTURE

Committing to Children

The conversation between the angelic messenger and the woman who will become the mother of Samson prompts us to think about the commitments we make to children both before and after their births. It is interesting that the issue of the woman's physical condition during her pregnancy is addressed. While it may have been ritualistic cleanliness concerns on the part of the angel, in our own circumstances we see different aspects. One of the serious health issues of our own society is the damage that can be done to fetuses by their mothers' substance abuse and other risky behaviors. Surely one of the basic commitments that we should make to our children is to provide healthy prenatal conditions for their development. It is humbling, even frightening, to learn that infant mortality statistics indicate that the United States ranks surprisingly low in comparison to other nations as a safe place for the birth of healthy infants. The church has a responsibility to use its influence in the political arena to lobby for the kinds of physical, psychological, and spiritual support that parents must have. The church is also challenged to get into the business of directly providing these kinds of support.

As persons in the community of faith, we need to be deeply committed to the spiritual preparation that we provide for our children. I frequently advise pastors to hold prebaptismal classes for expectant parents so that they seriously consider the spiritual aspects of their and their child's lives at the same time that they are preparing for birth in other ways. In most parts of Christianity, parents are counseled to have their infants or young children baptized. In this sacrament, we believe that God claims the child as God's own and that the child is launched on the lifelong journey of salvation. Parental commitment is an important part of the baptism of an infant. The United Methodist ritual, which I will use as an example, expresses the commitment that all churches seek. Parents profess their own Christian faith and then are asked:

Will you nurture these children
in Christ's holy church,
that by your teaching and example
    they may be guided
    to accept God's grace for themselves,
    to profess their faith openly,
    and to lead a Christian life?

An affirmative response is a daunting commitment.

We have heard it said "it takes a village to raise a child." I suggest that in the community of faith we say "it takes a church to raise a Christian." Children are deeply influenced not only by parents but also by the other adults to whom they are exposed. The whole body of Christ must make a commitment to raising Christians. This is why the baptismal ritual also includes opportunities for the congregation to pledge itself to the task. The pastor charges the congregation to "Do all in your power to increase their faith, / confirm their hope, and perfect them in love." The congregation affirms:

We will surround these persons
    with a community of love and
        forgiveness,
    that they may grow in their trust of
        God,
    and be found faithful in their service
        to others.

When Commitments Fail

Persons in believer's baptism churches sometimes object to infant baptism on the grounds that no one else can speak for the child. Of course, we do not speak for our children; we speak for ourselves—our faith, our intention. We follow up on that commitment by nurturing and forming our children in the faith both at church and at home. But sadly, no matter how sincere our commitments may be and how faithfully we keep them, we cannot control or guarantee their outcomes. Some of us know how Samson's mother must have felt in later years when, in spite of her efforts, he failed to be the person God had called him to be. It was not her fault. As far as the Scripture indicates, she did her part in preparing him for the life of consecrated service to which he was called. That is all that parents can do, and when we do it we have fulfilled our commitments. Ultimately, maturing children become responsible for themselves. They must make and live their own commitments.

Within the church we prepare our children for what United Methodism calls profession of faith/confirmation. This is the occasion when children, now grown to an age of responsibility for their own moral decisions, declare their faith in Christ and their commitment to live as faithful Christians. Afterward we continue to guide and shape them, but the choices are theirs. Our commitments to and for other people can go only so far. Finally everyone must make and live out his or her own.

In one of my seminary classes recently, I taught a young Korean man who mentioned several times that he was committed to being an ordained minister no matter how he felt about the vocation. When I asked him more about this, he told me that his mother had suffered the death of two children who were born before him. She had promised God that if God would give her a healthy son, he would become a Christian minister. The young man had been brought up being constantly reminded of his mother's vow and the result was that he believed that he had no choice but to fulfill it. He said to me repeatedly, "I don't have a choice." Finally I replied, "Yes, yes, you do have a choice. It would be very difficult, but it must ultimately be your own choice." He was caught in the dilemma of conflicting commitments, of the disparity between his mother's and what he wanted to make his own.

Commitments of Nameless Women

In the story of Samson's coming birth, it is his nameless mother who is the model of faithfulness. She accepted with joy the unexpected change in her life that this surprising pregnancy created. She was attentive to God's Word delivered by the angel and willing to adopt what we might call an alternative lifestyle in order to be physically and ritually prepared for motherhood.

In Mark 14:3-6, we read the account of another nameless woman who expends something of great value to express the depth of her commitment to Christ: "A woman came with an alabaster jar of very costly ointment of nard, and she broke open the jar and poured the ointment on his head" (14:3). Immediately there was loud and vehement criticism from those who were dining with Jesus. They complained that this very valuable ointment had been wasted. They pointed out that it could have been sold and the profits given to the poor, although none of them were selling their possessions for that purpose. Jesus did not denigrate giving to the poor; he simply pointed out that his tablemates had the opportunity to do that whenever they wished. He praised the woman who "has performed a good service for me" (14:6). He recognized that her action, while impractical and extravagant, was a genuine expression of her commitment to him. Indeed, Jesus cited her as an example of the profound commitment that he wanted from his disciples: "Truly I tell you, wherever the good news is proclaimed in the whole world, what she has done will be told in remembrance of her" (14:9).

These two nameless women, one in the Old Testament and one in the New, exemplify for us the life-transforming commitments to God that God's people are to make.

SHARING THE SCRIPTURE

Preparing Our Hearts

Meditate on this week's devotional reading, found in Psalm 91. How does it assure you of God's protection, even in the face of difficult or dangerous circumstances? The psalmist exudes great confidence in God. Recall a situation in which you depended on God as your refuge. Was God your first choice for help—or a last resort? What happened? Record your thoughts about God as a protector in your spiritual journal.

Pray that you and the adult learners will commit yourselves completely into God's care.

Preparing Our Minds

Study the background from Judges 13 and the lesson Scripture from verses 1-13, 24. Ponder this question: How are people challenged to make new commitments?

Write on newsprint:
❑ information for next week's lesson, found under "Continue the Journey."
❑ activities for further spiritual growth in "Continue the Journey."

Option: Read Numbers 6:1-21 and present it as a brief lecture for "Examine the Circumstances Surrounding Samson's Birth." You may want to do some additional research to explain what it means to be a Nazirite.

Have a small candle (perhaps tealights or votives) available for each participant. Also have one or more lighters on hand.

LEADING THE CLASS

(1) Gather to Learn

❖ Welcome the class members and introduce any guests.

❖ Pray that today's participants will be open to new commitments that God may set before them.

❖ Read the third paragraph of "When Commitments Fail" from Interpreting the Scripture.

❖ Discuss these questions:

(1) **Given the mother's grief and disappointment over the loss of two children, it is easy to see why she made this commitment to God. Do you think it is fair, however, for one person to make a vocational commitment for another? Why or why not?**

(2) **Had you been the son, what would you have done? Why?**

❖ Read aloud today's focus statement: **Promise and commitment may arise out of great disappointment. How are people challenged to make new commitments? God sent an angel to prepare Samson's mother for his coming birth.**

(2) Examine the Circumstances Surrounding Samson's Birth

❖ Choose volunteers to read Judges 13:1-13, 24. One person is to read the narrator's part; another that of the angel; another, Samson's mother; and a fourth to read Manoah's words. Encourage the readers to be as dramatic as possible.

❖ Read or retell the information from Judges 13:1 in Understanding the Scripture. Be sure to emphasize the pattern of Israel's relationship to God.

❖ Point out that just as Sarah (wife of Abraham), Rebekah (wife of Isaac), Rachel (wife of Jacob), and Hannah (mother of Samuel) were unable to bear children, so too the unnamed mother of Samson was barren. Yet, God acted in each of these women's lives and announced that they would have a son.

❖ Ask someone to read again Judges 13:4-5, which are the angel's words to the woman. Also note that in Judges 13:8 and again in verse 12, Manoah asks about how

the boy is to live. Choose someone else to read Numbers 6:1-21, where the law sets forth the rules for living as a Nazirite.

❖ **Option:** Summarize Numbers 6:1-21 yourself and present it as a brief lecture. You may wish to include additional information regarding the Nazirite lifestyle.

❖ Invite the class to imagine the commitments Samson's mother would have to make to carry and raise this child. What challenges can they envision her facing?

(3) Sense God's Promise Amid Disappointments

❖ Recall that Samson's mother and father must have felt deep disappointment because they did not have a child. In modern America, some couples choose not to have children and other couples who want to have children but cannot are referred to fertility clinics for medical treatment. Such options were not possible in the society of Samson's parents, where childlessness was seen as a sign of God's disapproval of the woman. Samson's mother likely felt marginalized among her family and the society at large. Life would have been bittersweet for her—until God's angel promised her a son.

❖ Distribute a candle to each participant. Give these directions: **Think of a disappointment you faced or are facing and have been able to overcome with God's help. Here are some examples:** *having to live with a chronic illness, losing a job, being passed over for a promotion, divorcing, being unable to retire, having a child who has not lived up to your expectations.* **You will have some time to meditate on this situation. Then, I will pass around the lighter(s). If you have experienced God's promise of blessing in this situation, please light your candle to let God's light shine. If for whatever reason you choose not to light your candle, please just pass the lighter to the next person.**

❖ Provide quiet meditation time, and then pass the lighter(s). When all have had an opportunity to light their candles, ask them to extinguish the candles carefully.

(4) Accept New Challenges and Act on Them

❖ Point out that one challenge facing most Christian congregations is figuring out how to make a commitment to children.

❖ Read or retell "Committing to Children" in Interpreting the Scripture.

❖ Invite the adults to comment on how they see the congregation responding to this challenge. List their ideas on newsprint.

❖ Encourage the students to identify ways that the church is not "child-friendly" and suggest ways to improve in those areas.

❖ Review the lists. Ask class members what they can do to bolster any of the activities listed, or create new opportunities to demonstrate the church's commitment to children. List these ideas on newsprint.

❖ Distribute paper and pencils. Invite the adults to write one step they will take this week to commit themselves to the children of the congregation, or to reach beyond the congregation to bring new children into the church.

❖ Encourage volunteers to tell what they plan to do. Perhaps several people are thinking along the same lines and could work together.

(5) Continue the Journey

❖ Pray that those who have gathered today will recognize that new commitments can emerge from disappointments.

❖ Read aloud this preparation for next week's lesson. You may also want to post it on newsprint for the students to copy.

■ **Title: A Shunammite Woman Helps**

■ **Background Scripture: 2 Kings 4:8-17**

■ **Lesson Scripture: 2 Kings 4:8-17**

■ **Focus of the Lesson: Some people make commitments that do not seem to benefit them. What kind of person will commit freely without requiring anything in return? The Shunammite woman was glad to serve Elisha without reward, but she received one anyway.**

❖ Challenge the students to complete one or more of these activities for further spiritual growth, which you will write on newsprint for the students to copy.

(1) **Research "Nazirite" in a Bible dictionary. What actions can you take to be "set apart" and yet still able to serve others?**

(2) **Review your church's baptism ritual. If you are the parent of a minor, how are you fulfilling the vows you made on behalf of your child? What else do you need to do? If you have no children at home, how can you support parents who are trying to raise their children in the faith?**

(3) **See what your church is doing to support young parents. Do you offer a "Parents' Day Out," "Adopt-a-Grandparent," or support group for parents? Do you knit blankets or create other gifts when a new baby arrives in the congregation? What could your class do to help?**

❖ Sing or read aloud "Our Parent, by Whose Name."

❖ Conclude today's session by leading the class in this benediction, taken from Luke 1:38: **Here am I, the servant of the Lord; let it be with me according to your word.**

UNIT 2: OLD TESTAMENT PEOPLE OF COMMITMENT
A SHUNAMMITE WOMAN HELPS

PREVIEWING THE LESSON

Lesson Scripture: 2 Kings 4:8-17
Background Scripture: 2 Kings 4:8-17
Key Verses: 2 Kings 4:9-10

Focus of the Lesson:
Some people make commitments that do not seem to benefit them. What kind of person will commit freely without requiring anything in return? The Shunammite woman was glad to serve Elisha without reward, but she received one anyway.

Goals for the Learners:
(1) to recall the relationship between Elisha and the Shunammite woman.
(2) to explore the possibility of commitment without apparent benefits.
(3) to make commitments without thought of personal gain.

Pronunciation Guide:
Elisha (i li' shuh)   Shunammite (shoo' nuh mite)
Gehazi (gi hay' zi)   Shunem (shoo' nuhm)

Supplies:
Bibles, newsprint and marker, paper and pencils, hymnals, index cards (or slips of paper)

READING THE SCRIPTURE

NRSV

2 Kings 4:8-17

⁸One day Elisha was passing through Shunem, where a wealthy woman lived, who urged him to have a meal. So whenever he passed that way, he would stop there for

NIV

2 Kings 4:8-17

⁸One day Elisha went to Shunem. And a well-to-do woman was there, who urged him to stay for a meal. So whenever he came by, he stopped there to eat. ⁹She said to her

a meal. ⁹She said to her husband, **"Look, I am sure that this man who regularly passes our way is a holy man of God. ¹⁰Let us make a small roof chamber** with walls, and put there for him a bed, a table, a chair, and a lamp, **so that he can stay there whenever he comes to us."**

¹¹One day when he came there, he went up to the chamber and lay down there. ¹²He said to his servant Gehazi, "Call the Shunammite woman." When he had called her, she stood before him. ¹³He said to him, "Say to her, Since you have taken all this trouble for us, what may be done for you? Would you have a word spoken on your behalf to the king or to the commander of the army?" She answered, "I live among my own people." ¹⁴He said, "What then may be done for her?" Gehazi answered, "Well, she has no son, and her husband is old." ¹⁵He said, "Call her." When he had called her, she stood at the door. ¹⁶He said, "At this season, in due time, you shall embrace a son." She replied, "No, my lord, O man of God; do not deceive your servant."

¹⁷The woman conceived and bore a son at that season, in due time, as Elisha had declared to her.

husband, **"I know that this man who often comes our way is a holy man of God. ¹⁰Let's make a small room on the roof** and put in it a bed and a table, a chair and a lamp for him. **Then he can stay there whenever he comes to us."**

¹¹One day when Elisha came, he went up to his room and lay down there. ¹²He said to his servant Gehazi, "Call the Shunammite." So he called her, and she stood before him. ¹³Elisha said to him, "Tell her, 'You have gone to all this trouble for us. Now what can be done for you? Can we speak on your behalf to the king or the commander of the army?'"

She replied, "I have a home among my own people."

¹⁴"What can be done for her?" Elisha asked.

Gehazi said, "Well, she has no son and her husband is old."

¹⁵Then Elisha said, "Call her." So he called her, and she stood in the doorway. ¹⁶"About this time next year," Elisha said, "you will hold a son in your arms."

"No, my lord," she objected. "Don't mislead your servant, O man of God!"

¹⁷But the woman became pregnant, and the next year about that same time she gave birth to a son, just as Elisha had told her.

UNDERSTANDING THE SCRIPTURE

Introduction to 2 Kings 4:8-17. In this Scripture passage we become acquainted with a colorful Old Testament character—the prophet Elisha, whose story fills much of the first thirteen chapters of the Book of Second Kings. Elisha was the disciple and successor to the prophet Elijah, who anointed him for this task in accordance with God's command.

Elijah was an Israelite prophet who became so famous that his deeds were legendary. Even today Jewish people look for

his return as a sign of the dawning of the messianic age. Elijah is probably best remembered for his struggle against the Baals and other false gods who were competing for the loyalty of the Israelites. He performed a variety of miracles that showed the power of the true God of Israel. Most famous is his contest with the prophets of Baal on Mount Carmel, when fire descended from heaven and consumed the sacrifice that the prophet had prepared (1 Kings 18). As Elijah became aware that his time to leave the earth was near, he arranged for Elisha to be his successor, which God had told him to do (1 Kings 19:16).

Elisha must have possessed considerable wealth; he was plowing with twelve yoke of oxen when Elijah called him, and he gave their meat to the people in an elaborate farewell feast (1 Kings 19:19-21). This prophet's dramatic reception of authority was a part of the familiar story of the fiery chariot from heaven that came to get Elijah when he was taken from the earth without experiencing death (2 Kings 2). (The spiritual "Swing Low, Sweet Chariot" celebrates this event.) Prior to the descent of the chariot to get his mentor, Elijah, Elisha had asked, "Please let me inherit a double share of your spirit" (2 Kings 2:9). After Elijah disappeared Elisha took his mantle and performed a miracle of parting the waters of the Jordan, just as Elijah had done earlier. The mantle was the sign of Elisha's succession and the other prophets affirmed, "The spirit of Elijah rests on Elisha" (2 Kings 2:15).

2 Kings 4:8-10. Apparently it was common for Elisha to pass through the town of Shunem as he traveled about on his prophetic duties. The woman took the initiative in inviting him to eat with her and her husband and doing so became a regular part of his routine. The woman was a strong and admirable personality, and she was probably a part of the landed gentry of the area and considerably wealthy. The Shunammite woman was spiritually sensitive enough to recognize that Elisha was a man of God. Interestingly, verse 9 is the only place in the Old Testament where a prophet is referred to as "holy." With the agreement of her husband, the woman had comfortable accommodations for Elisha constructed on the roof of their home and invited him to stay there whenever he was in the area.

2 Kings 4:11-13. After enjoying her hospitality, Elisha wanted to do something to repay the woman's kindness and sent his servant to bring her to his room. Gehazi served as the prophet's traveling companion. Elisha asked her what favors he might be able to do for her. By this time the prophet had become quite influential in the kingdom and had the ear of the king. He probably could have helped protect her from excessive taxes and from the military units who often took property from the people. The woman indicated that she was quite secure in her community and not in need of help from anyone else.

2 Kings 4:14-15. When the woman left, Gehazi made a suggestion—a rather obvious one, but based on something that Elisha had apparently not noticed. There is no indication in this Scripture that the Shunammite woman had yearned for a child, as there is in so many similar accounts of barren women. However, it was a safe assumption on the part of the prophet and his servant that she desired a son. Without an heir, the family name would end and the family properties pass to someone else. Gehazi had pointed out that the woman's husband was old, assumedly much older that she was, and therefore unlikely to father a child. A widow left without a son would be in a precarious position in that society, having no male to depend upon.

2 Kings 4:16-17. The woman's emotional response when Elisha told her that she would have a son demonstrated the deep disappointment and desire that she had long felt. Although she had not talked about being childless or asked Elisha for anything, she was overwhelmed by this wonderful news, even reluctant to believe it lest it not be true. The word of the prophet came to fruition with the birth of the promised son.

As Chapter 4 of 2 Kings continues, we learn more about Elisha's involvement with the Shunammite woman and her family. Immediately after the verse announcing the child's birth, we read that the boy suffered some kind of stroke while in the field with his father and the reapers. He was carried to his mother and died in her arms. The mother laid her son's body on Elisha's bed in the room built for the prophet. Without telling her husband what had happened, the woman took a servant and rode her donkey to find Elisha. When she told the prophet about her son's death, he sent Gehazi to take the prophet's staff to the home and lay it on the boy's face. The grieving mother was doubtful that this would work and she insisted that Elisha come home with her. As she feared, Gehazi met

them and reported no results from using the stick. When Elisha reached the house, he secluded himself in the room with the child's body and prayed. Then he stretched his own body out on the boy. As he lay there, warmth returned to the child. Finally, the child sneezed seven times and opened his eyes. Elisha restored the child—now alive and healthy—to the arms of his mother. This account is among the numerous miraculous acts attributed to Elisha.

INTERPRETING THE SCRIPTURE

The Woman Who Had Everything

The commitments that people make are influenced by their circumstances, what they have and what they desire. The Shunammite woman in this Scripture was a woman of means and position. She owned a home and fields. She must have had a loving, congenial husband. She was well regarded in her community and lived in harmony with her neighbors. She appeared to have everything that she needed, even all that she desired. In addition, this woman must have been a person of faith, for she recognized Elisha as a holy man and provided for him generously. Her commitment to the prophet, and implicitly to the prophet's God, was without qualification or expectation. There were no strings, no tit for tat. This is one way in which we should all examine the commitments that we make: Are our commitments motivated by a desire to get something that we want in return? If so, they are not truly commitments at all; they are investments. God is not in the investment banking or brokerage business. We are not to be motivated by hope for profits or dividends.

In the story of the Shunammite woman, we eventually learn that something was missing in her life after all. The woman had

hidden this missing part so well that even the prophet did not immediately perceive it. She had no child, and her heart yearned for one. We know this by her joy when Elisha told her that she would soon be a mother. It was news so marvelous that she was afraid to believe it. We can imagine that by the point in her life when she met Elisha she had given up hope because her husband, as Gehazi noted, was aged. She did not really have everything after all. There was deep pain in her heart over her childlessness. There may have been nagging fear over how she would face the future alone after the death of her husband, who must have been older than she was. Remember that in ancient societies women without male relatives were very vulnerable.

I see this story as a warning not to evaluate people simply by the qualities that are obvious but to recognize that there may be deep pain within. I have a poster that says, "Be kind, for everyone you meet carries a heavy burden." The needs of many people we encounter are plain. But for others, even more consuming deprivation and emptiness may be present, but not obvious. We live, work, and play with many persons who, on the outside, seem at have it all but who harbor profound needs within. This is an important reminder for us as we seek to live out our commitments to Jesus Christ by loving and serving other people.

Commitment Without Expecting Gain

As we have noted in earlier lessons, the question of motive is very important in understanding and evaluating commitments. What is the Shunammite woman's motive for ministering to Elisha? The answer is not at all clear. Let us compare her situation to that of other women whom we have studied earlier. First, the Hebrew midwives who refused to carry out Pharaoh's order to kill the newborn male children of the Hebrews. These women risked their own lives by not only disobeying but also deceiving Pharaoh. Their motive was not to gain something for themselves. They were committed to their people and to their God. Their motive and their reward were knowing that they had saved their people from destruction. In later decades they were further rewarded by the retelling of the story in which they were heroes. Even their names were passed on to posterity—something not always true for women.

When the Israelite spies came to Rahab's house, she hid them and helped them escape from the city safely. What was her motive? She had become convinced that God was on the side of the Israelites and that she should be on their side too. Her motive was protection for herself and her family. If she had chosen to betray the spies to the king of Jericho, she might have gotten a reward as well as protection, but she knew that her safety lay in being on God's side. What about the unnamed mother of Samson? She is motivated almost completely by her desire for a child, and she received what she yearned for.

Each of these women was at least partly motivated by her hope for some kind of benefit or gain for herself personally and for those she cared about. This is not to ignore their faith in God, but it is to emphasize that they saw something to be gained by their actions. By comparison, what about the Shunammite woman? In her case, there really seems to be no expectation or hope for gain. She never asked Elisha for anything; she never spoke to her husband about how they might benefit from having the prophet in their home. She did not view serving Elisha as a religious duty that she should perform. There is no indication in the story that she was trying to gain something either for herself or anybody else. As far as the story allows us to judge, she was motivated solely by her desire to provide hospitality and comfort to a man of God.

Heaven When I Die

In *The Communist Manifesto*, Karl Marx wrote that Christianity was the "opium of the people." By this he meant that the promise of life in heaven had been used by oppressive rulers to restrain and repress suffering people by encouraging them to believe in the coming joys of the future. History reveals clearly that this charge was accurate. Kings and emperors, as well as popes and priests, often assured the suffering that their heavenly rewards would be so great that they would forget all the misery of this life. Critics of the faith throughout history have claimed that Christians are chiefly motivated by hope for "pie in the sky by and by." Can this be true?

It is sometimes said that the true test of a person's character is what that person would do if they absolutely knew that no one, even God, would ever know about it. This can be understood to refer to what a person might try to get away with, something he or she might do that is illegal or immoral, if protected from the possibility of being found out. Let's look at it from another perspective. What would you do or not do that is good if you absolutely knew that no one, even God, would ever know about it? Would your morality change, your spiritual disciplines, your altruistic actions?

What if there were absolutely nothing in it for you? The hope of heaven and fear of hell have frequently been preached as motivations for Christian living. But what if there were no heaven or hell, no rewards or punishments of any kind either in this life or in the life to come? How would knowing this affect your actions? Perhaps this is, indeed, the authentic test of Christian commitment and character.

SHARING THE SCRIPTURE

Preparing Our Hearts

Meditate on this week's devotional reading, found in Luke 6:32-36. Here, Jesus teaches us how to be grace-filled people, even as God is. This teaching to love one's enemies seems contrary to common sense. Why would we choose to love someone who hurts us? Yet, this is what Jesus calls us to do. When have you helped someone who did not care for you, knowing that your assistance would not be reciprocated? Why did you do this? How did you feel about yourself and the other person afterward?

Pray that you and the adult learners will be willing to make a commitment to others, even those who you call enemies, without expecting a reward for your behavior.

Preparing Our Minds

Study the background and lesson Scripture, both of which are taken from 2 Kings 4:8-17. Ask yourself: What kind of person will commit freely without requiring anything in return?

Write on newsprint:
❑ information for next week's lesson, found under "Continue the Journey."
❑ activities for further spiritual growth in "Continue the Journey."

LEADING THE CLASS

(1) Gather to Learn

❖ Welcome the class members and introduce any guests.

❖ Pray that the adults who gather today will find a fresh perspective on generosity.

❖ Ask the class this question. List their ideas on newsprint: **Why do people give?** (You need not limit the giving to time or money, or to any specific group. Let this be a broad question.)

❖ Provide a moment for the students to review the list and mentally check off the reasons that they choose to give.

❖ Read aloud today's focus statement: **Some people make commitments that do not seem to benefit them. What kind of person will commit freely without requiring anything in return? The Shunammite woman was glad to serve Elisha without reward, but she received one anyway.**

(2) Recall the Relationship Between Elisha and the Shunammite Woman

❖ Select volunteers to read 2 Kings 4:8-17 as a drama. You will need students to act as a narrator, the Shunammite woman, Elisha, and Gehazi.

❖ Discuss these questions:
  (1) **What do you learn about the Shunammite woman?** (Read "The Woman Who Had Everything" from Interpreting the Scripture to expand the discussion.)
  (2) **What do you learn about the prophet Elisha?**
  (3) **What do you learn about the way God works?**
  (4) **Think back over the people we have studied so far this quarter.**

How would you compare these people to the Shunammite woman? (Read or retell "Commitment Without Expecting Gain" in Interpreting the Scripture after the students have responded.)

(5) **Who in the last fifty years or so has offered the kind of commitment without expectation of reward that we see in this woman?**

❖ Choose two people to role-play an imaginary discussion between the Shunammite woman and her son at age ten in which she tells him about Elisha, what she and his father did for Elisha, and how their commitment to this man of God was unexpectedly rewarded.

❖ Wrap up this portion of the lesson by discussing this question: **How can the Shunammite woman be a role model for you?**

(3) Explore the Possibility of Commitment Without Apparent Benefits

❖ Encourage the students to tell brief stories about people who committed themselves to a cause or gave money without any apparent benefits to themselves.

❖ Read or retell this story. **In May 2007, East High School in Des Moines, Iowa, inducted Ben Witten, an 89-year-old alumnus of the school, into their Hall of Fame for his service to humanity. He had learned lessons of giving from his parents, who gave away food from their grocery store during the Depression. Mr. Witten had been writing checks for charities in multiples of $18—a number with symbolic meaning in Judaism—for decades. On the basis of a handshake, he gave a younger East High School graduate an interest-free $500 loan in 1959 to finance his college education. A few months after Mr. Witten suffered a stroke in January 2007, the loan recipient, a retired surgeon, was finally able to make contact with him to repay the loan. Instead of accepting the money, Witten's son asked that the money be given to someone else. Agreeing to "pay it forward," the surgeon contacted a music teacher and gave a generous, undisclosed amount to finance music programs and orchestra trips. When asked about his father's giving, Witten's son Dwayne said, "It's nothing fancy, just the typical story of the son of an immigrant, growing up poor and becoming successful and wanting to give back."**

❖ Discuss this question. List ideas on newsprint: **As you consider Mr. Witten's story and the stories of the class members, what do you think motivates people to give without thought of reward?**

❖ Compare and contrast these ideas with the ones listed earlier in the "Gather to Learn" portion of the lesson.

(4) Make Commitments Without Thought of Personal Gain

❖ Encourage the students to consider a class project in which they can give without seeking recognition or reward.

❖ Distribute index cards (or slips of paper) and pencils. Ask each participant to write one idea for a project that the class could do together. These ideas may benefit the church itself (for example, hold a "baby shower" to replace toys and furniture in the church nursery), or a group in the church (for example, sponsor a family dinner that does not require anyone to bring a dish), or members of the community (for example, staff a booth at a community event). The important point here is that the project is something that the group would do without expectation of reward or recognition, though that may come.

❖ Collect the cards and read (or have others read) the ideas.

❖ Try to reach a consensus with the class as to which one project they would like to do. Assure the adults that everyone will have a role to play. Some people will be able to do physical activity, others may be able to make phone calls, others may be able to donate money.

❖ Form a task force to determine what needs to be done, for whom, by whom, when, for what purpose, with what resources, and for what cost. Ask this task force to report back at an agreed upon date.

❖ Plan to evaluate the project in several months to see how the intended recipients benefited and if those who participated benefited, even in unintended ways.

(5) Continue the Journey

❖ Pray that all in attendance today will see the Shunammite woman as a role model whose commitment without expectation of reward they may emulate.

❖ Read aloud this preparation for next week's lesson. You may also want to post it on newsprint for the students to copy.

■ **Title: Nathan Challenges David**
■ **Background Scripture: 2 Samuel 12:1-15**
■ **Lesson Scripture: 2 Samuel 12:1-7, 13-15**
■ **Focus of the Lesson: Some commitments we make involve people who have no part in agreeing to the decision. How do we consider how our commitments affect everyone involved? Nathan's commitment to God led him to confront King David.**

❖ Challenge the students to complete one or more of these activities for further spiritual growth, which you will write on newsprint for the students to copy.

(1) **Write a thank-you note to someone in the congregation who has been a "selfless saint." Let this person know how much he or she means to you and the congregation.**

(2) **Offer hospitality to someone in need. You may be able to do this in your home, a shelter, a soup kitchen, or elsewhere in the community where people who need assistance gather.**

(3) **Give a donation of money or goods to an agency that serves those in need or those who are traveling and need help.**

❖ Sing or read aloud "Go Now in Peace."

❖ Conclude today's session by leading the class in this benediction, taken from Luke 1:38: **Here am I, the servant of the Lord; let it be with me according to your word.**

UNIT 2: OLD TESTAMENT PEOPLE OF COMMITMENT

NATHAN CHALLENGES DAVID

PREVIEWING THE LESSON

Lesson Scripture: 2 Samuel 12:1-7, 13-15
Background Scripture: 2 Samuel 12:1-15
Key Verses: 2 Samuel 11:27–12:1

Focus of the Lesson:
Some commitments we make involve people who have no part in agreeing to the decision. How do we consider how our commitments affect everyone involved? Nathan's commitment to God led him to confront King David.

Goals for the Learners:
(1) to study Nathan's commitment to God that results in a confrontation with King David.
(2) to explore how they can confront evil and injustice.
(3) to take action to speak truth to power.

Pronunciation Guide:
Absalom (ab' suh luhm)   Tamar (tay' mahr)
Adonijah (ad uh ni' juh)   Uriah (yoo ri' uh)
Amnon (am' non)

Supplies:
Bibles, newsprint and marker, paper and pencils, hymnals

READING THE SCRIPTURE

NRSV
2 Samuel 11:27; 12:1-7, 13-15

11:27But the thing that David had done displeased the LORD, 12:1and the LORD sent Nathan to David. He came to him, and said to him, "There were two men in a certain city, the one rich and the other poor. 2The rich man had very many flocks and herds; 3but the poor man had nothing but one little

NIV
2 Samuel 11:27; 12:1-7, 13-15

11:27But the thing David had done displeased the LORD.

1The LORD sent Nathan to David. When he came to him, he said, "There were two men in a certain town, one rich and the other poor. 2The rich man had a very large number of sheep and cattle, 3but the poor man had ewe lamb, which he had bought. He brought it up, and it grew up with him and with his children; it used to eat of his meager fare, and drink from his cup, and lie in his bosom, and it was like a daughter to him. ⁴Now there came a traveler to the rich man, and he was loath to take one of his own flock or herd to prepare for the wayfarer who had come to him, but he took the poor man's lamb, and prepared that for the guest who had come to him." ⁵Then David's anger was greatly kindled against the man. He said to Nathan, "As the LORD lives, the man who has done this deserves to die; ⁶he shall restore the lamb fourfold, because he did this thing, and because he had no pity."

⁷Nathan said to David, "You are the man!" . . . ¹³David said to Nathan, "I have sinned against the LORD." Nathan said to David, "Now the LORD has put away your sin; you shall not die. ¹⁴Nevertheless, because by this deed you have utterly scorned the LORD, the child that is born to you shall die." ¹⁵Then Nathan went to his house.

The LORD struck the child that Uriah's wife bore to David, and it became very ill.

nothing except one little ewe lamb he had bought. He raised it, and it grew up with him and his children. It shared his food, drank from his cup and even slept in his arms. It was like a daughter to him.

⁴"Now a traveler came to the rich man, but the rich man refrained from taking one of his own sheep or cattle to prepare a meal for the traveler who had come to him. Instead, he took the ewe lamb that belonged to the poor man and prepared it for the one who had come to him."

⁵David burned with anger against the man and said to Nathan, "As surely as the LORD lives, the man who did this deserves to die! ⁶He must pay for that lamb four times over, because he did such a thing and had no pity."

⁷Then Nathan said to David, "You are the man!"

¹³Then David said to Nathan, "I have sinned against the LORD."

Nathan replied, "The LORD has taken away your sin. You are not going to die. ¹⁴But because by doing this you have made the enemies of the LORD show utter contempt, the son born to you will die."

¹⁵After Nathan had gone home, the LORD struck the child that Uriah's wife had borne to David, and he became ill.

UNDERSTANDING THE SCRIPTURE

Introduction. The encounter between David and the prophet Nathan can be understood only if we are reminded of the events that precipitated it. The scene was the nation of Israel when it was being ruled by the great King David, roughly one thousand years before the birth of Christ. From the roof of his palace in Jerusalem, David saw a woman named Bathsheba bathing in the courtyard of a nearby home. The king was strongly attracted to her and sent his servants to bring her to the palace so that he

could have sexual intercourse with her. Later Bathsheba sent word to David that she was pregnant. Bathsheba's husband, Uriah, was a soldier in the king's army, which was engaged in warfare with a neighboring nation. In order to make it appear that the child was Uriah's, David had Uriah brought home for a brief furlough. The king's plan was foiled when Uriah remained faithful to his oath of sexual abstinence during warfare and refused to go to his home and be with his wife. David sent Uriah back to the army, unknowingly carrying his own death warrant—an order to his general that Uriah be placed in a battle position where he would be killed. After Uriah's death and his widow's period of mourning, David married Bathsheba and she had his son.

2 Samuel 11:27–12:1. The last verse of Chapter 11 introduces this verse: "But the thing that David had done displeased the LORD." Months had passed, and David probably thought that this unseemly episode was over, but God was about to intervene. Nathan was a court prophet whose job it was to advise the king. He approached David as God's messenger and, instead of accusing the king directly, told him a powerful parable that led him to recognize his guilt. The parable is a literary form best known to us in the parables of Jesus. It is a story that makes one major point, illuminating a truth by portraying it in metaphorical language.

2 Samuel 12:2-4. Nathan's parable set up a sharp contrast between the man who had almost nothing and the man who had almost everything. Notice how skillfully the prophet portrayed the poor man's affection for the little female lamb that he had nurtured. Similarly, the callousness and selfishness of the rich man was manifest in his action. The story was brilliantly constructed so as to evoke the king's sympathy and anger. Perhaps it was significant that David had himself been a shepherd as a youth and cared for the lambs of his father's flock.

2 Samuel 12:5-6. The parable had the emotional impact that Nathan intended. The king became very angry at the rich man and ordered that he compensate the poor man fourfold. The words "As the LORD lives" were an oath formula, similar to "I swear to God." Note that David was especially infuriated because the rich man "had no pity." To David such a misuse of power without mercy or concern about the pain caused to someone else was particularly bad. He sympathized with the powerless one who had become the victim of another

person's selfish desire. Of course, these feelings were precisely what Nathan had intended to produce in the king.

2 Samuel 12:7-8. In his climactic sentence, Nathan suddenly switched to direct accusation. In four short words he delivered a devastating blow when he informed the king that David himself was the man who had done this reprehensible thing. Using the power of surprise, Nathan bluntly told the king that the action he had so condemned in the rich man in the story was really what he himself had done. Then the prophet began to speak as the messenger of God's words. God reminded David of how he came to be king by divine action and of how much God had given him. Strikingly God even declared, "if that had been too little, I would have added as much more." David was not in need, and God would have provided for him whatever he desired. Instead, the king had ignored God and God's law by cruelly taking what he wanted for himself without regard to anyone else.

2 Samuel 12:9. David's action was a betrayal of God, blatant disobedience to God's will by doing something that he knew was wrong. God's words portrayed David as directly responsible for Uriah's death as surely as if he had taken the sword in his own hand and killed him.

2 Samuel 12:10-12. As a result of David's sin, "the sword shall never depart from your house." These chilling words from God foreshadowed the conflicts between David and his sons in which the king would be publicly humiliated by one son taking his harem. God emphasized that the secret sin of the king would be revealed and avenged by very public displays of his punishments. In other parts of the narrative, we read about the troubles that came to David's house. In Chapter 13, David's son Amnon raped his half-sister Tamar and then threw her out. Two years later, another son, Absalom, a full brother of Tamar, murdered Amnon in revenge. Absalom fled to another nation and his father "mourned for his son day after day" (13:37). Later Absalom was allowed to return to Jerusalem, but not to David's presence until two years had passed (14:28). Immediately, Absalom began to plot rebellion against the king, his father. Even though he was the natural heir to the throne, he was unwilling to wait for his father's death. Absalom was a very attractive man (14:25) and a shrewd politician (15:6). Absalom led a revolt, and David and his household were forced to flee from Jerusalem. The king's forces triumphed in battle. David had given orders that Absalom not be harmed, but one of his generals disobeyed and killed the young rebel. When David heard of his son's death, he mourned deeply (18:33). Even after David's death, the bloody rivalry between his sons continued. Solomon, who succeeded David as king, had his brother Adonijah executed to remove him as a threat (1 Kings 2:25). Clearly, the sword did not depart from David's house.

2 Samuel 12:13-15. An indication of David's authentic character was his immediate willingness to acknowledge and confess his sin without making excuses. God forgave David, but the sin still had its consequences. Rather than take David's life, God's judgment was executed upon David and Bathsheba's child, who would die.

INTERPRETING THE SCRIPTURE

Nathan's Difficult Commitment

Most of us can feel sympathy for Nathan. He was in a very tight spot! Like all of the true prophets of the Old Testament he was God's spokesman. But, saying what God wanted said was not always easy. We remember the trouble that other prophets got into when their messages from God were not what people wanted to hear. Jeremiah was taunted, accused of treason, and arrested. Amos came into conflict with the religious authorities of his day and was forbidden to speak publicly. Like them, Nathan was God's man, and God had given him a task: to speak God's Word. He also had a commitment to the king. As a court prophet he was relied upon to be the spokesman for God, to give sound and honest advice. Even so, speaking an unpopular message to the king was dangerous. The king had power to expel him from his position, to imprison him, and even to have him killed. He had to have the courage to confront his ruler no matter what the risk was. Nathan was courageous, but he was also smart. First, he did not confront David until God told him to do so. Nathan must have known for months about the king's transgression, but he had remained silent, waiting for God. Second, Nathan did not rush into the king's audience room and blurt out his accusation. His approach kept David from becoming angry and defensive. With great skill, the prophet got the king to indict himself. No room was left for pretense or argument. Nathan's courage and wisdom enabled him to fulfill his commitment to the king and, above all, to God.

Speak Truth to Power

The words "speak truth to power" have become widely used in the twenty-first century. They are the titles of books, blogs, and articles. The expression is not new. It can be traced back to a charge given to Quakers by one of their leaders in the eighteenth century. Quakers have long been characterized by their willingness to defy earthly powers in order to be faithful to their principles. Nathan certainly spoke truth to power when he confronted King David.

Speaking truth to power is the task of the Christian church in secular society. Like Nathan's task it is not easy, but it is necessary if we are to be faithful. The church must gather its courage to confront the evils around it. In their baptismal vows, United Methodists are challenged to promise "to resist evil, injustice, and oppression in whatever forms they present themselves."

Too often, rather than resisting, the Christian church has become comfortable with evil, injustice, and oppression, even complicit in them. The church does not have a very good record of committing itself to confront wrongs and work for change. Indeed, historically the church has had to be dragged, sometimes kicking and screaming, into struggles for justice and peace. In the face of the evil of human slavery in the United States, most churches failed to speak Christian truth. Instead, several denominations split along geographic lines even earlier than the nation did, as people in the slave states were determined to defend their "peculiar institution." The churches were at best silent, more often supportive. In the fight for equal rights for women, the church has frequently resisted and even been the most conservative influence against equality in the society. The same is true in the efforts for equal civil rights for African Americans and now for gay, lesbian, and other sexual minority persons. Hilary Swank won an Academy Award for her role in the movie "Boys Don't Cry" about the life and murder of a transgender teenager. When she accepted the Oscar, Swank said that she looked for a time when we could celebrate diversity. What a challenge to the church!

What are other situations in which the contemporary church is challenged to emulate Nathan and speak truth to power? We live in the richest society that the world has ever known and yet deprivation, poverty, and need are ever-present realities. Many Americans work full time, sometimes at more than one job, and yet cannot earn enough to provide for their families. Thousands of Americans, including many children, cannot get adequate medical care because they cannot afford health insurance. What will God say to us in judgment about the specter of homeless people living on the streets of our cities and in the woods around our suburbs? The twin horrors of slaughter and starvation destroy the lives of thousands of African people while Western governments and the United Nations bemoan but do not act. The United States, among other countries, devotes huge portions of its spending to weaponry and other paraphernalia of warfare. These nations engage in military action that kills thousands of innocent civilians and dismisses them as "collateral damage." Who will speak truth to power? It is the task of Christian people and of the Christian church—God's spokespersons today as were the prophets in the Old Testament.

The kind of change that makes the world more like the kingdom of God only happens when faithful and courageous people speak truth to power. The words of Martin Luther King, Jr., concerning the silence of decent people in the face of evil should haunt the church.

"Cleanse Me From My Sin"

When the prophet Nathan spoke truth to power, power listened and repented. The king's response to the prophet's declaration of guilt revealed the basic goodness of David's character. Despite his grievous moral lapse, he was fundamentally a man committed to God. David remembered how God had chosen him as king and empowered him to take the throne. He could not have forgotten how God had protected him during war with his rivals and with his enemies, the Philistines. He was aware that he had a pivotal role in God's plan for salvation. Nathan's words seem to have reawakened the real David. As the Gospel of Luke says about the prodigal son, "he came to himself" (Luke 15:17). And when he did, he was ashamed, guilt-ridden, and deeply sorrowful. Psalm 51 has traditionally been identified as the psalm that David composed to express his remorse and repentance. It is a powerful and poignant plea to God:

> Have mercy on me, O God,
>   according to your steadfast love;
> according to your abundant mercy
>   blot out my transgressions." (51:1)

Having come to himself, David called upon God to be God—to evince God's covenant loyalty and forgiving nature. David asked God to change him and to restore him to saving relationship: "Create in me a clean heart, O God, / and put a new and right spirit within me" (51:10). "Restore to me the joy of your salvation" (51:12). There are perhaps no finer words to express repentance. They should be very familiar to the Christian church and to individual Christians.

David's sin had been horrid in its effects upon other people: Uriah had been killed; Bathsheba had been violated, widowed, and bereaved; their child had died. David was keenly aware of all of this and deeply sorry. And yet when he mourned his sin, he realized that the greatest offense had been done to God: "Against you, you alone, have I sinned, / and done what is evil in your sight" (51:4). It was his crime against God that underlay and enabled all his wrongdoing. In a society and a church that too often fail to recognize the prevalence and power of human evil, David is an instructive example.

SHARING THE SCRIPTURE

Preparing Our Hearts

Meditate on this week's devotional reading, found in Psalm 51:1-9. David supposedly wrote this penitential psalm after Nathan had confronted him about his sin with Bathsheba. What does this psalm imply about David's understanding of his sin and God's forgiveness? In what ways is David's psalm your own psalm?

Pray that you and the adult learners will be aware of your own sins and pray repentantly for pardon.

Preparing Our Minds

Study the background from 2 Samuel 12:1-15 and the lesson Scripture from verses 1-7, 13-15. Note that 2 Samuel 11:27–12:1 constitute the key verses for this week. As you read, think about how our commitments affect everyone involved.

Write on newsprint:

- ❏ names and addresses of elected officials for "Take Action to Speak Truth to Power."
- ❏ information for next week's lesson, found under "Continue the Journey."
- ❏ activities for further spiritual growth in "Continue the Journey."

Locate a list of names and addresses of elected officials who represent your area, locally and nationally. Post this information on newsprint. The e-mail address for the White House is comments@whitehouse.gov. The mailing address is The White House, 1600 Pennsylvania Avenue NW, Washington, DC 20500. Phone comments may be directed to 202-456-1111.

LEADING THE CLASS

(1) Gather to Learn

❖ Welcome the class members and introduce any guests.

❖ Pray that all who attend will be open to God's Spirit as you study and learn together.

❖ Suggest that the class think about situations in which one person makes a commitment that affects others, often adversely. List these ideas on newsprint. Here are several examples: *A spouse or parent chooses a career that requires extended periods away from home; a family member jeopardizes financial security by gambling; a top executive's dishonesty causes a company to fold; second-hand smoke affects the health of family members and co-workers.*

❖ Ask: **How do you feel about commitments others make that affect you, even though you were never given an opportunity to voice your opinions and concerns?**

❖ Read aloud today's focus statement: **Some commitments we make involve people who have no part in agreeing to the decision. How do we consider how our commitments affect everyone involved? Nathan's commitment to God led him to confront King David.**

(2) Study Nathan's Commitment to God That Results in a Confrontation With King David

❖ Read or retell the "Introduction" for Understanding the Scripture to prepare the class for today's Scripture lesson.

❖ Choose three volunteers—a narrator, King David, and Nathan—to read 2 Samuel 11:27; 12:1-7, 13-15 as a drama.

❖ Discuss these questions with the class:
   (1) **What does David's response reveal about him?** (Expand the discussion by reading or retelling "Cleanse Me From My Sin" in Interpreting the Scripture.)
   (2) **What effect did David's choice to**

engage in adultery have on parties who had no role in his decision? (Note that Uriah was killed, Bathsheba lost her husband, the child to be born from the illicit union would die, and "the sword shall never depart from [David's] house" [12:10].)
   (3) **What does this passage reveal to you about the prophet Nathan and his commitment to God?** (To add to the discussion, read or retell "Nathan's Difficult Commitment" from Interpreting the Scripture.)

(3) Explore How the Learners Can Confront Evil and Injustice

❖ Recall that Nathan was willing to "speak truth to power," in spite of the fact that David could have had the prophet killed. Likewise, we are called to make commitments to speak truth in the face of injustice and evil.

❖ Read the first and second paragraphs under "Speak Truth to Power" in Interpreting the Scripture.

❖ Discuss the following questions. You can find examples in "Speak Truth to Power" to add to the discussion.
   (1) **What situations can you name in your community, country, and the world in which evil and injustice need to be overcome?** (List these ideas on newsprint.)
   (2) **In what specific ways is your congregation resisting evil, injustice, and oppression?** (List these ideas on newsprint. When you have finished, post the two lists side by side.)
   (3) **Compare what you are doing with the situations you have listed. How do you think God would rate your congregation as "Nathans" who speak truth to power?**

❖ Read the following questions and ask the students to discuss them with a small group:

    (1) How do you individually, like Nathan, speak truth to overcome evil and injustice?

    (2) If you are not acting like Nathan, what reasons can you give for not confronting injustice?

    (3) How does the reluctance of individuals to speak up affect the church and its commitment to justice?

(4) Take Action to Speak Truth to Power

❖ Distribute paper and pencils. Invite the students to choose an issue, preferably from the lists they have created. Encourage them to write a draft of a letter, e-mail, or phone message they would like to send to an elected official about the injustice that concerns them.

❖ **Option:** Several students interested in the same issue may want to work together to send one correspondence as a group.

❖ Call for volunteers to read or retell what they have written.

❖ Challenge the adults to hold themselves accountable to revising what they have written and actually sending a letter or e-mail or making a phone call. One way to do this is to ask the students to choose a partner. During the week, partners are to contact each other to report on action they have taken.

(5) Continue the Journey

❖ Pray that each participant will, like Nathan, keep commitments to God, even if they must challenge powerful leaders to do so.

❖ Read aloud this preparation for next week's lesson. You may also want to post it on newsprint for the students to copy.

    ■ **Title: Esther Risks Her Life**

    ■ **Background Scripture: Esther 4–5**

    ■ **Lesson Scripture: Esther 4:1-3, 9-17**

    ■ **Focus of the Lesson: Some persons are willing to make commitments that break rules and may imperil themselves. To what do people commit even at personal risk? Queen Esther was willing to sacrifice her life for the people of God.**

❖ Challenge the students to complete one or more of these activities for further spiritual growth, which you will write on newsprint for the students to copy.

    (1) Identify a "Nathan" in your own life, someone who has made you aware of something you did that displeased God. How did you respond to this person?

    (2) Meditate on Psalm 51, in which David confesses his sin. As you identify sins in your own life, ask God for forgiveness.

    (3) Write or revise a letter begun in class, send an e-mail, or make a phone call to an elected official to speak out against an injustice. Encourage others to take similar action.

❖ Sing or read aloud "Move Me."

❖ Conclude today's session by leading the class in this benediction, taken from Luke 1:38: **Here am I, the servant of the Lord; let it be with me according to your word.**

UNIT 2: OLD TESTAMENT PEOPLE OF COMMITMENT
ESTHER RISKS HER LIFE

PREVIEWING THE LESSON

Lesson Scripture: Esther 4:1-3, 9-17
Background Scripture: Esther 4–5
Key Verse: Esther 4:16

Focus of the Lesson:

Some persons are willing to make commitments that break rules and may imperil themselves. To what do people commit even at personal risk? Queen Esther was willing to sacrifice her life for the people of God.

Goals for the Learners:

(1) to explore passages in the Book of Esther to identify its messages of commitment, including that of Mordecai.
(2) to consider the implications of making commitments without respect to potential personal harm.
(3) to make commitments in spite of personal risk.

Pronunciation Guide:

Ahasuerus (uh hash yoo er' uhs)   Purim (pyoo' rim)
Haman (hay' muhn)   Susa (soo' suh)
Hathach (hay' thak)   Vashti (vash' ti)
Mordecai (mor' duh ki)   Zeresh (zihr' ish)

Supplies:

Bibles, newsprint and marker, paper and pencils, hymnals, optional children's book *Queen Esther: The Morning Star*

READING THE SCRIPTURE

NRSV
Esther 4:1-3, 9-17

¹When Mordecai learned all that had been done, Mordecai tore his clothes and put on sackcloth and ashes, and went through the

NIV
Esther 4:1-3, 9-17

¹When Mordecai learned of all that had been done, he tore his clothes, put on sackcloth and ashes, and went out into the city,

city, wailing with a loud and bitter cry; ²he went up to the entrance of the king's gate, for no one might enter the king's gate clothed with sackcloth. ³In every province, wherever the king's command and his decree came, there was great mourning among the Jews, with fasting and weeping and lamenting, and most of them lay in sackcloth and ashes.

⁹Hathach went and told Esther what Mordecai had said. ¹⁰Then Esther spoke to Hathach and gave him a message for Mordecai, saying, ¹¹"All the king's servants and the people of the king's provinces know that if any man or woman goes to the king inside the inner court without being called, there is but one law—all alike are to be put to death. Only if the king holds out the golden scepter to someone, may that person live. I myself have not been called to come in to the king for thirty days." ¹²When they told Mordecai what Esther had said, ¹³Mordecai told them to reply to Esther, "Do not think that in the king's palace you will escape any more than all the other Jews. ¹⁴For if you keep silence at such a time as this, relief and deliverance will rise for the Jews from another quarter, but you and your father's family will perish. Who knows? Perhaps you have come to royal dignity for just such a time as this." ¹⁵Then Esther said in reply to Mordecai, ¹⁶"Go, gather all the Jews to be found in Susa, and hold a fast on my behalf, and neither eat nor drink for three days, night or day. I and my maids will also fast as you do. After that I will go to the king, though it is against the law; and if I perish, I perish." ¹⁷Mordecai then went away and did everything as Esther had ordered him.

wailing loudly and bitterly. ²But he went only as far as the king's gate, because no one clothed in sackcloth was allowed to enter it. ³In every province to which the edict and order of the king came, there was great mourning among the Jews, with fasting, weeping and wailing. Many lay in sackcloth and ashes.

⁹Hathach went back and reported to Esther what Mordecai had said. ¹⁰Then she instructed him to say to Mordecai, ¹¹"All the king's officials and the people of the royal provinces know that for any man or woman who approaches the king in the inner court without being summoned the king has but one law: that he be put to death. The only exception to this is for the king to extend the gold scepter to him and spare his life. But thirty days have passed since I was called to go to the king."

¹²When Esther's words were reported to Mordecai, ¹³he sent back this answer: "Do not think that because you are in the king's house you alone of all the Jews will escape. ¹⁴For if you remain silent at this time, relief and deliverance for the Jews will arise from another place, but you and your father's family will perish. And who knows but that you have come to royal position for such a time as this?"

¹⁵Then Esther sent this reply to Mordecai: ¹⁶"Go, gather together all the Jews who are in Susa, and fast for me. Do not eat or drink for three days, night or day. I and my maids will fast as you do. When this is done, I will go to the king, even though it is against the law. And if I perish, I perish." ¹⁷So Mordecai went away and carried out all of Esther's instructions.

UNDERSTANDING THE SCRIPTURE

Introduction to Esther 4–5. The Book of Esther is set in the historical period when the Jews were under the authority of the Persian Empire. The events take place largely in the city of Susa, the winter residence of the Persian king. The story opens with an account of a great banquet given by the king Ahasuerus (known in Greek as

Xerxes) where "he displayed the great wealth of his kingdom and the splendor and pomp of his majesty" (1:4). This great feast is said to have lasted for six months! Here is an early hint that the Book of Esther is a fictionalized legend or tall tale. There is a lot of humor and much of it comes through exaggeration. The feast for nobility was followed by a banquet for the ordinary people of Susa, and it was here that the king's problems with women began. Under the influence of too much wine, Ahasuerus sent for his queen Vashti to come to the banquet hall so that he might display her beauty before the crowd. Vashti refused to come! For this act of defiance Vashti has become a prototype of the liberated woman. The king's advisors warned: "this deed of the queen will be made known to all women, causing them to look with contempt on their husbands" (1:17). The description of the men's agitation is quite overstated and amusing. For her defiance Queen Vashti was banished from the king's presence, and official letters were sent throughout the empire, "declaring that every man should be master in his own house" (1:22). When he began to grieve over Vashti, the king's advisors organized an elaborate beauty contest. Lovely young maidens from all over the empire were brought to Susa and, after a year of cosmetic treatments, each "went in to the king" (2:13). Esther won the contest and was made queen. Esther was a Jewish woman who was the cousin and adopted daughter of Mordecai, a minor official at the Persian court. She did not reveal her Jewish ethnicity to the king or his court.

In Chapter 3 we learn that Haman had been elevated to a high position in the royal court. Haman was a pompous man and was infuriated when Mordecai, whose Jewishness was well known, refused to bow down to him. For revenge Haman plotted to destroy all the Jews. He bribed and persuaded the king to issue a decree that on a certain day people throughout the empire were to attack and kill their Jewish neigh-

bors. At the beginning of Chapter 4, Mordecai had found out about this decree.

Esther 4:1-3. Mordecai dressed himself in sackcloth and ashes and wailed bitterly—typical expressions of mourning in that culture. The Jewish population joined him in these demonstrations. The king's gate was the main gate of the city. It functioned as a place where commercial transactions took place and legal matters were settled. As an official in the government, Mordecai was probably there regularly, but at this point his mourning made him ritually unclean.

Esther 4:4-8. The women of a king's harem were attended and guarded by eunuchs—men who were incapable of sexual activity, either naturally or as a result of castration. A trusted eunuch was used by Esther as her liaison with Mordecai. Isolated in the harem, Esther was unaware of the king's decree and wanted to learn the reason for Mordecai's actions. Mordecai knew that only Esther was in a position to do anything to thwart the decree of which he sent her a copy.

Esther 4:9-11. Apparently the king's ardor for Esther had cooled and she had not been called to him in a month. Because of the risk of assassinations, which were common, palace security rules forbade anyone who had not been summoned from approaching the king.

Esther 4:12-14. Mordecai's assertion that if Esther will not intervene, "relief and deliverance will rise for the Jews from another quarter" is cryptic and ambivalent. Ordinarily one would assume that the reference is to God, but the Book of Esther makes no explicit mention of the Deity. The most famous words in the book are Mordecai's statement to Esther that she may have become queen, "for just such a time as this."

Esther 4:15-17. Esther's call for a fast is the only mention in the book of anything that might be considered a religious activity. Persuaded by Mordecai's appeal, Esther was preparing herself for dangerous action.

Esther 5:1-3. Esther dressed so as to

appear most attractive to Ahasuerus and courageously violated both custom and law, literally risking her life. The golden scepter or rod was a sign of the royal authority. The king's promise to give Esther "even to the half of my kingdom" was typical hyperbole of the culture and clearly conveyed his pleasure at her appearance before him.

Esther 5:4-5. Rather than raising her concern directly, Esther invited the king and Haman, his prime minister and enemy of the Jews, to a banquet. We might assume that she thought that a dinner party was the best setting in which to make her plea. The occasion would be in the women's quarters of the palace where she would feel secure.

Esther 5:6-8. We expect Esther's request to be raised at the banquet, but the author deliberately prolongs the suspense of the tale. The second banquet has no significance except as a literary embellishment to the story.

Esther 5:9-11. Haman had been flattered by these two invitations to dine alone with the king and queen. He was feeling even more pompous and arrogant than usual but was abruptly brought down by Mordecai's disrespect. His shallowness was revealed plainly in his expansive boasting to his wife and friends. Later in the book we learn that Haman had ten sons—a source of great pride in this patriarchal culture.

Esther 5:12-13. Haman could not enjoy his status and wealth because his hatred for Mordecai poisoned his whole mind.

Esther 5:14. In his lust for vengeance, Haman prepared to put Mordecai to death by public hanging on a gallows 75 feet high. This excessive height is another touch of oriental hyperbole.

INTERPRETING THE SCRIPTURE

A Rationale for Merrymaking

The Book of Esther was one of the last books to be accepted into the biblical canon by Jews and by Christians. It is not hard to see why: It contains no mention of God or of religious practices, no mention of the law or the covenant. The action takes place in a purely Gentile environment and a woman whose morals were subject to question is the heroine. It is a thoroughly secular piece of writing. Worse, it praises actions of violent revenge. The book is the only one in the Old Testament that is not found among the Dead Sea Scrolls; it is not quoted or even referred to in the New Testament.

Esther is one of the Five Scrolls—books that are read on certain Jewish festival days. It contains the explanation of the origin of the popular feast of Purim, which Jews celebrate in early spring. Purim was probably a festival that was borrowed from neighboring people in some area of the Persian Empire. The name is taken from the Hebrew word for "lot." In Esther 9:24, Haman cast lots to determine on what day the extermination of the Jews would be scheduled. Purim is a thoroughly secular holiday; a time for riotous celebration. We might think of it as Jewish Mardi Gras. An old proverb says: "On Purim, anything is allowed." That is an exaggeration, but it is true that there is great feasting, exchanging of gifts of food, charitable giving, and partying. Another old proverb exhorts: "Drink until you cannot distinguish 'Cursed be Haman' from 'Blessed be Mordecai.'" Costume parties are popular and reading aloud of the Book of Esther is punctuated with acclamation, cheers, hisses, and boos. Of course, the holiday is a great favorite of Jewish children.

The Book of Esther provides a rationale for Purim, which is mentioned nowhere else in Scripture. This fact, however, does not mean that the book has no theological value. Purim celebrates the Jews' victory over those who would have destroyed them. That reality has deep meaning in understanding God's plan for salvation.

"For Just Such a Time as This"

The story is told in third person, and we are not given any insight into what was going on in Esther's mind except as expressed in her words and actions. We cannot ascertain precisely why she acted as she did, contrary to all common sense and self-interest. Esther was one of the king's favorites. She likely could have remained secluded and safe in the palace, regardless of what happened to her people. Instead she chose to act to save the Jews. We do not know what commitments motivated her. Was it her love for her cousin and adoptive father Mordecai? Was it love for her people? Or was it perhaps her own integrity and sense of duty? We are reminded of the story of Joseph after he had been sold into slavery by his brothers and taken to Egypt. Having risen to a high position in the Egyptian government, he was able to care for them and their families in time of famine. When they apologized, he replied, "God sent me before you to preserve life. . . . It was not you who sent me here, but God" (Genesis 45:5, 8).

What Haman had planned was what has since been called pogroms—violent attacks on the Jews by mobs with at least tacit government support. The history of the Jewish people has been replete with this kind of persecution. This book includes an interesting explanation for anti-Semitism: "Their laws are different from those of every other people, and they do not keep the king's laws, so that it is not appropriate for the king to tolerate them" (3:8). The Jews have suffered a long, bloody history of persecution that has not yet ended. Yet they survive and retain their identity as a people. One of the messages of the Book of Esther is surely that God's chosen people are ultimately indestructible. They will suffer, but they will not be exterminated, because they are a part of the divine plan for human salvation. This truth is embedded in the book in the warning of Haman's wife Zeresh, who said to him: "If Mordecai, before whom your downfall has begun, is of the Jewish people, you will not prevail against him, but will surely fall before him" (6:13).

Although God does not appear in the Book of Esther in the prominent, active role that the divine plays in most of the rest of the Old Testament, we should not think that God is absent. God is "in the wings" in this drama, arranging the props, supplying the lines, directing the actors. In one way or another, God is hidden behind all events; God is present even when seemingly absent. We know it by faith and experience, even when we have no concrete evidence to prove it. The Jewish and the Christian hope, indeed confidence, is that God's purposes will ultimately be fulfilled. The witness of the Book of Esther is that God works through human beings to direct the events of history. Because God has so chosen, human action is important in accomplishing the divine purpose and fulfilling the divine will.

Commitment at the Risk of Life

Esther risked her life when she agreed to approach the Persian king on behalf of her people. She is an example for us of the dangers and uncertainties of deep commitment. Fortunately, most Christians in North America today will never be in positions where we will be called upon to assume such dire risks. However, we must not be unaware that there are Christians in other parts of the world who are, indeed, risking their lives daily in order to be faithful to Christ. Christians in China and under other totalitarian governments are persecuted for their faith just as surely as were the early Christians in the Roman Empire. In some Muslim nations that are ruled by extreme fundamentalist Islamists (certainly this does not include all Muslim societies), conversion to Christianity is a crime punishable by death. A good spiritual exercise for all for us would be to regularly and prayerfully consider what we would do if we were literally risking our lives in order to be faithful to Christ. What would you do? How would you find the strength to be faithful? What might happen if you were unable to face the costs?

I am writing this on the eve of *Yom HaShoah*, Holocaust Memorial Day, which is observed every spring by Jews and by many Christian churches. In worship services commemorating this horrible occurrence, six candles may be lit—honoring the six million Jews who were killed. For those of us who are Christian, there is powerful significance in another symbol. During some commemorations six yellow tulips are placed on the altar table in honor of the "righteous Gentiles"—those Christians who risked their lives, and in many cases lost their lives, to rescue and protect their Jewish neighbors. Here is a striking expression of the cost of commitments that we may undertake without knowing what the consequences will be but willing to pay the highest price if necessary.

SHARING THE SCRIPTURE

Preparing Our Hearts

Meditate on this week's devotional reading, found in Philippians 1:20-30. Here, Paul writes about "speaking with all boldness" (1:20), even if that forthrightness costs him his life. In that way he is like Esther, whose story we will encounter this week. When it comes to speaking out about your faith, just how candid are you? Are there things you will say only to certain people, fearing ridicule or reprisals from others? How can Paul be a role model for you in speaking fearlessly on behalf of Christ?

Pray that you and the adult learners will be willing to risk everything for God.

Preparing Our Minds

Study the background from Chapters 4 and 5 of Esther and the lesson Scripture from Esther 4:1-3, 9-17. Ponder what people are willing to commit themselves to, even at personal risk.

Write on newsprint:

❑ information for next week's lesson, found under "Continue the Journey."

❑ activities for further spiritual growth in "Continue the Journey."

Option: Locate *Queen Esther: The Morning Star* by Mordicai Gerstein, which is a children's book that portrays Esther's story.

LEADING THE CLASS

(1) Gather to Learn

❖ Welcome the class members and introduce any guests.

❖ Pray that those who have come today will be challenged to take risks for God.

❖ Read this information: **Imagine attending a worship service where police officers routinely broke into the church, beat and arrested worshipers, destroyed church buildings, and confiscated Bibles. We are not recalling the days of ancient Rome but are talking about the contemporary church in China, as reported on January 18, 2007, on *World Net Daily*. Despite vigorous persecution of those engaged in "a cultic and illegal activity," an estimated 3,000 people come to know Jesus every day. About 90 percent of these**

Christians worship in house churches, which stand firm in preaching the gospel despite the enormous cost. Government action, amazingly, is not enough to deter those who continue to seek Christ.

❖ Discuss this question: **Why do you think people are willing to pledge themselves so unreservedly to Christ even though they know there is a high probability they will suffer for their commitment?**

❖ Read aloud today's focus statement: **Some persons are willing to make commitments that break rules and may imperil themselves. To what do people commit even at personal risk? Queen Esther was willing to sacrifice her life for the people of God.**

(2) Explore Passages in the Book of Esther to Identify Its Messages of Commitment, Including That of Mordecai

❖ Begin the Bible exploration by reading or retelling the Introduction to Esther 4–5 in Understanding the Scripture. Then read Esther 3:8-11, 13-14 so that the adults can clearly understand the reason for Mordecai's distress in Chapter 4.

❖ Ask a volunteer to read today's Scripture lesson from Esther 4:1-3, 9-17.

❖ **Option:** Read *Queen Esther: The Morning Star* by Mordicai Gerstein. This beautifully illustrated children's book retells the story of Esther. Remind the class that the Purim holiday, which celebrates Esther's triumph in saving the Jews, is a beloved holiday among Jewish children. Class members may enjoy seeing the story as they hear it. Note that two additions to the biblical story have been made in this book.

❖ Distribute paper and pencils. Note that we have no way of knowing what is going through Esther's mind, or Mordecai's. Encourage some students to write a diary/journal entry for Esther on the night before she tries to see the king.

Include her thoughts on her own life, the threat to her Jewish people, how she intends to persuade the king, and the risks she is willing to take on their behalf. Encourage other students to write a diary/journal entry for Mordecai, noting what he expects Esther to be able to do, his own concerns for the Jewish people, and his commitments.

❖ Invite the students to read their entries to a partner and to discuss how Esther and Mordecai are fulfilling their respective commitments to God.

(3) Consider the Implications of Making Commitments Without Respect to Potential Personal Harm

❖ Read the second paragraph of "Commitment at the Risk of Life" in Interpreting the Scripture.

❖ Note that according to The Southern Institute for Education and Research, **"significantly less than one percent of the non-Jewish population in Nazi-occupied Europe embarked upon the path of Jewish rescue. Many people were afraid to help the Jews, knowing well the Nazi penalties. Many were indifferent to the Jewish destruction. Many were delighted by it."**

❖ Discuss these questions:
   (1) What would you individually and as a congregation be willing to do to help those who are being persecuted?
   (2) Who can we help now?
   (3) What can we do? (You may be able to send money, support a missionary, or provide Bibles.)

❖ **Option:** Plan a get-together with the class during which you watch and then discuss the movie *Schindler's List*.

(4) Make Commitments in Spite of Personal Risk

❖ Read the following: **In an interview, former Muslim, now Christian teacher at a Baptist seminary, Dr. Emir Caner spoke** with Wendy Griffith of the Christian Broadcasting Network about the price Muslims pay for converting to Christianity. According to Dr. Caner, author of *The Costly Call*, "they lose their family, they risk their lives, they lose their jobs; they're ostracized from their culture." Consequences for Christian conversion include being disowned, as Dr. Caner was, seeing one's parents killed or severely beaten, and exile.

❖ Invite the students to meditate on this question: **If being a Christian were that costly, would you take the risk and pay the price? Why or why not?**

❖ Encourage the students to talk about whether or not they would be willing to make such a risky commitment. Be careful, though, that class members do not judge one another. What we agree to in a hypothetical situation we may find impossible to fulfill in an actual situation. On the other hand, some who think such commitment is impossible may find great courage in such a difficult situation.

(5) Continue the Journey

❖ Pray that today's participants will be willing to make risky commitments to others in order to serve God.

❖ Read aloud this preparation for next week's lesson. You may also want to post it on newsprint for the students to copy.

■ **Title: Isaiah Answers God's Call**
■ **Background Scripture: Isaiah 6**
■ **Lesson Scripture: Isaiah 6:1-8**
■ **Focus of the Lesson: Some people may be required to give up a way**

of life and to relocate in order to fulfill their commitment. How much are we willing to sacrifice for a commitment? Isaiah answered God's call to commitment by giving up everything and moving on.

❖ Challenge the students to complete one or more of these activities for further spiritual growth, which you will write on newsprint for the students to copy.

(1) **Research some Righteous Gentiles of World War II, those who aided Jews in spite of potential dire consequences. Oskar Schindler, Raoul Wallenberg, and Frank Foley are names you will be able to locate. What do you suppose motivated them to take such dangerous risks?**

(2) **Read a book or article about Christians who have been persecuted for their faith. *Tortured for Christ* (first published in 1967) tells author Richard Wurmbrand's now classic story of his own abduction and imprisonment in Romania for his refusal to deny Christ.**

(3) **Spend time in prayer and fasting about a situation in which you or others are at risk for faith in Christ.**

❖ Sing or read aloud "Trust and Obey."

❖ Conclude today's session by leading the class in this benediction, taken from Luke 1:38: **Here am I, the servant of the Lord; let it be with me according to your word.**

UNIT 2: OLD TESTAMENT PEOPLE OF COMMITMENT
ISAIAH ANSWERS GOD'S CALL

PREVIEWING THE LESSON

Lesson Scripture: Isaiah 6:1-8
Background Scripture: Isaiah 6
Key Verse: Isaiah 6:8

Focus of the Lesson:

Some people may be required to give up a way of life and to relocate in order to fulfill their commitment. How much are we willing to sacrifice for a commitment? Isaiah answered God's call to commitment by giving up everything and moving on.

Goals for the Learners:

(1) to discover the motivation for Isaiah's commitment.
(2) to explore the limits of their commitment to God.
(3) to identify and respond to situations in which God is calling them to move beyond the present limits of their commitments.

Pronunciation Guide:

Ahaz (ay' haz)
Hezekiah (hez uh ki' uh)
Uzziah (uh zi' uh)

Supplies:

Bibles, newsprint and marker, paper and pencils, hymnals

READING THE SCRIPTURE

NRSV
Isaiah 6:1-8

¹In the year that King Uzziah died, I saw the Lord sitting on a throne, high and lofty; and the hem of his robe filled the temple. ²Seraphs were in attendance above him; each had six wings: with two they covered their faces, and with two they covered their

NIV
Isaiah 6:1-8

¹In the year that King Uzziah died, I saw the Lord seated on a throne, high and exalted, and the train of his robe filled the temple. ²Above him were seraphs, each with six wings: With two wings they covered their faces, with two they covered their feet,

feet, and with two they flew. ³And one called to another and said:

"Holy, holy, holy is the LORD of hosts;
the whole earth is full of his glory."

⁴The pivots on the thresholds shook at the voices of those who called, and the house filled with smoke. ⁵And I said: "Woe is me! I am lost, for I am a man of unclean lips, and I live among a people of unclean lips; yet my eyes have seen the King, the LORD of hosts!"

⁶Then one of the seraphs flew to me, holding a live coal that had been taken from the altar with a pair of tongs. ⁷The seraph touched my mouth with it and said: "Now that this has touched your lips, your guilt has departed and your sin is blotted out."

⁸Then I heard the voice of the Lord saying, "Whom shall I send, and who will go for us?" And I said, "Here am I; send me!"

and with two they were flying. ³And they were calling to one another:

"Holy, holy, holy is the LORD Almighty;
the whole earth is full of his glory."

⁴At the sound of their voices the doorposts and thresholds shook and the temple was filled with smoke.

⁵"Woe to me!" I cried. "I am ruined! For I am a man of unclean lips, and I live among a people of unclean lips, and my eyes have seen the King, the LORD Almighty."

⁶Then one of the seraphs flew to me with a live coal in his hand, which he had taken with tongs from the altar. ⁷With it he touched my mouth and said, "See, this has touched your lips; your guilt is taken away and your sin atoned for."

⁸Then I heard the voice of the Lord saying, "Whom shall I send? And who will go for us?"

And I said, "Here am I. Send me!"

UNDERSTANDING THE SCRIPTURE

Introduction to Isaiah 6. Most scholars believe that the Book of Isaiah contains the writings of at least three different prophets from different periods of Jewish history. The first thirty-nine chapters are designated as the work of Isaiah of Jerusalem; he is the prophet with whom this lesson is concerned. He is considered the greatest of the writing prophets. This passage comes from the portion of the book that is the prophet's memoir and is often referred to as the call of the prophet Isaiah. Although he may have started his prophetic activity prior to this experience, he certainly understood this to be the occasion of his commissioning to the work of calling his people to account for their sins. Isaiah's career was in the eighth century before Christ, in the southern kingdom of Judah. He was a contemporary of other Old Testament prophets such as Amos, Hosea, and Micah. The period was

one of great challenge and significance. The Israelite nation had reached its height of power and influence during the kingships of David and his son Solomon. After Solomon's death, the nation was divided into two kingdoms—Israel in the north with its capital at Samaria and Judah in the south with its capital at Jerusalem. Both of these small kingdoms were constantly threatened by the powerful empires of the Middle East who were their neighbors. The Northern Kingdom of Israel had fallen under the control of the Assyrian Empire in 721 B.C. Its land was annexed to the empire and its people dislocated. Judah had hung on precariously but was always in danger.

Isaiah 6:1. The setting of this dramatic experience was the great Temple built by Solomon. It was a beautiful, elaborate, and lavishly adorned building in the capital city of Jerusalem. The Temple was divided into several sections. The innermost was the Holy of Holies or Most Holy Place where the presence of God was believed to dwell most powerfully. Beyond that was the Holy Place. Isaiah may have been in one of these inner sanctums and, if so, this indicates that he was a priest, since no one else was allowed there. The prophet's vision in the Temple of Solomon was of the heavenly temple of God. This encounter with the Lord probably occurred in the year 742 B.C. King Uzziah had ruled Judah wisely and well for more than forty years. His death marked the end of the nation's glory and prosperity. Isaiah was elsewhere credited with having written a history of the reign of Uzziah (see 2 Chronicles 26:22). He was likely depressed and discouraged over the death of his monarch.

Isaiah 6:2. In the vision of the heavenly temple, God sat enthroned with his heavenly court. God was attended by seraphs (plural is also "seraphim"), who are mentioned nowhere else in the Bible. They were angelic creatures, rather serpent-like in appearance, with multiple wings. The root word "seraph," which means "to burn" is translated as "fiery serpent" in Isaiah 14:29. According to later writers who tried to interpret the positioning of the wings, covering the eyes was a sign of *poverty*, because a veiled face signified *humility*. Since "feet" was a well-known euphemism for genitals, the covering of the feet was a sign of *chastity*. The two wings the seraphim used to fly wherever God sent them to carry out God's orders signified *obedience*. The seraphim are the highest of the nine orders of angels.

Isaiah 6:3. For Isaiah, holiness is the defining quality of God. His favorite title for God was "The Holy One of Israel." (The term "Israel" is commonly used to refer to the whole Jewish people even after the conquest of the Northern Kingdom.) The threefold repetition of "holy" is for emphasis. The seraphim sang an antiphonal hymn of praise to God.

Isaiah 6:4. Smoke was a sign of the divine presence and recalled the smoke of incense and burnt offerings used in Temple worship. The precise meaning of the Hebrew word that the NRSV translates as "pivots" is unknown, but the NIV rendering as "doorposts" seems reasonable. An earthquake during the reign of Uzziah was remembered by Amos (1:1) and Zechariah (14:5) and small tremors were not unusual in the area. Such quakes were thought of as signs of the presence of God. The scene is reminiscent of the manifestations of the divine presence at Mount Sinai when the Hebrew people were on their journey from Egypt through the desert wilderness (Exodus 19:18-19; 20:18-19).

Isaiah 6:5. Isaiah was terrified by the sense of his own unworthiness. He knew that no sinful person could stand before God and that anyone who saw God was expected to die. Not only was he personally sinful but he was also aware of the unfaithfulness of his people. The theme of this and the following verses is the contrast between divine holiness and human sinfulness.

Isaiah 6:6-8. The coal was apparently so hot that the seraph had to use tongs to remove it from the altar where the sacrifices were burning. The touching of Isaiah's mouth with the coal was a ritual of purification. Fire is often used in the Scripture as a metaphor for cleansing and refining. In the call accounts of both Jeremiah (1:9) and Ezekiel (3:2), God touched the mouths of the prophets in order to put the divine message within them. God spoke for the first time in the vision, but to the heavenly council, not to the prophet. The climax of the account occurred when Isaiah overheard the divine question and responded affirmatively. The prophet's acceptance of God's call was in the tradition of Abraham, Moses, Samuel, and others in the Old Testament who responded the same way.

Isaiah 6:9-13. The prophet was made to understand that his words would not change the hearts of his people and they, their houses, and their cities would be destroyed. Only the last part of verse 13 offers any hope and the text of the manuscripts from which translators work are so damaged that the meaning is unclear.

INTERPRETING THE SCRIPTURE

"Holy, Holy, Holy"

Isaiah's favorite designation for God is "The Holy One of Israel." "Holy, Holy, Holy! Lord God Almighty" is one of the most widely used of our hymns. However, I would argue that the holiness of God is a concept with which many contemporary Christians struggle. We are, unfortunately, more comfortable with a view of God as our "copilot," "the man upstairs," or "big daddy in the sky." Perhaps it is because those of us who are Americans are innately anti-hierarchical in our thinking. We resist recognition of anything or anyone so superior to ourselves that our only proper response is awe and adoration. Karl Barth (1886–1968), an eminent theologian of the twentieth century, taught that we should think and speak of God as "the Wholly Other." Rudolf Otto (1869–1937), a German theologian, wrote a famous book entitled *The Idea of the Holy*. He emphasized that authentic religious feeling far transcends rationality: "[The holy is] the deepest and most fundamental element in all strong and sincerely felt religious emotion." It may "come sweeping like a gentle tide, pervading the mind with a tranquil mood of deepest worship. . . . It may burst in sudden eruption up from the depths of the soul with spasms and convulsions, or lead to the strangest excitements, to intoxicated frenzy, to transport, and to ecstasy." Perhaps these words express something of the feeling that Isaiah felt in the Temple. It is this kind of intensity of experience, transcending rationality and calculation, that enables us to make and keep the kind of commitments that God desires.

Isaiah was likely a priest; he was connected to the aristocracy of his society; he served as a kind of secretary of state to King Ahaz and King Hezekiah. In defiance of this status, Isaiah was commissioned by God to proclaim a very unpopular message, one that was counter to the desires and behavior of the society in which he lived. He was even commissioned to announce that inevitable disaster was approaching his people. A tradition recorded in a Jewish writing "The Ascension of Isaiah" says that the prophet was sawed in half by order of the evil king Manasseh. He was able to fulfill this commission only because he had personally and powerfully experienced the presence of the God whose glory filled the Temple and fills the whole earth. Would that God's people today could open ourselves to the realization that the nature and will of God far exceed our finite human capacities to comprehend!

"Here I Am, Lord"

One of the most popular new hymns in many Christian communities is "Here I Am, Lord," which speaks of God "calling in the night." Surely the writer, Dan Schutte, must have been inspired by Isaiah 6, as well as similar call accounts in the Bible. Numerous people testify that they have been powerfully moved by this hymn to commit themselves to Christ and Christian service in deeper, more powerful ways. Many experiences of call and commitment occur in the context of worship, as did Isaiah's. Indeed, one of the purposes of worship for Christians is that it provides an arena in which we can open ourselves to hear what God has to say to us. In the midst of the busyness of life, we may too seldom be sensitive to the divine presence and message. In public and private worship, we have the opportunity to listen and answer.

For many of us the call to respond to the needs of the world is experienced in the context of worship. It is the responsibility of pastors, musicians, and other liturgical leaders to confront worshipers with the realities of racism, poverty, prejudice, oppression, and discrimination. Worship can present a challenge and call forth a response. Indeed, I contend that worship that does not raise awareness and concern for the deprivation in which so many live is shallow and hollow. Worship that does not call forth transformation is a charade. Our society, our world, is in desperate need of prophetic voices today. While few of us are able to enjoy the grandeur of a worship setting comparable to the Temple, the issue is not the majesty of the place, but the majesty of the Lord. God can reveal the divine self and call us into prophetic service within any worship experience. Lines from a Franciscan benediction express it well: "May God bless you with anger at injustice, oppression, and exploitation of people, so that you may work for justice, freedom, and peace. . . . And may God bless you with enough foolishness to believe that you can make a difference in the world so that you can do what others claim cannot be done." That is the spirit with which we are to leave worship.

Faithfulness, Not Success

Too often, we evaluate our work, even our lives, by noting the successes that we have accomplished. The biblical message is different: It is our failures that may be the best indicators of our faithfulness. We are responsible for our commitments and for the conscientiousness with which we fulfill them. We are not responsible for the results,

which may well be beyond our control. Judged by the usual standards of success, the preaching of most of the prophets was a failure. Judged by similar standards, the ministry of Jesus was not at all successful.

In light of God's call and Isaiah's commitment, verses 9 and 10 of Isaiah 6 are confusing to most readers. God seems to be instructing the prophet not to warn the people, but to make certain that they do not become aware of the divine warning of impending judgment. Portions of these verses are quoted by Jesus in Matthew 13:13-15, Mark 4:12, and Luke 8:10, in his explanation to the disciples of the parable of the sower. He was making the point that the disciples were able to understand his message but that the crowds of hearers were unwilling to do so. There are other passages in both the Old and New Testaments which make clear that God's words through God's spokespersons are going to be rejected.

I do not claim to have ultimate wisdom about how these passages should be understood, but my opinion is this: God knows the future as well as the past and present. All time is alike to God; there is no difference. God knows what the response to a prophet's proclamation, to the teachings of Jesus, or to the preaching of the gospel will be, because for God it has already happened. God's foreknowledge, though, is not the same as predestination. God's knowledge of what humans will do does not cause us to act that way. We possess God-given freedom of will to make moral choices.

When God commissions Isaiah to proclaim the divine message to the people of Judah, God knows and tells the prophet that his efforts will not succeed. When we commit ourselves to the work of God, we are not guaranteed success or sometimes even expected to succeed. In the final analysis, the response of others to our message and work is not our responsibility. Instead, the depth of Isaiah's commitment, and of ours, is measured by our willingness to answer and obey God's call.

SHARING THE SCRIPTURE

Preparing Our Hearts

Meditate on this week's devotional reading, found in Revelation 4, where we glimpse a peek of worship in heaven. Who do you see here? What are they doing? How would you feel to be part of such an assembly? As you read today's lesson from Isaiah 6, keep in mind this picture in Revelation so that you can compare the two.

Pray that you and the adult learners will experience the mystery and awe of God as you worship.

Preparing Our Minds

Study the background from Isaiah 6 and the lesson Scripture from verses 1-8. Evaluate how much you are willing to sacrifice to fulfill a commitment.

Write on newsprint:
❑ small group discussion questions for "Identify and Respond to Situations in Which God Is Calling the Learners to Move Beyond the Present Limits of Their Commitments."
❑ information for next week's lesson, found under "Continue the Journey."
❑ activities for further spiritual growth in "Continue the Journey."

Practice reading aloud Isaiah 6:1-8.

LEADING THE CLASS

(1) Gather to Learn

❖ Welcome the class members and introduce any guests.
❖ Pray that everyone who has come today will be open to experiencing God in fresh and exciting ways.
❖ Read this story, which is true, though the names have been changed. **Emily and John had retired to a beautiful home on a golf course in a country club community.** **They were looking forward to enjoying their time together and well-earned rest when their daughter who lived in another state was diagnosed with multiple sclerosis (MS). As her condition worsened, Emily and John made the decision to sell their lovely home and move to a smaller house close to their daughter to help care for her and the grandchildren.**
❖ Discuss with the class what they believe motivates people to make such a huge commitment. Invite the students to tell stories of families they know who have also made major commitments.
❖ Read aloud today's focus statement: **Some people may be required to give up a way of life and to relocate in order to fulfill their commitment. How much are we willing to sacrifice for a commitment? Isaiah answered God's call to commitment by giving up everything and moving on.**

(2) Discover the Motivation for Isaiah's Commitment

❖ Prepare the class for the reading of today's Scripture by asking them to close their eyes and envision themselves in the setting of the passage. Ask them to imagine what they can see, hear, taste, touch, and smell as you read Isaiah 6:1-8 expressively.
❖ Encourage the adults to identify the sights, sounds, tastes, odors, and things they could touch in this Temple scene.
❖ Discuss how this rich sensory environment made them feel. Were they awed, frightened, ready to leave, fascinated? Ask them to consider how their emotions were similar to and different from those of Isaiah that are reported in the text.
❖ Discuss Isaiah's description of God as holy and the call Isaiah received from the Holy One by reading or retelling "Holy, Holy, Holy" in Interpreting the Scripture.
❖ Encourage the students to think for a

few moments about their own vocational calling. Ask them to talk with a partner or small group about what God called them to do and how they knew it was God speaking to them. (Point out that "vocation" does not necessarily refer to one's career. Raising children or caring for aging family members, for example, may also be one's vocation.)

❖ Read aloud this information and discuss these questions with the class. **Humans are created in God's own image, but we easily fall short of the mark of living up to that image. Yet, often today even stalwart church members do not want to own up to sinful behavior. In verse 5, Isaiah acknowledged his sinfulness ("man of unclean lips") and the sinfulness of the Israelites ("people of unclean lips"). Why do you suppose Isaiah would confess when we so often fail to? What do you think would motivate contemporary people to recognize sin and repent more often than probably most of us do?**

(3) Explore the Limits of the Learners' Commitment to God

❖ Invite the students to read in unison today's key verse, Isaiah 6:8.

❖ Note that Isaiah put no limits on his commitments. He did not ask where God would send him, when, or with whom, or maybe without someone dear. He just responded.

❖ Ask: **Suppose you had been Isaiah. Would you have been willing to give God carte blanche (a blank check, so to speak) with your life? Why or why not?**

❖ Distribute paper and pencils. Tell the adults that this activity is for their eyes only. Ask them to write these words on the left side of the page: *time, money, talents, spiritual disciplines.* Go through the following steps, one at a time, allowing the class members enough time to complete each segment.

◼ Instruct the adults to think about how many hours they are willing to

give in service to God per week and write that figure in next to *time.*

◼ Ask them to consider the amount of money they give back to God through the church or perhaps through agencies that serve the poor, sick, or imprisoned, and write that figure in beside *money.* Also ask them, if possible, to compute the percentage of their weekly income they are contributing and add that figure.

◼ Invite them to list next to *talents* the gifts and skills they have that they are willing to use on a regular basis for God.

◼ Encourage them to estimate the number of hours per week they spend on *spiritual disciplines,* such as prayer, reading the Bible devotionally, Bible study, or meditation, and include that figure.

❖ Provide a few moments for the students to ponder the amount of commitment they have identified in each category. Then ask: **What do you think Jesus would say to you about the commitments you have made? If you think he would not be satisfied, what would you say regarding why your commitments are so limited?** Most students will likely prefer to answer these questions silently.

❖ Spend some time talking about why it is so difficult for many of us to make sacrificial commitments to God. See if the group can discern any strategies for increasing commitment.

(4) Identify and Respond to Situations in Which God Is Calling the Learners to Move Beyond the Present Limits of Their Commitments

❖ Brainstorm answers to this question with the class and list ideas on newsprint: **What challenges has God set before our congregation that may stretch us beyond our current limits of commitment?** (Here are some ideas: *reaching out to residents in a new housing development; wisely spending or investing a contribution made by a deceased parishioner; partnering with a church doing a special ministry, such as a congregation with a soup kitchen; undertaking the support of a missionary; adding a weekday ministry, such as child care or preschool.)*

❖ Divide into small groups and consider these questions, which you will post on newsprint. If you have identified several possible commitments, assign each group a different one.

    (1) What indications do we have that God is calling us to this ministry?

    (2) How will this new commitment stretch us as the people of God?

    (3) What can our class, as a group and as individuals, do to answer this call?

❖ Provide time for the groups to report on their findings.

❖ Take whatever action is necessary to enable the class to move forward with this potential commitment.

(5) Continue the Journey

❖ Pray that all those who have come today will be willing to answer God's call, even if that means making major changes in their lives.

❖ Read aloud this preparation for next week's lesson. You may also want to post it on newsprint for the students to copy.

    ■ **Title: A New Spirit**

    ■ **Background Scripture: Ezekiel 11:14-21**

    ■ **Lesson Scripture: Ezekiel 11:14-21**

■ **Focus of the Lesson: The frustrations of life, especially problems of our making, may entice us to give up hope for change. Is everything truly lost because we must reap the rewards of our own folly? Absolutely not, claims the prophet, for the God who never abandons us promises to give us a fresh start by providing a new heart and spirit.**

❖ Challenge the students to complete one or more of these activities for further spiritual growth, which you will write on newsprint for the students to copy.

    (1) Go to a place where you feel close to God—your church, an area of your home, nature. Meditate on the glory and majesty of God. Respond to any commitments that God may call you to make.

    (2) Research Isaiah of Jerusalem, whose call is recorded in Isaiah 6. How did he fulfill the commitment he made to God? In what ways can you be like Isaiah?

    (3) Assist someone who has had to make a major life change to fulfill commitments. Offer to support and help this person (or family) in any way you can.

❖ Sing or read aloud "Here I Am, Lord."

❖ Conclude today's session by leading the class in this benediction, taken from Luke 1:38: **Here am I, the servant of the Lord; let it be with me according to your word.**

THIRD QUARTER
New Creation in Christ

MARCH 1, 2009–MAY 31, 2009

The fourteen lessons for the spring quarter stretch across the Bible from Ezekiel through Luke and Acts to Ephesians to illustrate the newness of life—the new creation—that was promised to the Israelites and became a reality through Christ.

Unit 1, "The Promise of New Life," considers five passages from Ezekiel during the month of March. Although Ezekiel's prophecies are generally grim, the ones we will explore offer hope for new life. Our study on March 1 focuses on Ezekiel 11:14-21, which promises "A New Spirit." Ezekiel 34, the background text for March 8, decries Israel's ineffective leadership and promises "New Leadership." In "God's People Restored Again," the lesson for March 15 from Ezekiel 36:22-32, we learn how God intends to reverse the fortunes of Israel to demonstrate God's holiness. Taken from the familiar passage of the valley of dry bones in Ezekiel 37, we see on March 22 how God intends to renew the exiled Israelites in "Prophesying New Life." The image of the life-giving river in Ezekiel 47:1-12 helps us meet the challenge of "Envisioning New Life."

In April we focus on Jesus' death, resurrection, and postresurrection appearances, and ways in which the disciples bring new life to others in the name and through the power of Christ. The first lesson of Unit 2, "The Path to New Life," is on Palm/Passion Sunday, April 5. "Suffering Unto Death" is an apt title for this exploration of Luke 23:32-46, which tells the story of Jesus' crucifixion. The Easter story for April 12 from Luke 24:1-12, "Resurrected Unto New Life," describes the women's startling discovery at the empty tomb. On April 19 we encounter the last appearance of the resurrected Jesus to the disciples as reported in Luke 24:36-53 in the session entitled "Witnesses to New Life." The unit ends on April 26 with "Bringing New Life to Those in Need," a study of Peter's healing of Aeneas and raising of Tabitha (Dorcas) as told in Acts 9:32-43.

During the month of May we explore five concepts from the letter to the Ephesians: church as family, life, revelation, home life, and equipping ourselves for Christian living. Unit 3, "The Way of New Life," begins on May 3 with "New Family in Christ," a lesson rooted in Ephesians 1:3-14 that assures us that we are God's adopted children through Jesus. On May 10, we move to Ephesians 2:1-10 to learn about the "New Life in Christ" that is ours by grace through faith. "New Revelation in Christ," the session for May 17 from Ephesians 3:1-13, reveals how Christ is good news for all people—Jew and Gentile. Ephesians 5:1–6:4 is the basis for the lesson on May 24, "New Life in the Home," which emphasizes mutual submission. The unit ends on May 31 with "Equipped for New Life," a lesson from Ephesians 6:10-18 where we find the familiar image of the whole armor of God.

MEET OUR WRITER

DR. KAY E. HUGGINS

In 2003, I took an early retirement from pastoral ministry in order to devote time and care to our family. That year we relocated from Tucson, Arizona, to Albuquerque, New Mexico, and our family expanded to include my mother, then 93 with minor health issues and progressive dementia. Mom lived a full and rich life with us for the next three years, dying at our home in November 2006. It was a completely different form of ministry for me . . . one that I will always treasure.

So, what does an early-retired Presbyterian pastor do? She teaches Christology and Systematic Theology at the Ecumenical Institute for Ministry, an Albuquerque-based program of St. Norbert College (De Pere, Wisconsin) providing an ecumenical setting for students pursuing a masters in theological studies. She writes adult educational materials for the Presbyterian and United Methodist denominations. She accepts a part-time call to interim ministry. Essentially, she juggles the ministry demands of three part-time ministry opportunities.

However, she is "retired." By "retired" I understand that my everyday life of tending garden and home is an exercise in spiritual practice. In retirement, I have discovered wisdom through bird watching and flute practicing. The boundaries of my days are small: one trip to the grocery store, a few e-mails to answer, and lots of still silence. At some point every day, I have a book in my hands. I read for pleasure, research, and spiritual devotion. At some point every day, I have a pen in my hand. I write prayers and poems, sermons and lists, short stories and long letters. I thoroughly enjoy reading and writing; both activities draw me closer and closer to the person God calls me to be.

I confess, I never wanted to be "retired"—I scorned the easy life of self-indulgence so well advertised in our culture. I have discovered, however, that I appreciate the feel of retirement. It can be a time for healthy self-indulgence, especially for those of us who abused ourselves with out-of-control work habits. I am learning to honor God's gift that is my aging body; I'm learning that there are wise and harmful ways to use this gift. Retirement can also be an easy time. Not easy in the sense of trouble free, but easy in terms of appreciation and acceptance. Yes, these days, it is easy for me to say "thank you" and "let it be."

So, I find myself as a retired pastor in the wonderful position of continuing my ministry: by small contributions of teaching, writing, and pastoring. As a retired pastor, I also find myself learning God's grace close to home, among family and friends, and through the ebb and flow of health and happiness. I am grateful for every opportunity to share my faith—as I hope you will be grateful to receive my testimony in these lessons. I am relaxing into my new rhythm, even as I know that this more relaxed me is appreciated by our God. These retired days come with strong blessings to share with people like you.

THE BIG PICTURE:
BECOMING A NEW CREATION

I am a preacher, which is shorthand for saying I love stories. My husband is a navigator, which means he understands directions, maps, and precise reconnoitering. Can you imagine the challenges we pose to each other? Husband, George, asks me, "Kay, how far to the next town?" I reply, "Well, I went there last when I was invited to the Harvest Festival. I never would have considered going, but this invitation seemed so sincere and the people were so engaging that I thought, just for this time." At this point, George's eyes glaze over. He does not want stories, he wants miles, preferably in tenths of the mile. Eventually, I recognize this. I answer, "Ten and two-tenths miles due west."

From my husband I have learned the importance of north, south, east, and west. Because of him in my life, I can give directions using these coordinates. From me, my husband learned the sweetness of stories. After many years of marriage, he can laugh and smile at the endless tales that circulate in our household.

Our differences are not unlike the circumstances of the early Christian community. In that gathering of believers were members who wanted to know the specifics of the "way of Jesus." Also, in that community were Christians who soaked in the stories about Jesus. Both were necessary in the formation of the earliest Christian congregations. It was imperative that some remembered the directions that Jesus gave: Love your neighbor, pray for your enemies, seek out the poor, and give to others without counting the cost. It was also imperative that others remembered the ancient promises of good shepherds and restored creation, as well as the stories of passion, encounter, and empowerment.

In this quarter, you have the privilege of listening to the storytellers *and* the navigators. From the storytellers, you will glean a renewed appreciation for familiar texts. From the navigators you will receive the directions able to show you true north. Remember, both are necessary on this path of new life in Jesus Christ.

The Promise of New Life

The promise we are about to study began in exile, a situation we will likely never know. A preacher, with a style and approach foreign to our contemporary experience, gave shape, substance, and voice to a completely new word from God, and delivered the promise. Amazingly, although hundreds of generations have come and gone, students of Scripture continue to be roused from despair to hope by the promise of new life delivered through the prophetic literature of the exile. This happens despite ample evidence of the extreme differences between the Israelites of the Babylonian exile and contemporary Christians. The challenge to step out of the security of one's own known world and into the difficult-to-imagine world of exile is extraordinary. Yet, this challenge continues to draw students of the Bible into deeper and deeper reflection on God's words and ways. Why are we so attracted? Perhaps it is as simple as the promise itself. Ezekiel spoke a promise of new life to the exiles in Babylon; contemporary people continue to yearn for the same promise.

In order to understand the promise, students of Scripture seek to understand the conditions of life for the original audience and the specific call to ministry of the speaker. In this case, the conditions of life were grim. Hopelessness settled on the people like a suffocating blanket. First, there were military defeats and losses as Israel tumbled to the power of Babylon. Next came the humiliation of the forced eviction of the elite from Jerusalem and Judah. Then the end came: In 587 B.C., Jerusalem was razed. This series of events devastated the culture of Israel and shattered its religious life. The people were not only conquered by a foreign power but also lost all the symbols of God's constant care. In the holy city, familiar buildings became piles of rubble and rocks. The Temple walls were breached, and, in the Holy of Holies, images of foreign gods stood. The priesthood fled to the hills or endured the deadly march across the desert. There were no words adequate to the tragedy. The land, those left behind, and those marched off to Babylon, all were in a state of mourning. All the dependable sources of strength were compromised or broken; all that remained was a small community of those bound by sorrow and failure.

Yet God, in abundant grace and constant love, called out prophets to speak a new word to those who despaired of everything. The words of these men are collected in Isaiah (Chapters 40–55, sometimes called Second Isaiah or Deutero-Isaiah), Jeremiah, and Ezekiel. Each man adopted a different approach in response to his prophetic call. Isaiah, considered by scholars to have the widest perspective on God's salvation, used the broad poetic language of the faith community at worship. Jeremiah, referred to as the "weeping prophet," offered his life as a symbol for God's persistence and pleading. Ezekiel, a prophet with a gift for concentration and focus, shared a rich series of visions in order to communicate God's promise of new life.

Ezekiel's approach is the most confounding for the contemporary reader. Although his audience naturally understood the symbolism of his visions, Ezekiel's words demand a background. Contemporary students of Ezekiel must use resources and references in order to understand the intricacies of his message. The passages selected for the first unit of this quarter include Ezekiel's visions, oracles (that is, the Lord's words cushioned by images and metaphors), and extended reflections on the applicability of these visions and oracles. When dealing with such difficult forms of writing, it is wise to practice simplicity. Train yourself to ask, What is the promise of new life in this passage? With this thematic question as your guide, the effort to understand will be eased. In fact you, as I, may conclude this unit saying, "Ezekiel promises believers a new spirit, a new set of leaders, a new inner life, a new setting, and a new season of fruitfulness."

The Path to New Life

As Ezekiel used odd forms of expression and strong language to shape God's promise of new life, so the path to new life runs through the unique experiences of Jesus' passion and resurrection and into the lively demonstrations of power that characterized the early Christian community. These stories were initially testimonies colored by awe. A reverent approach is appropriate for the contemporary student. Consider the development of Christian theology from the earliest creed, "Jesus is Lord," to our contemporary and varied confessions of faith. What began with simplicity, today fills libraries. What started as a whispered account of Jesus' death, today is a story known around the world. The first to believe and the first to tell the stories could not imagine the consequence of their words and commitments. Yet, because they recorded a few words and joined together in small communities of trust, the world changed. The influence of Jesus, as mediated by his followers, is literally incalculable. Yet, the path to new life remains a mystery that each generation of Christians must unravel.

In the second unit of study, we face the mystery of Jesus' death, appearances, and continuing presence in the community of faith. Demanding concepts mark the path of new life: suffering, believing, witnessing, and serving. At each stopping point along the path, a familiar story provides the text. Beneath each text, a question pulses, What has this to do with me? These are not texts to be read and understood abstractly; rather, these intimate texts actually invite readers to listen with untutored ears and to look with untrained eyes. It just may be that most of us "know" too much about these texts—and that all of us "know" too little about their directions for following Jesus. Thus, this second section should be studied as a standard for faithfulness.

Each student of Jesus' path to new life walks through the Good Friday-to-Pentecost story of Jesus. On this path, each must settle for herself or himself the role that suffering, believing, witnessing, and serving plays in personal faith. None of these elements can be dismissed; all must be reckoned into the vibrant Christian faith. Without suffering, Jesus' story is only half told. Without the challenge of belief—is God able to raise Jesus from the dead?—we only "make believe." Whoever is incapable of telling the truth of Jesus has yet to be fully formed as one of his followers. Where there is no service to the poor, the neglected, the unloved, and the enemy, there is no obedient following of Jesus' path.

This unit addresses the familiar concepts of suffering, believing, witnessing, and serving in order to assist Christians in considering their individual path of faithfulness. However, the approach is not heavy-handed; these passages invite rather than command. With an emphasis on reverent studying, these passages are capable of inspiring awe similar to that possessed by the earliest Christians. As they followed Jesus, recorded his words, suffered their own humiliations, and honored his commitments to the poor and outcast, those Christians mapped out the path to new life. Your opportunity as a student is to follow their map and discover for yourself the route of Jesus' path.

The Way of New Life

The final unit allows a glimpse into a Christian community actually living "the way of new life." The Letter to the Ephesians provides a case study in the development of a community that has received the promise, the path, and the experience of new life. The congregation behind the letter is a healthy congregation. They are known to the author of the letter, and they are familiar with the broader community of small congregations. They have not yet faced persecution, but there are signs of danger in their context. Lively, worshipful, caring, and, at times, confused, this congregation is both similar to and wildly different from contemporary congregations. Their love of worship, respect for one another (even the difficult others), and their joy in the Lord are qualities found in contemporary North American Christian congregations. Their conflict over Jewish-versus-Gentile practices, their minority status (and subsequent cultural isolation), and the possibility of persecution make their experience foreign to the contemporary student. Again, there is a great divide between the first-century experience of faith and the twenty-first-century Christian experience. Again, by careful attention to setting, authorship, and, in this case, specialized vocabulary, students are able to walk alongside the Ephesians on their way of new life.

The setting of the Letter is the trade city of Ephesus, a cosmopolitan center where Far East and Near East met. The religious center of Ephesus was the Temple of Diana. The synagogue and new Christian community were very small in comparison to the cult of Diana. Insignificance in numbers and economic status provided a shadow of protection in which the Christian community developed without interference from the power and culture of Rome. Being small meant being safe; growth invited attention. Eventually, that attention would turn hostile. However, at the time the Letter to the Ephesians reached the congregation, there was a quiet peace surrounding.

It is, actually, impossible to authenticate the author of the Letter to the Ephesians. On the surface, there is internal evidence that Paul was the author (see 1:1; 3:1; 4:1). However, many scholars have compared the vocabulary of Ephesians to authenticated letters of Paul, and their discoveries make it unlikely that Paul is the author. Indeed, scholarship is equally divided between those who affirm Pauline authorship and those who deny his authorship. It is not a question that can be easily settled, but it is a question that can be easily set aside. This much is clear:

- the author knew and respected the congregation;
- the author wrote from a theological perspective on grace;
- the author trusted the congregation to receive the letter as an authoritative teaching.

Whether or not this author was Paul, I cannot say; in this unit I refer to the author as Paul, but I am holding open the scholarly question on authorship. Nevertheless, this much is sure: The Letter to the Ephesians was written and received by Christians endeavoring to make their way, with care and correction, along the path of Jesus.

The specialized vocabulary of the Letter to the Ephesians requires some attention. At the center of this letter is "mystery"—a mystery revealed in Jesus Christ. For the author of Ephesians, "mystery" means the unity of all creation in Christ. This mystery is a present reality that has an impact on the future. In the Letter to the Ephesians, mystery is sufficient to unite Jews and Gentiles in Christ, which is the goal of the whole letter. The second word that is specific and important is "power." In the Letter to the Ephesians, "power" refers to the presence of the resurrected Jesus among the community. When "mystery" and "power" combine, the community of Jesus Christ recognizes the fullness of Jesus' path. They are a community able to recognize the remarkable potential among them. Indeed, by the mystery of unity in Christ the congregation experiences the power of resurrection.

An Afterword

I have a personal disclaimer that accompanies this set of lessons. While I was researching, writing, editing, and enjoying these lessons, I was also applying, being considered, and finally selected for a new ministerial position. The name of the congregation is "New Life Presbyterian." As I wrote those words, "new life," over and over, I was also considering what my "new life" at New Life might be.

- Would I be sufficiently wise to lead a congregation named by Jesus' resurrection power?
- Would I be sensitive enough to accompany members who gave themselves permission to be continually "new" in Christ Jesus?
- Would I have the strength to release the familiar and the comfortable in order to truly receive a new life?

These lessons helped me recall the promise of God that God, and God alone, gives the gift of new life. That helped me to relax. Through my writing, I also contemplated that Jesus walked toward his own death possibly without fully understanding the new life that awaited beyond death. That helped me to trust. Finally, as I studied Ephesians, I was powerfully reminded of the potential within every congregation for new life. I knew that whatever the outcome of my journey, I would be associated with a congregation that treasured new life in Christ. As I completed these lessons, the congregation of New Life called me as their interim pastor. As I accepted this call, I felt prepared through this course, "New Creation in Christ." I hope that you will have a similarly significant experience.

CLOSE-UP:
IMAGES OF DEATH
AND NEW LIFE

In this quarter's lessons we encounter images of both death and new life. The promise of new life seen in Ezekiel becomes a reality in the New Testament.

Ezekiel 37, which is the basis of the lesson for March 22, presents a familiar image. Many school children learned the spiritual "Dem Bones," which is both an anatomy lesson set to a catchy tune and a vivid illustration of how God is able to take lifeless, scattered bones, reconnect them, and breathe life into them. The prophet's vision of this valley of dry bones has been depicted by numerous artists, whose work can help this image become vivid for us. (See examples at http://www.biblical-art.com/biblicalsubject.asp?id_biblicalsubject=339 &pagenum=1.) It seems incredible to the prophet that this "army of the Lord," dead and wasting, could ever rise up again. But they do. The prophet speaks as God commands, and it is so. The dead shall be brought to life, given God's Spirit, and returned to their homeland. In Ezekiel, though, this vision is just that—a vision of the future.

In the lesson for March 29, we encounter another image of life: the river that flows by the throne of God. A hymn familiar to many of us, "Shall We Gather at the River," describes "the river that flows by the throne of God" as it appears in Revelation 22:1-5. In the Gospel of John, as he talks with the woman of Samaria at the well, Jesus speaks of the water that he gives and says it "will become . . . a spring of water gushing up to eternal life" (4:14). In Ezekiel (47:1-12), this water that flows from the Temple appears in a vision, but the effectiveness of this life-giving water becomes apparent in Jesus, who fulfills the promise of new life.

In Ephesians 2:1-2, which opens our study on May 10, we read: "You were dead through the trespasses and sins in which you once lived." Like the vast army in the valley of the dry bones, the members of the church to which Paul writes had experienced death because of disobedience to God. But, thanks be to God, the promise of new life is fulfilled, for "even when we were dead through our trespasses, [God] made us alive together with Christ" (2:5). Just as God raised up the dry bones, God also took the initiative to save us through faith by grace. Even as the bones had no power to reconnect themselves and come to life, so too the members of the church had no means of coming to life were it not for the gracious gift of God. Note that in Ephesians 2:10, Paul writes: "we are what he [God] has made us, created in Christ Jesus for good works, which God prepared beforehand to be our way of life." As people who have been given the gift of new life, we are called to act in ways that glorify God and show forth to others that we are living in the way of Christ Jesus.

Talk with the class about these images. Sing the songs. Look at the art. Study the Bible passages. Invite the students to reflect on how these images enable them to perceive themselves as new creations in Christ.

FAITH IN ACTION: LIVING THE NEW LIFE IN CHRIST

During this quarter we are exploring the promise of new life, the path to new life, and the way of new life in Christ. We also need to think about concrete actions we can take to live this new life. Here is a strategy for doing that with the class members. You may want to read these steps aloud and provide time for completion of each one, or write the steps on newsprint and set a time limit for completing the entire assignment.

Step 1: Distribute paper and pencils. Tell the students that they will be asked to identify ways in which they live out their discipleship.

Step 2: Ask the students to list spiritual disciplines they engage in, such as prayer, Bible study, meditation, or worship.

Step 3: Invite the students to list actions they take within your congregation to live the new life in Christ and to help others do the same. These actions might include serving on a committee, ushering, singing in the choir, or assisting with fellowship events.

Step 4: Encourage the adults to identify ways that they practice their faith at work (paid or volunteer) by thinking about questions such as these: Do I give my full effort when on the job? Do I speak well of my employer and co-workers? Am I fair? In what ways can others see Christ in me?

Step 5: Prompt the learners to consider ways in which they show their Christian faith at home. Ask the adults to grapple with questions such as these: When there is conflict, am I able to control my temper and work things out in a Christ-like way? If people saw how I treated my spouse and children behind closed doors, what conclusions would they draw about my relationship with Christ?

Step 6: Recommend that the students review their lists and ask themselves: Where is my light brightly shining for Christ? In what situations have I hidden my light under a basket? Suggest that they take a few moments to jot down some corrective action they feel they need to take.

Step 7: Challenge the students to consider some ministries beyond the walls of the church where they can be a witness as they do something for which they have the gifts and passion. Here are some ideas among many for them to ponder. Encourage them to select a ministry and make a commitment to it.

Pet therapy. Many hospitals and nursing homes are looking for pet/handler teams to cheer and encourage patients. Schools, libraries, and bookstores appreciate pet teams that can read to children. Check the Delta Society (www.deltasociety.org) or Therapy Dog International (www.tdi-dog.org) for more information about this very rewarding ministry.

Meal delivery. Many areas have programs where drivers deliver meals to people who are homebound, giving the recipient not only fresh food but also an opportunity to interact with a friendly person who is interested in their well-being.

Building projects. Habitat for Humanity, missions groups, and community organizations build or renovate homes for people in need of safe, secure housing. Often those in need have been the victims of a natural disaster.

UNIT 1: THE PROMISE OF NEW LIFE
A NEW SPIRIT

PREVIEWING THE LESSON

Lesson Scripture: Ezekiel 11:14-21
Background Scripture: Ezekiel 11:14-21
Key Verse: Ezekiel 11:19

Focus of the Lesson:
The frustrations of life, especially problems of our making, may entice us to give up hope for change. Is everything truly lost because we must reap the rewards of our own folly? Absolutely not, claims the prophet, for the God who never abandons us promises to give us a fresh start by providing a new heart and spirit.

Goals for the Learners:
(1) to explore God's promise of new life made to the Israelite captives in Babylon.
(2) to recognize that hope and seeds of new life are often planted in the soil of punishment.
(3) to seek the new heart and spirit that God promises.

Supplies:
Bibles, newsprint and marker, paper and pencils, hymnals, Bible commentaries

---

READING THE SCRIPTURE

NRSV
Ezekiel 11:14-21

14Then the word of the LORD came to me: 15Mortal, your kinsfolk, your own kin, your fellow exiles, the whole house of Israel, all of them, are those of whom the inhabitants of Jerusalem have said, "They have gone far from the LORD; to us this land is given for a possession." 16Therefore say: Thus says the Lord GOD: Though I removed them far away among the nations, and though I scattered them among the countries, yet I have been a sanctuary to them for a little while in the

NIV
Ezekiel 11:14-21

14The word of the LORD came to me: 15"Son of man, your brothers—your brothers who are your blood relatives and the whole house of Israel—are those of whom the people of Jerusalem have said, 'They are far away from the LORD; this land was given to us as our possession.'

16"Therefore say: 'This is what the Sovereign LORD says: Although I sent them far away among the nations and scattered them among the countries, yet for a little countries where they have gone. [17]Therefore say: Thus says the Lord GOD: I will gather you from the peoples, and assemble you out of the countries where you have been scattered, and I will give you the land of Israel. [18]When they come there, they will remove from it all its detestable things and all its abominations. **[19]I will give them one heart, and put a new spirit within them;** I will remove the heart of stone from their flesh and give them a heart of flesh, [20]so that they may follow my statutes and keep my ordinances and obey them. Then they shall be my people, and I will be their God. [21]But as for those whose heart goes after their detestable things and their abominations, I will bring their deeds upon their own heads, says the Lord GOD.

while I have been a sanctuary for them in the countries where they have gone.'

[17]"Therefore say: 'This is what the Sovereign LORD says: I will gather you from the nations and bring you back from the countries where you have been scattered, and I will give you back the land of Israel again.'

[18]"They will return to it and remove all its vile images and detestable idols. **[19]I will give them an undivided heart and put a new spirit in them;** I will remove from them their heart of stone and give them a heart of flesh. [20]Then they will follow my decrees and be careful to keep my laws. They will be my people, and I will be their God. [21]But as for those whose hearts are devoted to their vile images and detestable idols, I will bring down on their own heads what they have done, declares the Sovereign LORD."

UNDERSTANDING THE SCRIPTURE

Introduction. The five passages selected for this unit, "The Promise of New Life," come from one of the more difficult prophetic books of the Hebrew Scriptures. The Book of Ezekiel includes intricate descriptions of visionary experiences, profound theological declarations, and pointed oracles against Jerusalem and Judah, as well as judgments against the "enemies" of God. Words of hope and encouragement are few. Ezekiel never speaks about grace in a casual manner; his words come from the most despairing period in ancient Israel. The prophet Ezekiel was a Judean priest sent to Babylon in the deportation of 597 B.C. (See 2 Kings 24:10-16 for background.) As a prophet called to deliver God's word, Ezekiel disclosed God's anger and offered God's grace. He described the horrors of Israel's persistent rebellion against God and the opportunities for a new life with God based on repentance and obedience. To a

contemporary audience, Ezekiel's words are harsh and his visions mystifying. However, his original audience of exiles understood his message—whether or not they chose to live accordingly. Ezekiel's words supported the key theological principles of Israel's faith; he affirmed the justice inherent in all God's dealings with the nations and with Israel, even as he offered a future to God's exiled chosen people. At a critical moment of divine judgment on Israel, Ezekiel reminded the people of their responsibilities as a community of faith and of God's sovereignty over all history. These are lessons appropriate to all generations.

Ezekiel 11:14-15. This text begs a context. The eleventh chapter of Ezekiel contains the conclusion of Ezekiel's second vision (Ezekiel 8:1–11:25). According to this passage, Ezekiel was transported, spiritually, to the Temple in Jerusalem and confronted by the abominations of pagan worship artifacts within God's holy dwelling place. This vision included a painful question: "Ah Lord GOD! will you make a full end of the remnant of Israel?" (11:13). This question provides the immediate context for our passage. In Ezekiel 11:14-15, the prophet affirmed his credentials as a mortal who received and shared the word of the Lord. His audience was, first and foremost, the exiles languishing in Babylon. The faith of these exiles was being challenged by the theological accusations from the current residents of Jerusalem. The charge to the exiles was painfully direct: Since God sent you into exile, you are no longer considered a part of God's chosen people. It followed logically that the Promised Land belonged to the current residents. This assertion echoed in Ezekiel's lament of 11:13 as the emotional, political, and theological challenge of the exile.

Ezekiel 11:16-17. The Book of Ezekiel is composed of three sections: Chapters 1–24 contain oracles of doom against Judah and Jerusalem; Chapters 25–32 are oracles against the foreign nations; Chapters 33–48 offer oracles of hope concerning the restoration of God's exiled people. The word that Ezekiel delivers in 11:14-21 is one of the few glimpses of God's grace toward the exiles in the first thirty-two chapters of the book. In characteristic style, the prophet affirmed God's authority over the events of deportation and exile. The people's situation was not accidental: God judged their disloyalty and scattered them. However, God did not break the covenant to be "their God" (11:20). God became a sanctuary to the exiled people. Scholars debate the exact meaning of the term "sanctuary," but Ezekiel's intent is clear. Although the people were geographically distant from the Temple in Jerusalem, God remained in a close spiritual relationship with them. Moreover, God intended to gather and return the scattered exiles to the Promised Land of Israel. Wholeness, return, and restoration were the future for the exiles according to God's word through the prophet Ezekiel.

Ezekiel 11:18-20. The return to Jerusalem necessitated a cleansing of the land, the city, and the Temple. This task was assigned to those who lived and learned fidelity to God while in exile. This is a remarkable expectation. For generations, Israel turned a blind eye on the commingling of the worship of Yahweh and the worship of the local gods of the land of Canaan. Moreover, during the exile some exiles casually shifted their loyalty away from Yahweh and toward the gods of Babylon. Ezekiel's word from God was clear: No foreign gods were welcome in Jerusalem. The returning exiles must destroy all signs of idolatry in the land, city, and Temple. God, however, realized the difficulty of this assignment for the exiles. Removing all the enticements of others gods and religious practices was too difficult for the exiles to do—without a radical change of heart. God, therefore, vowed to provide the exiles with a new spirit and a new heart. God's spiritual providence made possible the fidelity of the restored community. The past, with all its human doubts and despairs, led to a future secured by God's intervention. The people who failed to honor God and who endured exile as a punishment for this failure were to be gathered, led, and renewed by God. By God's grace they had another chance.

Ezekiel 11:21. As swiftly as Ezekiel's words offered a glimpse of grace, so quickly did Ezekiel return to his dominant theme: God's judgment. There is no easy grace in this passage. The people who were granted the second chance of restoration must become obedient. No one failing the loyalty exam survived. Indeed, God's punishment touched all whose hearts went after foreign gods and false teachers. Ezekiel's words were harsh; he expressed himself as a prophet utterly devoid of sentimentality. As a deeply spiritual man, Ezekiel heard God's word and saw visions sent by God's Spirit. As a member of a broken community, Ezekiel knew there was no wiggle room before God. He announced a clear choice:

Either the people chose obedient lives or they received God's severe judgment. Thus, the interlude of grace in Ezekiel 11:14-20 was sealed by a warning in verse 21.

Ezekiel's prophetic calling was confirmed, once again, by his persistence in delivering the whole word from God—a word of grace and a word of judgment.

INTERPRETING THE SCRIPTURE

In a Time of Lamentation

There are times when Christians, individually or corporately, raise a voice in lamentation. Strangely, those outside the faith community often misinterpret such sad refrains as despair. Rather than a lack of faith, our saddest prayers authentically affirm our faith. As we lament the lack of justice for the poorest of the poor, we announce God's compassion for the weak. As we lament the untimely death of an adult or a child, we affirm God's judgment on the preciousness of all life. As we lament the fear that paralyzes nations and diminishes individual courage, we admonish one another to love as boldly as Christ loved.

Lamentation is a particular form of faithful speech, and faithful speech was the particular calling of the prophet Ezekiel. He was commissioned to speak to the exiles from Jerusalem, a sad collection of people who had lost everything. Not only were they separated from their homeland by deserts, rivers, and mountains but the exiles also experienced the spiritual pain of separation from God. They found it difficult to make sense of their circumstances, and their thoughts were full of contradictions. Were they experiencing a temporary judgment, or a profound divine rejection? Was exile an odd test of faithfulness, or a brief interlude to a new chapter of promise and blessing? Should they accommodate themselves in the new land by marrying and planting vineyards, or should they remember their homeland and patiently await a return to their precious past? Their confusion is obvi-

ous in a psalm from the period of exile, Psalm 137. Reading this psalm is a fitting introduction to the emotional tenor of the times; Ezekiel spoke words of lamentation to and with the exiled chosen people of God. Because their confusion echoes in contemporary lamentations, Ezekiel's message reaches into our most lamentable circumstances. There is a time to lament; Ezekiel helps us make sense of that time.

God's Choice Reconsidered

The most shocking words within the community of faith are "You don't belong." Sometimes this message is delivered by an offhand remark, a disapproving glance, or an unintended slight. Many seekers walk away from a "first visit" with an indistinct sense of rejection. Whether they were actually told "you don't belong" or they brought that message imprinted on their psyche does not matter. The truth is rejection by a religious community is a painful experience.

In today's passage, one group within God's chosen people has decided that another group no longer belongs. The residents of Jerusalem (those not taken into exile) were mainly individuals from the lower, less-educated classes. After the exile, the responsibility to maintain the holy city and worship fell to them. They became heady with their new importance; it seemed obvious that God loved them and rejected the exiles. From this observation, the residents of Jerusalem drew a religious (or was it a political?) conclusion: God chose us and rejected you; therefore, we get the land. The community in exile understood the logic and the conclusion. Emotionally, the painful message they received was "You don't belong." It was to this pain that the prophet spoke. He addressed the exiles as members of "the whole house of Israel" (11:15). Ezekiel affirmed that the relationship to God was not geographic. Then, Ezekiel offered a tender reminder: Although the people were previously comforted by a physical structure—the Temple—during this exile, God was a "sanctuary" for them. Indeed, God's spiritual presence stayed with the people despite their scattered locations. Moreover, Ezekiel announced God's intention to unite all the scattered and restore the people to their rightful inheritance. Thus, Ezekiel assured the exiles that God's choice was (and is and always will be) God's choice. One group within the community of faith had no authority to exclude another group. That was God's work. Only God's judgment mattered and the exiles, though scattered, still lived under the sanctuary of God's authority.

God's Choice Reaffirmed

Have you ever felt the heavy sadness of disappointing God and finding yourself outside the joy of divine communion? Most adults remember such circumstances, and many adults brood over the sins of the past. Evidently, some of Ezekiel's audience brooded excessively over their sins. The bitterness of exile polluted every aspect of life; the recognition that the exile as punishment of past sins canceled hope for the future. Most exiles felt stuck in an exile caused by their own deeds of unfaithfulness.

Ezekiel's challenge, therefore, was to reorient the exiles' perspective from the past (with its heavy weight of sin) to the future (with its promise of restoration). He did that with two grand, and surprising, announcements. First, Ezekiel announced that God had not forgotten the exiles. Though they were living in a foreign land and under the domination of an enemy, God recognized the actual circumstance of all the scattered Israelites. Indeed, God not only remembered and recognized but God also intended to gather and restore them to the land of Israel. This physical change of circumstances surely was good news. But was it believable good news? From the brooding perspective of the exiles, God was correct in casting them out of the land; they were sinners to the core. Probably, Ezekiel's first announcement did not bring a cheer—most exiles assumed that past sins placed them beyond God's grace.

The second announcement, however, sparked energy. Ezekiel also announced there was work for the exiles to do in Jerusalem. They were to be in charge of cleansing the land: removing and destroying all signs, artifacts, and edifices devoted to foreign gods. This announcement intrigued the exiles; they could roll up their sleeves and work for the Lord. In their minds, perhaps, the task offered a path of self-redemption. By cleaning up the land and the holy city, the exiles would prove their commitment to God and demonstrate their sorrow about past sins.

In a Time of Restoration

God's grace never comes by bargain, overachievement, or perfect behavior. God's grace is gracious; it comes from God's great heart and enfolds the human community in divine pleasure. While the exiles may have prepared to earn their restoration, Ezekiel continued delivering God's word.

There was a third announcement: God was about to give the people spiritual resources for a whole new way of living. These resources were "one heart" and a "new spirit." One heart signified unity among the restored people. This common commitment was to be complemented by a common passion: God's own spirit energizing and comforting the people. Thus God prepared the people for a physical change of circumstances and offered the exiles the spiritual resources to live obedient lives in their new setting. Indeed, the people were promised more than they expected. Their hope was to return home; they were promised restoration, meaningful work, and spiritual resources fit for their future. Still, this was not easy grace; the people were expected to be vigilant. In the final verse, Ezekiel 11:21, the prophet reminded the exiles that although God's grace was amazing, the temptations of foreign gods and disloyalty were persistent. Solemnly, Ezekiel concluded his vision with a word of judgment: God will punish all whose hearts go astray. By this last word, Ezekiel affirmed that God's grace and judgment always include a choice for life or death.

SHARING THE SCRIPTURE

Preparing Our Hearts

Meditate on this week's devotional reading, found in 2 Corinthians 3:1-11. Notice the wonderful image in verses 2 and 3: We are letters written with the Spirit on the tablets of one another's hearts. We are, indeed, "ministers of a new covenant" (3:6), one that is glorious and permanent. Ponder Paul's words. If you are a letter, what do you think that other people are "reading" about God as they observe and interact with you? How do you need to "edit" the letter so as to be more Christ-like?

Pray that you and the adult learners will keep your hearts soft and malleable so that you will be outstanding letters of recommendation on behalf of Christ.

Preparing Our Minds

Study the background and lesson Scripture, both found in Ezekiel 11:14-21. As you read, think about whether everything is truly lost because we must reap the rewards of our own folly.

Write on newsprint:

❏ information for next week's lesson, found under "Continue the Journey."
❏ activities for further spiritual growth in "Continue the Journey."

Read "Introduction: New Creation in Christ," "The Big Picture," "Close-up," and "Faith in Action." Determine how you will use these supplements throughout the quarter.

Locate several Bible commentaries. Your church or local public library will likely have these resources.

LEADING THE CLASS

(1) Gather to Learn

❖ Welcome the class members and introduce any guests.

❖ Pray that all of today's participants will be listening for a fresh word from God to empower them to live with a new spirit of hope.

❖ Challenge the class to think of some difficult circumstances that people encounter, particularly ones that may have arisen as a result of poor choices they have made. List their ideas on newsprint. Here are some examples: *a driver chooses to handle the car recklessly and seriously injures a friend or family member; an honor student cheats to stay at the top of the class and fails a course when the cheating is discovered; an employee knowingly commits fraud and not only loses a job but also spends years in prison.*

❖ Ask: **If you were to be involved in one of the situations we have identified, how would you feel about the future?**

❖ Read aloud today's focus statement:

The frustrations of life, especially problems of our making, may entice us to give up hope for change. Is everything truly lost because we must reap the rewards of our own folly? Absolutely not, claims the prophet, for the God who never abandons us promises to give us a fresh start by providing a new heart and spirit.

(2) Explore God's Promise of New Life Made to the Israelite Captives in Babylon

❖ **Option:** Use all or part of "The Big Picture: Becoming a New Creation" to introduce this quarter's course of study.

❖ Read or retell the introduction in Understanding the Scripture to familiarize the students with this difficult prophetic book.

❖ Choose a volunteer to read aloud Ezekiel 11:14-21.

❖ Distribute Bible commentaries, paper, and pencils. Divide the students into groups of three or four to answer this question: **What is God saying to the people through the prophet Ezekiel?** Suggest that the adults study the commentary together and then individually write the gist of God's message in their own words.

❖ Invite several volunteers to read what they have written. If appropriate, use information from Understanding the Scripture to clarify Ezekiel's message.

❖ Discuss these questions with the class:
  (1) **Had you been one of the exiles, what ideas would have grabbed your attention most as you listened to Ezekiel?**
  (2) **How would you have felt about yourself and your fellow exiles as you listened?** ("God's Choice Reaffirmed" in Interpreting the Scripture will provide additional information.)
  (3) **If you had been present and could have asked Ezekiel one question about his message, what would it be?**
  (4) **What does this passage teach us**

about the correlation or discrepancy between current dire circumstances and future hope?

❖ Provide a few moments of quiet time for the adults to reflect on ways in which this passage might provide hope for a situation they are currently facing.

(3) Recognize That Hope and Seeds of New Life Are Often Planted in the Soil of Punishment

❖ Call the class back together and read this summary of Charles (Chuck) Colson's life. **Born in 1931, Chuck Colson became a lawyer who served as Special Counsel to President Richard Nixon. Although he had a wide range of duties, Colson is best remembered for his role in the conspiracy to cover up the Watergate burglary. Just before his arrest, he read C. S. Lewis's *Mere Christianity* and gave his heart to Christ. Convicted of obstruction of justice, Colson served seven months in prison. Disbarred, he was unable to return to his profession upon his release. He founded a Christian organization, Prison Fellowship, and worked diligently to reform the U.S. prison system so that prisoners could truly be rehabilitated rather than just warehoused. Colson is a strong voice not only for prisoners but also on behalf of the Evangelical wing of the church.**

❖ **Option:** Encourage the students to name other well-known figures who have found new hope in the soil of punishment.

❖ Make a list on newsprint of the range of feelings and thoughts of people who have experienced a crisis, been punished for it, and then stabilized their lives.

❖ Challenge the adults to identify ways that they can help people respond to a crisis so as to give them hope for the future.

(4) Seek the New Heart and Spirit That God Promises

❖ Invite the participants to read today's key verse, Ezekiel 11:19, in unison.

❖ Note that in today's lesson God is giving a new heart and spirit to the whole faith community, not just a few individuals.

❖ Brainstorm answers to this question with the class. Write their ideas on newsprint. **How would our church be different if we experienced a new heart and new spirit?**

❖ **Option:** If the class brainstormed ideas that they can actually begin to work on, encourage them to do so. For example, if they said a new spirit would make the congregation friendlier, encourage them to each make it a point today of talking to someone new or someone they do not know well. Little changes can make a huge difference.

❖ Challenge all of the class members to pray daily for a new spirit for themselves individually and for the church as the body of Christ.

(5) Continue the Journey

❖ Pray that all who have come today will depart with a new spirit of hope.

❖ Read aloud this preparation for next week's lesson. You may also want to post it on newsprint for the students to copy.

- **Title: New Leadership**
- **Background Scripture: Ezekiel 34**
- **Lesson Scripture: Ezekiel 34:23-31**
- **Focus of the Lesson: Sometimes people become very disappointed with leaders who are self-serving and disconnected from their con-**

stituents. **What remedy can be found when such a person is in a leadership position? Ezekiel tells us that God will provide new servant-leaders who care tenderly for their flock, just as God the Good Shepherd does.**

❖ Challenge the students to complete one or more of these activities for further spiritual growth, which you will write on newsprint for the students to copy.

(1) **Think of a time when your actions caused you to feel separated from God. What had you done or not done? What gave you hope for the future?**

(2) **Reach out in whatever way you can to someone living in exile. Perhaps you can assist with financial contributions or a letter-writing campaign to ease the plight of these persons, who are often victims of war or political oppression.**

(3) **Talk with someone who seems crushed by life's circumstances. Do what you can to offer this person the hope that Christ gives us.**

❖ Sing or read aloud "Spirit of God, Descend Upon My Heart."

❖ Conclude today's session by leading the class in this benediction: **Give us new hearts filled with your Spirit, O Lord, that we may live as new creations in Christ. Amen.**

UNIT 1: THE PROMISE OF NEW LIFE
NEW LEADERSHIP

PREVIEWING THE LESSON

Lesson Scripture: Ezekiel 34:23-31
Background Scripture: Ezekiel 34
Key Verse: Ezekiel 34:31

Focus of the Lesson:
Sometimes people become very disappointed with leaders who are self-serving and disconnected from their constituents. What remedy can be found when such a person is in a leadership position? Ezekiel tells us that God will provide new servant-leaders who care tenderly for their flock, just as God the Good Shepherd does.

Goals for the Learners:
(1) to explore the promise of a new David who will lead God's people as a good shepherd.
(2) to identify traits of servant-leaders, both in others and in themselves.
(3) to commit to joining and to supporting God's servant-leaders.

Supplies:
Bibles, newsprint and marker, paper and pencils, hymnals

READING THE SCRIPTURE

NRSV
Ezekiel 34:23-31

²³I will set up over them one shepherd, my servant David, and he shall feed them: he shall feed them and be their shepherd. ²⁴And I, the LORD, will be their God, and my servant David shall be prince among them; I, the LORD, have spoken.

²⁵I will make with them a covenant of peace and banish wild animals from the land, so that they may live in the wild and sleep in the woods securely. ²⁶I will make them and the region around my hill a

NIV
Ezekiel 34:23-31

²³I will place over them one shepherd, my servant David, and he will tend them; he will tend them and be their shepherd. ²⁴I the LORD will be their God, and my servant David will be prince among them. I the LORD have spoken.

²⁵" 'I will make a covenant of peace with them and rid the land of wild beasts so that they may live in the desert and sleep in the forests in safety. ²⁶I will bless them and the

blessing; and I will send down the showers in their season; they shall be showers of blessing. [27]The trees of the field shall yield their fruit, and the earth shall yield its increase. They shall be secure on their soil; and they shall know that I am the LORD, when I break the bars of their yoke, and save them from the hands of those who enslaved them. [28]They shall no more be plunder for the nations, nor shall the animals of the land devour them; they shall live in safety, and no one shall make them afraid. [29]I will provide for them a splendid vegetation so that they shall no more be consumed with hunger in the land, and no longer suffer the insults of the nations. [30]They shall know that I, the LORD their God, am with them, and that they, the house of Israel, are my people, says the Lord GOD. [31]**You are my sheep, the sheep of my pasture and I am your God, says the Lord GOD.**

places surrounding my hill. I will send down showers in season; there will be showers of blessing. [27]The trees of the field will yield their fruit and the ground will yield its crops; the people will be secure in their land. They will know that I am the LORD, when I break the bars of their yoke and rescue them from the hands of those who enslaved them. [28]They will no longer be plundered by the nations, nor will wild animals devour them. They will live in safety, and no one will make them afraid. [29]I will provide for them a land renowned for its crops, and they will no longer be victims of famine in the land or bear the scorn of the nations. [30]Then they will know that I, the LORD their God, am with them and that they, the house of Israel, are my people, declares the Sovereign LORD. [31]**You my sheep, the sheep of my pasture, are people, and I am your God, declares the Sovereign LORD.'"**

UNDERSTANDING THE SCRIPTURE

Ezekiel 34:1-10. The opening section of this lesson's passage could be entitled "Woe to shepherds." Ezekiel, following the pattern of his prophet-colleague Jeremiah, used the image of a shepherd to cover a wide range of leaders. His sharp words were directed toward all the leaders of the chosen people: kings and princes, as well as scribes, elders, Levites, and priests. The failure of leadership was pervasive; thus, the image of the shepherd was widely applied. Although the leaders targeted for judgment were many, Ezekiel was quite specific in the charges against the leaders of Israel. He boldly accused them of sins of commission and omission. With the flair of self-interest, these leaders were guilty of deriving gain from their supervision of the "flock"; they ate the fat lambs, sheared the young, slaughtered and abused the flock in an irresponsible manner. As reprehensible as were

these deeds, the sins of omission were even more troublesome. The supposed "shepherds" of Israel failed to do the most basic task of shepherding: They had not tended the flock. Rather, they allowed the lost to be lost, the sick to be sick, the weak to become weaker. Because of their self-serving approach to leadership, the whole flock was scattered "over all the face of the earth" (34:6). Speaking with divine authority, Ezekiel announced that God's own flock was in peril. The sadness within Ezekiel's words judged the shepherds of Israel guilty of betraying the divine responsibility to care for God's people. Therefore, what the leaders of Israel failed to do, God intended to accomplish. God would depose the shepherds and take up the cause of the flock.

Ezekiel 34:11-16. After such specific charges of corruption, a sharp word of judgment or rebuke seems appropriate. Yet,

Ezekiel did not deliver a divine curse on the shepherds. Rather, Ezekiel disclosed the significance of the failed shepherding responsibility by stating that God was assuming personal responsibility for the flock. With God as the shepherd, the circumstances of the flock would change: Whereas once the flock was scattered, abused, and vulnerable, God intended to seek the lost, to tend the sick, and to provide pasture and protection for the whole flock. Instead of vulnerability and death, the flock would grow strong and healthy through God's guidance. As the prophet spoke, his words broke through the agony of the exiles' daily life and ignited a small flicker of hope among those in captivity. Using the prophetic image, "day of clouds and thick darkness" (34:12), Ezekiel connected his audience with the anticipated Day of the Lord when God would right all wrongs by restoring justice and peace in the land. Using the powerful phrase, "I will bring them out" (34:13), Ezekiel associated the impending rescue with the greatest event in Israel's salvation history: the exodus from Egypt. Additionally, Ezekiel proclaimed that this divine deed was greater than the former exodus since the scattered people of Israel were to be rescued from many locations, not from the singular domination of the Egyptian pharaoh. Finally, Ezekiel's imagery climaxed as he described God's shepherding the flock to good pasture where neither fear nor deprivation threatened. This description of God as the shepherd of Israel echoed Psalm 23 and foreshadowed Jesus' self-disclosure as the Good Shepherd (John 10). These poetic descriptions of the shepherding God resonate with our contemporary understanding of God as the source and guarantor of all life.

Ezekiel 34:17-24. God's declaration to be the shepherd of Israel did not, however, exempt the people from judgment. Indeed, Ezekiel's prophetic task was to explain God's purpose within the exile in such a way that the people would understand God's judgment, repent, and turn their hearts to God. Thus, even as God's grace toward the "flock" of Israel was affirmed, Ezekiel reminded the people that internal dangers persisted. Among the people some grew greedy and some took advantage of the weak. To these, Ezekiel stressed God's judgment: Persistent sinners would be eliminated from the flock. To all, Ezekiel declared that God intended to establish both internal and external justice. Ezekiel employed an ancient promise to signify the unity and peace characteristic of God's future. With the promise, "I will set up over them one shepherd, my servant David" (34:23), Ezekiel affirmed the restoration of the whole people of God as promised in the original covenant with David (see 2 Samuel 7:16). Amazingly, this restoration was to be greater than the golden days of David's rule. In God's future with Israel, the leader would be spiritually mature. None of the sins that David confessed would ensnare this new leader. Rather, the one shepherd would always lead according to God's direction.

Ezekiel 34:25-31. Thus, a judged people led by a divinely appointed shepherd entered into a restored life—a life made spiritually complete with a new "covenant of peace" (34:25). This remarkable description of God's intervention described the transformation of all creation. Wild animals were banished. Seasonal rains were dependable. The earth yielded abundant grain, vegetables, and fruits. There were neither slave owners nor slaves; indeed, there was no form of oppression. Humanity lived in complete freedom from fear. With such idyllic and idealistic words, the prophet offered solid hope to the exiles. All the circumstances they were powerless to change—political, social, environmental, and spiritual—God would transform. Although Ezekiel cast the covenant of peace in visionary terms, he offered it to his audience with intimacy and tenderness. The true import of this peaceful transformation resided in a new relationship between Israel and God. It was not enough that God was willing to rescue the people. God's intentions were greater than another rescue; God intended that the people know God's presence and power consistently and personally. This unique relationship, "You are my sheep . . . and I am your God" (34:31) made peace possible. By such a strong bond, Israel was prepared to fulfill its calling as a witness to all nations. The covenant of peace described by Ezekiel was, therefore, a full disclosure of God's ultimate purpose: a peaceful, just, and righteous creation.

INTERPRETING THE SCRIPTURE

When Leaders Set the Wrong Example

Whether in the family, politics, or business, every leader faces opportunities and temptations. When rightly received, opportunities lead to success; when wrongly pursued, temptations bring failure. Religious leaders also distinguish between opportunities and temptations, but their choices include an additional dynamic: Religious leaders are constantly announcing or denying their faith by the choices they make.

Every public choice, direction, intention, and deed becomes an announcement of an inner conviction—or the lack thereof. If a religious leader has disappointed you, you understand the additional dynamic within the role of a religious leader. Perhaps a pastor failed to be a faithful steward of the financial resources of the congregation or a nationally known evangelist was caught in a sexual scandal. Whether the disappointment was experienced within a small country congregation or spread across the mass media of the nation, the impact is singular: The sin of a religious leader may weaken the faith of the followers.

In our text, the scale of the wronghearted leadership described by Ezekiel is almost incomprehensible. The leaders he condemned used their positions for personal profit and well-being. These leaders feasted upon the young of the flock, sheared and slaughtered randomly, and ignored the needs of the whole flock. Surely, the people noticed these actions. Surely, some in Israel were outraged. Yet, the text is silent on the peoples' response to their selfish leaders. In this silence is a terrible sorrow. Those who ignored the sins of the leaders also slid into sin. It is absolutely true that leaders set an example; when the leaders are self-serving, the people gradually begin serving their own needs as well. In other words, the people followed the leaders by mimicking their values, decisions, and deeds. Thus, as the people followed their leaders, their hearts turned from God. The leaders were greedy, and the people swiftly conformed. As the leaders neglected the weak, the lost, or the sick in order to fulfill their own desires and passions, the people learned to look out for their own needs of food, clothing, and health. Thus, a people once trained to depend upon God for all the blessings of life became greedy. Just as the leaders ignored the special opportunities and temptations of religious leadership, so the people forgot how to depend upon God, the source of their well-being.

God's Way of Leading

The leadership failure in Israel was pervasive and persistent. The people were on the verge of extinction. Thus the remedy was dramatic and deep. There was one way, and only one way, to restore justice and peace: God must become the leader of Israel. Ezekiel described God's leadership as a comprehensive approach for the welfare of the whole flock. God assumed the responsibility to rescue, nurse, heal, feed, water, and provide security to all the sheep of the flock. To the contemporary reader this image is captivating, but it is also easily dismissed. In order for us to hear Ezekiel's words as more than lovely poetry, an ancient scriptural perspective on faith must inform our hearing. In the Hebrew Scriptures, the promises of God and the actions of God are tightly interwoven. What God had done in the past and what God promised to do in the future is a single story of a just and peaceful creation. In the past, God's deeds of rescue were complemented by God's gracious provision of the law. In the present exile, God's prophets announced judgment and blessing. In the future, God's grace would right all injustices and cleanse all infidelity.

In Hebrew theology time is unified—all circumstances eventually are transformed in God's salvation. Thus, as Ezekiel described God as Israel's shepherd-leader, time literally stood still. Israel's heritage of divine rescue joined with their present situation of exile and became salvation. In this unity of time, God's actions were both memory and hope. The people understood Ezekiel's words because they remembered the stories of rescue and divine blessing. The people accepted Ezekiel's promises because in exile they lost all but the most precious elements of faith, that is, a confident hope in God. Accordingly, Ezekiel's description of God's leadership was neither poetic nor visionary; it was, rather, an affirmation of the essence of the Hebrew faith.

Common Responsibilities

The relationship between a leader and his or her followers is multidimensional. Leaders are expected to understand the opportunities and challenges that surround their followers. Followers trust their leaders to make decisions based on the welfare of the whole. Leaders know their actions have immediate and long-term consequences. Followers absorb the values of their leaders and imitate their actions.

Within the faith community, leaders and followers have a common responsibility to live just and peaceful lives in communion with God. When leadership fails, as it did prior to the exile of Israel to Babylon, it is insufficient to blame the leaders; blaming does not restore right relationships. When followers are poisoned by the greed or irresponsibility of their leaders, it is insufficient to condemn their sins; condemnation does not promote peace. Rather, leaders and followers share a common responsibility to understand and to maintain a healthy relationship with God. No one is exempt from cultivating an honest heart and a righteous lifestyle. All are expected to contribute to the welfare of the whole: Leaders contribute through breadth of visions, and followers contribute through attention to the details of justice and righteousness. Each contributes to the common good, and both common responsibilities shape the spiritual life of the whole. Together they present a unity of responsibility and compassion, of diligence and justice, and of service and reconciliation.

A Vision for All

How do you envision creation's reconciliation? Do you see happy, healthy babies everywhere—even across the famine-swept deserts of Africa? Do you see workers able to afford health insurance for their families? Do you see the end of all form of tyranny—even the tyranny of drugs and alcohol? Do you see mutual respect among all peoples and nations? Do you see pure rivers and clean skies?

Ezekiel saw God's restored creation reflected through the concerns of his time and his people. For example, he envisioned all wild and dangerous animals chased from the inhabited land and sent to the woodlands to live. He saw a circle of blessing radiating out from God's holy mountain; within that circle there was sufficient rain and sunshine to produce an abundant harvest of grains and fruits. Ezekiel saw a changed physical environment able to sustain a restoration of peace among the nations. Wars ceased. Plunder no longer threatened. Every yoke of domination was broken. National humiliation and public shame ended. And at the very center of Ezekiel's vision was reconciliation between people and God. No longer did the people doubt or fear; instead, they lived with God in complete security and joy. Finally, Ezekiel's descriptive words fail his prophetic intentions. With a tenderness born of grieving and comforting, Ezekiel spoke for God saying, "You are my sheep, the sheep of my pasture and I am your God" (34:31). Having tested this image against the failed leaders of Israel and having filled the image with God's new intentions, Ezekiel's words affirmed the psalmist's declaration: The Lord is our shepherd, we shall not want.

SHARING THE SCRIPTURE

Preparing Our Hearts

Meditate on this week's devotional reading, found in John 10:11-18. In verse 11 of this familiar passage we hear Jesus say, "I am the good shepherd." What does that mean to you? What expectations do you have of Jesus in his role as shepherd? What expectations do you have of those who have leadership positions in the church? How do you feel when those expectations are not met?

Pray that you and the adult learners will be ready to follow servant-leaders who shepherd their flocks as Jesus did.

Preparing Our Minds

Study the background from Ezekiel 34 and the lesson Scripture from Ezekiel 34:23-31. As you read, ponder the kind of remedy that can be found when those who are self-serving and disconnected from their constituents are in leadership positions.

Write on newsprint:
❏ information for next week's lesson, found under "Continue the Journey."
❏ activities for further spiritual growth in "Continue the Journey."
Prepare to present the brief lecture suggested for "Explore the Promise of a New David Who Will Lead God's People as a Good Shepherd."

LEADING THE CLASS

(1) Gather to Learn

❖ Welcome the class members and introduce any guests.

❖ Pray that today's participants will discern and act on God's word for them from today's lesson.

❖ Invite the students to think of leaders in any arena (for example, business, government, church, education, nonprofit organizations) who have disappointed their supporters because they served themselves rather than those they were called to lead. The students are not to name these people aloud.

❖ List on newsprint how these failed leaders affected the class members. Use general terms, such as "caused me to lose faith in government," "made me question whether all Christian leaders were hypocrites," "prompted me to stop giving money to charities."

❖ Ask for a show of hands to indicate how many class members have been affected in one or more of the negative ways listed. (It is likely that most, if not all, of the students will have had an experience with a bad leader.)

❖ Read aloud today's focus statement: **Sometimes people become very disappointed with leaders who are self-serving and disconnected from their constituents. What remedy can be found when such a person is in a leadership position? Ezekiel tells us that God will provide new servant-leaders who care tenderly for their flock, just as God the Good Shepherd does.**

(2) Explore the Promise of a New David Who Will Lead God's People as a Good Shepherd

❖ Present a brief lecture using the information from Ezekiel 34:1-10 in Understanding the Scripture to help the adults understand the contrast between the unscrupulous leaders who were in place and the change that God will bring about in leadership. "When Leaders Set the Wrong Example" and "God's Way of Leading" in Interpreting the Scripture also highlight contrasts between these two types of leaders.

❖ Explain that according to verses 11-22, God will be the Good Shepherd.

❖ Ask a volunteer to read Ezekiel 34:23-31.

❖ Identify the aspects of the vision of the world that will exist when God's servant David (understood to be someone from the house of David) takes over as leader. List ideas on newsprint. Use "A Vision for All" from Interpreting the Scripture as needed to round out the discussion.

❖ Pause for a few moments to reflect on this vision and pray silently for it to be fulfilled.

(3) Identify Traits of Servant-Leaders, Both in Others and in the Learners

❖ Read these words from the first chapter of Robert K. Greenleaf's fascinating book, *Servant Leadership* (1977):

If one is a *servant*, either leader or follower, one is always searching, listening, expecting that a better wheel for these times is in the making. . . .

I am hopeful for these times, despite the tension and conflict, because more natural servants are trying to see clearly the world as it is and are listening carefully to prophetic voices that are speaking *now*. They are challenging the pervasive injustice with greater force and they are taking sharper issue with the wide disparity between the quality of society they know is reasonable and possible with available resources, and, on the other hand, the actual performance of the whole range of institutions that exist to serve society.

. . . A new moral principle is emerging which holds that the only authority deserving one's allegiance is that which is freely and knowingly granted by the led to the leader in response to, and in proportion to, the clearly evident servant stature of the leader. Those who choose to follow this principle will not casually accept the authority of existing institutions. *Rather, they will freely respond only to individuals who are chosen as leaders because they are proven and trusted as servants.* To the extent that this principle prevails in the future, the only truly viable institutions will be those that are predominantly servant-led.

❖ Encourage the students to respond to Greenleaf's words.

    (1) Do you think people will accept leaders who are first servants? Why or why not?

    (2) How does Greenleaf's idea of servant leadership relate to current power structures?

    (3) How does Greenleaf's idea support or stand in tension with Ezekiel's words, especially in 34:23-24?

❖ Invite the adults to share stories with the class or a small group concerning servant-leaders who have been significant in their own lives. What is it about these people that makes them so special?

❖ Create a list on newsprint of traits that servant-leaders seem to have in common.

❖ Provide time for quiet reflection on these questions: **Which of these traits do I already have? Which of these traits could I work to develop?**

(4) Commit to Joining and Supporting God's Servant-Leaders

❖ Point out that although the vision of the "covenant of peace" (34:25) is not yet a reality, servant-leaders are working to bring about peace, to end oppression, to end fear, to end suffering, and to end hunger.

❖ See if the class can name any famous—or not so famous—people working to bring about this vision. Ask: **What impresses you about one or more of these servant-leaders?**

❖ Encourage the adults to think about ways that they, too, could be servant-leaders for those who are hungry, suffering, oppressed, or afraid.

❖ Invite those willing to commit themselves to working as servant-leaders on behalf of these people to raise their hands.

(5) Continue the Journey

❖ Pray that those who have participated in today's class will go forth to act as servant-leaders and support others who have assumed these leadership positions.

❖ Read aloud this preparation for next week's lesson. You may also want to post it on newsprint for the students to copy.

■ **Title: God's People Restored Again**
■ **Background Scripture: Ezekiel 36:22-32**
■ **Lesson Scripture: Ezekiel 36:22-32**
■ **Focus of the Lesson: Although the fruits of action are often visible, the reasons for an action taken in a particular time and at a certain place are more difficult to discern. What motivates actions? According to Ezekiel, God's promise to restore Israel is not motivated by Israel itself but rather for the sake of God's holy name.**

❖ Challenge the students to complete one or more of these activities for further spiritual growth, which you will write on newsprint for the students to copy.

   (1) **Send a letter or e-mail to someone who acts as a servant-leader. Thank this person for his or her effective work.**

   (2) **Examine your own leadership style. Do you exhibit traits of the servant-leader? If not, what attributes do you need to develop in order to lead as a servant?**

   (3) **Look for articles in the media that explore the actions of self-serving leaders as well as servant-leaders. How do people respond to these different types of leadership?**

❖ Sing or read aloud "Savior, Like a Shepherd Lead Us."

❖ Conclude today's session by leading the class in this benediction: **Give us new hearts filled with your Spirit, O Lord, that we may live as new creations in Christ. Amen.**

UNIT 1: THE PROMISE OF NEW LIFE

GOD'S PEOPLE RESTORED AGAIN

PREVIEWING THE LESSON

Lesson Scripture: Ezekiel 36:22-32
Background Scripture: Ezekiel 36:22-32
Key Verse: Ezekiel 36:23

Focus of the Lesson:
Although the fruits of action are often visible, the reasons for an action taken in a particular time and at a certain place are more difficult to discern. What motivates actions? According to Ezekiel, God's promise to restore Israel is not motivated by Israel itself but rather for the sake of God's holy name.

Goals for the Learners:
(1) to delve into God's plans and intentions to restore Israel.
(2) to repent of their sins and to recognize that God forgives them.
(3) to display evidence of the new life that results from God's gracious restoration.

Supplies:
Bibles, newsprint and marker, paper and pencils, hymnals, optional music and appropriate player

---

READING THE SCRIPTURE

NRSV
Ezekiel 36:22-32

²²Therefore say to the house of Israel, Thus says the Lord GOD: It is not for your sake, O house of Israel, that I am about to act, but for the sake of my holy name, which you have profaned among the nations to which you came. ²³I will sanctify my great name, which has been profaned among the nations, and which you have profaned

NIV
Ezekiel 36:22-32

²²"Therefore say to the house of Israel, 'This is what the Sovereign LORD says: It is not for your sake, O house of Israel, that I am going to do these things, but for the sake of my holy name, which you have profaned among the nations where you have gone. ²³I will show the holiness of my great name, which has been profaned among the nations,

among them; and **the nations shall know that I am the** Lord, **says the Lord** God, **when through you I display my holiness before their eyes.** [24]I will take you from the nations, and gather you from all the countries, and bring you into your own land. [25]I will sprinkle clean water upon you, and you shall be clean from all your uncleannesses, and from all your idols I will cleanse you. [26]A new heart I will give you, and a new spirit I will put within you; and I will remove from your body the heart of stone and give you a heart of flesh. [27]I will put my spirit within you, and make you follow my statutes and be careful to observe my ordinances. [28]Then you shall live in the land that I gave to your ancestors; and you shall be my people, and I will be your God. [29]I will save you from all your uncleannesses, and I will summon the grain and make it abundant and lay no famine upon you. [30]I will make the fruit of the tree and the produce of the field abundant, so that you may never again suffer the disgrace of famine among the nations. [31]Then you shall remember your evil ways, and your dealings that were not good; and you shall loathe yourselves for your iniquities and your abominable deeds. [32]It is not for your sake that I will act, says the Lord God; let that be known to you. Be ashamed and dismayed for your ways, O house of Israel.

the name you have profaned among them. **Then the nations will know that I am the** Lord, **declares the Sovereign** Lord, **when I show myself holy through you before their eyes.**

[24]" 'For I will take you out of the nations; I will gather you from all the countries and bring you back into your own land. [25]I will sprinkle clean water on you, and you will be clean; I will cleanse you from all your impurities and from all your idols. [26]I will give you a new heart and put a new spirit in you; I will remove from you your heart of stone and give you a heart of flesh. [27]And I will put my Spirit in you and move you to follow my decrees and be careful to keep my laws. [28]You will live in the land I gave your forefathers; you will be my people, and I will be your God. [29]I will save you from all your uncleanness. I will call for the grain and make it plentiful and will not bring famine upon you. [30]I will increase the fruit of the trees and the crops of the field, so that you will no longer suffer disgrace among the nations because of famine. [31]Then you will remember your evil ways and wicked deeds, and you will loathe yourselves for your sins and detestable practices. [32]I want you to know that I am not doing this for your sake, declares the Sovereign Lord. Be ashamed and disgraced for your conduct, O house of Israel!

UNDERSTANDING THE SCRIPTURE

Ezekiel 36:22-23. The passage for this lesson is an oracle of Ezekiel intended to strengthen both the hope and understanding of the Israelites in captivity in Babylon. Although the passages selected for this unit, "The Promise of New Life," emphasize hope and new beginnings, it is important to remember that the vast majority of Ezekiel's words, visions, and oracles announced judgment on Israel, its leaders (religious and political), enemies, and captors. Grace notes of hope, such as those studied in this unit, are rare; thus, they should be examined as precious insights.

In Ezekiel 36:1-21, the prophet offered a succinct explanation for Israel's exile: violence (resulting in the shedding of innocent blood) and idolatry (resulting in the pollution of the Temple and the land). These twin sins not only spread corruption among the Israelites but also polluted the land.

The prophet addressed these sins with three statements. First, Ezekiel prophesied to the mountains God's intention to restore the land to its former blessed state (Ezekiel 36:1-15). Next, Ezekiel recorded a personal oracle (Ezekiel 36:16-21) that revealed a new insight: The restoration of Israel, both the people and the land, vindicated God's holy name. Finally, the reason for God's grace toward Israel, as first promised in Ezekiel 34, had only one purpose: to prove to the nations the glory of the Lord (Ezekiel 36:22-23). By these three statements, Ezekiel confirmed that the judgment and grace experienced by Israel were part of God's larger intention to be known and glorified throughout creation.

Ezekiel 36:24-27. Having set a new theological framework, Ezekiel began to detail God's vindication through the rescue of the exiles. The key words, "take," "gather," and "bring," indicated a new exodus. Whereas the impetus for the exodus from Egypt was the suffering of the people, the inspiration for this exodus from Babylon was God's own holiness. Since God's identity was at stake, the act of restoration was comprehensive. Not only would the people be gathered together and returned to their land but they also would be transformed by divine intention. Initially, Ezekiel addressed Israel's twin sins of uncleanness (violence resulting in murder) and of pollution (idolatry resulting in unfaithfulness). Ezekiel's words may sound strange to contemporary ears. Yet, there are many current illustrations of violence sparking increased violence (Ezekiel's word "unclean" applies here). Likewise, those who nibble from the contemporary feast of spiritualities often discover the core of their own faith compromised. (Ezekiel would say "profaned.") Thus, Ezekiel's message is as current as today's newspaper. Because of such sins, God must act. Next, Ezekiel revealed God's promise to perform an external sign, a purifying rite of

water/cleansing (see Exodus 29:4 and Numbers 8:7). This external ritual begged an internal change. Continuing the oracle, Ezekiel announced God's gifts to the restored nation of a new heart and a new spirit. With a new heart the people could live from a divine rather than a human perspective. With a new spirit they could live obediently within God's expectations.

Ezekiel 36:28-30. Having explained God's plan for the restoration of people and land, Ezekiel turned to a new topic: the qualitative change accomplished by divine rescue and restoration. Echoing the closing promise of Ezekiel 34, the prophet spoke of the return of blessings. Whereas once Israel experienced God's judgment in famine and exile, a restored people received God's blessing in abundant food. The prophet offered this wide description of a restored future because captivity included both physical and spiritual oppression. Indeed, as the exiles attended to the prophets and thoughtfully reflected on their past conduct, they were deeply convinced of their sinfulness. This conviction became a type of spiritual captivity: The people could not imagine themselves able to please God. Thus, the prophet showed them God's future—not a future that the exiles "earned" or "deserved." Notice the preciseness of Ezekiel's speech as he described the comprehensiveness of God's rescue of Israel. The divine pronoun "I" introduced every change; God initiated, conducted, and concluded every aspect of the restoration. The people, in contrast, passively received every changed circumstance, gift, and opportunity. In other words, the prophet declared, again, that God would accomplish those things the people dared not imagine—let alone do for themselves.

Ezekiel 36:31-32. Two consequences accompanied God's promised deeds of restoration. First, the people remembered their former sins, and second, they loathed themselves because of their past. Again, Ezekiel's words sound overly harsh to contemporary readers. Yet his intention echoes in the contemporary caution that those who forget the past are condemned to repeat the past. Indeed, explained the prophet, God offered the exiles a new future, but the people must accept the offer with a distinct recollection of their sins and the bitter consequence of exile. To fully live in God's future, the people cultivated their memory of the shameful truths learned during the exile. Without this memory, they could not receive and use the gifts of God (a new heart, a new spirit, a cleansed land, and a restored future). As the people remembered and loathed all forms of sinfulness, the true character of God emerged. God was the powerful savior of Israel who intended to spread divine glory through this once ragtag and scattered people. This rescue was not for Israel's sake alone; this mighty deed was a sign of the holiness and glory of God that would one day encompass all creation. Finally, the prophet had fully published the divine word. Clearly, God was acting for the sake of the divine, not the sake of the Israelites. With the formula phrase in verse 32, "let that be known to you," the prophet concluded his message. The final sentence (Ezekiel 36:32) indicated the emotional weight of this message on Ezekiel and the Israelites. The experience, lessons, and truths of exile were poignant; neither the prophet nor the people hid from the shame of exile. Surprisingly, however, within this stark experience was the spiritual protection necessary to live in the restored and transformed world God offered. By remembering their exile and by hating their former sins, Israel prepared to live in God's new future.

INTERPRETING THE SCRIPTURE

To Glorify God

One of the most difficult tasks in human experience is to understand the past and learn its lessons. While the people of Israel were in exile, this difficult task was their daily bread. Prior to the exile, their leaders (those prophesied against in Ezekiel 34) cultivated a false security based on their status as "chosen." These leaders taught that since God chose Israel, God protected the nation; because God chose the Temple, God guarded the holy city Jerusalem; because God promised the land to Abraham, Israel was secure on its land. One by one, history contradicted these lessons. First Israel, then Judah and Jerusalem, fell to enemies. The Temple was looted and defiled. Famine spread across the land as the elite were marched off to Babylon.

During the exile, the traditional theology of Israel was reexamined. Slowly, under the guidance of prophets like Ezekiel, Israel acknowledged her sins that had provoked the exile. Gradually, words like "sin," "judgment," and "punishment" sank into the exiles' vocabulary. Indeed, these took control of the people's theological reflection with such tenacity that Ezekiel identified a new theological issue. While Israel bewailed her past deeds of unfaithfulness and violence, she grew despondent. The nation lost all hope of regaining God's affection.

In Ezekiel 36, the prophet spoke to this despondency. His words were critical and precise: God's judgment was just, but God's intentions were glorious. The same God who judged Israel's sins would show mercy, in abundance, on the scattered nation. Why? The answer was remarkably unrelated to Israel and her claims of worthlessness or worthiness. Simply said, God desired all nations and peoples to recognize the glory of the Lord. This was a new formulation of the ancient truth that glory motivated all God's deeds. Essentially, the prophet attempted to teach the people a new theological approach: God's acts are glorious, and human circumstances must be interpreted through God's glory.

Changed People

How would Israel apply this new theological approach? Before the exile, Israel trusted that her status with God was guaranteed by God's covenant. During the exile, the people learned the profound connection between sin and judgment. Now, the prophet challenged the people to experience all of life through God's glory. This new theology seemed beyond the people. How could a broken, sin-soaked, mournful people approach God's glory? The situation swiftly spiraled into hopelessness. And then, as is often the case, when all human effort failed, there was God. In this case, God promised to restore Israel by giving her a "new heart." The Hebrew word is singular because it referred to a common gift divinely bestowed upon all the restored of Israel.

God took the initiative to change the people so that they would appreciate and live in the glorious, new future. This change involved, first and foremost, a change of perspective. No longer would Israel know God through the rough and ready experiences of judgment and blessing. With a new heart, Israel experienced the compassion of God toward creation and was able to appreciate, to care for, and to cherish creation as a manifestation of God's glory. Likewise, by the gift of a new spirit, the people discovered a new capacity for loyalty and obedience. With a new heart and a new spirit, Ezekiel described a corporate renewal—with individual consequences. For the people as a whole to receive this gift of a new heart and a new spirit, each individual Israelite had to experience an inner transformation. By turning the nation's eyes from sin and sin's consequences and toward God's glory, Ezekiel announced God's intention to change the nation—person by person.

Changed Circumstances

Have you ever known someone whose circumstances turned from grave to glorious? Perhaps a friend was near death but suddenly grew strong and steady. Or maybe a scattered, broken family experienced reunion and reconciliation. Or possibly the nearly broke became the benefactor to many. Such changed circumstances prompt the questions, Why? How? Frequently, the reflection on changed circumstances becomes theological. Often a simplistic analysis concludes with a judgment of worthiness: Circumstances change for the better because God blesses the good, the wise, the careful, the faithful, the righteous, or the obedient.

This analysis is the exact opposite of Ezekiel's teachings to the exiles. Ezekiel did not hold a theology of rewards. True, he exposed the sin of Israel and explained that it was necessary for God to punish that sin. However, even in his harsh words of judgment, Ezekiel was careful to stress that God's judgment was a manifestation of God's glory. In the passage for this session, God's glory is the reason for judgment and rescue. So that people and the land would be purified from the corruption of sins, God scattered the people. So that the nations would be awed by God's glory, God intended to return the people to a transformed homeland. In this new setting, neither wild animals nor foreign militaries threatened; the land of Israel was safe and peaceful. No longer did famine kill the youngest victims or drought dry up the future; the land of Israel was fertile and the rains were dependable. By God's glory the land was transformed.

Predictably, the people were amazed by this prophecy of transformation. Just as contemporary people feel giddy when circumstances suddenly shift from grim to great, Israel caught her corporate breath as Ezekiel described their renewed homeland. Could God do this? Would God do this? And if God could and would, how should the people respond?

Remember!

Ezekiel knew the exiles' wonderings, both practical and theological. He knew, after the experience of exile in Babylon, they understood the link between sin and punishment. He hoped they glimpsed God's glory through his prophetic words. He assumed they accepted his caution to be faithful in the future God was preparing. Thus, as Ezekiel drew this oracle to a close he offered direct advice to the exiles. Their challenge, as they received God's gifts of a new heart, a new spirit, and a renewed homeland, was to remember.

This direction strikes me, initially, as odd. I don't know about you, but there are sins in my past I'd rather forget. Wisely, cautioned by preachers such as Ezekiel, I have learned the wisdom of remembering the sins of former days. As Christians we release our sins to God's redeeming grace, but we remember the deceptions, rebellions, lies, and ignorance that were those sins. Such remembrance, when linked to the desire to live in God's grace, is a form of spiritual protection.

Although Ezekiel offers this spiritual guidance in his usual harsh vocabulary—"loathe yourselves," "abominable deeds," "be ashamed and dismayed"—the pace of these parting lines is slow and the tone is tender (36:31-32). If only the people remembered accurately and intensely, then God's glorious future might have a chance. But, if the people forgot their past—with secret idolatries or cultivated lusts for violence—then God's glory would seek another manifestation. Strongly, Ezekiel challenged the people to remember their past, to recommit to the law, and to return to God. If they did so, not only Israel but all nations, peoples, and creation would know the glory of the Lord.

SHARING THE SCRIPTURE

Preparing Our Hearts

Meditate on this week's devotional reading, found in Psalm 25:11-22. In this acrostic psalm ascribed to David, the writer prays for God's guidance and deliverance. Notice in verse 11 that the psalmist asks God for pardon "for your name's sake." The idea of God forgiving human guilt for God's own sake is seen again in today's Scripture passage from Ezekiel 36:22-32. Ponder those words. Ask yourself, Why should God want to forgive my guilt for the sake of God's name?

Pray that you and the adult learners will change your attitudes and behavior not only for your sake but also for the sake of God.

Preparing Our Minds

Study the background and lesson Scripture, both found in Ezekiel 36:22-32. As you ponder this passage, think about what motivates people's actions.

Write on newsprint:

❑ topics related to repentance for "Repent of Sins and Recognize That God Forgives."

❑ information for next week's lesson, found under "Continue the Journey."

❑ activities for further spiritual growth in "Continue the Journey."

Locate somber, instrumental music appropriate for contemplating one's sins.

Have the appropriate player available. Bach's "Come, Sweet Death" and Handel's "Largo" would be appropriate choices.

LEADING THE CLASS

(1) Gather to Learn

❖ Welcome the class members and introduce any guests.

❖ Pray that the participants will have open hearts and minds to receive whatever God would have for them today.

❖ Read aloud these quotations on the subject of motivation.

- **God considers not the action, but the spirit of the action.** (Peter Abelard, 1079–1142)
- **God strikes at the core of our motivations. He is not interested in merely applying a new coat of paint, imposing a new set of rules. He wants to rebuild our minds and give us new values.** (Erwin Lutzer, 1941–)
- **God does not care What good you did But why you did it.** (Angelus Silesius, 1624–1677)
- **It is not what a man does that determines whether his work is sacred or secular, it is why he does it.** (A. W. Tozer, 1897–1963)
- **Man sees your actions, but God your motives.** (Thomas à Kempis, about 1380–1471)

❖ Invite the students to comment on any of these quotations that particularly grabbed their attention. Also discuss with the class the importance of motivation. Note that the same actions can be the result of very different motivations.

❖ Read aloud today's focus statement: **Although the fruits of action are often visible, the reasons for an action taken in a particular time and at a certain place are more difficult to discern. What motivates actions? According to Ezekiel, God's** promise to restore Israel is not motivated by Israel itself but rather for the sake of God's holy name.

(2) Delve Into God's Plans and Intentions to Restore Israel

❖ Choose a volunteer to read aloud Ezekiel 36:22-32.

❖ **Option:** If the students all use the same version of the Bible, ask half to read the even-numbered verses and half to read the odd-numbered ones as a responsive reading.

❖ Ask these questions. If you wish to add to the discussion, check "To Glorify God," "Changed People," and "Changed Circumstances" in Interpreting the Scripture for ideas.

1. **What does this passage tell you that God is going to do?**
2. **What motivates God's actions?**
3. **How will these actions affect the exiles?**
4. **What effect will the restoration of the fortunes of the exiled Israelites have on other people who are observing these dramatic changes?**

(3) Repent of Sins and Recognize That God Forgives

❖ Divide the class into groups of three or four. Ask each group to read together the first portion of the parable of the prodigal son, Luke 15:11-24. Encourage the groups to discuss these topics, which you will post on newsprint:

- the sins of the prodigal.
- what prompted him to "come to himself."
- what most people would expect the father's reaction to be.
- what the father's reaction actually was.

❖ Invite the groups to report on insights they gleaned from their discussions.

❖ Distribute paper and pencils. Tell the

class that this is an individual activity for their eyes only. Encourage them to write a conversation with God in which they name sins they have committed this week and hear God's words of forgiveness. Perhaps they, like the prodigal, will hear words from God that they would not expect.

❖ **Option:** Play some serious music that sets an appropriate mood to contemplate sin and forgiveness.

❖ Suggest that some students may want to put these conversations in their Bibles for later review. Others may want to shred them as a sign that the sins of their lives are now forgiven and before them no more.

(4) Display Evidence of the New Life That Results From God's Gracious Restoration

❖ Point out that the behavior of Christians creates a perception of God for observers.

❖ Follow these steps to write a litany that highlights new life as a result of God's gracious forgiveness. Remember that a litany is usually read responsively with a leader reading different ideas and the rest of the group repeating a refrain.

- **Step 1:** Write a line that will be repeated by everyone throughout the litany. Here's an example: **We give thanks, O Holy One, for the new life you give us.**
- **Step 2:** List on newsprint the kinds of behaviors that will show to the world that God has restored those who have fallen. Some examples can be found in Galatians 5:22-23, which lists fruit of the Spirit.
- **Step 3:** Write lines that highlight each of the examples you want to include. For example, **Help us keep ourselves under control so that people might see your holiness within us.**
- **Step 4:** Read the litany aloud to close the session.

(5) Continue the Journey

❖ Pray that each person will experience restoration and forgiveness.

❖ Read aloud this preparation for next week's lesson. You may also want to post it on newsprint for the students to copy.

- ■ **Title:** Prophesying New Life
- ■ **Background Scripture:** Ezekiel 37
- ■ **Lesson Scripture:** Ezekiel 37:1-14
- ■ **Focus of the Lesson:** Sometimes situations seem so overwhelming that we fall into despair. Where can we find hope? Ezekiel's prophecy of the valley of dry bones vividly illustrates how God enlivens people and fills them with the breath of life and hope.

❖ Challenge the students to complete one or more of these activities for further spiritual growth, which you will write on newsprint for the students to copy:

(1) Be aware of how your actions and attitudes are sending messages to others about who God is. Use whatever opportunities you can to give glory to God.

(2) Review the day in your mind, as if watching a DVD. Hone in on things you should not have done but did, and things you should have done but didn't. Seek God's forgiveness and pray for guidance to do better next time.

(3) Think about a good act that you did recently. Why did you do this? What do you think Jesus would say about your motivation, even if the act itself was helpful?

❖ Sing or read aloud "Give Me a Clean Heart," found on page 2133 in *The Faith We Sing.*

❖ Conclude today's session by leading the class in this benediction: **Give us new hearts filled with your Spirit, O Lord, that we may live as new creations in Christ. Amen.**

UNIT 1: THE PROMISE OF NEW LIFE
PROPHESYING NEW LIFE

PREVIEWING THE LESSON

Lesson Scripture: Ezekiel 37:1-14
Background Scripture: Ezekiel 37
Key Verse: Ezekiel 37:6

Focus of the Lesson:
Sometimes situations seem so overwhelming that we fall into despair. Where can we find hope? Ezekiel's prophecy of the valley of dry bones vividly illustrates how God enlivens people and fills them with the breath of life and hope.

Goals for the Learners:
(1) to unpack the metaphor of the valley of dry bones as it applies to the captives in Babylon.
(2) to examine their own faith communities for signs of both "dry bones" and new life.
(3) to pray that God's Spirit will enliven them, individually and as a community of faith.

Supplies:
Bibles, newsprint and markers, paper and pencils, hymnals, picture of the valley of dry bones

---

READING THE SCRIPTURE

NRSV
Ezekiel 37:1-14

¹The hand of the LORD came upon me, and he brought me out by the spirit of the LORD and set me down in the middle of a valley; it was full of bones. ²He led me all around them; there were very many lying in the valley, and they were very dry. ³He said to me, "Mortal, can these bones live?" I answered, "O Lord GOD, you know." ⁴Then he said to me, "Prophesy to these bones, and say to them: O dry bones, hear the word of the LORD. ⁵Thus says the Lord GOD to these

NIV
Ezekiel 37:1-14

¹The hand of the LORD was upon me, and he brought me out by the Spirit of the LORD and set me in the middle of a valley; it was full of bones. ²He led me back and forth among them, and I saw a great many bones on the floor of the valley, bones that were very dry. ³He asked me, "Son of man, can these bones live?"

I said, "O Sovereign LORD, you alone know."

bones: I will cause breath to enter you, and you shall live. [6]I will lay sinews on you, and will cause flesh to come upon you, and cover you with skin, and **put breath in you, and you shall live; and you shall know that I am the LORD."**

[7]So I prophesied as I had been commanded; and as I prophesied, suddenly there was a noise, a rattling, and the bones came together, bone to its bone. [8]I looked, and there were sinews on them, and flesh had come upon them, and skin had covered them; but there was no breath in them. [9]Then he said to me, "Prophesy to the breath, prophesy, mortal, and say to the breath: Thus says the Lord GOD: Come from the four winds, O breath, and breathe upon these slain, that they may live." [10]I prophesied as he commanded me, and the breath came into them, and they lived, and stood on their feet, a vast multitude.

[11]Then he said to me, "Mortal, these bones are the whole house of Israel. They say, 'Our bones are dried up, and our hope is lost; we are cut off completely.' [12]Therefore prophesy, and say to them, Thus says the Lord GOD: I am going to open your graves, and bring you up from your graves, O my people; and I will bring you back to the land of Israel. [13]And you shall know that I am the LORD, when I open your graves, and bring you up from your graves, O my people. [14]I will put my spirit within you, and you shall live, and I will place you on your own soil; then you shall know that I, the LORD, have spoken and will act," says the LORD.

[4]Then he said to me, "Prophesy to these bones and say to them, 'Dry bones, hear the word of the LORD! [5]This is what the Sovereign LORD says to these bones: I will make breath enter you, and you will come to life. [6]I will attach tendons to you and make flesh come upon you and cover you with skin; I will **put breath in you, and you will come to life. Then you will know that I am the LORD.'"**

[7]So I prophesied as I was commanded. And as I was prophesying, there was a noise, a rattling sound, and the bones came together, bone to bone. [8]I looked, and tendons and flesh appeared on them and skin covered them, but there was no breath in them.

[9]Then he said to me, "Prophesy to the breath; prophesy, son of man, and say to it, 'This is what the Sovereign LORD says: Come from the four winds, O breath, and breathe into these slain, that they may live.'" [10]So I prophesied as he commanded me, and breath entered them; they came to life and stood up on their feet—a vast army.

[11]Then he said to me: "Son of man, these bones are the whole house of Israel. They say, 'Our bones are dried up and our hope is gone; we are cut off.' [12]Therefore prophesy and say to them: 'This is what the Sovereign LORD says: O my people, I am going to open your graves and bring you up from them; I will bring you back to the land of Israel. [13]Then you, my people, will know that I am the LORD, when I open your graves and bring you up from them. [14]I will put my Spirit in you and you will live, and I will settle you in your own land. Then you will know that I the LORD have spoken, and I have done it, declares the LORD.'"

UNDERSTANDING THE SCRIPTURE

Ezekiel 37:1-10. Well-known passages, such as this text, present unique challenges to the student of Scripture. One challenge is to release all conclusions previously made about the passage. Another challenge is to read the exact words of the text, slowly and carefully. Our passage begins as the prophet felt the hand of God transporting him to an unnamed valley. A close translation of the Hebrew text includes an article, "the." This article indicated that this valley was, perhaps, easily identified and well-known. This vision was, therefore, particular: given to a particular person (Ezekiel), at a particular time (a point in the exile where hopelessness overwhelmed hope), and employing a particular setting (recognized by the audience). Scholars see this valley as a battlefield where the unburied bones of the Israelites who endured the Babylonian invasion lay strewn. Once Ezekiel saw this valley, God conducted a tour of the many dry bones lying about the valley. Only after the magnitude of the vision impressed Ezekiel did God speak. God questioned Ezekiel about the viability of these bones. Of course, based on every scrap of human experience, dry bones are unquestionably dead bones; the answer to this question was no. Yet, the question posed by God was also a challenge to imagine God's power. Respectfully, Ezekiel did not answer. Then, God instructed the prophet to speak to the bones so that the bones might live and acknowledge God. As Ezekiel prophesied a loud rattling signaled the impossible. As Ezekiel watched, bones assembled into skeletons and sinews, flesh, and skin appeared. However, there were no signs of life. Next God directed Ezekiel to prophesy to the four winds (this Hebrew word may be translated "wind," "spirit," or "breath") to enliven the restored bodies. As Ezekiel spoke to the wind, the bodies came alive.

Ezekiel 37:11-14. After this amazing vision, God interpreted to Ezekiel the vision's significance. First, God explained that the vision was meant for the whole house of Israel. After the death of Solomon, the nation Israel was divided into two kingdoms, Judah and Israel. With the fall of Israel, and then of Judah, the people were scattered throughout the surrounding countryside, nations, and peoples. Yet the vision addressed all the chosen people, regardless of their current status of exiled, alienated, or assimilated in foreign nations. The audience for this vision was as vast as the vision itself. Moreover, it was a vision designed to refute a popular lament among the exiles found in verse 11: "Our bones are dried up, and our hope is lost; we are cut off completely." The sorrow in this lament was palpable. Independently, each phrase signified a hopeless situation—"dried up," "lost," and "cut off." Together they described the finality of death. God's word aimed directly at this finality; God declared an intention to restore the whole people of Israel—by opening graves. These dead people would live by God's own gift of spirit. Moreover, God would "place" (also translated, "establish") the people in their homeland. In God's future the whole people of Israel was revived. Why? Once again, God desired only to be known.

Ezekiel 37:15-24a. Just as God provided Ezekiel with a visual presentation of the restoration of Israel, so God instructed Ezekiel to visually demonstrate the restoration to the people. The props for this demonstration were simple sticks of wood. On each stick was a name: Israel, signifying all the house of Joseph, and Judah, indicating the remaining tribes. Ezekiel bound these two sticks together so that they appeared to be a single unit. Only after this symbolic demonstration was Ezekiel allowed to speak. Notice, this is the same pattern experienced by Ezekiel in the valley. First he saw what God desired him to see, and then God explained to him the significance of the vision. Once the people saw what Ezekiel presented to them, Ezekiel spoke according to God's word. The first word was a powerful presentation of hope: God intended to "take," "gather," and "bring" the people to their homeland. Again, scale was significant: This promise applied to the whole people of God. Restoration, however, was only the beginning of God's promise. Indeed, the nation, as a political entity, would be restored under the leadership of one king. God intended to cleanse the nation of corporate pain, sorrow, defeat, separation, and sin. With the grand phrase "never again," the unity and purity of the nation was restored by God's word. Finally, a long-awaited word was spoken: "[God] will save them" (37:23). Salvation for Israel entailed restoration, reunion, and reconciliation. Such salvation was meant to be seen and understood—first, by the symbolic joining of two sticks into one, and second, by the reestablishment of the reign of David's lineage.

Ezekiel 37:24b-28. The final words of this passage paint a grand picture of God's salvation. As a restored nation, Israel was, first and foremost, obedient to God's law. Such obedience included not only the ethical behavior of the community but also the religious and liturgical life of the nation as well. The law of God was understood as a guide enabling the nation to live abundantly and blessedly with God. The new condition of human-divine communion gave Ezekiel's words grandeur. Indeed, Ezekiel's final speech crossed temporal, communal, and spiritual boundaries. Ezekiel emphasized God's amazing grace in the gift of land and life "forever." His words affirmed God's ultimate goal with an "everlasting" covenant of peace. He spoke lavishly to future generations by announcing that God blessed Israel's "children's children." With prophetic insight Ezekiel tenderly described how God was sanctuary to Israel forevermore. Finally, Ezekiel explained why God's salvation was so expansive. The prophet declared, once again, that God desired to be known by the people and acknowledged by the nations. This last vision, broad and wide as Ezekiel's words, was not, however, a glimpse into the future. It was, rather, the future in complete wholeness. God's salvation stretched to fill all time, to include all the scattered, and to overcome every sin, obstacle, and frailty—and the guarantor of this salvation was the only power able so to speak and do: God.

INTERPRETING THE SCRIPTURE

Where's the Vision?

For most contemporary Christians, the type of visionary experience described in Ezekiel 37 is suspect. Although such a strange occurrence may have happened long ago to a prophet like Ezekiel, the chances of such a visionary experience occurring in our times are slim. Quite likely, if your next-door neighbor or even your pastor reported being transported by the hand of the Lord and guided through a seemingly realistic vision, such a report would provoke a chuckle, a sigh of disbelief, or both.

We have become a Christian community estranged from Ezekiel-type visions. However, we continue, simultaneously, to be hungry for spiritual communion with our God. Could it be that Ezekiel's experience and our hunger have something in common? As I struggled with Ezekiel's vision, I understood that significance was in both the style *and* content. Ezekiel received a visual shock. This shock was communicated as a vision that provoked something unexpected—hope for life in the presence of death.

Stop for a moment and consider the contemporary visual shocks that inspire hope. Some are quite small: the sight of children playing in the park, geese flying in formation, light flashing through a stained-glass window, or the intricacy of a snowflake. Other visions are quite large: a painting or movie depicting reconciliation, an unexpected peace between former international enemies, or the graceful reclamation of a forest following a devastating fire. Wonderful sights to encourage the downcast heart surround us, yet frequently these go unnoticed. We do not see the messages God embeds in nature or splashes throughout the human community.

Whatever the reason, we are spiritually hungry people with eyes shut tight. The spiritual practice designed to correct this condition is attention. Open your eyes; look carefully at your surroundings; ask, from your hungry heart, What is God showing to me? Practice such attention for a week, a month, a year and you will be as eager as Ezekiel to see what God is doing. But do not be surprised if, one day, something that feels like God's hand is actually leading you to see even more.

The Work Within the Vision

Ezekiel's vision of the valley of dry bones seems shockingly simple to comprehend. This is a vision of God's capacity to bring life out of death. However, in Ezekiel's recounting of this vision, the obvious conclusion was not so obvious. Notice how God led Ezekiel all around the valley of bones. It is almost as if God wanted Ezekiel to acknowledge each and every sign of sorrow, despair, and death. God purposefully slowed Ezekiel's response to the vision. The vision's intentionally slow pace reminded Ezekiel to give full attention to his actual situation. Surely, Ezekiel could have found words of encouragement forged out of his own prophetic vocabulary.

People of faith usually have something positive or encouraging to say. God's intention, however, was greater than a quick, "Everything will be all right" affirmation; God wanted Ezekiel to inventory the exact dimension of suffering before rushing to a kindly word of encouragement. The necessary first step in understanding the vision was (and is) to patiently see every aspect.

After Ezekiel toured the whole valley and counted every dry bone, God posed a question: "Mortal, can these bones live?" (37:3). It was an absurd and tantalizing question. It was an ultimate question of hope posed by God, the only power able to make possibilities out of impossibilities. Ezekiel was wise enough to refrain from speaking his own mind; humbly, he deferred to the wisdom of God. Once again, God kept the pace of the vision slow by explaining to Ezekiel what he should say and do. Carefully, Ezekiel spoke. Surprisingly, bones rattled and sinews, flesh, and skin appeared. Still, the bones were not alive. Once again, God directed Ezekiel to speak, and once again, Ezekiel fulfilled God's direction by prophesying to the winds. The breath of God's Spirit enlivened the "assembled" bones. Now, Ezekiel faced a living, breathing, standing multitude. The impossible, symbolically, became a reality. By a dreamlike rehearsal, God prepared Ezekiel to speak a new word.

A Command to Speak

Ezekiel's audience was as vast as the number of bones in his vision. The scattered nation was either assimilated or dominated by conquering empires. Yet, God appointed Ezekiel to address the "whole house of Israel" (37:11). How could Ezekiel fulfill this command? There was no place on earth that the whole of Israel could be assembled. Moreover, even if such a gathering could be arranged, there remained inner tensions among tribes, clans, and leaders, as well as between those who fled to hills and those who were exiled. There was little opportunity to speak a word of hope to the "whole house of Israel"; yet, God commanded Ezekiel to speak to all.

Then, God provided an entry point for Ezekiel's vast audience. Evidently, there was a hopeless saying gaining popularity in Babylon that described the exiles as already dead (37:11). This saying was Ezekiel's point of connection between God's word and the situation of the whole house of

Israel. God instructed Ezekiel to recast the vision of dry bones into a prophetic word of God's power to bring life even to the dead and buried. It was not necessary for Ezekiel to recount his vision to the people. Rather, he was to testify to God's power to create life. In a sense, Ezekiel's words conjured up another vision. As Ezekiel spoke, his audience heard and saw the graves they feared. As Ezekiel prophesied, according to God's precise direction, the exiles saw their brothers, sisters, mothers, fathers, relatives, and friends emerging from the grasp of death. Indeed, the Spirit of God active in Ezekiel's prophetic preaching bound the community together and gave them the will to imagine God's future. Ezekiel's prophetic preaching created community, inspired hope, and provided a path into the future.

The Spiritual Trump Card

The promise to renew the life of the whole house of Israel was sealed by God's declarations. The actions in Ezekiel 37:12-14 are strong and charged with power. God *will* open graves, bring the dead to life, return the people to their land. These dramatic changes confirmed God's promises; moreover, the confirmation also created a new form of knowledge. Finally, the whole house of Israel knew God. In the past they lurched from rescue to rebellion and from obedience to idolatry. God's new chance for life included a spiritual dynamic unavailable in previous mighty deeds of God.

Contemporary believers might easily overlook the spiritual "trump card" Ezekiel played. We are comfortable with the idea of God's Spirit working and moving among us. We have learned Jesus' promises and received the blessed comfort of the Spirit. We have sensed the Spirit's presence in baptism, communion, and services of worship. We have been led, forgiven, inspired, and transformed by God's Spirit. In contrast, Ezekiel's audience was neither acquainted with nor prepared to receive God's Spirit. Thus, the word of the Lord, "I will put my spirit within you" (37:14), was unexpected. The exiles had no theological category to hold the concept of God's Spirit living actively among the whole house of Israel. Ezekiel's announcement trumped every system to earn or deserve God's grace. God was about to do the unprecedented: bless the whole people of God with God's own Spirit.

SHARING THE SCRIPTURE

Preparing Our Hearts

Meditate on this week's devotional reading, found in Romans 6:1-14. Here Paul writes about dying and rising with Christ. Through baptism we enter into his death and then are raised to a new life. We are, as the apostle indicates in verse 11, "dead to sin and alive to God in Christ Jesus." What has been your experience in light of this idea of dying to sin and rising in Christ? How does this baptismal image empower you to feel as if God has renewed your life?

Pray that you and the adult learners will recognize the renewed life that is yours in Christ.

Preparing Our Minds

Study the background from Ezekiel 37 and the lesson Scripture from Ezekiel 37:1-14. As you read this well-known passage, think about where we can find hope, particularly in an overwhelming situation.

Write on newsprint:

❏ information for next week's lesson, found under "Continue the Journey."

❏ activities for further spiritual growth in "Continue the Journey."

Locate a picture of the valley of dry bones in a book or on the Internet. Check www.biblical-art.com/biblicalsubject.asp?id_biblicalsubject=339&pagenum=1. Many artists throughout history have illustrated this scene.

LEADING THE CLASS

(1) Gather to Learn

❖ Welcome the class members and introduce any guests.

❖ Pray that those in attendance today will be ready to face new challenges and find new life in Christ.

❖ Read aloud this paragraph concerning New Orleans after hurricane Katrina from the "National Guard" newsletter for August 29, 2006 (http://www.ngb.army.mil/news/archives/2006/08/082906-Katrina_remembered.aspx). **With the levees temporarily patched and everybody evacuated from the Super Dome and Convention Center, journalists and fresh troops walk through the dome one last time, and suddenly through the damaged roof of the Super Dome a beam of sun light pierces through the dark interior as if God sends a message of renewal to those who are beginning to lose hope that this city can ever be restored to its former splendor.**

❖ Discuss these questions: **Have you ever experienced a devastating situation, such as hurricane Katrina? If so, what gave you hope to believe that God would bring about renewal in the midst of what appeared to be a hopeless situation?**

❖ Read aloud today's focus statement: **Sometimes situations seem so overwhelming that we fall into despair. Where can we find hope? Ezekiel's prophecy of the valley of dry bones vividly illustrates how God enlivens people and fills them with the breath of life and hope.**

(2) Unpack the Metaphor of the Valley of Dry Bones as It Applies to the Captives in Babylon

❖ Choose three volunteers to read the parts of a narrator, the prophet, and God. Ask them to read Ezekiel 37:1-14 with as much vocal and physical expression as possible.

❖ Show whatever illustrations you have located of the valley of dry bones. Invite the students to comment on the following points:

■ emotions that well up as they view the scene.

■ how the color or lack of color affects the intensity and realism of the scene.

■ what they might have thought had they been Ezekiel confronted by this scene.

■ ways this art illustrates for them dry bones as a metaphor for those who are spiritually dead and raised to new life.

❖ Discuss these questions:

(1) What does this passage say to you about God, especially about how God acts in human history? (Refer to "The Spiritual Trump Card" in Interpreting the Scripture for ideas.)

(2) God gave Ezekiel this vision for a purpose. What role was the prophet to play on behalf of the exiles? (Use "A Command to Speak" in Interpreting the Scripture to add to the discussion.)

(3) What hope might this passage give the church?

❖ **Option:** Discuss the issue of visions, such as the one Ezekiel saw. While some students will have no problem with the idea of someone seeing such a detailed vision attributed to God, others may find it too fantastic to comprehend or take seriously. "Where's the Vision?" in Interpreting the Scripture can help you address skepticism, though do not insist that students change their point of view.

(3) Examine the Learners' Own Faith Communities for Signs of Both "Dry Bones" and New Life

❖ Divide the class into groups and give each group a sheet of newsprint and marker. Assign half of the groups to answer this question: **What signs of "dry bones" do we see in our congregation or denomination?** Assign the other half of the groups to answer this question: **What signs of new life do we see in our congregation or denomination?**

❖ Allow time for the groups to work and then bring everyone together to report. See if the class can come to consensus on two or three "dry bones."

❖ Talk together about what action they can take individually and collectively to address the problems. List ideas on newsprint.

❖ Encourage the class to come to consensus on two or three signs of new life within the congregation or denomination. Discuss what they can do as individuals and collectively to strengthen and support this new life. List these ideas on newsprint.

❖ **Option:** Invite the learners to tell stories of times when God has breathed new life into something that seemed dead. These stories may reflect the experience of an individual or the collective history of this (or another) congregation.

(4) Pray That God's Spirit Will Enliven the Learners, Individually and as a Community of Faith

❖ Spend time in prayer concerning the "dry bones," inviting the students to pray aloud as they feel led to do so.

❖ Encourage volunteers to note any insights they experienced during the prayer. Perhaps at least one person will have gleaned a new direction.

❖ Invite the adults to look again at the signs of hope they see and pray for God's continuing renewal.

(5) Continue the Journey

❖ Conclude the group prayer by asking God to empower the participants with the breath of new life that they may go forth to serve and share the message of new life with others.

❖ Read aloud this preparation for next week's lesson. You may also want to post it on newsprint for the students to copy.

■ **Title: Envisioning New Life**
■ **Background Scripture: Ezekiel 47:1-12**
■ **Lesson Scripture: Ezekiel 47:1-12**
■ **Focus of the Lesson: Humankind depends on the water that covers the vast areas of earth's landscape. What impact do these bodies of water have on humanity and all creation? In a vision, Ezekiel sees a sacred river that flows freely from God's throne, sustaining life.**

❖ Challenge the students to complete one or more of these activities for further spiritual growth, which you will write on newsprint for the students to copy:

(1) **Encourage someone in a difficult situation to consider how God can breathe new life into an apparently hopeless situation. Do whatever you can to assist this person.**

(2) **Research the meanings of the word "spirit." The word has at least three different meanings in the passage we studied today.**

(3) **Pray and journal about a situation in your own life or the life of a beloved one that is causing feelings of hopelessness and despair. Be open to whatever God is telling you about this situation and what you may need to do.**

❖ Sing or read aloud "Breathe on Me, Breath of God."

❖ Conclude today's session by leading the class in this benediction: **Give us new hearts filled with your Spirit, O Lord, that we may live as new creations in Christ. Amen.**

UNIT 1: THE PROMISE OF NEW LIFE
ENVISIONING NEW LIFE

PREVIEWING THE LESSON

Lesson Scripture: Ezekiel 47:1-12
Background Scripture: Ezekiel 47:1-12
Key Verse: Ezekiel 47:9

Focus of the Lesson:
Humankind depends on the water that covers the vast areas of earth's landscape. What impact do these bodies of water have on humanity and all creation? In a vision, Ezekiel sees a sacred river that flows freely from God's throne, sustaining life.

Goals for the Learners:
(1) to explore the significance of the river of life that flows from the throne of God as seen by Ezekiel in a vision.
(2) to consider how this metaphorical water, flowing fresh from God, sustains their spiritual lives.
(3) to make a commitment to order their spiritual lives so as to remain close to the source of this life-giving water.

Pronunciation Guide:
Arabah (air' uh buh)   En-gedi (en ged' i)
En-eglaim (en eg' lay im)

Supplies:
Bibles, newsprint and marker, paper and pencils, hymnals, unlined paper, pitcher and basin

---

READING THE SCRIPTURE

NRSV
Ezekiel 47:1-12

¹Then he brought me back to the entrance of the temple; there, water was flowing from below the threshold of the temple toward the east (for the temple faced east); and the water was flowing down from below the south end

NIV
Ezekiel 47:1-12

¹The man brought me back to the entrance of the temple, and I saw water coming out from under the threshold of the temple toward the east (for the temple faced east). The water was coming down from

of the threshold of the temple, south of the altar. ²Then he brought me out by way of the north gate, and led me around on the outside to the outer gate that faces toward the east; and the water was coming out on the south side.

³Going on eastward with a cord in his hand, the man measured one thousand cubits, and then led me through the water; and it was ankle-deep. ⁴Again he measured one thousand, and led me through the water; and it was knee-deep. Again he measured one thousand, and led me through the water; and it was up to the waist. ⁵Again he measured one thousand, and it was a river that I could not cross, for the water had risen; it was deep enough to swim in, a river that could not be crossed. ⁶He said to me, "Mortal, have you seen this?"

Then he led me back along the bank of the river. ⁷As I came back, I saw on the bank of the river a great many trees on the one side and on the other. ⁸He said to me, "This water flows toward the eastern region and goes down into the Arabah; and when it enters the sea, the sea of stagnant waters, the water will become fresh. ⁹Wherever the river goes, every living creature that swarms will live, and there will be very many fish, once these waters reach there. It will become fresh; and **everything will live where the river goes.** ¹⁰People will stand fishing beside the sea from En-gedi to En-eglaim; it will be a place for the spreading of nets; its fish will be of a great many kinds, like the fish of the Great Sea. ¹¹But its swamps and marshes will not become fresh; they are to be left for salt. ¹²On the banks, on both sides of the river, there will grow all kinds of trees for food. Their leaves will not wither nor their fruit fail, but they will bear fresh fruit every month, because the water for them flows from the sanctuary. Their fruit will be for food, and their leaves for healing."

under the south side of the temple, south of the altar. ²He then brought me out through the north gate and led me around the outside to the outer gate facing east, and the water was flowing from the south side.

³As the man went eastward with a measuring line in his hand, he measured off a thousand cubits and then led me through water that was ankle-deep. ⁴He measured off another thousand cubits and led me through water that was knee-deep. He measured off another thousand and led me through water that was up to the waist. ⁵He measured off another thousand, but now it was a river that I could not cross, because the water had risen and was deep enough to swim in—a river that no one could cross. ⁶He asked me, "Son of man, do you see this?"

Then he led me back to the bank of the river. ⁷When I arrived there, I saw a great number of trees on each side of the river. ⁸He said to me, "This water flows toward the eastern region and goes down into the Arabah, where it enters the Sea. When it empties into the Sea, the water there becomes fresh. ⁹Swarms of living creatures will live wherever the river flows. There will be large numbers of fish, because this water flows there and makes the salt water fresh; **so where the river flows everything will live.** ¹⁰Fishermen will stand along the shore; from En Gedi to En Eglaim there will be places for spreading nets. The fish will be of many kinds—like the fish of the Great Sea. ¹¹But the swamps and marshes will not become fresh; they will be left for salt. ¹²Fruit trees of all kinds will grow on both banks of the river. Their leaves will not wither, nor will their fruit fail. Every month they will bear, because the water from the sanctuary flows to them. Their fruit will serve for food and their leaves for healing."

UNDERSTANDING THE SCRIPTURE

Ezekiel 47:1. Our text begins with the prophet's vision of a mysterious spring of water; it concludes with the wonderful impact of this water on the earth and on humanity. It is a broad and rich vision, but one that demands our careful attention. To understand this passage, a specific context is necessary. While in Babylon, every aspect of life was strange to the exiles: climate, local foods, language, architecture, government, and, of course, religions. Each provoked the pains of homesickness; however, separation from the Temple brought the deepest sorrow. The vision in our passage is built upon the exiles' emotional connection to the Temple in Jerusalem. More than a physical structure, the Temple held God's presence and, therefore, ensured God's availability to the people. Sadly, Jerusalem's Temple had been defiled. Since God and impurity could not coexist, the exiles believed that God's presence had departed from the Temple. The exiles thus bore two sorrows: separation from their beloved Temple and defilement of that sacred space resulting in God's departure. In 43:1-5, Ezekiel recorded a vision that addressed the exiles' twin sorrows. Artfully, Ezekiel described the mighty gathering of God's glory and its purposeful return to the Temple. This passage provides the context for our text. Once God reclaimed the Temple, the amazing future began. In our text, this future, symbolized by an unexplained trickle of water, began in the Temple—the place where God and humans met.

Ezekiel 47:2-6a. In a desert, water is precious. After a disaster, whether caused by war or natural calamity, finding clean water becomes a necessity. During illness, water cleanses and soothes. In everyday life, water supports the growth of plants for food. But in the Bible, water symbolizes God's gracious gift of life. In the first account of creation (Genesis 1), God ordered the chaos of waters and the conditions for life emerged: dry land, vegetation, fruit trees, and grains. In the second creation account (Genesis 2:4b-25), the earth and the heavens were steamy and moist. God used this damp earth to fashion a man (the Hebrew word, *adam*, means "from arable land") and placed him in a pleasant garden. A river flowing out of Eden (the Hebrew word means "delight") watered the garden, and then divided into four branches giving life to the world. As Ezekiel observed the trickle of water at the Temple, biblical associations bubbled up. However, Ezekiel refrained from drawing any conclusions. Rather, he followed his guide from the Temple, pausing four times to measure the trickle's growth from ankle deep to a river difficult to cross. Then, the prophet was questioned, "Mortal, have you seen this?" (47:6). With this question, Ezekiel's audience was invited to reflect on the theological consequences of the return of God's glory to the Temple. The trickle that began in the Temple grew to amazing proportions; surely, this growth encouraged the exiles to expect mighty changes from small shifts within their circumstances of exile.

Ezekiel 47:6b-11. In the vision, a guide led the prophet back to the Temple along the same riverside path. His guide explained the course of the river and pointed out the river's impact on the land and seas. The sight of a transformed environment amazed Ezekiel. There were numerous trees and vegetation on the riverbanks. Moreover, the fresh water purified the stagnant seas. Many kinds of fish filled the stream and fishermen worked their nets from the banks. Indeed, the Dead Sea was a living environment. Although the springs at En-gedi and En-eglaim (47:10) continually fed the Dead Sea with fresh water, the quantity (and quality) of their water was insufficient to correct the imbalance of salt in the whole sea. Yet, the water from this Temple river purified the sea and restored it with fish. The sight Ezekiel beheld, coupled with the words of his guide, revealed the full impact of God's restoration. Not only was the day coming when God would gather his people as a shepherd gathers a flock (Ezekiel 34), not only would God lead the people to a peaceful homeland (Ezekiel 37) but by God's might the desert would blossom and salty seas would be refreshed. The water flowing from the

Temple was not only mysteriously abundant but also purifying and life-giving as well. Yet, to demonstrate God's attention to detail in this restoration some swamps and marshes were left salty. This detail reminded the audience of the many uses of salt: for preserving, for seasoning, for healing, and for Temple rituals (Ezekiel 43:24). The salt swamps and marshes reminded the exiles that life in the restored land was for living! In God's future, the human community would labor, take delight in physical pleasures, experience diseases and healings, and conduct rituals intended to strengthen the human/divine relationship. The restored land of Israel was not a whisper of poetry; it was an opportunity to live again.

Ezekiel 47:12. The last verse of Ezekiel's vision departed from the practicality of the previous verse. In a vision of the end times, the natural order of seasons no longer applied. Remarkably, the trees kept their leaves and produced fresh fruit every month. Moreover, the leaves and fruit of these trees had healing properties. As the vision concluded, the prophet confidently declared that God had redeemed Israel, both the land and the people. This announcement was intended for all the scattered of Israel. It was not offered, as similar visionary assurances from Isaiah and Jeremiah were, to all nations and people. Ezekiel was pointedly parochial; the restoration he announced was limited to the chosen people, the land of Israel, and the Temple in Jerusalem. Much later, however, the beautiful images from Ezekiel were woven into another prophet's vision. In the final chapter of his book, John saw the river "of the water of life" (Revelation 22:1). Concurring with Ezekiel's vision, John saw the river "flowing from the throne of God." He also saw trees with leaves with healing power. However, in John's vision the healing leaves are for *all* the nations (22:2). What began in Ezekiel as a limited salvation became in Revelation an all-encompassing salvation. God's gifts of renewal, life, healing, and delight are abundantly provided throughout creation.

INTERPRETING THE SCRIPTURE

Water in a Dry Land

When the prophet Ezekiel spoke, his audience understood his message. Ezekiel's words rested on shared sorrow and common faith. The exiles were suffering; Ezekiel understood their grief. The exiles were confused about their beliefs; Ezekiel taught a theology fit for their past, their present, and their future. Ezekiel spoke from his heart to the heart of the exiles. This connection is not easy for a contemporary audience to understand. We know little of the experience of exile. Of course, we are familiar with the ostracism of prejudice or the estrangement of broken vows. We know that some people select a lifestyle that excludes them from family or community. We also know that some estrangements are painfully perpetuated by rumor and deceit. Still, the experience of corporate exile is uncommon, and we have difficulty entering into a mind-set of a displaced people.

There are ways, however, to experience the circumstances of homesickness. Even through the dance of translation, conversations with recent immigrants provide insight. Literature helps. Personal reflection and imagination are invaluable tools. At the heart of the experience of exile one discovers the essentials of life: familiarity, freedom, and focus. In exile, familiar objects from home become precious. Israel, for example, clung to the poetry and songs of the Temple. These familiar objects or memories inspire an inner freedom unknown by the physically or politically free. The exiles' freedom comes from living on the other side of loss. From this perspective, an intense focus develops. The people of Israel knew God was involved in their exile, and Ezekiel knew God was preparing their restoration. His poetic words of prophecy satisfied the exiles as a cool drink of water on a scorching hot day. Indeed, he offered the image of water to people exiled in a dry land.

From Trickle to River

Ezekiel's words intended more than refreshment; they intended amazement. Yet, Ezekiel knew if he quickly painted grand images, the people would ignore him. Thus, the prophet led the people, slowly, through his own spiritual experiences. He hoped that by revealing his own growing awareness of God's grace the exiles would also mature in their faith. The best illustration of Ezekiel's methodology is his careful description of the growth of a divine trickle from the Temple threshold. What began as bemused wonderment concluded in amazement. In between, the audience is led deeper and deeper into the mystery of God's grace. The exiles knew the stories of those life-giving waters flowing from the garden of Eden. They also sang about a river flowing from God's holy city and Temple (Psalm 46:4). Indeed, Ezekiel's water image was not "new" information about God's grace. He was, however, offering the abundance of grace.

As Ezekiel described his walk along the stream, the audience experienced the physical change from a small trickle to a mighty river. This, Ezekiel taught, was the true nature of God's grace. God's goodness may seem initially small—so small a trickle under the Temple's threshold might be ignored. However, because the source of this trickle is divine, the results were greater than expected. Ezekiel's image sparked hope among the exiles. His words address our experiences as well. While we are not a peo-

ple taught by exile to treasure the familiar, nurture inner freedom, or theologically focus our lives, we still long for God's amazing grace. With the exiles, we look for the small signs of God's grace. With Ezekiel, we travel slowly along the path of grace to measure its impact. With all creation, we stand in amazement at what God has completed, is doing, and intends to create. As a visionary trickle became a mighty river, so our ordinary lives are blessed by God's amazing grace.

A Renewed Environment

The change that Ezekiel observed in the river was more than quantitative. As Ezekiel was led back to the Temple, he noted the qualitative change wrought by the river. First, there were trees. In the vision, these trees mysteriously appeared as the river streamed along. Evidently, Ezekiel walked out on a bare riverbank and returned among mature trees. The change happened in vision time—a time similar to dream time. Have you ever had a dream that mixed times and ages? For example, a dream begins with your current family constellation then suddenly twists to include long-dead grandparents and you as a little child? Time is fluid in both dreams and visions. In Ezekiel's vision time collapsed: The river's new course and the maturity of the trees happened in the space of an afternoon walk.

The second qualitative change was the purifying of the Dead Sea by the Temple river. Where previously salty waters failed to nourish fish, now fishermen caught fish of astonishing variety.

The final qualitative result came as a surprise: God allowed the swamps and marshes to remain salty. In this small detail was the connection to everyday life and time. In ordinary life, salt was necessary for preservation, seasoning, bartering, and health. Salt was also necessary in Temple rituals. Ezekiel's vision included a reminder that although God's restoration was mighty, in the restored land people would continue to labor and rest, eat and drink, become ill and be healed, remember their sins and gather for worship. The abundance of God's grace was the invitation to full life.

A Healed People and Land

Ezekiel's vision perfectly matched the sorrow of the exiles. To the dryness of their lives, he offered the image of a freshwater stream. To the pointlessness of their exile, he offered a glimpse of the tiny, almost insignificant, beginning of change. To their restless homesick hearts, he offered the Temple filled with the glory of the Lord. To their experience of "being stuck," he offered a vision of God's future. To their inability to appreciate life, he offered a second chance to return to the familiar routines of labor, family, community, and faith. His vision matched the despair and lifted the hopes of the exiles.

Contemporary students of the Bible, however, may find Ezekiel's vision too parochial. After all, this vision speaks to Israel alone. There is no suggestion that God intended anything more than the salvation of the chosen people. There is no expansion of grace to touch and restore the enemies of Israel. Even the river that flows from the sanctuary does not meander beyond the land of Israel. When compared with the deep and wide visions of Isaiah and Jeremiah, Ezekiel's vision seems small and nationalistic.

Indeed, Ezekiel was a focused and resolute prophet. Called to his ministry by an empowering vision, Ezekiel spent half of his prophetic career prophesying against Jerusalem and Judah (Chapters 1–24). After the exile, Ezekiel spoke out against the enemies of God's chosen people (Chapters 25–32). Finally, when the time was ripe, Ezekiel preached the hope of restoration to the exiles (Chapters 33–48). Ezekiel's visions are parochial; however, his inspiration was developed by subsequent theologians, prophets and preachers. In Revelation 22:1-2, Ezekiel's image of healing leaves applies to all nations. In John 4:13-15, the refreshing of God's water becomes a spiritual gift available to all people. And in John 7:38, Jesus describes holy streams of water flowing not out of the physical Temple in Jerusalem but from the hearts of believers. Thus contemporary Christians continue to be blessed by Ezekiel's image of God's refreshing, purifying, and delightful river of life.

SHARING THE SCRIPTURE

Preparing Our Hearts

Meditate on this week's devotional reading, found in John 4:7-15. In this familiar passage we hear Jesus ask a woman of Samaria to give him water from Jacob's well. As the conversation unfolds, Jesus uses the metaphor of living water to describe himself. We will encounter the same idea of life-giving water in today's passage from Ezekiel. Think about how you use, conserve, and waste water. How would you handle this resource differently if you always thought of it in terms of being life-giving?

Pray that you and the adult learners will give thanks to God for water and use this gift wisely.

Preparing Our Minds

Study the background and lesson Scripture, both found in Ezekiel 47:1-12. As you consider this passage, think about water and the impact that it has on humanity and all creation.

Write on newsprint:
❑ information for next week's lesson, found under "Continue the Journey."

❏ activities for further spiritual growth in "Continue the Journey."

Locate a pitcher and basin or other receptacle. If possible, choose a clear glass pitcher for greater visual effect.

Prepare a lecture for "Imagine the River of Life That Flows From the Throne of God as Seen by Ezekiel in a Vision." Use any information from Understanding the Scripture or Interpreting the Scripture that you think will help the students better understand Ezekiel's vision.

Be prepared to discuss spiritual disciplines. You are likely familiar with these already, but if not, consult one of the numerous books on this topic, such as Richard Foster's *Celebration of Discipline*, or discuss this with your pastor.

LEADING THE CLASS

(1) Gather to Learn

❖ Welcome the class members and introduce any guests.

❖ Pray that today's participants will experience transformation through the word of God.

❖ Go around the room and ask each person in turn to name one thing that comes to mind when they hear the word "water." List ideas on newsprint. (If the class is large, invite volunteers to call out ideas.)

❖ Review the list. Put a plus (+) next to positive aspects of water, and put a minus (-) next to destructive aspects of water.

❖ Discuss for a few moments the impact that water has on humanity and on all creation.

❖ Read aloud today's focus statement: **Humankind depends on the water that covers the vast areas of earth's landscape. What impact do these bodies of water have on humanity and all creation? In a vision, Ezekiel sees a sacred river that flows freely from God's throne, sustaining life.**

(2) Imagine the River of Life That Flows From the Throne of God as Seen by Ezekiel in a Vision

❖ Distribute paper (preferably unlined) and pencils. Tell the students that as you slowly read Ezekiel 47:1-12 aloud, they are to sketch whatever they hear. They may choose to create several different scenes. Emphasize that their artistic ability is not important, and their work will not be shared. Your purpose is to help them imagine Ezekiel's vision.

❖ Talk with the adults about what they have imagined. Ask:

(1) What does this vision reveal to you about God?

(2) How does this vision make you feel? (You may mention that the vision shows how God can turn the barren wastelands of one's life into fertile land. Recognition of this transformation may elicit some emotions.)

❖ Present the lecture you have prepared to help the students understand what Ezekiel envisioned and its meaning. Be sure to note the following qualitative changes discussed under "A Renewed Environment."

■ Trees appeared along the formerly barren riverbank.

■ The waters of the Dead Sea were purified.

■ God allowed swamps and marshes to remain salty because salt was necessary for life.

❖ Close this portion of the session by asking the adults to suggest how this vision might have affected them had they been exiles. End their discussion by reading the first paragraph of "A Healed People and Land."

(3) Consider How This Metaphorical Water, Flowing Fresh From God, Sustains the Learners' Spiritual Lives

❖ Pour water from a pitcher into a basin or other receptacle. Raise the pitcher high so that all of the students can see and hear the water as it falls.

❖ Invite the students to talk with a partner or small group about these questions, which you will read aloud, allowing time for the learners to answer:

(1) **In what ways do you think of water as symbolically refreshing your spiritual life?**

(2) **Which spiritual disciplines do you practice?**

(3) **Which of the disciplines that you practice seem to most revitalize your spiritual life?**

❖ Discuss with the class the kinds of spiritual practices that they have identified as most helpful. These practices may include but are not limited to: *worship, prayer, meditation, Bible study, journaling, walking a labyrinth, simple living, tithing, fasting,* and *service.*

(4) Make a Commitment to Order One's Spiritual Life so as to Remain Close to the Source of This Life-giving Water

❖ Distribute lined paper and pencils (if you have not already done so). Invite the students to select at least one spiritual discipline that they do not currently practice that may enliven and refresh their own faith journey. Ask them to write a commitment to God stating what they will do in the coming week to incorporate this discipline into their spiritual lives. Note that this may be a beginning step, such as locate a labyrinth, buy a notebook to use as a spiritual journal and write one entry, or talk with someone who could become a spiritual mentor.

❖ Suggest that the adults talk with the same partner or group as in the previous section to state what they plan to do during the coming week.

❖ **Option:** Recommend that partners or team members exchange phone numbers or e-mail addresses to contact one another by Thursday to see what action has been taken toward fulfilling their commitment.

(5) Continue the Journey

❖ Pray that today's participants will go forth will a new appreciation for the resources God gives to sustain and enhance their lives.

❖ Read aloud this preparation for next week's lesson. You may also want to post it on newsprint for the students to copy.

■ **Title: Suffering Unto Death**

■ **Background Scripture: Luke 23:32-46**

■ **Lesson Scripture: Luke 23:32-46**

■ **Focus of the Lesson: The death event can feature a mix of emotions from suffering to joy. How, then, can we face death? Luke's account of the last week in the life of Jesus reveals that his trust in God led Jesus through triumph and sustained him in suffering.**

❖ Challenge the students to complete one or more of these activities for further spiritual growth, which you will write on newsprint for the students to copy:

(1) **Take a walk, preferably in a park or along a nature trail. What vegetation do you see? How would you rate its health? What sources of water do you find? What affect does the water have on the vegetation? Marvel at God's creation.**

(2) **Write a prayer or psalm of thanksgiving for God's gift of abundant life. Pray or recite what you have written each day this week.**

(3) **Plant a flower in a garden or pot. As it grows and flourishes, let this plant be a metaphor for you of the fruitfulness God wills for your life.**

❖ Sing or read aloud "Shall We Gather at the River."

❖ Conclude today's session by leading the class in this benediction: **Give us new hearts filled with your Spirit, O Lord, that we may live as new creations in Christ. Amen.**

UNIT 2: THE PATH TO NEW LIFE
SUFFERING UNTO DEATH

PREVIEWING THE LESSON

Lesson Scripture: Luke 23:32-46
Background Scripture: Luke 23:32-46
Key Verse: Luke 23:46

Focus of the Lesson:
The death event can feature a mix of emotions from suffering to joy. How, then, can we face death? Luke's account of the last week in the life of Jesus reveals that his trust in God led Jesus through triumph and sustained him in suffering.

Goals for the Learners:
(1) to explore the people and events associated with Jesus' crucifixion as recorded in the Gospel of Luke.
(2) to consider suffering and death in their own lives.
(3) to affirm that God is with them at all times, even in their suffering and death.

Supplies:
Bibles, newsprint and marker, paper and pencils, hymnals

READING THE SCRIPTURE

NRSV
Luke 23:32-46

³²Two others also, who were criminals, were led away to be put to death with him. ³³When they came to the place that is called The Skull, they crucified Jesus there with the criminals, one on his right and one on his left. [[³⁴Then Jesus said, "Father, forgive them; for they do not know what they are doing."]] And they cast lots to divide his clothing. ³⁵And the people stood by, watching; but the leaders scoffed at him, saying, "He saved others; let him save himself if he is the Messiah of God, his chosen one!" ³⁶The

NIV
Luke 23:32-46

³²Two other men, both criminals, were also led out with him to be executed. ³³When they came to the place called the Skull, there they crucified him, along with the criminals—one on his right, the other on his left. ³⁴Jesus said, "Father, forgive them, for they do not know what they are doing." And they divided up his clothes by casting lots.

³⁵The people stood watching, and the rulers even sneered at him. They said, "He saved others; let him save himself if he is the Christ of God, the Chosen One."

soldiers also mocked him, coming up and offering him sour wine, ³⁷and saying, "If you are the King of the Jews, save yourself!" ³⁸There was also an inscription over him, "This is the King of the Jews."

³⁹One of the criminals who were hanged there kept deriding him and saying, "Are you not the Messiah? Save yourself and us!" ⁴⁰But the other rebuked him, saying, "Do you not fear God, since you are under the same sentence of condemnation? ⁴¹And we indeed have been condemned justly, for we are getting what we deserve for our deeds, but this man has done nothing wrong." ⁴²Then he said, "Jesus, remember me when you come into your kingdom." ⁴³He replied, "Truly I tell you, today you will be with me in Paradise."

⁴⁴It was now about noon, and darkness came over the whole land until three in the afternoon, ⁴⁵while the sun's light failed; and the curtain of the temple was torn in two. ⁴⁶Then Jesus, crying with a loud voice, said, **"Father, into your hands I commend my spirit." Having said this, he breathed his last.**

³⁶The soldiers also came up and mocked him. They offered him wine vinegar ³⁷and said, "If you are the king of the Jews, save yourself."

³⁸There was a written notice above him, which read: THIS IS THE KING OF THE JEWS.

³⁹One of the criminals who hung there hurled insults at him: "Aren't you the Christ? Save yourself and us!"

⁴⁰But the other criminal rebuked him. "Don't you fear God," he said, "since you are under the same sentence? ⁴¹We are punished justly, for we are getting what our deeds deserve. But this man has done nothing wrong."

⁴²Then he said, "Jesus, remember me when you come into your kingdom."

⁴³Jesus answered him, "I tell you the truth, today you will be with me in paradise."

⁴⁴It was now about the sixth hour, and darkness came over the whole land until the ninth hour, ⁴⁵for the sun stopped shining. And the curtain of the temple was torn in two. ⁴⁶Jesus called out with a loud voice, **"Father, into your hands I commit my spirit." When he had said this, he breathed his last.**

UNDERSTANDING THE SCRIPTURE

Luke 23:32. Each Gospel author used the narrative of Jesus' crucifixion to summarize a specific theological perspective. The uniqueness of each account is more a matter of emphasis and small detail than of radical differences. Most of the events of Jesus' death are shared by all four Gospels: Roman soldiers crucified Jesus along with two others; the charge against Jesus is recorded as a title, "King of the Jews"; a mixed crowd witnessed his death; Jesus spoke from the cross. Mark set the pattern for the Synoptic Gospels; Luke and Matthew pressed their own material and emphases upon his narra-

tive. John, in uncharacteristic style, also built his narrative upon Mark's brief account. For Luke, the most polished storyteller, the passion presented the last opportunity to show Jesus engaged in ministry. Thus, the story included more details on the people who were involved in Jesus' dying hours. As in life, Jesus was with the needy, so in death he shared his final breath with criminals excluded from proper society. Luke used these two men to connect the community of Jesus' ministry with the community of his death. Their names are unknown; they were simply two men.

Likewise, their guilt, but not charges against them, was stated. Yet Luke used this small community of need and this much-wounded Savior to demonstrate God's grace in the midst of utter horror. From the perspective of the three lifted up on crosses Luke's story of the death of Jesus expanded to include the widest range of human conditions: the sorrowful, the respectful, the frightened, the belligerent, the needy, the humble, the callous, and the hopeful.

Luke 23:33-38. In the Gospels, surprisingly few physical details of the crucifixion were recorded. Scripture does not disclose the height, shape, or manner of affixing humans to the cross. Based on research, literature, and visual dramatizations we have a stark, visual image. Evidently, the authors of the Gospels did not believe the actual crucifixion to be the heart of the story. Instead, each Gospel set the crucifixion within a context. Mark used the mocking, jeering crowd and the dramatic natural and supernatural events to provide context. Matthew followed the same pattern, expanding with details necessary for his emphasis as an educator. John's Gospel placed the passion within two lines of authority: that of Pilate and that of Jesus, with Jesus' authority undiminished throughout his dying. Luke, however, slowly drew his audience into the actual events of Jesus' death. The first act of Jesus from the cross was prayer. After the context of criminals and soldiers was established, Jesus begged his Abba (better translated intimately as "Poppa" or "Daddy," rather than the formal "Father") to forgive the unknowing actions of those around him. Was he praying for the soldiers, the criminals, the Jewish leaders, the mocking crowd, or the fearful disciples? The text does not specify. Surely, each segment of the population participating in, observing, or avoiding the crucifixion stood in need of God's forgiveness. However, the prayer had no impact on those around the cross: The soldiers mocked and gambled, the religious leaders scoffed and, ironically, the soldiers ultimately blasphemed as they taunted Jesus to act like the King of the Jews.

Luke 23:39-43. At this point in the narrative, Luke folded in a story not incorporated in the other Gospel accounts. Continuing Luke's emphasis on forgiveness, the scene tightened to the space between the three crosses. There one criminal had picked up the tenor of the soldiers and the leaders; he mocked Jesus even as he asked for help. The second criminal redressed him explaining that they were judged "justly" but that Jesus was righteous, for he had "done nothing wrong" (23:41). Luke's audience would not have missed the verbal hints highlighting the difference between the two men and Jesus: Two were sinners and one was without sin. Then, the criminal addressed Jesus by name and asked Jesus to remember him in his kingdom. Possibly the criminal knew the Psalter by heart. In Psalm 25:7, there is a similar appeal:

> Do not remember the sins of my youth
>   or my transgressions;
> according to your steadfast love
>   remember me,
> for your goodness' sake, O LORD!

The plea to be remembered was also on the lips of Hannah (1 Samuel 1:11), Job (Job 14:13), and Jeremiah (Jeremiah 15:15); in each case the profound desperation of the petitioner was balanced by humility before God. Jesus responded directly to the man by vowing that on that very day the criminal would join Jesus in paradise (literally, the garden; allegorically, the garden of Eden; symbolically, a new beginning). Based merely on the request, without any sign of contrition or repentance, Jesus offered the criminal hope for a new beginning. This offer disclosed God's forgiveness to those who turned to Jesus—even a justly condemned criminal. In this brief encounter, Luke emphatically proclaimed the theology of forgiveness as a gracious gift.

Luke 23:44-46. To demonstrate the significance of Jesus' death, Luke expanded the perspective from the intimacy of the three dying men to the cosmic extravagance of God. The skies grew dark; the sun's light failed; the Temple curtain was torn in two (the passive tense implied God's action). The cosmic dimension of Jesus' death manifested God's presence in the midst of this human tragedy. Luke, emphasizing Jesus' confidence in God, turned the loud cry of Mark's Gospel (15:34) into an articulate prayer as Jesus offered himself to God's care. The word translated "spirit" was linguistically related to the verb "breathed" in the concluding phrase. Luke's audience understood Jesus' last prayer to be a petition to God to receive his life. From a Hebrew perspective, "my spirit" stood for "me" (see Psalm 31:5). Likewise, the last phrase, "he breathed his last," testified to his death. Luke wove themes from Jesus' ministry—forgiveness, confident trust in God, and the ever-available pathway to God—into the story of Jesus' death. Following the burial of Jesus (Luke 23:50-56), the narrative paused; after a two-day silence, it continued with Jesus' resurrection appearances, ascension, and inspiration of the disciples.

INTERPRETING THE SCRIPTURE

Beginning at the Ending

In Matthew, Mark, and John, the crucifixion and the resurrection appearances of Jesus conclude the Gospel. In Luke, however, the crucifixion and resurrection initiate a new beginning. Since this Gospel is linked by authorship to the Acts of the Apostles, the final scenes from Luke's Gospel introduce the themes to be developed in Acts. In order to understand this transition, Luke's Passion Narrative may be approached structurally. Relevant questions include, What communities are present? How do these communities relate to Jesus? How does Jesus minister throughout his death? What keeps the story moving forward? Rather than delving into the layers of meaning and mystery, in this lesson we sift and measure the components of the story. By so doing, the transition from the ministry of Jesus to the ministry of his disciples becomes clearer. This slower, structured approach yields surprisingly fresh material.

The first verse of the assigned reading, Luke 23:32, is concise but significant. According to Luke, three men were led away, presumably from Jerusalem by Roman soldiers, to be put to death. Of the three men, two were criminals and one was Jesus. This little community of prisoners faced the same captors and punishment. The three, however, experienced their deaths differently. Luke's account invited his audience to attend to the simple facts: soldiers in charge of prisoners to be executed by crucifixion. The first verse conveyed neither surprise nor mystery.

The second verse, Luke 23:33, was likewise terse. The place of the crucifixion carried a name contemporary readers fill with gruesome imagery; however, to the original audience, "The Skull" was a geographic rather than a symbolic reference. The site was named but no other details were given to the audience. Luke set before the reader nameless soldiers, three crosses, and Jesus dying between two strangers.

The Direction of Prayer

In this stark setting, Jesus prayed. Again, Luke's audience received few details. Indeed, from the text, it is difficult to identify the "them" of Jesus' prayer. Perhaps Luke intended his readers to ponder the question of who the unknowing ones in need of forgiveness were. The answer to this question was settled centuries ago; most interpreted that Jesus prayed for the soldiers who nailed him to the cross to die. Luke, however, allowed the prayer to float over the crucifixion scene as the story continued.

At this point the perspective moves from the community of three on their crosses to those who surrounded the crosses. Notice the various responses Luke described. The soldiers gambled and grumbled as men comfortable with their assigned task as executioners. An unnamed crowd watched; their emotional response was not noted. Luke's audience surely wondered about the impact of the events witnessed. The leaders, presumably the religious leaders, mocked Jesus as a failed, dying, false messiah. Gradually, the soldiers took up the mocking; their Gentile diction strangely out of cadence with the Jewish leaders. Thus the action below the dying men was ordinary and passive, as well as mean and mocking. There was no singular emotion or response; the community beneath the crosses was a community of confusion.

At this point the author carefully guided the reader's attention up to the crosses; the title on Jesus' cross, "This is the King of the Jews," proclaims the irony of the crucifixion. The dying Jesus was a source of confusion to all who looked up at his cross. Affixed to his cross was the truth of his identity. His prayerful petition to forgive them had the potential to give new meaning to the title hanging above his head. Yet, at this point in the story, newness was only a small hint.

Christ's Gracious Response

Thus the story was told with sparse details and a shifting point of view from the crucified men to the community below and back to the crucified man in the middle. Luke refrained from explanations; rather, by deed, prayer, confusion, and ironic hint, the story invited the audience to carefully observe Jesus' death.

With the attention redirected to the men dying on the crosses, Luke presented a final ministry vignette. As Jesus and the two criminals were dying, one criminal found solace in joining the chorus of mockers. His attack was brutal, but it provoked something beautiful. Whereas no one below had the courage to counter the mocking, the other dying man did. He saw Jesus not as a failed messiah but as a righteous man unjustly condemned to death. Did the proximity of his own death heighten his insight? Was he a pious and spiritually wise man? Luke did not explain; rather, as shepherds, Galileans, old men, and a young woman recognized divinity in the baby Jesus at the beginning of the Gospel, so a criminal condemned to death saw Jesus clearly as he died.

After rebuking the other criminal, the dying man spoke directly to Jesus. He called him by name, not by title or claim. He guessed Jesus' divine destination to be paradise. He asked only to be remembered. With grace sufficient to forgive the convicted sinner and the unknowing murderers, Jesus responded. He did not offer a pie-in-the-sky possibility dependent on a yet-to-be-reckoned judgment. Rather, according to Luke, Jesus did what he had done many times throughout his ministry (see Luke 4:21 and Luke 19:9). He offered God's salvation as a present reality to a man who never expected such a blessing.

Now pause to take inventory: Are you confused? Do you believe a convicted criminal was saved in a moment? Do the mockers make you mad? Could you pray for them as Jesus prayed for the unknowing ones? These questions provoked by Luke's account have only one answer: God's grace is sufficient. Regardless of complicity in sin or insight into spiritual matters, God's grace offered (and continues to offer) a new beginning. Everyone—the watching crowd, the mocking leaders, the rough soldiers, the dying criminals, and Luke's ancient and ever expanding audience—was invited into this grace. Yet, at this point in Luke's passion, only one man believed Jesus was God's Messiah.

To Be Continued

From this inviting and intimate exchange, Luke moved the story forward with dramatic forcefulness. Suddenly, the insight of a criminal was replaced by cosmic signs and symbolic shifts. The images Luke employed suggested the "Day of the Lord" when God would right all wrongs, redress all unrighteousness, and save all the chosen ones. The imagery was terrifying and, undoubtedly, Luke's original audience

trembled. Then, Jesus prayed again. This prayer was loud—competing, perhaps, with the rumble of thunder. This prayer was confident—articulated for the crowd's benefit. This prayer was Jesus' last act of obedience—by it he returned his spirit (meaning himself) to God's care.

Then Jesus died. He died in the same manner the criminals on his left and right died. He breathed his last breath in the same way every dying person stops breathing. His death was as fully human as the life he lived. Yet, in that loud, bold prayer something else was present. It was something woven into the sparse details, confusion, and hints of Luke's Passion Narrative. Jesus' last prayer opened the possibility of the continuation of the story. In God's hands the impossible became possible for soldiers, bystanders, religious leaders, criminals, and even God's Messiah.

SHARING THE SCRIPTURE

Preparing Our Hearts

Meditate on this week's devotional reading, found in 1 Corinthians 15:1-11. In verse 3 Paul proclaims "that Christ died for our sins." He goes on in verse 4 to say that Christ was buried and "raised on the third day," all in accordance with the Scriptures. His resurrection was attested to by people who had seen the risen Lord, including Paul himself. As you look ahead to Holy Week, what do you think and feel when you hear that Christ died on your behalf? What response are you willing to make to this amazing news?

Pray that you and the adult learners will focus on Jesus' passion in the week ahead.

Preparing Our Minds

Study the background and lesson Scripture, both found in Luke 23:32-46.

Think seriously about how you can face death.

Write on newsprint:
❏ information for next week's lesson, found under "Continue the Journey."
❏ activities for further spiritual growth in "Continue the Journey."

LEADING THE CLASS

(1) Gather to Learn

❖ Welcome the class members and introduce any guests.

❖ Pray that all who have come today will be willing not only to sing Hosanna on this Palm Sunday but also confront the fact of Jesus' suffering and death.

❖ Prompt the students to begin thinking about suffering and death by reading aloud this excerpt from a sermon preached on

Easter, 2006, at the Rollins Chapel of Dartmouth College by Chaplain Richard R. Crocker:

Isn't it remarkable that Christian faith is strongest . . . among people who have suffered? Isn't it remarkable that what is perhaps the strongest Christian community . . . is found among people who experienced slavery here? . . . We can probably agree that suffering is a universal part of the human condition. . . . I am not saying that suffering in itself produces faith. . . . Many people who suffer come to a different faith, or they conclude that no faith is possible for them. But . . . , of the people who believe in the resurrection of Christ . . . , the beginning of faith very often is suffering.

❖ Ask: **What enables people to face suffering and death? Do you agree that "of the people who believe in the resurrection of Christ . . . the beginning of faith very often is suffering"? Explain your answer.**

❖ Read aloud today's focus statement: **The death event can feature a mix of emotions from suffering to joy. How, then, can we face death? Luke's account of the last week in the life of Jesus reveals that his trust in God led Jesus through triumph and sustained him in suffering.**

(2) Explore the People and Events Associated With Jesus' Crucifixion as Recorded in the Gospel of Luke

❖ Select individuals to read the parts of Jesus, a narrator, and two criminals, and choose groups of at least two readers to act as the leaders and the soldiers. Ask the actors to read Luke 23:32-46 as expressively as possible.

❖ Divide the class into three groups: criminals, religious leaders, and soldiers. Invite each group to talk about what they believed about Jesus, why they acted as they did toward him, and how they felt about his crucifixion. Then encourage the groups to report back to the class. Talk

about how the differences in perceptions about Jesus prompted people to act differently than, or similar to, one another.

❖ Encourage the adults to look at the words of Jesus found in verses 34, 43, and 46. Ask these questions. You may wish to add information from Understanding the Scripture and Interpreting the Scripture, particularly "The Direction of Prayer."

    (1) What do these words reveal about Jesus, even as he is suffering and near death?

    (2) How might these words help you as you think about your own death?

❖ Direct the students' attention again to Luke 23:44-45. Use "To Be Continued" from Interpreting the Scripture to help the class examine the cosmic effects of Jesus' death.

(3) Consider Suffering and Death in the Learners' Lives

❖ Note that we have explored how Jesus handled his own suffering and death. Point out that while we believe he was truly God with us, he was also truly human. Thus, he experienced suffering and the emotional turmoil of impending death just as any human being would.

❖ Distribute paper and pencils. Encourage the adults to write answers to these questions as you read them aloud. Be sure to pause long enough for them to provide thoughtful answers. Tell them to be honest; they will not be asked to share these very personal answers with anyone else.

    (1) How spiritually and emotionally prepared are you for death?

    (2) Have you made a last will and testament and other documents that will help your family know what your wishes are in the event of catastrophic illness and then when you are deceased? If your answer is no, what keeps you from doing this work?

    (3) Most of us have experienced the

loss of dear ones. Who for you has been a model of how to handle serious illness and impending death with grace and dignity? What is it about this person's journey that you could emulate?

(4) Affirm That God Is With the Learners at All Times, Even in Their Suffering and Death

❖ Distribute hymnals. Suggest that the adults page through them to find hymns that relate to the themes of suffering, death, and God's continuing presence. You may recommend "Abide with Me," "Be Thou My Vision," "I Want Jesus to Walk With Me," or "Stand by Me."

❖ List on newsprint what the adults perceive to be the stance of the hymn writers in the face of suffering and death. Once the list has been completed, invite the students to agree or disagree with the hymn writers. Encourage the adults to state their own perspectives on suffering and death. How do they envision God as being present with them?

❖ **Option:** Sing a few of the selections, if time permits.

(5) Continue the Journey

❖ Pray that even as the participants consider Jesus' suffering and death they will also prepare for their own death, knowing that God is always present.

❖ Read aloud this preparation for next week's lesson. You may also want to post it on newsprint for the students to copy.
- ■ **Title: Resurrected Unto New Life**
- ■ **Background Scripture: Luke 24:1-12**

- ■ **Lesson Scripture: Luke 24:1-12**
- ■ **Focus of the Lesson: Death seems final, totally defeating, irreversible. Are these widely held assumptions really true? No; Luke's record of Easter morning assures us that new, resurrected life is possible because Jesus rose from the dead.**

❖ Challenge the students to complete one or more of these activities for further spiritual growth, which you will write on newsprint for the students to copy:

(1) **Plan to attend Holy Week services at your church or in your community. Let the events of Maundy Thursday and Good Friday help you grapple not only with the death of Jesus but also with the death of loved ones and the prospect of your own death.**

(2) **Read the accounts of Jesus' crucifixion as they appear in all four Gospels. Which Gospel story is most compelling for you? Why?**

(3) **Visit someone who is said to be terminally ill. Listen to this person's concerns and, where appropriate, share the hope and faith that you have in Christ through his resurrection.**

❖ Sing or read aloud "Go to Dark Gethsemane."

❖ Conclude today's session by leading the class in this benediction: **Give us new hearts filled with your Spirit, O Lord, that we may live as new creations in Christ. Amen.**

UNIT 2: THE PATH TO NEW LIFE

RESURRECTED UNTO NEW LIFE

PREVIEWING THE LESSON

Lesson Scripture: Luke 24:1-12
Background Scripture: Luke 24:1-12
Key Verse: Luke 24:5

Focus of the Lesson:
Death seems final, totally defeating, irreversible. Are these widely held assumptions really true? No; Luke's record of Easter morning assures us that new, resurrected life is possible because Jesus rose from the dead.

Goals for the Learners:
(1) to encounter the story of Easter morning, as told in the Gospel of Luke.
(2) to explore the meaning of Jesus' resurrection for their lives.
(3) to make a commitment to live as if they really believe that new life is possible through the resurrected Christ.

Pronunciation Guide:
Arimathea (air uh muh thee' uh)
zeteo (dzay teh' o)

Supplies:
Bibles, newsprint and marker, paper and pencils, hymnals

READING THE SCRIPTURE

NRSV
Luke 24:1-12

¹But on the first day of the week, at early dawn, they came to the tomb, taking the spices that they had prepared. ²They found the stone rolled away from the tomb, ³but when they went in, they did not find the

NIV
Luke 24:1-12

¹On the first day of the week, very early in the morning, the women took the spices they had prepared and went to the tomb. ²They found the stone rolled away from the tomb, ³but when they entered, they did not

body. ⁴While they were perplexed about this, suddenly two men in dazzling clothes stood beside them. ⁵The women were terrified and bowed their faces to the ground, but the men said to them, **"Why do you look for the living among the dead? He is not here, but has risen.** ⁶Remember how he told you, while he was still in Galilee, ⁷that the Son of Man must be handed over to sinners, and be crucified, and on the third day rise again." ⁸Then they remembered his words, ⁹and returning from the tomb, they told all this to the eleven and to all the rest. ¹⁰Now it was Mary Magdalene, Joanna, Mary the mother of James, and the other women with them who told this to the apostles. ¹¹But these words seemed to them an idle tale, and they did not believe them. ¹²But Peter got up and ran to the tomb; stooping and looking in, he saw the linen cloths by themselves; then he went home, amazed at what had happened.

find the body of the Lord Jesus. ⁴While they were wondering about this, suddenly two men in clothes that gleamed like lightning stood beside them. ⁵In their fright the women bowed down with their faces to the ground, but the men said to them, **"Why do you look for the living among the dead? ⁶He is not here; he has risen!** Remember how he told you, while he was still with you in Galilee: ⁷"The Son of Man must be delivered into the hands of sinful men, be crucified and on the third day be raised again.' " ⁸Then they remembered his words.

⁹When they came back from the tomb, they told all these things to the Eleven and to all the others. ¹⁰It was Mary Magdalene, Joanna, Mary the mother of James, and the others with them who told this to the apostles. ¹¹But they did not believe the women, because their words seemed to them like nonsense. ¹²Peter, however, got up and ran to the tomb. Bending over, he saw the strips of linen lying by themselves, and he went away, wondering to himself what had happened.

UNDERSTANDING THE SCRIPTURE

Luke 24:1-3. In the Gospel of Luke, only the women disciples witnessed Jesus' crucifixion, burial, and resurrection. The women are listed, along with "all his acquaintances," in Luke 23:49 as witnesses to Jesus' crucifixion and death. Following Jesus' death, Joseph of Arimathea, a pious and powerful member of the Jewish council, appealed to Pilate for Jesus' body and arranged for the burial. Luke specified in 23:55 that only the women observed the burial. Because the Sabbath was near, there was insufficient time to anoint the body or to tuck the spices into the linen cloths. Thus, upon returning to the disciples, the women prepared spices and ointments used in burial.

Then, without transition other than Sabbath rest, the scene moved forward in Luke 24:1 to the early morning experience of the women. Luke's theological perspective emphasized the power of the resurrection on individual lives. Thus, Luke focused this scene on the women's experience. There was neither sealed tomb (as in Mark) nor earthquake (as in Matthew). Rather, using the passive voice indicating divine action, the women found the stone rolled away. Upon closer inspection, they discovered that the body of Jesus was missing. Luke's description, up to this point, is completely devoid of emotion or subjectivity. The women intended to perform a proper burial for Jesus, but the empty tomb ended their pious intentions.

Luke 24:4-7. Finally, Luke acknowledged the women's mental and emotional state: They were perplexed. Their experience did not lead immediately to faith but required further revelation and education. The perplexed women next encountered two men. Luke does not use the word "angels"; rather, by the suddenness of their appearance and the dazzling radiance of their clothing, the audience assumed these two to be divine messengers.

Appropriately, the women fearfully bowed down in the presence of the divine. These messengers omitted the formula "do not be afraid" (see Luke 1:13; 1:30; and 2:10) in order to question, reeducate, and remind the women of what they already know. The angels' question was posed with a specific word, *zeteo*, carrying a range of meanings from the casual "to look for" to the theologically charged "to seek," indicating a passionately motivated activity. Luke introduced *zeteo* into his Passion Narrative as the Jewish leaders sought a way to put Jesus to death (Luke 19:47). Luke's audience understood the irony in the messenger's question. Subtly the women were questioned on the success of the plot to kill Jesus.

Next the "two men" succinctly announced their message, "He is not here, but has risen" (24:5). The passive tense, again indicating divine action, is best rendered "has been raised." Finally, the angels asked the women to consider Jesus' teachings about his death throughout his Galilean ministry (see Luke 9:22; 9:44; and 18:32-33). This empty tomb should be no surprise for women educated by Jesus' own voice.

Luke 24:8-10. Everything turns on one brief statement in verse 8: "Then they remembered his words." As a teacher and a theologian, Luke was optimistic. Not only did he trust his narrative to demonstrate the truth of the women's experience from perplexity to faith to action but he also expected his audience to remember and respond with similarly faithful conclusions and deeds. Thus, Luke was not compelled

to include an angelic command. The women remembered Jesus' teaching and without further instruction returned to tell the disciples.

This simple remembrance and return was Luke's demonstration of the power of Jesus' death. By his death, his teachings were confirmed. Nothing more was needed; the women now believed. To further substantiate the witness of the women who went to the tomb that first Easter morning, Luke provided names. These names, immediately recognized by Luke's first-century audience, present a puzzle to contemporary readers. The first woman's name was Mary Magdalene; she was also included in the other three accounts of the empty tomb (see Matthew 28:1; Mark 16:1; and John 20:1). Moreover, Mary Magdalene and Joanna were among the women who followed Jesus in Galilee (see Luke 8:2-3). Mary the mother of James is also mentioned in Mark's account (Mark 16:1) and may be indicated by Matthew's phrase "the other Mary" (Matthew 28:1). To these three, Luke added "the other women." These were women known to the early church as true disciples: They were selfless in their service and devotion to Jesus and the disciples (8:2-3 and 23:49). Thus, the authenticity of their words was confirmed by (1) eyewitness account of the events of Easter morning, (2) agreement of several witnesses, and (3) being known as devoted, disciplined, and generous members of the community of Jesus' followers. Traditionally, scholars have not extended the word "disciple" to include women; this text, with the emphasis on the women as taught by Jesus, acknowledged by the community of male disciples and reliable witnesses to the empty tomb, suggests otherwise. Women were members of Jesus' community throughout his ministry, during his death, and at his burial. Women provided the reliable link between "Jesus' words," remembrance, and faith.

Luke 24:11-12. Interestingly, the words of the women, although judged as authentic, did not provoke faith among the other disciples. Three distinct responses are featured in the text. First, some disciples dismissed the women's witness as "an idle tale" (24:11, one word in Greek; this is the only use of the word in the New Testament). Evidently this response did not persist within the Christian community. The second response, however, persisted: Some did not believe them. Throughout the history of Christian faith, the point and purpose of doubt had a place. From doubt came dialogue (24:13-27). With their doubts, disciples saw their risen Lord (24:36-38), and because of doubt, the Holy Spirit continued to minister in the hearts of disciples (24:40-45). The final response was Peter's run to the tomb; he intended to confirm the women's report. But his experience took him no further than amazement. Once again Luke emphatically demonstrated that an empty tomb does not provoke belief. The events of Easter morning required more reflection, remembrance, and revelation before all the disciples came to believe, "He is not here, but has risen" (24:5).

INTERPRETING THE SCRIPTURE

From Ordinary to Empty

The women returned to Jesus' tomb with spices and ointments. Their intentions were ordinary. They only expected to do for Jesus what they had not done at the time of his burial. Because of the Sabbath, with its mandate to rest and refrain from work, the women had only a short time to gather the necessary items. Prior to dawn on Sunday, they returned to the cave where on Friday they witnessed Jesus' burial. Grief undoubtedly muddied their plan and actions. Yet, as mourning women throughout the centuries have done, these women pressed forward to do the right thing. They were not exemplary in this early morning attention to detail; they were ordinary. Even though Jesus' life ended dramatically, these women carried on.

"Dogged" might best describe their approach to the tomb. According to Luke, the women were not surprised that the stone was rolled away from the tomb. Likewise, Luke included no emotional content (in contrast with Mary Magdalene weeping in John 20:11). Instead, the women investigate and discover that Jesus' body is missing. They were face-to-face with the emptiness of the tomb. The empty tomb was a fitting metaphor for these women whose lives were emptied of love, meaning, and purpose. What remained were the ordinary actions that get people through the experience of death. In our world, the first few days of grieving are predictable: There are decisions to make regarding service arrangements; there are phone calls and e-mails to inform family and friends; there will be social calls made and received, as well as hospitality from neighbors and to visiting relatives. We get through the first few days by following the ordinary rhythm of mourning. Still, we, like the women at the tomb, often face emptiness.

From Perplexity to Action

In the experience of the women at the tomb, emptiness was filled with gentle revelation. They encountered angels, and the angels' encounter provoked memories and thoughts that filled their emptiness. Let's observe this process with care, for it contains a guideline for your encounters with mourning friends and relations.

The appearance of angels inspired a dramatic response: The women bowed down and trembled. Although your visit with individuals in the first stages of mourning may not provoke divine fear, still you will stir strong emotions. The sight of a dear friend usually brings tears or fears to the recently bereaved.

The angels began with a question, "Why do you look for the living among the dead?" (24:5). They basically asked, Do you think God's plans were defeated? You probably don't want to begin with that line, but consider a gentle statement such as, "You probably feel you've lost everything." In the face of death, everyone needs encouragement to appreciate the aliveness that continues to surround them.

Next, the angels briefly stated the foundation of Christian belief and moved swiftly to challenge the women to remember. It is important to share your faith with your grieving friends; it is not appropriate to preach a twenty-five-minute sermon in the space of a condolence visit. Before you visit, prayerfully reflect on the one or two Scriptures or succinct statements of faith that your friend might be able to hear. Weave a faith affirmation into the middle of your visit. Then, always, always, always encourage the mourner to remember. Use the angels' pattern: Lift up a significant memory able to unleash a positive recollection. Depart, as did the angels, quickly and without fanfare. Trust the mourner to resolve the perplexity of grief.

From Remembrance to Reality

As the women reflected on the words of the angels, they remembered Jesus' teaching about his own death, the core values of his life and how they had been in his presence. It was more than an intellectual "aha!" that brought them to their feet with an eagerness to return to the disciples. No, their minds, their spirits, and their hearts were involved in the recollection. Ideas, even the most

lofty of theological thought, do not create Christian faith. Spiritual experiences, even the most profound mystical revelations, are not the substance of Christian insight. Christian love shared between a married couple or in breadth of the community of believers is an incomplete expression of Christian belief. If we are to move from remembrance to reality, we must combine ideas, feelings, and actions into an intricate and integrated pattern.

It does not matter how an individual enters into faith—whether she comes, as did the women at the tomb, through thoughtful reflection of Jesus' teachings or whether he comes, as did the women at the tomb, through a mystical encounter with the divine, or whether we arrive at faith by the process of being loved by Christians. To grow into mature Christians, each believer must explore the theological truths of faith, must be open to the inspiration of the Holy Spirit, and must practice the art of loving others as Christ loved. Once such maturity begins to blossom, regardless of the length of gestation, believers become active witnesses. For the women at the empty tomb, the transformation was swift. They moved from the ordinary experience of caring for the dead through revelation, remembrance, and reflection to faith. And then, they returned to give their witness.

From Reliability to Disbelief

There's a disappointing ending to Luke's account of the first Easter morning. After the profound and faith-filled experience of the women at the empty tomb, the reader anticipates a joyful "Alleluia" conclusion. Instead, the other disciples make light of the women's testimony or openly refuse to believe. The one exception is Peter, who runs to the tomb to confirm the women's witness. He comes back amazed but not full of faith.

Some have used this story as an argument against women as interpreters or teachers of Christian faith. Indeed, it is easy to read the text and think "missed opportunity." But I believe Luke was presenting more than the future difficulties to be faced by women in leadership in the Christian community. I believe Luke was quietly reminding each and every believer that there is no such thing as secondhand faith. Every man, woman, teen, child, or older adult must come to faith personally. Testimonies as powerful as those of the women returning from the empty tomb may be inspiring. Passion as bright as the gleam in the women's eyes can be contagious. This type of risky behavior, women's voices speaking hope to a circle of mourning disciples, often moves the immoveable.

But, sometimes a passionate, risky testimony fails. Why? Because faith is, first and foremost, a gift from the Holy Spirit. The disciples were called to belief; they were taught and formed by Jesus himself; they witnessed his death, and they heard about his resurrection. They still required the movement of the Holy Spirit to spark mature faith in them. Jesus warned them that believing would not come easily to all. The women were a divine exception; faith came more slowly and more predictably to the rest of the disciples. Perhaps that is why most chose disbelief. Perhaps it was simply a question of timing. For when the time was right the women's reliable word was believed. By the power of the Holy Spirit, the disciples became apostles who witnessed with their lives and their deaths to their Lord. Those disciples, who mourned and feared and disbelieved, established the church from which we have drawn our faith.

SHARING THE SCRIPTURE

Preparing Our Hearts

Meditate on this week's devotional reading, found in 1 Corinthians 15:12-26. After writing about the resurrection of Christ in the first eleven verses of this chapter, Paul goes on to assert that because Christ is raised, so too there is a resurrection of the dead. As you read Paul's argument, consider what you believe to be true about Christ's resurrection—and your own prospects for resurrection. How does your belief influence what you do in this life?

Pray that you and the adult learners will give glory to God for the events of Easter and what they mean for you and those you love.

Preparing Our Minds

Study the background and lesson Scripture, both found in Luke 24:1-12. Consider that death seems so final and irreversible. Ask yourself, Are these widely held assumptions really true?

Write on newsprint:
❑ questions for "Explore the Meaning of Jesus' Resurrection for One's Life."
❑ information for next week's lesson, found under "Continue the Journey."
❑ activities for further spiritual growth in "Continue the Journey."

LEADING THE CLASS

(1) Gather to Learn

❖ Welcome the class members and introduce any guests.

❖ Pray that those who have come today will experience great joy upon hearing the news that Christ is risen; he is risen indeed.

❖ Invite the students to recall a funeral they attended where some of the guests clearly had a hope of resurrection and others saw death as an irreversible finality. Encourage the adults to talk with the class, or in small groups, about the reactions of those who were present. To protect privacy, suggest that they not mention specific names.

❖ Read aloud today's focus statement: **Death seems final, totally defeating, irreversible. Are these widely held assumptions really true? No; Luke's record of Easter morning assures us that new, resurrected life is possible because Jesus rose from the dead.**

(2) Encounter the Story of Easter Morning as Told in the Gospel of Luke

❖ Select a volunteer to read the part of the narrator and another to read the part of the "men in dazzling clothes" in Luke 24:1-12. Before the readers begin, ask the students to think about the sights, sounds, smells, tastes, and things they could touch as they listen to this familiar story.

❖ Discuss with the adults what their senses perceived in this story. List their ideas on newsprint. Such an exercise will enable the students to enter into the story and "walk around" with the characters.

❖ Encourage the adults to define the roles played by the women. Here are some possible ones: *mourners, close friends who had come to prepare Jesus for burial, recipients of a divine message, keepers of the collective memory of the disciples ("rememberers"), and witnesses.*

❖ Read or retell "From Ordinary to Empty" and "From Perplexity to Action" in Interpreting the Scripture to help clarify the women's responses.

❖ Note that the women heard the word and responded. They told the men, but the men did not believe them. Ask these questions:

(1) **Why didn't the other disciples believe them?** (Per Jewish law, women were not allowed to testify as witnesses. Therefore, the disci-

ples heard their report as "an idle tale.")

(2) **How do you think the women might have felt when their report was so brashly dismissed?**

(3) **What did Peter's action indicate?** (We don't know whether Peter actually believed the women, but he was willing to go to the tomb immediately and have a look. We are told he was "amazed" but do no know what other response he might have made.)

❖ Read aloud again Luke 24:6-8. Ask the students to meditate silently on these questions: **If you were asked to remember something Jesus said or did, what would it be? What kind of response does this action bring forth in you?**

❖ Bring the class together and invite volunteers to share insights from their meditations.

(3) Explore the Meaning of Jesus' Resurrection for One's Life

❖ Encourage the students to read in unison today's key verse, Luke 24:5.

❖ Divide the class into discussion groups. Post these questions on newsprint where everyone can see them on this Easter Sunday:

(1) **What does this scriptural encounter with Jesus' resurrection suggest to you about the possibility of your own resurrection?**

(2) **What implications does the knowledge of Christ's resurrection have for us concerning our priorities as a church? Do they need to be altered? If so, in what ways?**

(3) **What implications does the knowledge of Christ's resurrection have for us as the church in relation to the concerns that Jesus had, such as caring for the poor, sick, and marginalized people?**

❖ Call the groups together and ask each of them to summarize their discussion of one of the questions.

(4) Make a Commitment to Live as if the Learners Really Believe That New Life Is Possible Through the Resurrected Christ

❖ Distribute paper and pencils. Encourage the students to write a brief paragraph, for their eyes only, concerning commitments they have made, or need to make, to live as Easter people. That is, what do they need to do to live as if they truly believe that new life is possible for them because Jesus is resurrected? This question involves consideration of ways in which believers' lives need to be different from other people's lives.

❖ Call the students back together. To remind students of the historical witness of the church to Jesus' resurrection, ask the class to affirm their faith by reciting "The Apostles' Creed" or "The Nicene Creed." Distribute hymnals and direct the students to the appropriate page.

(5) Continue the Journey

❖ Pray that each one who has come today will recognize implications for the new life that already exists in the resurrected Christ and is promised to them.

❖ Read aloud this preparation for next week's lesson. You may also want to post it on newsprint for the students to copy.

- ■ **Title: Witnesses to New Life**
- ■ **Background Scripture: Luke 24:36-53**
- ■ **Lesson Scripture: Luke 24:44-53**
- ■ **Focus of the Lesson: People are often willing to give testimonials on behalf of products or services**

they believe in. What—or who—are we willing to endorse? According to Luke's Gospel, Jesus appeared to his disciples and commissioned them to witness to the new life they have in him, for the Scriptures affirm that he is the Messiah.

❖ Challenge the students to complete one or more of these activities for further spiritual growth, which you will write on newsprint for the students to copy:

(1) **Talk with someone engaged in hospice work. Ask this volunteer or professional to share observations concerning how people who clearly believe in Christ's resurrection and those who report no such belief react to their impending death or the death of a loved one.**

(2) **Search the Scriptures to locate at least two passages that reflect the hope you have in the resurrected Christ. Can you pinpoint reasons that your particular choices give you comfort and strength whenever you deal with issues surrounding physical death?**

(3) **Note that the women are the first not only to hear the good news of the resurrection but also to share it. Consider the role of women in ministry. If you are a woman, how does this passage empower you to take on new ministry roles?**

❖ Sing or read aloud "He Rose."

❖ Conclude today's session by leading the class in this benediction: **Give us new hearts filled with your Spirit, O Lord, that we may live as new creations in Christ. Amen.**

UNIT 2: THE PATH TO NEW LIFE
Witnesses to New Life

PREVIEWING THE LESSON

Lesson Scripture: Luke 24:44-53
Background Scripture: Luke 24:36-53
Key Verses: Luke 24:48-49

Focus of the Lesson:
People are often willing to give testimonials on behalf of products or services they believe in. What—or who—are we willing to endorse? According to Luke's Gospel, Jesus appeared to his disciples and commissioned them to witness to the new life they have in him, for the Scriptures affirm that he is the Messiah.

Goals for the Learners:
(1) to reflect on Luke's account of Jesus' commissioning his disciples.
(2) to identify ways that God has blessed them and to feel gratitude for those blessings.
(3) to witness to others about the new life they have in Christ Jesus.

Supplies:
Bibles, newsprint and markers, paper and pencils, hymnals, ads from any printed source

---

READING THE SCRIPTURE

NRSV
Luke 24:44-53

⁴⁴Then he [Jesus] said to them, "These are my words that I spoke to you while I was still with you—that everything written about me in the law of Moses, the prophets, and the psalms must be fulfilled." ⁴⁵Then he opened their minds to understand the scriptures, ⁴⁶and he said to them, "Thus it is written, that the Messiah is to suffer and to rise from the dead on the third day, ⁴⁷and that repentance and forgiveness of sins is to be proclaimed in his name to all nations,

NIV
Luke 24:44-53

⁴⁴He [Jesus] said to them, "This is what I told you while I was still with you: Everything must be fulfilled that is written about me in the Law of Moses, the Prophets and the Psalms."

⁴⁵Then he opened their minds so they could understand the Scriptures. ⁴⁶He told them, "This is what is written: The Christ will suffer and rise from the dead on the third day, ⁴⁷and repentance and forgiveness of sins will be preached in his name to all

beginning from Jerusalem. **⁴⁸You are witnesses of these things. ⁴⁹And see, I am sending upon you what my Father promised;** so stay here in the city until you have been clothed with power from on high."

⁵⁰Then he led them out as far as Bethany, and, lifting up his hands, he blessed them. ⁵¹While he was blessing them, he withdrew from them and was carried up into heaven. ⁵²And they worshiped him, and returned to Jerusalem with great joy; ⁵³and they were continually in the temple blessing God.

nations, beginning at Jerusalem. **⁴⁸You are witnesses of these things. ⁴⁹I am going to send you what my Father has promised;** but stay in the city until you have been clothed with power from on high."

⁵⁰When he had led them out to the vicinity of Bethany, he lifted up his hands and blessed them. ⁵¹While he was blessing them, he left them and was taken up into heaven. ⁵²Then they worshiped him and returned to Jerusalem with great joy. ⁵³And they stayed continually at the temple, praising God.

UNDERSTANDING THE SCRIPTURE

Luke 24:36-43. All four Gospels include accounts of Jesus' appearances to the disciples. In the Gospel of Mark, the appearances are in the shorter and longer conclusions (Mark 16:8 and 16:9-20) to the Gospel; both include Jesus' commission to the disciples. Matthew briefly describes one appearance in Jerusalem (Matthew 28:9-10) and another in Galilee (Matthew 28:16-20), again concluding with a commission to the disciples. John fills two chapters with appearance stories. Jesus first appeared to Mary Magdalene (John 20:14-17); then, three times to the disciples as a group (John 20:19-23; 20:26-28; 21:1-8). Luke devotes several verses to the two disciples on the road to Emmaus (Luke 24:13-33), and he briefly states that Simon Peter has also seen Jesus (Luke 24:34-35). Easter day concluded with a final appearance to all the disciples (Luke 24:36-43). Luke's theological treatment of the appearances is unique among the Gospels. In Matthew and Mark, there are no stories, but only the mention of the appearances and the commissioning. John's appearance narratives emphasized that seeing or being with Jesus was sufficient to spark ministering faith in the disciples (see John 20:17; 20:27; 21:7-8). In Luke, however, belief was not immediate. Faith came after

physical experience with Jesus: In Luke 24:13-33, two disciples walked, talked, and ate with Jesus. In our passage today, the disciples were commanded to examine Jesus' body and to observe him eating as confirmation that he was no apparition. These proofs provided the necessary firsthand experiences that established the apostles' authority to testify to the continuity between the crucified Jesus and the resurrected Jesus. Luke's Gospel pointed to the next spiritual reality: the church as the body of Christ in the world.

Luke 24:44-47. Luke's Gospel began with a bow to Scripture. In Luke 1:1-2, Luke explained that this Gospel was an "orderly account of the events that have been fulfilled among us" according to the testimony of "eyewitnesses and servants of the word." Throughout the Gospel, the Hebrew Scriptures illuminated Jesus' life, and his teachings clarified the intent of God's law. At the conclusion of the Gospel, Luke introduced a new dynamic to Scripture. As the resurrected Jesus spoke to the disciples, he "opened their minds" (24:45) in a manner similar to his conversation with the two disciples on the Emmaus road. This "opening" of the disciples was the promised power of the Holy Spirit deepening the spiritual insight of the disciples. Luke used these two passages to remind his audience that Scripture was not self-evident but required the spiritual guidance of Jesus to be fully comprehended. This first aspect of scriptural interpretation was complemented by a second even more amazing one. Jesus taught, once again, that his death and resurrection were specified in Scripture. He also proclaimed that the purpose of his death was "that repentance and forgiveness of sins is to be proclaimed in his name to all nations, beginning from Jerusalem" (24:47). This unique link between the Messiah's death in Scripture and the preaching of repentance and forgiveness provided a mandate for the disciples' mission. With a characteristic concern for the change in human hearts (repentance), the new life created by forgiveness, and the universal purpose of the gospel, Luke expanded the disciples' authority from Scripture and inspiration to Jesus' own commandment.

Luke 24:48-49. There are five accounts of Jesus' commissioning of the disciples in the New Testament. In Mark 16:15, the disciples are to preach the gospel; in Matthew 28:19-20 they are to make disciples and teach them; in John 20:21, the disciples are sent into the world as the Father has sent the Son; in Acts 1:8 they are to be Spirit-empowered witnesses. In our passage, the disciples are commissioned to wait. Evidently, Luke was not impressed by the spontaneous onset of faith. Rather, Luke deliberately slowed the process of the disciples' transformation to apostles. Since Luke painted the broadest picture of God's reconciling work through Jesus—a work encompassing the whole world—the pace provided time for thought and assimilation. The disciples were indeed commissioned for a worldwide ministry; however, before they were permitted to begin that ministry they were commanded to wait. Moreover, they were to stay in Jerusalem, the holy city,

the site of the holy Temple. There, as the disciples spent days in prayer and reflection, the Holy Spirit would continue to open their minds and inspire new insights until these eyewitnesses grasped the significance of Jesus' life, death, and resurrection and were able to communicate this as the core of Christian faith.

Luke 24:50-53. The Gospel of Luke is the only Gospel to describe the departure of Jesus from the disciples; in fact, the author of Luke describes two ascensions: Luke 24:51 and Acts 1:9-11. Accordingly, an ascension closed Jesus' earthly ministry and a second ascension opened the apostles' ministry in his name. The elements of each ascension narrative are the same: Jesus blessed his disciples; they witness him being lifted up into heaven; they respond to his departure with an act of obedience. In this first scene, Jesus led the disciples out of Jerusalem; this last walk with Jesus ended in Bethany, the village where Jesus' friends Mary, Martha, and Lazarus provided him and his disciples with hospitality. Together, the disciples and the risen Lord walked from the heart of the Jewish religious community to the heart of the new community of those who loved and followed Jesus. Next, Jesus' departure was integrated into his final blessing, implying that his departure was for the benefit of the disciples (see John 16:7). Finally, the response of the disciples was twofold. First, they immediately worshiped Jesus; this is the first association of the verb "to worship" with Jesus in this Gospel (see Luke 2:37; 4:7; and 4:8 for other examples of "to worship"). Then, in obedience, the disciples returned to Jerusalem to wait for the promised power from on high. They were joyful (as Jesus predicted in John 15:11), and they were prayerful. With these two spiritual gifts the Gospel concluded. The disciples waited forty days, and then the Acts of the Apostles began.

INTERPRETING THE SCRIPTURE

What's in an Appearance?

When it comes to the conclusion of the Gospel narratives, Luke and John are clearly the most engaging. Both of these Gospels include stories that feature named and unnamed disciples and events that allow the resurrected Jesus to interpret his life, ministry, death, and resurrection. Contemporary readers are often confounded by the stories of Jesus' appearances. Although the resurrection is the key element in Christian faith, these appearances are bothersome. How does one explain a risen Lord who suddenly appears and just as suddenly disappears? How does one explain the resurrected Jesus fixing breakfast or eating with his disciples? First-century believers answered such questions with ease: Jesus appeared to his disciples in order to prepare them for their ministry.

Contemporary Christians often miss this emphasis on Jesus' resurrection as an invitation to ministry. Because the disciples were convinced of the continuity of the crucified Jesus and the glorified Jesus, they found courage to continue his ministry. Jesus' appearances were not troublesome for the earliest believers. Rather, the appearance turned fearful disciples into bold apostles. When we focus on the "how, what, and wherefore" of the appearances, we miss the amazing transformation that is taking place: The disciples are being reinvented as apostles. This reinvention happened because their experience with Jesus did not end at the crucifixion or even in the empty tomb. Like Christians in every age, we need to pull back from the appearances to see the "whole picture." What's in an appearance? Not a sighting. More than a miracle. Jesus appeared so that the disciples would move from fearful hiding to bold witnessing.

What's Left to Teach?

Have you ever imagined yourself to be one of Jesus' original disciples? I have. I've imagined myself walking the dusty roads of Galilee listening to every word spoken by Jesus. I've imagined long talks after a day of intense ministry. I've imagined quiet time for disciples with Jesus. And I've imagined the stories, directions, and guidance given by my Lord. I am able to imagine so freely because the Gospels provide a rich description of Jesus' interactions with his disciples. At times I feel they had all the advantages, whereas I am left with only the stories. But, in some ways, I value my position over that of the disciples: I have the opportunity to read and reread the words of the disciples while they had to "get it" as they walked by his side.

In these last encounters with the risen Lord, the disciples still had a need for Jesus' words and instruction. Moreover, Jesus was sensitive to their need and continued to teach them. The Gospel of Luke gives a summary of Jesus' final teaching in 24:44-47. First, Jesus reminded his disciples of his previous teaching that his life and death were a fulfillment of Scripture. Notice that Jesus does not quote chapter and verse; rather, he reminds the disciples of the wide sweep of Scripture. "Everything written" was a code phrase indicating God's comprehensive reconciliation.

Yet, even a wide and deep understanding of Scripture was not sufficient to equip the disciples for their future roles as apostles. Therefore, Jesus "opened their minds" to the Scriptures. Quite likely, he taught them again what they already knew: the significance of mercy, justice, peace, and love.

Finally, Jesus gathered what they knew (all the truth from the Hebrew Scriptures and from Jesus' own interpretation of Scripture) and connected those truths with the central goal of his ministry: to call all to repentance and to proclaim forgiveness for everyone. When the old was linked to the new, something unexpected was taught. The disciples were instructed to proclaim the possibility of new life in Jesus to the whole world! This was Jesus' last and most important lesson.

Will You Be a Witness?

In the school of Jesus, learning was only significant if it led to ministry. Thus, as Jesus offered his final lesson to his disciples—just moments before he mysteriously left them—he challenged the disciples to become his witnesses. Interestingly, Jesus did not ask if the disciples felt comfortable as witnesses. Neither did Jesus inquire if the disciples were willing to assume this role. Rather, Jesus stated the obvious: You are witnesses of these things. From the arrest and trial to the crucifixion and burial, the disciples observed how Jesus was treated and how he responded. From the discovery of the empty tomb to the spontaneous interruptions of the disciples on travels, at meals, or out in their boats fishing, the disciples encountered Jesus again and again. They could not deny their new category as "witnesses." The only question hanging in the air was, What kind of witnesses will these disciples become? In many ways that same question hangs in the air over every contemporary Christian community.

We have all witnessed strangers made friends in Christ. We have all known the blessings of "giving a cup of water" in Christ's name. We have prayed and been forgiven; we have waited and been blessed. We, too, are witnesses of Christ's continuing love in the church and in the world. Thus, the question is for us, What kind of witnesses will we be? The answer for the first disciples, and the answer for contemporary believers, is the same. We will be empowered by the Holy Spirit. The first disciples were instructed to wait in Jerusalem until they received spiritual power to proclaim Jesus' way. Contemporary disciples are also encouraged to wait for the Spirit's guidance. Without the energy of the Spirit, all attempts at witnessing fail. But in the power of the Spirit, disciples become apostles, believers become evangelists, and Christians offer Christ's love to a hungry, hurting world.

A Way to Wait

The final verses in the Gospel of Luke read like stage directions in a screenplay. It is easy to visualize—although difficult to comprehend—the scene. Jesus walked and talked with his disciples, then lifted up his hands in a final blessing. With hands thus uplifted, mysteriously he was taken up into the clouds. The disciples worshiped him. Then, with joy etched on every face, they returned to Jerusalem to join evening worship. It was an amazing Easter day, one that began with the confusing testimony of the women and concluded with Jesus' final blessing and ascension.

Just as amazing as the events of the day was the profound emotional shift within the disciples. They began the day full of doubt, and they ended the day joyfully praising God in the Temple. Moreover, they had a plan. Jesus told them to wait. Something more was going to happen before they were fit to be apostles. Surprisingly, these disciples, who during Jesus' earthly life questioned him about the timetable and content of the coming reign of God, now were content to do what they did best: praise God. They no longer worried about their own safety; they blended into the congregation. They no longer felt the sting of the sight of Jesus' dying on the cross. They joyfully thanked God for the gift of seeing their risen Lord. They no longer fretted over their next steps. They sang and prayed and listened to God's word. Jesus' final words entered their hearts freeing them to worship fully, in spirit and in truth. This was their way to wait: to worship at the Temple morning, midday, and evening. Their waiting was and is an example to the Christian community: When the future is yet-to-be-revealed, worship. What a powerful way to witness to the new life that awaits us.

SHARING THE SCRIPTURE

Preparing Our Hearts

Meditate on this week's devotional reading, found in Acts 2:22-32. This passage recounts, in part, Peter's speech to the crowd on Pentecost. Verse 32 states: "This Jesus God raised up, and of that all of us are witnesses." The Greek word for "witness" is the same one from which we derive our English word "martyr." Write in your spiritual journal about what it means to be a witness (even a martyr) for the sake of Christ. What challenges do you face as you try to be a faithful witness?

Pray that you and the adult learners will be willing to share the good news with others.

Preparing Our Minds

Study the background from Luke 24:36-53 and the lesson Scripture from verses 44-53. Think about what—or who—you are willing to endorse.

Write on newsprint:
❑ information for next week's lesson, found under "Continue the Journey."
❑ activities for further spiritual growth in "Continue the Journey."

Collect some advertisements from newspapers, magazines, junk mail, or other places to bring to class on Sunday. Look especially for ones that include testimonials. Weight loss plans, for example, often give before and after pictures with a few words from a satisfied customer.

Prepare a brief lecture for "Reflect on Luke's Account of Jesus' Commissioning His Disciples" to introduce today's lesson Scripture.

LEADING THE CLASS

(1) Gather to Learn

❖ Welcome the class members and introduce any guests.

❖ Pray that those who have gathered today will be blessed by the good news of Jesus Christ.

❖ Distribute or display advertisements you have located. Point out the ones where people have endorsed a specific product or service. Ask these questions:
   (1) What about the advertisement makes the product or service appealing to you?
   (2) Would you be willing to try the product or service it touts? Why or why not?
   (3) What kinds of products or services would you be willing to endorse? Why?

❖ Read aloud today's focus statement: **People are often willing to give testimonials on behalf of products or services they believe in. What—or who—are we willing to endorse? According to Luke's Gospel, Jesus appeared to his disciples and commissioned them to witness to the new life they have in him, for the Scriptures affirm that he is the Messiah.**

(2) Reflect on Luke's Account of Jesus' Commissioning His Disciples

❖ Use information from Luke 24:36-43 in Understanding the Scripture to prepare the students to read today's lesson. Present a brief lecture.

❖ Select a volunteer to read Luke 24:44-49.

■ Encourage the class members to comment on what they perceive Jesus taught the disciples. "What's Left to Teach?" in Interpreting the Scripture includes ideas that will add to the discussion.

■ Ask the students to imagine that they were there with Jesus. **What questions would you want to ask him about (a) his message, (b) his expectations that they will be his witnesses, and (c) what he means by the phrase "clothed with power from on high" (24:49)?**

■ Read information from Luke 24:48-49 in Understanding the Scripture to help the adults see how Luke's account of commissioning the disciples is similar to and different from the accounts found in other passages.

❖ Choose someone to read the story of Jesus' ascension from Luke 24:50-53.

■ Ask someone else to read the ascension as reported in Acts 1:6-11. Discuss the similarities and differences between these two accounts. (You will find information to assist you in Understanding the Scripture, Luke 24:50-53).

■ Read these words from Interpreting the Scripture: **Jesus' final words entered [the disciples'] hearts freeing them to worship fully, in spirit and in truth. This was their way to wait: to worship at the Temple morning, midday, and evening. Their waiting was and is an example to the Christian community: When the future is yet-to-be-revealed, worship. What a powerful way to witness to the new life that awaits us.**

■ Invite the adults to comment on this excerpt. Particularly ask them to report on their own experiences of waiting and worshiping.

(3) Identify Ways That God Has Blessed the Learners and Feel Gratitude for Those Blessings

❖ Set out markers and post several sheets of newsprint entitled "Count Your Blessings." Invite the students to each write one or more blessings on one sheet. Talk with them about commonalities they see, such as blessings of family, church, relationship with Christ, or other similar notations.

❖ **Option:** If the class is too large to work comfortably with newsprint, ask the students to call out blessings and write them on newsprint yourself. Be sure to talk about commonalities that they see.

❖ Set up a role-play in which one person is complaining about life. He or she is dissatisfied with family, work, neighbors, even the church. Ask a second person to try to encourage this person to look at God's blessings in his or her life, perhaps naming some that the class has listed.

❖ Debrief the role-play by asking those who watched to identify ways in which the second speaker acted as a true witness for Christ.

❖ **Option:** Divide into groups and have several pairs present the role-play, each to a different group.

❖ Conclude this portion of the lesson by providing a few moments of quiet time for the adults to offer silent prayers of thanksgiving for their blessings. Cue the class that the prayer time has ended by saying "amen."

(4) Witness to Others About New Life in Christ Jesus

❖ Read aloud this statement: **Active witnessing for the Lord provides a checkpoint for one's inner commitment and an outward life focus for believers as they invite others to follow Jesus.**

❖ Encourage the students to comment on the previous statement, indicating how they have—or have not—found it to be true in their own lives.

❖ Distribute paper and pencils. Read this quotation by Dan Greene: **Witnessing is not a spare-time occupation or a once-a-week activity. It must be a quality of life. You don't go witnessing, you are a witness.** Invite the students to write briefly, for their own eyes, how they believe that their life is—or is not—a witness for Christ. Encourage them to address these two questions as they write: **What evidence supports their conclusion? If they could make one change that would strengthen them as witnesses, what would that change be?**

❖ Provide a few moments for silent prayer and meditation, based on the findings of this question.

(5) Continue the Journey

❖ Conclude the meditation time by praying that today's participants will go forth to witness to the new life available in Christ to all.

❖ Read aloud this preparation for next week's lesson. You may also want to post it on newsprint for the students to copy.

■ **Title: Bringing New Life to Those in Need**
■ **Background Scripture: Acts 9:32-43**
■ **Lesson Scripture: Acts 9:32-43**
■ **Focus of the Lesson: Various cries**

for physical and spiritual assistance clamor for the world's attention. **Where do we turn for help in times of physical illness and death? Through the power of Christ, Peter was able to heal Aeneas and raise Tabitha from the dead.**

❖ Challenge the students to complete one or more of these activities for further spiritual growth, which you will write on newsprint for the students to copy:

(1) **Share your witness for Christ this week in word and deed. Invite your listener to attend church with you on Sunday, if he or she seems ready to do so.**

(2) **Recall the impact a word of witness made on your life. Who proclaimed this word? How did it affect you? How did you "pass it on" to others?**

(3) **Let someone know how much of a blessing he or she has been to you. A word of thanks or token of appreciation will suffice. Be as specific as possible in stating the blessings you have received from this person.**

❖ Sing or read aloud "Pass It On."

❖ Conclude today's session by leading the class in this benediction: **Give us new hearts filled with your Spirit, O Lord, that we may live as new creations in Christ. Amen.**

UNIT 2: THE PATH TO NEW LIFE

BRINGING NEW LIFE TO THOSE IN NEED

PREVIEWING THE LESSON

Lesson Scripture: Acts 9:32-43
Background Scripture: Acts 9:32-43
Key Verse: Acts 9:38

Focus of the Lesson:
Various cries for physical and spiritual assistance clamor for the world's attention. Where do we turn for help in times of physical illness and death? Through the power of Christ, Peter was able to heal Aeneas and raise Tabitha from the dead.

Goals for the Learners:
(1) to relate the miracles of new life given to Aeneas and Tabitha.
(2) to feel the power of Christ's presence in times of need.
(3) to demonstrate the kind of care and concern that Peter showed.

Pronunciation Guide:
Aeneas (i nee' uhs)   Lydda (lid' uh)
Dorcas (dor' kuhs)   Tabitha (tab' i thuh)

Supplies:
Bibles, newsprint and marker, paper and pencils, hymnals, optional unlined paper and colored pencils

---

READING THE SCRIPTURE

NRSV

Acts 9:32-43

³²Now as Peter went here and there among all the believers, he came down also to the saints living in Lydda. ³³There he found a man named Aeneas, who had been bedridden for eight years, for he was paralyzed.

NIV

Acts 9:32-43

³²As Peter traveled about the country, he went to visit the saints in Lydda. ³³There he found a man named Aeneas, a paralytic who had been bedridden for eight years. ³⁴"Aeneas," Peter said to him, "Jesus Christ

³⁴Peter said to him, "Aeneas, Jesus Christ heals you; get up and make your bed!" And immediately he got up. ³⁵And all the residents of Lydda and Sharon saw him and turned to the Lord.

³⁶Now in Joppa there was a disciple whose name was Tabitha, which in Greek is Dorcas. She was devoted to good works and acts of charity. ³⁷At that time she became ill and died. When they had washed her, they laid her in a room upstairs. **³⁸Since Lydda was near Joppa, the disciples, who heard that Peter was there, sent two men to him with the request, "Please come to us without delay."** ³⁹So Peter got up and went with them; and when he arrived, they took him to the room upstairs. All the widows stood beside him, weeping and showing tunics and other clothing that Dorcas had made while she was with them. ⁴⁰Peter put all of them outside, and then he knelt down and prayed. He turned to the body and said, "Tabitha, get up." Then she opened her eyes, and seeing Peter, she sat up. ⁴¹He gave her his hand and helped her up. Then calling the saints and widows, he showed her to be alive. ⁴²This became known throughout Joppa, and many believed in the Lord. ⁴³Meanwhile he stayed in Joppa for some time with a certain Simon, a tanner.

heals you. Get up and take care of your mat." Immediately Aeneas got up. ³⁵All those who lived in Lydda and Sharon saw him and turned to the Lord.

³⁶In Joppa there was a disciple named Tabitha (which, when translated, is Dorcas), who was always doing good and helping the poor. ³⁷About that time she became sick and died, and her body was washed and placed in an upstairs room. **³⁸Lydda was near Joppa; so when the disciples heard that Peter was in Lydda, they sent two men to him and urged him, "Please come at once!"**

³⁹Peter went with them, and when he arrived he was taken upstairs to the room. All the widows stood around him, crying and showing him the robes and other clothing that Dorcas had made while she was still with them.

⁴⁰Peter sent them all out of the room; then he got down on his knees and prayed. Turning toward the dead woman, he said, "Tabitha, get up." She opened her eyes, and seeing Peter she sat up. ⁴¹He took her by the hand and helped her to her feet. Then he called the believers and the widows and presented her to them alive. ⁴²This became known all over Joppa, and many people believed in the Lord. ⁴³Peter stayed in Joppa for some time with a tanner named Simon.

UNDERSTANDING THE SCRIPTURE

Acts 9:32-35. The theme of this unit is "The Path to New Life." That theme has been developed through a close examination of the disciples' experience of Jesus' death, resurrection, and appearances. Through their eyes, we have seen Jesus' suffering, felt the cold shroud of his burial, and known the joy of his resurrection. We have observed their despair, confusion, doubts, and fears. We have noted their spirits transformed and their purposes refined.

In short, we have studied the very first steps of the disciples on "The Path to New Life." In this final passage, the disciples are further along that path. Our passage comes from the Acts of the Apostles. The author of this collection of stories of the birth and development of the early church is probably the author of the Gospel of Luke. Indeed, these two works are designed to be read as one story. As Luke is a compilation from various sources (the framework provided by Mark, material shared by Matthew and Luke, and the stories specific to Luke), so the Acts of the Apostles stitches together independent traditions concerning the early church leaders: Peter, Stephen, Philip, and Paul. In our passage, Peter was moving among the Christian communities in Judea. His travels took him to communities of believers in Lydda, Joppa, and Caesarea. The opening phrase, "Now as Peter went here and there among all the believers," indicated but did not describe the rich ministry of Peter during this trip. Undoubtedly most of his time was spent teaching, preaching, and advising the community on matters of morality and community life. Peter's spiritual power, however, was also attested to during this trip. Our passage includes two healing accounts, each highlighting Peter's spiritual authority. Aeneas, a paralyzed man, was healed by Peter's invocation of the power of Jesus Christ. This healing bears a remarkable similarity to Jesus' miracle recorded in Luke 5:24-25. Both healings demonstrate spiritual authority and result in widespread amazement and conversions.

Acts 9:36-38. Following a pattern developed in the Gospel of Luke, accounts of healings were grouped together. In this case, the healing of a man was complemented by a mighty deed performed for a woman. The account of Dorcas's healing contained more detail than the sparse account of Aeneas. Dorcas received the identification of "disciple," a word reserved for an eyewitness of Jesus' ministry, death, and resurrection. This woman's discipleship was further demonstrated by her many good deeds and charitable works. Because the community's grief at the death of Dorcas was so great, they sent messengers to Peter petitioning him to come immediately to Joppa. Whether this message was a request for Peter to join (and lead) the community in mourning or for a miracle is unknown. It seems likely that having prepared Dorcas for burial, the request for Peter had to do with the burial and mourning of this distinguished woman disciple.

Acts 9:39-41. Peter did not hesitate; he accompanied the messengers to Joppa. Upon arrival, Peter went to the upstairs room in which Dorcas's body lay. The mourning community was present, including the poorest members of the community, the widows. These women were particularly aggrieved by Dorcas's death as she provided the widows with clothes that she made. Clearly, Dorcas was a disciple who fulfilled Jesus' command to clothe the naked. As Peter comprehended the situation, he acted with authority and dismissed the mourners. Whatever was to happen was not a public spectacle but a private and intense spiritual experience. Alone, Peter followed the pattern of the early Christian community: He knelt down in prayer. After he prayed, he turned to the body of Dorcas and using her Hebrew name commanded, "Tabitha, get up." Once again, the author of Luke/Acts referenced a miracle of Jesus. In Mark 5:41-42 (a story also recorded in Luke 8:51-56) the tone of Jesus' words, "Talitha cum," which means "Little girl, get up!" was a verbal connection the original audience immediately recognized. Once again, spiritual authority was the issue and a healing confirmed the power of the healer. In the Gospels, Jesus was confirmed, while in Acts the power of Jesus was confirmed as operative through Peter. The miracle was authenticated as Peter assisted Dorcas to her feet and returned her to the community and to the widows. Using the same words found in Acts 1:3 to describe Jesus' appearance, Peter "showed her to be alive." Dorcas's physical life was confirmed as the community embraced her; her spiritual aliveness was described as the very aliveness present in Jesus when he appeared to his disciples following his death. Indeed, both Aeneas and Dorcas were recipients of the new life possible through faith in Jesus.

Acts 9:42-43. The consequence of these two demonstrations of Peter's spiritual power was the growth of the circles of believers in the region surrounding Joppa. Unlike Jesus, for whom itinerant ministry meant ministry on the move, Peter devoted significant time to the believers in Joppa. This devotion of time was characteristic of the development of the early church. Evangelists, apostles, teachers, and preachers did not make brief and powerful appearances; rather, they joined into the life of the community fully. Because the disciples had "caught" faith through their intimate association with Jesus, the leaders of the early church employed a similar communal intensity to establish new communities of faith. Interestingly, Peter spent his time in Joppa at the home of Simon, a tanner rejected by more orthodox Jews. As a tanner, an occupation that required handling the carcasses of animals, Simon was continuously ritually unclean according to Jewish law. Yet, Peter stayed with him. Perhaps it was in Simon's home that the Holy Spirit prepared Peter for his remarkable baptism of the first Gentile, Cornelius (Acts 10:44-48). Evidently, Peter and the whole community were on a path of ever-expanding new life—from Jerusalem to the whole world.

INTERPRETING THE SCRIPTURE

The Lame Walk

When the disciples of John the Baptizer approached Jesus' disciples, they wanted to know if, indeed, Jesus was the Messiah. Jesus told them, "Go and tell John what you have seen and heard: the blind receive their sight, the lame walk, the lepers are cleansed, the deaf hear, the dead are raised, the poor have good news brought to them. And blessed is anyone who takes no offense at me" (Luke 7:22-23). In the Gospels, mighty deeds—deeds accomplished through the power of God—attested to Jesus' identity as God's Son and the world's Savior. This same authentication was applied within the early Christian communities; miracles and mighty deeds signified that God was with the apostles. Thus, The Acts of the Apostles was a book written as a proof of the continuity between the ministry of Jesus and the life of the early Christian community. The path to new life was lined with miracles.

Sadly, in our contemporary approach to faith, miracles provoke more questions than settle issues related to authority. The modern, scientific mind seeks explanations according to physical laws. Unfortunately, rarely does the biblical witness contain sufficient "facts" to judge the event according to a scientific methodology. In the Bible the intention of a miracle is more important than the physical event. In the Acts of the Apostles, miracles demonstrate the spiritual authority of leaders. Thus, Peter visited the saints in Lydda, met a paralyzed man, and healed him by the powerful name of Jesus Christ. Neither a request for healing nor a community decision is included in the story. Rather, a man was healed and many, many people from the region turned to the Lord. A lame man walking was a sufficient sign of God's power at work in the world. Just as John's disciples sought evidence from Jesus so the early Christian community observed miracles that brought men and women to faith in Jesus.

The Poor Receive Good News

Throughout the Gospel of Luke, the poor were blessed by Jesus. Consistently, Jesus welcomed those whom others rejected, gave his time to the unworthy (women and children), and declared that God's love especially favored the "little ones." This attentiveness to the poor continued in the early church as they compassionately cared for widows. The situation of widows in the first century was most difficult. The words used by Greek and Hebrew reveal the difficulty. In Hebrew, the root of the word "widow" is the verb "unable to speak." In Greek, "widow" means "forsaken" or "left empty." In the time of Jesus, most widows had no legal rights and were dependent upon familial charity. Widows were at the very bottom of the social scale. Thus it was that the early Christian community provided the security of food, shelter, and clothing for widows. This ministry flowed directly from Jesus' reach toward the poor. By caring for the widows, early Christians demonstrated their comprehension of Jesus' path and extended his teachings to the least among the community.

Evidently Dorcas excelled in her compassion and generosity toward the widows of Joppa. At her death, the widows' grief was palpable. Not only was a true disciple of Jesus dead but the widows also feared the end of her ministry of compassion and support. Have you been in such a circumstance? A leader of a particular ministry dies and the congregation quietly wonders who will continue the ministry. Often a leader's death (or move away from the community of faith) initiates a change in ministry style and direction, but if the ministry was gospel-inspired, it continues. One of the difficult lessons the early church had to learn was trust. Step by step, project by project, death by death the early communities learned to trust God's providential inspiration of leaders. Such trust continues to be a challenge for the contemporary church even as God continues to supply leaders to bring good news to the poor.

The Dead Are Raised

The strongest proof of spiritual power was the ability to bring life to the dead. In Jesus' ministry this power was demonstrated in the raising of the widow's son at Nain (Luke 7:11-17), again in the raising of a little girl (Mark 5:41-42 and Luke 8:51-56) and once more in the raising of a dear friend, Lazarus (John 11:1-57). In the Acts of the Apostles, the raising of Dorcas (Acts 9:36-42) is one of only two instances of life being restored to the dead. The other instance occurs after Eutychus fell out of a third-story window and Paul picked him up and restored him (Acts 20:7-12). Turning to the Old Testament, we see the dead brought to life in 1 Kings 17:17-24, when the prophet Elijah revives the son of a widow, and again in 2 Kings 4:34-35 when Elisha revives the Shunammite woman's dead son. As a biblical sign, these mighty deeds are scarce. And yet, these stories should not be dismissed. Although we cannot examine these texts with a critical, scientific approach to fully understand how the dead are raised, we can see the power of God mightily at work.

We meet Dorcas only after her death, but the reports about her indicate that she was a beloved disciple known for her charitable good works. Her friends have washed her body in preparation for burial. This is an important detail, for there can be no question that Dorcas was truly dead. Peter, who was in nearby Lydda, was sent for, and he came "without delay" (9:38). Alone in the room with her, Peter prayed and commanded Dorcas to "get up" (9:40). The dead woman opened her eyes and sat up. An individual was restored to life through the power of the Holy Spirit, and as news of this miracle spread, her return to life also prompted many to believe in Jesus.

And Blessed Are the Believers

The description of the early Christian community in our text is subtle but rich. First, from our text we imagine the hospitality provided by the early church that enabled a church leader, such as Peter, to go "here and there among all the believers" (Acts 9:32). Leaders were blessed by staying in the homes of believers, and believers were blessed by receiving the company of their leaders. Second, the community was not only distinguished by hospitality given and received but it was also an economically and socially diverse community. Aeneas, a paralyzed man, had been bedridden for eight years; his condition probably meant that he had few resources to contribute to the community. Dorcas not only ministered to the widows but she also included them within the community of believers. Finally, we can observe that the community specialized in communication. They must have talked openly and joyfully about the mighty deeds performed by Peter.

The news of Aeneas's healing spread throughout Lydda and Sharon. News of Dorcas's revival also spread through the city of Joppa. Many people were converted because of the enthusiastic testimony of community members.

Thus the description of the early church emphasized hospitality, radical inclusivity, and enthusiastic testimonies. The contemporary church would do well to examine itself by these three traits. How does our congregation extend and receive hospitality? Are "the poor" welcomed? How enthusiastically do our members tell the blessings of Christian faith? Our answers to these questions provide a gauge by which we can measure how effective we are in bringing new life to those in need.

SHARING THE SCRIPTURE

Preparing Our Hearts

Meditate on this week's devotional reading, found in John 14:8-14. In Jesus' response to Philip, who wants to see the Father, Jesus makes the astonishing remark that those who believe in him will do greater works than he has done. How can we possibly do the kinds of things Jesus has done, much less "top" his actions? This seems impossible until you read today's lesson from Acts and recognize that the disciples were, in fact, able to heal and raise the dead. What kinds of actions have you been asked to take that seemed impossible but which worked out anyway because God provided?

Pray that you and the adult learners will be open to new paths of service and life.

Preparing Our Minds

Study the background and lesson Scripture, both from Acts 9:32-43. Think about where you turn for help in times of physical illness and death.

Write on newsprint:
❏ information for next week's lesson, found under "Continue the Journey."
❏ activities for further spiritual growth in "Continue the Journey."

Have unlined paper and colored pencils on hand if you choose to work with them.

LEADING THE CLASS

(1) Gather to Learn

❖ Welcome the class members and introduce any guests.

❖ Pray that those who have joined with the class today will experience God's presence and help.

❖ Distribute paper and pencils to each student. Read aloud these questions and ask them to jot down the number of the question and the first answer that comes to mind:

(1) Who would you call for help if you were experiencing chest pains?

(2) Suppose you or a family member

is diagnosed with **AIDS** or is **HIV positive. Where would you turn for help?**

(3) **Where would you turn if a co-worker said that he or she wanted to commit suicide?**

(4) **Where would you seek help if a family member died at home?**

(5) **Suppose that a loved one is terminally ill with cancer. Where would you turn for help?**

❖ Invite the adults to talk with a small group or the entire class about their answers. Some answers will be generic, such as paramedics or an emergency room. Others may be quite specific, naming an organization or individual who can help. This kind of networking can be useful as students may have a need later and recall this discussion.

❖ Read aloud today's focus statement: **Various cries for physical and spiritual assistance clamor for the world's attention. Where do we turn for help in times of physical illness and death? Through the power of Christ, Peter was able to heal Aeneas and raise Tabitha from the dead.**

(2) Relate the Miracles of New Life Given to Aeneas and Tabitha

❖ Invite a student to read the story of the healing of Aeneas in Acts 9:32-35.

❖ Choose another volunteer to read the story of Peter raising Dorcas, also known as Tabitha, found in Acts 9:36-43.

❖ Ask the students to discuss this question with a partner: **What would you have thought about Peter and the Christ in whose name he healed had you witnessed either of these miracles?** (Recognize that while many people have believed and continue to believe in miracles, for some Christians the idea of miracles is difficult to accept. Students with differing opinions may be in this class.)

❖ **Option:** Look at the story of Jesus raising the daughter of Jairus in Matthew 9:18-19, 23-26; Mark 5:21-24, 35-43; Luke 8:40-42, 49-56.

Compare at least one of the Gospel accounts with the story of Peter raising Dorcas.

❖ Read or retell "The Dead Are Raised" from Interpreting the Scripture.

❖ Discuss these questions:

(1) **Peter is following in the footsteps of Jesus by performing these miracles. What stories can you think of in the Gospels that report on Jesus' healings?**

(2) **How are Peter's actions similar to or different from the actions of Jesus in these stories?**

❖ Conclude this portion of the lesson by noting that as wonderful as these stories are, they do represent miracles. People pray persistently for miraculous healings, but we know that often these healings do not occur. Some things are just a mystery that we have to accept by faith.

(3) Feel the Power of Christ's Presence in Times of Need

❖ Do the following guided imagery activity with the group:

■ Encourage the adults to close their eyes and recall a time when they had a need, particularly a time when they were ill or had just lost a loved one. (pause)

■ Suggest that they think about how they felt at that time, how others supported them, and how they believe Christ was—or was not—present in a way they could identify. (pause)

■ Ask the adults to envision how they would express this presence of Christ in art, music, or dance. Is there an image, artwork, color, hymn, or tune that comes to mind when they think about experiencing Christ's presence? (pause)

■ Invite the students to open their eyes when they are ready.

❖ Encourage the learners to state whatever comes to mind when they experience

Christ's presence. See if there are common perceptions in the class, or if each person has a unique idea.

❖ **Option:** Distribute unlined paper and colored pencils (or other drawing equipment). Invite the students to draw the image or make lines with the colors they have identified during the guided imagery activity. You may also want to distribute hymnals and invite those who imagined a hymn or tune to point that out and invite the class to sing a verse or hum the tune.

(4) Demonstrate the Care and Concern That Peter Showed

❖ Brainstorm with the class ideas as to how they could help persons who are acutely or chronically sick or terminally ill. Write their responses on newsprint. Here are some possible answers: *volunteer at a hospital, hospice, or nursing home; do pet therapy at such a facility; run errands; write cards or pay bills for an ill person; prepare food; babysit; or transport the patient to medical appointments.*

❖ See if the church actually sponsors any of these activities. For example, perhaps your church conducts worship one night a month at a nursing home. See which of these ministries individuals in the class can connect with and provide contact information, if possible.

❖ Talk about where in the community other ministries on the list occur. Perhaps some members of the class engage in these ministries and could speak about them and serve as liaisons for those who may be interested in participating.

❖ Challenge the students to commit themselves to looking into a possible ministry with those who are ill or dying. They may wish to join with an existing ministry or consider starting a new one within the congregation or ecumenically in the community.

(5) Continue the Journey

❖ Pray that all who have participated in today's lesson will recognize that they can both seek help in times of need and offer such help to others.

❖ Read aloud this preparation for next week's lesson. You may also want to post it on newsprint for the students to copy.

- ■ **Title: New Family in Christ**
- ■ **Background Scripture: Ephesians 1:3-14**
- ■ **Lesson Scripture: Ephesians 1:3-14**
- ■ **Focus of the Lesson: Family life offers opportunities for rewards and challenges, for close ties and for estranged relationships. How do we see ourselves within the context of our families? In the Letter to the Ephesians, Paul celebrated and gave thanks for those whom God had adopted into a new family in Christ.**

❖ Challenge the students to complete one or more of these activities for further spiritual growth, which you will write on newsprint for the students to copy:

(1) **Offer a prayer for specific people who are in need of healing. Do what you can to assist these people in their time of need.**

(2) **Volunteer at a hospital, hospice, health clinic, nursing home, or other facility where people are ill. How does your work affect those you assist? What affect does this kind of ministry have on you?**

(3) **Read a book about the connection between faith and healing. Larry Dossey's books are thought-provoking and yet accessible to a layperson.**

❖ Sing or read aloud "O Christ, the Healer."

❖ Conclude today's session by leading the class in this benediction: **Give us new hearts filled with your Spirit, O Lord, that we may live as new creations in Christ. Amen.**

UNIT 3: THE WAY OF NEW LIFE

New Family in Christ

PREVIEWING THE LESSON

Lesson Scripture: Ephesians 1:3-14
Background Scripture: Ephesians 1:3-14
Key Verse: Ephesians 1:5

Focus of the Lesson:
Family life offers opportunities for rewards and challenges, for close ties and for estranged relationships. How do we see ourselves within the context of our families? In the Letter to the Ephesians, Paul celebrated and gave thanks for those whom God had adopted into a new family in Christ.

Goals for the Learners:
(1) to examine Paul's words of thanksgiving for the family of faith.
(2) to recognize their blessings and responsibilities as God's children.
(3) to make a commitment to live harmoniously with all God's children.

Supplies:
Bibles, newsprint and marker, paper and pencils, hymnals

READING THE SCRIPTURE

NRSV
Ephesians 1:3-14

³Blessed be the God and Father of our Lord Jesus Christ, who has blessed us in Christ with every spiritual blessing in the heavenly places, ⁴just as he chose us in Christ before the foundation of the world to be holy and blameless before him in love. **⁵He destined us for adoption as his children through Jesus Christ, according to the good pleasure of his will,** ⁶to the praise of his glorious grace that he freely bestowed on us in the Beloved. ⁷In him we have redemption

NIV
Ephesians 1:3-14

³Praise be to the God and Father of our Lord Jesus Christ, who has blessed us in the heavenly realms with every spiritual blessing in Christ. ⁴For he chose us in him before the creation of the world to be holy and blameless in his sight. In love **⁵he predestined us to be adopted as his sons through Jesus Christ, in accordance with his pleasure and will—**⁶to the praise of his glorious grace, which he has freely given us in the One he loves. ⁷In him we have redemption

through his blood, the forgiveness of our trespasses, according to the riches of his grace [8]that he lavished on us. With all wisdom and insight [9]he has made known to us the mystery of his will, according to his good pleasure that he set forth in Christ, [10]as a plan for the fullness of time, to gather up all things in him, things in heaven and things on earth. [11]In Christ we have also obtained an inheritance, having been destined according to the purpose of him who accomplishes all things according to his counsel and will, [12]so that we, who were the first to set our hope on Christ, might live for the praise of his glory. [13]In him you also, when you had heard the word of truth, the gospel of your salvation, and had believed in him, were marked with the seal of the promised Holy Spirit; [14]this is the pledge of our inheritance toward redemption as God's own people, to the praise of his glory.

through his blood, the forgiveness of sins, in accordance with the riches of God's grace [8]that he lavished on us with all wisdom and understanding. [9]And he made known to us the mystery of his will according to his good pleasure, which he purposed in Christ, [10]to be put into effect when the times will have reached their fulfillment—to bring all things in heaven and on earth together under one head, even Christ.

[11]In him we were also chosen, having been predestined according to the plan of him who works out everything in conformity with the purpose of his will, [12]in order that we, who were the first to hope in Christ, might be for the praise of his glory. [13]And you also were included in Christ when you heard the word of truth, the gospel of your salvation. Having believed, you were marked in him with a seal, the promised Holy Spirit, [14]who is a deposit guaranteeing our inheritance until the redemption of those who are God's possession—to the praise of his glory.

UNDERSTANDING THE SCRIPTURE

Introduction. In the first century there were three distinct types of letters, each with a specific style and vocabulary. Business letters, written for reasons of commerce, were characterized by formal greetings, clearly offered information, and a sincere closing. A second type of letter was exchanged between close friends; these letters contained recollections of past times and featured the exposition of ideas, especially ideas of ethical or religious content. Finally, chatty letters bound families together; these letters included the author's insight into issues in family and culture, but rarely rose to the level of expression characteristic of letters exchanged by friends. Letters exchanged by church leaders and congregations, some of which are included

in our New Testament, did not fit any established pattern of letter writing. Rather the Epistles, both pastoral and congregational, combined elements of all three types. Most New Testament letters began with formal praise of God and offered thanksgiving for the community of faith addressed. The Epistles featured theological and ethical issues, as well as directions on practical matters of Christian living. These letters broke previous patterns as the authors wrote from a perspective of faith to a community of faith. In discussing faith, both the formality of theological insight and the intimacy of community life should be carefully examined.

Ephesians 1:3-6. In Ephesians 1:3-14, words and phrases designed to remind the readers of the height, depth, length, and breadth of faith were lifted from the intimate and well-known vocabulary of worship. Ephesians opens with a blast of richly expressive but tersely compact liturgical language. In three verses (1:3-6), six theological ideas were referenced: Christology, spiritual gifts, election, righteousness, salvation, and perfection of God's will. In rapid succession these ideas were mentioned but not commented upon. By using the familiar language of worship the author introduced the letter's theological purpose: the community's obligation and opportunity to praise God.

Ephesians 1:7-10. Once the congregation caught the author's enthusiasm for God's graciousness, it was appropriate to list some of the many benefits of salvation. Again, images and ideas were strung together with little explanation, yet the audience received each phrase as familiar, precious, and worthy of contemplation. Rather than well-formed sentences presenting logical truth, the opening verses of Ephesians were designed to provoke a recollection of faith. Indeed, since verses 3-14 have no punctuation and are actually one long sentence in Greek, the audience was propelled forward. Along the way, the benefits of salvation were listed: redemption through Christ's blood, forgiveness of personal sins, and lavish grace seasoned with wisdom and insight. These ideas were linked with the actual experience of the audience in worship. Thus, the language of worship provoked a rich theological recollection.

For example, redemption brought to mind the freedom price of a slave, as well as the final righting of wrongs anticipated by Israel. Likewise, forgiveness of personal sins released believers to live boldly and faithfully. The concept of God's grace as freedom from the physical conditions of bondage was complemented by the liturgical release of guilt and the acceptance of Christ's forgiveness. Next, Christ's grace, as mediated in worship, inspired wisdom and

insight through the teaching ministry of the congregation. Finally came the mystery at the heart of creation/redemption and the fullness of time as Christ unified heaven and earth. Thus, in rapid succession, the author placed the personal benefits of God's redemption beside Christ's universal reconciliation. The theological import of all these words must have stunned the original audience. Still, the words flowed on.

Ephesians 1:11-12. Just as the previous verses balanced the personal and universal aspects of Jesus' saving work, so the next two verses balanced the future and present grace of his life, death, and resurrection. Using the code phrase "in Christ" to indicate the present experience of grace, the author linked the present to the future by the word "inheritance." Inheritance was a benefit that came to the living after the death of someone. In this case, believers put their trust "in Christ" and understood that all of life—physical, material, communal, and spiritual—was an inheritance secured by Jesus' death. Moreover, this inheritance was grounded in the eternal purposes of God. There was nothing accidental or temperamental about salvation in Christ. Indeed, it was an essential aspect of God's purpose in, with, and throughout creation. All the words of salvation—*reconciliation, redemption, adoption, cleansing, forgiveness,* and *predestination*—had a singular direction: Believers were to praise God throughout all life!

Ephesians 1:13-14. Finally came the pause. The author slowed down the rapid pace of theological language to focus on the audience individually. First came a sketch of the development of faith: the word was preached ("you had heard the word of truth"), the word became saving truth ("the gospel of your salvation"), salvation expanded into Christian belief ("had believed in him"), and finally was confirmed by the Holy Spirit ("the seal of the promised Holy Spirit"). This pattern was the dependable evangelism approach of the first century. Preaching led to salvation; salvation led to wisdom and understanding of Christ's way; Christian wisdom and understanding was confirmed by the testimony of the Holy Spirit.

The significance of salvation, however, had both a present and a future significance. In the present, those who heard, believed, matured, and were blessed by the Holy Spirit became members of God's own family. They were joined together into a spiritual community that displayed all the dynamics of a family. With God as the parent of all and Christ as the eldest son securing the standing of the siblings, the early believers accepted one another as equals in Christ. This new reality of a spiritual community foreshadowed a universal reconciliation yet to be completed by God. Indeed, the community of believers was a pledge toward the future when all creation would join in praise of God. Thus, the verses for this lesson's study form a single thought: The God who gathered and blessed the community in Christ intended to use that community to reconcile the whole creation.

INTERPRETING THE SCRIPTURE

The Blessing of New Life

The early church was a dynamic and experimental community. Each congregation grew out of a particular context and a specific demonstration of the gospel. As Jews and Gentiles heard the words of the first-century evangelists, preachers, prophets, and teachers, they stretched their previous religious experience to comprehend the amazing grace proclaimed by the followers of Jesus. Not every new community was a success. Some slipped into heresy by failing to mature in Christian teachings while others allowed bitter power struggles to quench the Holy Spirit. Despite the failures, many bands of Christians were faithful. They received the teachings of itinerant leaders, they practiced hospitality toward all, they confessed Jesus as their Lord and Savior, and they employed their material and spiritual gifts for the benefit of the poor. The corporate gathering for worship, praise, and prayer was the touchstone of their common life. Thus, the language of worship was a natural choice for the Letter to the Ephesians. Here is a simple way to "read" the densely packed first chapter of Ephesians. Take out a sheet of paper and list all the hymn titles you can think of that include the word "blessing." Now read the list out loud. Consider the impression formed by these hymn titles: Are you smiling, confused, bored? In a similar way, the opening verses of Ephesians are packed with the words and ideas regularly used in worship. As these words streamed by, the audience heard one idea: God blessed them with new life in Jesus. Therefore, as you study this densely packed passage, lighten up and hum hymns of blessings. The Letter to the Ephesians begins with a burst of blessings rather than a lecture. Allow the worship words of Ephesians 1:3-14 to sing blessings to you.

The Blessing of Salvation

Every Christian has two vocabularies of faith. The first vocabulary is intensely personal. It is the experiential side of salvation; this language is used to tell *your* story of God's grace. Some stories abound with suggestive adjectives or adverbs. For example, when John Wesley wrote that his heart was "strangely warmed," he implied but did not define his experience of salvation. Other stories point to specific divine interventions. For example, many people come to faith after an experience of healing or physical rescue. Some stories detail prayerful encounters with Jesus Christ. Other stories describe mystical moments beyond human language. All these experiences are personal. Some are, frankly, confusing while others are clearly Christ-focused.

Regardless of the personal experience of salvation or divine blessing, in the Christian community we share our faith by using a second vocabulary: the language of God's revelation as captured in Scripture. Scriptural language is broad: It recounts the history of the chosen people (the Torah and Histories); sings songs of worship and offers wise teaching (Psalms and the Writings); declares blunt judgments and offers gracious promises (the Prophets); describes the life, death, resurrection, and appearances of Jesus (from four distinct Gospels); attends to the corporate work of the Holy Spirit (Acts and the Epistles); and concludes with the heightened images of apocalyptic writing (Revelation to John). By such breadth the Bible offers a common language for describing the blessing of salvation. Through a careful weave of individual experience and the corporate story of faith, Christians fill words such as redemption, adoption, forgiveness, and grace with a double meaning. The blessing of salvation is twofold: It is *your* testimony and the testimony of Scripture.

The Blessing of Worship

In the early church everything happened at once! There were no discrete times for education, worship, new member orientation, private counseling, mission preparation, and long-range planning. There were no special programs for the education of children, youth, women, or leaders. There was not even a common worship book or approved format for congregational organization. Instead, everything happened at the weekly gathering for worship. Gradually, early congregations evolved to offer classes

for communicants, a particular pattern for worship, ministry organizational models, education for children and youth, and defined responsibilities for leaders (elders, deacons, pastors, teachers, and evangelists). But, no matter the breadth of the congregational organization, worship remained the central experience of the community.

This centrality of worship has persisted from the first-century church to the contemporary church. Contemporary Christians experience a particular closeness to God, the world, and one another in worship. As they worship, the community remembers and relives the megastory of God's redemption. By their worship, the community encounters and encourages particular members through the personal and corporate confession of sins, prayers for one another, and spiritual nourishment for the pilgrimage of faith. Worship inspires the community to dream great dreams, challenge common assumptions, create novel ministries, and expect spiritual empowerment. In worship, everything happens at once—and everything that happens becomes a reason to praise God.

The Blessing of God's Own People

Consider the blessings of this lesson. First, the blessing of new life begins as Christians recognize Christ as one who establishes a spiritual and loving relationship with God. Second, the blessing of salvation personally links the believer with the grand sweep of God's redemption. Next, the blessing of worship develops the new life of salvation. Finally, all three blessings—new life, salvation, and worship—are secured by the blessing of being a part of God's own people. These blessings begin with the "aha" that there is a whole new way to live and concludes with the sustaining practices that support a Christian lifestyle.

Christian communities survive because they have a sure and certain foundation on God's grace. Every congregation is a collection of people who "get it"—emotionally, intellectually, spiritually, and physically. Christians are people who, recognizing the new life offered in Christ, have been converted as his followers. Likewise, every congregation provides two essential supports for Christians. These are the last two blessings of today's study. The first is the blessing of worship and the second is the blessing of community. As already noted, without the weekly services of worship, Christianity would be reduced to an intellectual insight or a warm fuzzy emotional connection to God. Worship is essential because in worship something more than humanly possible happens. In worship the Holy Spirit sways the congregation.

But, worship—even the most inspired and inspiring worship—depends on the last blessing described in this lesson, the blessing of God's own people. To know this blessing is to live in the world with hope and freedom. Being a part of "God's own people" is more than a human membership in a particular congregation; it is a deep spiritual incorporation in God's redemptive plan for all creation. Christians recognize one another as family; they trace the image of Christ's face on the faces of believers, both those well-known and those unknown. This family identity implies a common purpose: to love the world as Christ loved the world. Thus, Christians are blessed with the experience of being "at home" in God's world. Wherever Christians go, they are members of God's own people. Whatever Christians do in the name of Christ, a great cloud of witnesses surround and support their ministry. Thus, comfort and boldness derive from and are sustained by this final blessing; being a part of God's own people provides both security and strength.

SHARING THE SCRIPTURE

Preparing Our Hearts

Meditate on this week's devotional reading, found in Exodus 19:1-8. Here at Mount Sinai God promises Moses that if the people will obey, then they will be God's "treasured possession out of all the peoples" (19:5). In essence, God is establishing the Israelites as God's own family, God's special people. As you think about the household of God, what images come to mind? How do you envision the church as the people of God? How do you see yourself as fitting into this spiritual family?

Pray that you and the adult learners will give thanks for the blessings they receive as members of the family of God.

Preparing Our Minds

Study the background and lesson Scripture, both found in Ephesians 1:3-14.

As you prepare, consider how you see yourself within the context of your family.

Write on newsprint:
❏ information for next week's lesson, found under "Continue the Journey."
❏ activities for further spiritual growth in "Continue the Journey."

LEADING THE CLASS

(1) Gather to Learn

❖ Welcome the class members and introduce any guests.

❖ Pray that all who have gathered today will experience the warmth of the family of God.

❖ Read these quotations and invite class members to comment on ones that for whatever reason ring true to them.

■ **A family is a unit composed not**

only of children, but of men, women, an occasional animal, and the common cold. (Ogden Nash, 1902–1971)

■ **A happy family is but an earlier heaven.** (Sir John Bowring, 1792–1872)

■ **Govern a small family as you would cook a small fish, very gently.** (Chinese proverb)

■ **If your father and mother, your sister and brother, if the very cat and dog in the house, are not happier for your being Christian, it is a question whether you really are.** (James Hudson Taylor, 1832–1905)

■ **It is impossible to overstate the need for prayer in the fabric of family life.** (James C. Dobson, 1936–)

■ **Nobody's family can hang out the sign Nothing the Matter Here.** (Chinese proverb)

■ **Nothing stops a family quarrel more quickly than the arrival of an unexpected guest.** (Anonymous)

❖ Read aloud today's focus statement: **Family life offers opportunities for rewards and challenges, for close ties and for estranged relationships. How do we see ourselves within the context of our families? In the Letter to the Ephesians, Paul celebrated and gave thanks for those whom God had adopted into a new family in Christ.**

(2) Examine Paul's Words of Thanksgiving for the Family of Faith

❖ Choose a volunteer to read Ephesians 1:3-14 expressively. Ask the students to imagine themselves as part of an early congregation as they hear these words.

❖ Discuss these three questions, which you will note relate to the headings in Interpreting the Scripture. Use information from the appropriate section of Interpreting the Scripture to augment the discussion.

    (1) In what ways is new life a blessing to you?

    (2) In what ways is salvation a blessing to you?

    (3) In what ways is worship a blessing to you?

(3) Recognize the Learners' Blessings and Responsibilities as God's Children

❖ Read these words of a hymn written in 1897 by Johnson Oatman, Jr. Some may know the tune, penned by Edwin Excell in 1897, and can lead others in singing this refrain.

> **Count your blessings, name them one by one,**
> **Count your blessings, see what God hath done!**
> **Count your blessings, name them one by one,**
> **And it will surprise you what the Lord hath done.**

❖ Post a sheet of newsprint. Go around the room and ask each person to add one blessing to the list. A fun way to do this activity is to start with "Mary," add her idea, and ask her to call out someone else's name. "John" volunteers his idea and then calls on "Fran." The list will likely include material and spiritual blessings and perhaps others that cannot be easily categorized.

❖ Invite the students to look at the sheet. Perhaps several people share similar blessings. Suggest that the class members discuss why these blessings that have been repeatedly named seem important to several people.

❖ Ask the learners to identify those blessings that are spiritual and put a check beside those. Note that in the lesson Paul speaks to us about spiritual blessings.

❖ Read these words from Luke 12:48, which conclude Jesus' parable of the faithful or unfaithful slave: **"From everyone to whom much has been given, much will be required; and from the one to whom much has been entrusted, even more will be demanded."**

❖ Discuss these questions with the entire class or in groups:

(1) **What do you think Jesus teaches us about being accountable for the blessings bestowed upon us?**

(2) **How does your church as a body practice this kind of accountability?**

(4) Make a Commitment to Live Harmoniously With All God's Children

❖ Invite the class to recall high points from their church's history. Consider how people pulled together, perhaps to achieve a goal such as erecting a new building or undertaking a major new ministry. Encourage those who were present to remember how they felt personally and how members of the congregation acted toward one another.

❖ Note that we don't continually live on the mountaintop; the newness of a special project or event fades, and sometimes we need to recommit ourselves to living harmoniously together.

❖ Distribute paper, pencils, and hymnals. Suggest that the students page through them to find hymns about their unity in Christ. (If you have *The United Methodist Hymnal*, pages 545-566 are devoted to this theme.) Ask them to choose one hymn that particularly speaks to them about this unity and jot down words or phrases from the hymn that grab their attention.

❖ Divide into small groups. Encourage the students to talk with one another about why the hymns they have selected are meaningful to them.

❖ Call the class together and challenge the adults to commit themselves to grace-filled living by recalling their hymn selection whenever discord seeks to threaten the harmony of Christ's body.

(5) Continue the Journey

❖ Pray that students will go forth with a renewed appreciation for the family life that they have in Christ.

❖ Read aloud this preparation for next week's lesson. You may also want to post it on newsprint for the students to copy.

■ **Title: New Life in Christ**

■ **Background Scripture: Ephesians 2:1-10**

■ **Lesson Scripture: Ephesians 2:1-10**

■ **Focus of the Lesson: Before we invest our time, our money, or ourselves, we want to be certain that our outlay will repay us well. How do we know that a potential investment will yield a good return? Paul claims that when we by faith invest our lives in Christ, we receive new life, the unparalleled benefit of God's love.**

❖ Challenge the students to complete one or more of these activities for further spiritual growth, which you will write on newsprint for the students to copy:

(1) **Interview someone this week who has been adopted. Inquire about the joys and challenges of becoming assimilated into a family not originally one's own. (If you were adopted, write about this topic in your spiritual journal.)**

(2) **Invite someone into a group in your church. Do whatever you can to make this person feel welcomed.**

(3) **Think about your own faith journey. Perhaps you have always felt connected to the family of God, but if you have not, compare your life prior to your entrance into the family with your life as a believer. What are the most important differences you note?**

❖ Sing or read aloud "Jesus, United by Thy Grace," or use "Family of God" by William and Gloria Gaither if you can locate it.

❖ Conclude today's session by leading the class in this benediction: **Give us new hearts filled with your Spirit, O Lord, that we may live as new creations in Christ. Amen.**

UNIT 3: THE WAY OF NEW LIFE
NEW LIFE IN CHRIST

PREVIEWING THE LESSON

Lesson Scripture: Ephesians 2:1-10
Background Scripture: Ephesians 2:1-10
Key Verse: Ephesians 2:8

Focus of the Lesson:

Before we invest our time, our money, or ourselves, we want to be certain that our outlay will repay us well. How do we know that a potential investment will yield a good return? Paul claims that when we by faith invest our lives in Christ, we receive new life, the unparalleled benefit of God's love.

Goals for the Learners:

(1) to investigate Paul's proclamation that we have moved from death to life by means of the gracious gift of God.
(2) to witness to their experiences of salvation by grace through faith.
(3) to give thanks for the bountiful benefits of God's gracious salvation.

Pronunciation Guide:

Aquila (ak' wi luh)

Supplies:

Bibles, newsprint and marker, paper and pencils, hymnals, optional Bible dictionaries

---

READING THE SCRIPTURE

NRSV
Ephesians 2:1-10

¹You were dead through the trespasses and sins ²in which you once lived, following the course of this world, following the ruler of the power of the air, the spirit that is now at work among those who are disobedient. ³All of us once lived among them in the passions of our flesh, following the desires of

NIV
Ephesians 2:1-10

¹As for you, you were dead in your transgressions and sins, ²in which you used to live when you followed the ways of this world and of the ruler of the kingdom of the air, the spirit who is now at work in those who are disobedient. ³All of us also lived among them at one time, gratifying the

MAY 10

flesh and senses, and we were by nature children of wrath, like everyone else. [4]But God, who is rich in mercy, out of the great love with which he loved us [5]even when we were dead through our trespasses, made us alive together with Christ—by grace you have been saved—[6]and raised us up with him and seated us with him in the heavenly places in Christ Jesus, [7]so that in the ages to come he might show the immeasurable riches of his grace in kindness toward us in Christ Jesus. **[8]For by grace you have been saved through faith, and this is not your own doing; it is the gift of God**—[9]not the result of works, so that no one may boast. [10]For we are what he has made us, created in Christ Jesus for good works, which God prepared beforehand to be our way of life.

cravings of our sinful nature and following its desires and thoughts. Like the rest, we were by nature objects of wrath. [4]But because of his great love for us, God, who is rich in mercy, [5]made us alive with Christ even when we were dead in transgressions—it is by grace you have been saved. [6]And God raised us up with Christ and seated us with him in the heavenly realms in Christ Jesus, [7]in order that in the coming ages he might show the incomparable riches of his grace, expressed in his kindness to us in Christ Jesus. **[8]For it is by grace you have been saved, through faith—and this not from yourselves, it is the gift of God**—[9]not by works, so that no one can boast. [10]For we are God's workmanship, created in Christ Jesus to do good works, which God prepared in advance for us to do.

UNDERSTANDING THE SCRIPTURE

Ephesians 2:1-3. Of all the congregations to whom Paul wrote, he was closest to the Ephesian congregation. He had labored there extensively with Priscilla and Aquila, preaching and teaching. Moreover, the congregation in Ephesus was a strong congregation. It was not divided by factional loyalties nor was it embroiled in disputes over morality, Christian conduct, or theology. Unlike other congregations that received pastoral letters, this congregation was a "model" congregation internally and externally.

There were, however, issues still to be addressed and chief among them was the meaning of "new life" in Christ. In the early church, the gift of new life in Christ was tested, over and over and over again, by the cultural distinctions between former Jews and Gentiles. Paul, like any first-century preacher and teacher, had to address the problems related to the different lifestyles and beliefs held by Jewish Christians and Gentile Christians.

In these verses, Paul appeared to be speaking to the Gentile believers. As he writes the opening words of this section, "You were dead through," his attention focused squarely on the Gentiles. He noted three characteristics from the past that are particular stumbling blocks for Gentile Christians. First, because they did not have the precious gift of God's law, they lived a lawless life characterized by sins and trespasses. Their primary guide for life came from their cultural setting. But there was something more dangerous than the cultural mix. The second stumbling block for Gentile Christians was astronomy. In the Hellenistic culture, astronomy was everywhere and used by everyone to understand everything. If there was illness, failure in business, or personal conflicts, a "reasonable answer" could be discovered by consulting the stars. (Astronomy and astrology were not seen as separate sciences at this time. What the people practiced is probably more akin to astrology.) According to Paul, astronomy was a dangerous and deceptive religion. Finally, the Gentile Christians were tempted by their own passions. This potential temptation touched the Jewish Christians as well. Paul's tone was gentle as he wrote, "all of us once lived . . . in the passions of our flesh."

Ephesians 2:4-7. Without a transition and, presumably, still addressing the Gentile Christians, Paul declared the great salvation offered to all Christians. His description of this salvation perfectly matched the needs of the Gentile Christians. First, with great love and mercy, God gave life to sinners who were dead in their sins and trespasses. This was the primary quality of Christian conversion: Believers got more than a second chance; they received a whole new life. With the new life came a new perspective on life in Christ: Believers were "raised up." Perhaps there was a hint of irony in Paul's words, for essentially he declared that Christians were able to see the world from a perspective greater than all the information gleaned by all the scholars and teachers of astronomy. The new perspective on life flowed from and reflected God's great mercy and love. Life was not controlled by the orderly or amazing patterns of planets, stars, sun, and moon. Rather, all life was under God's control. Christians were, by Christ's teachings, raised up to God. With Christ-like love and mercy, believers understood the world as the object of God's love and the subject of God's reconciling power. Still, there was more to the new life Paul described. Salvation in Christ meant that Christians shared in his exalted life. They were "seated" with Christ in the heavenly places. Paul's language was appropriate to his culture, but difficult for contemporary readers. This image of being raised up and seated with Christ offered a comprehensive sweep of salvation. Believers were not only rescued from their past but they also were given a whole new vantage point on life. Nevertheless, everything depended on a relationship with Christ.

Ephesians 2:8-9. Next, Paul turned to the source of all the benefits of salvation: new life, new perspective on creation, and new relationship with Christ. At this point, his words broadened to include all believers: both those who came to faith through their Jewish faith and those who were converted from a Gentile lifestyle. The words Paul penned are at the heart of his gospel preaching and teaching: "For by grace you have been saved through faith." As a result of his personal conversion and his intense immersion in Christian community Paul understood that salvation was first and foremost a spiritual gift from God. This gift could not be earned; it was, rather, received in faith. The God who was rich in mercy and abundant with love freely offered the faith (that is the capacity) by which believers received Christ's grace. Salvation was not related to the legal requirements of the law, an idea cherished by some Jewish Christians. Nor was salvation a matter of right thinking, a path proposed by some Gentile Christians. Rather, salvation was a matter of faith, and faith as grace was a gift from God. No one was able to "make believe" Christ's salvation; undoubtedly, such a belief fell short of the height, length, breadth, and depth of Christ's salvation as described by Paul.

Ephesians 2:10. With great awe, Paul's final words affirmed his own attitude toward Christ. After he declared the benefits, stated the source, and renounced all boasting, he proceeded to announce to his audience that their salvation was also purposeful. Paul wrote that all Christians were created—or, to be more exact, spiritually created—for "good works." The preciousness of each believer was determined by God's expectation that every believer contributed to the world's redemption. Christ's salvation moved over, in, with, and through the whole community of believers to call the world to praise God. Such was the Christian way of life. It was a way of life created, sustained, and blessed by Christ. Through God's gift of faith, each believer received a new life. By a steadfast relationship to Christ in the faith community, all believers matured in wisdom and in practice. With the amazing, yet tangible, shift of perspective, the Christian community beheld the world from God's own perspective. Thus, salvation developed from a personal to a corporate experience and from an individual to a universal perspective. Indeed, salvation bestowed on the believer, the faith community, and the whole world grace upon grace—until all joined in praise.

INTERPRETING THE SCRIPTURE

Saved From . . .

Paul's letter to the Ephesians may be read as a primer in spiritual direction. With profound spiritual insight and sensitivity, he addressed his friends' desires to mature in Christ. Rather than counseling the Ephesians regarding sins, signs of brokenness, or theological ignorance, Paul looked into the corporate soul of the congregation. He saw there the fissure lines that existed in the congregation. As he wrote, he carefully attended to the tender places where congregational strife or corporate grief might sidetrack their full maturity. Such careful observation and expression is worthy of our contemporary attention.

First, Paul addressed one of the subtle divisions in the congregation: the different cultural backgrounds between Gentile and Jewish converts. Beginning with words to the Gentiles, Paul listed what they already knew: the depths of sin, confusion, and forsakenness experienced by Gentiles prior to conversion. Paul did not belittle the Gentile converts, but he helped them remember the actual impact Christ had, was having, and would have on their lives.

Paul, however, did not write to one group only; he expanded his comments to include the Jewish converts. Although these converts had the precious gift of God's law, they also faced their human inclinations toward self-absorption. Indeed, Paul had been just that sort of Jew before his conversion. As a law-abiding Pharisee, Paul was proud of his religious accomplishments. However, Paul came to understand that the pride inspired by his rigorous obedience was "rubbish" (see Philippians 3:8). Using his own experience, in three brief verses, Paul disclosed the past sins, bondage, and distance from God experienced by both Jews and Gentiles. Then he announced: Christ saved everyone from a particular past.

Saved To . . .

Salvation, according to Paul, was more than a rescue; salvation was a new way of life. In order to express succinctly the forward motion of salvation, Paul stated that conversion not only rescued nonbelievers from a meaningless life but also replaced the past ways of living with new possibilities and perspectives. For example, those who were dead in their sins (Ephesians 2:1) were made alive in Christ (2:5). Likewise, those who were "following the course of this world" (2:2) were raised up with Christ (2:6) to a heavenly perspective. Finally, those who once were dominated by the passions of flesh and senses (2:3) now were seated with Christ in glory, sharing his authority over all creation and spiritual powers (2:6).

The impact of Paul's words must have been profound in the Ephesian congregation. Remember, everyone who entered that congregation came by a costly conversion. Gentiles gave up the respect of their community as they renounced the "power of the air" (2:2) and turned from astrology to Christ. Jewish converts broke with their spiritual community as they affirmed that Christ's love was greater than Torah. Everyone had a past; everyone knew that from which they were saved.

Paul, however, wanted all believers to know that salvation was more than a past-tense experience. Salvation brought the believers to a new way of living. As forgiven sinners, a free life opened before believers. Moreover, because they were maturing within a community focused upon Christ's teaching, their wisdom and vision expanded. And finally, through the spiritual experience of union with the risen Christ, believers recognized that the absolute authority in the world belonged to God. They were alive, they were learning, and they were liberated from all fears. Salvation brought believers to life—and was, literally, a new life in Christ.

Saved By . . .

In the opening section of this passage, Paul's words addressed the Gentile members directly and expanded in verse 3 to include both Jewish and Gentile converts. In the second section, Paul described the benefits of salvation as the new life provided to all believers. In the third section, verses 8 and 9, Paul's words pointed toward the Jewish converts. Underlying his affirmation of "by grace alone" was the pride of works righteousness. For generations, the Jewish people were taught the importance of full, rigorous, and constant obedience to the law. During the ministry of Jesus, the Pharisees often interrogated him regarding the law. Too often contemporary Christians fail to appreciate the passion of the Pharisees; they have become the punch line of preachers' jokes. However, rather than laughable, the Pharisees were models of faithfulness. Their diligence sprang from a heightened desire to make themselves (as individuals) and

their nation righteous. They invested everything—heart, mind, and soul—in the pursuit of right living.

Unfortunately, such effort, despite a commendable goal, easily made one judgmental toward others and fanatical toward self. Although the intent of the law was establishment of a peaceable community, the "doing side" of the law corrupted the divine gift. As the law became something to accomplish rather than an insight into God's ways, obedience became a personal effort, an accumulation of credits, and a weapon wielded against others. Contrary to the religious education of Paul, and of all his former religious allies, God did not offer salvation to those with long lists of righteous deeds nor to those with perfect attendance at Temple services. God gave salvation to those who responded in faith toward God's Chosen One, Jesus. "Salvation by grace through faith in Christ" was Paul's caution to believers prone to boast about their spiritual accomplishments.

Saved For . . .

In this brief passage, Paul demonstrated his gifts as a gospel teacher. He addressed the community as mature Christians, even as he hinted at their former sins and their current temptations. He spoke eloquently about the gift of salvation. However, if he had stopped writing at verse 9, the community might have fallen into one of the most persistently mistaken beliefs about salvation. Up to verse 9, salvation can be interpreted narrowly, as applying only to individuals or to specific communities of faith. But Paul did not stop there. In verse 10, Paul taught the gospel breadth of salvation. Just as no individual earned God's gift of salvation, so salvation was never intended for an individual. Salvation was God's way of redeeming creation. Thus, Paul taught that salvation initiated a qualitative rather than a quantitative change.

God was working through believers the

"good works" necessary for reconciliation. Surely, this was amazing good news to the early Christian community. They were few in numbers, yet God purposefully saved them for participation in the great and glorious work of restoring the world. They had neither social standing nor political power, yet they were invited to share in Christ's reign over all creation. They were rejected, belittled, excluded, and finally persecuted, yet through those whom God saved twenty-one centuries ago, your faith, your Scriptures, your church, and even your salvation was ensured. And why has God saved you? For the same reason: so that you could participate in God's great good work of salvation. According to Paul, salvation may begin as an individual experience, but, propelled by grace and growing in Christian maturity, salvation expands to embrace all of creation. Salvation is God's gracious choice of individuals and communities to become what they were created in Christ to be: those who do God's good work of restoration, redemption, and reconciliation.

SHARING THE SCRIPTURE

Preparing Our Hearts

Meditate on this week's devotional reading, found in Psalm 86:1-13. The psalmist prays for God to save him "in the day of [his] trouble" (86:7). The thrust of the psalm changes in verses 8-13 as the psalmist sings God's praises. In verse 13, the writer acknowledges God's love and the fact that God has delivered, or saved, his soul from Sheol. Christians, too, speak of salvation, though our understanding of it is different. If someone were to ask you to define "salvation" or explain that term, what would you say?

Pray that you and the adult learners will choose a new way of life in Christ.

Preparing Our Minds

Study the background and lesson Scripture, both taken from Ephesians 2:1-10. Think about how you invest your time and money and the criteria you use to determine whether your investment will yield a good return.

Write on newsprint:
❑ information for next week's lesson, found under "Continue the Journey."
❑ activities for further spiritual growth in "Continue the Journey."

Locate several Bible dictionaries. For "Investigate Paul's Proclamation That We Have Moved From Death to Life by Means of the Gracious Gift of God," you will be given the option to ask the students to work in groups to define the word "grace," or prepare a definition yourself to present in a brief lecture.

LEADING THE CLASS

(1) Gather to Learn

❖ Welcome the class members and introduce any guests.

❖ Pray that everyone who has come today will find new opportunities for discipleship in Christ.

❖ Distribute paper and pencils. Read this list of criteria and invite the students to respond using a three-point scale: 1 means "strongly agree"; 2 means "neutral, or do not care"; 3 means "strongly disagree."

(A) When I am deciding whether or not to take on a volunteer responsibility, I think about how

this experience might help me in my regular job.

(B) When asked to use my time for a church or charitable cause, I want to know what effect my work could potentially have on people.

(C) When I have money to invest, I check carefully to see how well a particular investment has performed in the past.

(D) When invited to volunteer, I try to be sure that the job I am being asked to do will use the best talents I have to offer.

(E) I am often persuaded to take on a job or donate money, even if I'm not interested in the job or do not feel my money is being well spent.

❖ Spend a few moments asking the students to share their answers to each question. Encourage them to state why they chose the answer they selected.

❖ Read aloud today's focus statement: **Before we invest our time, our money, or ourselves, we want to be certain that our outlay will repay us well. How do we know that a potential investment will yield a good return? Paul claims that when we by faith invest our lives in Christ, we receive new life, the unparalleled benefit of God's love.**

(2) Investigate Paul's Proclamation That We Have Moved From Death to Life by Means of the Gracious Gift of God

❖ Select a volunteer to read Ephesians 2:1-10.

❖ Encourage the students to look at the passage and identify characteristics of one who is "dead." List these traits on the left side of a sheet of newsprint. Then ask them to identify the characteristics of one who is "alive." List these traits on the right side of the sheet of newsprint. The sections in Interpreting the Scripture entitled "Saved

From . . ." and "Saved To . . ." will be helpful for this discussion.

❖ Help the class define "grace" by doing one of these activities:

■ **Option 1:** Present a brief lecture on the meaning of "grace."

■ **Option 2:** Divide the students into groups. Distribute Bible dictionaries, paper, and pencils. Ask the students to research the concept of "grace." Provide time for them to report back to the class.

❖ Conclude this portion of the lesson by inviting the students to read today's key verse, Ephesians 2:8, in unison.

(3) Witness to the Learners' Experiences of Salvation by Grace Through Faith

❖ Point out that different people have different experiences of salvation. Some come to faith gradually after a long process of prayer, reflection, and being immersed in a family or group of Christians. Others have an immediate conversion experience when they, at a certain time and place, know that they have been saved. Make sure the class members understand that there is no "correct" way; God calls us as God will.

❖ Suggest that a pattern of salvation, whether over time or immediately, often involves these verbs: *hear, believe, repent, confess, be baptized.*

❖ Encourage the adults to talk with the class as a whole or a small group about their own experiences as they came to salvation. Some may want to choose just one of the verbs previously mentioned and talk about how they heard the word, for example, or why they chose to believe.

❖ **Option:** Read these words from the journal of John Wesley, the founder of Methodism, written on May 24, 1738: **"In the evening I went unwillingly to a society in Aldersgate Street, where one was reading Luther and preface to the Epistle to the Romans. About a quarter to nine, while he** was describing the change which God works in the heart through faith in Christ, I felt my heart strangely warmed. I felt I did trust in Christ, Christ alone for salvation, and an assurance was given me that he had taken away my sins, even mine and saved me from the law of sin and death." Invite the students to recount their own experiences of being assured of God's salvation, which may or may not be anything like Wesley's experience.

(4) Give Thanks for the Bountiful Benefits of God's Gracious Salvation

❖ Ask the students to turn in their Bibles to Psalm 103 and read it silently. Note the benefits listed there (*forgives, heals, redeems, crowns, satisfies, renewed youth, works vindication and justice*).

❖ Provide time for them to meditate on this psalm and consider how the benefits listed here relate to the salvation they experience in Christ.

❖ Break the silence and invite volunteers to reflect aloud on any insights they gleaned as they meditated.

(5) Continue the Journey

❖ Pray that as the students go forth they will give thanks for God's saving grace.

❖ Read aloud this preparation for next week's lesson. You may also want to post it on newsprint for the students to copy.
- ■ **Title: New Revelation in Christ**
- ■ **Background Scripture: Ephesians 3:1-13**
- ■ **Lesson Scripture: Ephesians 3:1-13**

■ **Focus of the Lesson: Mysteries pique interest because most people want to uncover "the rest of the story." What mysteries would we like to have uncovered? New Testament apostles believed that the revelation of Jesus unlocks mysteries concerning God's eternal and all-inclusive plan for salvation.**

❖ Challenge the students to complete one or more of these activities for further spiritual growth, which you will write on newsprint for the students to copy:
1. **Write a psalm or offer a prayer in which you praise God for new life in Christ.**
2. **Talk with someone else about the benefits you have experienced as a result of new life in Christ. Encourage this person to consider such benefits in his or her own life.**
3. **Think about your life before you made a serious commitment to Christ. Contrast the way you lived then to the way you live now. What differences do you note?**

❖ Sing or read aloud "Let Us Plead for Faith Alone," which is based on Ephesians 2:8-10.

❖ Conclude today's session by leading the class in this benediction: **Give us new hearts filled with your Spirit, O Lord, that we may live as new creations in Christ. Amen.**

UNIT 3: THE WAY OF NEW LIFE

NEW REVELATION IN CHRIST

PREVIEWING THE LESSON

Lesson Scripture: Ephesians 3:1-13
Background Scripture: Ephesians 3:1-13
Key Verses: Ephesians 3:8-9

Focus of the Lesson:

Mysteries pique interest because most people want to uncover "the rest of the story." What mysteries would we like to have uncovered? New Testament apostles believed that the revelation of Jesus unlocks mysteries concerning God's eternal and all-inclusive plan for salvation.

Goals for the Learners:

(1) to discern Paul's understanding of the role that God's revelation in Jesus plays in salvation history.
(2) to acknowledge and appreciate the revelation of Jesus to the world.
(3) to make Jesus known to others outside their comfort zone.

Supplies:

Bibles, newsprint and marker, paper and pencils, hymnals

READING THE SCRIPTURE

NRSV
Ephesians 3:1-13

¹This is the reason that I Paul am a prisoner for Christ Jesus for the sake of you Gentiles—²for surely you have already heard of the commission of God's grace that was given me for you, ³and how the mystery was made known to me by revelation, as I wrote above in a few words, ⁴a reading of which will enable you to perceive my understanding of the mystery of Christ. ⁵In former generations this mystery was not made known to humankind, as it has now been

NIV
Ephesians 3:1-13

¹For this reason I, Paul, the prisoner of Christ Jesus for the sake of you Gentiles—

²Surely you have heard about the administration of God's grace that was given to me for you, ³that is, the mystery made known to me by revelation, as I have already written briefly. ⁴In reading this, then, you will be able to understand my insight into the mystery of Christ, ⁵which was not made known to men in other generations as it has now been revealed by the Spirit to God's holy

revealed to his holy apostles and prophets by the Spirit: [6]that is, the Gentiles have become fellow heirs, members of the same body, and sharers in the promise in Christ Jesus through the gospel.

[7]Of this gospel I have become a servant according to the gift of God's grace that was given me by the working of his power. [8]Although I am the very least of all the saints, this **grace was given to me to bring to the Gentiles the news of the boundless riches of Christ, [9]and to make everyone see what is the plan of the mystery hidden for ages in God who created all things;** [10]so that through the church the wisdom of God in its rich variety might now be made known to the rulers and authorities in the heavenly places. [11]This was in accordance with the eternal purpose that he has carried out in Christ Jesus our Lord, [12]in whom we have access to God in boldness and confidence through faith in him. [13]I pray therefore that you may not lose heart over my sufferings for you; they are your glory.

apostles and prophets. [6]This mystery is that through the gospel the Gentiles are heirs together with Israel, members together of one body, and sharers together in the promise in Christ Jesus.

[7]I became a servant of this gospel by the gift of God's grace given me through the working of his power. [8]Although I am less than the least of all God's people, this **grace was given me: to preach to the Gentiles the unsearchable riches of Christ, [9]and to make plain to everyone the administration of this mystery, which for ages past was kept hidden in God, who created all things.** [10]His intent was that now, through the church, the manifold wisdom of God should be made known to the rulers and authorities in the heavenly realms, [11]according to his eternal purpose which he accomplished in Christ Jesus our Lord. [12]In him and through faith in him we may approach God with freedom and confidence. [13]I ask you, therefore, not to be discouraged because of my sufferings for you, which are your glory.

UNDERSTANDING THE SCRIPTURE

Ephesians 3:1-4. The first phrase of chapter 3, "This is the reason" was written to connect the theme of the previous chapter with Paul's life experiences. In Chapter 2:11-22, Paul described with polished eloquence the incorporation of Gentile believers into the church. However, it was surely neither a polished nor an eloquent experience that actually brought about such unity. Paul realized that his audience, although externally united as a community of believers, still carried ancient prejudices and suspicions. Neither Jews nor Gentiles were completely at ease with their unity in Christ. The Jewish Christian converts, however, experienced the most discomfort. Thus, Paul called the audience to attention by the shocking affirmation that his imprisonment was the direct

result of his ministry "for the sake of you Gentiles." Imagine those words received by a mixed congregation. The Jewish converts were shocked that Paul attributed his imprisonment not to hostile authorities but to his faithful conduct of ministry. The Gentile converts were stunned that they were the cause of Paul's imprisonment. Rhetorically, the opening sentence worked perfectly: The whole audience paid close attention to the most difficult (and rarely discussed) issue among them. Into this attentive audience, Paul poured a brief account of his ministry. He stated that his commission, given by God's grace, to preach to the Gentiles was received by a revelation. Paul did not dream up the mission to the Gentiles or the shocking proposition that Gentile believers were equal partners with Jewish converts. Indeed, a man formed in the crucible of educated Jews and having the privilege of Roman citizenship could not have imagined such a calling.

Ephesians 3:5-6. Next Paul began to disclose the mystery of the gospel. This mystery was not a "new" revelation; however, it was a revelation that waited for the proper time. Just as Jesus began his ministry with the phrase, "the kingdom of God is at hand" (Mark 1:15 KJV), so Paul understood the revelation of God's mysterious plan as being accorded to a divinely appointed time. Although ancient prophetic words approached the mystery of unity, that mystery was not fully revealed to the prophets. However, with the gift of Jesus—in his life, ministry, death, and resurrection—a glimpse of God's mystery was offered to humanity. Then, by the inspiration of the Holy Spirit, that mystery was fully revealed to "holy apostles and prophets." Notice how carefully Paul led the audience. He began with a shocking first verse; he presented his credentials (2-4); then he boldly announced that in God's own time and to God's commissioned apostles and prophets, the fullness of truth was revealed. Then, he simply stated the mystery: Gentiles are heirs, members, and sharers in the gospel of Christ Jesus. Although brief and almost mundane, this mystery Paul disclosed was a revelation as old as creation. Indeed, God's redemptive purposes were always a part of creation. Just as God separated the light from darkness, God reconciled these opposites by naming one day and the other night. These two separate entities belonged together: God united daytime and nighttime into a single unit of time, a whole day. In a similar manner, God intended all humanity to be united as a distinct entity, namely the church.

Ephesians 3:7-9. The unity of Jews and Gentiles in Christ's body, that is the church, was Paul's particular share in God's reconciliation of creation. Because of this min-

istry, he labored as a missionary throughout the Roman Empire. His preaching and teaching won converts from Jewish and Gentile communities and created new congregations composed of former strangers and enemies. His ministry overflowed in letters that addressed young congregations of believers. Paul's ministry also brought him face-to-face with the political power of Rome and eventually landed him in a prison cell. His work was the most carefully documented and significant ministry of the first century. Yet, despite these many contributions and successes, Paul steadfastly understood that God, and God alone, gifted and empowered his ministry. Although his phrase in verse 8, "I am the very least of all the saints," may sound like false modesty to contemporary ears, this was a common rhetorical technique to point out the source of an author's authority or power. Just as the revelation of the unity of Gentile and Jew in the spiritual body of Christ came to Paul from God, so did the physical, emotional, intellectual, and spiritual power to conduct this ministry.

Ephesians 3:10-13. The final three verses of our passage are a grand declaration of the purpose of the church. First, the church witnessed to the wisdom of God by its rich variety. In the early Christian community, boundary lines that previously separated humanity were bridged. Not only did Jew and Gentile worship side-by-side but also so did males and females, slaves and owners, widows and Roman citizens, those privileged with education and those condemned to live as outcasts. Indeed, most early congregations exhibited such diversity that they became the topic of gossip. Yet this rich diversity revealed the mystery of unity in Christ to the world. Still, the impact of the church's witness was greater than neighbors and local communities. Paul affirmed that their witness revealed God's purpose to spiritual powers and authorities. This claim may be obscure to contemporary readers; our world is not as cosmologically complex as was the world of the first-century believer. However, contemporary believers do recognize the force of evil in the world. With Paul and the earliest Christians, contemporary believers also affirm that Christ's power is greater than any other force in creation—be the force political, material, physical, psychological, or spiritual. As believers understood the breadth of their witness, they also recognized the wondrous way of God's redemp-

tion. God used what was small and insignificant in the world to redeem the world. God empowered socially marginalized communities of believers to preach and to live the gospel of Jesus Christ. God even welcomed prayers and strengthened believers in boldness. Because of all this, even when "all this" included sufferings, Paul reminded the church in Ephesus not to lose heart, for in Christ they were united, secure, and clothed in glory.

INTERPRETING THE SCRIPTURE

A New Commission

Are you a credential checker? I confess that I am. I like knowing a person's background, education, and life experiences. Although I generally approach people with a welcoming acceptance, when I am dealing with people in authority, something in me wants to check them out. I assume most people ask these same questions, so when I find myself in a new position or community I introduce myself with my credentials (see the introductions of the authors in this book!).

Among the early Christians establishing credentials was not easy. As long as the first disciples were alive they were granted authority by their status as "apostles." An apostle was an individual sent by Jesus to preach, teach, and make disciples. Most of the apostles were Jesus' disciples during his ministry. Paul, however, was granted the title of apostle through his personal encounter with the risen Lord (see Acts 9).

In addition to apostles, the early Christians welcomed itinerant preachers and teachers into their homes and congregations. Usually, two "tests" helped the community to decide whether these guests were truly sent by Christ. The first test was to judge the message against the community's understanding of Jesus' teaching. The

second test concerned the spiritual power of the teacher. Early Christian communities were charismatic; they expected evidence of spiritual charisma in each and every leader. Passionate commitment to the gospel and bold proclamation indicated a spiritual gift, as did the demonstration of "signs and wonders" or ecstatic speech with interpretation. Authority was also "tested" informally as a congregation considered a teacher's reputation and the accomplishments or risks encountered in gospel work. With no seminary credentials, standards for ordination, or church personnel files, early congregations exercised their judgment carefully. Thus, when a preacher with obvious spiritual gifts who was sound of teaching and respected among the greater church community explained that his "commission" to preach was a mysterious gift from God, the congregation accepted his word. Paul deferred to mystery as one of his credentials; his ministry was a new commission from God.

A New Revelation

Imagine the most tiresome difficulty facing your congregation. Is it an aging or an ethnically shifting congregation? Is your church marginalized by the community or even by your larger church structure?

Perhaps your congregation is saddled with an old facility constantly in need of repairs, or perhaps there are voices within your congregation recommending relocation. Does your congregation long for the "good old days" or dream of a "what if" future?

In most early congregations the difficulty that would not go away was the relationship between converted Jews and Gentiles. Early Christians understood, theologically, the inclusion of Gentiles within previously "Jewish only" communities. However, when this theological reality took on flesh and blood—when members had to rub shoulders and share meals with each other—the ancient tensions and prejudices arose. It was into this hidden and unmentionable congregational issue that Paul poured out the gospel mystery of his commission. It was dramatically brief: The Gentiles are fellow heirs, members and sharers in Jesus Christ. This verse, Ephesians 3:6, is the heart of Paul's letter. Everything that preceded and every word that followed assumed this mysterious foundation. Imagine the impression on the congregation: The issue they wished would just go away was the precise point of the gospel.

Contemporary congregations need such dramatic calls to attention. Could it be that your aging congregation is precisely the congregation that reveals Christ to the world? Could it be that the shifting ethnicity of your community is a gospel call for outreach and unity? Could it be that old building is to be loved to wholeness even as the congregation rejoices in the gift of a place from which to provide hospitality? Could the status of marginalized be a reminder that the gospel came first to the disaffected, the weak, the marginalized, and the poor? Could it be that God's mysterious desire for unity is always discovered in the persistent and tiresome difficulties in congregational life? This was the mystery given to Paul. This was the mystery declared to the Ephesians: God desires Christ's unity in your current situation. Imagine.

A New Boldness

If the Ephesians were to live their unity in Christ, Paul had to encourage them in an extraordinary manner. Thus he shifted from poetic language (Ephesians 3:5-6) to personal testimony. Paul presented his ministry as a gift and a power given by God. Indeed, he considered himself "the very least of all the saints" (3:8) and yet God gave him a huge commission. That commission included: (1) revealing God's mysterious plan of reuniting creation, (2) preaching the good news of the gospel to the Gentiles, and (3) nurturing the church to a wise self-understanding.

The breadth of Paul's insight into his call was stunning. A commission to reveal "the plan of the mystery hidden for ages" (3:9) was magnificent. It would have been daunting (not to mention dangerous) to preach the gospel to the dominant culture, the Gentiles. Surely bringing small congregations into awareness of their ultimate significance to God was a lifelong task. But, combining all three seemed beyond any single human, which indeed it was! Paul understood the poverty of his wisdom, leadership, and rhetoric. Yet, Paul also knew his commission was a portion from God's eternal purpose. Because Paul accepted his importance to God, understood Jesus' loving care, and trusted in the Holy Spirit's empowerment, Paul stepped out in faith. He was faithful (exhibiting a complete trust in Jesus), confident (a mental attitude based on a sound grasp of the gospel), and bold (a spiritual capacity founded on constant prayer). By his own life story, Paul displayed to the congregation in Ephesus exactly what God called them to be: a faithful, wise, and bold witness to Jesus Christ.

A New Heart

Because Paul was first and foremost a pastor, he was compassionate toward the members of the congregations he visited, founded, and guided. Because Paul was first and foremost a pastor, he also cherished high hopes for what God in Jesus Christ could accomplish within and through congregations. Thus, Paul approached congregations with compassionate hope. He, as a servant of Jesus, sympathized with their situations, challenges, and weaknesses. He, as one commissioned to preach the gospel, exhorted congregations to mature in wisdom and understanding, to confess and seek forgiveness, and to witness with boldness to Jesus Christ.

In the last verse of the passage we are studying, verse 13, Paul offered tender words to the Ephesians. These words whisper Paul's constant theme in prayer: that congregations be given new hearts sufficient to their witness. The greatest danger for early Christian communities was not heresy, although false teachers plagued Christian communities. Nor were the greatest dangers moral and ethical failures, although temptations and sins were persistent and damaging. The greatest danger in the earliest Christian community was a failure of courage—and courage was a condition of the heart. Thus, Paul tenderly prayed that the Ephesians not lose heart when they learned of his sufferings and when they themselves were suffering. Rather, Paul offered them something tangible: a glimpse of their own glory. Everything—the challenges of congregational life shared by Jews and Gentiles, the marginalized status of the congregation, the mysterious call of the gospel and the likelihood of suffering—everything leads to glory. The glimpse of glory Paul offered to the Ephesians was nothing more or less than salvation in Christ.

SHARING THE SCRIPTURE

Preparing Our Hearts

Meditate on this week's devotional reading, found in Isaiah 40:1-11. Writing to the people who are in exile, the prophet speaks words of peace and comfort. Isaiah proclaims that after the highway has been prepared for the exiles to return home, "the glory of the LORD shall be revealed, / and all people shall see it together" (40:5). "All people" are included in this revelation. Imagine yourself as a Jewish exile in Babylon. How would you have responded had you heard that not just your own chosen people but everyone will be able to know God?

Pray that you and the adult learners will be open to diverse people who may relate to and worship God differently than you do.

Preparing Our Minds

Study the background and lesson Scripture, both from Ephesians 3:1-13.

Consider this question: What mysteries would we like to have uncovered?

Write on newsprint:
❏ information for next week's lesson, found under "Continue the Journey."
❏ activities for further spiritual growth in "Continue the Journey."

Familiarize yourself with the information in Understanding the Scripture in order to lead a discussion or present a lecture for "Discern Paul's Understanding of the Role That God's Revelation in Jesus Plays in Salvation History."

LEADING THE CLASS

(1) Gather to Learn

❖ Welcome the class members and introduce any guests.
❖ Pray that all who have come today will be ready to explore the mystery of new revelation in Christ.

❖ Invite the students to name mystery writers, book titles, or characters that they enjoy reading about. Also encourage them to speak about nonfiction mysteries that are of interest, such as what happened to a particular lost civilization.

❖ Ask: **Why do so many of us find mysteries, both real and fictional, appealing?**

❖ Read aloud today's focus statement: **Mysteries pique interest because most people want to uncover "the rest of the story." What mysteries would we like to have uncovered? New Testament apostles believed that the revelation of Jesus unlocks mysteries concerning God's eternal and all-inclusive plan for salvation.**

(2) Discern Paul's Understanding of the Role That God's Revelation in Jesus Plays in Salvation History

❖ Choose a volunteer to read Ephesians 3:1-13 as the adults follow along in their Bibles. (Do not be concerned if not everyone is using the same translation.)

❖ Start at verse 1 to do a careful analysis of this passage. Use information from Understanding the Scripture to help you present this as a lecture or as additional information for a class discussion. Here are three words to highlight:

- *Mystery:* The first part of the mystery, Paul reveals, is that the Gentiles are included among God's people. They, as part of one body, share in the promise of Jesus; they are part of the plan of salvation. The second part of the mystery is that the church is charged with the responsibility of announcing to all people that they are included in the household of God.
- *Grace:* Invite the students to recall the definitions or descriptions of grace they discussed last week.
- *Revelation:* Note that God, through the work of the Holy Spirit, makes known mystery to apostles and prophets. Paul is one to whom mystery has been revealed, and he, in turn, is to share what he knows with others, especially Gentiles.

(3) Acknowledge and Appreciate the Revelation of Jesus to the World

❖ Invite two or three pairs of students to enact this scene, which you will need to read aloud. The rest of the class will witness these two or three conversations. **A co-worker who has no relationship to the church or Christ joins you for lunch. This person is seeking "something more" in life. The conversation turns to religion and you feel led to speak to this person about who Jesus is and why he came. Your co-worker may resist, so you need to make clear that Jesus has come for everyone.**

❖ Debrief each conversation by asking the class to consider these questions:

(1) **Had you been the "seeker," would the Christian's comments have motivated you to at least find out more? Why or why not?**

(2) **Had you been the one who was speaking to the "seeker" what other points would you have made? Why do you feel these are important?**

❖ Provide time for those who did not participate as role-players to say why the revelation of God in Jesus is so important to their own lives.

(4) Make Jesus Known to Others Outside the Learners' Comfort Zone

❖ Read or retell "A New Revelation" from Interpreting the Scriptures. Note the challenges suggested in the first paragraph. Encourage the students to name challenges that their own congregation faces and list these ideas on newsprint.

❖ See if the group can identify "a difficulty that won't go away" in your own setting. Look at the geographic location and demographics of your congregation, for example. Have you become a "commuter" church because the population around the church is changing? Are you a "rural" church in what was once farmland but now is sprawling housing developments?

❖ Challenge the class to develop a plan that they could implement on their own, or present to the congregation, which would enable the congregation to reach out to people in the community who may not be "like us." Think, for example, about how the middle-class commuters might reach out to disenfranchised urban youth around the church campus.

❖ **Option:** Assign one or more class members the task of developing the plan and presenting it to the appropriate committee in your congregation for approval and action.

(5) Continue the Journey

❖ Pray that all who have participated today will appreciate the new way of life that they have in Christ and will invite others to experience this gracious salvation for themselves.

❖ Read aloud this preparation for next week's lesson. You may also want to post it on newsprint for the students to copy.

■ **Title: New Life in the Home**
■ **Background Scripture: Ephesians 5:1–6:4**
■ **Lesson Scripture: Ephesians 5:21–6:4**
■ **Focus of the Lesson: Family life is often disrupted by internal conflict. How can families learn to live together in harmony? In Ephesians, Paul urges believers to** serve one another in the home in the name and Spirit of Christ.

❖ Challenge the students to complete one or more of these activities for further spiritual growth, which you will write on newsprint for the students to copy:

(1) **Think about how your congregation welcomes people. Are there changes that need to be made so that everyone knows he or she is included? If so, what steps can you take to help make those changes?**

(2) **Research congregations in your area. Plan to visit one that has a diverse congregation in terms of race, ethnicity, language, and age. What lessons can you learn from such a congregation? (If you cannot find such a church in your area, search the Internet for diverse congregations or contact your denominational office in your area.)**

(3) **Participate in some kind of ecumenical event. This could be a worship service, but it might be a community project, such as building a Habitat for Humanity house. What insights do you gain about Christ's inclusion of all people as you gather with others whose worship style or beliefs may not be the same as yours, but who all claim the name of Christ?**

❖ Sing or read aloud "Spirit of Faith, Come Down."

❖ Conclude today's session by leading the class in this benediction: **Give us new hearts filled with your Spirit, O Lord, that we may live as new creations in Christ. Amen.**

UNIT 3: THE WAY OF NEW LIFE
NEW LIFE IN THE HOME

PREVIEWING THE LESSON

Lesson Scripture: Ephesians 5:21–6:4
Background Scripture: Ephesians 5:1–6:4
Key Verse: Ephesians 5:21

Focus of the Lesson:

Family life is often disrupted by internal conflict. How can families learn to live together in harmony? In Ephesians, Paul urges believers to serve one another in the home in the name and Spirit of Christ.

Goals for the Learners:

(1) to examine Paul's teaching about life in the Christian household.
(2) to explore the meaning of being subject to others in the family.
(3) to work toward healing conflict in their homes and families.

Supplies:

Bibles, newsprint and marker, paper and pencils, hymnals

READING THE SCRIPTURE

NRSV
Ephesians 5:21-33

21Be subject to one another out of reverence for Christ.

22Wives, be subject to your husbands as you are to the Lord. 23For the husband is the head of the wife just as Christ is the head of the church, the body of which he is the Savior. 24Just as the church is subject to Christ, so also wives ought to be, in everything, to their husbands.

25Husbands, love your wives, just as Christ loved the church and gave himself up for her, 26in order to make her holy by cleansing her with the washing of water by

NIV
Ephesians 5:21-33

21Submit to one another out of reverence for Christ.

22Wives, submit to your husbands as to the Lord. 23For the husband is the head of the wife as Christ is the head of the church, his body, of which he is the Savior. 24Now as the church submits to Christ, so also wives should submit to their husbands in everything.

25Husbands, love your wives, just as Christ loved the church and gave himself up for her 26to make her holy, cleansing her by the washing with water through the word, the word, ²⁷so as to present the church to himself in splendor, without a spot or wrinkle or anything of the kind—yes, so that she may be holy and without blemish. ²⁸In the same way, husbands should love their wives as they do their own bodies. He who loves his wife loves himself. ²⁹For no one ever hates his own body, but he nourishes and tenderly cares for it, just as Christ does for the church, ³⁰because we are members of his body. ³¹"For this reason a man will leave his father and mother and be joined to his wife, and the two will become one flesh." ³²This is a great mystery, and I am applying it to Christ and the church. ³³Each of you, however, should love his wife as himself, and a wife should respect her husband.

Ephesians 6:1-4

¹Children, obey your parents in the Lord, for this is right. ²"Honor your father and mother"—this is the first commandment with a promise: ³"so that it may be well with you and you may live long on the earth."

⁴And, fathers, do not provoke your children to anger, but bring them up in the discipline and instruction of the Lord.

²⁷and to present her to himself as a radiant church, without stain or wrinkle or any other blemish, but holy and blameless. ²⁸In this same way, husbands ought to love their wives as their own bodies. He who loves his wife loves himself. ²⁹After all, no one ever hated his own body, but he feeds and cares for it, just as Christ does the church—³⁰for we are members of his body. ³¹"For this reason a man will leave his father and mother and be united to his wife, and the two will become one flesh." ³²This is a profound mystery—but I am talking about Christ and the church. ³³However, each one of you also must love his wife as he loves himself, and the wife must respect her husband.

Ephesians 6:1-4

¹Children, obey your parents in the Lord, for this is right. ²"Honor your father and mother"—which is the first commandment with a promise—³"that it may go well with you and that you may enjoy long life on the earth."

⁴Fathers, do not exasperate your children; instead, bring them up in the training and instruction of the Lord.

UNDERSTANDING THE SCRIPTURE

Ephesians 5:1-14. The material presented in today's text rests upon the last verse of chapter 4: "and be kind to one another, tenderhearted, forgiving one another, as God in Christ has forgiven you." These words frame the ethical teachings of Chapters 5 and 6. First, the tenderness and familial closeness experienced from God was to be shared among believers. Second, the community's love was to evidence Christ's self-giving and pure love. Thus, the forceful ethical instructions were wrapped in tenderness, forgiveness, purity, and love. The first set of prohibited activities was drawn from the excesses of the Hellenistic culture.

Fornication, for example, implied a variety of illicit activities prevalent in Roman culture ranging from adultery to child prostitution. Added to these were the more general sins of greed and vulgar talk that obviously stood in opposition to a Christ-like lifestyle. The final warning concerned the Christian's responsibility to stay away from people and practices able to diminish Christ's light in the world. Paul encouraged the congregation members to expose such "works of darkness." The goal of the Christian community was to shine Christ's light as individuals, throughout the church, and for the benefit of the larger community.

Ephesians 5:15-20. After the list of prohibitions, an admonishment set a new tone: "Be careful." Christians were to become wise, mature, and effective testimonies to Christ. Such maturity was required because the congregation lived within a culture alienated from God's way, word, and wisdom. Their cultural context was neither easy nor neutral. In fact, within a few decades Christians would experience prejudice and economic boycott, as well as blame for social unrest and persecution as enemies of the state. With great insight, Paul pointed the congregation toward a sure and certain resource: communal worship. In verses 16-20, ethical cautions are followed by positive recommendations grounded in congregational worship. Instead of continuing in ignorance or foolish thinking, Christians sought to understand the will of the Lord. Rather than getting drunk for the sake of being drunk, in worship Christians experienced the fullness of the Holy Spirit. Finally, as Christians worshiped by singing psalms, hymns, and spiritual songs, they sang from their hearts. Remember the conclusion of the last lesson, 3:13? In that passage, Paul prayed that the congregation not lose heart but persist in bold and confident prayer. Here, as spiritual music lifted worship from mundane to sacred, Paul commanded the congregation to sing their bold and confident prayers. Communal worship offered wise instruction for the ignorant, spiritual power to the weak, and emboldened hearts to the whole congregation. But most of all in worship, the church fulfilled the calling of all creation: ceaseless praise of God in Christ's name.

Ephesians 5:21. Paul's purpose in writing to the Ephesians was to nurture the Christian community in Christ-like love. He used an emphasis on worship to encourage the community's faith. In worship as the community heard wise teachings, they learned to care for one another in tender and forgiving ways. The highest command Paul presented was the command to love

brothers and sisters as Christ loved. This was both a practical and a spiritual duty. The word translated "be subject" carried various implications for the original audience. Paul's audience understood that being subject was an active, not a passive, stance that an individual assumed. In other words, they heard Paul encouraging each individual to determine his or her role in relationships. Rather than being subjected to the domination of others, Christians willingly sought to serve one another as Christ had modeled. Their choice allowed the needs, concerns, and expectations of the church (composed of equal members with different roles, gifts, and maturities) to shape each individual relationship. Being subject to one another was a stunning way to experience Jesus' command to his disciples to be servants to one another (see Matthew 20:25-28). However, Paul added another dynamic to Jesus' words. Paul recommended Christians choose the welfare of the community over their individual needs as a way of honoring Jesus. Indeed, the phrase Paul used, "out of reverence for Christ," implied the attitude of worship. Being subject to one another was a practical and a spiritual choice.

Ephesians 5:22–6:4. Three sets of relationships were fundamental in the first century: husbands and wives, parents and children, slaves and masters. Teachers of philosophy and ethics frequently gave instructions on these relationships; thus, as the early Christian community matured in gospel living, Christian teachers were expected to offer instructions regarding these basic roles. Contemporary teachers refer to these instructions as "household codes," although such a category was unknown to early Christians. Rather, the earliest communities of Christians sought advice for applying the Christ-like virtues practiced in the congregational life to a family context. The key to understanding the instructions to family members is Ephesians 5:21 (today's key verse), "Be subject to one another out of reverence for Christ." Thus, the advice was both practical and spiritual. Moreover, in each set of relationships addressed, there is a subtle demonstration of the gospel.

The gospel emphasis of "good news to the poor" allowed Paul the freedom to address his words first to the weaker member of each relationship. Thus in the section on marital roles, the wife was addressed first and then the husband; when family roles were presented, children were instructed before fathers. Even slaves were allowed the first position, while instructions to masters followed.

Although this does not seem earthshaking in contemporary standards, according to the practice of rhetoric in the first century, Paul's order of address was shocking. The gospel not only was surprising in the structure of the instructions but also informed the content of each set. Each individual role had a spiritual dimension. Wives were encouraged to serve their husbands with the same love and dedication by which they serve Christ; husbands were to tenderly love their wives as Christ loves his body, the church. Children were instructed to fulfill the commandment to honor their parents, while fathers were directed to raise their children to be knowledgeable disciples of the Lord. In the family, as in every aspect of life, Christians were to witness Christ's love by loving and serving others.

INTERPRETING THE SCRIPTURE

Reverence to Christ

Reverence is a rare word in our contemporary culture. Only a few decades ago, children were taught to be reverent in worship settings, at cemeteries, before national memorials, and toward religious leaders. Contemporary children are instructed in similar ways, however the word "respect" has replaced reverence. Although the outward conduct of reverence and respect may look similar, the inner content is quite different. To reverence a person, place, or object contains an acknowledgment of the holy. To respect a person, place, or object acknowledges a special achievement or attribute. Reverence leads to God; respect leads to human accomplishment.

When Paul wrote to the Ephesians that they should conduct their interpersonal relationships out of reverence for Christ, his words assumed the sacredness of every human relationship. The Letter to the Ephesians described an ideal Christian community wherein every need was supplied, every joy celebrated, and every broken spirit restored by the members' mutual concern and attention. In this ideal community, as each member loved as Christ loved, all were secured, restored, and blessed.

One phrase, "Be subject to one another," captured the Christ-like character of the community. Unfortunately, this phrase is easily misunderstood. Rather than a direction to an individual to offer holy service within the community of faith, "be subject" became a condition. When subjection (to be under another's power or authority) replaced service (the free exercise of spiritual practice), domination corrupted the phrase. However, the gospel is not about domination; the gospel is about freedom. A free individual is able to see and respond to the holy in another; a dominated individual lives in fear. "Be subject to one another" was first-century shorthand for mutuality and encouragement within the Christian community. Sadly, this phrase became a battleground of rights, entitlements, and power plays. We are as religiously impoverished by this misreading of Ephesians 5:21, as we are by the loss of the word "reverence" in everyday speech.

A First-century Household

Christians are trained to study God's word in context by understanding the life situation of the original actors, authors, and audience. Because generations separate contemporary Christians from their religious forebears, students of the New Testament imaginatively re-create the original context. Perhaps because there is so much to research, when a word such as "family" or "home" pops up, contemporary Christians assume familiarity. Home is where you live in safety and love; family is the circle of relatives who surround you with love. However, these two words, family and home, had first-century shades of meaning we dare not ignore. For example, most early Christians were urban rather than rural; some lived in large cities (such as Jerusalem) or in trading centers (such as Ephesus). Homes were more than the residence of a family; most homes were also centers of economic activity. In cities, "home" was one of a series of apartments above shops and workspace. In smaller towns, "home" was a collection of rooms with some designated for family living and others for commerce or production. Thus, a "home" was also an economic institution and the "family" worked together to run the business, produce goods for sale, or provide needed labor, skill, or craft.

The family consisted of all the members of the household, including parents, grandparents, children, in-laws, hired workers, servants, and slaves. It would not be unusual for a household to include ten members living and working together. Some households were much larger; up to fifty people could dwell together in a series of apartments or a rambling set of rooms and still be considered one household providing one service or product to the local economy.

Our image of home as the sanctuary from work and family as those gathered around the Thanksgiving table does not accord with the context of the early Christian communities. They lived in larger families and worked together as an economic entity. Moreover, the likelihood of mixed families (composed of Christians and nonbelievers) was great. Although some families converted en masse, many believers lacked the support of other believers in their home. As we study Paul's teachings on family life, let us remember the original context.

Words to Married Couples

Christian marriage was based on a free choice: the choice to love and serve the partner as one loved and served Christ. This choice was not forced or imposed; rather, it flowed from the good news of salvation in Jesus Christ. As believers understood their individual forgiveness, call, and empowerment, they experienced a new zest for living. No longer was the mundane simply mundane; with the blessing of Christ in their hearts, believers experienced the mundane as holy. A visit with a friend, a day of labor, a walk through the town, a casual encounter on the street—all of these became an opportunity to love, serve, bless, and witness as a Christian.

Thus it was natural that early Christians sought to convert their family life to Christ's pattern. They requested and received instructions on Christian family living. When considering married couples, Paul addressed the wife first. She was encouraged to model her fidelity to her husband on her faithfulness to Christ. As she served Christ, so she served her husband. As Christ, the head of the church, offered salvation to all the members, so the husband, as the head of the household, provided security to all family members.

In contrast with contemporary culture, few first-century women had the privilege of supporting a family and claiming the title of head of household. First-century women were dependent upon their fathers, husbands, or sons for security and support. However, their status as "dependent women" did not negate the importance of their Christian service within the home. Christian wives chose to serve their husbands out of reverence for Christ.

In a similar way, Christian husbands were to love their wives out of reverence for Christ. Wives were as precious to husbands as the church was precious to Christ. Just as Christ loved the church without reservation, so, too, Christian husbands accepted the full responsibility of loving their wives. The spiritual relationship of wife and husband was, finally, another revelation of the great mystery at the heart of the Letter to the Ephesians: unity in Christ.

Words to Children and Parents

The instructions to children are brief and based upon the development of their independence. Children are to honor their parents not as an obligatory sign of respect but as a way of understanding the holiness of the child/parent relationship. Imagine, in a culture that deferred valuing children until they came of age (usually twelve years of age), children being raised by Christians were encouraged to seek knowledge of God. Within the Christian community, children were taught to honor their parents in order to understand the spiritual nature of a whole and abundant life. Once children understood the sacredness of their parents, they were prepared to love and serve others out of reverence for Christ.

Naturally, the instructions to the children were complemented by instructions to the fathers (the first-century heads of households). Fathers were to refrain from provoking their children through unfair, mean, or ignorant treatment; rather, fathers were to accept the spiritual task of bringing up children "in the discipline and instruction of the Lord" (6:4). Once again, a few words implied a great challenge: The fathers were commanded to evangelize their children in much the same way that Christ commanded his disciples (see Matthew 28:18-20).

SHARING THE SCRIPTURE

Preparing Our Hearts

Meditate on this week's devotional reading, found in 1 Corinthians 1:4-17. Here Paul expresses concern about divisions in the church. Quarrels among factions are disturbing the peace. Paul pleads for unity. How would you rate your own congregation in terms of unity? If there are divisions, what do you perceive to be the cause of the discord? What can you do to bring about reconciliation?

Pray that you and the adult learners will do all in your power to make the church unified.

Preparing Our Minds

Study the background from Ephesians 5:1–6:4 and the lesson Scripture from Ephesians 5:21–6:4. Think about how families learn to live together in harmony.

Write on newsprint:
❏ information for next week's lesson, found under "Continue the Journey."
❏ activities for further spiritual growth in "Continue the Journey."

Warning: As you discuss this passage, which is seen by some as controversial in our day, be sensitive to the possibility that abuse may have occurred (or be occurring) in families where the idea of subjection has been distorted and one person has attempted to dominate the family. Try to focus on Paul's idea of mutual submission.

Invite a professional or experienced volunteer who deals with family conflict if you choose to do the optional activity under "Work Toward Healing Conflict in the Learners' Homes and Families." Suggest that this guest speak about causes of family conflict and strategies for resolving these conflicts. Be sure to set a time limit.

LEADING THE CLASS

(1) Gather to Learn

❖ Welcome the class members and introduce any guests.

❖ Pray that those who have come today will find harmony within the church and their homes.

❖ Invite the class to call out fictional families that have appeared on television. Here are some titles to jog memories: *Leave It to Beaver, Father Knows Best, The Simpsons, The Brady Bunch, All in the Family, Married With Children.* List ideas on newsprint.

❖ Review the list and ask the adults to use words or phrases to describe the families in these shows.

❖ Ask: **Which families seem most true to life? Why?**

❖ Read aloud today's focus statement: **Family life is often disrupted by internal conflict. How can families learn to live together in harmony? In Ephesians, Paul urges believers to serve one another in the home in the name and Spirit of Christ.**

(2) Examine Paul's Teaching About Life in the Christian Household

❖ Choose readers for the following portions of today's lesson: Ephesians 5:21, entire class; 5:22-24, men; 5:25-33, women; 6:1-4, oldest two people in the class. If the class is all men or all women, then just divide those parts in half.

❖ Provide background by reading aloud "A First-century Household" from Interpreting the Scripture. Encourage the students to compare and contrast this portrait of an early household with the one in which they live. Students need to be aware that there are many different household structures today and that our structures are different again from the families of the first century.

❖ Make the point that at one time men and women had very different roles in the household, at least in the United States. Those roles, however, have been evolving and blending since at least World War II. Ask these questions:

(1) How do you perceive that the roles of men and women have changed?

(2) In what ways do you think these new roles are positive?

(3) In what ways do you think they are negative?

(4) In light of what Paul wrote two thousand years ago to people who lived in household structures different from most of ours, what do you think he would say to Christians today regarding family roles?

(5) How are Paul's comparisons between the wife and the church and the husband as the head of the church still useful today—or are they?

(6) What effect might Paul's comments have on parent-child relationships today?

(3) Explore the Meaning of Being Subject to Others in the Family

❖ Talk about today's key verse by (1) asking the class to state what it means in their own words, (2) retelling information from Ephesians 5:21 in Understanding the Scripture, and (3) using information from

"Reverence to Christ" in Interpreting the Scripture.

❖ Ask these questions:

(1) What factors in our society make it difficult for us to hear these words without interpreting them in a way that makes people feel belittled?

(2) How does the phrase "out of reverence for Christ" change our understanding?

❖ Invite the learners to think about their own families and the fictional families they identified in "Gather to Learn." Suggest that they talk with a partner or small group about how any of these families could be different if they were willing to be subject to one another because they reverenced Christ.

❖ Divide the class into groups of three or four. Challenge each group to identify concrete ways that people can act and relate to others that would show reverence for Christ.

(4) Work Toward Healing Conflict in the Learners' Homes and Families

❖ Distribute paper and pencils. Assure the participants that their work will remain confidential. Direct them to divide the paper into three columns, labeled as follows: *Subject of Conflict; Person Most Likely to Create Conflict; Person Most Likely to Resolve Conflict or Back Away From It.* Encourage the students to jot down ideas in each column as they relate to their own home lives. Suggest that they think about this question as they work: **What can I do to bring harmony to our home?**

❖ Break the silence by asking volunteers to comment on any insights they have gained from this activity.

❖ **Option:** Introduce the guest you have invited and ask him or her to talk about family conflict and strategies for resolving it. If time permits, encourage the students to raise questions of a general nature. The guest may be willing to give contact information for those who feel that a visit to this speaker's agency would be helpful.

(5) Continue the Journey

❖ Pray that all who have come today will practice mutual commitment in their homes as a sign of reverence for Christ.

❖ Read aloud this preparation for next week's lesson. You may also want to post it on newsprint for the students to copy.

■ **Title: Equipped for New Life**

■ **Background Scripture: Ephesians 6:10-18**

■ **Lesson Scripture: Ephesians 6:10-18**

■ **Focus of the Lesson: Life is challenging because competing voices beckon us to follow different paths. How can we stand firm in the face of opposition to what we believe? Paul teaches that God arms us to fight spiritual battles.**

❖ Challenge the students to complete one or more of these activities for further spiritual growth, which you will write on newsprint for the students to copy:

(1) Do something nice for a family member "just because." Buy a little gift, write a card of appreciation, or treat someone to lunch.

(2) Explore options with your spouse or other family members as to how everyone can show respect for the needs of each other. Implement your ideas.

(3) Research abuse in your community. Abuse of children, women, and animals is unfortunately common in U.S. society. What strategies can you find for helping families to respect one another so that abuse no longer occurs?

❖ Sing or read aloud "Happy the Home When God Is There."

❖ Conclude today's session by leading the class in this benediction: **Give us new hearts filled with your Spirit, O Lord, that we may live as new creations in Christ. Amen.**

UNIT 3: THE WAY OF NEW LIFE

EQUIPPED FOR NEW LIFE

PREVIEWING THE LESSON

Lesson Scripture: Ephesians 6:10-18
Background Scripture: Ephesians 6:10-18
Key Verse: Ephesians 6:13

Focus of the Lesson:
Life is challenging because competing voices beckon us to follow different paths. How can we stand firm in the face of opposition to what we believe? Paul teaches that God arms us to fight spiritual battles.

Goals for the Learners:
(1) to investigate the metaphorical armor needed for life as a Christian.
(2) to become equipped for a life of spiritual warfare.
(3) to fight spiritual battles as they arise.

Supplies:
Bibles, newsprint and marker, paper (preferably unlined) and pencils, hymnals

---

READING THE SCRIPTURE

NRSV
Ephesians 6:10-18

[10]Finally, be strong in the Lord and in the strength of his power. [11]Put on the whole armor of God, so that you may be able to stand against the wiles of the devil. [12]For our struggle is not against enemies of blood and flesh, but against the rulers, against the authorities, against the cosmic powers of this present darkness, against the spiritual forces of evil in the heavenly places. [13]Therefore **take up the whole armor of God, so that you may be able to withstand on that evil day, and having done everything, to stand firm.** [14]Stand therefore, and fasten the belt of truth around your waist, and put on the breastplate

NIV
Ephesians 6:10-18

[10]Finally, be strong in the Lord and in his mighty power. [11]Put on the full armor of God so that you can take your stand against the devil's schemes. [12]For our struggle is not against flesh and blood, but against the rulers, against the authorities, against the powers of this dark world and against the spiritual forces of evil in the heavenly realms. [13]Therefore **put on the full armor of God, so that when the day of evil comes, you may be able to stand your ground, and after you have done everything, to stand.** [14]Stand firm then, with the belt of truth buckled around your waist, with the

of righteousness. ¹⁵As shoes for your feet put on whatever will make you ready to proclaim the gospel of peace. ¹⁶With all of these, take the shield of faith, with which you will be able to quench all the flaming arrows of the evil one. ¹⁷Take the helmet of salvation, and the sword of the Spirit, which is the word of God.

¹⁸Pray in the Spirit at all times in every prayer and supplication. To that end keep alert and always persevere in supplication for all the saints.

breastplate of righteousness in place, ¹⁵and with your feet fitted with the readiness that comes from the gospel of peace. ¹⁶In addition to all this, take up the shield of faith, with which you can extinguish all the flaming arrows of the evil one. ¹⁷Take the helmet of salvation and the sword of the Spirit, which is the word of God. ¹⁸And pray in the Spirit on all occasions with all kinds of prayers and requests. With this in mind, be alert and always keep on praying for all the saints.

UNDERSTANDING THE SCRIPTURE

Ephesians 6:10. Our passage begins with the word translated by the NRSV as "Finally." According to rhetorical patterns, this word fits the context—Paul was "finally" at the conclusion of his words to the congregation in Ephesus. However, there are two other equally appropriate possibilities to consider when translating the Greek term. "Finally" may also mean "from now on." Some scholars think that the conclusion of this letter was an exhortation to the newly baptized members of the congregation. As Paul addressed those at the beginning of their Christian journeys, "from now on" marked a transition from darkness to light and introduced resources for living in the light. The other possibility exposed the spiritual time of God's salvation. In the letter, Paul alluded to God's final redemption with two themes. First, by the power of Christ's cross, Jews and Gentiles were reconciled into one family, God's own people. This was a sign of the new age of reconciliation. Second, by revelation God made known the mystery of redemption: creation's unity in Christ. This revelation signified the importance of the church in the coming redemption. These two signs indicated that the new age had begun. All that remained was the return of Christ to gather

his church and to execute final judgment. If Paul eyed the horizon of redemption at the letter's conclusion, then the translation "for the remaining time" was fitting. Thus, three translations were layered in the word "finally." However, regardless of context, Paul's message directed the church to receive and be empowered by God's own strength. Whatever followed "finally" required something greater than human strength and achievement.

Ephesians 6:11-13. In this section Paul directed the congregation as a whole (the verb tense indicates second person plural) to "put on the whole armor of God." The word "armor" referred to the protective and decorative garb of the military. However, this armor was donned not for military action but for solidarity with God. Two verbs disclosed the purpose of the armor: "able to stand" (6:11) and "able to withstand" (6:13). The danger described did not come from "enemies of blood and flesh" (6:12). Surely, the Ephesian congregation expected a political response to their community and, just as surely, they received a political response in the forms of official condemnation and persecution. Such circumstances, although full of danger, did not reach the level of danger described in verse

12 as "the rulers," "the authorities," "the cosmic powers of this present darkness," "the spiritual forces of evil in the heavenly places." Paul's assessment of the time was blunt: The spiritual forces defeated by Christ's death and resurrection retained a fraction of craftiness (wiles of the devil) and continued to conspire together to bring "that evil day" (6:13). In the space of three verses, Paul summoned all the fears of the small and politically insignificant congregation. He did so, however, not to belittle or dismiss these fears but to acknowledge the struggles that the congregation would face. Into these struggles Paul poured the image of the armor of God, the spiritual resources available to the community as a whole and to each individual within that community.

Ephesians 6:14-17. Next, Paul called the congregation to attention, "Stand therefore," and instructed them about the armor of God. First came the belt, a sign of preparedness. The spiritual belt for the Christian was truth, specifically the truth of the gospel. Next came the breastplate, a scriptural allusion to a prophetic stand against social evil (see Isaiah 59:17), but here described as righteousness, a term used by Paul to describe not morality but a right relationship with God. Following these two elements came gospel shoes, which probably reminded the hearers of the sandals with cleats worn by the Roman army so that they could stand firm. With these sandals strapped on, the community was ready to "proclaim the gospel of peace" (6:15). Next, in verse 16, came "the shield of faith." These large, Roman shields were designed to catch a barrage of ignited arrows. They locked together to form a single and solid line of defense. Paul used this common and dreaded shield to describe the sufficient and interlocking faith of a Christian community.

The last two items of God's providential armor distinguished the Christians from all other warriors. First, the decorative helmet worn by Christians was their salvation. In ancient times the rank and commission of soldiers was indicated by their headgear; for Christians only one type of helmet was offered. The helmet of salvation signified the acceptance of each individual, with his or her particular gifts and calling, into the community. Finally, God provided an offensive weapon: the sword of the Spirit, the Word of God. Thus, dressed in God's protective garb and armed with God's Word, the community stood at attention as they faced the future.

Ephesians 6:18. The image was complete: The congregation saw themselves dressed in God's protection, standing at attention, facing a fearsome future, and preparing to withstand all manner of evil. One more gift remained, the gift of prayer. Paul's final instruction to the congregation was to pray—to pray fervently in the Spirit at all times. Moreover, Paul directed those prayers to include supplication for all the saints. This subtle direction packed an enormous spiritual insight: In times of danger, the human response was (and is!) fear. People tended to huddle together and to narrow their concerns to immediate dangers. Paul warned the Ephesians not to limit their prayers according to their particular needs, but to expand prayer to cover the whole church. By such prayerful attention to the greater community of Christians, the small and fearful congregation of Ephesus would keep alert. The mystery of the gospel, the unity of creation in Christ, demanded such a comprehensive view. Paul's final gift of encouragement equipped the congregation with God's own strength and reminded the congregation of their part in God's redemption. They were a small collection of believers, but they were gifted by the Spirit, incorporated into their risen Lord, and essential to God's great intention of a peaceful, praising creation united by the body of Christ.

INTERPRETING THE SCRIPTURE

Be Strong in the Lord

Undoubtedly you've heard the proverb "God helps those who help themselves." Quite likely, you believe the proverb to be true. Our North American perspective on life certainly supports the initiative and determination of that proverb. Perhaps you've even heard these words attributed to the Bible. However, problems occur when this proverb is tested by the gospel. First, it is not a direct quotation from the Bible but is generally attributed to Ben Franklin, author of *Poor Richard's Almanac*. There is scriptural support for hard work and personal initiative, as for example, in the Letter to the Ephesians, even thieves are encouraged to get a job (Ephesians 4:28).

However, God's help is available to both the first worker on the job and the last to arrive (see Matthew 20:1-16). Strangely and mercifully, God's help does not match our popular proverb. God's help is available in circumstances beyond human self-help and at the point of personal exhaustion. At the conclusion of the Letter to the Ephesians, the strength of the Lord was presented as the only refuge for the community. The Ephesian congregation knew themselves to be small in numbers and insignificant in political power. They also recognized the signs of danger spreading within the government and community of Ephesus. Moreover, by the instruction of teachers such as Paul, they understood that the future afflictions would shake the faith of the strong. This congregation, literally, could not help themselves in such circumstances—nor were they expected to use their own power, ingenuity, or strength. There was a greater strength available to them: the spiritual power of Christ's presence among them. This power was described in Ephesians 1:20 as the power God put to work in Christ's resurrection and ascension. The sure and certain strength available to the Ephesians was resurrection power.

Take Your Stand

A friend who worked as a nurse in a busy emergency room at a county hospital shared the most important lesson taught by the charge nurse in the ER. It came packaged in familiar words, yet it packed a surprising spiritual punch. The charge nurse introduced every new nurse to the chaos and pace of the emergency room by advising—sometimes at the top of her lungs—"Don't just do something, stand there!" These wise words give interpretation to Paul's final directions to the Ephesians. He does not minimize the impending chaos; he declares that this struggle involves every aspect of life, from local politicians to spiritual forces of evil. Before such dangers, Paul expected the Ephesians not to "do something" but to stand there.

Have you ever experienced a spring of peace while others were giving in to hysteria? Such remarkable moments can be as small as grabbing a child from danger or as monumental as standing against unjust treatment of aliens or strangers. God's spiritual gift of calm and peace sometimes surprises Christians. However, Paul taught the Ephesians to expect this divine intervention. He offered them a spiritual practice: to stand firm. The history behind this practice is sung in the Psalms as the prayerful activity of waiting on the Lord (see Psalms 27:14; 130:5-6). By standing firm or waiting, Christians not only observed the exact circumstances surrounding them but also restrained their own impulse to "do something." When God's people stand together and wait, God is able to use them in unexpected ways. Just as the charge nurse expected all the nurses to wisely assess the chaos of emergency before "doing something," so Paul cautioned the Ephesians to wait upon God's strength and direction before doing anything.

Dress Accordingly

The metaphorical "whole armor of God" included four defensive items, one status symbol, and one offensive element. The belt, breastplate, shoes, and shield of the Roman military were known in every Roman city and protectorate. These items were not only necessary in battle, they also distinguished soldiers from ordinary citizens. Roman soldiers were the visual symbol of the Empire; when these soldiers marched through a city, everyone understood the power of Rome.

Paul's dress code for Christians also announced to the world the characteristics of believers. Christians were bound to God's truth, protected by Christ's righteousness, and swift to proclaim the gospel of peace. Just as Roman soldiers were the visual symbol of the Roman Empire, so Christians were distinguished as men and women living according to God's will and directed by a discipline of love. In their everyday conduct, Christians testified to God by their eagerness to share their faith in Christ's righteousness.

Moreover, Christians wore on their heads the sign of God's approval. Metaphorically, Paul used the military helmet to symbolize salvation. Perhaps he was thinking of the waters of baptism that sealed a believer as God's own child. Or, perhaps, he was remembering the crown of thorns that Jesus wore during his own passion and death. In either case, Paul reminded his readers that salvation was not a hidden or secret condition; it was as obvious as a Roman soldier's helmet.

Finally, Christians were equipped for battle with a spiritual sword, the Word of God. This was the clearest indication that Paul did not support a strictly military interpretation of the armor of God. The Word of God had no physical power. Rather, this sword wielded spiritual power to preach, convict, call, convert, and reconcile. Like any weapon, this sword was used against enemies; but unlike a weapon designed to harm, this weapon gave life. From the Word of the Lord came hope, new opportunities, forgiveness, purposeful work, and praise.

Pray at All Times

Ephesians strengthened, equipped with spiritual resources, and called to attention those who heard this letter. Throughout the letter, Paul's teachings bounced back and forth between practical concerns of everyday life and critical spiritual challenges. However, each lesson found a resting place of worship. The language of worship supported this letter and added depth to the simplest of instructions. Paul understood that in worship the community was intentional. Worship provided the quiet and focus that allowed God to be known. Paul also knew that in worship the Spirit was able to heal hurts within the community. As the congregation sang songs of praise, the broken pieces of life were restored. Moreover, Paul anticipated that the prayers said in worship reverberated throughout the week in every believer's home.

Thus, his last direction to the congregation was to keep on praying. Personal prayers kept the community whole. Mutual concern expressed in prayer extended the compassion of the congregation. Specific intercessions reminded believers that the communion of saints surrounded and supported them—regardless of time or place. By encouraging prayer in all circumstances and at every imaginable time, Paul directed the congregation to reverence their gatherings for worship. Indeed, because believers' prayers were offered for all the saints it was impossible to isolate a believer from corporate worship. Ceaseless prayer mysteriously held the community together. This final gift testified to the mystery revealed in the Letter to the Ephesians: "There is one body and one Spirit, just as you were called to the one hope of your calling, one Lord, one faith, one baptism, one God and Father of all, who is above all and through all and in all" (Ephesians 4:4-6). Let all God's people say, Amen!

SHARING THE SCRIPTURE

Preparing Our Hearts

Meditate on this week's devotional reading, found in Luke 11:14-23. Notice that in the context of a discussion with opponents concerning the source of his power, Jesus refers to "a strong man, fully armed" who ensures that "his property is safe" (11:21). How are you prepared to stand up to onslaughts against your beliefs? Are you fully prepared to defend your beliefs? If not, what do you feel is lacking? How can you obtain this "missing piece"?

Pray that you and the adult learners will be ready at all times to stand up for Christ and his church.

Preparing Our Minds

Study the background and lesson Scripture, both from Ephesians 6:10-18. Ponder how we can stand firm in the face of opposition to what we believe.

Write on newsprint:
❑ information for next week's lesson, found under "Continue the Journey."
❑ activities for further spiritual growth in "Continue the Journey."

LEADING THE CLASS

(1) Gather to Learn

❖ Welcome the class members and introduce any guests.

❖ Pray that all who attend today will be ready to follow where God leads them.

❖ Encourage the students to think about advertisements for vehicles (or another product). Ask them to discuss the virtues of a specific car or truck that its manufacturer touts. Next, prompt them to discuss the virtues of a competitor, as claimed by its advertisers.

❖ Ask: **How can we decide which product to choose when competing commercials all claim that their product is the best choice?**

❖ Read aloud today's focus statement: **Life is challenging because competing voices beckon us to follow different paths. How can we stand firm in the face of opposition to what we believe? Paul teaches that God arms us to fight spiritual battles.**

(2) Investigate the Metaphorical Armor Needed for Life as a Christian

❖ Distribute paper and pencils. Ask the students to draw the outline of a human figure. They are to add armor to their drawing as you read aloud from Ephesians 6:10-18. Assure them that artistic ability is not important, and they will not be asked to show their drawings to classmates.

❖ Read Ephesians 6:10-18 aloud, allowing time for the students to sketch the armor.

❖ Read or retell "Dress Accordingly" from Interpreting the Scripture to provide a perspective on today's Scripture passage.

❖ Look again at Ephesians 6:10-13. Invite the students to comment on Paul's perception of spiritual warfare, which is conducted on a cosmic level. Ask: **Do you agree or disagree with Paul's understand-**

ing? **Give reasons to support your answer.** (Be aware that an image of battle may be troubling to some Christians. Note the sharp contrast between the warfare image and the image of the gospel of peace in 6:15.)

❖ Encourage the class members to identify other images to suggest how they can stand up for Christ in the midst of opposition.

(3) Become Equipped for a Life of Spiritual Warfare

❖ Write these words that describe the Christian's spiritual armor on newsprint: *truth, righteousness, readiness to proclaim the gospel of peace, faith, salvation, Word of God.* Invite the students to talk about each piece of armor by discussing these questions. As an option, distribute paper and pencils and read the questions aloud so that the students may write their answers.

(1) **How do you know that something is authoritatively true?**

(2) **What kinds of behaviors and attitudes indicate that you are living righteously?**

(3) **What evidence can you give to show that you are ready to proclaim the gospel of peace?**

(4) **How do you define "faith"? If you were to rate your faith on a scale of 1 to 10, with 10 being the highest, where would you say you are?**

(5) **What does it mean to you to say that you are "saved"?**

(6) **How do you approach the Word of God, interpret it, and use it as a guide for your Christian journey?**

❖ Challenge the students to think of something that they generally wear, perhaps a watch or a ring, which can be a symbol for them of the whole armor of God. Suggest that whenever they are confronted by a situation that challenges their faith they touch the watch or ring as a reminder that they are spiritually clothed and prepared to stand firm. Give the students a moment to identify whatever this symbol will be.

(4) Fight Spiritual Battles as They Arise

❖ Divide the class into two groups, Group A and Group B. Read aloud these stories and ask each group to discuss how they would finish each story so that the character is seen as winning a spiritual battle. (If the class is large, have several groups work on story A and other groups work on story B.)

■ **Story A: Ingrid has been a dedicated bookkeeper at Acme Widgets for more than thirty years. She has prided herself on her accuracy and honesty. A new Chief Financial Officer came on board last year, and, through his mismanagement, the company is not doing as well as it was financially. He has been providing Ingrid with documentation of expenses that she knows is false. She must work, and she does not want to look for a job elsewhere at this stage in her life. Here's how Ingrid handles the situation so as to be true to her Christian beliefs.**

■ **Story B: Jerry's spouse, Maxine, always seems to have work to do on their computer. Jerry respects the fact that she is a professional with many responsibilities. Still, it doesn't seem to him that she needs to spend so many hours at home tending to her work. One day he receives a notice that their checking account is overdrawn. Initially he assumes it's a bank error, but, as he talks with Maxine, the story gradually unfolds. She has been gambling online. It started innocently enough, she claims, but then the stakes got** bigger and bigger. She confesses that their savings are almost gone, too. While Jerry is understandably upset, here's how he handles the situation so as to be true to his Christian beliefs.

❖ Conclude this portion of the session by asking the students to pray silently that they may be equipped and ready to stand firm in situations that are testing their faith.

(5) Continue the Journey

❖ Break the silence by praying that today's participants will be fully armed and prepared to stand firm against attacks on their faith.

❖ Read aloud this preparation for next week's lesson. You may also want to post it on newsprint for the students to copy.

■ **Title: God Calls Moses**

■ **Background Scripture: Exodus 2:23–3:12**

■ **Lesson Scripture: Exodus 3:1-12**

■ **Focus of the Lesson: Sometimes a special person is called to help another person or a people to overcome difficulties and to survive in times of hardship. Who has the power and position to help us? God chose Moses to save God's**

people and promised to give Moses all the help he needed.

❖ Challenge the students to complete one or more of these activities for further spiritual growth, which you will write on newsprint for the students to copy:

(1) Practice standing firm in your faith this week. Be alert for situations that beckon you to step away from your beliefs, and then respond as one who wears the whole armor of God.

(2) Review Ephesians 6:18. Offer intercessory prayers for the church and "all the saints." Consider keeping a prayer journal in which you list your requests and then make notes as they are answered.

(3) Explain the idea of the "whole armor of God" to a child. Help him or her understand what can be done to prepare oneself for spiritual battle.

❖ Sing or read aloud "Soldiers of Christ, Arise," which is based on Ephesians 6:13-18.

❖ Conclude today's session by leading the class in this benediction: **Give us new hearts filled with your Spirit, O Lord, that we may live as new creations in Christ. Amen.**

FOURTH QUARTER
Call Sealed With Promise

JUNE 7, 2009–AUGUST 30, 2009

During the final quarter of the 2008–2009 Sunday school year, entitled "Call Sealed With Promise," we will focus on the theme of God's call of a covenant community as reflected in four Old Testament books of the law: Exodus, Leviticus, Numbers, and Deuteronomy.

Unit 1, "Called Out of Egypt," includes four lessons concerning God's call to Moses, the response of Moses and Aaron, Pharaoh's refusal to heed God's call, and God's call to the people to leave Egypt. "God Calls Moses," the lesson from Exodus 2:23–3:12 for June 7, records the familiar conversation between Moses and God as God enlists Moses to lead the people out of Egypt. On June 14, we hear "Moses and Aaron Respond" in the lesson rooted in Exodus 4:10-16, 27-31. In the session for June 21, based on Exodus 5:1–6:1, "Pharaoh Ignores God's Call" because he is unwilling to recognize God's authority. The unit ends on June 28 with "God Calls the People Out of Egypt," a study of Exodus 13:17–14:30.

The second unit, "Called to Be God's People," which also consists of four lessons, explores how God's call led to the establishment of a new covenant, how the people responded to that call in celebration and worship, ways the people committed themselves to special service, and the institution of Jubilee. The session for July 5, "God Calls People to Covenant," rooted in Deuteronomy 5:1-27, focuses on rules for living. Passover, the most sacred holiday of the Jewish calendar, is a time of remembrance as recorded in Deuteronomy 16:1-8, which we will study on July 12 in a lesson entitled "God Calls People to Remember." On July 19 we turn to Leviticus 8:1-13, which is the story of Aaron being commissioned to the priesthood, to discover how "God Calls People to Special Service." Leviticus 25:8-24, the basis for the lesson for July 26, explores the concept of stewardship in "God Calls People to Jubilee."

Unit 3, "Called to Choose Life," reflects on God's ongoing call to obedience and defines what actions demonstrate faithfulness and rebelliousness. These five lessons demonstrate that God remains faithful to divine promises whether or not we choose to obey. Of course, our choices do have consequences. This final unit begins on August 2 with a study of the people's complaints in the wilderness as we examine Numbers 11 in "People Grumble." We continue in Numbers 14:1-25 on August 9 with "People Rebel," in which the freed slaves want to return to Egypt. Numbers 20:1-13, the Scripture for August 16, demonstrates that even a great leader may fail to follow God's commands, as we see in "Moses Disobeys." On August 23, we read in Deuteronomy 6 of how "God Calls for Obedience" as the people are directed to love God with all of their being. This Sunday school year concludes on August 30 with a look at Deuteronomy 30, where "God Calls for Decision," and the choice one makes will result in blessings or curses.

Meet Our Writer

THE REVEREND DR. REBECCA ABTS WRIGHT

Rebecca Abts Wright is a United Methodist minister and the daughter, sister, and great niece (twice) of ministers. She received her master of divinity degree from Wesley Theological Seminary in Washington, D.C., and served parishes in West Virginia and Maryland before returning to school for a Ph.D. in Old Testament from Yale University. While in Connecticut, she was copastor for a five-point and then a two-point charge. She is now Professor of Old Testament and Hebrew at the School of Theology, the University of the South, Sewanee, Tennessee, which is a seminary of the Episcopal Church. Although most of the seminarians are Episcopalian, there are also Lutherans, Cumberland Presbyterians, and United Methodists in the student body. She delights in returning to Wesley Seminary every summer to teach in the Course of Study School.

Her greatest joy is in her two daughters, Helen Kate and Anna Miriam. Her household companions are a dog, Gailor, a cat, Heri, and innumerable worms that compost her garbage. She lives in a straw-bale house and enjoys gathering and splitting wood for the woodstove, though she does admit to using the backup furnace, especially when she has company. Gardening is a continuing interest although it seems to mean mostly trying to salvage a few vegetables from the deer and some fruit from the birds. An increasing academic interest is in team-teaching courses for combined classes of undergraduates and seminarians in the fields of biodiversity, ecological economics, and sustainability.

THE BIG PICTURE: GOD'S CALL

This quarter, "Call Sealed With Promise," covers some of the foundational stories of both Judaism and Christianity, beginning with the call of Moses and Aaron and continuing through the exodus from Egypt, the giving of the law at Mount Sinai, and the long wilderness wanderings of the Israelites. The quarter is divided into three units. Unit 1, "Called Out of Egypt," starts with God's call of Moses at the burning bush and Moses' (and Aaron's) response to the call. We then see Pharaoh's refusal to heed God's call to him or to acknowledge God's authority through Moses and Aaron, and finally God's calling the Israelites out of Egypt. The next four weeks in Unit 2, "Called to Be God's People," examine some of the results of God's calls, especially in the establishment of a covenant, the people's response in celebration, worship, remembrance, and special service, and the introduction of the notion of Jubilee as a part of the ongoing life of the community. We finish the quarter with a five-week Unit 3, "Called to Choose Life." In these weeks we look at God's relentless faithfulness despite various sorts of rebellion on the part of the people and even their leaders.

Interestingly, some of the more familiar episodes you may remember from childhood Sunday school are not here in these weeks. There is no discussion of the plagues in Egypt or the motif of Pharaoh's hard heart, for example, nor will we have a lesson on the golden calf. Rather than focusing only on familiar stories, there is much more emphasis on theological matters and especially how they intersect with our contemporary lives. The call of Moses, for instance, leads us to consider how God calls people today and for what purposes they may be chosen. The ordination of Aaron and his sons provides a catalyst for us to consider how the church today separates, sets apart, and consecrates certain people for particular roles. Some of the stories we will consider are not especially cheerful. There was much complaining by the people in the wilderness, for example, and they did not hesitate to express their hearty dissatisfaction with the reliable supply of food God provided for them. In the end they rebelled both against Moses as their leader and against God. But neither rebellion nor any sort of sin can have the last word with our most gracious God. Despite their fussing, God tends them throughout the wilderness wanderings and finally the next generation comes to the Jordan River. We leave them at the end of this quarter on the brink of entering the Promised Land.

In some ways is this not where we find ourselves living—in the "almost but not quite" space between Jesus' resurrection and ascension and the final culmination of God's end-time grace and the completeness of the kingdom? We have glimpses today of what life in Christ's kingdom is like, but we also know all too well what life in a fallen world is like. We will see, over and over again in these thirteen weeks, how our ancestors in the faith wavered between living out their faith in God and wanting to go back to their (mis)remembered life in Egypt.

It is important to be especially clear this quarter about a particular concept, embodied in the familiar word "covenant." This vitally important word within the Bible has been used by some scholars as the central point around which to describe the entire biblical message. But because the word is also used in the wider culture as a synonym for agreement, contract, treaty, promise, and pledge, we would do well to spend a few paragraphs defining its biblical meaning. For biblically speaking, "covenant" is not simply a fancy churchy word for any of those synonyms listed in the previous sentence.

In the matter of covenants as in several other things, biblical writers made use of forms that were familiar from the larger society of their own time and invested those forms with new kinds of meanings. Archaeologists have discovered treaties from the second millennium B.C. in the ancient Near East that in their *form* show many similarities to some biblical texts. This particular form has these five parts:

(1) Preamble ("These are the words. . .")
(2) Historical Prologue (A recounting of events leading up to the treaty)
(3) Stipulations (A list of the responsibilities of the covenant partners, particularly what the losers are required to give to the winners)
(4) Divine Witness (A list of the gods who are called to witness the treaty and ensure that it will be followed)
(5) Blessings and Curses (A notation of the positive results for those who follow the covenant and the punishments for those who break it)

We can see this form in short pieces of text, such as Exodus 20, and in longer pieces, such as the entire book of Deuteronomy. In this latter case you can identify the five major sections as follows:

(1) Preamble (Deuteronomy 1:1-5)
(2) Historical Prologue (1:6–4:49)
(3) Stipulations (5–26)
(4) Witnesses (30:19; 31:19; 32:1-43)
(5) Blessings and Curses (27–28)

One major characteristic of this treaty is that it is always offered by the stronger party on an "agree to it or else" basis to the weaker party. This comes about nearly always as the result of warfare and the defeat of one group by another. There was never a real choice involved; the winners took what they wanted and imposed whatever conditions—usually a matter of tribute to be paid on a regular basis—they cared to on the losers. The losers had no recourse.

God with Israel takes this widely known form and makes some surprising changes. Of course there are not several gods called upon to be witnesses since Israel is always called to acknowledge that there is only one true God. More important, God makes no threats against the people should they decide not to agree to the covenant. There are consequences for disobeying once they have agreed to it, of course, but insofar as possible, God wants Israel to make a free choice. God invites and persuades but does not coerce. Nor does God dangle the Promised Land as a carrot in front of the people while concealing the stick of punishment for potential covenant breaking from them. Yet, the people respond with eager acceptance to their first hearing of God's covenantal offer at Mount Sinai (Exodus 19:8). They are, in fact, being called into covenant with God.

Another matter that needs to be mentioned is that of time horizons. Readers will notice quickly that the lessons in this quarter do not cover texts in biblical order. Not only is the Bible not laid out in strict chronological order but there also are three distinct times to keep in mind when reading it. First there is the time of the events themselves. Then, there is the time the incidents were remembered and collected and passed to succeeding generations. Finally, there is the time in which the collected memories were edited into the version we now have before us in our Bibles. For much of the Old Testament, especially the early books, there are centuries separating one time horizon from another. It may initially seem confusing to have the material this way instead of in a single concise chronological account, but in the end we have a greater richness because of the collection of voices than if the Bible consisted of just one line of vision. (There is actually a *Reader's Digest Bible* that removes all duplications and "extra" and "boring" passages. I am glad it has not become particularly successful because it misses the point of Scripture entirely!)

Finally, in these introductory comments, I would like to say something about one more issue: How is the Bible to be used responsibly both by the body of Christ and by individual Christians? This is a matter of ongoing interest for the church today, especially since so many controversies are swirling around different interpretations of particular verses. I readily admit that there have been times when I would prefer to have a simple answer book to which I could turn with every question and find there a clear verse that would tell me exactly what to do in any given situation. But, we believe, this is not how the Bible functions within the church. We need to interpret what we read, praying for the guidance of the Holy Spirit and testing our interpretations within the group. We need to listen for the voice of God in one another and encourage one another in the venture.

In a time of shifting cultural values I know that I often long for absolutes. But the church is clear in its witness that there is only one absolute, and that is God. Nothing else—not church doctrine, not even an interpretation of the Bible itself—is absolute. In part, this is because everything we know is filtered through our finite human consciousness, and thus everything we know is subject to error, to misinterpretation, and even to willful blindness and sin. Part of the wondrous grace of God shows itself in the reality that God deals with us where we are and as we are, albeit always encouraging us to move forward toward a more complete realization of the image of God within us. Our recurring issues elicit recurring response and input from God.

I believe that God speaks to us in all our diversity and particularity. And when one faith community (ancient Israel, for example) is inspired to write of their encounters with God, and people of a faith community in a far different time and place (us, for example) are inspired to read of those encounters with God, some "translation" will be necessary. By this I mean not only the move from the Old Testament's Hebrew and Aramaic to our English but also matters such as cultural assumptions held in ancient times but believed no longer.

There are three kinds of ancient wisdom. There are those things discovered millennia ago that we know still to be true. The square of the hypotenuse of a right triangle is equal to the sum of the squares of the other two sides. That has been known since almost six centuries before Jesus' birth when Pythagoras proved it, and it is still true today. Then there are things that used to be believed but have been discovered to be false. We know, as the ancient peoples did not, that the sun does not actually rise up from under the earth in the morning, travel across the sky, and then go down under the earth at night. We know, as our ancestors did not, that the earth is round and rotates on its axis, which merely gives the appearance of sunrise and sunset. And yet we continue to use the words "sunrise" and "sunset" to describe what still appears to our eyes to be the case, although our minds understand the matter differently. That the biblical writers were wrong in some of what they believed to be factual does not detract in the least from the truths they proclaimed. (And as a matter of humility, we would do well to remember that generations after us will discover many of our closely held viewpoints to be wrong.)

The final sort of ancient wisdom is that which we still know is true but have as much trouble living as did our ancestors. The Great Commandment (Deuteronomy 6:4-5) is just as true as it ever was and just as hard for us to maintain as ever before. Sin, rebellion against God, seems no less rampant today than what we see in the pages of the Bible. Our campus bookstore has a poster with a traditional picture of Jesus on it, and at the bottom a caption reading, "He died to take away your *sins*, not your *mind*." Many people today are not sure whether it is really possible to love God with their minds or appropriate to subject the Bible to the same sort of scrutiny as other ancient literatures. Many seem to think that religion and serious thought are really two quite different parts of life and that they should not be mixed. Other people think that religious convictions can be true if and only if they can be demonstrated scientifically to be factual. These folks consider religious people to be either gullible or foolish. They would agree with Mark Twain's definition of faith as "believing what you know isn't true" and contend that it has no positive place in human life.

Then there are those who want to use their minds and at the same time recognize that there are some matters that human brains simply do not understand. They are comfortable with a certain degree of ambiguity and with mystery. I happen to think that humility in this position is a positive good. Both the person who demands complete proof and the one who refuses to consider any evidence that contradicts his or her own understandings are setting up their own minds as the final arbiters of reality. Argument is probably not going to convince a member of any camp to switch positions. The argument of a faithful life, however, can speak louder than any number of words, however brilliant and eloquent they may be.

Ancient peoples believed that slavery was acceptable; we do not. I believe that God always starts with us where we are and then patiently prods and calls and pushes and cajoles and invites us to deeper understandings and more abundant life. No human community will ever get everything totally right; we always have more to learn from God. Such learning may be painful when it means we have to give up one cherished idea for another. But such learning can also be freeing and exciting as we move closer to the life we were created for, the fuller life within the body of Christ.

A final reminder before we get on with the lessons themselves: We are saved neither by our knowledge nor by our respect for the Bible. We are saved by God's grace, made known to us most fully in the life, death, resurrection, and ascension of Jesus Christ. The creative and creating power of God manifested in the Holy Spirit inspired the biblical writers. That same creative and creating power is still at work, inspiring us as we read and study and interpret God's Word. Thanks be to God for the marvelous gift of Scripture.

Close-Up:
God Calls Moses
and God Calls You

Moses is the main character in the story of the Hebrew people's liberation from slavery in Egypt. Traditionally, he is thought to have been the author of Genesis, Exodus, Leviticus, Numbers, and Deuteronomy, all of which tell the story of God's encounter with those who are called to be the chosen people.

Moses is called by God to help set the captives free. He not only leads the people away from their oppressed lives under Pharaoh but also continues to follow God's directives as they move through the wilderness for forty years toward God's ultimate goal for them: the land promised to their ancestors Abraham, Isaac, and Jacob. Moses ultimately undertook numerous roles: mediator, priest, prophetic teacher, and scribe. He was so highly revered that the author of the Gospel of Matthew took great care to draw numerous parallels between Jesus and Moses.

Yet, if we look at Moses' response to God's call, we may see some similarities between ourselves and this spiritual giant. Like most of us, Moses was working, going about the usual business of life—in his case tending sheep—when God called him. Surely most of us do not hear voices emanating from a burning bush, and yet the bush itself was simply a device God used to get Moses to pay attention. Moses hears God calling his name and telling him that he is on holy ground. This speaker is the one God who had a relationship with Moses' ancestors. Understandably, Moses responds with fear, hiding his face.

God goes on to give Moses a specific task to do: lead the Israelites "out of Egypt" (Exodus 3:10). Overwhelmed, Moses cannot imagine how he will be able to do this. God, however, never calls us without equipping us to do the job and promising, "I will be with you" (3:12). Moses continues to converse, wanting to know God's name (3:13). Furthermore, God gives Moses a glimpse of the miraculous power that is available to him (4:1-9). Interestingly, although Exodus 7:7 reports that Moses is eighty years of age, he does not include "old age" in his list of numerous excuses to decline the job. Instead, he focuses on the fact that he is not a good public speaker (4:10). Only after God promises that Moses' brother Aaron will assist him does Moses begin to answer God's call (4:28-31). The Bible records that his faithful response to that call changed the course of history.

As you and the students think about Moses' call, read aloud these questions and allow time to ponder them:

1. **When has God called you?**
2. **How did you respond to that call?**
3. **What reasons did you give to avoid the call, even if, like Moses, you eventually agreed?**
4. **How did you know that it was God who was calling you to a particular task?**
5. **In what ways did God gift and equip you?**
6. **As you review your life, are there opportunities that you have missed to answer a call?**
7. **What is God calling you to do right now?**
8. **How will you respond?**

FAITH IN ACTION: HEARING AND HEEDING GOD'S CALL

During this quarter we are considering God's call of the covenant community. Our sessions, which focus on Exodus, Leviticus, Numbers, and Deuteronomy, enable us to see how God called people—and how they responded. The treasures these lessons have for us reflect not only on God's history with the people who were once slaves in Egypt and then wanderers in the wilderness but also on God's relationship with us today.

Encourage the students to consider God's call on their congregation or class by suggesting that they complete this activity together at a time of your choice, preferably toward the end of this quarter. Lead the class in completing these steps:

Step 1: Remember some of the calls you heard during this quarter.

List on newsprint their answers, which may include: God's call of Moses to lead the people, of Aaron to assume responsibility as a priest, of the people to become a covenant community.

Step 2: Ask: What have you been hearing God call your congregation or class to do?

List on newsprint any actions that the adults can identify to move the church forward in mission and ministry. For example, the church may be considering a major construction project or a new ministry to the community such as a tutoring program or the sponsorship of a missionary.

Step 3: Choose one or two of these calls and consider the tangible steps the congregation has taken to obey the call(s).

Encourage the adults to name actions taken, even if they have not yet completed the task. For example, a building committee may be considering the needs of the church so as to create useful space to undertake its ministries or someone may be in the process of recruiting volunteer tutors.

Step 4: Encourage the students to identify ways in which they hear God calling them as individuals to become involved in any of the missions or ministries that you have been discussing.

Distribute paper and pencils and invite each person to write at least two tasks that he or she could undertake to help the congregation answer this call. Urge them to consider their own gifts and graces as they ponder what they could do. For example, one person may have the expertise to chair the building committee, whereas another may be able to make visits to invite people to contribute to this construction project.

Step 5: Covenant together with the students to do whatever they can individually and as a class to hear and heed God's call.

Guide the students in writing a litany in which they express what they intend to do. Encourage individuals to add what they have written in step 4 so that as many actions as possible may be included. The group response to each of these actions may be words such as, *"With God's help we will heed the call to act as God's covenant people."* End this activity by reading the litany. Perhaps you or a student can type it for the group and photocopy it or send it to each class member, possibly by e-mail.)

UNIT 1: CALLED OUT OF EGYPT
GOD CALLS MOSES

PREVIEWING THE LESSON

Lesson Scripture: Exodus 3:1-12
Background Scripture: Exodus 2:23–3:12
Key Verse: Exodus 3:10

Focus of the Lesson:
Sometimes a special person is called to help another person or a people to overcome difficulties and to survive in times of hardship. Who has the power and position to help us? God chose Moses to save God's people and promised to give Moses all the help he needed.

Goals for the Learners:
(1) to examine God's call for Moses to lead God's people.
(2) to recognize that God's work is often done as they respond to God's call.
(3) to listen for and respond to God's call in their lives.

Pronunciation Guide:
Amorite (am' uh rite)   Jebusite (jeb' yoo site)
Canaanite (kay' nuh nite)   Jethro (jeth' roh)
Hittite (hit' tite)   Midian (mid' ee uhn)
Hivite (hiv' ite)   Perizzite (per' uh zite)
Horeb (hor' eb)

Supplies:
Bibles, newsprint and marker, paper and pencils, hymnals

READING THE SCRIPTURE

NRSV
Exodus 3:1-12

¹Moses was keeping the flock of his father-in-law Jethro, the priest of Midian; he led his flock beyond the wilderness, and came to Horeb, the mountain of God. ²There

NIV
Exodus 3:1-12

¹Now Moses was tending the flock of Jethro his father-in-law, the priest of Midian, and he led the flock to the far side of the desert and came to Horeb, the mountain of

the angel of the LORD appeared to him in a flame of fire out of a bush; he looked, and the bush was blazing, yet it was not consumed. ³Then Moses said, "I must turn aside and look at this great sight, and see why the bush is not burned up." ⁴When the LORD saw that he had turned aside to see, God called to him out of the bush, "Moses, Moses!" And he said, "Here I am." ⁵Then he said, "Come no closer! Remove the sandals from your feet, for the place on which you are standing is holy ground." ⁶He said further, "I am the God of your father, the God of Abraham, the God of Isaac, and the God of Jacob." And Moses hid his face, for he was afraid to look at God.

⁷Then the LORD said, "I have observed the misery of my people who are in Egypt; I have heard their cry on account of their taskmasters. Indeed, I know their sufferings, ⁸and I have come down to deliver them from the Egyptians, and to bring them up out of that land to a good and broad land, a land flowing with milk and honey, to the country of the Canaanites, the Hittites, the Amorites, the Perizzites, the Hivites, and the Jebusites. ⁹The cry of the Israelites has now come to me; I have also seen how the Egyptians oppress them. **¹⁰So come, I will send you to Pharaoh to bring my people, the Israelites, out of Egypt."** ¹¹But Moses said to God, "Who am I that I should go to Pharaoh, and bring the Israelites out of Egypt?" ¹²He said, "I will be with you; and this shall be the sign for you that it is I who sent you: when you have brought the people out of Egypt, you shall worship God on this mountain."

God. ²There the angel of the LORD appeared to him in flames of fire from within a bush. Moses saw that though the bush was on fire it did not burn up. ³So Moses thought, "I will go over and see this strange sight—why the bush does not burn up."

⁴When the LORD saw that he had gone over to look, God called to him from within the bush, "Moses! Moses!"

And Moses said, "Here I am."

⁵"Do not come any closer," God said. "Take off your sandals, for the place where you are standing is holy ground." ⁶Then he said, "I am the God of your father, the God of Abraham, the God of Isaac and the God of Jacob." At this, Moses hid his face, because he was afraid to look at God.

⁷The LORD said, "I have indeed seen the misery of my people in Egypt. I have heard them crying out because of their slave drivers, and I am concerned about their suffering. ⁸So I have come down to rescue them from the hand of the Egyptians and to bring them up out of that land into a good and spacious land, a land flowing with milk and honey—the home of the Canaanites, Hittites, Amorites, Perizzites, Hivites and Jebusites. ⁹And now the cry of the Israelites has reached me, and I have seen the way the Egyptians are oppressing them. **¹⁰So now, go. I am sending you to Pharaoh to bring my people the Israelites out of Egypt."**

¹¹But Moses said to God, "Who am I, that I should go to Pharaoh and bring the Israelites out of Egypt?"

¹²And God said, "I will be with you. And this will be the sign to you that it is I who have sent you: When you have brought the people out of Egypt, you will worship God on this mountain."

UNDERSTANDING THE SCRIPTURE

Exodus 2:23-25. What we have here is the background and introduction not only for the call of Moses but also for the entire exo-

dus event. We do not know precisely how much time has passed since 2:22, only that it is "a long time" and that the old king, the one who sought Moses' life for killing an Egyptian overseer, is dead. Moses has a new life now in Midian; Egypt may well be fading from his memory. It is not so with God, however. The four verbs used of God in verses 24-25 are highly significant. They are all simple words, and in the Hebrew text they are used in their simplest forms: God heard. God remembered. God saw. God knew. In the Bible, when God hears, remembers, sees, or knows, it is likely that something noteworthy is about to happen. And here we have all four verbs together. What is coming next will surely be something spectacular!

Because this is a familiar text to most of us we may miss some important points. It is the people's distress and their outcry that captures God's attention. They are not said to be calling specifically to God, just crying out in their misery. And they certainly are not petitioning the divine in measured, polite, church-service language. They are hurting, and they cry out. In some ways they remind us of Bartimaeus (Mark 10:46-52) and his crying out to Jesus even when those around him tried to keep him polite and quiet. Whether or not the slaves in Egypt know God, God surely knows them.

Introduction to Exodus 3:1-12. These verses are the beginning of the literary form that scholars have named "prophetic call narrative." By the arrangement of the pieces of the story and the way it is told, those early hearers would have recognized that God was calling Moses for a specific task. It was also usual for the prospective prophet to object—often in a "why me?" manner. God's first promise is almost always the simple, "I will be with you."

Exodus 3:1-5. After the buildup of 2:23-25, this section seems something of a letdown. God has taken note of the oppression of the people in Egypt and has remembered the covenant with Abraham, Isaac, and Jacob, but suddenly we are back with Moses in Midian. Not only that, Moses seems to have settled into his new life as a shepherd

and is tending to his father-in-law's sheep. In the NRSV's phrasing, he is "beyond the wilderness." That is, he is far away from home, far from all human contact. His attention is caught suddenly by a bush that is on fire, yet does not seem to be burned up. He goes closer to take a look at this phenomenon and hears God call him by name from out of the bush. Notice that as soon as God has Moses' attention, there is no more mention of the burning bush. It may indeed have been a miraculous bush, but the bush is not the focus of the story. The point of the encounter is the encounter itself—the conversation between God and Moses.

God's command to Moses, "Remove the sandals from your feet, for the place on which you are standing is holy ground," may strike us as odd. We can understand removing shoes at the entrance of a building in order to keep from tracking dirt onto the floor, but how could Moses' sandals get the ground dirty? This is a case of a cultural tradition that had meaning for the biblical characters and the early readers and hearers of these stories. Because our culture is different, we may miss the significance of God's command here. In many ancient Mediterranean cultures, including Israel, slaves and servants were barefoot and only free people wore shoes. Thus, God is telling Moses that, here in this encounter with God, Moses is not in charge. (For another example of this same cultural symbol, look at Luke 15:19-22. The returning son has prepared a speech offering to be a servant in the household, but his father does not even wait to hear the whole speech before calling for someone, among other things, to "put . . . sandals on his feet." Thus everyone would know, just by looking at him, that this "prodigal" son was back as a member of the family and not as a servant.)

Exodus 3:6. God's self-introduction is in terms of history and continuity. In a time when many people believed that gods were territorial, that the "God of Maryland" and the "God of Tennessee" were entirely different beings, it is important for Moses to learn that it is one and the same God of his ancestors who is speaking to him, even though the conversation is taking place in a location far from his home. God's mentioning the patriarchs Abraham, Isaac, and Jacob, would surely also call to Moses' mind the covenant God made with those ancestors. What God is going to do may well be new, but it will be built on the relationships God has developed with previous generations.

Exodus 3:7-9. God then recounts to Moses what the narrator has already told us in 2:23-25, that God knows of the oppression of the people in Egypt and is going to do something about it. God will not only deliver them from their bondage but also give them a place of their own to live. It will not be just any place either, but one that is "good and broad" and "flowing with milk and honey."

Exodus 3:10-12. The first verse here comes as a shock. In verse 8, God has said, "I have come down to deliver them," but God is now saying that Moses will be the instrument of that deliverance. Moses makes what sounds like a reasonable objection: "Who am I?" It makes little human sense that God would call one individual, one lone shepherd, for such a huge task. But the lone shepherd will not be alone, for God promises, "I will be with you."

INTERPRETING THE SCRIPTURE

Uncomfortable Background

The Bible has many passages that exhort us to "call upon the LORD" or "wait upon the LORD." (See, for example, Psalms 27:14; 37:34; 130:5; Isaiah 40:31; Zephaniah 3:8.) Clearly, however, that is not what the Hebrew slaves are doing in Exodus 2:23-25. There is not even any indication that the slaves know the Lord at this point in the story, and they certainly are not presented as acting in an orderly manner. They are not having prayer vigils or worship services. Instead they are groaning and crying out, whether or not they believe anyone will hear them or can do anything to help them. They remind me of Bartimaeus in Mark 10 or of the widow in Jesus' parable in Luke 18:1-5. Such people are not always pleasant to be around. I am much more comfortable sending a check to a project of the Board of Global Ministries than being accosted on a street corner by someone asking for money. But God does not tell the people they must petition in an orderly fashion or send their grievances up through the proper channels.

We already know the outcome of this story, that the oppressors of those Hebrew slaves endured mighty punishments because of how they oppressed others. Might this be in the back of our minds as we read these texts and as we are confronted by suffering in our world? We may be able to be blind and deaf to suffering in our world. But we cannot believe that God will not see and hear. And God will also act.

Minding His Own Business

Moses has had a difficult life up to this point. He narrowly escaped death as an infant and has had to flee his home country because he killed an Egyptian overseer. He has found refuge in Midian and now even has a wife and son, though he names the son a combination of two Hebrew words meaning "alien there," as a commentary on his life as an alien in a foreign land (2:22). He certainly is not presented as searching out some kind of deeper ministry with God. Neither is he shown as trying to run away from God (as Jonah certainly did). No,

Moses is an ordinary man apparently living his life in an ordinary way when he is confronted by something extraordinary.

At every point until this one Moses has been free to make a choice. When he noticed the strange behavior of the bush, he could have shrugged and walked in the other direction. He might even have rationalized his decision by saying it would be dangerous to let the sheep get so close to such strange fire, that the only responsible thing to do would be to go quickly in the opposite direction. Even when he hears his own name being called from the midst of those flames, he could have pretended not to hear. As we will see in next week's lesson, Moses does not take to this assignment from God without a great deal of argument. My point here is this: God *invites* but does not *compel* Moses to enter into the conversation.

What Is the Miracle?

A bush that burns without being consumed would surely be a boon to our world today as we are using up petroleum and other nonrenewable energy supplies at prodigious rates. Yet that bush is not the point of the story. The "miracle" is something that on the surface is much less flashy, much more prosaic. The miracle is that God wants to be in communication with us. The miracle is that—at least in the biblical accounts—God does not start with people who have all the wisdom and skills and abilities and power to do whatever the pressing task may need.

God seems to call unlikely people, people who appear weak or foolish or otherwise unprepared for mighty tasks. Notice also that God's call is not to a generalized and indeterminate ministry or to an otherwise unspecified obedience, but to a very precise job. Notice as well that Moses is not being called to a "religious" as distinct from a "secular" occupation. We may categorize jobs in this way, but God's call tends to be to whatever needs to be done at a particular

time and place, regardless of the vocational distinctions we humans may make. Today ministers and pastors may speak of their "call," but the rest of us should in no way think that God does not also call people to other tasks. A bus driver or nursery school teacher may have no less a sacred call than a minister. In fact, partly because of all the other lives involved, such jobs should never be done by people who do not want to do them.

In whatever ways we "tend our sheep" as Moses was doing, God may interrupt with the startling news of another occupation in store for us. Notice too that God does not say Moses is a bad shepherd or that tending sheep is not a worthwhile and honorable occupation. Hearing God's call to something new does not have to mean what we have been doing up to that point is not also a worthwhile occupation. It may simply mean that God has something else in store for us now.

Is God's Presence Enough?

For whatever reasons, Moses is not immediately thrilled by God's invitation that he return to Egypt, confront Pharaoh, and lead the Israelites out of their bondage. He certainly must remember the reason he fled to Midian in the first place was that Pharaoh wanted to have him killed. God's first promise in response to Moses' startled "Why me?" is one of divine presence.

But is that enough? When faced with a difficult task, I would so much more like to hear, "Don't worry about anything; it will be easy; nothing can possibly go wrong." Of course, we all know that is not how life in this world unfolds most of the time. Given the reality of life in a fallen world, the assurance of the presence of God is not a trivial matter. Neither in this week's text nor next week's continuation of this conversation does God scold Moses or tell him he should just "have faith" or put more trust in God. The Lord knows our frailties and is patient with us. No one in the Bible is ever scolded by God or by Jesus for asking honest questions. We do the disciple Thomas a great disservice to call him "Doubting Thomas" because he wanted to see what the other disciples had already seen (John 20:24-29).

The opposite of faith is not doubt, but indifference on the one hand or certitude on the other. God knows we are frail; God knows we cannot handle the tasks on our own. And God promises the greatest gift of all: divine presence.

SHARING THE SCRIPTURE

Preparing Our Hearts

Meditate on this week's devotional reading, found in Hebrews 3:1-13. The first six verses of this passage compare Moses and Jesus. Note that Moses is commended for faithfulness, but in the end he is God's servant, whereas Jesus is God's son. Based on what you know about Moses, how would you describe him? In what ways do you see him as faithful? To what tasks or ministries are you called by God? How have you answered?

Pray that you and the adult learners will be ready to hear and respond faithfully to God's call on your lives.

Preparing Our Minds

Study the background from Exodus 2:23–3:12 and the lesson Scripture from Exodus 3:1-12. As you read, consider who has the power and position to help us overcome difficulties and survive in times of hardship.

Write on newsprint:
❑ question under "Recognize That God's Work Is Often Done as the Learners Respond to God's Call."
❑ information for next week's lesson, found under "Continue the Journey."
❑ activities for further spiritual growth in "Continue the Journey."

Prepare a brief introductory lecture for "Examine God's Call for Moses to Lead God's People."

LEADING THE CLASS

(1) Gather to Learn

❖ Welcome the class members and introduce any guests.

❖ Pray that those who have come today will be open to the word God has for them.

❖ Read this information from Nobelprize.org to the class. **Lech Walesa, an electrician who worked in the Gdansk shipyards in Poland, was willing to take a risky stand on behalf of workers and free trade unions. As a result of his activities that catapulted him to prominence as the leader of a labor movement, he was seen as a threat by the government. His actions were closely monitored and he was often detained. A shipyard strike in 1980 emboldened workers throughout the country to strike. Awarded the Nobel Peace Prize in 1983, Walesa "has always regarded his Catholicism as a source of strength and inspiration." From 1990 until 1995 he served as the President of the Republic of Poland, having been freely elected to this position in the formerly Communist-controlled country.**

❖ Ask this question: **What difference did the leadership of this one man make for individual workers and for his country?**

❖ Read aloud today's focus statement: **Sometimes a special person is called to help another person or a people to overcome difficulties and to survive in times of** hardship. **Who has the power and position to help us? God chose Moses to save God's people and promised to give Moses all the help he needed.**

(2) Examine God's Call for Moses to Lead God's People

❖ Use information for Exodus 2:23-25 from Understanding the Scripture and "Uncomfortable Background" from Interpreting the Scripture to set the stage for today's lesson in a brief lecture.

❖ Choose three volunteers—one as the narrator, one to play the part of Moses, and one to read the words of God—to read the lesson Scripture from Exodus 3:1-12.

❖ Discuss these questions:
  (1) What does this passage suggest to you about God?
  (2) What does it suggest to you about Moses?
  (3) What does it suggest about God's relationship with the Hebrew people?

(3) Recognize That God's Work Is Often Done as the Learners Respond to God's Call

❖ Read "Minding His Own Business" from Interpreting the Scripture. Also read aloud the last paragraph of "What Is the Miracle?" in Interpreting the Scripture.

❖ Ask the students to comment on times when they or people they know were going about the ordinary business of life when they felt God was calling them. What happened?

❖ Read aloud again today's key verse, Exodus 3:10.

❖ Note that Moses' response to God's call was a question: "Who am I?" (3:11). Invite the students to talk with a partner or small group about their own reactions when they feel God has called them to a task. Ask them to consider the doubts, fears, and questions they may have when faced with a challenging task.

❖ Point out that in Exodus 3:12 God assures Moses with these words: "I will be with you."

❖ Distribute paper and pencils. Invite the students to write answers to this question, which you will read aloud and post on newsprint: **How does the assurance that God will be present enable you to engage in the work you are called to do, even though you do not know exactly what is involved or how you are supposed to do the job?**

❖ Call the class together and encourage volunteers to read or retell what they have written.

❖ Conclude this portion of the lesson by asking: **Is God's presence enough?** You may want to augment the discussion by reading "Is God's Presence Enough?" from Interpreting the Scripture.

(4) Listen for and Respond to God's Call

❖ Note that Moses was called to liberate others from oppression. He was, with God's guidance, able to get the Hebrew slaves out of Egypt. However, millennia later oppression, poverty, and powerlessness still exist.

❖ Ask: **In what situations in our community and around the world are people crying out for help?** (List these ideas on newsprint.)

❖ Invite the students to look at the list for a moment and then close their eyes as you read this guided imagery exercise.

  ■ **Listen as one of the groups we have identified calls out to you. What are they saying about their situation?** (pause)
  ■ **See Jesus approach you and begin to talk with you about how you can help these people. Listen as he suggests to you ways you can use your skills and talents to assist.** (pause)
  ■ **Respond silently to Jesus, making whatever commitment you can to him to help in this situation.** (pause)

■ **Please open your eyes when you are ready.**

❖ Call the class back together. Solicit volunteers to report their ideas to others. Encourage the adults to consider ways that they might make these images a reality. For example, if some heard victims of a natural disaster calling, could they organize a mission trip to help rebuild the area? Could others in the class do a fundraiser to sponsor those who can go?

(5) Continue the Journey

❖ Pray that all who have come today will not only hear but also heed the words of the Lord.

❖ Read aloud this preparation for next week's lesson. You may also want to post it on newsprint for the students to copy.

■ **Title: Moses and Aaron Respond**
■ **Background Scripture: Exodus 4:10-16, 27-31**
■ **Lesson Scripture: Exodus 4:10-16, 27-31**
■ **Focus of the Lesson: Because some people believe they are not adequate to a task, they are fearful of and resistant to accepting it. How can people who are afraid be encouraged to do the work**

assigned them? Moses resisted God's call, but then he accepted aid from his brother Aaron, according to God's command.

❖ Challenge the students to complete one or more of these activities for further spiritual growth, which you will write on newsprint for the students to copy:

(1) **Spend time in meditation each day, listening for God's word to you. Try focusing on Samuel's words, "Speak, for your servant is listening" (1 Samuel 3:10).**

(2) **Research a country where people are oppressed. How are they calling for help? Who is answering? As of this writing, Darfur in the Sudan would be a prime example of such oppression.**

(3) **Tell someone else about how God has responded to the cries of your own heart. Perhaps someone was listening who came to your aid.**

❖ Sing or read aloud "The Voice of God Is Calling."

❖ Conclude today's session by leading the class in this benediction: **We hear your call, O God, and ask that you send us forth empowered by your Spirit to live and serve as your covenant people.**

UNIT 1: CALLED OUT OF EGYPT
MOSES AND AARON RESPOND

PREVIEWING THE LESSON

Lesson Scripture: Exodus 4:10-16, 27-31
Background Scripture: Exodus 4:10-16, 27-31
Key Verse: Exodus 4:30

Focus of the Lesson:

Because some people believe they are not adequate to a task, they are fearful of and resistant to accepting it. How can people who are afraid be encouraged to do the work assigned them? Moses resisted God's call, but then he accepted aid from his brother Aaron, according to God's command.

Goals for the Learners:

(1) to delve into the account of Moses' resistance to God's commands and Aaron's acceptance of his role in leading the people.
(2) to explore personal feelings of inadequacy.
(3) to take responsibility for the tasks to which God has called them.

Pronunciation Guide:

Abihu (uh bi' hyoo)   Ithamar (ith' uh mahr)
Amram (am'ram)   Jochebed (jok' uh bed)
Eleazar (el ee ay' zuhr)   Levite (lee' vite)
Elisheba (i lish' uh buh)   Nadab (nay' dab)

Supplies:

Bibles, newsprint and markers, paper and pencils, hymnals, optional Bible commentary

---

READING THE SCRIPTURE

NRSV
Exodus 4:10-16, 27-31

¹⁰But Moses said to the LORD, "O my Lord, I have never been eloquent, neither in the past nor even now that you have spoken to your servant; but I am slow of speech and slow of tongue." ¹¹Then the LORD said to

NIV
Exodus 4:10-16, 27-31

¹⁰Moses said to the LORD, "O Lord, I have never been eloquent, neither in the past nor since you have spoken to your servant. I am slow of speech and tongue."

¹¹The LORD said to him, "Who gave man

him, "Who gives speech to mortals? Who makes them mute or deaf, seeing or blind? Is it not I, the LORD? [12]Now go, and I will be with your mouth and teach you what you are to speak." [13]But he said, "O my Lord, please send someone else." [14]Then the anger of the LORD was kindled against Moses and he said, "What of your brother Aaron, the Levite? I know that he can speak fluently; even now he is coming out to meet you, and when he sees you his heart will be glad. [15]You shall speak to him and put the words in his mouth; and I will be with your mouth and with his mouth, and will teach you what you shall do. [16]He indeed shall speak for you to the people; he shall serve as a mouth for you, and you shall serve as God for him.

[27]The LORD said to Aaron, "Go into the wilderness to meet Moses." So he went; and he met him at the mountain of God and kissed him. [28]Moses told Aaron all the words of the LORD with which he had sent him, and all the signs with which he had charged him. [29]Then Moses and Aaron went and assembled all the elders of the Israelites. [30]**Aaron spoke all the words that the LORD had spoken to Moses, and performed the signs in the sight of the people.** [31]The people believed; and when they heard that the LORD had given heed to the Israelites and that he had seen their misery, they bowed down and worshiped.

his mouth? Who makes him deaf or mute? Who gives him sight or makes him blind? Is it not I, the LORD? [12]Now go; I will help you speak and will teach you what to say."

[13]But Moses said, "O Lord, please send someone else to do it."

[14]Then the LORD's anger burned against Moses and he said, "What about your brother, Aaron the Levite? I know he can speak well. He is already on his way to meet you, and his heart will be glad when he sees you. [15]You shall speak to him and put words in his mouth; I will help both of you speak and will teach you what to do. [16]He will speak to the people for you, and it will be as if he were your mouth and as if you were God to him.

[27]The LORD said to Aaron, "Go into the desert to meet Moses." So he met Moses at the mountain of God and kissed him. [28]Then Moses told Aaron everything the LORD had sent him to say, and also about all the miraculous signs he had commanded him to perform.

[29]Moses and Aaron brought together all the elders of the Israelites, [30]and **Aaron told them everything the LORD had said to Moses. He also performed the signs before the people,** [31]and they believed. And when they heard that the LORD was concerned about them and had seen their misery, they bowed down and worshiped.

UNDERSTANDING THE SCRIPTURE

Exodus 4:10-13. The conversation between God and Moses at the burning bush, which we looked at last week, is continued here in this lesson. As you recall, Moses' first response to God was on the order of a simple "Why me?" He has raised several other objections in the intervening verses and comes now to what he must suppose will clinch his argument and compel God to choose someone else for this great

task instead of him. What he says, in essence in verse 10, is actually humorous: "I have not ever been a good speaker, and I certainly have not gotten any better since I have been talking with you." Of course we are not privy to Moses' inner thoughts and feelings, so we do not know if this was just one more excuse or if he actually believed himself to be a poor speaker. Perhaps he really did want this mission to succeed and was afraid that if he were the leader it would have very little chance of working out right. God reminds Moses that all our senses are part of the divine creation and reassures him that he will not be alone when he goes before Pharaoh. But the reassurance is for naught. "Please, please, please just send someone else," begs Moses.

A portion of verse 11 may be troublesome to some. Is it saying that God causes people to be blind or mute? (A very similar question is asked of Jesus by the disciples in John 9.) This is an important question and the answer is not a simple yes or no. If there is only one God—as Israel maintains throughout the Old Testament—then ultimately nothing can be done outside the divine providence. But if one carries this manner of thinking too far in a straight line, it could come out saying that we human beings finally bear no responsibility for our own actions, or even that since Pharaoh enslaved the Israelites, it must all have been part of God's will. No, many things remain mysteries to us and probably beyond our complete understanding in this life. In this verse God is reassuring Moses that his inability to speak well is not an insurmountable obstacle to God.

Exodus 4:14-16. Since Moses has been raising objection after objection for a chapter and a half, it does not seem surprising that God's patience seems to be wearing thin. "All right," says God, "Aaron can be the speaker." This pronouncement raises questions: Who is Aaron? Where has he come from? We know that Aaron was the brother of Moses and of Miriam. Exodus 6:20 records genealogical information about his family: "Amram married Jochebed his father's sister and she bore him Aaron and Moses." Numbers 26:59 records that Jochebed was the daughter of Levi, and that she and Amram had three children: Aaron, Moses, and Miriam. Moses' birth story tells us that Miriam watched to see what would happen to baby Moses, and even offered to get a Hebrew woman (their

mother) to nurse him (Exodus 2:4-8), so we can conclude that she was significantly older than Moses. Exodus 7:7 states that when God called, Moses was eighty and Aaron was eighty-three, so Aaron must have been the middle child, only three years older than Moses. Exodus 6:23 records that Aaron was married to Elisheba and that together they had four children: Nadab, Abihu, Eleazar, and Ithamar. From this genealogy we also learn that this family is descended from Levi (6:16), just as recorded in Exodus 2:1.

Exodus 4:14 raises another question: Why is Aaron "coming out to meet" Moses now? How does he even know where Moses is after all this time? These questions are perfectly legitimate, but the narrator has no interest in them. God needs to provide someone to be Moses' spokesman, and Aaron is chosen. It would be fascinating if we also had an account of Aaron's call in Egypt, wouldn't it? Bringing in another person at this point can teach us several important lessons. God is not saying, in introducing Aaron, that there is no further use for Moses. Rather, God is going to "Plan B" to take into account Moses' objections and fears. The strengths of one of them can fill in for the weaknesses of the other. In addition, neither of them needs to be fearful of what to say, because God will provide the words necessary at the appropriate time. (See also Jesus' several assurances to the disciples, as at Matthew 10:19-20, Mark 13:11, and Luke 12:11-12.)

Exodus 4:27-28. The actual meeting of Aaron and Moses is recounted after Moses has gone home to tell his father-in-law that he wants to return to Egypt to see his own family. Moses, his wife Zipporah, and their two sons set out from Midian with Jethro's blessing (4:18-20). The narrator, with great economy of words, tells us that Moses recounts everything he has heard and seen from the Lord to his brother and shows him the signs God taught him. Did Aaron already know what God had promised?

Was he excited? Was he reluctant? Was he just glad to have his brother back, even with this amazing commission from God? Again the narrator is silent about all these human details. Instead, the narrator focuses on the plot of the story, telling what is necessary to let the reader know what is happening.

Exodus 4:29-31. After they arrive back in Egypt, Moses and Aaron gather the leaders of the Israelites. They tell the people the momentous news that the Lord has heard their cries for help and has promised to deliver them from their bondage. The two of them even show the leaders all the signs God had taught Moses back at the burning bush (see Exodus 4:2-7). Who would not believe such wondrous news, especially when it is accompanied by strange supernatural signs? And so we are told that the people did believe what Moses and Aaron told them. In response to the news, they worshiped the Lord. Yes, we know the rest of the story, and we know they will raise objections of their own soon enough. But for now their response is exactly right: They hear and see, they believe, and they worship.

INTERPRETING THE SCRIPTURE

One More Excuse

When Moses tells God that he has never been a good speaker and has not gotten better since conversing with God, how does he mean it? That verse could be read in several tones of voice with many different meanings. Perhaps Moses believes that his halting speech will be a serious barrier to the task of freeing the slaves. Or maybe he is just making excuses. We really do not know. And what of the responses we make when we are asked to take on a task with great responsibility? We too may answer with mixed motives. "I am not good enough, not skilled enough, not energetic enough," are some common options. And we may be exactly right when we give those reasons for trying to turn down the job. We do need to ask ourselves, usually, whether we are trying to get out of doing something we don't want to do mostly because we just don't want to do it. All our objections cannot ever be answered totally, especially if the issues we are raising are not really honest questions but rather excuses to avoid responsibility. If we want to have all the facts before making a decision we will remain perpetual fence-straddlers. But, look at the way God responded to Moses by solving the particular problem. If we respond to the invitation with honest concerns, if we take those concerns to God and to other members of the body of Christ, it is possible a solution will be forthcoming that we had not thought of ourselves.

Anger With a Solution

Yes, the text says clearly that God became angry. But God's anger does not lash out at others the way human anger often does. Nor is God an emotionless machine. For whatever fathomless reason, God wants to be in relationship with us. God loves us and wants us—all of us—to have good and fulfilling lives on this earth. So when we wiggle and squirm and keep throwing objections back at God's requests, it is not surprising that God's response may at some points seem a little out of sorts. God cares passionately about this creation and therefore cares passionately about what we are doing to it and to one another. God did not want the Israelites to remain slaves in Egypt and, for whatever reason, needed Moses to help free them. We all want God to be patient with us, but maybe for the sake of other people God will let some of this sort of anger show once in a while. Maybe the anger was to get Moses' attention. Maybe it was a way of reminding Moses that what his kinfolk were experiencing back in Egypt was not a "Sunday school picnic." Maybe God was, in effect, saying that Moses had a pretty soft life, even out in the wilderness with a flock of sheep, compared to what the slaves were living through. The anger is short-lived, and God comes up with the solution to Moses' final objection to his call.

Others Are Called Too

The introduction of Aaron into the story raises several more questions. It is likely that many parallels to our own stories are raised as well. What if Aaron had not agreed to his own call? What if he did not have a good relationship (or *any* relationship) with his brother? What if he resented Moses' upbringing in Pharaoh's palace while he, Aaron, had to live and work as a slave? What if he did not want to be just the mouthpiece? What if he had had a relationship with God for many years and resented being only second in command instead of the leader? Anyone who has read the book of Genesis knows that biblical brothers do not always get along well with each other! And I can imagine many questions from Moses' side as well when God offers Aaron as the solution to Moses' difficulty with speech. Most of the preceding questions about Aaron could just as well be posed from the point of view of Moses.

It is probably especially difficult in our society, with the numerous culture heroes of lone cowboys, maverick crime fighters, and self-made men and women of every stripe, to put in a good word for cooperation at the highest levels. The image of "the individual" seems so strong at times that cooperation is almost a taboo, and compromise is seen as a bad thing. Yet this biblical passage shows another way: No one can have *all* the qualifications required for a large undertaking. Yet the culture proclaims that winning is everything, that no one remembers number two, and so forth. My biweekly newspaper seldom has an issue without pictures of winners: endless beauty pageants with a winner in each of several age categories, the real estate agent with the highest sales for the month, the boy with the most rebounds on the high school basketball team, the cutest baby at the fall festival. Rarely is a cooperative venture celebrated. I certainly do not mean to denigrate individual achievements; my point is that we need to pay attention to more than individual winners while dismissing everyone else as losers. Could the real estate agent, to take one example, have made all those sales without the support of an office staff? Or could the basketball player have rebounded so many times without four teammates on the court with him—to say nothing of an opposing five-person team? Although celebrating the *team* with the best winning record, or the real estate *office* with the most sales could be a step in a better direction, what about all the other basketball players and house sellers? Why do we not celebrate a game well played and work done well? Must everything be divided into winners and losers or leaders and followers?

Of course this is not a new problem, nor one found only in the United States. Jesus' disciples did a fair amount of jockeying for position also. (See, among other passages, Matthew 18:1-5; Mark 9:33-37; Luke 9:46-48.) This issue can raise questions for our life together within the body of Christ. How well do we cooperate in the church? How much do we realize our need for one another and our dependence on one another?

Following Instructions

When Moses and Aaron return to Egypt everything looks good for a while. That simple statement "the people believed" (4:31) must have been heartening to them. This is often the case. In the first wave of enthusiasm for a new project, a new political candidate, or a new emphasis in the church, much may be accomplished. We need not be cynical and always looking for the downside, the slipup, the mistakes. That first enthusiasm was real and is to be celebrated. In the strength of such moments we can go far in the work God has given us to do.

SHARING THE SCRIPTURE

Preparing Our Hearts

Meditate on this week's devotional reading, found in Proverbs 1:20-33. Wisdom, personified in this passage as a woman, is eager to share her knowledge but also ready to rain down disaster on those who refuse to listen to her. Think carefully about these questions: In what ways do you seek and heed God's wisdom? How can God's wisdom embolden you to accept confidently tasks God calls you to do?

Pray that you and the adult learners will be open to responding to the knowledge that God wants to give you to benefit yourself and others.

Preparing Our Minds

Study the background and lesson Scripture, both of which are found in Exodus 4:10-16, 27-31.

Write on newsprint:

❑ information for next week's lesson, found under "Continue the Journey."
❑ activities for further spiritual growth in "Continue the Journey."

Familiarize yourself with Understanding the Scripture so as to be able to help answer students' questions.

LEADING THE CLASS

(1) Gather to Learn

❖ Welcome the class members and introduce any guests.

❖ Pray that today's participants will be ready and willing to respond to God's call on their lives.

❖ Read this brief excerpt from the book *This I Believe: The Personal Philosophies of Remarkable Men and Women* edited by Jay Allison and Dan Gediman. Introduce Jody Williams as the founding coordinator of the International Campaign to Ban Landmines, an organization that was awarded the 1997 Nobel Peace Prize. **"I believe it is possible for ordinary people to achieve extraordinary things. For me, the difference between an 'ordinary' and an 'extraordinary' person is not the title that person might have, but what they do to make the world a better place for us all.**

" . . . My older brother was born deaf. Growing up, I ended up defending him, and I often think that is what started me on my path to whatever it is I am today.

"When I was approached with the idea of trying to create a landmine campaign, we were just three people in a small office in Washington, D.C., in late 1991. I certainly had more than a few ideas about how to begin a campaign, but what if nobody cared? What if nobody responded? But I knew the only way to answer those questions was to accept the challenge."

❖ Discuss these questions with the class:

(1) What do you suppose motivated Jody Williams and her colleagues to work so diligently on behalf of a cause?

(2) Jody obviously took a risk to support something she believed in, even though she said she really did not know how to begin. What lessons can you learn from her?

❖ Read aloud today's focus statement: **Because some people believe they are not adequate to a task, they are fearful of and resistant to accepting it. How can people who are afraid be encouraged to do the work assigned them? Moses resisted God's call, but then he accepted aid from his brother Aaron, according to God's command.**

(2) Delve Into the Account of Moses' Resistance to God's Commands and Aaron's Acceptance of His Role in Leading the People

❖ Choose three volunteers to read the parts of Moses, God, and a narrator in Exodus 4:10-16, 27-31.

❖ Invite the students to raise questions about this passage. What seems unclear or puzzling to them? List these questions on newsprint.

❖ Encourage class members to answer these questions. Add information from the lesson, particularly the Understanding the Scripture portion. If you have a Bible commentary on hand, ask one or more students to research the passage to see if answers can be found.

❖ Look at the situation from Aaron's point of view. Read aloud the first paragraph of "Others Are Called Too."

❖ Choose at least one team of two role-players to take the parts of Aaron and Moses. Ask these volunteers to have a conversation as if they are meeting for the first time in years. Have Moses tell Aaron what God expects them to do. Either or both may ask questions and raise objections.

❖ End this portion by inviting the students who observed this exchange to make comments about how they might have responded had they been Moses or Aaron.

(3) Explore Personal Feelings of Inadequacy

❖ Read aloud these quotations:
- **Anything I've ever done that ultimately was worthwhile . . . initially scared me to death.** (Betty Bender)
- **Do not let what you cannot do interfere with what you can do.** (John Wooden)
- **Nothing splendid has ever been achieved except by those who dared believe that something inside them was superior to circumstance.** (Bruce Barton)

❖ Invite the class members to discuss these ideas in small groups by commenting on how they respond to challenges that appear to be beyond their ability to fulfill.

❖ Point out that God answered Moses' concerns by having Aaron join him. Distribute newsprint and a marker to each group. Challenge the groups to make a list of tasks in your congregation where more people are needed to assist. Maybe you need more choir members, more Sunday school teachers, more missions team members, or more hospital visitors.

❖ Ask the groups to post their lists around the room. Encourage the adults to walk around and see the lists, if that is possible. If not, have each group read its list. Identify areas where several groups believe assistance is needed. Star (*) these areas.

(4) Take Responsibility for the Tasks to Which God Has Called the Learners

❖ Distribute paper and pencils. Provide quiet time for the adults to reflect on the lists, particularly the starred items. Encourage them to listen. Is God calling them to take responsibility for any of these tasks?

❖ Suggest that they write on their papers any actions they feel called to take. Suggest that they list all of the reasons they can think of as to why they should *not* accept these responsibilities. Recommend that they pray silently about these objections.

❖ Ask the adults to choose someone in the class who will be their prayer partner. Make sure that everyone has a partner. Be sure that the partners have a phone number or e-mail address so that they can check in during the week.

❖ Conclude by encouraging all of the adults to continue to pray about God's call and their own response, as well as the call and response of their prayer partner.

(5) Continue the Journey

❖ Pray that the students will go forth today ready to hear God's call and respond with confidence, knowing that God will provide all they need to accomplish the task.

❖ Read aloud this preparation for next week's lesson. You may also want to post it on newsprint for the students to copy.

■ **Title: Pharaoh Ignores God's Call**
■ **Background Scripture: Exodus 5:1–6:1**
■ **Lesson Scripture: Exodus 5:1-9, 22–6:1**
■ **Focus of the Lesson: Some people fail to recognize true authority and power, erroneously believing that the authority and power rest within themselves. What brings us to recognize a higher authority? When Pharaoh refused to obey God's command to release the Israelites from slavery in Egypt, God promised to force obedience with a mighty hand.**

❖ Challenge the students to complete one or more of these activities for further spiritual growth, which you will write on newsprint for the students to copy.

(1) **Recall that Moses and Aaron responded to God by accepting responsibility for a task. Where in the church or the world do you see tasks that you believe God is calling you to undertake? What is your answer?**

(2) **Pray for leaders that they might seek God's strength and guidance to fulfill their missions.**

(3) **Offer to assist a person who might need help in fulfilling a responsibility.**

❖ Sing or read aloud "Take My Life, and Let It Be."

❖ Conclude today's session by leading the class in this benediction: **We hear your call, O God, and ask that you send us forth empowered by your Spirit to live and serve as your covenant people.**

UNIT 1: CALLED OUT OF EGYPT
PHARAOH IGNORES GOD'S CALL

PREVIEWING THE LESSON

Lesson Scripture: Exodus 5:1-9, 22–6:1
Background Scripture: Exodus 5:1–6:1
Key Verse: Exodus 5:1

Focus of the Lesson:
Some people fail to recognize true authority and power, erroneously believing that the authority and power rest within themselves. What brings us to recognize a higher authority? When Pharaoh refused to obey God's command to release the Israelites from slavery in Egypt, God promised to force obedience with a mighty hand.

Goals for the Learners:
(1) to recount Pharaoh's refusal to obey God.
(2) to explore issues of authority and obedience in their lives.
(3) to recognize and respect God's authority.

Pronunciation Guide:
Septuagint (sep' too uh jint)

Supplies:
Bibles, newsprint and marker, paper and pencils, hymnals, optional pictures of people oppressed by those in authority

---

READING THE SCRIPTURE

NRSV
Exodus 5:1-9, 22–6:1

¹Afterward Moses and Aaron went to Pharaoh and said, **"Thus says the LORD, the God of Israel, 'Let my people go, so that they may celebrate a festival to me in the wilderness.'"** ²But Pharaoh said, "Who is

NIV
Exodus 5:1-9, 22–6:1

¹Afterward Moses and Aaron went to Pharaoh and said, **"This is what the LORD, the God of Israel, says: 'Let my people go, so that they may hold a festival to me in the desert.'"**

the LORD, that I should heed him and let Israel go? I do not know the LORD, and I will not let Israel go." ³Then they said, "The God of the Hebrews has revealed himself to us; let us go a three days' journey into the wilderness to sacrifice to the LORD our God, or he will fall upon us with pestilence or sword." ⁴But the king of Egypt said to them, "Moses and Aaron, why are you taking the people away from their work? Get to your labors!" ⁵Pharaoh continued, "Now they are more numerous than the people of the land and yet you want them to stop working!" ⁶That same day Pharaoh commanded the taskmasters of the people, as well as their supervisors, ⁷"You shall no longer give the people straw to make bricks, as before; let them go and gather straw for themselves. ⁸But you shall require of them the same quantity of bricks as they have made previously; do not diminish it, for they are lazy; that is why they cry, 'Let us go and offer sacrifice to our God.' ⁹Let heavier work be laid on them; then they will labor at it and pay no attention to deceptive words."

²²Then Moses turned again to the LORD and said, "O LORD, why have you mistreated this people? Why did you ever send me? ²³Since I first came to Pharaoh to speak in your name, he has mistreated this people, and you have done nothing at all to deliver your people."

⁶:¹Then the LORD said to Moses, "Now you shall see what I will do to Pharaoh: Indeed, by a mighty hand he will let them go; by a mighty hand he will drive them out of his land."

²Pharaoh said, "Who is the LORD, that I should obey him and let Israel go? I do not know the LORD and I will not let Israel go." ³Then they said, "The God of the Hebrews has met with us. Now let us take a three-day journey into the desert to offer sacrifices to the LORD our God, or he may strike us with plagues or with the sword." ⁴But the king of Egypt said, "Moses and Aaron, why are you taking the people away from their labor? Get back to your work!" ⁵Then Pharaoh said, "Look, the people of the land are now numerous, and you are stopping them from working."

⁶That same day Pharaoh gave this order to the slave drivers and foremen in charge of the people: ⁷"You are no longer to supply the people with straw for making bricks; let them go and gather their own straw. ⁸But require them to make the same number of bricks as before; don't reduce the quota. They are lazy; that is why they are crying out, 'Let us go and sacrifice to our God.' ⁹Make the work harder for the men so that they keep working and pay no attention to lies."

²²Moses returned to the LORD and said, "O Lord, why have you brought trouble upon this people? Is this why you sent me? ²³Ever since I went to Pharaoh to speak in your name, he has brought trouble upon this people, and you have not rescued your people at all."

⁶:¹Then the LORD said to Moses, "Now you will see what I will do to Pharaoh: Because of my mighty hand he will let them go; because of my mighty hand he will drive them out of his country."

UNDERSTANDING THE SCRIPTURE

Exodus 5:1-4. Moses and Aaron have joined forces and they now have an audience with Pharaoh. In what is probably one of the most familiar biblical phrases, they proclaim to the ruler: "Thus says the LORD, the God of Israel, 'Let my people go!' " (5:1). Except that is not quite what the Hebrew says. The verb root used here means "send."

What is more, the "variation" of the verb is an intensive alternative to the basic root and here it is in the imperative (command) form. Indeed, some forty-one times when this section of Exodus has a version of "Let my people go" in English, the Hebrew has this same intensive variation. Aaron and Moses, on behalf of God, are not simply saying, "Please let us take a bit of a stroll in the wilderness," but rather "Send us out." They are not even using the polite form of the imperative, but the stark, "Send out!" In addition to using an imperative to Pharaoh, they say they want to go into the wilderness to worship the Lord. Going into the wilderness would mean they would be outside Pharaoh's control. Worse, from Pharaoh's point of view, the worshiping of a non-Egyptian God would mean the people have a rival source of power in competition with their Egyptian ruler. Loyalty to anything other than imperial power will not be tolerated, and so it is no surprise that Pharaoh does not agree with their request/demand.

Not only does Pharaoh turn them down, he asks, "Who is the LORD?" (5:2). We cannot know what tone of voice the king used, but the sense is one of extreme condescension. Pharaoh is not asking for information, as the surface of the question might suggest. When Pharaoh says, "I do not know the LORD," he refers to more than a lack of factual knowledge. He is also asserting that he does not recognize any authority that can legitimately be granted to the Lord. "Knowing" the Lord is a major theme not only in the confrontations between Pharaoh and Moses but also throughout the Old Testament. To know the Lord is to have reverence for, to serve, and ultimately to give allegiance to the Lord rather than to any lesser power. Pharaoh will allow no rivals. He dismisses Moses and Aaron brusquely: "Get back to your work!" (5:4 NIV).

Exodus 5:5-18. To Pharaoh's way of thinking, if the people have anything else on their minds other than work, other than the economic contribution they make to his realm, then they clearly are not working hard enough. Too much free time allows dangerous ideas to sprout. His solution is to increase their labor by ceasing to provide straw, one of the raw materials they need for the production of bricks. Of course the daily production quota is not to be diminished in the slightest. When it is not possible to produce the required number of bricks, the Egyptian taskmasters beat the Hebrew overseers. Showing enormous courage, the overseers themselves go to Pharaoh and try to explain the situation, that if they have to gather their own straw, there will not be enough time to make the same number of bricks as before. Pharaoh again accuses them of being lazy and reiterates that they will not be allowed to leave the country to worship the Lord.

Exodus 5:19-21. The Israelite supervisors are caught in the middle between Pharaoh and Moses, and it is not a comfortable place to be. They may have been happy when they first learned that God had sent Moses and Aaron to bring about their emancipation (4:29-31), but they are anything but happy now. They are in the wretched position of having much responsibility but no power. They are still required to see that there is no decrease in the number of bricks produced by the Israelite slaves, but they have no authority to require that straw be supplied as it had been before. According to the Greek text (the Septuagint), they say to Pharaoh, "You are unjust" (5:16). When they gain nothing from their encounter with Pharaoh, they go to Moses and Aaron, likewise accusing them of making the situation worse. In the Hebrew idiom they say, "You have made us like a bad smell to Pharaoh and his officials" (5:21). This phrase is often used to mean "lesser" people have become "odious" to those above them, as in Genesis 34:30; 2 Samuel 10:6 and 16:21. (The Hebrew word is translated as "stench" in the NIV.)

Exodus 5:22–6:1. We are not told what, if anything, Moses and Aaron say to the outburst of the overseers. Rather, Moses turns with angry honesty to God. This outcome is certainly not what he bargained for before agreeing to leave his life in Midian and return to Egypt. The force of his argument may not come through as clearly in your English translation as it does in the Hebrew. The overseers are "in trouble" in 5:19 and in 5:22 Moses accuses the Lord of "mistreating" the people, but it is the same root in the original. Moses lays the trouble, literally "the evil," clearly at God's door. The situation is not better. It is not even the same as it had been but has become much worse. Not only that, as far as Moses can see, the Lord has "done nothing at all to deliver your people" (5:23). Moses may have protested that he is not eloquent (4:10), but he certainly makes his message clear at this point. The Lord's reply neither makes any excuses nor attempts to make light of the suffering that is indeed still continuing. God reiterates that Pharaoh will send the people out of the country, "by a mighty hand" (6:1). "Hand" is often used to refer to power or strength. Interestingly, there is no pronoun used in this verse to specify whose hand is mighty (although the NIV does add it). Still, it is clear to the reader that Pharaoh, who sneered at the beginning of today's reading, "Who is the LORD, that I should heed him?" (5:2), will not turn out to be the stronger of the two.

INTERPRETING THE SCRIPTURE

Says Who?

One of the reasons Pharaoh refuses to let the people of Israel go into the wilderness to worship is that he does not know who their God is. If Pharaoh does not know the Lord, then the Lord must not be worth knowing. And Pharaoh does not take orders from anyone. He is in charge. He is unwilling to allow any rivals.

Throughout all the intervening centuries, many leaders have been like Pharaoh. And such behavior is seen not only in leaders of nations but also in military generals, business owners and, alas, sometimes church and family leaders too. Power in any amount has a tendency to want to block out all competing voices, whether from those lower on the social ladder or higher up.

Things Get Worse Before They Get Better

Whether it is a matter of housecleaning or changing an unjust situation, the first few steps toward change often make the situation look worse than it was before. My bedroom looks relatively neat before I decide to do a major overhaul of the closet and all my drawers. Then there will be a period of relative chaos as everything is brought out and I decide what to keep and what to give away. In the middle of it I usually wonder why I even started such a project.

I do not mean to trivialize the matter. On the scale of social change, there can be great suffering as a result of some people who are being mistreated asking for better conditions. Some of us are old enough to remember when the civil rights movement began to come to general public awareness in the late 1950s. There were many voices urging caution and patience. And when violence did erupt in some areas, there were voices raised to say, "Aha! You see! We told you so! It is better to leave things as they are and not try to make changes." Such voices do not come from only one side of the issue. The oppressed and the oppressor can, and often do, use the same language, albeit with different ends in mind. Remember, it was not only Pharaoh who opposed Moses and Aaron in today's reading but the Israelite overseers as well. Change can be hard. Change can be uncomfortable. And when just a little bit of change brings on greater opposition, it can make the previous condition look better in retrospect than it had felt at the time.

What's the Point?

Are people only economic units? Pharaoh seems to think so, but then such a view is what one might expect from the person at the very top of the pyramid. What of the viewpoints current in our society? Is life only drudge work to scrape together enough money to pay the rent and utilities and food and maybe have enough left over for some new clothes? Those of us in the church, especially, are quick to say life is much more than economics, much more than what we have and what we produce. But to what degree do we live as if we believe in an alternative viewpoint? Do we allow ourselves time to enjoy what we are supposedly putting so much energy into acquiring? Or how many of us measure our self-worth by our busyness? Perhaps we receive no money at all for our efforts, but we feel guilty if we say no to anyone who asks our assistance, whether to teach Sunday school or help out with the high school band bake sale or to drive for Meals on Wheels.

In the fall of 2006 the Nobel Peace Prize was divided between the Grameen Bank and Muhammad Yunus, the founder of the bank. Dr. Yunus "invented" the concept of microcredit, lending amounts that seem tiny to us—$100 is considered a large loan—to poor people so that they can start or improve their home-based businesses. I was dismayed to read several articles at the time that gave his work a polite nod and then went on to say that people in poor areas could make even more money if they would just move to the cities and work in factories. They might indeed make more money, but at what social cost? Is it better to give up liv-ing with one's family and community to make more money? Is it better to disrupt and even destroy the social fabric for the sake of more cash? Pharaoh seemed to think so.

It's All Your Fault!

As far back in human history as we can go, there is a constant refrain of "It's not my fault!" accompanied by finger-pointing and accusations. Look, for example, at the first man in the Garden of Eden when God asked him why he was hiding. "The woman," he says, "whom you gave to be with me" (Genesis 3:12). It is not enough to blame the woman; the man even blames God for putting the woman with him in the first place.

Sometimes we are accused of things that are not our doing. But the point I want to emphasize here has to do with the exchange between Moses and God at the end of Exodus 5. Moses is clearly angry and upset, and he lashes out at God, saying in essence: "You have not done what you promised you would do!" No, that is not the politest way to speak to the deity, but Moses was being angrily honest. Hiding our emotions behind churchy words when we pray certainly will not fool God. And if we are unwilling to admit to our less-than-pleasant feelings, how can God begin to deal with them? It is greatly to our benefit, I believe, that we have such bits in Scripture, for they remind us that we do not have to protect God, or tiptoe around, or use only fancy words. God is seeking a relationship with us and if it is to be genuine, then, like any other relationship we may have, it needs to be grounded in honesty.

God Remembers

The situation may look worse than it did before, but God reiterates the promise that Israel will indeed be freed from its bondage in Egypt. But neither in the Bible nor in our world does God simply wave a magic wand and make everything better. For whatever reason, God chooses to work with and through human beings. God's assurance is important and at the same time we need to see whether we are doing our part. Change for the better usually comes about with what seem to us to be very slow and small steps. As Dr. Martin Luther King, Jr., reminded us, history has a long arc, but that arc always stretches in the direction of justice. When nothing seems to be improving, Christians can remember our Lord, can remember that he was crucified, and can remember that God raised him from the dead. God neither forgets nor ever breaks a promise.

SHARING THE SCRIPTURE

Preparing Our Hearts

Meditate on this week's devotional reading, found in Psalm 10:1-14. Actually, Psalm 9:1–10:18 forms an acrostic poem, which in this case means that every second verse begins with the next letter of the Hebrew alphabet. This prayer for deliverance in Psalm 10 is particularly apropos of today's lesson, for Pharaoh is certainly an enemy of God's people. Verse 12, in which God is asked to "rise up" and "not forget the oppressed" could easily have been prayed by the Hebrew people in bondage in Egypt. Where are enemies lurking in your life? Are you, like the psalmist, willing to call on God in times of trouble, or do you choose to act as if you were self-sufficient?

Pray that you and the adult learners will rely on God at all times, recognizing that God is, indeed, the only true authority.

Preparing Our Minds

Study the background Scripture from Exodus 5:1–6:1 and the lesson Scripture from Exodus 5:1-9, 22–6:1. Ask yourself: What brings us to recognize a higher power?

Write on newsprint:

❑ scenarios for "Explore Issues of Authority and Obedience in the Learners' Lives."
❑ information for next week's lesson, found under "Continue the Journey."
❑ activities for further spiritual growth in "Continue the Journey."

Locate magazine and newspaper pictures that depict groups or individuals being oppressed by those in authority. Mark or cut out these pictures for use in class, if you choose this option.

LEADING THE CLASS

(1) Gather to Learn

❖ Welcome the class members and introduce any guests.

❖ Pray that everyone will depend on God's grace and help in time of need.

❖ Read aloud these last two lines from the well-known poem "Invictus" by William Ernest Henley (1849–1903):

I am the master of my fate:
I am the captain of my soul.

❖ Pose these questions for discussion with the entire class or in small groups:

(1) **What conclusions can you draw about people who would assert that they are masters of their fate and captains of their soul?**

(2) **How does this attitude relate to the beliefs of those who claim to worship God?**

❖ Read aloud today's focus statement: **Some people fail to recognize true authority and power, erroneously believing that the authority and power rest within them-**

selves. What brings us to recognize a higher authority? When Pharaoh refused to obey God's command to release the Israelites from slavery in Egypt, God promised to force obedience with a mighty hand.

(2) Recount Pharaoh's Refusal to Obey God

❖ **Option:** Show pictures you have located of people who are being oppressed by someone who has personal, political, or economic power over them. Pictures of a political uprising to end a despotic rule would be particularly appropriate for this lesson. Talk with the class about the misuse of authority by those in power. Relate that discussion to Pharaoh's misuse of power over the Hebrew slaves by reading "Says Who?" from Interpreting the Scripture.

❖ Choose volunteers to read the parts of Pharaoh, Moses, Aaron, the Lord, and a narrator from Exodus 5:1-9, 22–6:1.

❖ Discuss these questions, using information from Understanding the Scripture to fill in gaps as appropriate:

   (1) **What do you learn about Pharaoh's authority?**

   (2) **What do you learn about Pharaoh's authority as it relates to God's authority?**

   (3) **What would you have done or said had you been Moses?**

   (4) **How might God's words in Exodus 6:1 continue to speak to oppressed people today? Who in the world needs to hear this reassuring message?**

❖ Read "Things Get Worse Before They Get Better" from Interpreting the Scripture.

❖ Wrap up this portion of the session by discussing challenges to changing the status quo.

(3) Explore Issues of Authority and Obedience in the Learners' Lives

❖ Post the following scenarios, which you have written on newsprint prior to the session. Read them aloud.

▪ A child disobeys her teacher by refusing to put her toys away.

▪ A teenager takes the keys to the car when he has specifically been told he may not drive that night.

▪ A salesperson tampers with numbers on a contract so as to receive more commission than the company allows for the transaction.

❖ Divide the class into three groups, assigning each one of the three scenarios. Ask each group to consider this question, which you will read aloud, in relation to their assigned scenario: **What are the potential rewards and punishments for the person who is disobeying the authority?**

❖ Bring the class back together. Invite someone from each group to summarize the group's discussion.

❖ Refocus the discussion by stating: **Suppose the authority being disobeyed is neither a teacher nor parent nor employer but God. What, then, are the potential rewards and punishments for someone who chooses to disobey God? What are the potential advantages and disadvantages for those who are willing to obey God?** (As the discussion progresses, be sure that the students recognize that sometimes obedience to God is quite costly in terms of popularity, financial gain, and so on. For that reason, some people may choose to ignore God's authority and do things their own way.)

(4) Recognize and Respect God's Authority

❖ Talk with the class about ways in which they discern God's authority in their daily lives. List ideas on newsprint. Here are some possible answers: *Bible study, prayer and discernment, a sermon, an encounter with nature, a conversation with a friend.*

❖ Distribute paper and pencils. Challenge the students to identify areas in their lives in which they do not see God as their authority. Perhaps they have a vice that violates divine authority over their bodies, such as substance or alcohol abuse, smoking, or overeating. Maybe they ignore their Christian values and ethics when on the job. Perhaps they do not treat those closest to them with the love and humility that Christ expects. The students are to list the areas that they have identified on their papers, understanding that whatever they have written will remain completely confidential.

❖ Ask the students to choose at least one area they have identified and write several sentences about changes they will make, with God's help, as they more fully recognize God's authority in this area of their lives.

❖ End this time of reflection by encouraging the adults to place their papers securely in their Bibles and continue to refer to them in the coming weeks to chart their progress.

(5) Continue the Journey

❖ Pray that all who have come today will recognize and heed only God's true authority.

❖ Read aloud this preparation for next week's lesson. You may also want to post it on newsprint for the students to copy.

■ **Title: God Calls the People Out of Egypt**

■ **Background Scripture: Exodus 13:17–14:30**

■ **Lesson Scripture: Exodus 14:15-25, 30**

■ **Focus of the Lesson: Many people have "protectors" to help them** through difficult, even perilous times. Where do we look for protection in difficult times? God protected the Israelites by parting the waters, leading them out of slavery in Egypt, and destroying their enemies.

❖ Challenge the students to complete one or more of these activities for further spiritual growth, which you will write on newsprint for the students to copy:

(1) **Look for news articles covering events where people are oppressed by someone in authority. Take whatever action you can take to stop this injustice. Writing a letter to the editor or calling an elected official can often be very helpful.**

(2) **Read a biography of a historical figure who was known for oppressing people. The lives of Nero, Hitler, or Herod the Great may give you insight into how the abuse of power creates situations that cry out for justice and liberation.**

(3) **Examine your own life to see if there are ways in which you treat others unjustly. What steps can you take to change this behavior?**

❖ Sing or read aloud "Go Down, Moses."

❖ Conclude today's session by leading the class in this benediction: **We hear your call, O God, and ask that you send us forth empowered by your Spirit to live and serve as your covenant people.**

UNIT 1: CALLED OUT OF EGYPT
GOD CALLS THE PEOPLE OUT OF EGYPT

PREVIEWING THE LESSON

Lesson Scripture: Exodus 14:15-25, 30
Background Scripture: Exodus 13:17–14:30
Key Verse: Exodus 14:30

Focus of the Lesson:
Many people have "protectors" to help them through difficult, even perilous times. Where do we look for protection in difficult times? God protected the Israelites by parting the waters, leading them out of slavery in Egypt, and destroying their enemies.

Goals for the Learners:
(1) to tell about the Israelites' miraculous escape from the Egyptians.
(2) to recognize ways that God has protected them.
(3) to trust God for help and to help others in times of trouble.

Supplies:
Bibles, newsprint and marker, paper and pencils, hymnals

READING THE SCRIPTURE

NRSV
Exodus 14:15-25, 30

¹⁵Then the LORD said to Moses, "Why do you cry out to me? Tell the Israelites to go forward. ¹⁶But you lift up your staff, and stretch out your hand over the sea and divide it, that the Israelites may go into the sea on dry ground. ¹⁷Then I will harden the hearts of the Egyptians so that they will go in after them; and so I will gain glory for myself over Pharaoh and all his army, his chariots, and his chariot drivers. ¹⁸And the Egyptians shall

NIV
Exodus 14:15-25, 30

¹⁵Then the LORD said to Moses, "Why are you crying out to me? Tell the Israelites to move on. ¹⁶Raise your staff and stretch out your hand over the sea to divide the water so that the Israelites can go through the sea on dry ground. ¹⁷I will harden the hearts of the Egyptians so that they will go in after them. And I will gain glory through Pharaoh and all his army, through his chariots and his horsemen. ¹⁸The Egyptians will know

know that I am the LORD, when I have gained glory for myself over Pharaoh, his chariots, and his chariot drivers."

[19]The angel of God who was going before the Israelite army moved and went behind them; and the pillar of cloud moved from in front of them and took its place behind them. [20]It came between the army of Egypt and the army of Israel. And so the cloud was there with the darkness, and it lit up the night; one did not come near the other all night.

[21]Then Moses stretched out his hand over the sea. The LORD drove the sea back by a strong east wind all night, and turned the sea into dry land; and the waters were divided. [22]The Israelites went into the sea on dry ground, the waters forming a wall for them on their right and on their left. [23]The Egyptians pursued, and went into the sea after them, all of Pharaoh's horses, chariots, and chariot drivers. [24]At the morning watch the LORD in the pillar of fire and cloud looked down upon the Egyptian army, and threw the Egyptian army into panic. [25]He clogged their chariot wheels so that they turned with difficulty. The Egyptians said, "Let us flee from the Israelites, for the LORD is fighting for them against Egypt."

[30]**Thus the LORD saved Israel that day from the Egyptians;** and Israel saw the Egyptians dead on the seashore.

that I am the LORD when I gain glory through Pharaoh, his chariots and his horsemen."

[19]Then the angel of God, who had been traveling in front of Israel's army, withdrew and went behind them. The pillar of cloud also moved from in front and stood behind them, [20]coming between the armies of Egypt and Israel. Throughout the night the cloud brought darkness to the one side and light to the other side; so neither went near the other all night long.

[21]Then Moses stretched out his hand over the sea, and all that night the LORD drove the sea back with a strong east wind and turned it into dry land. The waters were divided, [22]and the Israelites went through the sea on dry ground, with a wall of water on their right and on their left.

[23]The Egyptians pursued them, and all Pharaoh's horses and chariots and horsemen followed them into the sea. [24]During the last watch of the night the LORD looked down from the pillar of fire and cloud at the Egyptian army and threw it into confusion. [25]He made the wheels of their chariots come off so that they had difficulty driving. And the Egyptians said, "Let's get away from the Israelites! The LORD is fighting for them against Egypt."

[30]**That day the LORD saved Israel from the hands of the Egyptians,** and Israel saw the Egyptians lying dead on the shore.

UNDERSTANDING THE SCRIPTURE

Exodus 13:17-22. Much has happened since last Sunday's text when the Israelite slaves were required to gather their own straw for brick-making and Moses accused God of not making good on the promise to free the slaves from their bondage. Now Pharaoh is sending the Israelites out of the land. Where are all the plagues? Are they not what many people remember most

about the exodus story? Just as the point of the story we refer to as "the burning bush" is not really about that bush (see the lesson for June 7), so the narrative of the exodus from Egypt is not primarily about plagues. At least four theological points are summed up in these verses. First, the point is always primarily about what happens to *people*, not the means God may employ in bringing something about. Second, God's promise in its strictest sense has now been fulfilled. God had said they would be free, and now they are free. But God well knows our feeble frame and our weak resolve and, therefore, is not content with the mere letter of the promise. God is looking into the future, both the far future when they will inherit the Promised Land, and the near future when they may run into some opposition to their escape. If the fleeing slaves run into any opposition, God knows, they will be prone to return to the familiarity of their former life, even if it is one of slavery. Next, although God cannot be seen, there are symbols of God's presence with them at all times. The pillar of cloud by day and the pillar of fire by night are visible to the entire community. One does not have to be in an elite group or have any special training to see these signs of divine grace and protection; they are available at all times and for all the people. Finally, the notice that they took Joseph's bones with them ties in with the end of the book of Genesis and with their history. Those slaves were tied to their history even as they followed God into the future. Doing something new does not mean turning our back on the past or abandoning our own identity.

Exodus 14:1-9. Pharaoh changes his mind once again. As recently as Exodus 12:31-32, he had summoned Moses and Aaron and told them to take all the people and all their possessions and just *leave*. Now that that has happened and the slaves are really and truly gone, Pharaoh realizes the enormity of the change and tries his best to undo it. He sends his army with horsemen and chariots in wild pursuit after the Israelites, not realizing—or not caring—that in so doing he was headed for battle with the Lord, the God of Israel. He had not yet learned what the psalmist proclaimed centuries later: "A king is not saved by his great army; . . . / The war horse is a vain hope for victory" (Psalm 33:16, 17; see also Psalm 147:10-11).

Exodus 14:10-18. Israel is in a panic, not

exactly because they do not trust in God but because they can see all too clearly how things stand—from the human, common-sense point of view. They have water in front of them and the Egyptian army thundering toward them from behind. Surely they are done for! They cry out to God in a generalized way and to Moses in fine specificity. Their wails would be comic if they were not in such terrible straits. "Was it because there were no graves in Egypt that you have taken us away to die in the wilderness?" (14:11). They also proclaim loudly that they never really wanted to be free, that they were perfectly content with their life in Egypt before Moses showed up with his extravagant claims and promises, that anything at all would be better than their situation at this moment. Moses gives orders in a form that sounds strikingly like what scholars term "war of the Lord." They are given orders that are simultaneously possible and nonsensical from the human perspective. "Stand firm," Moses says (14:13). He encourages them to be quiet and see the salvation of the Lord. It is within the capability of every one of them to be quiet and stand still, although how that could contribute to their salvation would not be obvious. But when God is fighting for the people, the human tasks always seem odd and ineffectual in part so that everyone will know it was God who won the victory and not the strength of the army or the cunning of the leaders. Think, for example, of Joshua and the people marching around Jericho, or Gideon and his small band armed with torches and trumpets.

Exodus 14:19-30. Just how is it that God saves Israel from the twin dangers of water and army? The Bible does not say. Or, actually, it gives too many explanations. The water is divided when Moses holds his staff over it. The water is divided when a strong east wind blows it all night. The chariot wheels of the pursuing Egyptians come off. The chariot wheels are clogged in mud. There is no way to build one straight-line, chronological narrative of Israel's escape. And that, I think, is quite intentional. Once again we have to face the reality that the mechanics of the miracle are not of primary importance. God saved the people when all seemed to be lost, and we cannot explain how it was done. This may bother our sensibilities because we want so much to understand and explain everything within our world. Mystery is not a comfortable category for many of us. We are not asked to study the miracles in order to understand them, only to acknowledge them with the awe and reverence due the Lord. Once again we meet an overriding theme of the Bible: God has done for the people what they in no way could have done for themselves.

INTERPRETING THE SCRIPTURE

Freedom Is Hard

Habits are hard to break. And actually bad habits are not so much "broken" as replaced by other, more positive, habits. But that transition time, when you are trying to give up the old but the new is not completely in place—ah, that transition time is so difficult. Few people can go from the old to the new without some slips, whether trying to give up smoking or overeating or driving too aggressively. Over and over again the old ways seem not so bad in retrospect, and the new ways appear to be blocked by insurmountable obstacles. "I'm really pretty healthy for my weight," some might say. "And anyway I could be run over by a truck tomorrow. So why not have another dish of ice cream?" One of the most significant strengths of addiction-fighting groups such as Alcoholics Anonymous and its related groups Alanon and Alateen, as well as the similar groups for fighting narcotics and gambling and other harmful habits, is the very fact of being a group. Members support one another. No one has to go it alone, without the camaraderie and support of others who themselves have been through a similar process. When one person is ready to give up or has actually gone back to old ways, there are always friends to be of support in the continuing journey.

There is another thing that makes freedom hard: In most cases you lose the benefits of the old system before the benefits of the new system are in place. I think the example of trapeze artists in a circus fits well here: Before you can take hold of the new swing, you have to let go of the old one, and there is a moment when you are holding onto nothing at all. You have to trust that the momentum from your launch will take you to the next trapeze.

In the Face of the Evidence

Jesus talks about "counting the cost" (Luke 14:28-32) before embarking on a large project or great adventure. It looks for a while as if Moses and Aaron did not count the cost or did not count it accurately. And yet, for all our calculations, we can never really be 100 percent certain of what tomorrow will bring. If we wait for ironclad guarantees before stepping out in faith, well, what sort of definition of "faith" would that be? God, through Moses, tells the people to step out into the unknown, into their future. This is a place where church groups can get bogged down, and even come to serious disagreements and splits. If we have a bit of extra money this year wouldn't it be more prudent to save it for next year instead of sending it to a missionary or an Advance

Special project? Or, if some people would like to try a contemporary worship service, should we really do it before our numbers are higher? What if it takes too many people from the regular service? Rarely can we be assured of an outcome before we launch out into a new project. Yet there are countless stories of small groups, or even individuals, who trust God's leading and begin something small that grows into a significant work for the Lord. Remember Jesus' promise is not that "where hundreds are gathered together" but rather "where two or three are gathered in my name, I am there among them" (Matthew 18:20).

Mental Speed Bumps

We are fascinated by *how* things happen and want especially to know *how* God's miracles occur. (Remember the burning bush? If only we could figure out how God made that happen, we might have a solution to our energy crisis!) And yet the Bible never discloses God's methods so that we can duplicate them. In fact, the Bible seems often to go out of its way to confuse the matter. There are at least two separate and irreconcilable accounts of how the Israelites escaped from Pharaoh's army. The editors of the biblical material could see that there were internal contradictions in the accounts. Did the sea part because Moses held his rod over it (14:16) or because there was a "strong east wind all night" (14:21)? Rather than write one linear account that we would all be able to "understand," the inspired writers and editors were wise to include several versions from their several traditions. They can function as mental speed bumps for us, reminding us yet again that

as the heavens are higher than the earth,
　so are [God's] ways higher than [our]
　　ways
　and [God's] thoughts than [our]
　　thoughts. (Isaiah 55:9)

Support for each other and trust in God do not require our ability to explain or understand everything. There is nothing wrong with asking the "How?" questions, as long as we do not let ourselves get bogged down with them. Did the chariot wheels come off or get stuck in the mud? The text can be read either way. Several scholars have spent massive amounts of time and ingenuity explaining how all the events surrounding the exodus could have happened by "natural" events. They may well be right—or they may be wrong. In my opinion, they simply miss the point.

God Takes Sides

The last phrase of this week's text is disturbing to me: "and Israel saw the Egyptians dead on the seashore" (14:30). Does God take sides to the point of killing one group for the sake of another? It certainly appears to be so. And this assertion leads us into dangerous territory, for it is a tiny step indeed to go from "God was on Israel's side and so killed Israel's enemies" to "God is on our side and so it is all right for us to kill our enemies." How many wars have been fought in the belief that God wanted one side to kill the other? And this is scarcely limited to Christians fighting non-Christians. In several places in the world today, Christians of one sort are battling Christians who are different. Surely this cannot be pleasing to God because God is not interested in seeing anyone die. In Ezekiel 33:11, God tells the prophet to speak to the Israelites: "Say to them, As I live . . . I have no pleasure in the death of the wicked, but that the wicked turn from their ways and live; . . . for why will you die, O house of Israel?" Ezekiel 18:32 expresses a similar idea: "For I have no pleasure in the death of anyone, says the Lord GOD. Turn, then, and live."

Today's lesson has many troublesome or at least perplexing parts. I think we need to be careful to read these verses in the light of the rest of the story—including the story of the cross. God is ever calling us to new and abundant life, and that life may require leaving behind some things that may have become quite comfortable. God calls us to support one another in our faith journey. We do not always understand the ways God works in our world. And God does, most emphatically, take sides.

SHARING THE SCRIPTURE

Preparing Our Hearts

Meditate on this week's devotional reading, found in Exodus 15:1-13. In this song of Moses, which follows our lesson Scripture for today, we overhear him praising God for strength and salvation. Moses recounts how God acted to save the Hebrews as the sea loomed ahead and Pharaoh's troops pressed from behind. Surely God protected them in this dire situation. Under what circumstances have you experienced God's protection? Write your own song of praise for God's action on your behalf.

Pray that you and the adult learners will trust in God's power to care for you.

Preparing Our Minds

Study the background Scripture from Exodus 13:17–14:30 and the lesson Scripture from Exodus 14:15-25, 30. As you read, consider this question: Where do we look for protection in difficult times?

Write on newsprint:
❑ questions for "Recognize Ways That God Has Protected the Learners."
❑ information for next week's lesson, found under "Continue the Journey."
❑ activities for further spiritual growth in "Continue the Journey."

Plan a brief lecture to introduce the Scripture in "Tell About the Israelites' Miraculous Escape From the Egyptians."

Locate a copy of artist Marc Chagall's painting *The Parting of the Red Sea* in a book or on the Internet. Here is one website where you can find this picture: http://sunsite.icm.edu.pl/cjackson//chagall/p-chagal42.htm.

LEADING THE CLASS

(1) Gather to Learn

❖ Welcome the class members and introduce any guests.

❖ Pray that those who have gathered today will be ready to receive God's word for them.

❖ Encourage the adults to brainstorm a list of things that protect them. Write these ideas on newsprint. Include a wide range of possibilities that people rely on, such as: *surge protectors for electronics, guard dogs, security systems, antilock brakes, insurance, baby gates, walkers,* and *seatbelts.*

❖ Read aloud today's focus statement: **Many people have "protectors" to help them through difficult, even perilous times. Where do we look for protection in difficult times? God protected the Israelites by parting the waters, leading them out of slavery in Egypt, and destroying their enemies.**

(2) Tell About the Israelites' Miraculous Escape From the Egyptians

❖ Give a brief lecture based on Exodus 13:17-22; 14:1-9; and 14:10-18 from Understanding the Scripture to prepare the class for today's lesson.

❖ Choose two volunteers to read the

words of the Lord and the narrator in Exodus 14:15-25, 30. Ask the class to read in unison the Egyptians' words at the end of 14:25.

❖ Show a copy of Marc Chagall's surreal picture *The Parting of the Red Sea*. Note that Chagall is an important painter of the twentieth century. Invite the students to identify characters and setting in this painting. Ask: **Do you sense that the people in this picture are being protected? If so, what images create that impression?** (Note especially the figure of the angel of God, as well as Moses himself who is following God's commands.)

❖ Discuss the Scripture passage by asking these questions:

(1) **How does God save the Hebrews?** (Note information in Understanding the Scripture for Exodus 14:19-30.)

(2) **What does this passage suggest to you about God and how God works?**

(3) **What questions does this passage raise in your mind?** (God's control over the chaotic waters is understood as a miracle. Be prepared for the possibility that some students will not accept that and will prefer to seek other "natural" explanations. "Mental Speed Bumps" and "God Takes Sides" in Interpreting the Scripture might be helpful in dealing with some of the perplexing questions.)

(3) Recognize Ways That God Has Protected the Learners

❖ Distribute paper and pencils. If possible, display the Chagall picture as a focal point for meditation as the students complete the next activity.

❖ Invite the adults to recall a specific situation in which God protected them. Illness, potential accident, natural disaster, and war make us especially vulnerable and in need of protection. Suggest that the students write about this incident, though be sensitive to those who prefer to think about it or those for whom such memories are too painful to recall. Post these questions for them to consider as they write or remember.

(1) **What happened? Describe your recollection of the events in a short paragraph.**

(2) **How did you perceive God at work in this incident?**

(3) **In what ways did this event change or strengthen your relationship with God?**

❖ Divide the class into groups. Encourage volunteers within the groups to read or retell the incident.

❖ Wrap up the discussion by calling the class back together. Spotlight any particularly memorable incidents that the groups want to identify. (Caution: Sometimes people believe that God only helps "special" people. Comments such as "I'm blessed" lead others who were not so fortunate to wonder where they are in relation to God because they were "not blessed." Perhaps a reminder that God is always present, no matter the circumstances, may be helpful to those who feel that God didn't protect them to the degree they would have hoped for.)

(4) Trust God for Help and Help Others in Times of Trouble

❖ Ask the students to read responsively Psalm 23 by alternating verses, with half reading the odd-numbered verses and the other half of the class reading the even-numbered ones. If you have a hymnal with a Psalter, you may choose to use that. Psalm 23 is found on page 754 of *The United Methodist Hymnal*.

❖ Identify with the students ways in which God protects people according to this psalm.

❖ Poll the class members to see if they believe that the Hebrew people of the exodus would have agreed with this psalm's message had it been written in their historical period. If not, what objections would the people have raised?

❖ Shift the discussion to consider ways in which the students can help others in times of trouble. Prayer is certainly one important way. Ask: **What concrete action can we take to help those in need?** Obviously, the answers will depend on what the need is, but here are some general ideas: *provide hands-on help, offer in-kind donations, send financial contributions,* and *work to change public policy and political systems that have created the need or made it worse.*

❖ Provide a few moments of reflection time for students to consider ways that they might help others who are experiencing difficulties right now.

(5) Continue the Journey

❖ Break the silence by praying that all who have come today will trust God to protect them in times of trouble, even as they reach out to help others in difficult situations.

❖ Read aloud this preparation for next week's lesson. You may also want to post it on newsprint for the students to copy.
- **Title: God Calls People to Covenant**
- **Background Scripture: Deuteronomy 5:1-27**
- **Lesson Scripture: Deuteronomy 5:1-9, 11-13, 16-21**

■ **Focus of the Lesson: People make agreements to give structure and rules for their life together. What regulations are necessary to enjoy mutually beneficial lives? God set forth ten rules of conduct governing behavior, property, relationships, and worship.**

❖ Challenge the students to complete one or more of these activities for further spiritual growth, which you will write on newsprint for the students to copy:

(1) **Watch Cecil B. DeMille's 1956 movie, *The Ten Commandments*, starring Charlton Heston. Note how the crossing of the Red Sea is handled in this larger-than-life film.**

(2) **Browse the Internet for answers to this often asked question: Where was God during the Holocaust? How do people see God as protector during this grim chapter in human history?**

(3) **Pray for an oppressed group that yearns to be set free from its modern "Pharaoh."**

❖ Sing or read aloud "Come, Ye Faithful, Raise the Strain."

❖ Conclude today's session by leading the class in this benediction: **We hear your call, O God, and ask that you send us forth empowered by your Spirit to live and serve as your covenant people.**

UNIT 2: CALLED TO BE GOD'S PEOPLE
God Calls People to Covenant

PREVIEWING THE LESSON

Lesson Scripture: Deuteronomy 5:1-9, 11-13, 16-21
Background Scripture: Deuteronomy 5:1-27
Key Verse: Deuteronomy 5:1

Focus of the Lesson:
People make agreements to give structure and rules for their life together. What regulations are necessary to enjoy mutually beneficial lives? God set forth ten rules of conduct governing behavior, property, relationships, and worship.

Goals for the Learners:
(1) to recount how God gave the Ten Commandments to the people.
(2) to value laws and the structure they create.
(3) to make a covenant with class members.

Pronunciation Guide:
Horeb (hor' eb)

Supplies:
Bibles, newsprint and markers, paper and pencils, hymnals

READING THE SCRIPTURE

NRSV
Deuteronomy 5:1-9, 11-13, 16-21
   ¹Moses convened all Israel, and said to them:
   Hear, O Israel, the statutes and ordinances that I am addressing to you today; you shall learn them and observe them diligently. ²The LORD our God made a covenant with us at Horeb. ³Not with our

NIV
Deuteronomy 5:1-9, 11-13, 16-21
   ¹Moses summoned all Israel and said:
   Hear, O Israel, the decrees and laws I declare in your hearing today. Learn them and be sure to follow them. ²The LORD our God made a covenant with us at Horeb. ³It was not with our fathers that the LORD made this covenant, but with us, with all of us who

ancestors did the LORD make this covenant, but with us, who are all of us here alive today. [4]The LORD spoke with you face to face at the mountain, out of the fire. [5](At that time I was standing between the LORD and you to declare to you the words of the LORD; for you were afraid because of the fire and did not go up the mountain.) And he said:

[6]I am the LORD your God, who brought you out of the land of Egypt, out of the house of slavery; [7]you shall have no other gods before me.

[8]You shall not make for yourself an idol, whether in the form of anything that is in heaven above, or that is on the earth beneath, or that is in the water under the earth. [9]You shall not bow down to them or worship them.

[11]You shall not make wrongful use of the name of the LORD your God, for the LORD will not acquit anyone who misuses his name.

[12]Observe the sabbath day and keep it holy, as the LORD your God commanded you. [13]Six days you shall labor and do all your work.

[16]Honor your father and your mother, as the LORD your God commanded you, so that your days may be long and that it may go well with you in the land that the LORD your God is giving you.

[17]You shall not murder.

[18]Neither shall you commit adultery.

[19]Neither shall you steal.

[20]Neither shall you bear false witness against your neighbor.

[21]Neither shall you covet your neighbor's wife.

Neither shall you desire your neighbor's house, or field, or male or female slave, or ox, or donkey, or anything that belongs to your neighbor.

are alive here today. [4]The LORD spoke to you face to face out of the fire on the mountain. [5](At that time I stood between the LORD and you to declare to you the word of the LORD, because you were afraid of the fire and did not go up the mountain.) And he said:

[6]"I am the LORD your God, who brought you out of Egypt, out of the land of slavery.

[7]"You shall have no other gods before me.

[8]"You shall not make for yourself an idol in the form of anything in heaven above or on the earth beneath or in the waters below. [9]You shall not bow down to them or worship them.

[11]"You shall not misuse the name of the LORD your God, for the LORD will not hold anyone guiltless who misuses his name.

[12]"Observe the Sabbath day by keeping it holy, as the LORD your God has commanded you. [13]Six days you shall labor and do all your work.

[16]"Honor your father and your mother, as the Lord your God has commanded you, so that you may live long and that it may go well with you in the land the Lord your God is giving you.

[17]"You shall not murder.

[18]"You shall not commit adultery.

[19]"You shall not steal.

[20]"You shall not give false testimony against your neighbor.

[21]"You shall not covet your neighbor's wife. You shall not set your desire on your neighbor's house or land, his manservant or maidservant, his ox or donkey, or anything that belongs to your neighbor."

UNDERSTANDING THE SCRIPTURE

Deuteronomy 5:1-5. The largest portion of the book of Deuteronomy is in the form of speeches or sermons given by Moses to

the Israelites immediately before they cross the Jordan River into the Promised Land. It has been forty years since they escaped from Egypt and the entire generation who were adults at the time of the exodus has died. Moses is retelling the story of their deliverance and travels through the wilderness to people who were young children at the start or who were born since their parents left Egypt. This is one of the things that makes verse 3 so interesting. Moses is emphasizing that the covenant between God and Israel is not just a matter of history, of something that happened to other people long ago and far away, but that it is a living relationship between God and the people standing in front of Moses at that very moment. Moses has come to the part in the retelling of the basic story where God first gives the law to Israel. This foundational law is traditionally called the Ten Commandments, although the Hebrew both here and at Exodus 20 says merely, "God spoke all these words." Different religious bodies divide some of the laws differently, but interestingly we always have a total of ten. The form this basic law takes is quite similar to ancient vassal treaties that have been discovered. Most of the content, however, is unique to Israel.

Deuteronomy 5:6-11. The first laws have to do with who the Lord God is and what the people's relationship to God is supposed to be. The Lord is the one who rescued Israel from slavery in Egypt. Therefore, the Lord has the right to ask for Israel's complete faithfulness. Verse 7 troubles people sometimes because it appears that God is acknowledging the existence of other gods in saying "you shall have no other gods before me." The Lord is simply being practical. Instead of getting into arguments with their neighbors—all of whom did worship more than one god in those days—Israel is simply to worship the Lord and not have anything to do with any other gods, real or not. Since most of the neighboring gods were represented by carved images or statues, it is logical that such representations were also forbidden to Israel lest they succumb to worshiping any of

their neighbors' gods. Verse 9 contains a troublesome word, "jealous." Jealousy is an emotion that seems unworthy of God. Indeed it is. When the King James Version of the Bible was published in 1611, however, "jealous" was used synonymously in English with "zealous." Every instance of this Hebrew word in its noun form was translated in 1611 as "zeal," although most of the adjective forms were translated as "jealous." In the early seventeenth century, apparently, "zealous" and "jealous" meant the same thing. English has changed over the intervening years although the traditional rendering of this word has not. We would be closer to the original meaning if we would substitute "zealous" for "jealous" whenever it occurs in the Bible. What this verse is saying is that God takes our sin, especially our idolatry, with exceedingly great seriousness. God is *zealous* about these matters and remembers the people's loyalty to thousands of generations.

Deuteronomy 5:12-16. The next five verses have to do with the Sabbath and with family relationships. The setting apart of one day in seven in which no one has to work spells out in great detail that this commandment is meant for everyone. Neither gender nor state of servitude nor lack of citizenship is to keep one from enjoying the benefits of this rest. It extends even to the animals! And this commandment is the first that comes with a reason. The reason stated in verse 15 may come as a surprise because most people are more familiar with the version found in Exodus 20:11. Both reasons are important. In imitation of God we take one day in seven to enjoy creation (Exodus). And because God does not want anyone to be forced to unremitting labor, we take our Sabbath, and we are to make sure that everyone else is able to do so as well.

The next commandment begins literally, "Make heavy your father and your mother." To translate it "honor" is not wrong, but I think it is important to see what lies behind this word. To "make parents heavy" means, among other things, to continue to feed them even after they are no longer able to contribute to the economic well-being of the family. Why? So that our lives may be long as well. That is, our children will observe our taking good care of elderly parents, so that when it is our turn to be old, they will take good care of us. Their children will observe that behavior and, in their turn, take care of their parents.

Deuteronomy 5:17-21. Next come three sharp, staccato prohibitions containing only two words each: "Don't kill," "Don't adulterate," "Don't steal." It would be nice if the word used for "kill" had no ambiguities about it, but it does. The only thing that is certain is that it is not the word used for the slaughter of animals. It certainly means we are not to murder, but whether it also covers capital punishment and the killing involved in warfare is not clear and cannot be proved one way or the other from this vocabulary. "Not bearing false witness" includes not lying and also means we are to speak up when we know something germane to a case. It is possible to bear false witness with our silence. The final commandment is the prohibition of coveting. To covet is more than to want something desperately. In simplest terms to covet is to say not only "I want what you have" but also "and I do not want you to have it."

Deuteronomy 5:22-27. Moses reminds the people that God spoke the law to the entire population, and they were terrified. They were so frightened that they pleaded with Moses to be a go-between for them so that they would not have to experience God directly ever again. As yet another sign of graciousness, God agreed.

INTERPRETING THE SCRIPTURE

The Order Is Important

Notice when God first delivers this set of regulations to the people. They are no longer slaves in Egypt. They have seen how God provides drinkable water. They have been given a dependable supply of food in the manna that is available to gather for six days of every week. What is more, God remembers that the manna on day six must be a sort that can be left overnight, so that the people may eat it on the Sabbath. Only now, some three months after rescuing them from Egypt (Exodus 19:1), does God present this list of commandments. I imagine most of us would have arranged things somewhat differently had we been in charge. I probably would have given Moses the commandments at the burning bush and said, "Take these back to the Israelites and when 90 percent of the people can keep 90 percent of the commandments 90 percent of the time, *then* I will come and rescue you from your slavery." This is emphatically *not* how God acts, and we should be very thankful! For over and over again, God first does for us what we cannot do for ourselves. Only then are "rules and regulations" brought into the picture. Nor can one say God "extorted" the covenant by presenting it sooner. People might agree to almost anything if they thought such agreement would get them out of slavery. God is careful also not to threaten them with a return to slavery. There is no, "Agree or I will stop sending manna" or "Agree or I will simply leave you out here in the wilderness all by yourselves without the pillar of cloud by day, the pillar of fire by night, or any other sort of guidance." To be sure there is a tremendous power difference between God and the people, but God appears to do everything possible so that the people may make a free choice.

And what of agreements in human relationships? The difficulty can be glimpsed where there is a great disparity of power. A private would only in the most extreme instance ignore a general's wishes. The nurse follows the doctor's orders. The student writes a paper to conform to the teacher's instructions more than to express individual creativity. The cashier follows the routine prescribed by the store owner. In such instances there is nothing wrong with the "lower" person's following orders from the "higher" one. But what about less formal, more personal relationships? Does the parent want the child to respond only out of fear of punishment or fear of abandonment? Does one spouse want the other to stifle his or her own individuality in order to do what he or she thinks (or guesses) the spouse prefers? If there is a great difference in power and freedom, it may be difficult for each partner to have a truly free choice.

God certainly has the power and the authority to be in the place of the general, doctor, teacher, or store owner in contrast to the private, nurse, student, or cashier. But over and over again the Bible tells us that that is not the sort of relationship God would prefer to have with us. Jesus uses the well-known figure of speech "Father" to refer to God. While this still has some cultural overtones of "big boss," it is not as stark as "owner" would be. Try to pretend to be God for a moment. How can you make an offer to human beings in a way that allows for their truly free response? Is there any way at all that the huge power differential between the Almighty God and puny Israel can be overcome to allow for a genuinely free choice? One way, I believe, that God tries to bridge this gap is always to put grace before law, to do for us what we cannot do for ourselves, and only then to ask for our response.

The Law as Gift and Blessing

Many in our culture enjoy circulating lawyer jokes and are quick with phrases such as "It's a free country" or "You can't make me!" In our too-hasty reading of some New Testament passages, we make it seem as if all the religious leaders who opposed Jesus were nit-picking, gnat-straining legalists and that Jesus came primarily to free us from the excessive burdens of the law. This attitude is an unfortunate misreading of both the Old and New Testaments. Imagine waking up one day to a community with no laws at all. It might seem like fun for a few minutes, but soon the chaos would become apparent. Imagine electricity to heat the water for coffee, specific frequencies for radio and television and telephone—with no regulation how would these be apportioned? And if there were no agreement about which side of the road to use for travel, who would dare venture out in a car? You can easily multiply such examples.

Clearly, one benefit of law is to keep the chaos at bay and make many of the things we enjoy in life possible. In giving the law, God gives a great gift, for one of the messages is that God desires an ongoing relationship with us. God could have said, in effect, "I have gotten you out of slavery. Have a nice life. Good-bye." Against all logic, however, God said instead, "I have gotten you out of slavery. I want our relationship to continue, so here are some basic rules to help you live in proper relationship with one another and with me."

But What About People?

How do we relate law and covenant to our personal relationships? Is it even appropriate to combine these categories? Certainly not if we are thinking of "law" only in terms of legalism. Neither marriage nor friendship nor even a Sunday school class is best served by unrelenting recourse to *Robert's Rules of Order*. Yet the underlying principles we see in the commandments do seem to be appropriate. For example, we can see that all people are to be honored. Although not everyone becomes a parent, everyone begins life with parents, so it is not a stretch to care graciously for all elderly citizens, not just those who are blood kin to us. The Sabbath commandment, especially in this version in Deuteronomy, makes clear that no category of people is to be treated to a life of perpetual slavery. Even allowing for the ancient Israelites' cultural differences that permitted some sorts of slavery, *everyone* was allowed Sabbath rest.

I once had a parishioner who stopped attending Sunday school when her class moved from an upstairs room to one on the ground floor. I thought that was odd and, after missing her for a couple of weeks, visited and asked her about it. She finally explained the situation to me. "I'm glad enough not to have to climb the stairs, what with the arthritis," she began. "But I guess everyone forgot about 'Betty's chair,' and so they didn't move it to the new room. I'm so short that, on the regular chairs, my feet don't touch the floor and that gets uncomfortable and sometimes my legs go to sleep and then it's darn near impossible to get up and walk when the class is over. But I don't want to make a fuss." When we are paying attention to the attitudes in the Ten Commandments, then no one will need to "make a fuss" as we look out for the simple needs of one another.

SHARING THE SCRIPTURE

Preparing Our Hearts

Meditate on this week's devotional reading, found in Matthew 22:34-40. Here Jesus answers a question by an authority on Jewish law concerning which commandment is the greatest. Jesus quotes from Deuteronomy 6:5 and Leviticus 19:18, saying that everything else in the law hinges on love of God and love of neighbor. What do you do to show your love for God? How is your love for God revealed in the way you treat other people?

Pray that you and the adult learners will recognize the importance of loving God and loving neighbor.

Preparing Our Minds

Study the background Scripture from Deuteronomy 5:1-27 and the lesson Scripture from verses 1-9, 11-13, and 16-21. As you delve into these texts, consider this question: What regulations are necessary to enjoy mutually beneficial lives?

Write on newsprint:

❑ questions for "Recount How God Gave the Ten Commandments to the People."
❑ information for next week's lesson, found under "Continue the Journey."
❑ activities for further spiritual growth in "Continue the Journey."

Study Understanding the Scripture and be prepared to add information to today's discussions.

LEADING THE CLASS

(1) Gather to Learn

❖ Welcome the class members and introduce any guests.

❖ Pray that all of the participants will be ready to hear and respond to God's word for them today.

❖ Encourage the adults to think about the kinds of laws and unwritten agreements that give structure to life in your community. Think of things such as driving, pets, trash, noise, schools, and property.

❖ Discuss this question: **How would life**

be different in your community if these rules or laws did not exist?

❖ Read aloud today's focus statement: **People make agreements to give structure and rules for their life together. What regulations are necessary to enjoy mutually beneficial lives? God set forth ten rules of conduct governing behavior, property, relationships, and worship.**

(2) Recount How God Gave the Ten Commandments to the People

❖ Choose eleven volunteers to read Deuteronomy 5:1-5, 6-7, 8-9 (ending with "worship them"), 11, 12-13, 16, 17, 18, 19, 20, 21. If you do not have that many volunteers, at least alternate so that the students hear a different voice for each commandment.

❖ **Option:** Ask the students to turn to Exodus 20:1-17 to compare this account to the one in Deuteronomy where Moses is recalling all that has happened. Where do you note differences? Do these differences really make any difference?

❖ Divide the class into teams of three or four. Five groups would be ideal, assuming you assign two commandments to each group. Post the following questions for discussion within each group. Assign each group specific laws to consider as they address these questions.
  (1) **What do these laws say about God?**
  (2) **What do these laws say about humans?**
  (3) **What do these laws say about living together in covenant in God's world?**

❖ Call the students back together to hear answers to the questions about the laws the groups were assigned to consider. Add information from Understanding the Scripture as you deem appropriate.

❖ Wrap up this portion of the session by reading in unison today's key verse, Deuteronomy 5:1. Remind the class that the word "hear" means not only to "listen" but

also to "heed" or "obey." Hearing the laws was not enough; people were expected to live by them.

(3) Value Laws and the Structure They Create

❖ Set aside a few minutes for a "sound off" by class members concerning laws they think are "stupid" or not in the best interest of the public. If the class is large, consider doing this in groups so more people will have a chance to participate.

❖ See if the students can identify common threads in the laws they have blasted. Perhaps the problem is that some are antiquated and do not work well in today's world. If so, what can they do to get these laws off the books?

❖ Turn the discussion to laws that make your community a civil place to live. Ask: **What would happen if laws, some of which are rooted in the Ten Commandments, that govern how we treat one other and property were not on the books and enforced?**

❖ Read or retell "The Law as Gift and Blessing."

❖ Invite the students to comment on how laws give structure to their lives and, therefore, are valuable to them.

(4) Make a Covenant With Class Members

❖ Challenge the class members to think of rules for living together as a class that would help them be more faithful in their Christian discipleship. List their ideas on newsprint. Here are some areas to consider:
  ■ When people are absent, the class is diminished because not everyone is participating. What agreements can you make with one another about attendance, recognizing, of course, that people do fall ill, take vacations, and must be away on business?
  ■ When people are absent or are having a known problem, what steps

will the class take to support them and let them know they are cared for and loved?

■ In what ways can the group members hold one another accountable for spiritual growth? Is every person willing to practice at least one spiritual discipline each week?

■ How can the group agree to live out its profession of faith by the service it performs for others as a sign of loving God and loving neighbor?

❖ Look at the brainstormed ideas. Work with the adults to create a covenant that all can agree to. Write it on newsprint. Distribute paper and pencils so that each student can make a copy. The wording can simply begin, "We the members of the Bible Fellowship Class agree to" and then write the covenant in the form of a list.

❖ Conclude by asking the group to read the covenant aloud in unison. When the students are ready to leave the room, have markers available so that they can sign their names on the newsprint copy.

(5) Continue the Journey

❖ Pray that those who have come today will recognize the value of God's rules for living and strive to obey them.

❖ Read aloud this preparation for next week's lesson. You may also want to post it on newsprint for the students to copy.

■ **Title: God Calls People to Remember**

■ **Background Scripture: Deuteronomy 16:1-8**

■ **Lesson Scripture: Deuteronomy 16:1-8**

■ **Focus of the Lesson: Individuals and communities regularly remem-**

ber and celebrate great occasions with thanksgiving. How do we commemorate significant events in our lives? God commanded the Israelites to remember their deprivation by eating only unleavened bread and simple meat at sundown.

❖ Challenge the students to complete one or more of these activities for further spiritual growth, which you will write on newsprint for the students to copy:

(1) **Write in your spiritual journal your thoughts in answer to these questions: What value do you see in having rules for living together? How do you respond when someone else's refusal to heed a law causes problems for you?**

(2) **Do an Internet search on "antiquated laws on U.S. books" or a similar heading. Some of these are actually funny in today's world. As you think about the Ten Commandments, do you perceive any of them to be obsolete? Why or why not?**

(3) **Research controversies in the United States concerning public displays of the Ten Commandments. Where do you stand on this issue? Why?**

❖ Sing or read aloud "Help Us Accept Each Other."

❖ Conclude today's session by leading the class in this benediction: **We hear your call, O God, and ask that you send us forth empowered by your Spirit to live and serve as your covenant people.**

UNIT 2: CALLED TO BE GOD'S PEOPLE
GOD CALLS PEOPLE TO REMEMBER

PREVIEWING THE LESSON

Lesson Scripture: Deuteronomy 16:1-8
Background Scripture: Deuteronomy 16:1-8
Key Verse: Deuteronomy 16:1

Focus of the Lesson:
Individuals and communities regularly remember and celebrate great occasions with thanksgiving. How do we commemorate significant events in our lives? God commanded the Israelites to remember their deprivation by eating only unleavened bread and simple meat at sundown.

Goals for the Learners:
(1) to recount the directions for celebrating Passover.
(2) to recognize the significance of occasions that call for commemoration and praise.
(3) to plan a celebration of a significant event in the life of their faith community.

Pronunciation Guide:
Abib (ay' bib)
anamnestic (a nam nes' tik)

Supplies:
Bibles, newsprint and marker, paper and pencils, hymnals, Passover food

---

READING THE SCRIPTURE

NRSV
Deuteronomy 16:1-8

¹Observe the month of Abib by keeping the passover to the LORD your God, for in the month of Abib the LORD your God brought you out of Egypt by night. ²You shall offer the passover sacrifice to the LORD

NIV
Deuteronomy 16:1-8

¹Observe the month of Abib and celebrate the Passover of the LORD your God, because in the month of Abib he brought you out of Egypt by night. ²Sacrifice as the Passover to the LORD your God an animal

your God, from the flock and the herd, at the place that the LORD will choose as a dwelling for his name. ³You must not eat with it anything leavened. For seven days you shall eat unleavened bread with it—the bread of affliction—because you came out of the land of Egypt in great haste, so that all the days of your life you may remember the day of your departure from the land of Egypt. ⁴No leaven shall be seen with you in all your territory for seven days; and none of the meat of what you slaughter on the evening of the first day shall remain until morning. ⁵You are not permitted to offer the passover sacrifice within any of your towns that the LORD your God is giving you. ⁶But at the place that the LORD your God will choose as a dwelling for his name, only there shall you offer the passover sacrifice, in the evening at sunset, the time of day when you departed from Egypt. ⁷You shall cook it and eat it at the place that the LORD your God will choose; the next morning you may go back to your tents. ⁸For six days you shall continue to eat unleavened bread, and on the seventh day there shall be a solemn assembly for the LORD your God, when you shall do no work.

from your flock or herd at the place the LORD will choose as a dwelling for his Name. ³Do not eat it with bread made with yeast, but for seven days eat unleavened bread, the bread of affliction, because you left Egypt in haste—so that all the days of your life you may remember the time of your departure from Egypt. ⁴Let no yeast be found in your possession in all your land for seven days. Do not let any of the meat you sacrifice on the evening of the first day remain until morning.

⁵You must not sacrifice the Passover in any town the LORD your God gives you ⁶except in the place he will choose as a dwelling for his Name. There you must sacrifice the Passover in the evening, when the sun goes down, on the anniversary of your departure from Egypt. ⁷Roast it and eat it at the place the LORD your God will choose. Then in the morning return to your tents. ⁸For six days eat unleavened bread and on the seventh day hold an assembly to the LORD your God and do no work.

UNDERSTANDING THE SCRIPTURE

Deuteronomy 16:1-2. Before atomic clocks and regularized time zones, before everyone wore a wrist watch, community time tended to be measured more by seasons and months than by hours or even days. The recurring cycle of seasons, with the various agricultural activities appropriate for each one, was the primary method for chronicling the passage of time. Later, official time would be measured in terms of kings' reigns. See the recurring refrains in the books of 1 and 2 Kings, for example, or Isaiah's dating his vision of the Lord to "the year that King Uzziah died" (Isaiah 6:1). Even then, however, and certainly before

the rise of the monarchy, Israel measured time in terms of seasons.

During their years in the wilderness, the Israelites learn and practice some of the religious festivals that they will continue when they inhabit the Promised Land. The most important celebration, theologically, is that of Passover. It takes place in the spring, in the month of Abib, which corresponds to March-April in our calendar. The Israelites are to make a yearly celebration of God's delivering them from bondage in Egypt. There are several suggestions concerning the origin of the name "Passover." Some scholars say it comes from the night before their escape, when the angel of death "passed over" all the residences that had doorposts sprinkled with lamb's blood (Exodus 12:23). Others suggest that it refers to the "passing over" from one agricultural year to the next. A third possibility comes from a Hebrew root meaning "protect" that is spelled differently from, but sounds the same as, the word for the angel's "passing over" their houses. By now all the meanings are combined, with themes of God's deliverance and protection, Israel's beginnings as a nation, and the start of a new agricultural year joined together. Regardless of where the name comes from, and despite any borrowings from Canaanite practices, it is clear that for Israel the Passover is a time of national remembrance and thanksgiving to God. As the regulations are given within the liturgical calendar of Deuteronomy, they look ahead to the time when Israel is not only settled in the land but also has constructed a centralized place for worship. This is what is meant by the somewhat odd-sounding phrase "at the place that the LORD will choose as a dwelling for his name" (16:2). Remember that the biblical story is not usually told in a simple linear fashion but rather in layers and with flashbacks to portions of their shared history and glimpses ahead in anticipation of things to come. There is no temple in the wilderness, yet Moses is giving the rules as if it were already in existence.

Deuteronomy 16:3-4. Along with the Passover lamb the meal is to include unleavened bread. In fact, only unleavened bread is to be eaten for a full seven days. These two celebrations were probably originally separate festivals and remembrances. Indeed, the unleavened bread very likely comes from a Canaanite agricultural festival and is only later combined with the Israelite religious celebration and historical remembrance. From one point of view, the Passover lamb would be a festival of nomadic herders of sheep and goats, and unleavened bread would be a festival for

and about the settled agricultural practice of grain farming and the celebration at harvest time. Those of us who live in a temperate climate zone may not realize the amount of skill necessary to wrest a living, whether as herders or farmers, from the land of Canaan. With limited rainfall and without the technology for irrigation, the food supply was uncertain at best, and a good harvest was cause for great celebration.

It is not at all uncommon for a religion to incorporate secular practices into the religious observances. Many of our favorite details within Christianity's major festivals come not from the Bible at all but from secular sources or even other religions' traditions. Trees decorated with lights at Christmas and brightly colored eggs at Easter are only two of the most familiar examples. Having incorporated the practices, the religion then attaches a theological meaning to them. In this case the Canaanite unleavened bread celebration becomes for Israel a memory of their having to leave Egypt too quickly to let their bread rise. For all time, Israel is to remember their deliverance from slavery in Egypt. Clearly this is not a factual, historical remembrance for any but that first generation. Rather it is an "anamnestic" celebration—a remembrance of who they are as a people of God and an eternal reminder of what God did for them/for their ancestors. It is a way for each community member in the ensuing generations to become part of the story. This sort of remembering is precisely what Jesus was referring to at the Last Supper when he gave the bread and wine to his disciples and told them, "This is my body, which is given for you. Do this in remembrance of me" (Luke 22:19).

Deuteronomy 16:5-8. Religious observance is not entirely a matter of "local option"; some of the details are specified by God. In this case, the Passover is to be celebrated as an entire community, rather than only individually or by small family units. It seems likely according to scholars that by the time the scribes who compiled the book of Deuteronomy were doing their work, the observances of Passover had become haphazard and the details varied widely and wildly from place to place. In an attempt to regularize the celebration and to reinvest it with important theological meaning, they spell out details differently from what we read in Exodus. This is a pattern that can be found in nearly all religions. Over time the people may forget the original meanings of what they are doing, and they may pick up different practices from their neighbors. In order to return to the remembrance of God's acts, it may become necessary to redefine the celebration. When new practices are kept and others even grafted in, they are imbued with new meanings to remind the celebrants of both the original and the continuing realities of God's relationship with the community.

INTERPRETING THE SCRIPTURE

Remembering to Give Thanks

Giving thanks is a primary religious impulse, found in virtually all human religions. It is at the heart of both Judaism and Christianity. It is primary, it is simple, and it is often neglected. At other times it may be demoted to a sort of rote repetition of thanks for individual blessings, carried out with the same robotic attitude as the ten-year-old's dutifully written thank-you notes to relatives for birthday presents. Giving thanks may become a duty performed without much enthusiasm. Alternatively, such public acts of gratitude may be relegated to one official Thanksgiving Day in the year. With such an official day, one that is even a national holiday, it has become all too easy for the aspects of giving thanks to be overshadowed either by important football games or by marking of the start of the "Christmas shopping season."

One reason Deuteronomy had a section regulating national religious observances was that people had let just about everything else except God become the focus of their attention. This should be an easy situation to understand because I think it is not all that different from what we have in the United States now. Why would churches and other groups even think to mount campaigns to "Put Christ Back in Christmas" if we were already observing the holiday appropriately? However, I sometimes think the church invests an awful lot of time and energy in such public drives—time and energy that could be better spent elsewhere if we were doing a better job of basic Christian education. In some areas the church seems to have given over nearly all religious definitions to the wider culture. For example, if all the church members who want laws regulating commerce on Sunday would simply not shop on Sundays, retail stores would close for simple economic reasons. It is important that the church make its own definitions and not expect the government to do it for us.

Remembering Together

Our religious lives are both individual and corporate. Our very identities as individuals are simultaneously connected with many others. In our culture we seem to have the individual part pretty well ingrained in us. We have much more difficulty with the communal aspects of our lives. Finding the appropriate balance between "I" and "we" is not always an easy task. It seems especially hard in the twenty-first century. Even groups that use the word "community" a great deal do not always live it well.

Living as members of a community is more than mere geographical closeness. Community members look out for one another and are ready to forgive one another for all the inevitable lapses and aggravations that come from being human with other humans. Because our national history began with more than two centuries of people's being able to pick up and move away from individuals they did not get along with, the tendency is still strong within us to leave instead of staying to work out troublesome issues. Even though there is no more "empty" frontier into which discontented people can move, that is still one of the first things groups will do when there is internal dissension. I live in an exceedingly small town, and yet even here there are congregations formed by people who were not happy with some decision or other in one church and so they began their own congregation.

When we remember all that God has done for us, instead of focusing on some irritation caused by the person across the road or across the aisle, we might be able to come closer to ways God wants us to live together. From the very start of creation God declared that it is not good for humans to live in isolation (Genesis 2:18). The gift of companionship, of family, of community, can be enriched as we celebrate together not only what God has done in our history but also the milestones of our lives. Many Sunday schools mark the birthdays and anniversaries of members. Many congregations recognize the high school and college graduations of members. Congregations I have served have celebrated an annual "Homecoming Sunday" when former pastors and former members are invited back for worship and singing and eating and all manner of fellowship. The laughter and all the "remember the time when" conversations over tables laden with potluck fare are soul-sustaining. Especially in a time and place that tends toward fragmentation, the church's witness of thanksgiving for community can be powerful indeed.

Looking Backward and Forward

The Israelite tradition of marking time in terms of cycles of days (weekly Sabbath), months (new moon festivals), seasons (Passover), and years (new year) is a way for all of life to be lived in remembrance of who and whose we are. Our modern notion of time as undifferentiated units clicking by relentlessly strips us of some of these natural remembrances. And we are the poorer for it.

A basic task of religion is to keep its adherents mindful of their history and at the same time help them to be able to react to changing circumstances in their present. There is a continuity about our celebrations within the church, about the liturgical year, and yet it is not a series of endless repetitions. The Christian liturgical year, for example, begins on the first Sunday of Advent in a yearly cycle, and the biblical lectionary readings start there as well, but they are arranged in a three-year cycle. Does this mean we repeat the same things over and over again, either every year or every three years? Not at all. Rather than being a circle, whether of one or three years' duration, we might think of the shape of our liturgical lives as a spiral staircase. We come to the same spot on the circle (Advent, or Year B, for instance), but we are at a different elevation along the stairway. None of us is exactly the same from one year to the next, nor is our world unchanged. At the very least, we are a year older each Advent. Many years will have seen momentous changes: births and deaths within the family, graduations, new jobs, marriages, retirements. In each local United Methodist church there is the possibility of a new minister arriving on the first Sunday in July! The recurring cycles are a way of ordering the changes so that we do not feel that our lives are chaotic and without pattern. The recurring cycles are also a natural way to introduce children and new Christians into the story.

The central ritual of the Christian community, the Eucharist or Lord's Supper or Holy Communion, serves several of these functions. Especially because Jesus made use of common food and drink and said that each time the disciples ate and drank they were to remember him. (See Luke 22:19 for one example.) Our spiritual lives would be a good deal stronger if, instead of just annual and weekly celebrations and remembrances of our Lord, we included thanksgivings and recollections of who and whose we are in Christ at every single mealtime.

SHARING THE SCRIPTURE

Preparing Our Hearts

Meditate on this week's devotional reading, found in 1 Corinthians 5:1-8. In writing to the church at Corinth about a serious sexual impropriety committed by a man and his stepmother, Paul uses the metaphor of "cleaning out the old yeast" (5:7) to urge the congregation to dismiss this man from their fellowship. The metaphor of yeast calls to mind the Passover, which we will study today, during which yeast was not allowed in one's home. What "old yeast" do you need to toss out of your life? Take steps this week to cleanse your spiritual cupboard.

Pray that you and the adult learners will act as those who have been called to be God's people.

Preparing Our Minds

Study the background and lesson Scripture, both found in Deuteronomy 16:1-8. As you read, think about how you commemorate significant events in your life.

Write on newsprint:

❑ information for next week's lesson, found under "Continue the Journey."
❑ activities for further spiritual growth in "Continue the Journey."

Plan a lecture based on information in Understanding the Scripture to familiarize the class with Passover for "Recount the Directions for Celebrating Passover."

Bring food that would normally be eaten during the Jewish Seder. You may wish to contact class members who could each provide something. Here are possibilities, but you need not bring all of them:

- *Matzoh* (unleavened bread) symbolizes the unleavened bread. Matzoh may be purchased in boxes in many grocery stores or made at home.
- *Parsley* (green herb) symbolizes rebirth and spring.
- *Horseradish* (bitter herb) symbolizes the bitterness of slavery.
- *Salt water* symbolizes tears. Parsley is dipped into the salt water.
- *Roasted egg* symbolizes the perpetual cycle of life from birth to death. Using tongs, hold a hard-boiled egg over a gas burner or candle flame to roast.
- *Lamb* or lamb bone symbolizes the lamb that was sacrificed on the eve of the exodus.
- *Haroseth* (also spelled *charoset*) symbolizes the mortar the Hebrew slaves used to make bricks for Pharaoh. Combine one cup of chopped walnuts and one diced Granny Smith apple. (You may want to put the apples and walnuts in a food processor.) Mix two teaspoons of cinnamon, two teaspoons of sugar, and red wine (or grape juice) to sprinkle over nuts and apple. You will need to make enough to give each class member a taste.

LEADING THE CLASS

(1) Gather to Learn

❖ Welcome the class members and introduce any guests.

❖ Pray that all who have come today will celebrate God's presence in their lives.

❖ Make a list on newsprint of the events that your congregation celebrates. These may include holy days that all Christians commemorate, such as Christmas and Pentecost. They may also include special days in the life of this particular congregation, such as a homecoming; church anniversary; recognition of choir members, leaders, or Sunday school teachers; or events honoring youth or children.

❖ Ask the students this question: **Why are those days so significant that we celebrate them in special ways?**

❖ Read aloud today's focus statement: **Individuals and communities regularly remember and celebrate great occasions with thanksgiving. How do we commemorate significant events in our lives? God commanded the Israelites to remember their deprivation by eating only unleavened bread and simple meat at sundown.**

(2) Recount the Directions for Celebrating Passover

❖ Choose a volunteer to read today's Scripture passage from Deuteronomy 16:1-8, which is a review of how Passover is to be celebrated.

❖ Give a brief lecture based on Understanding the Scripture to help the students understand the purpose and meaning of the Passover celebration.

❖ Offer any of the food you have brought, explaining the symbolism of each item as described under "Preparing Our Minds."

❖ Discuss these questions:
    (1) Why do people of faith celebrate certain events on a regular basis?
    (2) How do such celebrations keep them connected with their religious heritage?

(3) Recognize the Significance of Occasions That Call for Commemoration and Praise

❖ Read "Remembering to Give Thanks" from Interpreting the Scripture.

❖ For emphasis, reread this sentence: **One reason Deuteronomy had a section regulating national religious observances was that people had let just about everything else except God become the focus of their attention.**

❖ Discuss these questions:
    (1) Do you think the same can be said of Christians today?
    (2) If so, in what ways do you believe that we have lost our focus of attention on God?
    (3) What steps do we need to take to refocus our celebrations on God?

❖ **Option:** Distribute paper and pencils. Look at a religious holiday that has become commercialized, such as Christmas. Invite the students to consider:
    ■ ways the religious significance has been lost.
    ■ ideas for making the holiday contemporary and relevant, while retaining its religious significance.

Bring the group back together and discuss any ideas. Encourage the adults to try to implement any ideas that seem feasible to them.

(4) Plan a Celebration of a Significant Event in the Life of the Learners' Faith Community

❖ Discuss any significant events that may be coming up in the next several months in your congregation. Talk about how the class might participate in this event. Be sure to list any ideas and assignments (who will do what) on newsprint so that this information will not be lost. Turn over the information to a task force willing to take responsibility for this effort.

❖ **Option:** Consider how the class might take leadership for Rally Day Sunday. Many churches hold Rally Day early in September to encourage Sunday school students to return to class. The adult class or a task force from the group would need to work with the superintendent and other teachers. Here are some ideas for you to read aloud:

■ Create and mail invitations to every member of the Sunday school inviting them to be present on Rally Day.

■ Underwrite the cost of something that will bring children and youth to the church, such as an inflatable Moon Bounce or a Christian rock group or storyteller or other person who will engage the young people.

■ Provide refreshments for the event.

■ Purchase small mementos of the day, such as pencils or bookmarks, for each student to take home.

■ If enough adults are available, let each child know that a special adult prayer partner will be praying for him or her during the coming year. Make arrangements to create these partnerships so that each student knows who his or her prayer partner is.

(5) Continue the Journey

❖ Pray that those who have participated today will remember and celebrate important events in the life of their church's faith journey.

❖ Read aloud this preparation for next week's lesson. You may also want to post it on newsprint for the students to copy.

■ **Title: God Calls People to Special Service**

■ **Background Scripture: Leviticus 8:1-13**

■ **Lesson Scripture: Leviticus 8:1-13**

■ **Focus of the Lesson:** Some individuals in a community are set aside for special service to the community. How do we discern, acknowledge, and affirm those people chosen for special service? God commanded that Aaron and his sons be recognized by consecrating them with water and holy garments.

❖ Challenge the students to complete one or more of these activities for further spiritual growth, which you will write on newsprint for the students to copy:

(1) Research the Jewish Seder. If possible, speak with a Jewish friend about what this celebration means to him or her.

(2) Research religious celebrations of a denomination or religion not your own to see how and why people of different faiths mark special occasions.

(3) Write brief descriptions of some memorable holiday traditions in your life to share with members of your family, particularly children.

❖ Sing or read aloud "What Gift Can We Bring."

❖ Conclude today's session by leading the class in this benediction: **We hear your call, O God, and ask that you send us forth empowered by your Spirit to live and serve as your covenant people.**

UNIT 2: CALLED TO BE GOD'S PEOPLE

GOD CALLS PEOPLE TO SPECIAL SERVICE

PREVIEWING THE LESSON

Lesson Scripture: Leviticus 8:1-13
Background Scripture: Leviticus 8:1-13
Key Verse: Leviticus 8:12

Focus of the Lesson:
Some individuals in a community are set aside for special service to the community. How do we discern, acknowledge, and affirm those people chosen for special service? God commanded that Aaron and his sons be recognized by consecrating them with water and holy garments.

Goals for the Learners:
(1) to retell the details of the dedication of Aaron's family for special service to God and community.
(2) to discern what the principles of ordination and consecration for service mean in their own lives.
(3) to accept roles of special service and to recognize persons called for service.

Pronunciation Guide:
ephod (ee' fod)   Urim (yoor' im)
Thummim (thum' im)

Supplies:
Bibles, newsprint and marker, paper and pencils, hymnals, picture of Aaron wearing his breastplate

---

READING THE SCRIPTURE

NRSV
Leviticus 8:1-13

¹The LORD spoke to Moses, saying: ²Take Aaron and his sons with him, the vestments,

NIV
Leviticus 8:1-13

¹The LORD said to Moses, ²"Bring Aaron and his sons, their garments, the anointing

the anointing oil, the bull of sin offering, the two rams, and the basket of unleavened bread; ³and assemble the whole congregation at the entrance of the tent of meeting. ⁴And Moses did as the LORD commanded him. When the congregation was assembled at the entrance of the tent of meeting, ⁵Moses said to the congregation, "This is what the LORD has commanded to be done."

⁶Then Moses brought Aaron and his sons forward, and washed them with water. ⁷He put the tunic on him, fastened the sash around him, clothed him with the robe, and put the ephod on him. He then put the decorated band of the ephod around him, tying the ephod to him with it. ⁸He placed the breastpiece on him, and in the breastpiece he put the Urim and the Thummim. ⁹And he set the turban on his head, and on the turban, in front, he set the golden ornament, the holy crown, as the LORD commanded Moses.

¹⁰Then Moses took the anointing oil and anointed the tabernacle and all that was in it, and consecrated them. ¹¹He sprinkled some of it on the altar seven times, and anointed the altar and all its utensils, and the basin and its base, to consecrate them. **¹²He poured some of the anointing oil on Aaron's head and anointed him, to consecrate him.** ¹³And Moses brought forward Aaron's sons, and clothed them with tunics, and fastened sashes around them, and tied headdresses on them, as the LORD commanded Moses.

oil, the bull for the sin offering, the two rams and the basket containing bread made without yeast, ³and gather the entire assembly at the entrance to the Tent of Meeting." ⁴Moses did as the LORD commanded him, and the assembly gathered at the entrance to the Tent of Meeting.

⁵Moses said to the assembly, "This is what the LORD has commanded to be done." ⁶Then Moses brought Aaron and his sons forward and washed them with water. ⁷He put the tunic on Aaron, tied the sash around him, clothed him with the robe and put the ephod on him. He also tied the ephod to him by its skillfully woven waistband; so it was fastened on him. ⁸He placed the breastpiece on him and put the Urim and Thummim in the breastpiece. ⁹Then he placed the turban on Aaron's head and set the gold plate, the sacred diadem, on the front of it, as the LORD commanded Moses.

¹⁰Then Moses took the anointing oil and anointed the tabernacle and everything in it, and so consecrated them. ¹¹He sprinkled some of the oil on the altar seven times, anointing the altar and all its utensils and the basin with its stand, to consecrate them. **¹²He poured some of the anointing oil on Aaron's head and anointed him to consecrate him.** ¹³Then he brought Aaron's sons forward, put tunics on them, tied sashes around them and put headbands on them, as the LORD commanded Moses.

UNDERSTANDING THE SCRIPTURE

Leviticus 8:1-5. People need basic rules for ordering their life together. We have seen one of God's provisions of rules in the giving of the Ten Commandments (see lesson on July 5). Communities also need ways of keeping track of time and for remembering important events. Last week we looked at some of the ways Israel dealt with time

and thanksgiving. Today we look at another basic need of communities: leadership. There is an almost infinite number of jobs that needs to be done, and each task needs to have a well-prepared person who can do it. We see in this portion of Leviticus both the ordaining of Aaron and his sons and the template for the setting aside of religious leaders in the future. One of the first things to notice is that the anointing of Aaron and his sons is not a private action. The instructions come from God and involve certain selected individuals, and at the same time the entire assembly of the people has a role to play. They will be observers of the rite that is shortly to take place, and yet this is not just a passive role for them. They both observe and give their assent to the action. The priesthood is being established not for the benefit of the priests exclusively but rather for the good of the entire community. Thus, the other members of the community need to play a role in the proceedings.

Leviticus 8:6-9. The rite begins with a ritual cleansing of Aaron and his sons. Then they are vested in the special garments that mark their office. We do not know what all the items mentioned in verses 7 through 9 looked like, or even what some of them were or why they were used. In all likelihood the clothing and other accoutrements were a combination of regular garments, such as the tunic, and special items, such as the ephod. There was probably decoration of some sort. The waistband, for example, is said to be "skillfully woven" (8:7 NIV). It is a natural impulse to use the best, the most special, for God's service. The Urim and Thummim (8:8) have fascinated scholars for centuries. Clearly they are items that are small enough to fit in a sort of pocket on the front of the priest's garment. They were used in some manner in some cases to help discern God's will. (See Numbers 27:21 for instance.) And yet we know practically nothing about them or precisely how they were used. One of the tantalizing details is that the words themselves are very close to the words for "light" and "uprightness," yet each one is in the plural form. Is this because there were several of them, or is it a mere quirk of the language, similar to our calling one object a "pair" of glasses or a "pair" of pants? We simply do not know. About all we can say with any certainty is that they do seem to have been used to answer questions that were put in a simple yes/no form.

If the Urim and Thummim were so important, why does the Bible give so little detail about them and how they were used? In all likelihood it is because they were so familiar to the writers and to the people in general that the author of this text thought it unnecessary to give any more detail. For example, I can write that I drive a "stick shift" car. That is all I need to say for you to understand that it does not have an automatic transmission, that I need to depress the clutch pedal and move the gear shift for the car to go from one gear to another. Might someone a long time from now when automobiles are a distant memory read that phrase "stick shift" and wonder if it had something to do with little tree branches? There have been many conjectures about the composition and use of Urim and Thummim, but the fact remains that we know practically nothing about them. Even the names are not translated; the Hebrew letters are simply put into our alphabet.

Leviticus 8:10-13. After the entire community has gathered and Aaron and his sons have been dressed in their special garments, Moses proceeds to anoint not only the new priests but also the priestly "equipment." This marks their being set aside for special use. The word "messiah" is our English pronunciation of the Hebrew word for "anointed." In the Old Testament, anointing was used in several circumstances. Kings as well as priests were anointed. Objects as well as people were anointed. For example, when Jacob awoke from his dream of God, he anointed a large stone to mark the experience (Genesis 28:18). In each case it was a matter of setting someone or something apart from the ordinary, to live or to be used in a special way or to function as an aid to remembrance for the people. That specialness was not a mark of privilege so much as a matter of relationship with God and service to the entire community.

The entire ordination process, both in the

Old Testament and in the church today, is recognition by the community that God has called these particular individuals to this particular service. There are three necessary sides to the relationship. God calls an individual, the individual agrees ("answers the call"), and the community ratifies the individual's response to God's call. The ordained person does not cease to be a fallible human being and a forgiven sinner. The ancient priests and also the ministers, pastors, and priests today function as signs to the community of the grace of God and serve as channels of God's blessings to the entire community, both those within the church and those outside of it. Ancient and contemporary people alike had trouble living up to God's call in its entirety. With the aid of the congregation, however, they are better able to live out their calling.

INTERPRETING THE SCRIPTURE

Who, Me?

As we saw in the story of Moses' call by God in Lesson 1 on June 7, the first response most people make to God is one of surprise and disbelief. Surely God cannot mean that *I* am called to ordination or some other specialized ministry! I find this reaction among the great majority of my students, both those in seminary and those preparing for ministries by way of the United Methodist Course of Study route. Some have spent many years in other careers, consciously trying to avoid the tug they feel toward ordination. Some have spent many years in other careers, believing they were using their gifts in the service of their Lord, but now feel a call to a different direction. Others may be fresh out of college but still believe it is almost too prideful to say they have been called by God into the ministry.

I want to make it very clear here that I do not believe God's call singles out individuals only for professionally religious lives. I believe truck drivers and salesmen, stay-at-home mothers and accountants, farmers and assembly-line workers can be called to their vocations just as surely as preachers. Each of us has been gifted by the Holy Spirit, and part of our call is to find and use our gifts both for our own satisfaction and for the good of the entire community.

There is but one ministry in Christ, but there are diverse gifts and evidences of God's grace in the body of Christ (Ephesians 4:4-16). The ministry of all Christians is complementary. No ministry is subservient to another. All United Methodists are summoned and sent by Christ to live and work together in mutual interdependence and to be guided by the Spirit into the truth that frees and the love that reconciles. (*The Book of Discipline of The United Methodist Church—2004* ¶129)

That said, because the Scripture lesson this week is about priestly ordination, that will be the primary focus of these comments.

Community

Before there can be ordained leaders there must be a community of faith. All the members have gifts and responsibilities. Traditionally, especially since the Protestant Reformation, within Christianity this idea has been called "the priesthood of all believers" or "the ministry of all Christians." In the official language of The United Methodist Church,

The church as the community of the new covenant . . . stretches out to human needs wherever love and service may convey God's love and ours. . . . Beyond the diverse forms of ministry is this ultimate concern: that all persons will be brought into a saving relationship with God through Jesus Christ and be renewed after the image of their creator (Colossians 3:10). This means that all Christians are called to minister wherever Christ would have them serve and witness in deeds and words that heal and free. (*The Book of Discipline of The United Methodist Church—2004* ¶126)

Through the sacrament of baptism we are incorporated into Christ's body and become ministers of Christ. If we were baptized as infants or children, with someone making vows for us and on our behalf, then, when we are old enough to speak for ourselves, we make the pledges for ourselves publicly in the rite of confirmation. These acts make us ministers of Christ just as much as any ordained person is a minister of Christ.

One of the jobs of the community is to help its members discern their gifts and how they can best use them in service to their Lord, whether that involves ordination or not.

Some Are Separated Out

Official statements of many denominations including Lutherans, Presbyterians, Episcopalians, and the United Church of Christ speak of ordained ministry in wording very similar to what we find in *The Book of Discipline of The United Methodist Church—2004:* "Ordination to this ministry is a gift from God to the church. In ordination, the church affirms and continues the apostolic ministry through persons empowered by the Holy Spirit" (¶303). Through years of preparation, most often in a master of divinity program at a seminary, or some other route prescribed by the denomination, a candidate studies those specialized topics required by the general church and perhaps some additional subjects mandated by the local authorities. Actually there is nothing in the preparation for ordination that would not be perfectly fine for laypeople to study as well. (Indeed, I wish more "ordinary" church members knew more Scripture and

more church history, had a basic grasp of theological and ethical notions, and so forth.) The official preparation is a combination of academic study and on-the-job training. This latter will probably include clinical pastoral education in some sort of medical setting as well as formal field education within one or more congregations. In the best of all situations, education is recognized as a lifelong process so that pastors will continue to read and think and attend training events long after their minimal required education is over.

Most denominations require a probationary period working full-time in a local congregation between seminary graduation and ordination. This can vary from six months in the Episcopal Church (sometimes waived) to three years for United Methodists. "Elder" is what United Methodists officially call their fully ordained clergy, although we do not use the word very much in ordinary conversation. Other denominations use words such as "priest" (Roman Catholic and Episcopal, for instance) or "pastor" (Lutheran). "Minister" and "pastor" are good, all-purpose designations to use, regardless of the denomination. In some contexts "preacher" is appropriate, but for most ordained folks, preaching is only a small portion of their regular responsibilities.

Local Celebrations

In many denominations, pastors are ordained in the congregation they will be serving. Since, in The United Methodist Church, ordinations take place at Annual Conference, congregations may find it difficult to participate fully. However, *The United Methodist Book of Worship* does include a service "An Order Recognizing One Who Has Been Ordained, Consecrated, or Certified" to take place in the local church. All the "mainline" denominations have similar services to celebrate new ministry.

There is lovely symbolism involved in the presentation of objects to the new leader of a congregation as tokens of what will be happening within that portion of the body of Christ. These objects may include a Bible, water, bread, a cup, a towel and basin, a hymnal, a worship book, a globe, and a stole. Words are spoken with each presentation, calling to mind for the congregation the significance of each object. For instance, the presenter of the Bible may say, "Accept this Bible, and be among us as one who proclaims the Word." The one giving a globe may say, "Receive this globe, and lead us in our mission to this community and all the world" ("An Order for the Celebration of an Appointment," *The United Methodist Book of Worship*).

Often, additional items are presented in recognition of particular circumstances of the situation. For example, a Lutheran friend of mine was handed a wastebasket and told, "Take this trash can and put it under the leak in the ceiling of your study in case it rains before we can get it fixed." The new minister of a tiny rural Episcopal church was given a plastic tablecloth and told, "Take this plastic and be sure to put it over the altar after each service to protect the altar cloth from the mice." Rather than detracting from the solemnity of the occasion, such presentations made the strong point that ministry is a shared occupation, that we are flawed people who live in an imperfect world, and, at the same time, that we are bound together in the grace of our Lord Jesus Christ.

SHARING THE SCRIPTURE

Preparing Our Hearts

Meditate on this week's devotional reading, found in Romans 11:33–12:2. This reading contains two very well-known New Testament verses: Romans 12:1-2. We are called to present ourselves to God as a holy, acceptable, living sacrifice. Today's lesson deals with those who are set apart for special service, but Paul reminds us that we are all called to present ourselves before God. In what ways have you presented yourself for service?

Pray that you and the adult learners will be open to God's call for you to take leadership responsibility within the community of faith.

Preparing Our Minds

Study the background Scripture and lesson Scripture, both found in Leviticus 8:1-13. Think about how we discern, acknowledge, and affirm those people who are chosen for special service.

Write on newsprint:
❑ information for next week's lesson, found under "Continue the Journey."
❑ activities for further spiritual growth in "Continue the Journey."

Plan a lecture from Understanding the Scripture for "Retell the Details of the Dedication of Aaron's Family for Special Service to God and Community."

Locate a picture of Aaron wearing his tunic with the breastplate. You may be able to find a picture on the Internet.

Invite the pastor to talk about the personal meaning of ordination for "Discern What the Principles of Ordination and Consecration for Service Mean in the Learners' Lives," if you choose to do this option.

LEADING THE CLASS

(1) Gather to Learn

❖ Welcome the class members and introduce any guests.

❖ Pray that those who are present today will recognize God's call on their lives and the lives of others who are called to engage in special service.

❖ Read this profile of The Rev. José Peña-Nazario, a United Methodist pastor (www.umc.org): **José Peña-Nazario began worshiping at The United Methodist Church in his hometown in Puerto Rico at age twelve but stopped attending as a teenager. While working on a masters degree in biology, he felt a deep tug to find meaning in his life. He returned to church, drew closer to Christ, and in 1987 went to seminary to become a pastor. He reported: "My life changed drastically when I felt the call to pastoral ministry and then to mission." From 1987–2000, he served "comfortable" churches in Puerto Rico but felt a call to serve those who lived in extreme poverty in Honduras, where he had participated in mission trips. In January 2001, he moved to Honduras, having been commissioned as a missionary by the United Methodist Board of Global Ministries.**

❖ Discuss this question: **What motivates people to set aside their own dreams to answer God's call?**

❖ Read aloud today's focus statement: **Some individuals in a community are set aside for special service to the community. How do we discern, acknowledge, and affirm those people chosen for special service? God commanded that Aaron and his sons be recognized by consecrating them with water and holy garments.**

(2) Retell the Details of the Dedication of Aaron's Family for Special Service to God and Community

❖ Choose two volunteers, one to read Leviticus 8:1-5 and another 8:6-13.

❖ Define ordination as "the ceremony to invest one who has been called to God's service with ministerial authority by the laying on of hands."

❖ Use information from Understanding the Scripture to help the class members understand the ordination rite and the symbolism associated with it.

❖ Show a picture of Aaron in his robe with the breastplate, if you have been able to locate one.

❖ Make a list on newsprint of the vestments and other accessories used for the ordination of Aaron as the high priest including: *tunic, sash, robe, ephod, breastplate with Urim and Thummim, turban, golden ornament, holy crown, anointing oil, tabernacle, altar, utensils, basin, bull of sin offering, two rams, and basket of unleavened bread. The whole congregation, which is those whom Aaron was to serve, was also to be present.*

❖ **Option:** Do a Bible study of some of the vestments and accessories listed. Assign different students to look up these passages and report their findings to the class.

■ Vestments: Exodus 39:1-31
■ Anointing oil: Exodus 30:22-31
■ Bull: Exodus 29:1
■ Holy crown: Exodus 29:6

❖ Compare Aaron's vestments and his ordination ritual with what your pastor wears and the ceremonies used in your congregation to recognize people for special service.

(3) Discern What the Principles of Ordination and Consecration for Service Mean in the Learners' Lives

❖ Read "Local Celebrations" from Interpreting the Scripture, which discusses ways a new ministry may be celebrated.

❖ **Option:** Invite the pastor to speak about his or her ordination and the meaning this ritual had and continues to have in ministry.

❖ Point out that all baptized members of the body of Christ have gifts and are called for service. (If time permits, read "Community" in Interpreting the Scripture.)

❖ Encourage the class members to talk about how a particular ministry that they feel called to engage in has enabled them to serve in a way that is meaningful to them.

(4) Accept Roles of Special Service and Recognize Persons Called for Service

❖ Brainstorm ministries offered through your congregation or ecumenically through the community. Write these ideas on newsprint. Ideas may range from work within the church on committees or as a choir member to work in the community in places such as a soup kitchen, shelter, hospice, or nursing home. The ministry may include people of all ages or focus just on children, youth, or adults. It may deal with helping church members grow or could be targeted toward pre-Christians who do not yet know Christ.

❖ Distribute paper and pencils. Provide quiet time for the adults to think about a ministry in which they are already engaged or a new ministry to which they feel called. Ask them to write on the paper **"I intend to engage in** _____ **ministry by** _____ **"** (and describe what they plan to do).

❖ Conclude this portion of the lesson by asking those who have discerned an area of new or renewed service to please raise their hands so that the class members might recognize and pray for them.

(5) Continue the Journey

❖ Pray that all who have participated today will be open to God's call in their own lives and affirm that call when they discern it in others.

❖ Read aloud this preparation for next week's lesson. You may also want to post it on newsprint for the students to copy.

- ■ Title: God Calls People to Jubilee
- ■ Background Scripture: Leviticus 25:8-24

- ■ Lesson Scripture: Leviticus 25:8-21, 23-24
- ■ Focus of the Lesson: The accumulation of property in the hands of a very few people means that some are wealthy while others have no chance to escape poverty. How can communities care for the poor in just ways? God gave laws for the just redistribution of wealth to provide for the poor and thereby to honor God, who provides all.

❖ Challenge the students to complete one or more of these activities for further spiritual growth, which you will write on newsprint for the students to copy.

(1) Talk with someone who has attended an ordination service, if you have never had the opportunity to attend. Find out what makes such a service so meaningful to the candidates for ordination and to those who are there to support them.

(2) Encourage a young person who may be hearing God's call to service to continue to discern that call and follow God's will.

(3) Note any special clothing that is worn or actions that are done during worship. Talk with your pastor about the meaning of any clothing or actions that you do not understand.

❖ Sing or read aloud "God the Spirit, Guide and Guardian."

❖ Conclude today's session by leading the class in this benediction: **We hear your call, O God, and ask that you send us forth empowered by your Spirit to live and serve as your covenant people.**

UNIT 2: CALLED TO BE GOD'S PEOPLE

GOD CALLS PEOPLE TO JUBILEE

PREVIEWING THE LESSON

Lesson Scripture: Leviticus 25:8-21, 23-24
Background Scripture: Leviticus 25:8-24
Key Verse: Leviticus 25:10

Focus of the Lesson:
The accumulation of property in the hands of a very few people means that some are wealthy while others have no chance to escape poverty. How can communities care for the poor in just ways? God gave laws for the just redistribution of wealth to provide for the poor and thereby to honor God, who provides all.

Goals for the Learners:
(1) to present the issues addressed in God's commands to redistribute property and to deal justly with one another in Jubilee.
(2) to value and appropriate the biblical principles of economic justice and stewardship of God's creation.
(3) to engage in an action that promotes economic justice and good stewardship.

Supplies:
Bibles, newsprint and marker, paper and pencils, hymnals

READING THE SCRIPTURE

NRSV
Leviticus 25:8-21, 23-24

⁸You shall count off seven weeks of years, seven times seven years, so that the period of seven weeks of years gives forty-nine years. ⁹Then you shall have the trumpet sounded loud; on the tenth day of the seventh month—on the day of atonement—you shall have the trumpet sounded throughout all your land. **¹⁰And you shall hallow the fiftieth year and you shall proclaim liberty throughout the land to all its inhabitants. It**

NIV
Leviticus 25:8-21, 23-24

⁸" 'Count off seven sabbaths of years— seven times seven years—so that the seven sabbaths of years amount to a period of forty-nine years. ⁹Then have the trumpet sounded everywhere on the tenth day of the seventh month; on the Day of Atonement sound the trumpet throughout your land. **¹⁰Consecrate the fiftieth year and proclaim liberty throughout the land to all its inhabitants. It shall be a jubilee for you; each one**

shall be a jubilee for you: you shall return, every one of you, to your property and every one of you to your family. [11]That fiftieth year shall be a jubilee for you: you shall not sow, or reap the aftergrowth, or harvest the unpruned vines. [12]For it is a jubilee; it shall be holy to you: you shall eat only what the field itself produces.

[13]In this year of jubilee you shall return, every one of you, to your property. [14]When you make a sale to your neighbor or buy from your neighbor, you shall not cheat one another. [15]When you buy from your neighbor, you shall pay only for the number of years since the jubilee; the seller shall charge you only for the remaining crop years. [16]If the years are more, you shall increase the price, and if the years are fewer, you shall diminish the price; for it is a certain number of harvests that are being sold to you. [17]You shall not cheat one another, but you shall fear your God; for I am the LORD your God.

[18]You shall observe my statutes and faithfully keep my ordinances, so that you may live on the land securely. [19]The land will yield its fruit, and you will eat your fill and live on it securely. [20]Should you ask, What shall we eat in the seventh year, if we may not sow or gather in our crop? [21]I will order my blessing for you in the sixth year, so that it will yield a crop for three years. . . . [23]The land shall not be sold in perpetuity, for the land is mine; with me you are but aliens and tenants. [24]Throughout the land that you hold, you shall provide for the redemption of the land.

of you is to return to his family property and each to his own clan. [11]The fiftieth year shall be a jubilee for you; do not sow and do not reap what grows of itself or harvest the untended vines. [12]For it is a jubilee and is to be holy for you; eat only what is taken directly from the fields.

[13]" 'In this Year of Jubilee everyone is to return to his own property.

[14]" 'If you sell land to one of your countrymen or buy any from him, do not take advantage of each other. [15]You are to buy from your countryman on the basis of the number of years since the Jubilee. And he is to sell to you on the basis of the number of years left for harvesting crops. [16]When the years are many, you are to increase the price, and when the years are few, you are to decrease the price, because what he is really selling you is the number of crops. [17]Do not take advantage of each other, but fear your God. I am the LORD your God.

[18]" 'Follow my decrees and be careful to obey my laws, and you will live safely in the land. [19]Then the land will yield its fruit, and you will eat your fill and live there in safety. [20]You may ask, "What will we eat in the seventh year if we do not plant or harvest our crops?" [21]I will send you such a blessing in the sixth year that the land will yield enough for three years.

[23]" 'The land must not be sold permanently, because the land is mine and you are but aliens and my tenants. [24]Throughout the country that you hold as a possession, you must provide for the redemption of the land.' "

UNDERSTANDING THE SCRIPTURE

Leviticus 25:8-13. There are actually three sections to the Jubilee, although only two of them come within today's section of Leviticus 25. There is Jubilee for the land itself (25:1-22). There is Jubilee for property, in that what has been sold reverts to its pre-vious owners (25:23-38). And there is Jubilee for people who have become slaves as they are to be given their freedom (25:39-55). The sabbatical year, as its name suggests, comes every seven years. It is a "Sabbath" for the land. There is to be no plowing, sowing, or reaping. This is similar to what had already been spelled out in Exodus 23:10-11. The Jubilee year comes after a "Sabbath of Sabbaths," after seven times seven, the fiftieth year. In that year, not only does the land rest but all property reverts to the original owner or to that person's descendants.

We can understand what is meant by the prohibition against planting in verse 11, but that against "reaping" needs to be looked at carefully. First, the absence of sowing does not mean that a particular plot of land would be without plants for the entire cycle. As anyone with a home garden knows, there will be "volunteer" plants that sprout either from roots left behind or from seeds that fell the previous year. These plants are to be left to themselves, without tending, until their fruit or seed is ripe. At that point it is entirely legal to walk through the field and pick and eat whatever is ripe. This is not considered "reaping." Reaping, rather, is the systematic picking of the crop and carrying it away in containers for storage. Grapes can be eaten in the vineyard from vines that have not been tended that year. No wine can be made from those particular grapes because that would necessitate "reaping" or "harvesting" the grapes, but eating them out there in the vineyard is perfectly legal.

Leviticus 25:14-19. The Torah teaches us that land cannot be sold in perpetuity. All that is actually being sold is the number of harvests from that piece of land until the next Jubilee year. Thus, the place in the cycle is to be calculated and is to determine the price. A piece of land that has twenty crop years left before the next Jubilee will fetch a much higher price than another field that is sold two years before a Jubilee, because the buyer will have only one-tenth the number of crops on the second field than on the first. Verse 17 is unambiguously clear: "You shall not cheat one another," using the same word for "cheat" as for "oppress" as in Leviticus 19:33: "You shall not oppress the alien." Even those persons who may have had to sell themselves into slavery because of overwhelming debt are to go free at the Jubilee. Frequently in the book of Leviticus, including three times in this chapter, we read the refrain "I am the LORD your God." God has the right, the standing, to make these rules for the people, to require that they treat the land and one another with respect and care.

Leviticus 25:20-22. God anticipates the people's likely and logical question: What will we eat if we follow this procedure? God promises that there will be enough produced from the year six crop and from the year seven "volunteer" growth to cover the time from one reaping to the next reaping. This should not be too difficult for God to accomplish, for the people certainly can remember the story of Egypt's seven good harvests that were enough to keep the population alive through the following seven years of famine (see Genesis 41). In addition, the Israelites could consider the manna they are receiving on a schedule of six days out of seven. The manna on day six is of a different sort from the other five days' "crop" in that it can be stored and eaten on day seven. The cycle of manna is a microcosm of what the Sabbath year for the land is to be. The people should be able to trust God's provisions since they have been seeing—and eating!—according to God's promise for their entire trek in the wilderness.

Leviticus 25:23-24. The theological center point of the chapter is in verses 23-24. The land is not to be sold forever; neither are people are to be enslaved forever, because all, ultimately, belongs to God. Because God is eternal and humans are transient, all people are "aliens and tenants" (25:23), even in the Promised Land. Thus, in a real sense, the land itself can never be sold, but only the crops the land can produce. And families are to look out for one another, so that even the crops of the land do not have to be sold or are not lost for long. If one part of an extended family falls deeply into debt and must sell a field, another relative is supposed to buy that field back, or "redeem" it, and return it to those who were forced to sell it in the first place. God's people are not supposed to take advantage of one another. They are not supposed to become rich at the expense of others. Especially because agriculture is an iffy matter in much of the Promised Land, the people are to be cooperative, lest any fall into such dire straits that they have to sell someone into slavery in order to feed the rest of the family. The world belongs to God and is given to the people for their use. God therefore has the right to stipulate how the people are to live on the land. Notice also that all of these rules and regulations are spelled out in detail long before the people take possession of their new land. There will not be any surprises when they reach Canaan. No one can claim God changed the rules. All is put forth by God for their benefit because "I am the LORD your God."

INTERPRETING THE SCRIPTURE

Just a Dream?

How could we possibly have a sabbatical year for the whole society today? It is different now, isn't it? An industrial society cannot operate in the same way as an ancient agricultural society. Yes, that is true, of course. But think for a moment: Would it really be more difficult for an industrial society to take time off than for a subsistence agricultural economy—such as ancient Israel—to refrain from planting for a year? When many people really do wonder where their next meal will come from, how could they think seriously of taking any land out of production?

We need to focus on the question of the real purpose of the sabbatical year. Remember that these regulations, when presented to the Israelites, are for the future, when the people who are presently out in the wilderness arrive in the Promised Land. Remember also the kind of Sabbath the people are experiencing while they are in the wilderness. On a completely regular basis, on day six they find twice as much manna as on days one through five. Not only that, the extra manna on day six lasts for them to eat on day seven. Manna spoils when they attempt to keep it overnight on any other day. Through this, God is trying to teach the people to trust the divine promises. Therefore it is not unreasonable to ask, If God can regulate the manna in that way, is it not possible that God could regulate the crops in year six so that between what can be stored from the year six harvest and what comes up by itself in year seven there would be enough to eat until the harvest in year eight?

Maybe a better question to ask goes back to the matter of purpose: Allowing that God can do whatever God wants to do, why would there be a sabbatical year even for the land? Think of the number of times Jesus tells his followers not to worry so much about material things. (See, among others, Matthew 6:25-33 and Luke 12:22-31.) He does not mean that no one should do any sort of work. Rather, if we are working together for God's kingdom, for righteousness here on earth, then the other things we need will be available.

What Do We Need?

Ah, here comes the crux of the matter. Most of us have far more in terms of physical goods than we could argue with a straight face that we *need*. I could eat for weeks without going to the grocery store. Of course I would miss milk and eggs and fresh produce after I finished what is in my refrigerator, but that lack would not compromise my health. I realize to my chagrin when swapping out summer and winter clothes that some of the garments I take from hangers and put in boxes for the attic have not been worn even once since they were taken out of the attic a few months before. Although my younger daughter is now in college, there are still two cars at our house.

An Experiment

When outlining this chapter several months before its due date, I decided I would try to reduce some of my excess as noted in the previous section. I report these results not to put a spotlight on myself, but to encourage other people to try something similar. As I was deciding to give away, at the very least, the clothes I had not worn in the past year, a family in the next community lost everything they owned in a house fire. The wife and oldest daughter "just happened" to be my size, and I was delighted to be able to deliver several bags of clothing for the family to their church. The second car is no longer just parked at our house. I have not sold it yet, but a student family that needed reliable transportation has it as a long-term loan.

There are still major issues remaining in each of these cases. Too many houses in this area are not safe. Too many families do not have homeowners' or renters' insurance. Actually, too many of them are without even basic health insurance. As for the transportation needs of our students, a more enduring solution, of course, must involve greater availability of public transportation and less reliance on individual automobiles.

My small actions have done nothing to address any of these larger issues. But I believe in the theme of John the Baptizer's instructions to those who came out to him in the wilderness and asked what they should do to "bear fruits worthy of repentance" (Luke 3:8). As recorded in the Gospel of Luke, John did not tell them they had to go back to Jerusalem and reform the entire economic and political system themselves. He told them, rather, to do what they could with what they had: They were to refrain from stealing and to share what they owned—little though it might be—with people who had even less (Luke 3:10-14).

But It Would Be Hard

I do not believe that there are insurmountable technical issues that have to be solved before a Jubilee could be possible. It is the issues of the human heart that seem insurmountable. As a culture, we seem to have lost any notion of what "enough" means. You can come up with examples of excess as easily as I can. We also have lost the concept that we are "aliens and tenants" on God's land (Leviticus 25:23). Consequently, we see ourselves as owners of the land, not as stewards. We clutch our "private property," be it land, a home, money, or something else dear to us. Jubilee reminds us that what we have is only ours for a season. But it is God's forever, and God will provide for us what we need.

When I was in seminary I learned what was then the well-accepted idea that the sabbatical and Jubilee Years were only theoretical constructs and had never been practiced in Israel. There had apparently been one abortive freeing of slaves, noted by Jeremiah, but as soon as that particular crisis had eased, the slaves were put again into servitude (see Jeremiah 34:8-11). And so we take ourselves off the hook, so to speak. If Israel never actually lived up to these ideals, how can we be expected to?

There is now some evidence, however, that there may actually have been sabbatical and Jubilee years celebrated in preexilic Israel and Judah. Regardless of what scholars ever decide on this issue, does not God still speak to us through these texts? At the very least, can we not still hear Jesus speaking to us through texts such as Matthew 25:31-46? Even with a population significantly larger than in biblical times, the earth still produces enough food to feed everyone. What is not possible is for everyone to have more than everyone else. A friend of mine has a bumper sticker on her car that captures the issue perfectly: "Insatiable is not sustainable."

SHARING THE SCRIPTURE

Preparing Our Hearts

Meditate on this week's devotional reading, found in Matthew 18:21-35. Here Jesus talks about forgiveness by using the parable of the servant who was forgiven a huge debt but who, in turn, demanded payment of a much smaller debt from someone else. God has forgiven us—and you. Are you willing to forgive others? Offer forgiveness this week to someone who has wronged you.

Pray that you and the adult learners will ask God's forgiveness and be ready to forgive someone else for a trespass against you.

Preparing Our Minds

Study the background Scripture from Leviticus 25:8-24 and the lesson Scripture from Leviticus 25:8-21, 23-24. As you read, think about how communities care for the poor in ways that are just.

Write on newsprint:

❑ information for next week's lesson, found under "Continue the Journey."

❑ activities for further spiritual growth in "Continue the Journey."

Check out some opportunities for increasing economic justice and stewardship in your community. Broad suggestions are given under "Engage in an Action That Promotes Economic Justice and Good Stewardship."

LEADING THE CLASS

(1) Gather to Learn

❖ Welcome the class members and introduce any guests.

❖ Pray that all who are participating today will rejoice in being called as God's people.

❖ Read aloud this information: **From 1789–1799 France experienced a major political and social upheaval. By the time the French Revolution ended, the Bourbon monarchy had been overthrown, the Roman Catholic Church had been restructured, and thousands lay dead. While social and intellectual causes fueled this revolution, one of the main causes was the poor economy and a very inequitable system of taxation. Not only the king but also the Roman Church, which was the largest landowner in the country, levied taxes. The clergy and nobles paid no tax at all, whereas taxes on the poor increased by 28 percent in some areas. The poor were struggling to survive while conspicuous consumption was the order of the day among the nobility. Riots took place in 1788–1789 among the poor due to the high cost of bread. The center could not hold and chaos ensued.**

❖ Ask: **Admittedly there were causes other than economic ones, but given the poor economy and huge government debt, the poor were squeezed to the point where revolt was their only hope. What does** their response suggest to you about the effects of inequality on a society? What remedies do you think are feasible when such gross inequity exists?

❖ Read aloud today's focus statement: **The accumulation of property in the hands of a very few people means that some are wealthy while others have no chance to escape poverty. How can communities care for the poor in just ways? God gave laws for the just redistribution of wealth to provide for the poor and thereby to honor God, who provides all.**

(2) Present the Issues Addressed in God's Commands to Redistribute Property and to Deal Justly With One Another in Jubilee

❖ Select a volunteer to read aloud Leviticus 25:8-21, 23-24.

❖ Discuss with the group the purpose of the Jubilee year, which was to return land to the family that first had possession. Note that unlike the sabbath (seventh) year where the land is simply allowed to rest, on the Jubilee year the land reverts to the clan that originally occupied it. God owns the land, which "shall not be sold in perpetuity" (25:23).

❖ Point out that unlike the way property is handled in the United States, where people are owners, people in the days of Leviticus were simply stewards. God owned the land. People just leased it. (See Leviticus 25:14-19 in Understanding the Scripture for a more thorough explanation of how this leasing worked.)

❖ Discuss these questions:

(1) **What does the inclusion of directions for a Jubilee year in the law suggest to you about God?**

(2) **What biblical evidence is there that Jubilee was actually practiced?** (Read "But It Would Be Hard" in Interpreting the Scripture.)

(3) **Suppose you had been one of the Israelites hearing this proclama-** tion of Jubilee. How would you have felt about the redistribution of land?

(3) Value and Appropriate the Biblical Principles of Economic Justice and Stewardship of God's Creation

❖ Read aloud "Just a Dream?" from Interpreting the Scripture.

❖ Solicit from the students their ideas as to the feasibility of celebrating Jubilee in a modern, developed nation.

(1) **Would Jubilee work today as the process is set forth in the Bible? Why or why not?**

(2) **If not, are there other ways that wealth could be redistributed aside from having property change hands?**

(3) **How would you feel about a redistribution of wealth if you were wealthy? If you were poor?**

(4) **What are the benefits of redistribution?**

(5) **What are the drawbacks to redistribution?**

❖ Invite the students to talk with a partner or team about how the world could be different if Jubilee were practiced. They may want to think about the effect of Jubilee on wars, which are often fought to gain territory, or the effects on relationships among neighbors as they realize that no one person is always on top of the economic ladder.

(4) Engage in an Action That Promotes Economic Justice and Good Stewardship

❖ Retell "What Do We Need?" and "An Experiment" from Interpreting the Scripture.

❖ Brainstorm with the students some ways that they could promote economic justice and good stewardship individually and corporately through the church. The group may want to think in terms of:

■ hands-on experiences, such as

building a home with Habitat for Humanity, an international organization that promotes biblical economics by providing interest-free loans for homebuyers who have contributed "sweat equity" to their homes.

- financial giving that will empower people to get on their feet, perhaps through a program that offers microcredit to poor people (often in developing countries) who lack collateral and credit history to get a loan that would enable them to start a business.
- changing habits, such as eating lower on the food chain in order to help ensure enough food for all the world's people, to promote better stewardship.
- reducing waste by only purchasing what is necessary.
- choosing environmentally friendly cleaning products for home and church.
- seeking "green" building products to use when replacing items in the church and at home.

❖ End this portion of the lesson by distributing paper and pencils. Provide quiet time for the adults to think about commitments they can make to promote Jubilee and better stewardship of creation. Ask them to write on their papers at least one step they will take this week to honor their commitments.

(5) Continue the Journey

❖ Break the silence by praying that the adults will find ways to increase their stewardship of the earth and their possessions so as to spread God's wealth to others.

❖ Read aloud this preparation for next week's lesson. You may also want to post it on newsprint for the students to copy.

- **Title: People Grumble**
- **Background Scripture: Numbers 11**
- **Lesson Scripture: Numbers 11:1-6, 10-15**
- **Focus of the Lesson: When people experience difficulties, they often forget their blessings. What happens when we forget our blessings during times of trouble? When God brought the people out of slavery in Egypt and provided for them in the desert, Moses and the people complained repeatedly.**

❖ Challenge the students to complete one or more of these activities for further spiritual growth, which you will write on newsprint for the students to copy:

(1) **Check out www.jubileeusa.org, which is an organization based on Leviticus 25 that strongly encourages debt cancellation, especially for poor countries. Consider offering your support to this group.**

(2) **Look through your belongings. Did you borrow something that you have forgotten to return? If so, round up those things that are not yours and return them to their owners.**

(3) **Take excess clothing and household items to a shelter or recycling agency such as the Salvation Army to be a good steward of your possessions.**

❖ Sing or read aloud "Blow Ye the Trumpet, Blow."

❖ Conclude today's session by leading the class in this benediction: **We hear your call, O God, and ask that you send us forth empowered by your Spirit to live and serve as your covenant people.**

UNIT 3: CALLED TO CHOOSE LIFE
PEOPLE GRUMBLE

PREVIEWING THE LESSON

Lesson Scripture: Numbers 11:1-6, 10-15
Background Scripture: Numbers 11
Key Verses: Numbers 11:4-6

Focus of the Lesson:
When people experience difficulties, they often forget their blessings. What happens when we forget our blessings during times of trouble? When God brought the people out of slavery in Egypt and provided for them in the desert, Moses and the people complained repeatedly.

Goals for the Learners:
(1) to recount the Israelites' grumbling about life in the wilderness.
(2) to explore the complexity of giving and receiving, of providing necessities and luxuries in their lives.
(3) to identify and give thanks for their blessings.

Pronunciation Guide:
Eldad (el' dad)
Medad (mee' dad)
Taberah (tab' uh ruh)

Supplies:
Bibles, newsprint and marker, paper and pencils, hymnals, suggested food, optional pictures from magazines, scissors, glue

---

READING THE SCRIPTURE

NRSV
Numbers 11:1-6, 10-15

¹Now when the people complained in the hearing of the LORD about their misfortunes, the LORD heard it and his anger was kindled. Then the fire of the LORD burned against them, and consumed some outlying parts of

NIV
Numbers 11:1-6, 10-15

¹Now the people complained about their hardships in the hearing of the LORD, and when he heard them his anger was aroused. Then fire from the LORD burned among them and consumed some of the outskirts of the

the camp. ²But the people cried out to Moses; and Moses prayed to the LORD, and the fire abated. ³So that place was called Taberah, because the fire of the LORD burned against them.

⁴**The rabble among them had a strong craving; and the Israelites also wept again, and said, "If only we had meat to eat! ⁵We remember the fish we used to eat in Egypt for nothing, the cucumbers, the melons, the leeks, the onions, and the garlic; ⁶but now our strength is dried up, and there is nothing at all but this manna to look at."**

¹⁰Moses heard the people weeping throughout their families, all at the entrances of their tents. Then the LORD became very angry, and Moses was displeased. ¹¹So Moses said to the LORD, "Why have you treated your servant so badly? Why have I not found favor in your sight, that you lay the burden of all this people on me? ¹²Did I conceive all this people? Did I give birth to them, that you should say to me, 'Carry them in your bosom, as a nurse carries a sucking child,' to the land that you promised on oath to their ancestors? ¹³Where am I to get meat to give to all this people? For they come weeping to me and say, 'Give us meat to eat!' ¹⁴I am not able to carry all this people alone, for they are too heavy for me. ¹⁵If this is the way you are going to treat me, put me to death at once— if I have found favor in your sight—and do not let me see my misery."

camp. ²When the people cried out to Moses, he prayed to the LORD and the fire died down. ³So that place was called Taberah, because fire from the LORD had burned among them.

⁴**The rabble with them began to crave other food, and again the Israelites started wailing and said, "If only we had meat to eat! ⁵We remember the fish we ate in Egypt at no cost—also the cucumbers, melons, leeks, onions and garlic. ⁶But now we have lost our appetite; we never see anything but this manna!"**

¹⁰Moses heard the people of every family wailing, each at the entrance to his tent. The LORD became exceedingly angry, and Moses was troubled. ¹¹He asked the LORD, "Why have you brought this trouble on your servant? What have I done to displease you that you put the burden of all these people on me? ¹²Did I conceive all these people? Did I give them birth? Why do you tell me to carry them in my arms, as a nurse carries an infant, to the land you promised on oath to their forefathers? ¹³Where can I get meat for all these people? They keep wailing to me, 'Give us meat to eat!' ¹⁴I cannot carry all these people by myself; the burden is too heavy for me. ¹⁵If this is how you are going to treat me, put me to death right now—if I have found favor in your eyes—and do not let me face my own ruin."

UNDERSTANDING THE SCRIPTURE

Numbers 11:1-9. Numbers 11 weaves two stories together: the people's complaints about their boring diet of manna, and Moses' exasperation and weariness from all his responsibilities. In both cases God provides a solution.

Once again the people are unhappy, dissatisfied with what God is doing for them.

They "complain" and God is not pleased. The form of the Hebrew verb used for their complaining indicates both an action repeated over and over and over again and an intensive recurring action. This is not a simple polite inquiry if something could not be changed but nagging and whining and, as we might phrase it today, getting on

God's last nerve. In many ways this chapter sounds like things we have heard before. Ever since Exodus 16:3, the people have had similar grievances. They ask why they ever left Egypt in the first place, even claiming that they had been perfectly happy in their slavery. That has been a refrain from Exodus 14:11 on.

Numbers 11:4 may be an attempt to soften the criticism of the people as a whole, for here the narrator blames the "rabble" among the people for raising the fuss about food. It was noted when the people left Egypt (Exodus 12:38) that the multitude was not only Israelites but a "mixed crowd" of anyone who wanted to escape Egypt for whatever reason. There is no evidence given that the carping came from any one segment of the population. Human nature, however, does like to point the finger at anyone who may be different from us.

Of course, we do not know what manna was or what it tasted like. And that is not really the point of the people's whining. They were tired of it, and they were probably tired of being out in the wilderness too. Maybe some of them were frightened that they were hopelessly lost. Others may have been uncomfortable with the whole notion of freedom. In times of anxiety and uncertainty, people will often pick up some otherwise small matter and harp on it endlessly.

"If only we had meat to eat!" they grumble (11:4). "We remember the fish we used to eat in Egypt for nothing, the cucumbers, the melons, the leeks, the onions, and the garlic" (11:5). Interestingly, the items they recall do not include the meat they are now crying for.

Numbers 11:10-15. This time it is not the people who are doing all of the complaining. Moses also grumbles about the people, more urgently than we have heard from him before. Moses hears the people's crying and complaining and turns to God. He is at the very end of his patience. We can almost hear Moses challenging God in these paraphrased words: "How is it that you have inflicted me with all these people? Did I create them or give birth to them? Why am I responsible for all their wants and needs? I cannot handle this burden by myself. If you are not going to do anything to improve the situation, LORD, you might as well just kill me now."

Numbers 11:16-25. God's initial response is not to the complaint about manna. Indeed, it scarcely seems to be responding to Moses at all. The answer starts with more instructions for Moses. He is to gather seventy of the elders and bring them all to the tent of meeting. The outline of the solution to both problems begins to be seen starting in verse 17. There God says that a portion of the spirit on Moses will be divided among the seventy leaders who are to come out with Moses. These leaders will share the burden of leading and governing the people. Then God moves on to the issue of meat. Not only will the people have meat to eat, but they will have so much of it they will get sick of the very sight of it. This meat will not be a one-day banquet but a whole month-long orgy. Now Moses does not believe his ears. Moses wants to know where God could possibly get enough meat to feed this horde for a whole month. God replies in a figure of speech, "Is the LORD's hand too short?" The hand or arm is often used as a symbol of power in biblical Hebrew. Thus the saying means, "Is the LORD's power limited?"

Once again the focus shifts away from food to the sharing of power and authority. The seventy elders have gathered outside the camp. The Lord comes in the cloud and speaks to them. When a portion of the spirit from Moses rests on the elders, they prophesy.

Numbers 11:26-30. Then someone runs out from camp with the news, "Eldad and Medad are prophesying in the camp" (11:27). Joshua, Moses' second in command, is outraged. "My lord Moses, stop them!" he demands (11:28). But Moses deflects the anger. Joshua's anger and upset is misplaced. Moses is interested in having not less of God's spirit among the people but more. In this episode, Joshua sounds very much like Jesus' disciples when they come upon a man who is healing people in Jesus' name, but is not part of their group. (See Mark 9:38-40; Luke 9:49-50.)

Numbers 11:31-35. There is one final shift of scene in this chapter, and a shift of wind brings quail into the camp, "two cubits [about thirty-six inches] deep" all around. As God had promised meat, the Israelites received meat. They likely did not expect to be hip-deep in quail! We are told that the person who gathered the least amount of meat had ten homers. How much is that? Since one homer is approximately six bushels or forty-eight gallons, ten homers would be the equivalent of four hundred eighty gallons of meat! The point is not the exact measurement, nor is it important to raise questions about how all that meat could be kept from spoiling during the month they ate it. No, the point is that God heard their cry and provided meat for them in unimaginable abundance. Perhaps in the superabundance there was actually difficulty in dealing with so much meat. God may have been trying to teach them a lesson about being satisfied with "enough" rather than always wanting, or demanding, more.

INTERPRETING THE SCRIPTURE

Yucky Manna

When we are truly hungry, any food will taste good. When we are well-fed, we may complain about plain or repetitious menus and not appreciate simple good nutrition. What was the manna like? Exodus 16:31 says it tasted like wafers made with honey. That verse and Numbers 11:7 compare it to coriander seed. In the Midrash there are stories telling that manna could taste like whatever you wanted to eat at that particular moment. Of course the real point of the people's complaining had little to do with the properties of the manna itself. It was a visible sign of God's continuing care for them. Day in and day out, week in and week out, it appeared for six consecutive days and then kept the Sabbath, never failing to return again on the following day. Whether the Israelites were bored or frightened or anxious, talking about their food was also a metaphor, as if they were asking, "What have you done for us lately, God?"

How many of us have all the material goods we truly need in our lives and yet are unsatisfied? How many of us are thankful for what we do have rather than irritated or peevish about some item that is just a bit out of reach? How many of us may be pleased with a new car or cell phone or pair of shoes only until we see the next model or a new color we do not yet own? Every one of the seventeen winters I have lived in my county some four or five houses have burned to the ground. Usually all the residents escape without injury. A family spokesman will be quoted in the newspaper saying something along the lines of, "Well, we lost everything we had, but no one got hurt. We praise the Lord for that. When you've got your family, you're all right." In our better moments, most people would probably agree with that sentiment. Still, so many of us adults embarrassingly often sound like whining children or complaining Israelites rather than grateful children of God.

Why Me?

It is easy to sympathize with Moses and to hear his long complaint in verses 11-15 with empathy. He did not ask for this job of leading the Israelites. Indeed, he tried to argue God out of choosing him for the task as we saw in the first two lessons this quarter. Over and over again the people show themselves to be impatient and unappreciative, and Moses can take no more of the responsibility. I think he does precisely the right thing at this point: He takes his troubles to God and pours out his frustrations with passionate honesty. That his frustrations were real and not just a prima donna act becomes clear when God offers to share the spirit with seventy elders. Moses jumps immediately into implementing God's suggestion, showing that it was genuine help Moses wanted and not just selfish attention. When we are in real trouble, God neither expects nor wants us to keep it all to ourselves. Taking our troubles to the Lord is one of the privileges we have as children of God. The difference between childish whining and deeply felt lament is seen in part in our reactions to God's response.

What Does "Enough" Mean?

I wonder sometimes if our country has forgotten the meaning of "enough." I wonder sometimes if there could ever be enough to satisfy some people. You probably know individuals who seem never to be satisfied with what they have. You may well have been such an individual at some point in your life. It seems so often that people do not know quite what they want, except that they want *more*, or at least bigger or newer. It is a near certainty that none of us can always be in first place in every comparison. If this is how we consider our lives and how we measure either success or satisfaction, then it is a near certainty that we will never be satisfied. This sounds rather like another variation of what I wrote in the "Yucky Manna" section. Obviously I think it is a large problem for our culture and, therefore, one that the church does not escape.

There is yet another aspect to be examined, and that is the relationship between desires or cravings and enslavement. The Israelites seem willing, eager even, to return to Egypt for the variety of food they remember, apparently forgetting that alongside their varied menu they were living lives of actual slavery. They could not have returned to one part of their previous lives in Egypt without also returning to that other condition of slavery. To what extent might the satisfaction of some of our wishes lead us into kinds of enslavement? A bigger house, a newer car, a more luxurious vacation—there is nothing intrinsically wrong with any such desires. But a growing proportion of the population is sinking further and further into debt, in part, to pay for such desires. More hours of work and even a second job may be taken on to pay the bills. More time at work means less time available for anything else, including family and church. Some parents try to substitute material goods for lack of time they can spend with their children. Children may not know how to articulate their preference for their parents' time and attention and may ask instead for more *things*. And so the cycle continues downward: more money for more stuff but less time for those things that matter even more than possessions.

What might make a difference? A combination of gratitude to God and the experience of the joy of sharing ourselves could probably do a lot for all of us. Gratitude is not a new concept, either in general or for this study series. The "Focus of the Lesson" today includes this question: "What happens when we forget our blessings during times of trouble?" That is meant to be not merely a rhetorical question but also a matter for serious consideration. If we do not say "thank you" often enough to God, will the divine cease to care about us? Of course not. But neither does that mean that God is indifferent to our responses. Forgetting our blessings does not change God's relationship to us, but it may cloud our vision of reality in the troublesome present. Remembering and thanking God for all the good that has been showered on us in past times may enable us to open our eyes to deeper parts of our present reality and give us strength to persevere into the good future that God wants for us.

SHARING THE SCRIPTURE

Preparing Our Hearts

Meditate on this week's devotional reading, found in Psalm 142. Here the psalmist tells God his troubles, pouring out complaints and praying for deliverance from those who persecute him. What concerns do you need to pour out to God today? List them in your spiritual journal. As you review the list, do you feel that these concerns are justified, or are you simply complaining to be noticed or get something you want but do not truly need?

Pray that you and the adult learners will give thanks to God for your blessings.

Preparing Our Minds

Study the background Scripture from Numbers 11 and the lesson Scripture from Numbers 11:1-6, 10-15. Consider what happens when we forget our blessings during times of trouble.

Write on newsprint:
- ❏ directions for the discussion under "Explore the Complexity of Giving and Receiving, of Providing Necessities and Luxuries in the Learners' Lives."
- ❏ sentences under "Identify and Give Thanks for Blessings," if you choose to post them.
- ❏ information for next week's lesson, found under "Continue the Journey."
- ❏ activities for further spiritual growth in "Continue the Journey."

Bring some favorite foods to arrange on a worship table. Include cucumbers, melons, leeks, onions, and garlic if you have access to these products. Prior to class, be sure to arrange these on a table where everyone can see them. Also bring plain crackers such as matzoh. You may wish to contact class members during the week to see if they can provide some food.

Prepare a brief lecture on the Scripture noted under "Recount the Israelites' Grumbling About Life in the Wilderness."

Gather pictures and art supplies for "Explore the Complexity of Giving and Receiving, of Providing Necessities and Luxuries in the Learners' Lives" if you choose to do this option.

LEADING THE CLASS

(1) Gather to Learn

❖ Welcome the class members and introduce any guests.

❖ Pray that all who have gathered today will learn from the experiences that the Israelites had with God.

❖ Read aloud this information: **In the Psalms, Job, and the Prophets, we find examples of people making complaints against God. Yet, did you know that according to a September 21, 2007, Associated Press release by Nate Jenkins, Nebraska state Senator Ernie Chambers of Omaha has filed a lawsuit against God? In his five-page suit, the self-avowed agnostic Senator claimed "that God has made** terroristic threats against him and his constituents, inspired fear and caused 'widespread death, destruction and terrorization of millions upon millions of the Earth's inhabitants.'" Chambers, who claims that his lawsuit is serious, is making the point that anyone can sue anyone, but he also hopes to get a permanent injunction against God.

❖ Invite the students to respond to Senator Chambers's specific claims and to the general idea of a lawsuit against God. You may want to note that there were two responses to the suit, one supposedly signed by God and witnessed by the archangel Michael arguing that "the court lacks jurisdiction over God" and another disputing Chambers's allegations. (Check out the article at www.law.com/jsp/article.jsp?id=1190278980163.)

❖ Read aloud today's focus statement: **When people experience difficulties, they often forget their blessings. What happens when we forget our blessings during times of trouble? When God brought the people out of slavery in Egypt and provided for them in the desert, Moses and the people complained repeatedly.**

(2) Recount the Israelites' Grumbling About Life in the Wilderness

❖ Choose two volunteers, one to read Numbers 11:1-6 and the other to read Numbers 11:10-15.

❖ Discuss these questions. Use information from Understanding the Scripture as appropriate.

    (1) **Why is the crowd complaining?**

    (2) **How are Moses's complaints different from those of the people?** (You may wish to read or retell "Why Me?" in Interpreting the Scripture to help answer this question.)

❖ Present a brief lecture on Numbers 11:16-25, 26-30, and 31-35 to enable the class to hear "the rest of the story." In these verses

God answers both the complaints of the people and the complaints of Moses.

❖ Direct the students' attention to the table where you have set up whatever food you have brought.

    ■ **Step 1:** Prompt several role-players to retell today's lesson Scripture by assuming the roles of several Hebrew people and Moses.

    ■ **Step 2:** Encourage the students to voice complaints using contemporary foods. For example, students may complain that homemade cookies are never served in class, even though they remember them being served when they were in the children's Sunday school. Or they might decry the removal of certain foods from store shelves because they pose a health risk.

(3) Explore the Complexity of Giving and Receiving, of Providing Necessities and Luxuries in the Learners' Lives

❖ Ask the participants to think about the gifts that they give and receive, perhaps at Christmas or on other occasions.

❖ Post these directions on newsprint for the adults to follow. Talk with a partner or small group about (a) how you decide who you will give a gift to and (b) how you decide what you will ask for. Do you generally give (a) to be recognized for your generosity, (b) just because you like the recipient, or (c) because you feel obligated to give?

❖ **Option:** Provide pictures from magazines and other sources that may be cut and pasted. Have glue sticks, scissors, and paper on hand. Encourage half of the students to work individually or with a partner to create collages of "necessities," and the other half to create collages of "wants." Invite the students to post their collages. Encourage the class to talk about why they classified certain items as "necessities" and others as "wants." Allow the adults to raise and justify disagreements over the classifications.

❖ Draw the class together and ask:

(1) **Why do you think God provides for our needs though not necessarily our wants?**

(2) **How do you know when you have enough?** ("What Does 'Enough' Mean?" in Interpreting the Scripture may be helpful here.)

(3) **How does God's motivation for giving differ from the reasons that often motivate our giving?**

(4) Identify and Give Thanks for Blessings

❖ Distribute paper and pencils. Ask the students to write down the first name or object that comes to mind when you read each of the following sentences. As an option, write these on newsprint and let the students respond at their own pace.

(1) **I am very thankful for all that _____ has done to help me become the person I am today.**

(2) **I am blessed by my relationship with _____.**

(3) **I am grateful that _____ is always there when I need someone to listen to my problems.**

(4) **I don't know what I would do without _____.**

(5) **God has spoken to me through _____.**

❖ Invite the students to spend a few moments in silent prayer, giving thanks for whomever they have identified.

(5) Continue the Journey

❖ Conclude the silent prayer time by praying that everyone present today will be mindful of blessings and able to recall these blessings when they feel like complaining.

❖ Read aloud this preparation for next week's lesson. You may also want to post it on newsprint for the students to copy.

■ **Title: People Rebel**

■ **Background Scripture: Numbers 14:1-25**

■ **Lesson Scripture: Numbers 14:1-12**

■ **Focus of the Lesson: When dissatisfaction grows great, people may rebel against their leaders and benefactors. What causes people to rebel against leadership and authority? The deprivation of the Israelites and the threats of destruction at the hand of others led the Israelites to seek new leadership and a return to Egypt.**

❖ Challenge the students to complete one or more of these activities for further spiritual growth, which you will write on newsprint for the students to copy.

(1) **Make a written list of your blessings each day this week. Give thanks to God. Note that when we take time to give thanks for what we do have, we have less time to complain about what we do not have.**

(2) **Recognize that just as Moses faced challenges from the people he was called to lead, so too it is likely that your church leaders feel inadequate to fulfill their tasks. Pray for each one by name at least once this week.**

(3) **Recall whatever for you were "the good old days." What was truly good about those days? What was not so good about them?**

❖ Sing or read aloud "Come, Ye Thankful People, Come."

❖ Conclude today's session by leading the class in this benediction: **We hear your call, O God, and ask that you send us forth empowered by your Spirit to live and serve as your covenant people.**

UNIT 3: CALLED TO CHOOSE LIFE
PEOPLE REBEL

PREVIEWING THE LESSON

Lesson Scripture: Numbers 14:1-12
Background Scripture: Numbers 14:1-25
Key Verse: Numbers 14:3

Focus of the Lesson:
When dissatisfaction grows great, people may rebel against their leaders and benefactors. What causes people to rebel against leadership and authority? The deprivation of the Israelites and the threats of destruction at the hand of others led the Israelites to seek new leadership and a return to Egypt.

Goals for the Learners:
(1) to investigate the Israelites' rebellion against Moses and God in the wilderness.
(2) to identify ways that complaining can lead the learners to rebellion.
(3) to find ways to confront and deal responsibly with dissatisfaction.

Pronunciation Guide:
Caleb (kay' luhb)   Nephilim (nef' uh lim)
Jephunneh (ji fuhn' uh)   Nun (nuhn)

Supplies:
Bibles, newsprint and marker, paper and pencils, hymnals, optional DVD of *Mutiny on the Bounty* and player

---

READING THE SCRIPTURE

NRSV
Numbers 14:1-12

¹Then all the congregation raised a loud cry, and the people wept that night. ²And all the Israelites complained against Moses and Aaron; the whole congregation said to them, "Would that we had died in the land of Egypt! Or would that we had died in this

NIV
Numbers 14:1-12

¹That night all the people of the community raised their voices and wept aloud. ²All the Israelites grumbled against Moses and Aaron, and the whole assembly said to them, "If only we had died in Egypt! Or in

wilderness! **³Why is the LORD bringing us into this land to fall by the sword?** Our wives and our little ones will become booty; **would it not be better for us to go back to Egypt?"** ⁴So they said to one another, "Let us choose a captain, and go back to Egypt."

⁵Then Moses and Aaron fell on their faces before all the assembly of the congregation of the Israelites. ⁶And Joshua son of Nun and Caleb son of Jephunneh, who were among those who had spied out the land, tore their clothes ⁷and said to all the congregation of the Israelites, "The land that we went through as spies is an exceedingly good land. ⁸If the LORD is pleased with us, he will bring us into this land and give it to us, a land that flows with milk and honey. ⁹Only, do not rebel against the LORD; and do not fear the people of the land, for they are no more than bread for us; their protection is removed from them, and the LORD is with us; do not fear them." ¹⁰But the whole congregation threatened to stone them.

Then the glory of the LORD appeared at the tent of meeting to all the Israelites. ¹¹And the LORD said to Moses, "How long will this people despise me? And how long will they refuse to believe in me, in spite of all the signs that I have done among them? ¹²I will strike them with pestilence and disinherit them, and I will make of you a nation greater and mightier than they."

this desert! **³Why is the LORD bringing us to this land only to let us fall by the sword?** Our wives and children will be taken as plunder. **Wouldn't it be better for us to go back to Egypt?"** ⁴And they said to each other, "We should choose a leader and go back to Egypt."

⁵Then Moses and Aaron fell facedown in front of the whole Israelite assembly gathered there. ⁶Joshua son of Nun and Caleb son of Jephunneh, who were among those who had explored the land, tore their clothes ⁷and said to the entire Israelite assembly, "The land we passed through and explored is exceedingly good. ⁸If the LORD is pleased with us, he will lead us into that land, a land flowing with milk and honey, and will give it to us. ⁹Only do not rebel against the LORD. And do not be afraid of the people of the land, because we will swallow them up. Their protection is gone, but the LORD is with us. Do not be afraid of them."

¹⁰But the whole assembly talked about stoning them. Then the glory of the LORD appeared at the Tent of Meeting to all the Israelites. ¹¹The LORD said to Moses, "How long will these people treat me with contempt? How long will they refuse to believe in me, in spite of all the miraculous signs I have performed among them? ¹²I will strike them down with a plague and destroy them, but I will make you into a nation greater and stronger than they."

UNDERSTANDING THE SCRIPTURE

Introduction. The Israelites have now come close enough to their destination, the Promised Land, the land of Canaan, that God instructs Moses to send spies across the Jordan River to see what the land is like. Moses chooses a representative from each tribe and tells them to see what they can see within the territory and especially to check what sort of resistance the people may meet from the current inhabitants of the land when they cross the river into it (13:17-20). After a forty-day excursion the men return, bringing back a mixed report. On the one hand they have found a land flowing with milk and honey and with spectacular produce (13:23, 27). On the other hand, most of them are afraid of the people in the land, saying that they felt like "grasshoppers" in their presence (13:33).

Numbers 14:1-10. Once more the Israelites complain, raising yet again their old cry, "Would that we had died in the land of Egypt!" (14:2). Just as they had clamored for Aaron to make them another god when Moses was delayed in returning from the top of Mount Sinai, now some of them even suggest choosing another leader and all of them returning to Egypt (14:4). In proposing such a plan, they are repudiating all that God has done for them, as well as all that God has promised them. They are turning their backs not just on God's promises for the future but are also counting as worthless everything they have seen that God has done for them up to this point in their journey. Moses and Aaron are in deep distress in front of the people and fall to the ground. Joshua and Caleb, two of the twelve spies, are so upset they tear their garments—an ancient action signifying the greatest upset and grief. The two spies then speak to the crowd and try once again to reason with them, to persuade them to move forward in obedience to God's command. They list all the splendid qualities of the land they have surveyed. They remind the congregation of God's promises and all God's faithfulness to them so far. But the people will have none of it and even threaten to kill them.

Numbers 14:11-21. The Lord then comes to the tent of meeting in the "glory" that is visible to the whole population. God speaks to Moses and repeats the offer made in Exodus 32:7-10. In language that sounds rather like psalms of lament, God says, in effect, "Enough of these complainers. They are never satisfied; they never believe in me and my care for them, despite all of the evidence I have shown them. So, Moses, out of my way. Let me kill them off and then I will make a better nation beginning with you." As he did in the conversation in Exodus 32, Moses is again able to argue God out of that idea. He does this in part by appealing to God, as before. Moses also reminds God of

the expanded name pronounced by the Lord in Exodus 34:6-7. The characteristics listed in Numbers 14:18 are considered to be part of God's name. Remember that in ancient Israel one's name was considered to indicate the deepest essence and identity of a being, whether human or divine. Therefore these qualities, as part of God's name, are also part of the very essence of the identity of God. Being long-suffering, full of compassion, and forgiving iniquity are not add-ons or occasional descriptions of how God might act. They are a portion of the very definition of God. Moses is making the argument that for God to destroy the people at this juncture would be to contradict the very divine nature. "Forgive the iniquity of this people according to the greatness of your steadfast love, just as you have pardoned this people, from Egypt even until now," he pleads (14:19).

Numbers 14:22-25. God agrees to Moses' prayer, up to a point. The people will be forgiven and not wiped out, but the generation of complainers will not be allowed to enter the Promised Land. Two exceptions are made to this ban. Because Joshua and Caleb gave a positive report and because they continued to urge the people to trust in the Lord and to cross the Jordan and go up into the land, they will be permitted to enter it. However, they will have to wait some forty years, until the entire generation who were adults when leaving Egypt has died.

As the report continues to the end of the chapter, God's responses actually give the people exactly what they have asked for, and on more than one occasion. They said, "Would that we had died in this wilderness" (14:2) and God replies, "Your dead bodies shall fall in this very wilderness" (14:29). The Israelites did not want to enter the Promised Land (14:3) and God says that indeed they will not (14:30). The people use concern for their women and children as a pretext not to advance across the river (14:3), and God promises that it will be the children who do enter the land (14:31-33). In this combined act of forgiveness and punishment, God is making a very important theological point: The sins of the parents will *not* be passed along to the children. Guilt does not accumulate from one generation to the next. Although the possession of the Promised Land is deferred until the following generation, this deferral is the end of the punishment for this particular sin.

The next response of the people would almost be funny if it were not so sad (14:39-45). Having been told by Moses that God has taken their complaints and fears about the mortal dangers awaiting them in the land of Canaan seriously and that God has now forbidden them to go into the Promised Land, they decide that they *will* go in. Moses warns them not even to try. But, ever rebellious, they try anyway, and immediately they are defeated.

INTERPRETING THE SCRIPTURE

The Future Is Just Too Frightening

It seems to me at times that the church is full of people like the ten scared spies and all those who followed them, people who yearn for the "good old days" and use whatever energy they can muster to try to bring back those former conditions as they exist in their memories. How much time and effort are expended by good and faithful Christians in trying to keep new conditions at bay, whether the "new" means ordained women or new wording of the Eucharistic prayer? Fear may be the most destructive power in the life of the contemporary church. How often in meetings do you hear—or have you said—"Well, yes, that sounds like a good idea, but . . ."? What follows the "but" is often a variation on the fear of losing money or losing members. Rarely do I hear people worry lest a particular decision might cause us to lose our vocation as members of the body of Christ, or forget that we are a people who are charged to take up our crosses and follow our crucified and risen Lord.

There has never been a shortage of naysayers, and we are certainly well supplied with them today. And there is rarely a shortage of matters that should concern us when we are taking a step into the future.

Blind "Pollyanna" optimism and living in a dream world are not worthy of our Lord either. And yet, how often do we turn concerns and potential problems into monsters? There were not really giants, Nephilim, in Canaan, although ten of the spies were able to convince the rest of the people that there were. We tend to make genuine potential difficulties that must be addressed into insurmountable obstacles. Worse than that is our all-too-human tendency to turn other people into enemies and monsters. They, too, even if they are opposed to our every notion and have no respect for our deepest faith, are beloved children of God for whom Christ died. If we continue to make people who are different from us into intractable enemies, we may be the ones God reluctantly requires to live out the rest of our lives and finally die in the wilderness.

We Cannot Do Everything

It is eminently true, of course, that we cannot solve, or even work hard on, all of the world's problems at once. But all too often we tend to play the issues off against each other, as if social justice and environmental concerns, for example, are in conflict with each other, as if we must choose one as the focus of our concern and thoroughly ignore the other. Here, I believe, is where part of the genius of Paul's analogy of the church as the body of Christ (1 Corinthians 12:12-31) and of the connectional systems of most mainline denominations—certainly including United Methodists, Lutherans, Presbyterians, and Episcopalians—comes into focus. Rather than playing on fears or being overly attentive to our weaknesses, it would be good to remember the God who called us into relationship in the first place, the God who has nurtured us, the God who promises good to us. The land in front of us is filled with both challenge and promise. Even more important than what is in the Promised Land is to remember that it is the Lord God who called us and promises never to leave us as we move into that future.

In the Meantime

There is actually a great difference between the ending of today's lesson Scripture and the rest of the background Scripture. We are charged in this lesson with identifying ways that complaining can lead to rebellion and with finding ways to confront and deal responsibly with anger. The "Focus of the Lesson" locates the causes of the Israelites' rebellion in their "deprivation" and "the threats of destruction at the hand of others." What is essential to recognize, however, especially as we relate these texts to our own lives, is that both the deprivation and the threats existed only in their minds and not in the reality of their external situation. At no time has God not provided for them an abundance of water and food. Not one of them has been lost to any enemy. To be sure, God has not acted like a cosmic Santa Claus, showering them with every little thing they whine for. Still they fuss and complain and finally rebel against their human leaders and ultimately against God. Added to their dissatisfaction with the present is their gross misremembering of their immediate past. They had been *slaves* in Pharaoh's Egypt, their only "abundance" being an overabundance of forced labor with ever harsher conditions imposed upon them.

When considering complaints, it is important to distinguish between the real and the imaginary or exaggerated problems. It is vital to discern what is actual and what is invented. Hyperbole is common with us: "I've told you a million times not to leave your bicycle outside at night" or "He never remembers to check that all the lights are turned out and all the doors locked when he is the last to leave the church." We often find it easier to repeat the cliché ("all politicians are greedy" or "teenagers are irresponsible") than to do the hard work of making adequate distinctions in real-life complicated situations. We can revert all too quickly to acting like petulant children, ever complaining that things are not to our liking.

The work of discernment is a great service class members can help one another with, before complaints lead to rebellion or dissatisfaction to anger. Having several viewpoints brought to an issue can be an immense help in clarifying what is actual and what is exaggerated or even imaginary. You have probably seen a standard "illusion" drawing of two people in profile facing each other that, with a slight shift of focus, looks instead like a vase. The eye and brain can shift back and forth between the two meanings of the picture but cannot hold the two of them simultaneously. There is no point in arguing that one is there and one is not when a slight shift of viewpoint can make now one and then the other pop into focus. Our lives are ever so much more complex than that simple drawing, and so it should not be surprising that different people will see the same situation differently. After all, Moses sent more than one man to spy out the land of Canaan, and we should seek out more than one opinion for important decisions, remembering always to ask for the guidance of the Holy Spirit as well.

Remembering those twelve spies will also remind us to be careful not to assume that a simple majority vote can always determine the truth!

SHARING THE SCRIPTURE

Preparing Our Hearts

Meditate on this week's devotional reading, found in Psalm 78:5-17. This psalm reminds listeners, just as a teacher of wisdom would, that God will continue to guide the next generation, even as God has led those in the past. The writer recalls not only the wonderful deeds that God has performed on behalf of the Israelites but also the ingratitude and rebellion of the people. Verse 17 relates directly to today's lesson, for it speaks of the people's rebellion "in the desert." Recall times when you feel that the church has rebelled against God. What attitudes or actions constituted sin? What happened (or needs to happen) to turn this situation around?

Pray that you and the adult learners will recognize the outcomes of rebellion against God and seek to live obediently.

Preparing Our Minds

Study the background Scripture from Numbers 14:1-25 and the lesson Scripture from Numbers 14:1-12. Ask yourself: What causes people to rebel against leadership and authority?

Write on newsprint:
- ❏ thought questions for "Find Ways to Confront and Deal Responsibly With Dissatisfaction."
- ❏ information for next week's lesson, found under "Continue the Journey."
- ❏ activities for further spiritual growth in "Continue the Journey."

If you choose to show a clip of *Mutiny on the Bounty* for "Gather to Learn," locate a DVD of the film, select the segment you want to use, and have a DVD player on hand.

LEADING THE CLASS

(1) Gather to Learn

❖ Welcome the class members and introduce any guests.

❖ Pray that all who have come today will hear and obey God's word for them.

❖ Read this information: **Webster's Collegiate Dictionary defines "mutiny" as "forcible or passive resistance to lawful authority." When we hear the word "mutiny," often the movie and story of *Mutiny on the Bounty*, a rebellion aboard a British naval ship in 1789, come to mind. History records many other mutinies as well. Often the cause was poor conditions or salaries that were due but never paid. Sometimes, a shipboard mutiny was part of a larger revolution. Penalties for mutiny, whether at sea or on land, are generally severe and often result in the death of the mutineers.**

❖ **Option:** Show a brief clip from *Mutiny on the Bounty* that demonstrates the rebellion of crew.

❖ Discuss this question with the group: **Why do you think people are willing to rebel against authority even though the resultant punishment may be death?**

❖ Read aloud today's focus statement: **When dissatisfaction grows great, people may rebel against their leaders and benefactors. What causes people to rebel against leadership and authority? The deprivation of the Israelites and the threats of destruction at the hand of others led the**

Israelites to seek new leadership and a return to Egypt.

(2) Investigate the Israelites' Rebellion Against Moses and God in the Wilderness

❖ Read "Introduction" in Understanding the Scripture to set the scene for today's lesson.

❖ Choose three volunteers to read, in turn, Numbers 14:1-4, 5-10a, and 10b-12. Encourage the listeners to try to imagine themselves in the crowd as this passage is read.

❖ **Option:** Have the passage read aloud from several translations. Invite the students to comment on words they heard in one translation that gave them new insight into the meaning of the text.

❖ Encourage the class members to identify the following and answer the accompanying questions:

■ the people's complaint.
  ○ **Does this complaint seem justified in light of God's recent actions with the people? Why or why not?**
■ the leaders' response. (Note that the response of Moses and Aaron is different from that of Joshua and Caleb.)
  ○ **What do these responses tell you about the leadership and how they respond to problems?**
■ the people's response to Joshua and Caleb.
  ○ **Why do you suppose the people responded the way they did?** ("The Future Is Just Too Frightening" in Interpreting the Scripture will provide some helpful clues here.)
■ God's response.
  ○ **In what ways, if any, does God's response surprise you?**

❖ Conclude by discussing this question: **What lessons do you think the church in general, or your church in particular, can** learn from the way the people approached the future?

(3) Identify Ways That Complaining Can Lead the Learners to Rebellion

❖ Read aloud "In the Meantime" from Interpreting the Scripture. Note especially that what the Israelites feared was only in their minds and did not represent the actual situation.

❖ Use this scenario to talk with the class about how we sometimes set up situations that can lead us into the sin of rebellion.

Mrs. Summerfield had been an active member of Community Church for all of her 74 years. She was well-liked and a good leader who had a lot of influence in shaping opinion among the congregation. In July, when a new pastor came whose preaching and leadership styles were not like those of a beloved former pastor, Mrs. Summerfield began making small, disparaging comments. Soon, other church members were also becoming dissatisfied with the new pastor. By January, church leaders had heard so much negative feedback that they were ready to ask for another pastor. The new pastor never really had a chance since people had not discerned his gifts and graces for ministry and encouraged him to use them.

❖ Discuss these questions with the entire class or in groups:

(1) **What role did Mrs. Summerfield play in the ouster of the new pastor?**
(2) **Do you think she believed that her small comments would have the effect that they did? Why or why not?**
(3) **In what ways was this congregation acting like the Israelites as we see them in Numbers 14?**
(4) **How could some "other voices," such as those of a Caleb or Joshua, within the church have made the difference—or could they?**

*(4) Find Ways to Confront and Deal
Responsibly With Dissatisfaction*

❖ Distribute paper and pencils. Ask the students to recall and write about a situation that caused them to become dissatisfied enough to complain. Here are some questions to read aloud to help the adults begin to think. You may prefer to post these questions on newsprint:

(1) **What was the situation?**

(2) **How did you handle this situation?**

(3) **Did you complain to someone who could actually do something to change the situation? If so, what happened?**

(4) **Did you adjust your own expectations? If so, in what ways?**

(5) **Had fear somehow entered into the situation? If so, how?**

(6) **How did this situation turn out in the end?**

(7) **What lessons did you learn?**

❖ Invite volunteers to read or retell what they have written.

❖ Encourage the students to affirm ways of dealing with dissatisfaction that are positive rather than leading to complaints and potential rebellion.

(5) Continue the Journey

❖ Pray that today's participants will go forth able to discern God's will and move ahead fearlessly toward that will.

❖ Read aloud this preparation for next week's lesson. You may also want to post it on newsprint for the students to copy.

■ **Title: Moses Disobeys**

■ **Background Scripture: Numbers 20:1-13**

■ **Lesson Scripture: Numbers 20:1-13**

■ **Focus of the Lesson: Even great leaders may fail to heed higher authority. Why do people disregard authority? Moses disobeyed God because he did not trust God to provide for the people.**

❖ Challenge the students to complete one or more of these activities for further spiritual growth, which you will write on newsprint for the students to copy:

(1) **Recall a "rebellion" against God that you experienced recently and repent of this sin by praying for God's forgiveness.**

(2) **Seek to be the Caleb or Joshua in a situation your church is currently experiencing. Perhaps people are afraid of moving into the future with a new worship style or building or ministry that feels unfamiliar. Do whatever you can to help people discern God's will and live into this future.**

(3) **Identify where a figurative Egypt might be in your life. Have you left a past to which you long to return? What was appealing about it? Why is that not the place where God would have you to be? Pray for strength to put these old ways behind you.**

❖ Sing or read aloud "I Want a Principle Within."

❖ Conclude today's session by leading the class in this benediction: **We hear your call, O God, and ask that you send us forth empowered by your Spirit to live and serve as your covenant people.**

UNIT 3: CALLED TO CHOOSE LIFE
MOSES DISOBEYS

PREVIEWING THE LESSON

Lesson Scripture: Numbers 20:1-13
Background Scripture: Numbers 20:1-13
Key Verse: Numbers 20:12

Focus of the Lesson:
Even great leaders may fail to heed higher authority. Why do people disregard authority? Moses disobeyed God because he did not trust God to provide for the people.

Goals for the Learners:
(1) to lay out the details of God's command and Moses' disobedience.
(2) to explore levels of authority and leadership and issues of obedience.
(3) to make a commitment to support leaders in prayer.

Pronunciation Guide:
Abiram (uh bi' ruhm)   Korah (kor' uh)
Dathan (day' thuhn)   Meribah (mer' i bah)
Kadesh (kay' dish)   Zin (zin)

Supplies:
Bibles, newsprint and marker, paper and pencils, hymnals, map of Israel at the time of the exodus, picture of Moses striking the rock

---

READING THE SCRIPTURE

NRSV
Numbers 20:1-13
¹The Israelites, the whole congregation, came into the wilderness of Zin in the first month, and the people stayed in Kadesh. Miriam died there, and was buried there.

²Now there was no water for the congregation; so they gathered together against Moses and against Aaron. ³The people quarreled with Moses and said, "Would that we

NIV
Numbers 20:1-13
¹In the first month the whole Israelite community arrived at the Desert of Zin, and they stayed at Kadesh. There Miriam died and was buried.

²Now there was no water for the community, and the people gathered in opposition to Moses and Aaron. ³They quarreled with

had died when our kindred died before the LORD! [4]Why have you brought the assembly of the LORD into this wilderness for us and our livestock to die here? [5]Why have you brought us up out of Egypt, to bring us to this wretched place? It is no place for grain, or figs, or vines, or pomegranates; and there is no water to drink." [6]Then Moses and Aaron went away from the assembly to the entrance of the tent of meeting; they fell on their faces, and the glory of the LORD appeared to them. [7]The LORD spoke to Moses, saying: [8]Take the staff, and assemble the congregation, you and your brother Aaron, and command the rock before their eyes to yield its water. Thus you shall bring water out of the rock for them; thus you shall provide drink for the congregation and their livestock.

[9]So Moses took the staff from before the LORD, as he had commanded him. [10]Moses and Aaron gathered the assembly together before the rock, and he said to them, "Listen, you rebels, shall we bring water for you out of this rock?" [11]Then Moses lifted up his hand and struck the rock twice with his staff; water came out abundantly, and the congregation and their livestock drank. **[12]But the LORD said to Moses and Aaron, "Because you did not trust in me, to show my holiness before the eyes of the Israelites, therefore you shall not bring this assembly into the land that I have given them."** [13]These are the waters of Meribah, where the people of Israel quarreled with the LORD, and by which he showed his holiness.

Moses and said, "If only we had died when our brothers fell dead before the LORD! [4]Why did you bring the LORD's community into this desert, that we and our livestock should die here? [5]Why did you bring us up out of Egypt to this terrible place? It has no grain or figs, grapevines or pomegranates. And there is no water to drink!"

[6]Moses and Aaron went from the assembly to the entrance to the Tent of Meeting and fell facedown, and the glory of the LORD appeared to them. [7]The LORD said to Moses, [8]"Take the staff, and you and your brother Aaron gather the assembly together. Speak to that rock before their eyes and it will pour out its water. You will bring water out of the rock for the community so they and their livestock can drink."

[9]So Moses took the staff from the LORD's presence, just as he commanded him. [10]He and Aaron gathered the assembly together in front of the rock and Moses said to them, "Listen, you rebels, must we bring you water out of this rock?" [11]Then Moses raised his arm and struck the rock twice with his staff. Water gushed out, and the community and their livestock drank.

[12]But the LORD said to Moses and Aaron, "Because you did not trust in me enough to honor me as holy in the sight of the Israelites, you will not bring this community into the land I give them." [13]These were the waters of Meribah, where the Israelites quarreled with the LORD and where he showed himself holy among them.

UNDERSTANDING THE SCRIPTURE

Numbers 20:1. Our text sets the stage by telling us the action takes place "in the first month," but it does not put "first month" in context for us. Most likely this refers to the first month of the fortieth year since the Israelites escaped from Egypt. Thus the pre-

scribed time of that generation's wandering in the wilderness is almost at an end. As if to signal this, we have a terse report of the death of Miriam. (A bit later in the chapter, 20:22-29, outside this lesson's assigned text, we will read of Aaron's death as well.) It is as if the deaths of the leaders stand for the dying of that entire generation who were forbidden to cross into the Promised Land after their abortive first attempt.

Numbers 20:2-5. It is almost too much to believe that the Israelites, faced with a water shortage, would once again gather against Moses and Aaron and reiterate their old complaints. We have heard fussing from them so many times before. Not one single time has God ever let the people down by ignoring their basic needs. Never in all their forty years in the wilderness have they ever been left hungry or thirsty. Some of the specific Hebrew words used here also connect this story to the account of the rebellion of Korah, Dathan, and Abiram in Numbers 16–17. In this episode it is almost as if we are being shown how the initial rebellion has spread throughout the population, and thus how undeserving this particular generation is to receive the gift of the Promised Land.

Whenever we hear the first hint of whining, we tend to assume the people's complaint is illegitimate, the attack on Moses and Aaron unjustified, and that God's righteous anger is just offstage, ready to be revealed within the next verses. And yet, there is something different about this account. Both the narrator in verse 2 and the people in verse 5 mention the lack of water. Unlike the cases of many of their other murmurings when they were expressing simple discontent, here the content of their complaint is not anything other than the bald truth.

Numbers 20:6-8. As they have done on previous occasions, Moses and Aaron appeal to God. As has happened in all the previous occasions, God gives them instructions to solve the crisis of the moment. Showing great forbearance, God makes neither complaint nor warning of impending judgment for the people's incessant fussing. The Lord merely tells the two leaders what they need to do to obtain water for the people.

Numbers 20:9-11. The story seems to be going along as before, with Moses and Aaron carrying out God's instructions. Moses does sound a bit exasperated as he calls the people "you rebels" before striking the rock with his staff. His words in verse 10 can be taken in many different ways. Since what we have on the page gives us no hint of his body language or tone of voice, it is not always a simple matter to decide the intended meaning from among several possible alternative interpretations. One possibility is that Moses might be asking a rhetorical question that assumes a positive answer: "Are you ready for water? Of course!" But since he does call them rebels, this seems an unlikely interpretation. A second possibility is that Moses is emphasizing the "we" who are to supply water, meaning Moses and Aaron rather than God. Or maybe he is toying with the people, saying in effect, "Do you really want us to bring out water? Remember what happened after you asked God for quails and you had so much meat you got sick on it. Be careful what you ask for." In this third interpretation Moses is not relating God's unqualified graciousness but almost taunting the people. Perhaps, as a fourth alternative, the question is not rhetorical at all and intimates that Moses and Aaron (and hence God too, of course) really cannot do such a thing. This would be a huge failure of trust on Moses' part. Finally, the words could be read as saying, "Of course we could produce water if we wanted to, but we don't want to." Once again, this would be denying God's undiminished graciousness that had been conveyed to Moses in God's instructions for obtaining water. Whichever of these possibilities is correct—and we really cannot tell from this distance—Moses and Aaron are implicated in one sort of unfaithfulness or another. Either they are trying to take credit for God's action, or they are implying that God is really not faithful after all.

Two hits on the rock and abundant water gushes out. There is enough to satisfy not only the people but all their livestock too.

Numbers 20:12-13. The story now takes a starkly surprising turn. God accuses Aaron and Moses of a lack of trust and says that, therefore, they will not be allowed into the Promised Land. Wherein lies their sin? This question has exercised the minds of countless generations of people who read this text. It may have something to do with Moses' words in verse 10 as explained above. It may involve his hitting the rock instead of following God's instructions in the detail of speaking rather than striking. One hint comes through in the Hebrew. The same phrase that is used in Numbers 14:11 is used here, that "this people" in the earlier account and the two leaders here "did not trust" God. Apparently they did not trust that God could or would continue to support them and fulfill all that had been promised. The Bible is nothing if not realistic about human beings, including great leaders. Even the most prominent and most influential, even someone as singular as Moses, has the potential to stumble and fall into sin.

The location is named "Meribah," a word from the Hebrew root for "strife" or "contention," memorializing this final wilderness conflict between the Israelites and God. With Exodus 17:7 it makes bookends of their experience and the murmuring tradition.

INTERPRETING THE SCRIPTURE

Partial Memory, or Filling in the Blanks

There are times we may remember and even repeat an action long after we have forgotten the reason for that action. According to many scholars, this is the case with Aaron and Moses not being allowed to enter the Promised Land. The tradition remembered that they did not cross the Jordan River with the people. There must have been a reason for their being left out and so, when compiling the written story of those days, the writers cast about for something, anything, that could explain their exclusion. Some people today are satisfied with the explanations put forth in the previous section. Others believe that the punishment is far too harsh for the supposed crime. What none of us seems capable of doing is admitting our ignorance by saying, "We do not know why Moses did not enter the Promised Land," and letting it go at that in terms of the details.

When we draw back from the details we see that no human being, not even someone as great as Moses, is immune to the possibility of sin. Neither the enthusiasm of the new Christian nor long years of ensuing faithfulness is a guarantee that someone will not succumb to any manner of significant disobedience.

How Much Does It Matter?

Part of me wants to say that our endless fascination with the nature of Moses'—or anyone else's—sin is misplaced. It reminds me of the conversation between the resurrected Jesus and Peter in John 21. Three times Jesus tells Peter what to do: "Feed my sheep." In the end Peter responds by looking over at the beloved disciple and asking, "Lord, what about him?" (21:21). It sounds as if he has been paying scarcely any attention to the instructions Jesus was giving to him but rather wondering about what someone else's tasks were to be (John 21:15-21).

When my daughters were much younger, I could almost always count on a similar response when I asked either of them to do some chore. "Aggie, would you please set the table?" "But what about Anna?" came the quick response from Aggie. "Anna, could you move the clothes from the washing machine to the dryer?" "But what about Aggie?" Anna countered immediately. With young children it is merely an annoyance. But with adults, such as Peter, it can be ever so much more serious.

Fascination with other people's business rather than with one's own responsibilities may also be part of the reason it seems so hard for some people to keep secrets or protect the confidences that are related to them. We are all so interested in what everyone else is about that we lose sight of legitimate boundaries.

Being Faithful Followers

Today's lesson is, on the surface, about leaders and their sin. But there is much here to learn about followers also. It is hard to be a leader. Leadership positions are made more difficult when those who are supposed to be following take it upon themselves to grumble and complain and second-guess decisions at every turn. How could such behavior not wear leaders down spiritually? Maybe Moses was finally fed up with the endless fussing that he had listened to since at least Exodus 17. Maybe he had simply reached his human limit. After all, he had interceded powerfully for the people on at least two occasions we read about and he had not received much appreciation from them.

How well do we support our leaders today? By "support" I certainly do not mean we should give any human being total and blind obedience. That would take us down a path toward idolatry. But do we pray for those in authority over us? And do we carry our share of the burden for the whole group? There are times when the political climate is so contentious, when the whole culture is awash in cynicism, that it is easy to slip into a sort of finger-pointing, joke-making mode. It becomes simpler to find

fault with everyone else than to offer paths to solutions. It becomes a habit of thought to lump all politicians together when some are exposed as cheaters or to say that all young people are irresponsible and rude when we have observed one behaving in that way. It is certainly easier than making careful distinctions among proposals simply to dismiss all suggestions out of hand.

But that is so far from God's way. When we are attempting to follow Jesus and we see one of our leaders in some sort of difficulty or think she may be going through an especially tough time, we can be even more supportive, more fervent in our prayer. Early on in my teaching ministry I had a mentor who fit nearly every stereotype of the kindly old parson. His face creased with smile lines, his snowy white hair, his gentle voice, and his ability to focus all his attention on whoever was speaking to him made him very easy to talk to. At various times in his career he had led congregations, been a seminary professor, and had a period of being a college chaplain. We visited each other regularly. I was pleased to share the joys and frustrations I found in the classroom and listened with fascination to his stories of what the school and town had been like many decades before. At times he would hint at some upsetting incidents in his ministry, times when he had been treated with great unfairness, mostly in the early days of desegregation in a small Southern town. Because I could not leave well enough alone, I asked another retired professor about some of those times and learned that my friend had been treated very badly indeed. Greatly indignant on his behalf I finally asked him point blank one day how he had managed to stay so calm and kind in the midst of such mistreatment. "I could say that looking to Jesus had made it all easy for me," he said quietly. "But that wouldn't be the whole truth. Often it was not easy. But early on in the troubles a student slipped me a folded piece of paper. It said simply 'I'm praying for you.' I discovered that made all the difference, to know I was being upheld in prayer."

In the end, our disobedience does not and cannot prevent God from working through us. On the other hand, such disobedience and sin may delay or prevent us from getting to the destinations that God intends for us to reach. God's admonition to Cain, "sin is lurking at the door" and that we must master it (Genesis 4:7) can fit our situations as well. Mutual encouragement to faithfulness will always be a more Christ-like path than grumbling against one another and against our leaders.

SHARING THE SCRIPTURE

Preparing Our Hearts

Meditate on this week's devotional reading, found in Psalm 95. In this hymn of praise we see a reference to an event found in today's Scripture lesson in Psalm 95:8-11. God speaks about being tested at Meribah and Massah. The reference here is to the people's complaints that led to God's anger. The psalmist is calling his generation—and ours—not to harden our hearts as the Hebrews had done in the wilderness. In what ways is your heart hardened? Under what circumstances might you disobey God? Write a prayer of repentance in which you ask God to forgive your disobedience and failure to listen to God's voice.

Pray that you and the adult learners will learn lessons from people's relationships with God in the past that you can apply to your own lives.

Preparing Our Minds

Study the background Scripture and lesson Scripture, both of which are taken from Numbers 20:1-13. Think about why people disregard authority.

Write on newsprint:
❑ information for next week's lesson, found under "Continue the Journey."
❑ activities for further spiritual growth in "Continue the Journey."
Locate a map, preferably large enough for the class to see or one that can be legally reproduced, showing possible routes of the exodus.

Find a copy of Joachim Anthonisz Wtewael's *Moses Striking the Rock* (1624) on the National Gallery of Art's website at www.nga.gov/cgi-bin/pimage?52858+0+0. Or, locate another picture of Moses hitting the rock at Meribah.

LEADING THE CLASS

(1) Gather to Learn

❖ Welcome the class members and introduce any guests.

❖ Pray that all who have gathered this morning will be ready to consider the importance of obedience to God.

❖ Encourage the students to recall well-known preachers who became involved in scandals. Names such as Jim Bakker, Jimmy Swaggart, Oral Roberts, and Ted Haggard may come to mind. Often these scandals involve misuse of money or extramarital sexual affairs.

❖ Discuss these questions:
1. **Why do you think these highly respected Christian leaders became involved in activities that they know are contrary to God's will?**
2. **How do you think the fall of such highly regarded figures affects those who already profess Christ?**

3. How do you think their fall affects those who may be searching but have not yet connected with Christ?

❖ Read aloud today's focus statement: **Even great leaders may fail to heed higher authority. Why do people disregard authority? Moses disobeyed God because he did not trust God to provide for the people.**

(2) Lay Out the Details of God's Command and Moses' Disobedience

❖ Read Numbers 20:1 and also information for that passage from Understanding the Scripture to orient the students to the situation of the Israelites.

❖ Continue the orientation by locating Kadesh and the wilderness of Zin on a map.

❖ Choose a volunteer to read Numbers 20:2-13.

❖ Show the Wtewael picture (or another you have located) of Moses hitting the rock. Ask the class these questions:

    (1) What words come to mind when you first see this picture?

    (2) What do you imagine the people are thinking as Moses strikes the rock?

    (3) How do the colors affect the scene?

    (4) What do the landscape and clothing tell you about the artist and his or her worldview? (If you are using the Wtewael painting, note that he was a Dutch painter who lived from 1566–1638.)

❖ Invite the students to turn to Exodus 17:1-7, which records a parallel story of angry people needing water. Discuss with the students any similarities and differences they discern between the two events. List their ideas on newsprint.

❖ Conclude by having two volunteers read Psalms 95:8-11 and 106:32-33. Ask the adults to consider the impact that this incident must have had on later Israelites. Note that Psalm 95 was written to praise God and call people to obedient faithfulness, whereas Psalm 106 records a communal confession of Israel's sins.

(3) Explore Levels of Authority and Leadership and Issues of Obedience

❖ Make a leadership chart for your denomination, local church, government, or the military. Begin at the top of a sheet of newsprint in the center and write the name or office of the person who has greatest authority. Just below that, write the name(s) or office(s) of those who are lesser authorities but equal to one another. Continue down the chain of command to the level of the "common worker."

❖ Note that not all organizations are structured in this way, but a hierarchical model is often used in business, government, and even the church. Another model is more collegial, where everyone has more or less equal power and authority.

❖ Discuss these questions:

    (1) Why do many of our institutions have a singular head?

    (2) How do you see power running both up and down the chain?

    (3) What happens when someone at a lower level disobeys higher authority?

    (4) What happens when someone who is at a high level misuses his or her authority?

    (5) What lessons do you think organizations, particularly the church, can learn from the actions of the Israelites and Moses at Meribah about who is really in charge?

❖ Read aloud "Being Faithful Followers" from Interpreting the Scripture. Note that leaders can be helped or hurt by the way those who are following them act.

❖ Ask: **What comparisons can you make between the way the complaints of the people affected Moses and the way the actions of contemporary church members may affect pastors and other leaders?**

(4) Make a Commitment to Support Leaders in Prayer

❖ List on newsprint leaders whose work affects the members of the class.

❖ Distribute paper and pencils. Ask each student to select one leader, perhaps one they know personally or one whose leadership has a direct impact on the participant and his or her family.

❖ Challenge the students to write a prayer in support of this leader. They may want to pray for courage, wisdom, strength, health, or guidance. The adults may also lift up specific challenges facing the leader, such as dealing with a potential factory closing or trying to revise the Sunday morning worship schedule.

❖ Gather the students together or ask them to divide into groups if the class is large. Encourage volunteers to read their prayers aloud.

❖ Suggest that the students continue to pray the prayers they have written throughout the week. Encourage them to lift up other leaders as well.

(5) Continue the Journey

❖ Pray that all who have participated today will encourage their leaders rather than complain about them.

❖ Read aloud this preparation for next week's lesson. You may also want to post it on newsprint for the students to copy.

- **Title: God Calls for Obedience**
- **Background Scripture: Deuteronomy 6**
- **Lesson Scripture: Deuteronomy 6:1-9, 20-24**

■ **Focus of the Lesson: When people obey laws, they expect that life will be good. Why do people care at all about laws and try to follow them? Deuteronomy states that God gives laws for our benefit.**

❖ Challenge the students to complete one or more of these activities for further spiritual growth, which you will write on newsprint for the students to copy:

(1) **Ponder your own relationship with authority. Do you normally accept the authority of those over you? If not, what past experiences have caused you to mistrust or disobey such authority?**

(2) **Do something this week to show your pastor or another church leader that you are supporting him or her. Consider a note of appreciation, a positive word at a meeting or after the sermon, or telling someone else how much a kindness by this leader meant to you.**

(3) **Consider a problem or stumbling block in your own life. Spend time in prayer and meditation this week, turning this situation over to God and trusting God to take care of it.**

❖ Sing or read aloud "Holy, Holy, Holy! Lord God Almighty."

❖ Conclude today's session by leading the class in this benediction: **We hear your call, O God, and ask that you send us forth empowered by your Spirit to live and serve as your covenant people.**

UNIT 3: CALLED TO CHOOSE LIFE
GOD CALLS FOR OBEDIENCE

PREVIEWING THE LESSON

Lesson Scripture: Deuteronomy 6:1-9, 20-24
Background Scripture: Deuteronomy 6
Key Verses: Deuteronomy 6:4-6

Focus of the Lesson:
When people obey laws, they expect that life will be good. Why do people care at all about laws and try to follow them? Deuteronomy states that God gives laws for our benefit.

Goals for the Learners:
(1) to explore the meaning of the Great Commandment.
(2) to connect the Great Commandment to their lives.
(3) to accept God's Great Commandment, to live accordingly, and to teach it.

Pronunciation Guide:
nephesh (nef' esh)
Shema (shuh mah')

Supplies:
Bibles, newsprint and markers, paper and pencils, hymnals

READING THE SCRIPTURE

NRSV
Deuteronomy 6:1-9, 20-24

¹Now this is the commandment—the statutes and the ordinances—that the LORD your God charged me to teach you to observe in the land that you are about to cross into and occupy, ²so that you and your children and your children's children may fear the LORD your God all the days of your life, and keep all his decrees and his commandments that I am commanding you, so

NIV
Deuteronomy 6:1-9, 20-24

¹These are the commands, decrees and laws the LORD your God directed me to teach you to observe in the land that you are crossing the Jordan to possess, ²so that you, your children and their children after them may fear the LORD your God as long as you live by keeping all his decrees and commands that I give you, and so that you may enjoy long life. ³Hear, O Israel, and be

that your days may be long. ³Hear therefore, O Israel, and observe them diligently, so that it may go well with you, and so that you may multiply greatly in a land flowing with milk and honey, as the LORD, the God of your ancestors, has promised you.

⁴Hear, O Israel: The LORD is our God, the LORD alone. ⁵You shall love the LORD your God with all your heart, and with all your soul, and with all your might. ⁶Keep these words that I am commanding you today in your heart. ⁷Recite them to your children and talk about them when you are at home and when you are away, when you lie down and when you rise. ⁸Bind them as a sign on your hand, fix them as an emblem on your forehead, ⁹and write them on the doorposts of your house and on your gates.

²⁰When your children ask you in time to come, "What is the meaning of the decrees and the statutes and the ordinances that the LORD our God has commanded you?" ²¹then you shall say to your children, "We were Pharaoh's slaves in Egypt, but the LORD brought us out of Egypt with a mighty hand. ²²The LORD displayed before our eyes great and awesome signs and wonders against Egypt, against Pharaoh and all his household. ²³He brought us out from there in order to bring us in, to give us the land that he promised on oath to our ancestors. ²⁴Then the LORD commanded us to observe all these statutes, to fear the LORD our God, for our lasting good, so as to keep us alive, as is now the case."

careful to obey so that it may go well with you and that you may increase greatly in a land flowing with milk and honey, just as the LORD, the God of your fathers, promised you.

⁴Hear, O Israel: The LORD our God, the LORD is one. ⁵Love the LORD your God with all your heart and with all your soul and with all your strength. ⁶These commandments that I give you today are to be upon your hearts. ⁷Impress them on your children. Talk about them when you sit at home and when you walk along the road, when you lie down and when you get up. ⁸Tie them as symbols on your hands and bind them on your foreheads. ⁹Write them on the doorframes of your houses and on your gates.

²⁰In the future, when your son asks you, "What is the meaning of the stipulations, decrees and laws the LORD our God has commanded you?" ²¹tell him: "We were slaves of Pharaoh in Egypt, but the LORD brought us out of Egypt with a mighty hand. ²²Before our eyes the LORD sent miraculous signs and wonders—great and terrible—upon Egypt and Pharaoh and his whole household. ²³But he brought us out from there to bring us in and give us the land that he promised on oath to our forefathers. ²⁴The LORD commanded us to obey all these decrees and to fear the LORD our God, so that we might always prosper and be kept alive, as is the case today."

UNDERSTANDING THE SCRIPTURE

Deuteronomy 6:1-3. On the eve of their arrival in the Promised Land, Moses reminds the people of the major events of the past forty years. He tells the story again of God's giving the law at Mount Sinai and reminds them that God has "charged" him with the responsibility of teaching the law

to them, for they are to "observe" it in the land that God is giving them.

Once again the law is presented not as a burden but as a gracious gift. The people are to live by the law, not just because God says so but "so that it may go well with you . . . in a land flowing with milk and honey, as the LORD, the God of your ancestors, has promised you" (6:3).

Deuteronomy 6:4-9. The two translations of verse 5 printed with this lesson are accurate in terms of being word-for-word translations, yet they are not sufficient to convey all that the verse means. There are four important and difficult words: "love," "heart," "soul," and "might/strength." The simple word "love" has as many shades of meaning in Hebrew as in English. Someone can say "I love my daughters," "I love books," and "I love broccoli" without fear of being seriously misunderstood, although these are three quite different uses of one word. For us, love tends to be something that either happens or doesn't. A mother cannot command her daughter's love in the same way she may demand bedtime at 9:00 p.m. She may force her son to eat broccoli, but she is powerless to make him love it. Similarly, a child cannot make a parent love Barney the TV character despite the child's affection for the stuffed dinosaur.

We find Jesus quoting Deuteronomy 6:5 in giving the "first and greatest commandment" (Matthew 22:37; Mark 12:29-30; Luke 10:27). But, if love cannot be commanded, how can we obey that commandment? Hebrew and surrounding cultures and languages gave a political dimension to the word "love," using it to mean "loyalty." The way to say slaves must be loyal to their masters was to say they must love their masters. Defeated rulers pledged fidelity to their conquerors using the word "love." It is not likely that many pleasant emotions were shared, but the vassals knew better than to sign up with another overlord.

This love/loyalty is to engage all our heart. Although "heart" is the correct translation for the Hebrew, the trouble is that when we hear "heart," we think of something different from what was meant by those Hebrew-speaking people. Human cultures tend to divide the body figuratively, to use particular body parts to stand for particular actions or characteristics. We speak of "loving with our whole heart," even though we know that the physical heart pumps blood and has nothing to do with the emotions we feel. So far, so good. The tricky part is that no two cultures/languages use the body parts in exactly the same way. We say we feel emotions in our heart; the Hebrews used "heart" to mean the place of thought and will, of decision-making and conscience.

The next important word is "soul." "Soul" is a Christian word with a long history, but the word used in Deuteronomy had a meaning long before Christianity. "Soul" (*nephesh* in Hebrew) has two parts. First, it is what makes people and animals alive, as distinct from plants. Second, *nephesh* indicates individuality. Your *nephesh* is not like anyone else's because you are a unique living being. Your *nephesh* makes you alive; your *nephesh* makes you *you*.

The last of our four words, "might," is equally tricky. A standard biblical Hebrew dictionary translates it "muchness, force, abundance, exceedingly." What is being commanded, thus, is a complete loyalty to God: a loyalty of thought and action and decision-making, a loyalty that will be individual and not just following some crowd, and a loyalty that may require hard work.

If you look at Jesus' words in Mark 12:29-30 or Luke 10:27, you may think he added something when he quoted the verse from Deuteronomy. Jesus' "expansion" was not in adding any different meaning, however. By using both "heart" and "mind" he was explaining for the Greek-speaking culture what was meant by the Hebrew concept of "heart" alone.

These words, and the ideas behind them, are so important that they are to be thought about at home and away from home, talked about with the children, tacked up on the doorposts so you see them every time you walk into your house or from room to room.

Deuteronomy 6:10-19. Then Moses issues a serious warning. The people are about to enter into the Promised Land. There they will move into houses other people built, eat produce from gardens and vineyards other people planted and tended, and use water from cisterns other people carved out. When that happens, when they have finally begun to realize the dream that sustained their ancestors for generations, they are not to forget God. They may not need God in the same way their parents needed to be freed from slavery in Egypt; they may not need God to guide them through the wilderness any longer once they have settled in the land. But God still wants to be in relationship with them. And God will notice, and respond, if they abandon God or if they decide to try out worship of some of the gods of their new neighbors.

Deuteronomy 6:20-25. Finally, what of the future? How are things to be continued into the next generations? Moses will not always be there to remind them of their history or of what God has asked of them. These verses contain a deceptively simple plan: When the children ask, tell them the story. And note two significant features of this plan. First, it is implied that children are to be included in the life of the community. Otherwise, how would they have anything to ask about? Second, the adults are to tell the story as their own story. That point is clearly seen in the wording: "*We* were Pharaoh's slaves" not "Your ancestors way back in the past were Pharaoh's slaves." What such a practice may lack in strict historical factuality, it more than makes up for in theological truth.

INTERPRETING THE SCRIPTURE

It's Just Words, Isn't It?

A major part of the previous section has been taken up in translating four words from verse 5. Some people have little patience for this kind of exercise, calling the making of such careful distinctions "just semantics" or "only words." But Christians, of all people, should be appreciative of words and their use, for we call the Second Person of the Trinity "the Word made flesh," and "the Living Word," and we refer to the Bible as "God's Word." Every human language changes as it is used so that if we are going to be faithful to the *meaning* of Scripture, we must be careful with our use of words. The schoolyard ditty "Sticks and stones may break my bones, but words will never hurt me" has it exactly backwards. Words are powerful beyond any physical weapon; words are potent for good or ill.

Beyond the Words

Important as it is to understand the words adequately, all the language study in the world is not a substitute for faithful living. Yet the two are not unrelated, for basic misunderstandings of words can get in the way of our living faithfully. For example, some people have great difficulty with the Great Commandment because they think that "love" must always include "thinking nice thoughts about" or "never being angry at." Realizing that "love" in Hebrew means acting with loyalty rather than feeling a particular emotion means that we can indeed be loyal to God even in times of disappointment or anger. Think of relationships of people close to you. Haven't we all said something on the order of "I love him, but I sure can't stand him today"? A solid and secure relationship cannot endure without honesty, including the honestly communicated negative feelings we all experience from time to time. In fact, if we are going to be truly loyal, whether to another person or to God, we must be honest with those negative feelings.

What possible definition of "loyalty" includes lying or being deceitful? We have many instances of such bold honesty reported in the Old Testament and never once does God scold someone for it. Nor does Jesus ever reprimand a critic or questioner for an honest statement. The book of Psalms has example after example of criticism of God, questioning of God, and other such reactions to what is going on in the psalmist's life. All those not-so-nice feelings we may have will fester within us if we do not deal with them. Who would be proud of asking God to deal with their enemies by imploring, "O God, break the teeth in their mouths" as we find in Psalm 58:6? That is scarcely a wish worthy of the people of God. And yet what better place is there to pour out our hurts and disappointments, our doubts and outrage, than in prayer to God? When we are able and willing to be honest in prayer, God can begin to help us through our difficulties. As long as we pretend that everything is just fine, our relationship with God will not be as deep as it could be. Once we are in a habit of being honest with God in prayer, we will probably discover that the more positive emotions our culture usually connects with the word "love" do come along too.

God wants, yearns for, relationships in which these positive emotions flourish. And God has shown us how to act, how to live, in such a way as to engender such relationships. The Great Commandment is both our starting place and the summary of all the law.

Not Just Another Add-on

Keeping the Great Commandment is far from being just one more thing on a seemingly endless "to do" list. Rather, it is the foundation that is to undergird all the rest of our actions. We humans do not make all our decisions randomly and without either coherent basis or pattern. Most of the decisions we make, however, are so automatic that we scarcely think of them as decisions at all, and yet they had to be learned at some point. When I am about to cross the street from the bank to the post office, I never go through the mental calculation, "Should I check to see if any cars are coming?" It would never occur to me to say that I "decide" to look for cars before stepping off the curb. It is even automatic for me to check for vehicles coming from the bank's drive-through lane, although that requires an extra turning not needed in most places I cross the street. Now I was not born with an instinct to watch out for cars and trucks. Instead, this practice was taught to me, drilled into me, by my parents and teachers over a several-year span. At first I paid attention not because I understood anything about traffic regulations but merely because I wanted to please my parents and then my teachers. When I was a bit older, the habit made sense to me in terms of safety. Then it was further cemented as a habit when I helped teach it to my younger brothers. What also helped me learn was seeing adults look carefully before they stepped into the street, whether or not they had children with them. There are innumerable examples like this of things we do each day, almost automatically, that at some point we had to learn. And if they are good practices, we have an obligation to teach them to the next generation both by specific lessons and by our continuing to live by them. (We all know the saying about actions speaking louder than words!)

This is how the Great Commandment is supposed to function for us. First we learn it, perhaps hearing about it over and over at home and in Sunday school and church. It is very helpful for the learner to see others obey it. Eventually it may become automatic, "second nature," to consider what loyalty to God entails in each individual decision. Of course, being with people who are also striving to follow God also will be a great help. And teaching such loyalty to our children, by our actions as well as by our words, will as a matter of course help us to keep it as a strong foundation of our

faith and life. These may be matters that we do not speak about easily, but it is our responsibility to pass these lessons on to the following generations, for that too is part of our complete loyalty to the one true God.

SHARING THE SCRIPTURE

Preparing Our Hearts

Meditate on this week's devotional reading, found in Proverbs 2:1-11. In today's lesson we will read the command to teach God's ways to our children. In this poem from Proverbs, the writer instructs "my child" about the value of wisdom. The child is encouraged to seek wisdom, just as one would seek precious metals. Here we see how the Hebrew Scriptures view heart and soul: According to verse 10, wisdom comes into one's heart, and knowledge pleases the soul. Ponder these words. Open yourself to receive God's wisdom. And be ready to teach that wisdom to a child who seeks it.

Pray that you and the adult learners will be always alert for God's wisdom.

Preparing Our Minds

Study the background Scripture from Deuteronomy 6 and the lesson Scripture found in verses 1-9, 20-24. Ponder why people care about laws and try to follow them.

Write on newsprint:
❑ information for next week's lesson, found under "Continue the Journey."
❑ activities for further spiritual growth in "Continue the Journey."

Plan the suggested lecture for "Explore the Meaning of the Great Commandment."

LEADING THE CLASS

(1) Gather to Learn

❖ Welcome the class members and introduce any guests.

❖ Pray that this week's participants will be eager to become familiar with God's law and obey it.

❖ Discuss these questions with the class:
   (1) How would you define "law abiding"? (Post ideas on newsprint. Words may vary but you want the idea of strict adherence to laws and rules.)
   (2) When people adhere to the law, what expectations might they have? (Consider things such as to live a good life, not to be wrongly accused, to be protected by law enforcement officers and the law, to assume that lawbreakers will be punished.)

❖ Read aloud today's focus statement: **When people obey laws, they expect that life will be good. Why do people care at all about laws and try to follow them? Deuteronomy states that God gives laws for our benefit.**

(2) Explore the Meaning of the Great Commandment

❖ Choose two volunteers, one to read Deuteronomy 6:1-9 and the other to read verses 20-24.

❖ Note that verses 4-6 include a very important confession of faith in Judaism. It is called the Shema, which means "hear," with the implied meaning that the words are to be obeyed as well.

❖ Discern what the people are confessing about God by asking the class members to look at verse 4. Encourage those who have alternate translations in their footnotes to read them aloud. Read these translations, which are found as footnotes in the NRSV, if none of the students volunteers them: **"The Lord our God is one Lord," or "The Lord our God, the Lord is one," or "The Lord is our God, the Lord is one."**

❖ Ask the students to consider how these slightly different sentences shade the meaning for them. (Be sure the students catch the significance of the "oneness" of God. The Israelites, unlike their neighbors, held fast to the belief that there is one God. Trinitarian Christians believe that as well, although we would say that there is one God who exists in three persons: Father, Son, and Holy Spirit.)

❖ Help the class understand the intended Hebrew meaning of verse 5 by presenting a lecture based on Deuteronomy 6:4-9 in Understanding the Scripture. Your focus will be on the words "love," "heart," "soul," and "might/strength."

❖ Invite the students to look, in turn, at the following three passages, Matthew 22:37, Mark 12:29-30, and Luke 10:27 to see how Jesus incorporated the Shema into his own teaching.

❖ End this section of the lesson by noting that Jesus obviously learned the Shema as had countless other generations of Jews whose families had taught it to them. Jesus himself follows the command to teach it to others.

(3) Connect the Great Commandment to the Learners' Lives

❖ Read aloud "Not Just Another Add-on" from Interpreting the Scripture.

❖ Read again this sentence: **"The Great Commandment is the foundation that is to undergird all the rest of our actions."**

❖ Divide the class into groups. Give each group a marker and sheet of newsprint. Ask them to brainstorm concrete examples of how loving God with all our heart, soul, and might provides the underpinning for everything else we do.

❖ Read these discussion starters if the groups need to "prime the pump." Make clear that these are just several examples among many possibilities.

■ If we love God completely, then we live in accordance with God's will and act obediently.

■ If we are giving our complete love and loyalty to God, then we are not swayed by the consumer mentality that beckons us to buy everything we see.

■ Because we love God unreservedly, we strive in word and deed to show others how to live as God's people.

❖ Call everyone together and ask each group to report to the class. Point out similar ideas among the groups.

(4) Accept God's Great Commandment, Live Accordingly, and Teach It

❖ Invite the students to read aloud today's key verses, Deuteronomy 6:4-6, using whatever translations they have available.

❖ Provide a few moments of meditation time for the adults to review these words silently and consider whether or not they are living according to this Great Commandment.

❖ Break the silence by asking the students to raise any questions they have about what this commandment means in terms of how they are to live. (You need not try to address their concerns yourself. Let the class respond to these questions.)

❖ Note that this Scripture not only calls us to obedience but also exhorts us to keep this Great Commandment ever before us and to teach it to our children.

❖ Discuss these questions:

(1) **In what ways do you keep God's commandment before you?** (You may consider how symbols such as a cross or dove remind the adults of their faith, just as the Jewish people wear reminders and have written reminders in their homes.)

(2) **In what ways are we as individuals telling the stories of our faith to children?**

(3) **What does our church do to communicate the stories of faith to children? How well do you think we are doing these activities?**

(4) **In what ways can we as a congregation be more open to children?**

❖ Conclude this portion of the lesson by distributing paper and pencil. Ask the students to do three things:

■ **First:** Copy Deuteronomy 6:4-6 from their Bibles as a way to reinforce its message.

■ **Second:** Write at least one concrete action they will take this week to live according to the Great Commandment.

■ **Third:** Place this paper in their Bibles for review during the week.

(5) Continue the Journey

❖ Pray that all who have come today will hear and obey the word of the Lord.

❖ Read aloud this preparation for next week's lesson. You may also want to post it on newsprint for the students to copy.

■ **Title: God Calls for Decision**

■ **Background Scripture: Deuteronomy 30**

■ **Lesson Scripture: Deuteronomy 30:1-10**

■ **Focus of the Lesson: People want to experience a satisfying life, to attain joy and prosperity. How do we get what we want out of life? Moses claimed that God wants us to love God so much that we want nothing more than to obey God.**

❖ Challenge the students to complete one or more of these activities for further spiritual growth, which you will write on newsprint for the students to copy:

(1) **Spend time this week with a child, teaching him or her something about Jesus that is appropriate to the child's level of understanding. Think about ways to teach this lesson by word and deed.**

(2) **Recall as many "memory verses" as you can. Try to remember who taught you these verses and when. Summarize in a brief paragraph the influence that this memorized Scripture has on your faith journey.**

(3) **Do an Internet search on the word "Shema." What can you learn about this extremely important Hebrew text? What meaning does it have for you as a Christian?**

❖ Sing or read aloud "Joyful, Joyful, We Adore Thee."

❖ Conclude today's session by leading the class in this benediction: **We hear your call, O God, and ask that you send us forth empowered by your Spirit to live and serve as your covenant people.**

UNIT 3: CALLED TO CHOOSE LIFE

GOD CALLS FOR DECISION

PREVIEWING THE LESSON

Lesson Scripture: Deuteronomy 30:1-10
Background Scripture: Deuteronomy 30
Key Verse: Deuteronomy 30:6

Focus of the Lesson:
People want to experience a satisfying life, to attain joy and prosperity. How do we get what we want out of life? Moses claimed that God wants us to love God so much that we want nothing more than to obey God.

Goals for the Learners:
(1) to restate Moses' promise that God will reward the Israelites' love and faithfulness with prosperity.
(2) to recognize the importance of loving and obeying God.
(3) to choose to obey God's call to obedience.

Pronunciation Guide:
Pentateuch (pent' tuh tyook)

Supplies:
Bibles, newsprint and marker, paper and pencils, hymnals

READING THE SCRIPTURE

NRSV
Deuteronomy 30:1-10

¹When all these things have happened to you, the blessings and the curses that I have set before you, if you call them to mind among all the nations where the LORD your God has driven you, ²and return to the LORD your God, and you and your children obey him with all your heart and with all your soul, just as I am commanding you today,

NIV
Deuteronomy 30:1-10

¹When all these blessings and curses I have set before you come upon you and you take them to heart wherever the LORD your God disperses you among the nations, ²and when you and your children return to the LORD your God and obey him with all your heart and with all your soul according to everything I command you today, ³then the

³then the LORD your God will restore your fortunes and have compassion on you, gathering you again from all the peoples among whom the LORD your God has scattered you. ⁴Even if you are exiled to the ends of the world, from there the LORD your God will gather you, and from there he will bring you back. ⁵The LORD your God will bring you into the land that your ancestors possessed, and you will possess it; he will make you more prosperous and numerous than your ancestors.

⁶Moreover, the LORD your God will circumcise your heart and the heart of your descendants, so that you will love the LORD your God with all your heart and with all your soul, in order that you may live. ⁷The LORD your God will put all these curses on your enemies and on the adversaries who took advantage of you. ⁸Then you shall again obey the LORD, observing all his commandments that I am commanding you today, ⁹and the LORD your God will make you abundantly prosperous in all your undertakings, in the fruit of your body, in the fruit of your livestock, and in the fruit of your soil. For the LORD will again take delight in prospering you, just as he delighted in prospering your ancestors, ¹⁰when you obey the LORD your God by observing his commandments and decrees that are written in this book of the law, because you turn to the LORD your God with all your heart and with all your soul.

LORD your God will restore your fortunes and have compassion on you and gather you again from all the nations where he scattered you. ⁴Even if you have been banished to the most distant land under the heavens, from there the LORD your God will gather you and bring you back. ⁵He will bring you to the land that belonged to your fathers, and you will take possession of it. He will make you more prosperous and numerous than your fathers. **⁶The LORD your God will circumcise your hearts and the hearts of your descendants, so that you may love him with all your heart and with all your soul, and live.** ⁷The LORD your God will put all these curses on your enemies who hate and persecute you. ⁸You will again obey the LORD and follow all his commands I am giving you today. ⁹Then the LORD your God will make you most prosperous in all the work of your hands and in the fruit of your womb, the young of your livestock and the crops of your land. The LORD will again delight in you and make you prosperous, just as he delighted in your fathers, ¹⁰if you obey the LORD your God and keep his commands and decrees that are written in this Book of the Law and turn to the LORD your God with all your heart and with all your soul.

UNDERSTANDING THE SCRIPTURE

Deuteronomy 30:1-5. God, through Moses, is looking far into the future here. Many things will happen to ensuing generations, both "blessings and curses." Nevertheless, God will never break the covenant promises made to the ancestral patriarchs Abraham, Isaac, and Jacob and reiterated even to this generation standing

on the brink of the Promised Land and to every generation yet to come. This sounds like good news, and indeed it is, but the people know that theirs is a history of fussing and falling away from their side of the promises, a nearly endless chain of going willfully after their own desires even when they knew full well it was not what God desired for them. Even if God is good and faithful, where is a hopeful future if God's covenant partner is nothing but a bunch of weak and willful humans?

Deuteronomy 30:6-10. The serious objection raised in the previous verses is answered in verse 6 by God. God will "circumcise [their] hearts."

Here indeed is a thorny figure of speech! Remember that "heart" stands for mind and will. God is here promising to cut away all that hinders the mind and will of the people, everything that makes it easy for them to disobey. This does not mean that humans are going to be transformed into puppets, into beings who have no choice but to do what God requires. Free will, and therefore sin, is not being abandoned. But God is doing everything possible from the divine side to enhance the possibility of our obedience. This passage brings us to the intersection of law and grace once again. That law should be an instrument of grace and that grace should help us to fulfill God's law is a recurring message throughout the Old and New Testaments and among later interpreters including Martin Luther and John Wesley.

Deuteronomy 30:11-14. Some of this section sounds as if Moses is anticipating still more objections from the people and is answering them before they even raise them out loud. It would certainly be in keeping with their previous behavior for the Israelites to complain, saying in essence, "Even this commandment is too hard; it is too far away. Who can possibly go up to heaven and bring it down to us? Who could ever make it all the way across the sea and come back and instruct us so that we may be obedient? Who could possibly live up to such a thing? It is for gods, not mere humans."

"On the contrary," we can imagine Moses saying, "what I am telling you is neither too difficult nor too remote. You have it all right here. And you have the ability to keep it if you so choose." Moses makes clear that obeying God is a matter not for the spiritual elite but for every member of the community.

Deuteronomy 30:15-20. In one final grand summation, Moses lays out the options before them. Life and the good are on one side; death and evil are on the other. How do they choose? How do they live out their choice? By loving (remember from last week this means "being loyal to") the Lord or by turning to other gods? The figure of speech is that of walking. Either they walk in the ways of God (30:16), or they go after other gods (30:17). That is, the "choice" is not merely a sort of intellectual assent. It is not enough for them to say the words; the words they say must be echoed in the way they live their entire lives.

The foundation of all other sin is idolatry. Idolatry is not limited to setting up statues and bowing down in front of them. Idolatry includes all actions that put something else in God's rightful place. According to Deuteronomy, that is the way of death. Choosing the Lord and the commandments of the Lord is the way that leads to life, for individuals and for their descendants. The choice is put before the people. It is a free choice; the matter of choice is their responsibility.

The description of the two options is important. The Hebrew calls the first choice "life and the good" (as seen in the KJV), but many English translations (including the NRSV and the NIV) render that as "life and prosperity" (30:15). It is a grave error, I fervently believe, to equate "the good" with "prosperity," especially if we limit the definition of prosperity to economic terms. But what are the synonyms of "prosperity" in English if not words such as "wealth," "affluence," "opulence," or "riches"? True enough. But if one considers the verb form "to prosper" instead of the noun, then other alternatives are easily apparent. There are still the economic alternatives such as make money or show a profit, but terms such as flourish or thrive are also available. Plants can flourish, a puppy can thrive. It is this flourishing and thriving sense of "the good" in verse 15 that is meant, a notion that has a much wider application than the merely economic.

In verse 20, Moses rounds out the promise. The land into which the people are about to cross is none other than the land that God promised generations ago to give to the descendants of Abraham, Isaac, and Jacob. At the end of Deuteronomy, which is also the end of the Pentateuch, we come to the fulfillment of the promise God had made all the way back in Genesis 12 in the calling of Abram/Abraham. Regardless of how much time may pass, despite any intervening obstacles, God's promises are kept.

There are three time horizons we need to keep in mind when reading any biblical passage. There is the time of the recorded events, the time the narrative about them was composed, and the time when all the elements came together in the form we now have in the Bible. The book of Deuteronomy did not reach its final form until the time of the exile, many centuries after the events it recounts. Even in the midst of the chaos of exile, the inspired authors reaffirm their trust in God's faithfulness with these ringing words of Moses.

INTERPRETING THE SCRIPTURE

What Sort of Choice Is This?

"Choose life and not death," Moses urges the Israelites. Is that a serious choice? What people in their right minds would ever choose anything other than life? Alas, people do it all the time, as individuals, as families, and as other groups including congregations. I am not referring here to options such as the terminally ill patient in intractable pain who chooses to halt treatment even though that will probably hasten his death. Nor do I mean cases of emergency where a police officer or firefighter may lose her life in the course of saving others. These and similar situations are understandable to most of us. Similarly, no person seeking to live will consciously step off the curb in front of an oncoming bus. Nor will an individual intent on long life knowingly ingest poison.

The issue Moses raises here has to do with those little, seemingly innocuous, choices that day by day can add up either to life or to death. Remember, too, that the categories of life and death are not limited to our physical bodies but also include the mental and spiritual and relational aspects of our being. Jesus put the same matter before us when he said he came that we might have "abundant" life (John 10:10).

Individual Life or Death

Most of our habits seem innocent enough that we give them little thought, and yet over time some can have fiercely negative consequences. I know I need to maintain a balance between the calories I eat and the calories I expend. I know some foods are inherently better for my body than others. I know to wear a helmet when riding my bicycle and always to fasten my seatbelt in the car. One individual piece of fudge will not make me morbidly obese nor will one uneventful drive without a seatbelt cause injury. But for most of us "choosing life" must include making good small choices so repetitively that they become automatic. My daughter had no idea she was going to have a bicycle accident the one day she did. It is probably only because putting on her helmet had become a habit that she is still alive and without brain damage.

Family Life or Death

Most people want to have a strong family life, and yet we allow little things, innocent in themselves, to keep us from that goal. We say we value conversation around the dinner table, and yet most families today find it difficult to share a daily meal. Worse, I think, is that when they do eat together, they do so around the television set. In addition, an astonishing seventy-one percent of children have a television set in their bedroom, according to a study that appeared in the July 2005 issue of *Archives of Pediatrics & Adolescent Medicine*. Now television is not evil in itself; there is much good educational and wholesome entertainment value available. But what is more important, family life or television? Are we habitually choosing abundant life or dullness?

Congregational Life or Death

I want to relate a relatively long example here because I think it illustrates the lesson of Deuteronomy 30. I also want to make it plain from the outset that I do not believe there are any villains in this piece. A congregation I knew well (I was not the pastor, although I knew her well also) had been struggling financially for many years. One of their members, who I'll call Mr. Tanner, owned a small printing business. His practice was to give nothing to the church until the middle of December. Then he would ask the treasurer how much money was needed to end the year in the black. Whatever the amount the treasurer told him, that was the amount of the check Mr. Tanner put in the offering plate on the last Sunday of the year. He did this without fanfare, although after a while most everyone in the congregation knew what he did and they were grateful to him. He did not chair any committees or exercise overt control over anything in that church, but little by little people began to defer to him when decisions were to be made. He did not think participating in the community soup kitchen was a good idea, so the church withdrew. He preferred wafers for Communion, so the pastor stopped using bread and bought wafers. He liked professionally arranged flowers on the altar, so people stopped bringing bouquets from their gardens in the summertime. Some of his choices involved greater expense for the church, but the common refrain was, "Mr. Tanner will pay for it."

By the time my friend was appointed there, the watchword for any choice became, "Check it out with Mr. Tanner." After she had been there for about a year, Mr. Tanner came to see her about her preaching. She took the Scripture readings for each Sunday from the lectionary, and he did not think that was a good idea. After all, none of her predecessors had done that. He handed her a list of texts he wanted her to preach on for the next six months. She explained what the lectionary was and why she used it. He politely told her to preach from his list of texts. She declined. He threatened to withdraw his financial support. She continued to preach from the lectionary. After she had been pastor there for two years, Mr. Tanner transferred his membership. Much of the congregation was terrified of what would happen to them financially. And yet, my friend reported, they pulled together and, to the amazement of most of them, ended the year in the black even without the big check on the final Sunday.

I want to be careful with this example, for I do not see any "bad guys" in this story. Mr. Tanner was not an evil man nor was that congregation made up of self-serving flatterers. But in abdicating their individual thoughts and voices, they had little by little chosen the path of death. Only when the membership stopped letting any one person have all the say, only when they tried again to listen to their Lord without worrying about a final year-end check, did they begin to regain the health they had not even realized they were missing. They never became robust financially and have since merged with another little congregation, but a spirit of community flourished among them that was delightful to see and heartening to experience.

The Circumcised Heart

When we take away, or allow God to remove, those things that cramp our thinking, we can begin to live the more abundant life God wills for the whole of creation. It may not be an easy process, but there are two things that work in its favor. First, we do not have to attempt everything alone because we are members of the body of Christ. Second, we do not have to attempt everything alone because our God is faithful. From Abraham to Moses to the biblical editors in exile, from Jesus to Paul to our own day, the unanimous testimony of the community of faith is that our God is faithful. God promises us life, but we are free to accept or reject that promise. The decision is ours to make. What will you choose?

SHARING THE SCRIPTURE

Preparing Our Hearts

Meditate on this week's devotional reading, found in Joshua 24:14-24. The theme of covenant pervades the Scriptures. It underlies our lesson from Deuteronomy 30, and, here in Joshua, we see a covenant renewal ceremony. Notice that, although God sets forth the covenant, people are free to choose or reject the life it brings. Jesus brings what we Christians refer to as the "new covenant," and we too may choose to accept or reject him. Are you willing to be in covenant and serve God alone, or do you choose to serve other gods? The Scriptures make it clear that we cannot have it both ways.

Pray that you and the adult learners will be able to say with Joshua, "as for me and my household, we will serve the LORD" (24:15).

Preparing Our Minds

Study the background Scripture from Deuteronomy 30 and the lesson Scripture found in verses 1-10. Identify ways in which we try to get what we want out of life.

Write on newsprint:

❑ sentence to be completed for "Gather to Learn."
❑ information for next week's lesson, found under "Continue the Journey."
❑ activities for further spiritual growth in "Continue the Journey."

LEADING THE CLASS

(1) Gather to Learn

❖ Welcome the class members and introduce any guests.

❖ Pray that the adults who have gathered today will hear God's Word and make good decisions.

❖ Post a sheet of newsprint with the words *To me, living a good life means . . ."* Invite the students to write something as they enter the learning area, or ask them to call out their ideas as you write them.

❖ Review the ideas. Encourage the students to put a plus (+) by the entries that they think Jesus would agree with and a minus (-) by the ones they think he would disagree with.

❖ Discuss why our ideas about "the good life" may be at odds with Jesus' teachings about "the good life."

❖ Read aloud today's focus statement: **People want to experience a satisfying life, to attain joy and prosperity. How do we get what we want out of life? Moses claimed that God wants us to love God so much that we want nothing more than to obey God.**

(2) Restate Moses' Promise That God Will Reward the Israelites' Love and Faithfulness With Prosperity

❖ Select a volunteer to read Deuteronomy 30:1-10 as if Moses were speaking these words to the people who were on the verge of entering the Promised Land.

❖ Point out that thus far in Deuteronomy Moses has been recalling the past. Now he looks into the future.

❖ Invite the students to notice that in verse 1, there is mention of "the blessings and the curses that I have set before you." Divide the class into three groups (or multiples of three). Ask one third of the groups to look at the blessings in Deuteronomy 28:1-14. Ask another third to consider the curses in Deuteronomy 28:15-37, and the final third to look at the curses in Deuteronomy 28:38-68. In all cases, the groups are looking to see what God intends to do. God's actions are based on the people's obedience or disobedience. Ask each group to name a recorder who will report to the class. Be sure to have paper and pencils available.

❖ Call the groups together and hear their reports about the blessings and curses.

❖ Point out that, as we know, the people often chose to disobey God. Ask:

   (1) Why do you think people deliberately disobeyed God when they knew beforehand what the consequences would be?

   (2) How do you see the church as being similar to and different from the people Moses addressed? (If time permits, read the long example from "Congregational Life or Death" in Interpreting the Scripture.)

(3) Recognize the Importance of Loving and Obeying God

❖ Read together in unison today's key verse, Deuteronomy 30:6. Compare that with Deuteronomy 6:4-6, which we studied last week. Use information from Understanding the Scripture for Deuteronomy 30:6-10 to help the class understand the meaning of verse 6. Note that whereas in 6:4-6 the people are commanded to love God unreservedly, in 30:6 God provides a way for that to happen.

❖ Ask the students to turn in their Bibles to John 13:34-35 as someone reads this passage aloud.

❖ Ask the adults to look also at 1 John 3:18-24 as another volunteer reads this passage aloud.

❖ Encourage the students to draw conclusions about the importance of loving and obeying God. (Some classes may include students who downplay the importance of the Hebrew Scriptures or have difficulty seeing continuity between the Old and New Testaments. Point out that this emphasis on loving and obeying God clearly runs throughout the entire Bible.)

❖ End this portion of the lesson by challenging the adults to identify ways that they can show their love and obedience to God. List their ideas on newsprint. Think not only of ways individual students can do that but also about ways that the class or entire congregation can act obediently out of love (loyalty) to God through Christ.

(4) Choose to Obey God's Call to Obedience

❖ Read "The Circumcised Heart" from Interpreting the Scripture.

❖ Invite the students to bear witness to the faithfulness of God as they have experienced it in their own lives. If the group is large, or if people are reluctant to speak, ask them to talk with a partner.

❖ Distribute paper and pencils. Read again these words and ask the students to write their decision. **God promises us life, but we are free to accept or reject that promise. The decision is ours to make. What will you choose?**

❖ Provide time for quiet meditation in which the adults consider the impact that their choice will have on their life and possibly on the lives of those closest to them.

(5) Continue the Journey

❖ Break the silence by praying that all who have participated today will continue to choose to obey God and live as God's people.

❖ Read aloud this preparation for next week's lesson. You may also want to post it on newsprint for the students to copy.

- **Title: Joshua: A Leader for the People**
- **Background Scripture: Joshua 1**
- **Lesson Scripture: Joshua 1:1-11, 16-17**
- **Focus of the Lesson: In the midst of change and uncertainty, we need leaders who can guide us in the right direction. What are the characteristics of such leaders? Joshua, who succeeded Moses, was a strong, courageous leader** whose obedience to God enabled the people to cross the Jordan into the Promised Land.

❖ Challenge the students to complete one or more of these activities for further spiritual growth, which you will write on newsprint for the students to copy:

(1) **Tell someone about how God has blessed you because you chose to obey God's will.**

(2) **Study Deuteronomy 12–26, where you will find details of God's covenant. How can you "translate" this information to the contemporary church? (Remember, we have our own idols, festivals, and laws.)**

(3) **Encourage someone who is having difficulties in life as a result of his or her poor choices to change priorities and follow the ways of God that lead to life.**

❖ Sing or read aloud "Sent Forth by God's Blessing."

❖ Conclude today's session by leading the class in this benediction: **We hear your call, O God, and ask that you send us forth empowered by your Spirit to live and serve as your covenant people.**